Lecture Notes in Computer Science 7807

Commenced Publication in 1973
Founding and Former Series Editors:
Gerhard Goos, Juris Hartmanis, and Jan van Leeuwen

More information about this series at http://www.springer.com/series/7410

Yvo Desmedt (Ed.)

Information Security

16th International Conference, ISC 2013
Dallas, Texas, November 13–15, 2013
Proceedings

 Springer

Editor
Yvo Desmedt
The University of Texas at Dallas
Richardson, TX
USA

ISSN 0302-9743   ISSN 1611-3349   (electronic)
Lecture Notes in Computer Science
ISBN 978-3-319-27658-8   ISBN 978-3-319-27659-5   (eBook)
DOI 10.1007/978-3-319-27659-5

Library of Congress Control Number: 2015957049

LNCS Sublibrary: SL4 – Security and Cryptology

This Springer imprint is published by SpringerNature
The registered company is Springer International Publishing AG Switzerland

Preface

The Information Security Conference (ISC), which started as a workshop (ISW) in 1997, is an international conference organized yearly. It has been held in five different continents.

ISC 2013 was organized in cooperation with the International Association for Cryptologic Research, and the Department of Computer Science, The University of Texas at Dallas, USA.

There were 70 submitted papers, which were considered by the Program Committee. This is roughly the same as for ISC 2012, which took place in Passau, Germany, and had 72 submissions. Owing to the large number of submissions, some papers that contained new ideas had to be rejected. Priority was given to novel papers. Of the 70 submissions, 16 were selected, which is a 23 % acceptance rate. We also accepted 14 short papers. Each paper was sent to at least three members of the Program Committee for comments. Submissions to ISC 2013 were required to be anonymous. EasyChair was used for submissions, refereeing, etc.

Beside the accepted papers, two invited presentations were given. Michael Reiter (University of North Carolina at Chapel Hill) spoke about "How to Misuse, Use, and Mitigate Side Channels in Virtualized Environments." G.R. Blakley (IACR Fellow) spoke about his joint work with Bob Blakley and Sean Blakley on "How to Draw Graphs: Seeing and Redrafting Large Networks in Security and Biology."

The proceedings contain all the regular papers and short papers accepted, except for the paper "Formal Analysis of ECC-Based Direct Anonymous Attestation Schemes in Applied Pi Calculus," by Li Xi, Yu Qin, and Dengguo Feng. Revisions of papers were not checked for correctness on their scientific aspects and the authors bear full responsibility for the content of their papers. Some of the papers may have been edited taking the comments of the Program Committee or external referees into account.

I am very grateful to the members of the Program Committee for their hard work and the difficult task of selecting the papers. The Program Committee appreciates the effort of the external referees who helped the Program Committee reach their decisions.

I thank the general chair, Bhavani Thuraisingham, and the local chair, Kevin Hamlen, for their help in organizing ISC 2013, and Stacy Morrison for some of the local organization aspects. Moreover, Julie Weekly helped with secretarial work and Jeyakesavan Veerasamy with the registration process.

Finally, I would like to thank everyone who submitted their work to ISC 2013.

September 2015   Yvo Desmedt

ISC 2013

The 15th Information Security Conference was held in in cooperation with the International Association for Cryptologic Research, and the Department of Computer Science, The University of Texas at Dallas.

General Chair

Bhavani Thuraisingham   The University of Texas at Dallas, USA

Local Chair

Kevin Hamlen   The University of Texas at Dallas, USA

Steering Committee Chair

Masahiro Mambo   Kanazawa University, Japan

Program Chair

Yvo Desmedt   The University of Texas at Dallas, USA; and University College London, UK

Local Organizing Committee

Yvo Desmedt
Kevin Hamlen
Stacy Morrison
Bhavani Thuraisingham

Program Committee

Alessandro Acquisti	Carnegie Mellon University, USA
Elisa Bertino	Purdue University, USA
Jean Camp	Indiana University, USA
K.P. Chow	University of Hong Kong, SAR China
Ed Dawson	QUT, Australia
Sabrina De Capitani Di Vimercati	University of Milan, Italy
Yvo Desmedt (Chair)	The University of Texas at Dallas, USA; and University College London, UK
Manuel Egele	Carnegie Mellon University, USA

Additional Reviewers

Albanese, Massimiliano
Alcaraz, Cristina
Alimomeni, Mohsen
Balasch, Josep
Bilgin, Begül
Camp, Jean
Chen, Jiageng
Cheng, Shu
Devigne, Julien
Fong, Philip
Futa, Yuichi
Gierlichs, Benedikt
Gupta, Aditi
Hayashi, Takuya
Hori, Yoshiaki
Jiang, Shaoquan
Kawai, Yutaka
Kobayashi, Tetsutaro
Liu, Zhenhua
Livraga, Giovanni
Min, Byungho
Morozov, Kirill
Ohata, Satsuya
Persichetti, Edoardo

Sakai, Yusuke
Sendrier, Nicolas
Shebaro, Bilal
Shin, Seonghan
Shirase, Masaaki
Sirvent, Thomas
Su, Chunhua
Sun, Kun
Tibouchi, Mehdi
Tupakula, Uday
Van Herrewege, Anthony
Varici, Kerem
Wang, Haining
Wang, Pengwei
Wei, Puwen
Xeng, Xifan
Yanai, Naoto
Yiu, Siu Ming
Yoneyama, Kazuki
Yoshino, Masayuki
Zhang, Hui
Zhang, Tongjie
Zhao, Fangming
Zhou, Lan

Contents

Cryptanalysis

Block Ciphers and Stream Ciphers

Entity Authentication

Security of Operating Systems

Integrity Checking of Function Pointers in Kernel Pools via Virtual Machine Introspection

Irfan Ahmed$^{(\boxtimes)}$, Golden G. Richard III, Aleksandar Zoranic,
and Vassil Roussev

Department of Computer Science, University of New Orleans,
Lakefront Campus, 2000 Lakeshore Dr., New Orleans, LA 70122, USA
{irfan,golden,azoranic,vassil}@cs.uno.edu

Abstract. With the introduction of kernel integrity checking mechanisms in modern operating systems, such as PatchGuard on Windows OS, malware developers can no longer easily install stealthy hooks in kernel code and well-known data structures. Instead, they must target other areas of the kernel, such as the heap, which stores a large number of function pointers that are potentially prone to malicious exploits. These areas of kernel memory are currently not monitored by kernel integrity checkers.

We present a novel approach to monitoring the integrity of Windows kernel pools, based entirely on virtual machine introspection, called HookLocator. Unlike prior efforts to maintain kernel integrity, our implementation runs entirely outside the monitored system, which makes it inherently more difficult to detect and subvert. Our system also scales easily to protect multiple virtualized targets. Unlike other kernel integrity checking mechanisms, HookLocator does not require the source code of the operating system, complex reverse engineering efforts, or the debugging map files. Our empirical analysis of kernel heap behavior shows that integrity monitoring needs to focus only on a small fraction of it to be effective; this allows our prototype to provide effective real-time monitoring of the protected system.

Keywords: Virtual machine introspection · Malware · Operating systems

1 Introduction

Malware (especially rootkits) often targets the kernel space of an operating system (OS) for attacks [1], modifying kernel code and well-known data structures such as the system service descriptor table (SSDT), interrupt descriptor table (IDT), and import address table (IAT) to facilitate running malicious code. In other words, malware of this type installs hooks, which enables it to control

This work was supported by the NSF grant CNS # 1016807.

Y. Desmedt (Ed.): ISC 2013, LNCS 7807, pp. 3–19, 2015.
DOI: 10.1007/978-3-319-27659-5_1

the compromised system. For instance, such malware might hide the traces of infection, such as a user-level malicious process, or introduce remote surveillance functionality into the system, such as a keylogger.

Microsoft (MS) has introduced kernel patch protection (a.k.a. PatchGuard) in 64-bit Windows (such as Windows 7/8) to protect the integrity of kernel code and the data structures often targeted by traditional malware. It is implemented in the OS kernel and protected by using anonymization techniques such as misdirection, misnamed functions and general code obfuscation. In the presence of PatchGuard, it is hard for malware to directly install stealthy hooks in kernel code or modify the data structures monitored by PatchGuard. In order to avoid detection, modern malware has modified its targets to previously unexplored data regions. In particular, it targets function pointers in the dynamically allocated region in kernel space (a.k.a. kernel pools) [15–17]. Function pointers refer to the entry point of a function or routine and by modifying a function pointer, an attacker can cause malicious code to be executed instead of, or in addition to, the intended code. A demonstration of this type of attack appears in Yin et al. [2]. They created a keylogger by simply modifying function pointers corresponding to a keyboard driver in a kernel pool. Moreover, there are thousands of function pointers in the Windows kernel pools, which provides an attractive opportunity for an attacker to install stealthy hooks [2].

Current solutions such as SBCFI [3], Gibraltar [4], SFPD [5], and HookSafe [6] check the integrity of function pointers by generating hook detection policy and extracting information about function pointers by performing static analysis of the kernel source code. For example, they obtain the definitions of the kernel data structures that contain the pointers, and subsequently generate the traversal graph used to reach the data structures containing the function pointers. Unfortunately, these solutions are dependent on the availability of kernel source code and thus not appropriate for closed source OSs such as MS Windows.

More recently, Yin et al. presented HookScout [2] for checking the integrity of function pointers in MS Windows. It uses taint analysis [7] to trace the function pointers in kernel memory, and generates a hook detection policy from the memory objects that hold the pointers. The tool learns about the function pointers from a clean installation of the OS with typical user applications installed on it. The effectiveness of HookScout depends on how much contextual information is obtained about the function pointers during the learning phase. During the detection phase, if a target machine is attacked via modification of a function pointer not evaluated by HookScout during its learning phase, it will be unable to check the function pointer integrity.

Importantly, HookScout was developed on a 32-bit Windows XP OS and its current approach cannot be readily extended to 64-bit Windows 7:

- For detecting hooks, HookScout adds a `jmp` instruction at the entry point of each function whose function pointer is being monitored. The `jmp` redirects the execution to its own detection code. In 64-bit Windows 7, such patching of functions is not possible due to PatchGuard.

- HookScout obtains a list of function pointers for analysis by disassembling the MS Windows kernel in IDA Pro and traversing through the relocation table to identify the absolute addresses of function pointers. This works on 32-bit Windows XP since Windows uses absolute addresses in the kernel to refer to functions and thus an entry for such addresses exists in the relocation table. However, 64-bit Windows 7 uses offsets from the current instruction to refer to functions, because the code in 64-bit Windows is guaranteed to be aligned on a 16-byte boundary [8]. Thus, the relocation table does not contain entries for all the function pointers in kernel code.
- Finally, HookScout is implemented as a kernel module, which runs in the kernel space being monitored in the target machine. Thus, it is prone to subversion like any other security solution running inside a compromised machine, a limitation acknowledged by the authors of HookScout.

In this paper, we present HookLocator for MS Windows, which checks the integrity of function pointers in a virtualized environment and identifies function pointers that are maliciously modified in a kernel pool. HookLocator runs in a privileged virtual machine and uses virtual machine introspection (VMI) to access the physical memory of a target virtual machine (VM) running MS Windows. Since HookLocator runs outside the target VM, it is less prone to subversion and can obtain the list of function pointers directly from reliable sources in the physical memory of the target machine (such as kernel code and data structures monitored by PatchGuard), without disassembling kernel code or traversing the relocation table. The list is then used to find the instances of function pointers in kernel pool data. HookLocator does not require hooking to obtain the kernel pool data; instead, it uses kernel data structures maintained by Windows to track memory allocations to locate appropriate dynamic allocations in kernel pools. Our tool does not require access to source code to learn contextual information about function pointers; instead, it obtains all the information directly from the physical memory of the target machine. Thus, it continues learning from the target machine even during the monitoring phase, in order to obtain new information about the pointers under scrutiny.

The main contributions of this work are as follows:

- We propose a new approach to obtain the list of function pointers to be monitored directly from physical memory. The approach takes two memory snapshots of kernel code that are loaded into two different locations in memory and uses the differences to locate candidate function pointers. The locations are marked and then used to obtain the function pointers from the in-memory kernel code of the target machine.
- We propose a VMI-based hook detection approach to check the integrity of function pointers in kernel pools. The approach obtains the list of function pointers and their context information directly from the physical memory of the target system.
- We present a proof-of-concept prototype, HookLocator, for 64-bit Windows 7 to evaluate the effectiveness and efficiency of the approach.

– We thoroughly evaluate HookLocator on Windows 7 and identify a region in kernel pool, which provides a non-pageable target-rich attack surface. Hook-Locator is able to perform real-time monitoring on the region with a negligible amount of memory overhead.

2   Related Work

In addition to HookScout, which represents the current state of the art, a number of other techniques have been developed to combat kernel hijacking techniques. Since the inclusion of PatchGuard within Microsoft Windows, rootkits are no longer able to hook to kernel objects by modifying kernel code. This, in turn, has changed malware hooking techniques by redirecting their subversion efforts to the previously unexploited kernel heap. Therefore, much prior work has become obsolete, and not up to the task of reliably detecting rootkits. Many of the techniques, which we outline below, have substantial practical limitations as they rely on source code availability and/or incur unacceptable performance penalties.

Riley *et al.* implemented PoKeR [18], a rootkit behavior profiling engine. It relies on the OS kernel source code for static analysis or debugging symbols and type information for binary analysis. Furthermore, certain modules in PoKeR, such as context tracking and logging, run inside the VM allowing malware to tamper with such modules. PoKeR utilizes a resource intensive profiling engine, which incurs a significant overhead and severely limits its practical deployment.

Yin *et al.* developed HookFinder [19], a method that uses dynamic analysis of kernel code to identify and analyze malware hooks. Designed mostly for analytical purposes, HookFinder does not constantly check for rootkit activity, but rather provides a controlled experimental environment to analyze rootkits in. The tool is relatively resource intensive and, therefore, potentially detectible by the malware using performance monitoring.

Carborne *et al.* [5] implements a system called KOP to perform systematic kernel integrity checking by mapping kernel objects. KOP operates in an offline manner by capturing Windows kernel memory dumps and using the Windows debugger to obtain information about the kernel objects. KOPs static analysis utilizes Vistas source code to identify relevant data types, variables and structures.

Wang *et al.* propose HookSafe [6] a solution that creates a shadow copy of non-movable function pointers, and return addresses mapped to a hardware protected page aligned area. Requests to modify this shadow copy are intercepted and forwarded to the hypervisor module that inspects the validity of these requests. It requires knowledge of OS source code, which is not always available, as in the case of Windows.

Nick *et al.*'s State Base Control Flow Integrity (SBCFI) [3] system conducts periodic kernel control flow integrity checks. To do so, it relies on knowledge of kernel source code and binary files. As stated before, OS kernel source code for commodity OSs is usually not readily available.

Baliga *et al.*'s Gibraltar [4] relies on a separate observer machine to capture periodic memory snapshots of the target machine for integrity analysis. This idea is similar in spirit to our approach; however, Gibraltar's implementation relies on constantly capturing memory snapshots via Direct Memory Access (DMA). This poses a significant performance overhead on the observer machine and increases training time to almost an hour; it also requires additional hardware just for monitoring. Another shortcoming is that Gibraltar requires kernel source code for the initial static analysis.

In summary, each of the prior efforts surveyed exhibit at least one of the following limitations: (a) reliance on source code; (b) execution at the same level of privilege as the malware; (c) significant performance overhead; and (d) incomplete coverage of kernel space. The HookLocator overcomes most of these limitations and present a viable solution to kernel heap integrity monitoring.

3 Integrity Checking for Function Pointers

3.1 Environment

In a modern virtualized environment, a virtual machine manager (VMM) allows multiple virtual machines (VMs) to run concurrently on the same physical hardware. The virtual machines are called guest VMs, and are isolated from each other by the VMM. However, some VMMs also provide virtual machine introspection (VMI) capabilities that allow a privileged VM to monitor the system resources (such as physical memory) of guest VMs. HookLocator works in such a virtualized environment, where it runs in a privileged VM and accesses the physical memory of guest VMs through VMI. We also assume that the kernel code and the well-known kernel data structures inside the guest VMs are protected by PatchGuard or an alternate solution, such as VICE [9], System Virginity Verifier [10], ModChecker [11] and IceSword [12].

The remainder of this section describes HookLocator's architecture in more detail.

3.2 HookLocator Architecture

Figure 1 shows the architecture of HookLocator, which consists of four modules: extraction, search, learning, and pool monitor. The extraction module builds a list of function pointers from reliable sources in the physical memory of a guest VM, which is used by the search module to locate candidate function pointers in the kernel pool data. The learning module uses heuristics to identify the genuine function pointers, which are then monitored for integrity by the pool monitor. The details for each module are provided in the following sections.

Extraction Module. The extraction module obtains function pointers from kernel code and well-known data structures residing in the physical memory of a guest VM and builds a list that is subsequently passed to other modules in HookLocator. The data structures are well organized and have specific fields that either contain or lead to function pointers, which are used by the module to

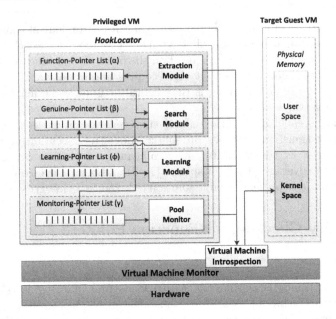

Fig. 1. HookLocator architecture. (Arrows directed towards the lists represent write operations; otherwise, they represent read operations).

extract the pointers. On the other hand, kernel code does not have such fields. Thus, extracting function pointers directly from the code requires a different approach. We employ two different methods to obtain function pointers from the code, which are described next.

The first method uses a cross-comparison approach and takes advantage of the relocatable property of Windows kernel code. Note that we cannot directly use the relocation table associated with kernel components, since the image loader often removes this table when the kernel is loaded[1]. Instead, we build a model from the kernel code, which identifies the absolute addresses in the code.

We accomplish this by comparing two snapshots of the kernel code loaded at two different locations in memory. The differences in the memory contents of the two loaded kernels are the identified absolute addresses, because the kernel has been loaded at different locations (the code itself is invariant). Figure 2 illustrates the process. If the addresses lie within the address range of kernel code, they are potentially kernel function pointers, and are tagged and stored within the protected VM. In order to extract function pointers from the kernel code of a target VM, the model is compared with the target VM's kernel code. The tags in the model identify the locations of the function pointers in the code, which are then obtained by the extraction module.

---

[1] While the `.reloc` section of the MS Windows kernel does contain the relocation table, the section is discardable as identified by the characteristic field in the section header.

```
00000000|  bc 44 2b 86 76 44 2b 86  f6 44 2b 86 44 45 2b 86   .D+.vD+..D+.DE+.
00000010|  7c 45 2b 86 f2 43 2b 86  64 44 2b 86 2c 44 2b 86   |E+..C+.dD+.,D+.
00000020|  ba 49 2b 86 24 b0 2b 86  bc 43 2b 86 62 48 2b 86   .I+.$.+..C+.bH+.
                          . . . .
0006c710|  30 01 83 f8 20 77 34 83  c1 04 3b 4d fc 72 eb 89   0... w4...;M.r..
0006c720|  55 10 ff 15 64 20 60 82  64 8b 0d 20 00 00 00 88   U...d `.d.. ...
                          . . . .
0011b8e0|  4e 8b 30 5b 46 d6 59 41  b8 71 17 c7 11 e7 34 0c   N.0[F.YA.q....4.
0011b8f0|  02 00 00 00 6e 74 6b 72  70 61 6d 70 2e 70 64 62   ....ntkrpamp.pdb
```

```
00000000|  bc 24 28 86 76 24 28 86  f6 24 28 86 44 25 28 86   .$(.v$(..$(.D%(.
00000010|  7c 25 28 86 f2 23 28 86  64 24 28 86 2c 24 28 86   |%(..#(.d$(.,$(.
00000020|  ba 29 28 86 24 90 28 86  bc 23 28 86 62 28 28 86   .)(.$.(..#(.b((.
                          . . . .
0006c710|  30 01 83 f8 20 77 34 83  c1 04 3b 4d fc 72 eb 89   0... w4...;M.r..
0006c720|  55 10 ff 15 64 00 65 82  64 8b 0d 20 00 00 00 88   U...d.e.d.. ....
                          . . . .
0011b8e0|  4e 8b 30 5b 46 d6 59 41  b8 71 17 c7 11 e7 34 0c   N.0[F.YA.q....4.
0011b8f0|  02 00 00 00 6e 74 6b 72  70 61 6d 70 2e 70 64 62   ....ntkrpamp.pdb
```

Fig. 2. Two snapshots of the .text section of the kernel code (ntoskrnl.exe) from 32-bit Windows 7. The kernel is loaded at the base addresses 00 10 60 82 and 00 f0 64 82.

The second approach is a simple pattern matching technique, which complements the first one in that it does not count on the relocation property of the kernel. It is specifically designed for 64-bit Windows to overcome the limitation of the first approach, due to the use of offsets rather than absolute addresses [8]. We analyzed a collection of kernel functions in the 64-bit Windows 7 kernel and found a useful pattern: after return instructions (opcode 0xC3), there are a number of NOP instructions (opcode 0x90) followed by the entry point of the next function. The extraction module uses the 0xC390 pattern to obtain a substantial list of function pointers.

Search Module. The search module performs three primary tasks. First, it obtains the kernel pool data from the kernel space in the physical memory of a guest VM; this involves extracting data structures that reference kernel pools in the memory, and identifying dynamic allocations in the pools.

Second, the search module searches for function pointers in the kernel pool data. To do this, it uses the function pointer list, built by the extraction module, and locates function pointers in the pool data.

Third, the search module decides whether to pass the pointer to the learning module or the pool monitor. This decision is based on the entries in the genuine pointer list, which contains contextual information about the pointers. This includes, among others, the name of the module that made the allocation containing the pointer, the size of the allocation, and the offset of the pointer from the base address of the allocation. When the search module finds a function pointer in a pool allocation, it obtains its information and searches for it in the genuine-pointer list. If it finds it in the list, it adds the pointer to the monitoring-pointer list so that the pool monitor will check the integrity of the pointer. If the search module does not find the pointer in the genuine pointer list, it adds it to the learning-pointer list so that the learning module can appropriately identify genuine pointers and add them to the genuine-pointer list.

Learning Module. A pointer located by the search module may or may not be genuine, because it can be confused with random data in the kernel pools that matches a pointer in the function pointer list. When the learning module receives a pointer via the learning-pointer list, it observes the pointer over its entire life span. Yin et al. [2] reported that 97 % of function pointers in Microsoft Windows do not change over their entire life span, which provides a basis to identify genuine pointers. If a pointer in the list does not change until the de-allocation of the memory where the pointer is located, the learning module assumes it is genuine.

HookLocator does not check the integrity of pointers that change during their life span. The rationale here is that attractive targets for attack are the pointers that: (a) have a long life span; and (b) do not change throughout their life span. This allows an attacker to create a persistent change in the control flow of the system. Such pointers may live in the system for long time, which apparently slows down the learning process, since the module cannot decide whether the pointer is genuine until its memory is deallocates. Thus, in order to identify such pointers efficiently, the learning module monitors the age of a candidate pointer and, if the age exceeds a given threshold, the learning module considers it to be genuine.

Pool Monitor. The sole purpose of the pool monitor is to check the integrity of function pointers and raise alerts upon any detected modifications. HookLocator maintains a monitoring-pointer list, which contains the pointers that are monitored by the module. Typically, the pointers being monitored do not change; however, if a pointer value is changed to another value within the address range of the kernel-code, or it is changed to NULL or from NULL to a value within the address range of the kernel code, the module considers the change in pointer value as legitimate; in all other cases, it raises an alert.

4   Implementation

HookLocator is fully implemented within a privileged VM and does not require modifications to the underlying VMM or running any components inside a guest VM. Thus, it works on any VMM (such as Xen, KVM, etc.) that has VMI support for physical memory analysis. Our current implementation is based on Xen (version. 4.1.2) on 64-bit Fedora 16 (version. 3.1.0-7). The Windows guests are Windows 7 SP1.

We use LibVMI [13] to introspect the physical memory of the guest VM to check the integrity of function pointers. Since LibVMI simply provides access to the raw physical memory of a guest VM, we need to bridge the semantic gap between raw memory and useful kernel data structures, which we further discuss in this section.

The extraction module builds a list of function pointers from kernel code (including kernel modules) and four tables: interrupt descriptor table, system service descriptor table, import address table, and export table. To extract information about function pointers from kernel code and import and export tables, the extraction module first gathers information about the in-memory kernel modules, including the name of each module, the module's base address, and the size of the module. Windows maintains a list of kernel modules in a doubly linked list. Each node in the list is represented by the data structure LDR_DATA_TABLE_ENTRY. The base address of the first node in the doubly linked list is stored in a system global variable PsLoadedModuleList, which is used by the extraction module to reach the list. Each LDR_DATA_TABLE_ENTRY also has FLINK and BLINK fields that contain pointers to the next and previous node in the list. The extraction module uses these fields to traverse the complete list of loaded modules.

For each module in the list, the extraction module uses the base address and size of the kernel module to extract the whole module from the memory. Each kernel module is in the portable executable (PE) format, which contains headers, code and data sections, and import and export tables. The extraction module parses each kernel module in the PE format to access the tables and the code. It further processes the code using the cross-comparison and pattern matching approaches discussed previously to obtain the list of function pointers. Moreover, the extraction module reads the base address and size of the IDT from the IDTR register and copies the entire IDT into a local buffer and further processes it to extract function pointers. It also obtains the system service descriptor table (SSDT) using the approach from a Volatility plugin [14]. The extraction module further processes the SSDT to obtain function pointers of system calls.

The search module locates function pointers in the Windows kernel pools by obtaining the data from each allocation in a pool and scanning it for matching function pointers. The allocations in a pool are classified into two types based on the allocation size: small chunks, and big allocations. A small chunk requires less than a page for an allocation. On the other hand, a big allocation requires more than a page for an allocation. MS Windows keeps track of these two types of allocations in separate data structures, which are also used by the search module to track and process kernel pool allocations. The big allocations are tracked through the PoolBigPageTable, with each entry represented by a POOL_TRACKER_BIG_PAGES structure. The search module finds the location of the PoolBigPageTable in the .data section of ntoskrnl.exe. A small chunk, on the other hand, resides completely within one page and an allocated page can have several small chunks (represented by POOL_HEADER structures), which are adjacently located in a sequence. The search module finds the allocated pages and further processes them to extract chunks.

The learning module observes pointers in the learning-pointer list. If a pointer does not change during its entire life span, i.e., until deallocation of the containing block, then the learning module considers it a genuine pointer. In order to discover the current validity of an allocation, the base address of the allocation can be examined, if the allocation is a big one. If the content of that address is not 1, it means it is a valid allocation. In case of a small chunk, the learning module looks at the 1st bit of the PoolType field in the chunk header POOL_HEADER. If it is set, it means the allocation is valid. There are some cases, e.g., when

Table 1. Number of function pointers found in the `.text` code section of kernel and its modules by HookScout's IDA plugin (H), our cross-comparison approach (C) and our pattern matching approach (P).

| Module name | Windows 7 | | | | |
| | 32-bit | | 64-bit | | |
	H	C	H	C	P
ntoskrnl.exe	5,388	5,390	401	200	2,960
hal.dll	537	537	0	0	537
ntfs.sys	147	147	0	0	416
i8042prt.sys	68	68	0	0	90
http.sys	212	212	0	0	518
disk.sys	11	11	0	0	65
volmgr.sys	18	18	0	0	35
kdcom.dll	21	21	0	0	20

a pointer has a long life span, which makes the first criteria less effective for learning. Thus, the learning module uses a threshold value based on the age of the pointer. If the age exceeds a certain threshold value, it considers the pointer as genuine. The learning-pointer list maintains the creation time of a pointer entry in the list, which the learning module uses to predict the age of a pointer.

The pool monitor observes the pointers from the monitoring pointer list until the allocation where the pointer is located is de-allocated. In this case, the module stops observing the pointer and also deletes the pointer entry from the list. If the pointer changes to `NULL` or to any other value within the address range of kernel code, the module considers such changes as legitimate and keeps observing the pointer. Otherwise, it raises an alert.

5   Evaluation

In this section we quantify the performance of each component of HookLocator. All experiments were performed on fresh installations of Windows 7 in VMs running on Xen (version. 4.1.2). We also installed several common applications: Skype, Google Chrome, MS Office 2010, Acrobat Reader, WinDbg, CFF explorer, and WinHex in order to understand the effects of user processes on kernel heap data.

5.1   Extraction Module

We use HookScout's IDA Pro plugin [2] as a baseline for our cross-comparison approach as both tools rely on the relocation property of Windows kernel. Table 1 summarizes the number of function pointers extracted from the code section of the Windows kernel by the different approaches.

Table 2. Number of function pointers from different sources in 64-bit Windows 7

Function pointer source name	Total number of function pointers
Kernel code	28,518
IDT	271
SSDT	401
IAT	12,142
Export table	4,887
TOTAL	46,219
Unique pointers	30,875

In the 32-bit case, the two methods are equally effective as they extract almost exactly the same number of function pointers (the number differs by 2 – and the exact reason for this is under investigation). In 64-bit Windows 7, HookScout and the cross-comparison approach do not work well, because the kernel code in 64-bit MS Windows 7 uses offsets to address the entry point of functions in instructions, instead of absolute addresses. Despite this fact, both the approaches showed one exception: they both obtained a small number of pointers from ntoskrnl.exe. HookScout finds 401 pointers (in ntoskrnl.exe) vs. 200 found by our cross-comparison approach. We further investigated the exception and it turns out that both methods find the pointers from the SSDT, however, HookScout analyzes the file, whereas we analyze the in-memory version. The file ntoskrnl.exe contains 401 absolute addresses for function pointers; however, when the kernel is loaded into memory, the addresses are adjusted according to where the kernel is loaded. After the adjustment, a new SSDT is created, which overrides the original. In the new SSDT, 201 of the 8-byte absolute pointers are replaced with 401 4-byte offsets from the base address of SSDT. Thus, half of HookScout's results are, in fact, false positives.

The byte pattern matching is much more effective and obtains an additional 2,960 pointers and this is the method we used to more accurately identify function pointers in 64-bit Windows 7. Table 2 shows a breakdown of the number of function pointers obtained from different sources. Since HookScout only works on 32-bit Windows, we present only our results for the 64-bit MS Windows 7. We found that 33.2 % of function pointers are duplicates; after excluding them, we are left with 30,875 distinct function pointers, which are used by the other modules of HookLocator.

5.2 Search Module

The search module goes through all memory allocations and scans for the function pointers identified by the extraction module. There are two types of allocations – small and big – in each of the paged and non-paged kernel pools. We used HookLocator to understand the number and distribution of pointers

Table 3. Correlation between the allocation size and the number of function pointers

Allocation type		Total size of allocations (MB)	Total number of pointers	Number of pointers per MB
Big allocations	Non paged pool	34.09	0	0
	Paged pool	79.13	1665	12
Small Chunks	Non paged pool	4.25	3201	753
	Paged pool	172.62	2297	13

in each of these cases. To obtain them, we ran HookLocator 10 times with a five-second delay between executions.

As shown in Table 3, we obtained the number of function pointers in each type of allocations and calculated the pointer density in each type of allocation. It is clear that allocations in the paged pool have a lower concentration of function pointers (12 per megabyte), which makes them less attractive for attack. More importantly, these allocations are pageable; if used by an attacker, there is always a chance that the page containing the modified pointer would be swapped out, which makes retaining control of the system flow more problematic.

Pages in the non-paged pool always reside in physical memory, so the pointers in the pool offer a more reliable means to subvert control flow. Our experiment shows that the big allocations in the non-paged pool have no function pointers, which leaves small chunks in the pool – with relatively high concentrations of function pointers – as the most target-rich attack surface. Thus, for the rest of our discussion, we narrow our focus to the small chunks in the non-paged pool as the area to be protected.

Table 3 shows that the small chunks in the non-paged pool consist of around 4 MB immediately after boot. Our first task is to understand whether there is a change in small chunk allocations and the number of pointers in the region when a user process is initiated. We obtained the total size of the small chunks in the pool before and after a user process is initiated. We ran HookLocator 10 times with a 5-s pause in between each run. The first four runs were performed before the initiation of a user process and obtained almost identical allocation sizes and number of pointers. After the fourth run, we initiated the process and obtained 6 more readings. The procedure was repeated for six different applications and their respective averages are given in Table 4.

Across the board, we see an increase of 1–2 % in the size of the small chunks and the total number of function pointers. Therefore, for the rest of our evaluation experiments we consider the system in both idle and active-user state.

5.3   Learning Module and Pool Monitor

The purpose of the learning module is to validate candidate pointers identified by prior modules and present them as genuine targets for integrity monitoring. The validation is based on age of the pointer and the observation that only a small number of kernel function pointers change over their life span [2]. Therefore,

Table 4. Effects of user process creation on small chunks in the non-paged pool.

Process name	Total size of allocations (in Kilo Bytes)			Total number of pointers		
	Before initiation	After initiation	%age increase	Before initiation	After initiation	%age increase
Skype	4,717.00	4,770.83	1.14	3,456	3,499	1.25
MS Word	4,751.25	4,793.33	0.89	3,491	3,512	0.61
MS Power-Point	4,769.25	4,789.33	0.42	3,503	3,515	0.34
Acrobat Reader	4,767.25	4,840.67	1.54	3,507	3,535	0.79
Windows Media Player	4,820.75	4,928.00	2.22	3,481	3,556	2.16
Chrome	4,789.75	4,863.33	1.54	3,472	3,533	1.76

to evaluate the false positives – our primary criterion for success – we study the life span of discovered function pointers and whether they are modified.

We consider two extreme cases: (1) when the machine is idle and there is no user activity; and (2) when the machine is actively in use. We use PCMark 7 [20] a performance-benchmarking tool to create a reproducible workload on the target machine, which is representative of user activities. It automatically performs several computational and IO activities on the system without any user intervention, including web browsing, image manipulation, video playback, and antivirus scanning.

We ran HookLocater for one hour to observe the function pointers in the small chunks of non-paged pool – the results are shown on Fig. 3(a/b). In the idle case, 8 % of function pointers end up de-allocated within the first six minutes, another 0.5 % are de-allocated by the end of the hour, and 91.5 % are still valid. None of the de-allocated pointers ever changed their value. In the active-user case, 69 % of pointers live no longer than 20 min, another 3 % are de-allocated by end of the experiment, and 28 % are still alive. Among pointers that have completed

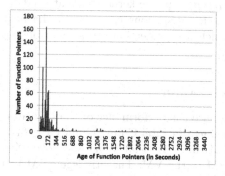
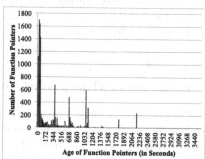

(a) VM is not in use by a user   (b) VM is actively in use by a user

Fig. 3. Life span of function pointers.

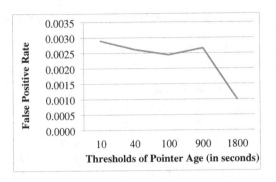

Fig. 4. False positive rate.

their life cycle, none changed their values. The interesting result here is that, it is easier to identify genuine pointers when the system is actively in use.

Evidently, for a practical system we need a time frame within which to make a decision whether a pointer is genuine, or not. When a genuine pointer is identified, it is included in the genuine pointer list, which is then handed over to the pool monitor for protection. If the assigned pointer is not genuine, it will generate false alarms and render our system less useful. In other words, we need to balance two requirements – *responsiveness* (identify breaches as soon as possible) and *accuracy* (have a low false positive rate).

We use a threshold parameter that determines how long we wait before we declare a pointer genuine. Figure 4 shows the measured false positive rate as a function of the age threshold of pointers. It is clear that even for a threshold of 10 s the false positive rate is 0.0028, which is a good starting point for tuning the system. Further investigation into the specific instances of false positives will, presumably, allow us to lower the rate even further but this study is outside the scope of this paper.

As a practical test of the effectiveness of the pool monitor we created a tool that synthetically mutates function pointers in the kernel pools at random. HookLocator raised an alert in all cases for suspicious changes. In the next section, we quantify the frequency at which the protection service can be run and these integrity checks be performed.

5.4   Performance Overhead of HookLocator

We built a small test environment to evaluate the performance of HookLocator. The physical machine that we used contained an Intel Core 2 Quad CPU (4 × 2.8 GHz) with 4 GB RAM. We used a VM running 64-bit Windows 7 over Xen (4.1.2), allocating one core and 1GB RAM to the VM. The privileged VM had Fedora 16 installed with the `3.1.0-7.fc16.x86_64` kernel.

We evaluated the HookLocator's execution performance on different types of memory allocations (big allocations/small chunks, paged/non-paged pools). We used two extreme test cases (1) when the target VM idle and (2) when it is

Table 5. Performance evaluation of HookLocator when VM is idle.

Allocation type	Memory overhead		No. of executions	
	MB^2	%age	per minute	per second
Big allocations	60	2.38	31	0.52
Small chunks (Paged Pool)	44	1.74	4	0.07
Small chunks (Non-paged pool)	24	0.94	115	1.91

Table 6. Performance evaluation of HookLocator when VM is actively being used.

Allocation type	Memory overhead		No. of executions	
	MB^2	%age	per minute	per second
Big allocations	65	2.58	31	0.52
Small chunks (Paged Pool)	47	1.87	4	0.07
Small chunks (Non-paged pool)	24	0.96	101	1.68

actively in use. Moreover, in both cases, we did not run any extra services on the privileged VM in order to allow HookLocator exploit all the available resources of the VM. We obtained the HookLocator's memory overhead and the speed of scanning a type of memory allocations.

We ran the HookLocator for a minute and counted the number of scans it performed. Tables 5 and 6 summarize the results for both the test case, which show that the HookLocator is able to scan the small chunks of non-paged pool more than once per second, which makes it suitable for even real-time monitoring. HookLocator also has a low memory overhead, compared to the typical physical memory available on a modern system.

6 Conclusion

In this paper, we argued that prior work does not provide reliable and practical protection against modern rootkits on Windows systems. Specifically, their shortcomings range from the need to analyze source code and execution in the same address space, to prohibitive overhead and no protection for the kernel heap. Also, they all focus on old, 32-bit Windows XP versions, and none is capable of working with 64-bit versions of Windows 7. To address these challenges, we developed a new approach based on VM introspection and implemented it in a tool called HookLocator. The main contributions of our work can be summarized as follows:

We address the biggest current threat to kernel hooking, which involves tampering with function pointers on the kernel heap. Microsoft's PatchGuard has effectively rendered most prior attack research ineffective, but does not protect the heap. Consequently, the kernel heap is becoming the primary vector for intercepting kernel control flow by current malware rootkits. Our approach conceptually works on both 32 and 64-bit versions of Windows. It does not rely on examining the source of the target OS; rather, it uses the relocatable property of Windows kernels as appropriate, supplemented by pattern matching to reliably identify kernel function pointers to be protected.

HookLocator works at a higher level of privilege than the potentially compromised VM, which makes it very difficult for any rootkit to cover its tracks. Further, since the tool runs in a separate VM and has a light performance footprint, it would be very difficult for a rootkit to detect that it is being monitored.

Our evaluation shows that our approach imposes minimal memory and CPU overhead, which makes it very practical. In particular, its light footprint enables real-time monitoring of the target VM, and easy path to scaling up the protection service.

References

1. Hoglund, G., Butler, J.: Rootkits: Subverting the Windows Kernel, 1st edn. Addison-Wesley Professional, Upper Saddle River (2005)
2. Yin, H., Poosankam, P., Hanna, S., Song, D.: HookScout: proactive binary-centric hook detection. In: Kreibich, C., Jahnke, M. (eds.) DIMVA 2010. LNCS, vol. 6201, pp. 1–20. Springer, Heidelberg (2010)
3. Nick, J., Petroni, L., Hicks, M.: Automated detection of persistent kernel control flow attacks. In: Proceedings of the 14th ACM Conference on Computer and Communications Security (CCS 2007), Alexandria, VA, USA, pp. 103–115 (2007)
4. Baliga, A., Ganapathy, V., Iftode, L.: Automatic inference and enforcement of kernel data structure invariants. In: Proceedings of the 24th Annual Computer Security Applications Conference (ACSAC 2008), Anaheim, California, USA, pp. 77–86 (2008)
5. Carbone, M., Cui, W., Lu, L., Lee, W., Peinado, M., Jiang, X.: Mapping kernel objects to enable systematic integrity checking. In: Proceedings of the 16th ACM Conference on Computer and Communications Security (CCS 2009), Chicago, IL, USA, pp. 555–565 (2009)
6. Wang, Z., Jiang, X., Cui, W., Ning, P.: Countering kernel rootkits with lightweight hook protection. In: Proceedings of the 16th ACM Conference on Computer and Communications Security (CCS 2009), Chicago, IL, USA, pp. 545–554 (2009)
7. TEMU. http://bitblaze.cs.berkeley.edu/temu.html
8. Russinovich, M., Solomon, D.: Windows Internals: Including Windows Server 2008 and Windows Vista, 5th edn. Microsoft Press, Redmond (2009)
9. Butler, J., Hoglund, G.: VICECatch the Hookers!, In: Black Hat USA, July 2004. http://www.blackhat.com/presentations/bh-usa-04/bh-us-04-butler/bh-us-04-butler.pdf
10. Rutkowska, J.: System virginity verifier: defining the roadmap for malware detection on windows systems. In: Hack in the Box Security Conference, September 2005
11. Ahmed, I., Zoranic, A., Javaid, S., Richard, G.G. III.: Mod-checker: kernel module integrity checking in the cloud environment. In: 4th International Workshop on Security in Cloud Computing (CloudSec 2012), pp. 306–313 (2012)
12. IceSword. http://www.antirootkit.com/software/IceSword.htm

13. LibVMI. https://code.google.com/p/vmitools/
14. SSDT   Volatility.   https://code.google.com/p/volatility/source/browse/trunk/volatility/plugins/ssdt.py?r=3158
15. Mandt, T.: Kernel Pool Exploitation on Windows 7. http://www.mista.nu/research/MANDT-kernelpool-PAPER.pdf
16. mxatone and ivanlef0u.: Stealth hooking: Another way to subvert the Windows kernel. http://www.phrack.com/issues.html?issue=65&id=4
17. Kortchinsky, K.: Real World Kernel Pool Exploitation. http://sebug.net/paper/Meeting-Documents/syscanhk/KernelPool.pdf
18. Riley, R., Jiang, X., Xu, D.: Multi-aspect proling of kernel rootkit behavior. In: The Proceedings of the 4th ACM European Conference on Computer Systems (EuroSys 2009), Nuremberg, Germany, pp. 47–60 (2009)
19. Yin, H., Liang, Z., Song, D.: HookFinder: identifying and understanding malware hooking behaviors. In: Proceedings of the 15th Annual Network and Distributed System Security Symposium (NDSS 2008), February 2008
20. PCMark 7. http://www.futuremark.com/benchmarks/pcmark7

Lightweight Attestation and Secure Code Update for Multiple Separated Microkernel Tasks

Steffen Wagner[✉], Christoph Krauß, and Claudia Eckert

Fraunhofer Institute AISEC, Munich, Germany
{steffen.wagner,christoph.krauss,claudia.eckert}@aisec.fraunhofer.de

Abstract. By implementing all non-essential operating system services as user space tasks and strictly separating those tasks, a microkernel can effectively increase system security. However, the isolation of tasks does not necessarily imply their trustworthiness. In this paper, we propose a microkernel-based system architecture enhanced with a multi-context hardware security module (HSM) that enables an integrity verification, anomaly detection, and efficient lightweight attestation of multiple separated tasks. Our attestation protocol, which we formally verified using the automated reasoning tool *ProVerif*, implicitly proves the integrity of multiple tasks, efficiently communicates the result to a remote verifier, and enables a secure update protocol without the need for digital signatures that require computationally expensive operations.

Keywords: Lightweight attestation · Microkernel tasks · Multi-context hardware security module · Trusted platform module

1 Introduction

To increase and ensure safety and security, microkernel-based systems provide separation mechanisms to isolate individual tasks from the rest of the system. The system enforces this strict separation by partitioning resources, e.g., CPU time or physical memory, and by virtualizing address spaces and devices. In addition, a microkernel such as *L4* [7] is very small in terms of code size and less complex compared to monolithic kernels, hence considered more trustworthy. However, a strong separation of potentially complex software components by a trusted microkernel does not necessarily imply the trustworthiness of the isolated tasks, which is a desirable property in most security-critical systems.

One approach to verify the trustworthiness of software components takes advantage of a hardware security module (HSM), such as a Trusted Platform Module (TPM) [14]. A TPM provides a cryptographic context and mechanisms to securely store integrity measurements, create (a)symmetric keys, and perform certain cryptographic operations, such as encryption. For a remote attestation, for example, load-time integrity measurements are signed with a private key inside the TPM and sent to a remote verifier together with a stored measurement log (SML) in order to prove the integrity of a system. However, since those digital

© Springer International Publishing Switzerland 2015
Y. Desmedt (Ed.): ISC 2013, LNCS 7807, pp. 20–36, 2015.
DOI: 10.1007/978-3-319-27659-5_2

signatures are based on asymmetric cryptography, more precisely RSA (with at least 2048 bit keys), they are quite large and rather expensive[1], even though the TPM includes dedicated cryptographic engines for signature calculation. The reason is that the TPM was never intended to be and, in general, does not act as a cryptographic accelerator. In addition, the TPM was also not designed to handle run-time integrity values, such as events or behavior scores generated by an anomaly detection, which thus cannot be used for a remote attestation.

Furthermore, TPMs do not support virtualization natively, since they only provide one cryptographic context for system-wide load-time integrity measurements and keys. That is why most existing concepts rely on the virtual machine monitor, also known as hypervisor, to virtualize the TPM [1,3,12]. However, as a consequence of the implementation in software, cryptographic secrets, e.g., keys, or integrity measurement values are not always handled inside the TPM. As a result, recent efforts explored and showed the feasibility to realize and manage multiple TPM contexts in hardware [4]. With multiple individual cryptographic contexts, a TPM-based HSM can provide each task with its own security context, which can be used to securely store, for example, keys and integrity measurements on a per-task basis. However, as a consequence of the isolated contexts, the number of digital signatures (and SMLs) in a remote attestation as specified by the Trusted Computing Group (TCG) increases with the number of contexts (i.e., tasks), which makes classical attestation even more expensive and also inefficient, especially on resource-constrained devices, e.g., smartphones.

To overcome these challenges, we first propose a microkernel-based architecture with an integrity verification and anomaly detection component that is enhanced with a multi-context HSM. Within the HSM, the load-time integrity values and events collected by an anomaly detection during run-time are stored in distinct contexts, so that task-specific keys, for instance, can be cryptographically bound to these values. As our main contribution, we then propose and formally verify a lightweight attestation mechanism, which mainly relies on symmetric cryptography and, thus, is able to efficiently verify multiple tasks in a microkernel-based system. Additionally, our attestation protocol is designed to enable secure code updates based on the integrity of existing security-critical tasks while eliminating the need for digital signatures.

The rest of the paper is structured as follows. In Sect. 2, we discuss related work on remote attestation with a focus on hardware-based attestation. In Sect. 3, we explain our scenario and attacker model. Section 4 describes the system architecture for the attestation and code update presented in Sect. 5. In Sect. 6, we analyze the security of our protocols. Finally, Sect. 7 concludes the paper.

2   Related Work

For a *hash-based remote attestation* as specified by the TCG [14], static load-time hash values of the components comprising the relevant software stack are

---

[1] That is because of the exponentiation operations used in RSA's encryption and compared to symmetric cryptography.

calculated during *authenticated boot* starting from a Core Root of Trust for Measurement (CRTM). That means the current software component in the boot chain measures the next one before executing it. Later, these integrity measurement values stored inside the TPM are signed and sent together with a SML to the remote verifier. However, since this approach primarily focuses on load-time integrity measurements for software binaries only, other schemes, such as *property-based* [8], *semantic* [5], or *logic-based attestation* [11], try to extend and generalize the attestation mechanism. For instance, property-based attestation aims at proving certain security characteristics rather than the integrity of certain software binaries. However, most of these attestation protocols still rely on quite expensive cryptographic operations—more precisely, digital signatures— which make them less suitable for an attestation of multiple separated tasks in a virtualized embedded system with limited resources, such as smartphones.

As a result, more recent efforts [10] proposed to increase the performance and efficiency by implementing a proxy component on the prover's system, which verifies that system locally and, thus, reduces the time between the attestation and the verification of the result. However, this approach still relies on traditional attestation mechanisms based on digital signatures to verify the hypervisor, virtualized device drivers, and the proxy component. Our mechanism, in comparison, focuses on a lightweight attestation, which relies on symmetric cryptographic operations rather than digital signatures and only requires very small messages to prove the integrity of multiple tasks including the microkernel.

3 Attestation Scenario and Attacker Model

In this section, we describe the scenario, which captures the settings for our attestation and secure code update protocol. We also specify the attacker model.

3.1 Scenario for the Attestation of Multiple Tasks

For our attestation and secure code update protocol, we define a $(\mathcal{P})$ and a $(\mathcal{V})$. The prover is a microkernel-based embedded system with different security- or safety-critical applications, such as a smartphone or a vehicle. $\mathcal{V}$, on the other hand, is a remote verifier, which is considered honest and trustworthy.

Without any loss of generality, we assume that the prover is a smartphone with a microkernel-based system architecture, which can execute various tasks in isolated virtualized environments. Typical tasks are the *baseband stack* for communications with a mobile network, *virtualized device drivers*, native tasks for *security-critical applications*, such as a secure email or VPN client, and *regular user applications* running on a rich *operating system*, e.g., a Linux-based Android. Since those tasks have different levels of criticality, they are strictly isolated by the separation mechanisms of the microkernel. However, an attacker might still be able to compromise tasks, e.g., by fuzzing their interfaces. That is why the prover has to provide verifiable evidence for the integrity of relevant security-critical tasks before the verifier grants access to restricted resources, such as emails, confidential documents, or updates for business applications.

For example, in our scenario, the smartphone might regularly connect to a company network via VPN, whenever the user needs access to company-internal resources. To establish a secure connection, the verifier in the company network first requires proof for the integrity of security-critical tasks, such as certain device drivers and the VPN client. Based on the attestation result, access to the company network is granted or denied. In case access is denied, e.g., because the VPN client was compromised, the verifier should be able to provide a code update based on the integrity of only the most basic security-critical tasks, such as the microkernel and the baseband stack. That way the prover is able to recover.

3.2 Attacker Model

In our scenario, the (A) can read and manipulate messages between the prover and the verifier as long as they are not encrypted or otherwise protected. More precisely, an attacker cannot decrypt an encrypted message or forge a correct message authentication code (MAC) for a modified message without the correct key. The attacker is also not able to invert cryptographic hash functions.

Additionally, as specified for most remote attestation protocols, we assume that hardware attacks are not possible. In particular, the security mechanisms of the HSM cannot be compromised by an attacker. That means we assume that the implementation of hardware-based security features, e.g., cryptographic engines, and firmware implemented in software are correct.

4 Microkernel-Based System Architecture with a Multi-context HSM

In security-critical systems such as described in the scenario, microkernel-based virtualization provides the necessary means to safely execute multiple tasks with different levels of criticality on the same hardware. Nevertheless, most critical systems require hardware-based security mechanisms, since they need to securely store cryptographic secrets, such as private keys, or integrity measurements. That is why those systems are often equipped with a HSM, which acts as a hardware-based security anchor and usually provides an internal context for the system-specific cryptographic information. However, most HSMs with a system-wide cryptographic context, such as a TPM, are not designed to separate and isolate security-sensitive information of individual tasks.

For this purpose, we propose a microkernel-based system architecture enhanced with an HSM that supports virtualization by providing multiple task-specific cryptographic contexts. As depicted in Fig. 1, which shows the system architecture that we designed and implemented using the $L4$-based $PikeOS$ [13], safety- and security-critical processes are realized as *native tasks*, whereas other non-critical components might be *POSIX tasks* or a *virtualized Linux instance*. All these individual tasks are isolated by the separation mechanisms of the kernel. However, the tasks are still able to communicate with other tasks in a controlled way, i.e., via kernel-based inter process communication (IPC) and individually distinct shared memory pages. The HSM proxy, for instance, receives commands via IPC and shared memory. It identifies the origin of the command, forwards it to the HSM, and receives the result, which in turn is communicated back to the respective source. Since all IPC channels and shared memory pages are isolated by the kernel, other tasks cannot read the commands or the result messages.

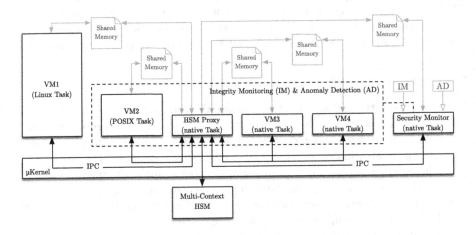

Fig. 1. Microkernel-based system architecture with multi-context HSM

There is, however, one exception: the *security monitor*. This component is one of the early tasks, which can start other tasks and is able to *measure the integrity* of a selection of tasks as indicated by the dashed box in Fig. 1. Since the security monitor, which is a critical task and hence realized as a native microkernel task, holds advanced capabilities, e.g., the right to directly access the memory of other tasks, it can effectively monitor their behavior and *detect anomalies*. As a result, the security monitor can store the integrity values measured at load-time in the task-specific context as well as keep a log of detected anomalies inside the HSM.

The design of our multi-context HSM, which is schematically depicted in Fig. 2, implements the functionality of a TPM and includes hardware-based security features, such as protected memory, a true random number generator (TRNG), and cryptographic engines for hash functions, MACs, and encryption algorithms like RSA or elliptic curve cryptography (ECC).

Based on the hardware components, the HSM firmware realizes *scheduling*, *multiplexing*, and *prioritizing of separate contexts*, which can handle cryptographic keys, store integrity measurements in shared and individual platform configuration registers (PCRs), and log atypical run-time events in per-context anomaly detection records (ADRs). That way each task can have its individual key hierarchy, anomaly detection status, and its very own set of hardware-based integrity measurement registers. However, the HSM also allows to (physically) share certain PCRs, e.g., to store common integrity measurements for the boot loader or the microkernel, in order to make the HSM design more efficient.

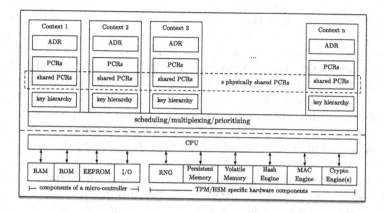

Fig. 2. Design of a multi-context HSM

5 Integrity Verification of Multiple Microkernel Tasks as Basis for a Secure Code Update

Based on the system architecture, we present our approach to implicitly verify the integrity of multiple separated microkernel tasks and communicate the result to a remote verifier without the need for expensive cryptographic operations. The attestation mechanism enables a secure code update of tasks based on the integrity of the system, in particular the microkernel and existing tasks.

The main idea of the attestation mechanism is to verify the integrity of a number of tasks locally rather than sending digitally signed integrity values to a remote verifier, which then has to check the signatures and evaluate the integrity values. Our attestation protocol, which we previously proposed for non-virtualized systems in [15], instead verifies the trustworthiness of tasks by loading task-specific keys into the key slots inside the HSM. This load operation is only possible if the specified tasks have not been tampered with, because the keys have been cryptographically bound to the correct integrity measurements of the tasks and their typical behavior, which is monitored by the anomaly detection component of the security task.

5.1 Notation

A *message authentication code (MAC)* is a cryptographic value, which is based on a shared symmetric key and can be used to verify the authenticity and integrity of a message. Formally, a MAC algorithm is a function that calculates a message digest dig with fixed length l for a secret key K and a given input m with virtually arbitrary size as $MAC(K, m) = dig = \{0,1\}^l$.

One method to construct a MAC algorithm is based on cryptographic hash functions, which are one-way functions with collision and pre-image resistance. Essentially, a hash function H compresses arbitrary-length input to an output with length l, that is $H : \{0,1\}^* \rightarrow \{0,1\}^l$. As an example for a hash-based

MAC, a *HMAC* generates a message authentication digest for data m based on key K as $HMAC(K, m) = H((K \oplus opad) \,\|\, H((K \oplus ipad) \,\|\, m))$, where $\|$ denotes a concatenation, $\oplus$ the exclusive or, *opad* the outer and *ipad* the inner padding.

For our attestation protocol, we presume that the load-time integrity of a microkernel task can be adequately described by a set of measurement values, which are securely stored in the PCRs of our multi-context HSM. Thus, the PCRs values, which cryptographically represent the task c, are referred to as *platform configuration* $P_c := (PCR_c[i_1], \ldots, PCR_c[i_k])$, where $i \in \{0 \ldots r\}$ and r is the number of physically available PCRs. To store an integrity measurement value μ in a PCR with index i that belongs to task/context c, the current value is combined with the new measurement value using $PCRExtend(PCR_c[i], \mu)$, which is specified as $PCR_c[i] \leftarrow SHA1(PCR_c[i] \,\|\, \mu)$ [14].

In addition to the load-time integrity measurements, the security task also monitors the run-time behavior of critical tasks. Based on machine learning algorithms [17,18], the anomaly detection component of the security task monitors, for instance, the order of system calls and assesses the probability for an attack. In case of an anomaly, an event $e = (m, p)$ is recorded by the security task using $ADRAdd(A_c, e)$, which securely stores a log message m in the ADR of task c and increases the *probability for an attack* stored in A_c with the value p. If the value in A_c exceeds a threshold T_c, the task must be considered compromised. In order to compensate for false-positives, the probability decreases over time very slightly, which might, however, be a security weakness and needs further research. As a consequence, we need to exclude false positives for now.

To cryptographically bind a key to a particular system state, which is also known as *wrapping*, the HSM links the key to the specified platform configuration and encrypts it with a public key (pk). A wrapped key, which is bound to a specific platform configuration P and encrypted with pk, is denoted as $\{K\}_{pk}^P$. This key can only be decrypted with the secret key (sk) and used by the HSM, if and only if the correct authentication value for the public wrapping key is provided and the current platform configuration P' equals the configuration P, which was specified when the key was wrapped. We extend this definition by also binding the wrapped key to an anomaly detection probability threshold T_c, that is $\{K\}_{pk}^{P_c, T_c}$. To load this wrapped key, the security monitor must also verify that the current probability stored in A_c is below T_c, which allows for more dynamic run-time verifications.

5.2 Cryptographic Keys

For each context c, an *integrity key* pair $K_c^{int} = (pk_c^{int}, sk_c^{int})$ is defined that needs to be loaded into the HSM for a successful attestation of the corresponding task. As shown in Fig. 3, the integrity keys are encrypted with the public portion of a shared non-migratable *wrapping key* $K^{wrap} = (pk^{wrap}, sk^{wrap})$ and cryptographically bound to a trusted platform configuration P_c and an anomaly detection probability threshold T_c, which is denoted as $\{K_c^{int}\}_{pk^{wrap}}^{P_c, T_c}$. The necessary authentication value, $Auth^{wrap}$, for loading the wrapping key is only known to the HSM and the remote verifier. The verifier also has access to the

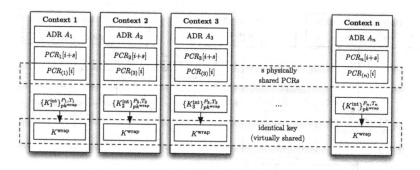

Fig. 3. Cryptographic keys, PCRs, and ADRs for multiple separated contexts

hash values of the wrapped integrity keys, which are combined with an *LoadKey* ordinal (*load*) and are denoted as $SHA1(load \,||\, \{K_c^{int}\}_{pk^{wrap}}^{P_c, T_c})$.

5.3 Integrity Verification and Attestation of Multiple Tasks

To verify the integrity of one or more microkernel tasks, a remote verifier $\mathcal{V}$ sends an *attestation request (req)* to the prover $\mathcal{P}$ as depicted in Fig. 4. The attestation request specifies k out of n microkernel tasks, which should be included into the attestation procedure, i.e., $req = \{c_i\}$ with $c, i \in \{1, \ldots, n\}$ and $|req| = k$.

Based on the request, $\mathcal{P}$ first transmits a set of random numbers $nonce_{\mathcal{P}_c}$, which are specifically calculated by the HSM for the selected tasks with context c. The random numbers are required to generate the authentication values $Auth_c$ and prevent replay attacks. $\mathcal{V}$ calculates the set of authentication values as

$$Auth_c = HMAC\big(SHA1(load \,||\, \{K_c^{int}\}_{pk^{wrap}}^{P_c, T_c}) \,||\, nonce_{\mathcal{P}_c} \,||\, nonce_{\mathcal{V}}, Auth^{wrap}\big), \quad (1)$$

where *load* is the ordinal for the *LoadKey* operation and $nonce_{\mathcal{V}}$ is a random number selected by the verifier (Fig. 4, step 1). This calculation of $Auth_c$ follows the authentication for TPM commands as specified by the TCG, more precisely for the load command [14, p. 72]. The authentication values $Auth_c$ and $nonce_{\mathcal{V}}$ are then sent to $\mathcal{P}$, which is now able to generate the command to load the task-specific integrity keys K_c^{int}. It is important to note that $\mathcal{P}$ has neither knowledge about nor access to $Auth^{wrap}$, which is only known to $\mathcal{V}$ and the HSM. As a consequence, $\mathcal{P}$ is not able to calculate the authentication HMACs without $\mathcal{V}$.

To load the keys K_c^{int} into the HSM and, thereby, generate the implicit proof for the trustworthiness of the corresponding tasks, $\mathcal{P}$ simply needs to generate a *LoadKey* command per context as shown in Fig. 4. When the HSM receives a command for context c, it verifies the authentication value $Auth_c$ and compares the current platform configuration P_c' with P_c, which has been specified when the integrity key was wrapped (Fig. 4, step 2). It also checks the anomaly detection record for any log entries (more precisely, whether the current probability value in A_c is above the probability threshold T_c specified during the wrapping step), which might indicate that the task was compromised during run-time. If the

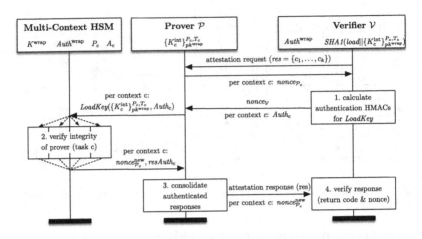

Fig. 4. Attestation protocol for multiple separated tasks

verification is successful and no anomalies were detected, the key is decrypted and loaded. However, if the key is already loaded into a key slot, an efficient HSM only verifies the wrapping conditions and omits the decryption.

After a successful load operation, the HSM generates HMAC-protected result messages and a set of new random numbers $nonce_{P_c}^{new}$ for each task c. The result messages mainly include a *return code (rc)*, which indicates the success of the load operation, the fixed command ordinal for the *LoadKey* operation (*load*), and the nonce selected by the verifier ($nonce_V$). Both values are protected by an HMAC, which is denoted as $resAuth_c$ and calculated as

$$resAuth_c = HMAC\big(SHA1(rc \,\|\, load) \,\|\, nonce_P^{new} \,\|\, nonce_V, Auth^{wrap}\big). \quad (2)$$

Again, it is important to note that the hash-based message authentication code (HMACs) are calculated based on $Auth^{wrap}$, which is the shared authentication value between the HSM and the verifier V. Before the prover P sends the new random numbers and the HMACs $resAuth_c$, which carry implicit proof that the attested tasks are still trustworthy, to V, the prover P can reduce the size of the *attestation response message (res)* by hashing the HMACs (Fig. 4, step 3), i.e.,

$$res = H(resAuth_c). \quad (3)$$

As a consequence, the efficiency of the transmitted attestation result can be increased without losing cryptographic information needed to verify the integrity of the selected tasks. However, if the attestation fail, the prover can also send the individual HMACs in a second attempt in order to allow for a recovery. In that case, the verifier only considers the most basic security-critical tasks and, in our scenario, grants access to a trusted version of the compromised software component as a failsafe. This recovery version can be provided using the secure code update protocol, which is described in more detail in the next section.

Finally, $\mathcal{V}$ verifies the response res by comparing it with a freshly generated hash res' (Fig. 4, step 4). First, $\mathcal{V}$ calculates a hash value $SHA1((rc' = 0) \,\|\, load)$, where $\mathcal{V}$ assumes that the load operation was successful, i.e., the return code, here rc', must be SUCCESS, which is defined as zero. Corresponding with Eq. 2, the hash value is then used to freshly calculate the task-specific HMACs based on the random numbers and the authentication value $Auth^{\mathrm{wrap}}$ as

$$resAuth'_c = HMAC\big(SHA1((rc') \,\|\, load) \,\|\, nonce_{\mathcal{P}}^{new} \,\|\, nonce_{\mathcal{V}}, Auth^{\mathrm{wrap}}\big). \qquad (4)$$

By hashing those values, i.e., $res' = H(resAuth'_c) \; \forall c \in req$ (cf. Equation 3), and comparing it to the attestation response, $\mathcal{V}$ can verify the implicit proof for the integrity of the selected tasks. The verifier can trust the individual attestation results, because they are protected by an HMAC and the shared secret $Auth^{\mathrm{wrap}}$, which is only known to the HSM and $\mathcal{V}$. In addition, the messages also include random numbers, which protect against replay attacks by providing verifiable proof that the attestation response message is indeed fresh.

5.4 Updating a Task After Verifying the Integrity of Existing Tasks

Based on the attestation protocol for existing microkernel tasks, we now describe our code update protocol, which allows to *update a task*, *creates verifiable proof*, and *maintains the ability to attest* both, the tasks and the system.

The main idea of the update protocol is that the prover creates and loads a new integrity key, which is specific to the new task, i.e., wrapped to the integrity values of the code update and the corresponding request. To ensure that the key is actually wrapped to the correct integrity measurements, the verifier provides a specific cryptographic authorization value, which only the verifier can calculate. When the HSM receives this authorization, it checks whether the new key will be wrapped to the correct integrity values before creating and wrapping the key. In combination with an efficient attestation of the code update, the verifier can ensure the authenticity of the initial update request and has verifiable evidence for the transaction. The prover, on the other hand, can use the new integrity key to create proof of a successful load operation in order to obtain the code update.

For a code update (U), the prover $\mathcal{P}$ initiates the protocol by sending a request (req) to the verifier $\mathcal{V}$ as depicted in Fig. 5 (step 1). Apart from the requested software update identified by ID_U, the message includes the cryptographic values to generate the authorization value referred to as $pubAuth_U$, which is used to create the new wrapped integrity key K_U^{int}. In more detail, the prover encrypts the authentication value to *use* and *migrate* the new integrity key, which are denoted as *usageAuth* (uA) and *migrationAuth* (mA) following the TCG specification [14]. The request also includes a nonce, which we refer to as $nonce_{\mathcal{P}}$ or $n_{\mathcal{P}}$ for short.

When the verifier receives the request from the prover $\mathcal{P}$, we assume that $\mathcal{V}$ might require to verify the trustworthiness of existing tasks for safety and security reasons before allowing to update or install a new software component. That is why $\mathcal{V}$ first initiates an attestation, which checks the authenticity and integrity of tasks running on $\mathcal{P}$'s system as described in the previous section.

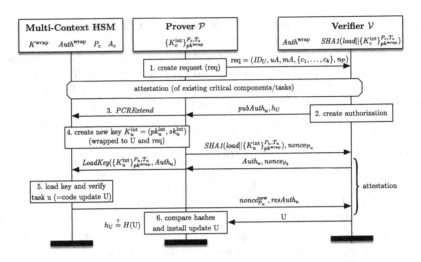

Fig. 5. Secure code update protocol

After a successful attestation of the relevant tasks, the verifier returns the encrypted authorization HMAC $pubAuth_U$ as well as a hash of the code update, denoted as h_U (Fig. 5, step 2). The HMAC authorizes the creation of the new integrity key and is calculated as

$$pubAuth_U = HMAC(sha1 \,||\, nonce_\mathcal{P} \,||\, nonce_{\mathcal{V}_1}, Auth^{\mathrm{wrap}}). \tag{5}$$

In this equation the hash value $sha1$ is generated as

$$sha1 = SHA1(wrap \,||\, usageAuth \,||\, migrationAuth \,||\, keyInfo), \tag{6}$$

where $wrap$ is the fixed ordinal for the command, which creates a wrapped key. The structure $keyInfo$ defines the cryptographic properties of the new key and follows the specification by the TCG [14, Part 2 Structures, p. 89]. In particular, the structure specifies the trusted platform configuration the key is wrapped to, which includes at least the integrity values of the *microkernel*, the *update* as well as the *request*. Additionally, the structure also specifies the threshold value T_c.

To create the new key, $\mathcal{P}$ first extends the PCRs of context U with the hash of the code update and the request (Fig. 5, step 3). After that, the prover creates the new integrity key K_U^{int}, which is encrypted with the wrapping key K^{wrap} and cryptographically bound to the trusted platform configuration, which is implicitly encoded into the HMAC $pubAuth_U$ (step 4).

After a successful generation of the wrapped integrity key, the prover $\mathcal{P}$ sends a hash of the key, $SHA1(load \,||\, \{K_U^{\mathrm{int}}\}_{pk^{\mathrm{wrap}}}^{P_u, T_u})$ and a random number $nonce_{\mathcal{P}_U}$ to the verifier, which initiates an attestation procedure for the code update (cf. Fig. 5). The verifier creates the authentication value $Auth_U$ and sends it to the prover together with a random number $nonce_{\mathcal{V}_2}$. $\mathcal{P}$ uses both values to load the new integrity key, which implicitly verifies the authenticity and integrity of the code update, more precisely the hash h_U (Fig. 5, step 5). The attestation response, in particular $resAuth_U$, is then sent to $\mathcal{V}$, which can check the result. If the attestation was successful, the verifier sends the actual code update to the prover. $\mathcal{P}$ can check the integrity of the code update by freshly generating the hash value $H(U)$ and comparing it to the previously received hash h_U, which has already been implicitly verified. If both values match, the code update is trustworthy and the prover can install the code update.

6 Security Analysis

In this section, we analyze the security of the proposed protocols.

6.1 Analysis of the Attestation Protocol

We start our analysis from the premise that hardware attacks, such as the TPM *cold boot attack* [6] or manipulations of the HSM communication bus [16], are out of scope. As specified in Sect. 3.2, we will mainly focus on software attacks.

Furthermore, we assume that the platform configuration reflects the load-time integrity of the system at any time, although this would require a periodic or on-demand integrity measurement architecture, such as IBM's IMA [9]. We also assume that the trusted platform configuration is created during authenticated boot and cannot be easily forged by exploiting software vulnerabilities, such as buffer overflows. In addition, we exclude the *time of check to time of use* (TOCTOU) problem, which might affect the validity of the attestation result.

Based on the attacker model and these assumptions, we now analyze our attestation protocol. In the first attack scenario, the $\mathcal{A}$ might try to extract and obtain the authentication values or cryptographic keys in order to compromise the attestation. However, the wrapping key K^{wrap} is non-migratable as specified in Sect. 5.2, which means it is always securely stored inside the HSM. In addition, the authentication value for the wrapping key $Auth^{\mathrm{wrap}}$, is only known to the verifier and never made public. Since this fact is very important for our attestation protocol, we will verify it formally in the next section.

$\mathcal{A}$ might also attempt to create and wrap a new integrity key to an insecure platform configuration, which does not include, for instance, any PCRs values, and replace the existing wrapped integrity key $\{K_c^{\mathrm{int}}\}_{pk^{\mathrm{wrap}}}^{P_c, T_c}$. However, this is not possible, because the wrapping key K^{wrap} is securely stored inside the HSM and the corresponding authentication value $Auth^{\mathrm{wrap}}$, is only known to the verifier (cf. previous attacks scenario). So in the formal verification, we will also check that the wrapping key K^{wrap} does not leave the HSM during the attestation.

In a different attack scenario, the adversary tries to compromise the task by manipulating the implementation. However, since the task is measured before it is executed, the verifier would detect the manipulation, because the integrity measurements in the PCR would be incorrect, the key could not be loaded, and an attestation would fail. The failure is indicated by the return code in the result message from the HSM. If the attacker compromises the binary and replays an old result message in order to convince the verifier that the load operation was successful, the verifier can detect the attack by checking the result, in particular the random number. Since this nonce is created by the verifier and does not match the old random number, the replay attack can be easily detected.

Finally, the attacker might try to compromise the behavior of a task during run-time. In this case, the security task detects an anomaly, e.g., in the number or order of certain system calls, by monitoring the behavior of the attacked task. As a result, the security adds an event (with a high probability, since it detected an attack) to the ADR, which is securely stored inside our HSM. So, if the prover tries to load the corresponding integrity key for the compromised task, the HSM prevents a successful load operation, since the current probability value is above the threshold T_c for any detected attack. As a consequence, the attestation fails.

6.2   Formal Verification of the Attestation Protocol

To substantiate our analysis, we have formally verified relevant security-critical properties of our attestation mechanism using *ProVerif* [2], an automated verifier for security protocols. We now discuss how our model implements certain aspects of the attestation protocol, which is also the core of the code update protocol.

The model for our remote attestation specifies a verifier, a prover, and an HSM, in this case with two contexts for simplicity (cf. Appendix A, Listing 1.1). To initiate the attestation protocol, the verifier creates a request and in turn receives the corresponding random numbers. The verifier then calculates the authentication values Authc1 and Authc2 (lines 9 and 11) based on the hash of the wrapped integrity keys, i.e., hWrappedKint1 and hWrappedKint2, the random numbers noncePc1 and noncePc2 as well as nonceV. The key for the both HMACs is AuthWrap. The prover receives the HMACs and loads the wrapped keys, wrappedKey1 and wrappedKey2 (lines 22 and 24). The HSM verifies the nonces (lines 34 and 39), compares the current platform configuration cpc with the trusted one tpc (lines 35 and 40), and checks if the probability value p matches T (lines 36 and 41; simplified with $T = 0$, i.e., no anomalies tolerated). Finally, the HSM generates the result message. The prover forwards the result and the nonces noncePc1New and noncePc2New to the verifier, which then checks the attestation result. So, the verifier assumes a successful load operation (hence the hardcoded value true in lines 14 and 15) and calculates a fresh result hash res (line 16), which verifies nonceV and the trustworthiness of the selected tasks.

In *ProVerif*, our formal verification is automated with queries, which check if the authentication value AuthWrap (line 1) or the wrapping key Kwrap (line 2) are disclosed during the attestation. A third query additionally checks whether the attestation was successful (line 3), which is indicated by an event that is created only if the attestation response can be successfully verified. The results show that *ProVerif* cannot find an attack path for the AuthWrap or Kwrap and that the attestation is successful if all verification steps are successfully passed.

6.3   Analysis of the Code Update Protocol

To analyze the security of the code update protocol, we now discuss different attack scenarios, where an adversary might try to compromise the code update.

For the first attack, we presume that $\mathcal{A}$ tries to compromise the integrity of the code update by replacing it with a manipulated version. However, this is not possible, since $\mathcal{P}$ generates a new integrity key, which is wrapped to the untampered code update by $\mathcal{V}$. To receive the actual code update, $\mathcal{P}$ needs to successfully load the new integrity key in order to be able to send the correct attestation result to $\mathcal{V}$. To verify the integrity of the code update, $\mathcal{P}$ compares a fresh hash of the code update with the previously received hash h_U, which must have been part of the wrapped key and the trusted platform configuration. $\mathcal{P}$ also implicitly verifies the authenticity, because only $\mathcal{V}$ knows the authentication value $Auth^{\mathrm{wrap}}$ for the wrapping key K^{wrap} and is able to generate the correct authorization value $pubAuth$ for creating the new wrapped integrity key.

To ensure the authenticity of the code update request, the verifier authorizes the creation of a new integrity key, which is cryptographically bound not only to the trusted platform configuration of the system and the task, but also the code update request. That way, the prover has to extend the hash of the code update request to PCRs of the task in order to be able to load the newly created integrity key during the attestation procedure. If an adversary manipulates the code update request, the verifier creates an authorization value $pubAuth$ for a false request and $\mathcal{P}$ cannot load the key, because $\mathcal{P}$ extended a different hash. As a result, the attestation fails and the verifier does not provides the actual code update in the final step of the protocol.

7   Conclusion

In this paper, we have presented a protocol for attesting the trustworthiness of multiple microkernel tasks. Compared to most existing attestation schemes, which mostly rely on expensive cryptographic operations, we show that our lightweight attestation mechanism can implicitly verify the integrity of multiple isolated microkernel tasks, securely communicate the result to a remote verifier, and enable secure code updates while eliminating the need for digital signatures.

As future work, we plan to evaluate our implementation in more detail. In comparison to existing attestation protocols, in particular classical remote attestation, we expect that our cryptographic integrity proof is more than ten times smaller, because our protocol mostly relies on symmetric cryptographic operations. When attesting more than one task with their own cryptographic contexts, this difference should become rather significant. Without even considering SMLs, we can already say that in this case our cryptographic integrity proof still only needs a constant size, whereas the number of digital signatures used in classical remote attestation increase with the number of tasks.

Acknowledgments. Parts of this work were funded by the *HIVE* project (GN: 01BY1200A) of the German Federal Ministry of Education and Research.

A ProVerif Code for the Attestation Mechanism

```
1   free AuthWrap:symKey [private].  query attacker(AuthWrap).
2   free Kwrap:sKey [private].       query attacker(Kwrap).
3   event successfulAttestation.     query event(successfulAttestation).
4
5   let Verifier(AuthWrap:symKey, hWrappedKint1:hash, hWrappedKint2:hash) =
6       new req:attestationRequest; out(c2, req);
7       in(c2, noncePc1:bitstring); in(c2, noncePc2:bitstring);
8       new nonceV:bitstring;
9       let Authc1= MAC(c(c(h2Bs(hWrappedKint1), noncePc1), nonceV), AuthWrap
            ) in
10      out(c2, Authc1);
11      let Authc2= MAC(c(c(h2Bs(hWrappedKint2), noncePc2), nonceV), AuthWrap
            ) in
12      out(c2, Authc2); out(c2, nonceV); in(c2, res:hash);
13      in(c2, noncePc1New:bitstring); in(c2, noncePc2New:bitstring);
14      let resAuth1 = MAC(c(c(h2Bs(SHA1(cBoolBs(true, load))), noncePc1New),
            nonceV), AuthWrap)  in
15      let resAuth2 = MAC(c(c(h2Bs(SHA1(cBoolBs(true, load))), noncePc2New),
            nonceV), AuthWrap)  in
16      if res = SHA1(c(MAC2Bs(resAuth1), MAC2Bs(resAuth2))) then
17          event successfulAttestation; 0.
18
19  let Prover(wrappedKint1:wKey, wrappedKint2:wKey, noncePc1:bitstring,
            noncePc2:bitstring) =
20      in(c2, req:attestationRequest); out(c2, noncePc1); out(c2, noncePc2);
21      in(c2, Authc1:mac); in(c2, Authc2:mac); in(c2, nonceV:bitstring);
22      let cmd1 = createLoadKeyCmd(wrappedKint1, Authc1, noncePc1, nonceV)
            in
23      out(c1, cmd1);
24      let cmd2 = createLoadKeyCmd(wrappedKint2, Authc2, noncePc2, nonceV)
            in
25      out(c1, cmd2);
26      in(c1, res:hash);
27      in(c1, noncePc1New:bitstring); in(c1, noncePc2New:bitstring);
28      out(c2, res); out(c2, noncePc1New); out(c2, noncePc2New); 0.
29
30  let HSM(AuthWrap:symKey, noncePc1:bitstring, noncePc2:bitstring, cpc1:
            PConf, p1:ADR, cpc2:PConf, p2:ADR) =
31      new noncePc1New:bitstring; new noncePc2New:bitstring;
32      in(c1, cmd1:LoadKeyCommand); in(c1, cmd2:LoadKeyCommand);
33      if getAuthc(cmd1) = MAC(c(c(h2Bs(SHA1(c(load, wKey2Bs(getWrappedKey(
            cmd1))))), noncePc1), getNonceV(cmd1)), AuthWrap) then
34      if noncePc1 = getNoncePc(cmd1) then      (* comment: check noncePc1
            *)
35      if cpc1 = pc(getWrappedKey(cmd1)) then   (* comment: check P_1 *)
36      if p1 = ard(getWrappedKey(cmd1)) then    (* comment: check ADR_1 *)
37      let resAuth1 = MAC(c(c(h2Bs(SHA1(cBoolBs(true, load))), noncePc1New),
            getNonceV(cmd1)), AuthWrap) in
38      if getAuthc(cmd2) = MAC(c(c(h2Bs(SHA1(c(load, wKey2Bs(getWrappedKey(
            cmd2))))), noncePc2), getNonceV(cmd2)), AuthWrap) then
39      if noncePc2 = getNoncePc(cmd2) then      (* comment: check noncePc1
            *)
40      if cpc2 = pc(getWrappedKey(cmd2)) then   (* comment: check P_2 *)
41      if p2 = ard(getWrappedKey(cmd2)) then    (* comment: check ADR_2 *)
42      let resAuth2 = MAC(c(c(h2Bs(SHA1(cBoolBs(true, load))), noncePc2New),
            getNonceV(cmd2)), AuthWrap) in
43      let res = SHA1(c(MAC2Bs(resAuth1), MAC2Bs(resAuth2))) in
44      out(c1, res); out(c1, noncePc1New); out(c1, noncePc2New); 0.
45
46  process
47      new noncePc1:bitstring; new noncePc2:bitstring;
```

```
48    new Kint1:intKey; new Kint2:intKey;
49    let wKint1 = wrapKey(Kint1, pk(Kwrap), tpc1, T1) in    (* cf. Sect.
      5.1 *)
50    let wKint2 = wrapKey(Kint2, pk(Kwrap), tpc2, T2) in    (* cf. Sect.
      5.1 *)
51    (!Verifier(AuthWrap, SHA1(c(load, wKey2Bs(wKint1))), SHA1(c(load,
      wKey2Bs(wKint2))))) | (!Prover(wKint1, wKint2, noncePc1, noncePc2
      )) | (!HSM(AuthWrap, noncePc1, noncePc2, tpc1, T1, tpc2, T2))
```

Listing 1.1. ProVerif Code for the Attestation Mechanism (excerpt)

References

1. Berger, S., Cáceres, R., Goldman, K.A., Perez, R., Sailer, R., Doorn, L.: vTPM: virtualizing the Trusted Platform Module. In: Proceedings of the 15th Conference on USENIX Security Symposium, vol. 15 (2006)
2. Blanchet, B.: An efficient cryptographic protocol verifier based on prolog rules. In: Proceedings of the 14th IEEE Workshop on Computer Security Foundations, CSFW 2001. IEEE Computer Society, Washington, DC (2001)
3. England, P., Loeser, J.: Para-virtualized TPM sharing. In: Lipp, P., Sadeghi, A.-R., Koch, K.-M. (eds.) Trust 2008. LNCS, vol. 4968, pp. 119–132. Springer, Heidelberg (2008)
4. Feller, T., Malipatlolla, S., Kasper, M., Huss, S.A.: dctpm: a generic architecture for dynamic context management. In: Athanas, P.M., Becker, J., Cumplido, R. (eds.) ReConFig, pp. 211–216. IEEE Computer Society (2011)
5. Haldar, V., Chandra, D., Franz, M.: Semantic remote attestation: a virtual machine directed approach to trusted computing. In: Proceedings of the 3rd Conference on Virtual Machine Research and Technology Symposium, Berkeley, CA, USA (2004)
6. Halderman, J.A., Schoen, S.D., Heninger, N., Clarkson, W., Paul, W., Calandrino, J.A., Feldman, A.J., Appelbaum, J., Felten, E.W.: Lest we remember: cold-boot attacks on encryption keys. Commun. ACM 52(5), 91–98 (2009)
7. Liedtke, J.: Microkernels must and can be small. In: Proceedings of the 5th IEEE International Workshop on Object-Orientation in Operating Systems (IWOOOS), Seattle, WA, October 1996. http://l4ka.org/publications/
8. Sadeghi, A.R., Stüble, C.: Property-based attestation for computing platforms: caring about properties, not mechanisms. In: Proceedings of the 2004 Workshop on New Security Paradigms, NSPW 2004, pp. 67–77. ACM, New York (2004)
9. Sailer, R., Zhang, X., Jaeger, T., van Doorn, L.: Design and implementation of a TCG-based integrity measurement architecture. In: Proceedings of the 13th Conference on USENIX Security Symposium, vol. 13, Berkeley, CA, USA (2004)
10. Schiffman, J., Vijayakumar, H., Jaeger, T.: Verifying system integrity by proxy. In: Katzenbeisser, S., Weippl, E., Camp, L.J., Volkamer, M., Reiter, M., Zhang, X. (eds.) Trust 2012. LNCS, vol. 7344, pp. 179–200. Springer, Heidelberg (2012)
11. Sirer, E.G., de Bruijn, W., Reynolds, P., Shieh, A., Walsh, K., Williams, D., Schneider, F.B.: Logical attestation: an authorization architecture for trustworthy computing. In: Proceedings of the Twenty-Third ACM Symposium on Operating Systems Principles, SOSP 2011, pp. 249–264. ACM, New York (2011)
12. Stumpf, F., Eckert, C.: Enhancing trusted platform modules with hardware-based virtualization techniques. In: Emerging Security Information, Systems and Technologies, pp. 1–9 (2008)
13. SYSGO AG: PikeOS. http://www.sysgo.com/
14. Trusted Computing Group: TPM Main Specification Version 1.2 rev. 116 (2011). http://www.trustedcomputinggroup.org/resources/tpm_main_specification

15. Wagner, S., Wessel, S., Stumpf, F.: Attestation of mobile baseband stacks. In: Xu, L., Bertino, E., Mu, Y. (eds.) NSS 2012. LNCS, vol. 7645, pp. 29–43. Springer, Heidelberg (2012)

16. Winter, J., Dietrich, K.: A Hijacker's guide to the LPC bus. In: Petkova-Nikova, S., Pashalidis, A., Pernul, G. (eds.) EuroPKI 2011. LNCS, vol. 7163, pp. 176–193. Springer, Heidelberg (2012)

17. Xiao, H., Eckert, C.: Lazy Gaussian process committee for real-time online regression. In: 27th AAAI Conference on Artificial Intelligence, AAAI 2013. AAAI Press, Washington, July 2013

18. Xiao, H., Xiao, H., Eckert, C.: Learning from multiple observers with unknown expertise. In: Pei, J., Tseng, V.S., Cao, L., Motoda, H., Xu, G. (eds.) PAKDD 2013, Part I. LNCS, vol. 7818, pp. 595–606. Springer, Heidelberg (2013)

Secret Sharing

The Security Defect of a Multi-pixel Encoding Method

Teng Guo[1]([✉]), Feng Liu[2], ChuanKun Wu[2], YoungChang Hou[3],
YaWei Ren[2,4,5], and Wen Wang[2,4]

[1] School of Information Science and Technology,
University of International Relations, Beijing 100091, China
guoteng.cas@gmail.com
[2] State Key Laboratory of Information Security,
Institute of Information Engineering, Chinese Academy of Sciences,
Beijing 100093, China
{liufeng,ckwu,wangwen,renyawei}@iie.ac.cn
[3] Department of Information Management, Tamkang University,
Taipei County 251, Taiwan
ychou@mail.im.tku.edu.tw
[4] University of Chinese Academy of Sciences, Beijing 100190, China
[5] School of Information Management,
Beijing Information Science and Technology University,
Beijing 100192, China

Abstract. A visual cryptography scheme (VCS) encodes a secret image into several share images, such that stacking sufficient number of shares will reveal the secret while insufficient number of shares provide no information about the secret. The beauty of VCS is that the secret can be decoded by human eyes without needing any cryptography knowledge nor any computation. Variance is first introduced by Hou et al. in 2005 to evaluate the visual quality of size invariant VCS. Liu et al. in 2012 thoroughly verified this idea and significantly improved the visual quality of previous size invariant VCSs. In this paper, we first point out the security defect of Hou et al.'s multi-pixel encoding method (MPEM) that if the secret image has simple contours, each single share will reveal the content of that secret image. Then we use variance to explain the above security defect.

Keywords: Visual cryptography · Variance · Security defect

1 Introduction

Naor and Shamir first introduced the concept of k out of n threshold visual cryptography scheme in [12], abbreviated as (k,n)-VCS, which splits a secret

This paper is previously posted on Cryptology ePrint Archive: Report 2012/315.

Y. Desmedt (Ed.): ISC 2013, LNCS 7807, pp. 39–48, 2015.
DOI: 10.1007/978-3-319-27659-5_3

image into n shares in such a way that the stacking of any k shares can reveal the secret image but any less than k shares should provide no information (in the information-theoretic sense) of the secret image. Ateniese et al. extended the model of Naor and Shamir to general access structure in [1]. Suppose the participant set is denoted as $P = \{1, 2, 3, \ldots, n\}$, a general access structure is a specification of qualified participant sets $\Gamma_{Qual} \subseteq 2^P$ and forbidden participant sets $\Gamma_{Forb} \subseteq 2^P$, where 2^P is the power set of P. Any participant set $X \in \Gamma_{Qual}$ can reveal the secret by stacking their shares, but any participant set $Y \in \Gamma_{Forb}$ cannot obtain any information of the secret image. Obviously, $\Gamma_{Qual} \cap \Gamma_{Forb} = \emptyset$ should always hold. In (k, n) threshold access structure, $\Gamma_{Qual} = \{B \subseteq P : |B| \geq k\}$ and $\Gamma_{Forb} = \{B \subseteq P : |B| \leq k - 1\}$.

Ito et al. introduced the concept of size invariant visual cryptography scheme (SIVCS) in [13], which has no pixel expansion. In SIVCS, both white and black secret pixels may be decoded as black, which results in deteriorated visual quality compared to VCS, in which a white (resp. black) secret pixel is surely decoded as white (resp. black). To improve SIVCS's visual quality, Hou et al. proposed the multi-pixel encoding method (MPEM) in [9]. Compared to VCS (see [12] and [1]), the main advantage of SIVCS and MPEM is that they are both of no pixel expansion, while the best pixel expansion of VCS is exponential large (e.g. the best pixel expansion of (n, n)-VCS is 2^{n-1}). In recent years, many researchers try to implement SIVCS with nice properties by an algorithm, referring to [3,4,7,8,14]. Other research lines include parameter optimization in VCS [2,15], color VCS [5,6,10].

Hou et al. introduced variance to compare the visual quality of SIVCS and that of MPEM in [9]. Liu et al. thoroughly verify, both analytically and experimentally, the idea of using variance to evaluate the visual quality of SIVCS in [11]. In this paper, we first point out the security defect of Hou et al.'s MPEM that if the secret image has simple contours, each single share will reveal the content of that secret image. Then we use variance to explain the above security defect. To the best of our knowledge, this is the first effort that uses variance to analyze a single share image, since all previous studies [9,11] use variance to analyze the decoded image. Besides, our study adds a new perspective about the security of VCS.

This paper is organized as follows. In Sect. 2, we give some preliminaries of VCS. In Sect. 3, we use variance to explain the security defect that we find in Hou et al.'s scheme. In Sect. 4, we discuss the influence of our result to real world application and future researches. The paper is concluded in Sect. 5.

2   Preliminaries

In this section, we first give the definition of SIVCS. Then we give a brief description of the MPEM proposed by Hou et al. in [9].

Before moving any further, we first set up our notations. Let X be a subset of $\{1, 2, \cdots, n\}$ and let $|X|$ be the cardinality of X. For any $n \times m$ Boolean matrix M, let $M[X]$ denote the matrix M constrained to rows of X, then $M[X]$ is a

$|X| \times m$ matrix. We denote by $H(M[X])$ the Hamming weight of the OR result of rows of $M[X]$.

Definition 1 (SIVCS [13, 16]). *The two $n \times m$ Boolean matrices (S_0, S_1) constitute a $(\{\Gamma_{Qual}, \Gamma_{Forb}\}, m, n)$-SIVCS if the following conditions are satisfied:*

1. *(Contrast) For any participant set $X \in \Gamma_{Qual}$, we denote $l_X = H(S_0[X])$, and denote $h_X = H(S_1[X])$. It should hold that $0 \leq l_X < h_X \leq m$.*
2. *(Security) For any participant set $Y \in \Gamma_{Forb}$, $S_0[Y]$ and $S_1[Y]$ are equal up to a column permutation.*

S_0 and S_1 are also referred to as the white and black basis matrices respectively. In a SIVCS [13], to share a black (resp. white) pixel, we randomly choose a column from the black (resp. white) basis matrix, and then distribute the i-th row of the column to participant i. In a $(\{\Gamma_{Qual}, \Gamma_{Forb}\}, n)$-SIVCS, considering qualified participant set $X \in \Gamma_{Qual}$, a black pixel is recovered as black with probability $\frac{h_X}{m}$, which is higher than the probability $\frac{l_X}{m}$ that a white pixel is recovered as black. Hence we can perceive the secret from the overall view. The average contrast of qualified participant set X is defined as $\bar{\alpha}_X = \dfrac{h_X - l_X}{m}$ and the average contrast of the scheme is defined as $\bar{\alpha} = \min\limits_{X \in \Gamma_{Qual}} \bar{\alpha}_X$.

In the following, the MPEM proposed by Hou et al. in [9] is described as Construction 1 for reader's convenience, which encrypts multiple pixels (non-adjacent for most cases) simultaneously.

Construction 1. *Let M_0 (resp. M_1) be the $n \times r$ white (resp. black) basis matrix. Each time, we take r successive white (resp. black) pixels as an white (resp. black) encoding sequence.*

1. *Take r successive white (resp. black) pixels, which have not been encrypted yet, from the secret image sequentially. Record the positions of the r pixels as $(p_1, p_2, \ldots, p_r)$.*
2. *Permute the columns of M_0 (resp. M_1) randomly.*
3. *Fill in the pixels in the positions $p_1, p_2, \ldots, p_r$ of the i-th share with the r colors of the i-th row of the permuted matrix, respectively.*
4. *Repeat step (1) to step (3) until every white (resp. black) pixel is encrypted.*

3 The Security Defect of MPEM

This section is divided into two parts: 1, our discovery of MPEM's security defect; 2, the explanation of the above security defect.

3.1 Our Discovery of MPEM's Security Defect

We use the (2,2)-MPEM proposed in [9] to encode image "Pythagoras" and image "Airplane", where the experimental results are given in Figs. 1 and 2.

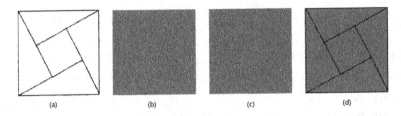

Fig. 1. Experimental results for (2,2)-MPEM: (a) the original secret image with image size 340×340, (b) share 1 with image size 340×340, (c) share 2 with image size 340×340, (d) stacked image with image size 340×340

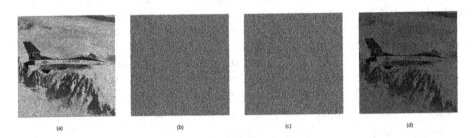

Fig. 2. Experimental results for (2,2)-MPEM: (a) the original secret image with image size 512×512, (b) share 1 with image size 512×512, (c) share 2 with image size 512×512, (d) stacked image with image size 512×512

From images (b) and (c) in Fig. 1, we can perceive the content of image (a), perhaps with some zooming, like 300 % or 400 %. Hence we claim that the MPEM proposed in [9] has security defect when it is used to encode simple contour images. However, for complex contour images (e.g. image (a) in Fig. 2), the shares generated by the (2,2)-MPEM look like noise images (e.g. images (b) and (c) in Fig. 2) and provide no visual information about the secret. Hou et al. only gave the experimental results for complex contour images and thus did not notice this security defect in [9].

3.2 Using Variance to Explain the Above Security Defect

The following two basis matrices for white and black pixels are the same as those in Sect. 2.1 of [9].

$$M_0 = \begin{bmatrix} \blacksquare\square \\ \blacksquare\square \end{bmatrix} = \begin{bmatrix} 10 \\ 10 \end{bmatrix}, M_1 = \begin{bmatrix} \blacksquare\square \\ \square\blacksquare \end{bmatrix} = \begin{bmatrix} 10 \\ 01 \end{bmatrix}.$$

In Hou et al.'s paper, the variance is defined separately on white and black regions. Readers can refer to the definition of encoding sequence in Construction 1 and the definition of standard deviation in Sect. 5 of [9]. However, we think the above definitions are improper, because the analysis results based on those definitions (referring to Table 1) cannot explain the above experimental results.

In this paper, we define variance on an encoding block of adjacent pixels. Similar to the encoding sequence in [9], the size of an encoding block is also two. In the following, we first give Hou et al.'s analysis based on encoding sequences, then we give our analysis based on encoding blocks.

Suppose the secret image contains the following sequence of pixels at the beginning,

$$\blacksquare\,\square\,\blacksquare\,\square\,\square\,\square\,\blacksquare\,\square$$

$$1\ \ 2\ \ 3\ \ 4\ \ 5\ \ 6\ \ 7\ \ 8$$

where numbers in the second line denote the positions of the pixels. The four encoding sequences are constituted by pixels in positions $\{1,3\},\{4,7\},\{2,5\}$ and $\{6,8\}$ respectively while the encoding blocks are constituted by pixels in positions $\{1,2\},\{3,4\},\{5,6\}$ and $\{7,8\}$ respectively. If we denote $\square$ by 0 and $\blacksquare$ by 1, all possible encoding sequences are "00" and "11" while all possible encoding blocks are "00", "01", "10" and "11".

We first gave the analysis of a single share from an encoding sequence's perspective. Denote the average and variance of the Hamming weights of the encoding sequences that are encoded from "00" by μ_{00} and σ_{00}, and similarly denote the average and variance of the Hamming weights of the encoding sequences that are encoded from "11" by μ_{11} and σ_{11}. Then μ_{00}, μ_{11}, σ_{00} and σ_{11} for a single share, which is generated by the (2,2)-MPEM, are summarized as Table 1.

Table 1. For each share image, the average and variance of the Hamming weights of the encoding sequences on it that are encoded from "00" and "11".

μ_{00}	μ_{11}	σ_{00}	σ_{11}
1	1	0	0

Remark: Table 1 follows from the fact that each row of M_0 and M_1, which are the basis matrices used by the (2,2)-MPEM, contains exactly one 1. Since the data in Table 1 provides no insight into the above security defect, we think the encoding sequence's perspective is improper.

In the following, we first give an encoding block's perspective of the MPEM proposed in [9]. The encoding process of secret pixels $\blacksquare\square\blacksquare\blacksquare\square\square\blacksquare\square$ by the (2,2)-MPEM contains the following steps:

1. The first block $\blacksquare\square$ is encoded by randomly drawing a column from M_1 and then randomly drawing a column from M_0;
2. The second block $\blacksquare\blacksquare$ is encoded by filling with the remaining column of M_1 from Step. 1 and then freshly and randomly drawing a column from M_1;
3. The third block $\square\square$ is encoded by filling with the remaining column of M_0 from Step. 1 and then freshly and randomly drawing a column from M_0;
4. The fourth block $\blacksquare\square$ is encoded by filling with the remaining column of M_1 from Step. 2 and the remaining column of M_0 from Step. 3.

The influence of the encoding of previous blocks over the encoding of the current block is summarized by an indicator, called *Encoding Situation*, which records the parity of the number of ■s having been encoded and the parity of the number of □s having been encoded. Since we encode a block of two successive pixels at a time, there are always even number of pixels having been encoded in total. Hence we only have the following two *Encoding Situations*:

Encoding Situation 1: There are even number of □s and even number of ■s having been encoded. In such a case, if the currently-processing block is □□ or ■■, the corresponding block on each share image will definitely have one ■ and one □; else if the currently-considered block is □■ or ■□, the corresponding block on each share image will have two □s with probability $\frac{1}{4}$, one ■ and one □ with probability $\frac{1}{2}$, and two ■s with probability $\frac{1}{4}$.

Encoding Situation 2: There are odd □s and odd ■s having been encoded. In such a case, no matter what the currently-processing block is (possibly □■, ■□, □□ and ■■), the corresponding block on each share image will have two □s with probability $\frac{1}{4}$, one ■ and one □ with probability $\frac{1}{2}$, and two ■s with probability $\frac{1}{4}$.

Remark: Every block is encoded under some *Encoding Situation*. In the previous example, the first block ■□ is encoded under *Encoding Situation 1*; the second block ■■ is encoded under *Encoding Situation 2*; the third block □□ is encoded under *Encoding Situation 2*; the fourth block ■□ is encoded under *Encoding Situation 2*.

We calculate the average and variance of the Hamming weight of an encoding block on a single share image by the following formulas,

$$\mu = \sum_{i=0}^{m} p_i \times i, \quad \sigma = \sum_{i=0}^{m} p_i \times (i - \mu)^2 \tag{1}$$

where m represents the size of an encoding block and p_i represents the probability of an encoding block of Hamming weight i appears. The variance is used to explain the variation of the Hamming weight (gray-level) of an encoding block on a single share,

Denote the average and variance of the Hamming weights of the encoding blocks that are encoded from "ij" under *Encoding Situation* k by μ_{ij}^k and σ_{ij}^k, where "ij" $\in \{00, 01, 10, 11\}$ and $k \in \{1, 2\}$. Then μ_{ij}^ks and σ_{ij}^ks for a single share, which is generated by the (2,2)-MPEM, are summarized as Table 2.

Table 2. For each share image, the average and variance of the Hamming weights of the encoding sequences on it that are encoded from "00", "01", "10" and "11" under *Encoding Situations* 1 and 2.

μ_{00}^1	μ_{01}^1	μ_{10}^1	μ_{11}^1	μ_{00}^2	μ_{01}^2	μ_{10}^2	μ_{11}^2	σ_{00}^1	σ_{01}^1	σ_{10}^1	σ_{11}^1	σ_{00}^2	σ_{01}^2	σ_{10}^2	σ_{11}^2
1	1	1	1	1	1	1	1	0	$\frac{1}{2}$	$\frac{1}{2}$	0	$\frac{1}{2}$	$\frac{1}{2}$	$\frac{1}{2}$	$\frac{1}{2}$

Remark: Generally speaking, contour area of the secret image contains encoding blocks of the form "01" and "10", while white and black areas of the secret image contain encoding blocks of the form "00" and "11". From Table 2, it is easy to see that for a single share, the variance of contour area is larger than that of the white and black areas in the overall sense, which may leak the contour information of the secret image.

The exact value of variance of contour area and those of black and white areas depend on the statistical character of the secret image. In the following, we aim to explain why share images encoded from image "Pythagoras" leak the secret while share images encoded from image "Airplane" do not.

Some statistical information of the encoding process of images (a) in Figs. 1 and 2 can be found in Table 3, where N_{ij}^k denotes the number of the encoding blocks that are encode form blocks that are encoded under *Encoding Situation* k and N denotes the total number of blocks in the image, where "ij" $\in \{00, 01, 10, 11\}$ and $k \in \{1, 2\}$.

Table 3. The number of "ij" form encoding blocks that are encoded under *Encoding Situation* k for images (a) in Figs. 1 and 2, where "ij" $\in \{00, 01, 10, 11\}$ and $k \in \{1, 2\}$.

Image	N_{00}^1	N_{01}^1	N_{10}^1	N_{11}^1	N_{00}^2	N_{01}^2	N_{10}^2	N_{11}^2	N
"Pythagoras"	28138	272	537	1539	25057	342	466	1449	57800
"Airplane"	22228	17196	17722	8393	22014	17322	17596	8601	131072

Remark: It should be noted that the above statistical information is related to the encoding process. We encode the original secret image line by line, from left to right.

Combining Tables 2 and 3, we can calculate the exact expected variance of "ij" form encoding block for images (a) in Figs. 1 and 2, where "ij" $\in \{00, 01, 10, 11\}$. The results are summarized by Table 4.

Table 4. For each share image, the expected variance of the Hamming weights of the encoding blocks on it that are encoded from "ij" for images (a) in Figs. 1 and 2, where "ij" $\in \{00, 01, 10, 11\}$.

Image	σ_{00}	σ_{01}	σ_{10}	σ_{11}
"Pythagoras"	0.23552	0.5	0.5	0.24247
"Airplane"	0.24879	0.5	0.5	0.25036

Remark: For image "Pythagoras", the expected variance of the Hamming weights of encoding blocks encoded from "00" is calculated by

$$\frac{28138}{28138 + 25057} \times 0 + \frac{25057}{28138 + 25057} \times \frac{1}{2} = 0.23552$$

For both image "Pythagoras" and image "Airplane", the variances over contour area is significantly larger than those over black and white areas. We infer the reason why share images for image "Pythagoras" leak secret while share images for image "Airplane" do not is due to the fact that image "Pythagoras" has very simple contours while image "Airplane" has very complex contours.

We use the MATLAB command, "*edge(f, 'sobel', 0.15)*", to extract the contour of image "Pythagoras" and image "Airplane". The experimental result can be found in Fig. 3. Since image "Airplane" is a halftone image, its contour image is very complex. Although for each share image of image "Airplane", the variances over contour area are significantly larger than those over black and white areas, the contour area and black and white areas are mixed together, which results in the invisibility of the visual unevenness.

4   Future Researches

Hou et al.'s MPEM has improved SIVCS's visual quality, but the security defect has limited its application in real world. In such a case, we may use Ito et al.'s SIVCS [13], which is more secure but has worse visual quality than MPEM.

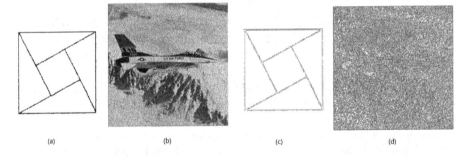

Fig. 3. Edge extraction: (a) image "Pythagoras" with image size 340×340, (b) image "Airplane" with image size 512×512, (c) contour image of "Pythagoras" with image size 340×340, (d) contour image of "Airplane" with image size 512×512

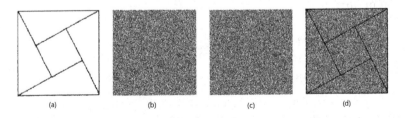

Fig. 4. Experimental results for (2,2)-SIVCS: (a) the original secret image with image size 340×340, (b) share 1 with image size 340×340, (c) share 2 with image size 340×340, (d) stacked image with image size 340×340

Figure 4 summarizes the experimental results for (2,2)-SIVCS, which demonstrates the above fact together with Fig. 1.

Following our results, an important topic in future research is how to combine the good visual quality of MPEM with the security properties of SIVCS and propose secure schemes with good visual quality.

5 Conclusions

In this paper, we first point out the security defect of Hou et al.'s multi-pixel encoding method. Then we point out that it is improper to define variance over an encoding sequence containing nonadjacent pixels. At last, we explain the above security defect by considering variance over an encoding block containing adjacent pixels.

Acknowledgments. This work was supported by 863 Program grant No. Y370071102, the "Strategic Priority Research Program" of the Chinese Academy of Sciences grant No. XDA06010701 and the "Fundamental Research Funds for the Central Universities" grant No. 3262015T20 (Topic: A new exploration of information research technology of Big Data environment, Project Leader: Yang LiangBin). Many thanks to the anonymous reviewers for their valuable comments.

References

1. Ateniese, G., Blundo, C., De Santis, A., Stinson, D.R.: Visual cryptography for general access structures. Inf. Comput. **129**, 86–106 (1996)
2. Bose, M., Mukerjee, R.: Optimal (k, n) visual cryptographic schemes for general k. Des. Codes Crypt. **55**, 19–35 (2010)
3. Chen, T.H., Tsao, K.H.: Visual secret sharing by random grids revisited. Pattern Recogn. **42**, 2203–2217 (2009)
4. Chen, T.H., Tsao, K.H.: Threshold visual secret sharing by random grids. J. Syst. Softw. **84**, 1197–1208 (2011)
5. Cimato, S., De Prisco, R., De Santis, A.: Optimal colored threshold visual cryptography schemes. Des. Codes Crypt. **35**, 311–335 (2005)
6. Cimato, S., De Prisco, R., De Santis, A.: Colored visual cryptography without color darkening. Theor. Comput. Sci. **374**, 261–276 (2007)
7. Guo, T., Liu, F., Wu, C.K.: Threshold visual secret sharing by random grids with improved contrast. J. Syst. Softw. **86**, 2094–2109 (2013)
8. Guo, T., Liu, F., Wu, C.K.: k out of k extended visual cryptography scheme by random grids. Sig. Process. **94**, 90–101 (2014)
9. Hou, Y.C., Tu, S.F.: A visual cryptographic technique for chromatic images using multi-pixel encoding method. J. Res. Pract. Inf. Technol. **37**, 179–191 (2005)
10. Kang, I.K., Arce, G.R., Lee, H.K.: Color extended visual cryptography using error diffusion. IEEE Trans. Image Process. **20**(1), 132–145 (2011)
11. Liu, F., Guo, T., Wu, C.K., Qian, L.: Improving the visual quality of size invariant visual cryptography scheme. J. Vis. Commun. Image R. **23**, 331–342 (2012)
12. Naor, M., Shamir, A.: Visual cryptography. In: De Santis, A. (ed.) EUROCRYPT 1994. LNCS, vol. 950, pp. 1–12. Springer, Heidelberg (1995)

13. Ito, R., Kuwakado, H., Tanaka, H.: Image size invariant visual cryptography. IEICE Trans. Fundam. Electron. Commun. Comput. Sci. **E82–A**(10), 2172–2177 (1999)
14. Shyu, S.J.: Image encryption by random grids. Pattern Recogn. **40**, 1014–1031 (2007)
15. Shyu, S.J., Chen, M.C.: Optimum pixel expansions for threshold visual secret sharing schemes. IEEE Trans. Inf. Forensics Secur. **6**(3), 960–969 (2011)
16. Yang, C.N.: New visual secret sharing schemes using probabilistic method. Pattern Recogn. Lett. **25**, 481–494 (2004)

Encrypted Secret Sharing and Analysis by Plaintext Randomization

Stephen R. Tate[1], Roopa Vishwanathan[1]([✉]), and Scott Weeks[2]

[1] Department of Computer Science, University of North Carolina at Greensboro,
Greensboro, NC 27402, USA
vishwanathan.roopa@gmail.com
[2] Department of Computer Science, George Mason University,
Fairfax, VA 22030, USA

Abstract. In this paper we consider the problem of secret sharing where shares are encrypted using a public-key encryption (PKE) scheme and ciphertexts are publicly available. While intuition tells us that the secret should be protected if the PKE is secure against chosen-ciphertext attacks (i.e., CCA-secure), formally proving this reveals some subtle and non-trivial challenges. We isolate the problems that this raises, and devise a new analysis technique called "plaintext randomization" that can successfully overcome these challenges, resulting in the desired proof. The encryption of different shares can use one key or multiple keys, with natural applications in both scenarios.

1 Introduction

During the past three decades, cryptography research has been very successful in developing clear notions of security and rigorous techniques for reasoning about security of cryptographic primitives and protocols. Formal notions of security in cryptography have evolved in essentially two main directions, with reduction-based proofs developing from the initial work of Goldwasser and Micali [9] and simulation-based proofs from the initial work of Goldreich, Micali, and Wigderson [8]. While we have a good understanding of how to reason about security in these settings, there are recurring issues with composability: using one secure protocol as a component of another protocol while retaining security inside the higher-level protocol. Somewhat counter-intuitively, some protocols (e.g., some zero-knowledge proofs) fail to maintain security even when multiple copies of the same protocol are run concurrently [7].

In this paper, we explore a combination of public-key encryption (PKE) with secret sharing, and in the process develop a general-purpose proof technique for analysis of cryptographic schemes and protocols that use public-key encryption (PKE) as a component. Perhaps the simplest example of such a system is the common practice of hybrid encryption: doing large scale encryption by

This material is based upon work supported by the National Science Foundation under Grant No. 0915735.

© Springer International Publishing Switzerland 2015
Y. Desmedt (Ed.): ISC 2013, LNCS 7807, pp. 49–65, 2015.
DOI: 10.1007/978-3-319-27659-5_4

first encrypting a random session key using a PKE scheme, and then using that session key with a symmetric cipher for bulk encryption. Due to the inefficiency of public key encryption, hybrid encryption has been standard practice since the 1980s, and our intuition tells us that if the PKE scheme and the symmetric cipher are both secure in some sense (e.g., against chosen ciphertext attacks) then the combination of these two components into a hybrid system should also be secure. However, despite widespread use of hybrid encryption, the security of hybrid encryption was not rigorously established until the 2003 work of Cramer and Shoup [5]. A key insight in Cramer and Shoup's analysis was the introduction of the notion of a "key encapsulation mechanism" (KEM), which can be built from a CCA-secure PKE scheme. The value of KEM does not come from the power of this new cryptographic primitive, but rather comes from the clarity it brings to the *analysis* of hybrid encryption. In this paper, we focus on improving the analysis process from the beginning, so that we obtain clear proofs directly, with no need to introduce a new primitive such as a KEM. While hybrid encryption is a very simple example of this, our analysis technique can be applied to any protocol that uses a PKE scheme to hide secrets used within the protocol — we use the term "PKE-hybrid" to refer to protocols like this.

Unfortunately, current proof techniques are not sufficient for some PKE-hybrid problems, including the very practical problem of secret sharing with encrypted shares. To understand this problem, consider a standard key escrow situation, in which a company escrows copies of keys for the company's officers so that keys can be recovered if a certain number of board members agree. This is a classic threshold secret sharing situation, but in the real world having board members keep copies of shares of all officer's keys (which might change somewhat regularly) locally would not be practical. A better solution would be to have each board member maintain their own long-term key (perhaps on a smartcard), and have the company store encrypted shares of the escrowed keys, encrypted with board members keys, on a central server. This way shares can be updated without interaction of the board members, but board members would still be needed in order to decrypt the shares for a key recovery.

To understand why standard proof techniques do not work for this problem, consider a situation in which a CCA-secure PKE is used to encrypt shares from a perfect k-of-n threshold secret sharing scheme. We mirror a CCA game by creating a game in which we provide two secrets to the game oracle, which encrypts shares of one of these secrets for the adversary who must guess which secret is used. Using standard techniques we would try to simulate this adversary and game oracle in a CCA PKE game to relate to the security of the PKE scheme. However, we must make multiple encryptions and they must be consistent across the shares that are provided. Multiple consistent encryptions suggests using a multi-query oracle such as the left-right or real-or-random security notions of Bellare *et al.* [2]; however, we must allow the adversary to decrypt *some* of the encrypted shares, only disallowing decryption of a set that would allow reconstruction of the secret. These two properties, consistent encryptions and allowing some decryptions, are fundamentally opposed in standard techniques, making analysis of this situation particularly difficult.

1.1 Plaintext Randomization

To overcome the problems described in the previous section, we have developed a new analysis technique that we call *plaintext randomization*, which we successfully use to prove a strong security result for the general "secret-sharing with encrypted shares" problem. We believe this technique will be useful in the analysis of a wide variety of PKE-hybrid protocols.

Consider a cryptographic problem in which security is defined using a game between an adversary and a game oracle — we don't make any assumptions about the goal of the adversary, so that it does not need to be a CCA-style distinguishability goal, but rather can be *any* adversary goal that is well-defined. The game oracle makes some use of a PKE scheme, but this is internal to the game and not something that the adversary necessarily sees. The adversary may in fact have no direct access to the PKE scheme at all, including key generation, encryption, or decryption, but only sees the effects of these operations as allowed by the game oracle definition. Internally, all access to the PKE scheme by the game oracle goes through a generic interface that neither depends on the precise PKE scheme being used nor gives access to randomness used internally to the PKE functions.

Plaintext randomization then is the following technique: internal to the game oracle, every time the PKE encryption function is called as $E_{PK}(p)$ (for plaintext p and public key PK) we replace the plaintext with a random string r of the same length and instead call $c = E_{PK}(r)$, using ciphertext c in place of what would have been the encrypted plaintext. To allow for consistent decryption, the game oracle remembers these "encryptions" by storing pairs (c, p) so that if the decryption function is used by the game oracle on ciphertext c, the plaintext p will be returned rather than the actual decryption of c (which would give r). By modifying the game in this way, we remove any use of meaningful ciphertexts, and the storage of pairs (c, p) allows the game to provide restricted and consistent decryptions, solving the two problems that we identified for secret sharing with encrypted shares. Furthermore, the use of ciphertexts that are unrelated to actual plaintexts "cuts" any hybrid use of the PKE from the rest of the protocol, exactly the property we need to enable or simplify proofs for PKE-hybrid problems.

There are a few technicalities that must be addressed for this to work, such as the ability to randomly sample the plaintext space (defined as a "plaintext-samplable PKE" in Definition 3) and a restriction on how the game in question uses PKE secret keys (defined as "sk-oblivious" in Definition 4). Once these formalities are established, we are able to prove a result which we call the "Plaintext Randomization Lemma" that bounds the difference between the adversary's success probability in the original game and the success probability in the modified game that uses plaintext randomization. This is the key to the subsequent proof for secret sharing with encrypted shares.

Based on the high-level description given above, two questions about related work come to mind: Is this anything more than the well-known "real-or-random" security definition? And if multiple decryptions of a set of ciphertexts are allowed, do selective opening attacks come into play? We address these two questions below.

Relation to Real-or-Random Security. In real-or-random (ROR) security, an adversary is tasked with distinguishing between the encryption of provided plaintext and encryption of randomized plaintext [2]. Our technique replaces plaintexts with randomized plaintexts in the same manner as ROR security, but our model takes chosen-ciphertext security (i.e., ROR-CCA) one step further by adding the ability to consistently "decrypt" some ciphertexts, regardless of whether the real or random plaintext was encrypted.

Consider an attempt to reduce the encrypted secret sharing (ESS) problem to ROR security: an ESS adversary could be used to create an ROR adversary in which shares of a challenge value are encrypted with the ROR adversary, and the resulting ciphertexts provided to the ESS adversary which must decide whether they are shares of the challenge value or unrelated ciphertexts. This is a natural definition of ESS security, but it is inherent in the definition of ESS that the adversary should be allowed to decrypt *some* of these ciphertexts. However, if the ciphertexts come from ROR-CCA oracle queries, then we are necessarily disallowed from decrypting *any* of the ciphertexts produced in this way. Furthermore, the ESS adversary doesn't even know the "real" side of the "real-or-random" encryption, as the real values are embedded within the ESS game and not revealed to the ESS adversary except through specific, controlled decryption requests. Therefore, allowing for consistent decryptions is not something that is under the control of the adversary — it must be embedded in the ESS game itself, which is precisely what plaintext randomization does.

In the absence of any decryptions that must be made consistent, our plaintext randomization technique can be used simply as an abstraction for replacing PKE within a game, although the benefit is really notational in this case. In particular, if only PKE encryptions are performed (i.e., only chosen plaintext queries), then plaintext randomization really does behave the same as ROR-CPA security, and in such a case a direct reduction to real-or-random security might be more appropriate, depending on how the PKE is exposed to the adversary. The examples we consider in this paper all rely on CCA security, and hence make full use of the plaintext randomization technique.

Selective Opening Attacks. The encrypted secret sharing problem provides a set of ciphertexts to the adversary and allows the adversary to open some subset of these ciphertexts. The underlying plaintexts are not independent since they are shares of a single secret, and this immediately raises a concern of selective opening attacks [6] and whether IND-CCA security is sufficient for the underlying PKE scheme. While this might be a concern for some applications, the encrypted secret sharing problem is based on trusted parties (either services or secure hardware such as a smartcard or trusted platform module) acting as both encryption and decryption oracles, where the randomness used in performing an encryption is never available external to the trusted party.

Our modular notation for PKE schemes ensures this property: Definition 2 defines the interface to a PKE scheme, and only encrypt/decrypt oracle calls are allowed, with no access to randomization used in encryption or revealed in decryption. Applications in which randomization might be revealed and made available to an adversary either directly or indirectly do not map to our definitions, and hence the plaintext randomization technique could not be applied to schemes in which selective opening attacks are a danger. The problems that we consider in this paper, natural and practical versions of encrypted secret sharing, *do* map to our definitions and selective opening is not an issue. We believe that many problems involving some type of escrow of secrets by trusted agents share these attributes.

1.2 Our Contributions

We briefly summarize the contributions of this paper below.

- We define notation that can be used in cryptographic games that use a PKE scheme inside the game oracle, for a uniform treatment and clear identification of how the PKE scheme is integrated into the protocol and game.
- We introduce the technique of *plaintext randomization* and prove the Plaintext Randomization Lemma, a powerful tool for analysis of PKE-hybrid systems.
- We formally define the "secret sharing with encrypted shares" problem, where shares are encrypted using public key encryption and a general key mapping function. We specify a PKE-hybrid scheme that uses a CCA-secure PKE in conjunction with a perfect secret sharing scheme, and prove the security of such a scheme.

While the original purpose of this work was to provide a security analysis for encrypted secret sharing, we believe that the plaintext randomization technique will be useful in a wide variety of situations, and will ease analysis of many protocols that make use of PKE as a component. As an example of this, we give a greatly simplified analysis (compared to prior work) of hybrid encryption.

2 Cryptographic Security and Games

All our schemes are parametrized by a security parameter λ. Specific parameters such as key sizes will depend on λ in operation-specific ways, and security is analyzed in terms of the probability of some event occurring as a function of λ — specifically, we want the probability of some bad event (related to a security compromise) to be a function that decreases as λ increases. Specifically, we use the standard notion of a negligible function.

Definition 1. *A function $f : Z \to R$ is **negligible in** λ (or just "negligible" when f is a function of a well-understood security parameter λ) if for every positive integer c_0 there exists an integer c_1 such that for all $\lambda > c_1$,*

$$|f(\lambda)| < \frac{1}{\lambda^{c_0}} \, .$$

If an event happens with probability $p(\lambda)$, we say that the event occurs "with overwhelming probability" if $p(\lambda) = 1 - f(\lambda)$, where $f(\lambda)$ is negligible.

Public-key cryptography is one of the foundations of modern cryptography, and is based on the idea that encryption and decryption can use different keys that are generated in pairs consisting of a public key (for encryption) and a secret key (for decryption). To formalize the idea of public-key encryption, we identify the three core operations that any public-key encryption scheme must provide, resulting in the following definition. Providing the full keypair, both public and secret keys, to the decryption function is slightly non-standard, but simplifies our presentation without changing the technical aspects.

Definition 2. *A **Public-Key Encryption (PKE)** scheme (referred to as "a PKE" for brevity) is defined by four sets and three probabilistic polynomial time operations. The sets are $\mathcal{PK}$, the set of public keys; $\mathcal{SK}$, the set of secret keys; $\mathcal{PT}$, the set of plaintexts; and $\mathcal{CT}$, the set of ciphertexts. The algorithms are the following:*

- *$KeyGen : 1^* \to \mathcal{PK} \times \mathcal{SK}$ — when called as $KeyGen(1^\lambda)$, where λ is a security parameter, produces a random public/secret pair (pk, sk) where $pk \in \mathcal{PK}$ and $sk \in \mathcal{SK}$.*
- *$Encrypt : \mathcal{PK} \times \mathcal{PT} \to \mathcal{CT}$ — when called as $Encrypt(pk, p)$, where $pk \in \mathcal{PK}$ and $p \in \mathcal{PT}$, produces ciphertext $c \in \mathcal{CT}$. It is not required that all plaintexts be valid for every public key, so we use $\mathcal{PT}(pk)$ to denote the set of valid plaintexts for a particular public key pk. If Encrypt is called with an invalid plaintext (i.e., $p \notin \mathcal{PT}(pk)$), then the operation fails and special value $\perp$ is returned.*
- *$Decrypt : \mathcal{PK} \times \mathcal{SK} \times \mathcal{CT} \to \mathcal{PT}$ — when called as $Decrypt(pk, sk, c)$, where $pk \in \mathcal{PK}$, $sk \in \mathcal{SK}$ and $c \in \mathcal{CT}$, produces plaintext $p \in \mathcal{PT}$. We can similarly restrict the ciphertext set to ciphertexts that are valid for a specific secret key sk, which we denote by $\mathcal{CT}(sk)$.*

We require that for any (pk, sk) produced by KeyGen, and for any plaintext $p \in \mathcal{PT}(pk)$, with overwhelming probability $Decrypt(pk, sk, Encrypt(pk, p)) = p$.

This definition provides the only way to interface with the PKE scheme, and so in particular neither the game oracle nor the adversary can have any access to randomization used during encryption. For the techniques described in this paper, we need PKEs that allow for random sampling from the set of valid plaintexts, a property of all widely-used PKE schemes. We call this property "plaintext-samplability," defined as follows.

Definition 3. *A **plaintext-samplable PKE** is a PKE scheme that, in addition to all operations of a standard PKE scheme, supports the following operation:*

- *PTSample : $\mathcal{PK} \times \mathcal{PT} \to \mathcal{PT}$ — when called as PTSample(pk, p), where $pk \in \mathcal{PK}$ and $p \in \mathcal{PT}$, produces a random plaintext of the same length as a supplied plaintext $p \in \mathcal{PT}$. Specifically, x is uniformly chosen from $\{x \mid x \in \mathcal{PT}(pk) \text{ and } |x| = |p|\}$.*

In reduction-based security proofs, security of cryptosystems is defined in terms of a game between a probabilistic polynomial time (PPT) adversary and a game oracle. The oracle sets internal, persistent state variables, and answers queries for the adversary. The goal of the adversary is typically to determine some information in the internal state of the game oracle (e.g., a hidden bit) based just on oracle queries. A game G is described in terms of the interface to the game oracle, as a set of functions of the following form:

- G.Initialize(1^λ): Sets up persistent variables that are maintained throughout the game based on a security parameter λ. This can involve generating one or more random keys, and picking a random bit that the adversary will need to guess.
- G.*OracleQuery*($\cdots$): One or more functions are defined that allow the adversary to query the oracle. These definitions are the heart of the security game.
- G.IsWinner(a): Takes a value a from the adversary at the end of the game, and returns true or false depending on whether a is a winning answer. This is always the "final answer" for the game, and once the adversary provides an answer a for IsWinner the game no longer accepts any more oracle queries.

A game typically relies on certain cryptographic operations, which we indicate by a superscript on the game name. For example, if some game G makes use of PKE scheme $\mathfrak{S}$, we indicate this specific version of G by writing $G^{\mathfrak{S}}$, and operations then might be denoted as $G^{\mathfrak{S}}$.Initialize(1^λ), etc. Games that use PKE schemes typically do so in a generic way, treating keys as opaque objects. We are specifically interested in protocols that treat secret keys in this way, so introduce the following terminology.

Definition 4. *A game G that uses a PKE scheme $\mathfrak{S}$ is **sk-oblivious** if, for any keypair (pk, sk) produced by $\mathfrak{S}.KeyGen$, the only way that G uses sk is to pass sk back unmodified in calls to $\mathfrak{S}.Decrypt$. In such a situation, we can say that "G makes sk-oblivious use of $\mathfrak{S}$".*

The goal of the adversary is to win the game (i.e., produce an answer a such that G.IsWinner(a) = true) with higher probability than simply guessing an answer randomly. Typically the "answer" is a single hidden bit that needs to be guessed, although our definition purposely avoids making this a requirement so that other goals could be accommodated. In the case where the answer is a single bit, the probability that a random guess would give a winning answer is $\frac{1}{2}$, and the goal is to win with probability non-negligibly larger than $\frac{1}{2}$, leading to the definition of the "advantage" against a game.

Definition 5. *The "advantage" of an adversary A in game G is denoted $Adv_{A,G}$, and defined as $Adv_{A,G} = |P(G.IsWinner(A^G(\lambda))) - \frac{1}{2}|$, where the probability is taken over both the random choices of A and the random choices of G. For some description of resource bounds B (e.g., time complexity, number of encryption or decryption queries, etc.), we also refer to the best possible advantage of any such adversary against a particular game, written $Adv_G(B)$, defined as $Adv_G(B) = \sup_A Adv_{A,G}$, where the supremum is taken over all adversaries A that meet the bounds requirements B.*

For a game G that defines the security of some type of cryptographic scheme, the goal is typically to find some specific scheme $\mathfrak{C}$ such that $Adv_{G^\mathfrak{C}}$ is negligible.

2.1   Multi-user CCA Security

As an extension to the better-known single key CCA security model for PKE, Bellare *et al.* considered security of public-key encryption when the system is used with multiple users (i.e., multiple keypairs) and multiple challenges are made that are answered consistently [1]. This is sometimes referred to as multi-user "left-right" security, since every encryption challenge is made with a pair of values, and the encryption oracle consistently encrypts either the left or the right value throughout the game. A key property of this model is that since encryption pairs are chosen by the adversary, plaintexts of the provided ciphertexts can be related in arbitrary ways, opening up the possibility of complex attacks. The following describes the multi-user CCA security game PK-MU$_n^\mathfrak{S}$ parametrized by the number of users n and a PKE scheme $\mathfrak{S}$.

- PK-MU$_n^\mathfrak{S}$.Initialize(1^λ): For $i = 1$ to n, the oracle generates keypairs $(pk_i, sk_i) = \mathfrak{S}.KeyGen(1^\lambda)$, picks a random bit $b \in \{0,1\}$, and sets C as an initially empty set of ciphertexts. $pk_1, \cdots, pk_n$ are returned to the adversary.
- PK-MU$_n^\mathfrak{S}$.Decrypt(i, x): If $(i, x) \in C$, the oracle returns $\bot$; otherwise, it returns $\mathfrak{S}.Decrypt(pk_i, sk_i, x)$.
- PK-MU$_n^\mathfrak{S}$.PEncrypt(i, x_0, x_1): The oracle calculates $c = \mathfrak{S}.Encrypt(pk_i, x_b)$, adds (i, c) to C, and returns c to the adversary.
- PK-MU$_n^\mathfrak{S}$.IsWinner(a): Takes a bit a from the adversary, and returns true if and only if $a = b$.

Note that PEncrypt ("pair encrypt") is similar to Challenge in the standard single-key CCA2 game, except that it can be called multiple times, and consistently encrypts either the first or second argument. While this is equivalent to the definition of Bellare *et al.*, we use a single multi-key oracle, as in the recent definition of Hofheinz and Jager [11]. When there is a single encryption user ($n = 1$), this definition turns into the standard notion of single-key CCA2 security, and so in that situation we will refer to this as "CCA2-security" in a single-user setting.

3   Plaintext Randomization

In this section, we present the technique of plaintext randomization. This technique creates a PKE scheme that can maintain some internal state between encryption and decryption requests. This stateful behavior would not be very useful in most real-life cryptographic uses of public key encryption, since the state would need to be protected and shared between encryption and decryption operations, which may be executed on separate systems. Nonetheless, it is possible to define such a stateful PKE scheme, and when this PKE is used inside a cryptographic game oracle — which can keep state secret from users of the oracle, and encryption and decryption are performed by the same party — it turns out to be a very useful concept.

Consider an adversary A that plays a game G that uses a plaintext-samplable PKE scheme $\mathfrak{S}$. We create a stateful PKE scheme that is based on $\mathfrak{S}$, but in which ciphertexts are meaningless, and cannot reveal any information about the corresponding plaintext other than perhaps its length. Specifically, ciphertexts are simply encryptions of random plaintexts of a given length, and the scheme uses internal state to keep track of plaintext/ciphertext pairs so that encryption followed by decryption gives the required result. We formalize this idea in the following definition.

Definition 6. *Given a plaintext-samplable PKE scheme* $\mathfrak{S}$, *the* **plaintext randomization** *of* $\mathfrak{S}$ *is a set of functions that acts as a PKE scheme, denoted* $\mathfrak{S}-rand$, *defined as follows:*

- $\mathfrak{S}-rand.KeyGen(1^\lambda)$ *computes* (pk, sk) = $\mathfrak{S}.KeyGen(1^\lambda)$ *and returns* (pk, sk).
- $\mathfrak{S}-rand.Encrypt(pk, p)$ *first computes* $r = \mathfrak{S}.PTSample(pk, p)$, *and then* $c = \mathfrak{S}.Encrypt(pk, r)$. *If a tuple of the form* $(pk, c, \cdot)$ *is already stored in* $\mathfrak{S}-rand's$ *internal state, then* $\perp$ *is returned (the operation fails); otherwise,* $\mathfrak{S}-rand$ *stores the tuple* (pk, c, p), *and returns* c *as the ciphertext.*
- $\mathfrak{S}-rand.Decrypt(pk, sk, c)$ *looks for a tuple of the form* (pk, c, x) *for some* x. *If such a tuple exists, then* x *is returned as decrypted plaintext; otherwise,* $p = \mathfrak{S}.Decrypt(pk, sk, c)$ *is called and* p *is returned.*

Note that the Encrypt function can fail if a duplicate ciphertext is produced, but since these ciphertexts are encryptions of random plaintexts then both the randomly chosen plaintext and randomness used in the encryption must be a repeat of a previous encryption, which happens with negligible probability. It is important not to confuse the above definition with an oracle that the adversary interacts with — the plaintext randomization of $\mathfrak{S}$ replaces calls to a PKE scheme that happen internal to a security game, and the adversary does not have direct access to these functions. Replacing a PKE scheme with its plaintext randomization typically results in a game that is much simpler to analyze, but is a good approximation to the original game. In particular, the following lemma shows that if the advantage against the plaintext-randomized game is negligible, then the advantage against the original game is also negligible.

Lemma 1 (Plaintext Randomization Lemma). *Let G be a game that makes sk-oblivious use of a plaintext-samplable public key encryption scheme $\mathfrak{S}$, and let $\mathfrak{S}-rand$ be the plaintext randomization of $\mathfrak{S}$. Then, for any probabilistic adversary A that plays $G^{\mathfrak{S}}$ so that the total game-playing time of A is bounded by t, the number of calls to $\mathfrak{S}.KeyGen$ is bounded by n, and the number of encryption and decryption requests for any individual key is bounded by q_e and q_d, respectively,*

$$\left| Adv_{A,G^{\mathfrak{S}}} - Adv_{A,G^{\mathfrak{S}-rand}} \right| \leq 2\, Adv_{PK\text{-}MU_n^{\mathfrak{S}}}(t', q_e, q_d), where\, t' = t + O(\log(q_e n))$$

Proof. Given adversary A that plays the game G we will construct an adversary A' that plays PK-MU$_n^{\mathfrak{S}}$, so A' converts A into an adversary that attacks the basic multi-user CCA security of the underlying PKE $\mathfrak{S}$. A' starts by calling PK-MU$_n^{\mathfrak{S}}$.Initialize(λ) and saves the list of public keys $pk_1, \cdots, pk_n$ for later use, setting $m = 0$ to track the number of public keys that are "in use" by G. A' next simulates the original adversary A and the game oracle G, replacing G's use of PKE $\mathfrak{S}$ with a specially constructed stateful PKE scheme $\widetilde{\mathfrak{S}}$ that has access to the public keys $pk_1, \cdots, pk_n$ and counter m, as well as the PK-MU$_n^{\mathfrak{S}}$ oracle. $\widetilde{\mathfrak{S}}$ provides the standard three PKE functions as follows:

- $\widetilde{\mathfrak{S}}.KeyGen(1^\lambda)$: If $m = n$ (i.e., we have already used n keypairs), this operation returns $\perp$ and fails. Otherwise, $\widetilde{\mathfrak{S}}$ increments m (the number of keys in use) and returns (pk_m, pk_m) as the generated "keypair." Note that the "secret key" is really just the public key, but this is not important since we can perform all the operations below with just this information, and G's use of $\mathfrak{S}$ is sk-oblivious.
- $\widetilde{\mathfrak{S}}.Encrypt(pk_i, p)$ for valid public key pk_i: $\widetilde{\mathfrak{S}}$ computes random plaintext $r = \mathfrak{S}.PTSample(pk_i, p)$, and then computes $c = $ PK-MU$_n^{\mathfrak{S}}$.PEncrypt(i, p, r). The tuple (pk_i, c, p) is saved in $\widetilde{\mathfrak{S}}$'s state, and c is returned.
- $\widetilde{\mathfrak{S}}.Decrypt(pk_i, pk_i, c)$: Note that the pk_i here is used as both the public and the secret key, despite the notation. The decrypt function first checks to see if $\widetilde{\mathfrak{S}}$'s state contains a tuple (pk_i, c, p) for some p, and if such a tuple is found p is returned as the plaintext. Otherwise, $p = $ PK-MU$_n^{\mathfrak{S}}$.Decrypt(i, c) is returned.

Note that all calls to PK-MU$_n^{\mathfrak{S}}$.PEncrypt store a tuple that includes the returned ciphertext, and the $\widetilde{\mathfrak{S}}.Decrypt$ function never calls the PK-MU$_n^{\mathfrak{S}}$.Decrypt oracle with such a ciphertext, so all *Decrypt* calls will succeed.

A' continues simulating A and $G^{\widetilde{\mathfrak{S}}}$ until A outputs its final result, a, for game G, at which point A' calls G.IsWinner(a) to check if A's output wins game $G^{\widetilde{\mathfrak{S}}}$. Based on this, A' outputs its guess b' for PK-MU$^{\mathfrak{S}}$'s secret bit b as follows:

- If A wins $G^{\widetilde{\mathfrak{S}}}$, A' outputs guess $b' = 0$.
- If A loses $G^{\widetilde{\mathfrak{S}}}$, A' outputs guess $b' = 1$.

Thus, A' wins if A wins and $b = 0$, or if A loses and $b = 1$. Since b is uniformly distributed,

$$P(A' \text{ wins}) = 0.5\, P(A \text{ wins } G^{\widetilde{\mathfrak{S}}} \mid b = 0) + 0.5\, P(A \text{ loses } G^{\widetilde{\mathfrak{S}}} \mid b = 1). \quad (1)$$

While our simulator does not know the bit b, the construction of $\widetilde{\mathfrak{S}}$ is such that when $b = 0$ the game played by A is exactly $\mathsf{G}^{\mathfrak{S}}$ (since in this case the encryption request is answered by an encryption of the real plaintext), and when $b = 1$ the game played by A is exactly $\mathsf{G}^{\mathfrak{S}-\mathrm{rand}}$ (since in this case the encryption request is answered using plaintext randomization). Using this observation we can simplify (1) as follows:

$$
\begin{aligned}
P(A' \text{ wins}) &= 0.5\, P(A \text{ wins } \mathsf{G}^{\mathfrak{S}}) + 0.5\, P(A \text{ loses } \mathsf{G}^{\mathfrak{S}-\mathrm{rand}}) \\
&= 0.5\, P(A \text{ wins } \mathsf{G}^{\mathfrak{S}}) + 0.5 \left(1 - P(A \text{ wins } \mathsf{G}^{\mathfrak{S}-\mathrm{rand}})\right) \\
&= 0.5 + 0.5\, P(A \text{ wins } \mathsf{G}^{\mathfrak{S}}) - 0.5\, P(A \text{ wins } \mathsf{G}^{\mathfrak{S}-\mathrm{rand}}).
\end{aligned}
$$

By definition, $Adv_{A',\mathrm{PK\text{-}MU}_n^{\mathfrak{S}}} = |P(A' \text{ wins }) - 0.5|$, and since A' only does some simple table lookups in addition to its simulation of A and G, which induces at most q_e and q_d encryption and decryption requests, respectively, we can bound $Adv_{A',\mathrm{PK\text{-}MU}_n^{\mathfrak{S}}}$ by $Adv_{\mathrm{PK\text{-}MU}_n^{\mathfrak{S}}}(t', q_e, q_d)$, where $t' = t + O(\log(n q_e))$. It follows that:

$$
\left|0.5\, P(A \text{ wins } \mathsf{G}^{\mathfrak{S}}) - 0.5\, P(A \text{ wins } \mathsf{G}^{\mathfrak{S}-\mathrm{rand}})\right| \leq Adv_{\mathrm{PK\text{-}MU}_n^{\mathfrak{S}}}(t', q_e, q_d),
$$

and so,

$$
\left|P(A \text{ wins } \mathsf{G}^{\mathfrak{S}}) - P(A \text{ wins } \mathsf{G}^{\mathfrak{S}-\mathrm{rand}})\right| \leq 2\, Adv_{\mathrm{PK\text{-}MU}_n^{\mathfrak{S}}}(t', q_e, q_d). \tag{2}
$$

Returning to the original problem, comparing the advantage of A with respect to $\mathsf{G}^{\mathfrak{S}}$ and $\mathsf{G}^{\mathfrak{S}-\mathrm{rand}}$,

$$
\left|Adv_{A,\mathsf{G}^{\mathfrak{S}}} - Adv_{A,\mathsf{G}^{\mathfrak{S}-\mathrm{rand}}}\right| = \Big| \left|P(A \text{ wins } \mathsf{G}^{\mathfrak{S}}) - 0.5\right| - \left|P(A \text{ wins } \mathsf{G}^{\mathfrak{S}-\mathrm{rand}}) - 0.5\right| \Big|,
$$

and so,

$$
\left|Adv_{A,\mathsf{G}^{\mathfrak{S}}} - Adv_{A,\mathsf{G}^{\mathfrak{S}-\mathrm{rand}}}\right| \leq \left| P(A \text{ wins } \mathsf{G}^{\mathfrak{S}}) - P(A \text{ wins } \mathsf{G}^{\mathfrak{S}-\mathrm{rand}}) \right| \tag{3}
$$

Combining bounds (2) and (3), we conclude that

$$
\left|Adv_{A,\mathsf{G}^{\mathfrak{S}}} - Adv_{A,\mathsf{G}^{\mathfrak{S}-\mathrm{rand}}}\right| \leq 2\, Adv_{\mathrm{PK\text{-}MU}_n^{\mathfrak{S}}}(t', q_e, q_d),
$$

which is the bound claimed in the lemma statement. $\square$

We next provide a corollary that gives two alternate forms for the Plaintext Randomization Lemma, which might be useful if a bound is desired in terms of traditional single-user, single-challenge CCA2 security. This corollary is stated without proof, as the bounds follow directly from the Plaintext Randomization Lemma and multi-user PKE bounds proved by Bellare *et al.* [1]. The second bound follows from the tighter multi-user security that is possible from the Cramer-Shoup PKE scheme.

Corollary 1. *Let G be a game that makes sk-oblivious use of a plaintext-samplable public key encryption scheme $\mathfrak{S}$, and let $\mathfrak{S}-\text{rand}$ be the plaintext randomization of $\mathfrak{S}$. Then, for any probabilistic adversary A that plays $\mathsf{G}^{\mathfrak{S}}$*

so that the total game-playing time of A is bounded by t, the number of calls to $\mathfrak{S}.KeyGen$ is bounded by n, and the number of encryption and decryption requests for any individual key is bounded by q_e and q_d, respectively,

$$\left| Adv_{A,G^\mathfrak{S}} - Adv_{A,G^{\mathfrak{S}-rand}} \right| \leq 2q_e n\, Adv_{PK\text{-}CCA2^\mathfrak{S}}(t', q_d),$$

where $t' = t + O(\log(q_e n))$. Furthermore, for the Cramer-Shoup PKE scheme, denoted $\mathcal{CS}$, we can bound

$$\left| Adv_{A,G^{\mathcal{CS}}} - Adv_{A,G^{\mathcal{CS}-rand}} \right| \leq 2q_e\, Adv_{PK\text{-}CCA2^{\mathcal{CS}}}(t', q_d).$$

4   Hybrid Encryption

In this section we provide an example of how plaintext randomization can simplify proofs other PKE-hybrid protocols, by giving a very simple proof for the security of hybrid encryption using a standard PKE rather than a KEM.

Definition 7. *A hybrid encryption scheme $\mathcal{H}(\mathcal{P}, \mathcal{S})$ combines the use of a PKE scheme $\mathcal{P}$ and an SKE scheme $\mathcal{S}$ to produce a public-key encryption scheme defined by the following functions:*

- *$KeyGen(1^\lambda)$: Compute $(pk, sk) = \mathcal{P}.KeyGen(1^\lambda)$ and return the keypair (pk, sk).*
- *$Encrypt(pk, p)$: Compute $k = \mathcal{S}.KeyGen(1^\lambda)$ and then ciphertexts $\psi = \mathcal{P}.Encrypt(pk, k)$ and $\phi = \mathcal{S}.Encrypt(k, p)$. The returned ciphertext is the pair $c = (\psi, \phi)$.*
- *$Decrypt(pk, sk, c)$: Ciphertext $c = (\psi, \phi)$ is decrypted by first finding the session key using $k = \mathcal{P}.Decrypt(pk, sk, \psi)$ and then computing the final plaintext $p = \mathcal{S}.Decrypt(k, \phi)$.*

Since the net effect of a hybrid encryption scheme is the same as a public key encryption system, security is defined by the multi-user CCA security notion that was given in Sect. 2.1. We also refer to the multi-user CCA security of a symmetric encryption scheme in the following analysis. The SK-MU game is a straightforward modification of PK-MU to a symmetric encryption setting, and is omitted here.

Theorem 1. *For any hybrid encryption scheme $\mathcal{H}(\mathcal{P}, \mathcal{S})$, if A is an adversary that runs in time t in a game that uses at most n keypairs and performs at most q_e and q_d encryption and decryption queries, respectively, then*

$$Adv_{A,PK\text{-}MU_n^{\mathcal{H}}} \leq 2\, Adv_{PK\text{-}MU_n^{\mathcal{P}}}(t', q_e, q_d) + Adv_{SK\text{-}MU_{q_e n}^{\mathcal{S}}}(t', 1, q_d),$$

where $t' = t + O(\log(q_e n))$.

Proof. Consider the plaintext randomization of $\mathcal{H}$, and an adversary A playing the PK-MU$_n^{\mathcal{H}-\mathrm{rand}}$ game: in this situation, a ciphertext (ψ, ϕ) is such that ψ is completely unrelated to ϕ — it is just an encryption of a random value. Therefore, any attack on $\mathcal{H}-\mathrm{rand}$ can be immediately turned into an attack on the SKE scheme $\mathcal{S}$ by simulating A and adding encryptions of random values to simulate the ψ portion of each ciphertext. Each use of the SKE scheme in this scenario uses a different random key, with a single encryption per symmetric key, and since the probability of winning the SKE game is the same as A winning the $\mathcal{H}-\mathrm{rand}$ game, we can bound the advantage of A in the PK-MU$_n^{\mathcal{H}-\mathrm{rand}}$ game as

$$Adv_{A,\text{PK-MU}^{\mathcal{H}-\mathrm{rand}}} \le Adv_{\text{SK-MU}_{q_{en}}^{\mathcal{S}}}(t, 1, q_d).$$

By the Plaintext Randomization Lemma, we know that

$$\left| Adv_{A,\text{PK-MU}^{\mathcal{H}}} - Adv_{A,\text{PK-MU}^{\mathcal{H}-\mathrm{rand}}} \right| \le 2 Adv_{\text{PK-MU}^{\mathcal{P}}}(t', q_e, q_d),$$

leading to the bound in the theorem. □

While we generally state bounds in terms of concrete security, we restate this bound as a simple statement about security with respect to a probabilistic polynomial-time (PPT) adversary. In particular, we say simply that a scheme is "PK-CCA2-secure" if $Adv_{A,\text{PK}-\text{CCA2}}$ is negligible for any PPT adversary A, and similarly for other games.

Corollary 2. *If $\mathcal{P}$ is a PK-CCA2-secure PKE scheme, and $\mathcal{S}$ is a SK-CCA2-secure SKE scheme, then hybrid scheme $\mathcal{H}(\mathcal{P}, \mathcal{S})$ is a PK-CCA2-secure PKE scheme.*

5   Secret Sharing with Encrypted Shares

Loosely speaking, a secret sharing scheme consists of a dealer, who knows some secret, and a set of participants who are given shares of this secret by the dealer in such a way that only authorized sets of participants can reconstruct the secret from their shares. Formalizing this intuitive notion is not difficult, and the formulation we use is a slight modification of the 1987 definition given by Ito, Saito, and Nishizeki [12].

Formally, an n-way secret sharing scheme is one in which a secret s comes from some space of secrets $\mathcal{SS}$, and a function MakeShares:$\mathcal{SS} \rightarrow \mathcal{PS}^n$ where $\mathcal{PS}$ is the "piece space" for shares of the secret. In particular, given $s \in \mathcal{SS}$, MakeShares(s) produces a vector $(s_1, s_2, \cdots, s_n)$ of shares, where $s_i \in \mathcal{PS}$ for all i, and shares are identified by their index in this vector. Using notation $[n] = \{1, \cdots, n\}$, an *access structure* $\Gamma \subseteq 2^{[n]}$ is a set of subsets of indices that are authorized to reconstruct the secret. For any subset $\{i_1, i_2, \cdots, i_m\} \in \Gamma$ we can use function Reconstruct$(s_{i_1}, s_{i_2}, \cdots, s_{i_m}) = s$ to reconstruct s from shares identified by an authorized subset of indices. We require that if $\{i_1, i_2, \cdots, i_m\} \notin \Gamma$ then it is infeasible to reconstruct s from shares $s_{i_1}, s_{i_2}, \cdots, s_{i_m}$, where "infeasible" can be defined either from a computational or an information theoretic standpoint. All of the secret sharing schemes we consider in this paper use the information theoretic model of security, meaning that for any $\{i_1, i_2, \cdots, i_m\} \notin \Gamma$ all secrets $s \in \mathcal{SS}$ are equally likely, so no algorithm can extract any information about s from these shares — such a secret sharing scheme is called *perfect*. Perfect secret sharing schemes are known and widely used for certain specific access structures, such as Shamir's secret sharing scheme for threshold access structures [13]. As is typical in secret sharing work, we require that Γ be monotone, so that if some $\mathcal{I} \in \Gamma$ then all supersets of $\mathcal{I}$ are also in Γ.

We are interested in schemes in which shares are encrypted using a public key scheme, so for a PKE with plaintext space $\mathcal{PT}$ we assume an embedding function $e : \mathcal{PS} \to \mathcal{PT}$ and a "de-embedding" function $d : \mathcal{PT} \to \mathcal{PS}$ so that $d(e(s_i)) = s_i$ for any share s_i. In what follows, use of the embedding and de-embedding functions is implicitly assumed when shares are encrypted or decrypted. Despite the widespread use of secret sharing, both as an independent cryptographic functionality and as a component of other cryptographic protocols, we have not located any formal work analyzing the situation in which shares are encrypted using a public key encryption scheme. Such a situation is similar to hybrid encryption, but with the ultimate secret computed using a combination of decryption and secret reconstruction. Traditional notions of indistinguishability games have serious challenges in this setting. Traditional games typically have the restriction that once a ciphertext is produced by a challenge oracle, the adversary is not allowed to request and receive a decryption of that ciphertext, so any reduction from a standard indistinguishability game should similarly avoid queries on ciphertexts produced by the challenge oracle. In the setting of secret sharing, we want to allow decryption of challenge ciphertexts as long as the full set of decryptions produced does not correspond to a set $\gamma \in \Gamma$ that can reconstruct the secret. Our plaintext randomization technique can handle this situation quite cleanly, while it is not clear how to start with a reduction from a traditional ciphertext indistinguishability game.

In our formalization, we consider an n-way perfect secret sharing scheme as defined above with monotone access structure Γ for which we will use k different keypairs (numbered 1 to k for convenience) to encrypt these shares according to a key mapping function $\mathcal{K} : [n] \to [k]$ so that share i will be encrypted using key number $\mathcal{K}(i)$. The scheme may depend on the access structure, and may in fact only work for some specific subset of access structures (such as threshold access structures), and we assume there is some appropriate and compact description $\mathcal{D}(\Gamma)$ of valid Γ's for a particular scheme.

Using this general key mapping function allows us to capture several different scenarios within one general definition. For example, with $k = 1$ and $\mathcal{K}(i) = 1$ for all i, we capture a scheme in which all shares are encrypted with the key of a single trusted authority and shares are distributed (either to a single party or multiple parties) so that decryption of shares is allowed based on some criteria determined by the trusted authority. For example, Γ might be a threshold structure with threshold t, and trusted hardware controls how many shares may be decrypted at any particular time (this is the case in Gunupudi and Tate's generalized oblivious transfer scheme based on trusted hardware [10]). As another example, consider $k = n$ escrow authorities, all with their own keys, and $\mathcal{K}(i) = i$ for all i. In this case, a single user could obtain all encrypted shares, and if the user needs to open the secret at some point the user could approach some subset $\gamma \in \Gamma$ of escrow authorities and convince them that they should decrypt the share that is encrypted with their key. This is the scenario described in the Introduction.

We define the following security game for secret sharing with encrypted shares.

- $\mathsf{ESS}^{\mathfrak{S}}.\mathsf{Initialize}(1^{\lambda}, k, n, \mathcal{K}, \mathcal{D}(\Gamma))$: If this scheme does not support access structure Γ, return $\bot$ and do not answer any further queries. Otherwise, the oracle generates keypairs $(pk_i, sk_i) = \mathfrak{S}.KeyGen(1^{\lambda})$ for $i = 1, \ldots, k$, picks a random bit $b \in \{0, 1\}$, and saves n, $\mathcal{K}$, and $\mathcal{D}(\Gamma)$ for later use. γ, used to track the set of shares that have been decrypted, is initialized to the empty set. Finally, set flag c to false, indicating that no challenge has yet been made, and return $pk_1, \ldots, pk_k$.
- $\mathsf{ESS}^{\mathfrak{S}}.\mathsf{Challenge}(x_0, x_1)$: If c is true, then return $\bot$. Otherwise, the oracle generates n shares $s_1, \ldots, s_n$ for x_b, creates share ciphertexts by computing $c_i = \mathfrak{S}.Encrypt(pk_{\mathcal{K}(i)}, s_i)$ for $i = 1, \ldots, n$, sets flag c to true, and returns the vector $(c_1, \ldots, c_n)$ to the adversary (keeping a copy for future reference).
- $\mathsf{ESS}^{\mathfrak{S}}.\mathsf{Decrypt}(i, x)$ (where $i \in [k]$ is a key number and x is a ciphertext): If $x \notin \{c_j \mid \mathcal{K}(j) = i\}$ (so c_j was not produced by encrypting with key i), then simply compute and return $\mathfrak{S}.Decrypt(pk_i, sk_i, x)$. Otherwise, $x = c_j$ for some j with $\mathcal{K}(j) = i$, so test whether $\gamma \cup \{j\} \in \Gamma$: if it is, return $\bot$; otherwise, set $\gamma \leftarrow \gamma \cup \{j\}$ and return $\mathfrak{S}.Decrypt(pk_i, sk_i, x)$.
- $\mathsf{ESS}^{\mathfrak{S}}.\mathsf{IsWinner}(a)$: Takes a bit a from the adversary, and returns true if and only if $a = b$.

Note that the test in $\mathsf{ESS}^{\mathfrak{S}}.\mathsf{Decrypt}(i, x)$ disallows decrypting shares for a share set that would allow reconstruction of the secret, while still allowing some decryptions. Furthermore, since Γ is monotone, if the ultimate set of shares that have been decrypted are from a set $\gamma \notin \Gamma$, then every subset of γ is also not in Γ and so this test does not restrict adversaries in any way other than not allowing them to receive a full share set.

Since the bounds in the Plaintext Randomization Lemma depend on the number of times each key is used, we define q_e to be the largest number of times any key is used according to our key mapping function. Specifically,

$$q_e = \max_{i \in [k]} |\{j \mid \mathcal{K}(j) = i\}|.$$

Theorem 2. *If ESS is a k-key perfect n-way secret sharing scheme using PKE $\mathfrak{S}$, with q_e and q_d defined as described above, then for any time t adversary A,*

$$Adv_{A, ESS^{\mathfrak{S}}} \leq 2\, Adv_{PK\text{-}MU_n^{\mathfrak{S}}}(t', q_e, q_d).$$

Proof. Consider the $\mathsf{ESS}^{\mathfrak{S}-\mathsf{rand}}$, the ESS game using the plaintext randomized version of $\mathfrak{S}$. Let b denote the secret random bit chosen during the initialization step, let x_0 and x_1 denote the challenge secrets selected by A, and let

$c_1, c_2, \cdots, c_n$ be the ciphertexts produced by the ESS oracle encrypting shares of x_b using $\mathfrak{S}-$rand. At any time while A is playing $\mathsf{ESS}^{\mathfrak{S}-\mathsf{rand}}$, its view consists of ciphertexts $c_1, c_2, \cdots, c_n$ as well as a set of shares that it has decrypted, $s_{i_1}, s_{i_2}, \cdots, s_{i_m}$, where $\{i_1, i_2, \cdots, i_m\} = \gamma \notin \Gamma$ (as enforced by the ESS game). Since the decrypted shares are not in Γ and the secret sharing scheme is perfect, and since plaintext randomization results in ciphertexts being independent of the actual shares (and hence the secret), each secret (x_0 or x_1) is equally likely given the adversary's view. Therefore, $Adv_{A,\mathsf{ESS}^{\mathfrak{S}-\mathsf{rand}}} = 0$.

Referring back to the Plaintext Randomization Lemma,

$$\left| Adv_{A,\mathsf{ESS}^{\mathfrak{S}}} - Adv_{A,\mathsf{ESS}^{\mathfrak{S}-\mathsf{rand}}} \right| \leq 2\, Adv_{\mathsf{PK}\text{-}\mathsf{MU}_n^{\mathfrak{S}}}(t', q_e, q_d),$$

and since $Adv_{A,\mathsf{ESS}^{\mathfrak{S}-\mathsf{rand}}} = 0$ we conclude with the bound stated in the theorem. □

6   Conclusions

In this paper we have examined the problem of encrypted secret sharing (ESS), developing a general and flexible definition, and solving challenges posed in the analysis by developing a new, general-purpose, and powerful technique called plaintext randomization. This technique modularizes the analysis PKE-hybrid cryptographic protocols, and separates out the dependence on the security of the PKE scheme in a way that is captured by the Plaintext Randomization Lemma that is proved in this paper. Beyond the immediate result for ESS, we believe that plaintext randomization holds great promise for additional applicability, given the prevalence of public-key encryption in cryptographic schemes and the efficient schemes that can be derived in the reduction-based security model.

References

1. Bellare, M., Boldyreva, A., Micali, S.: Public-key encryption in a multi-user setting: security proofs and improvements. In: Preneel, B. (ed.) EUROCRYPT 2000. LNCS, vol. 1807, pp. 259–274. Springer, Heidelberg (2000)
2. Bellare, M., Desai, A., Jokipii, E., Rogaway, P.: A concrete security treatment of symmetric encryption. In: Proceedings of the 38th Symposium on Foundations of Computer Science (FOCS), pp. 394–403 (1997)
3. Canetti, R.: Universally composable security: a new paradigm for cryptographic protocols. In: Proceedings of 42nd Symposium on Foundations of Computer Science (FOCS), pp. 136–145 (2001)
4. Canetti, R., Kushilevitz, E., Lindell, Y.: On the limitations of universally composable two-party computation without set-up assumptions. J. Crypt. 19(2), 135–167 (2006)
5. Cramer, R., Shoup, V.: Design and analysis of practical public-key encryption schemes secure against adaptive chosen ciphertext attack. SIAM J. Comput. 33, 167–226 (2003)
6. Dwork, C., Naor, M., Reingold, O., Stockmeyer, L.: Magic functions: in memoriam: Bernard M. Dwork 1923–1998. J. ACM 50(6), 852–921 (2003)

7. Goldreich, O., Krawczyk, H.: On the composition of zero-knowledge proof systems. SIAM J. Comput. **25**(1), 169–192 (1996)
8. Goldreich, O., Micali, S., Wigderson, A.: How to play any mental game. In: Proceedings of the 19th Symposium on Theory of Computing (STOC), pp. 218–229 (1987)
9. Goldwasser, S., Micali, S.: Probabilistic encryption. J. Comput. Syst. Sci. **28**(2), 270–299 (1984)
10. Gunupudi, V., Tate, S.R.: Generalized non-interactive oblivious transfer using count-limited objects with applications to secure mobile agents. In: Tsudik, G. (ed.) FC 2008. LNCS, vol. 5143, pp. 98–112. Springer, Heidelberg (2008)
11. Hofheinz, D., Jager, T.: Tightly secure signatures and public-key encryption. In: Safavi-Naini, R., Canetti, R. (eds.) CRYPTO 2012. LNCS, vol. 7417, pp. 590–607. Springer, Heidelberg (2012)
12. Ito, M., Saito, A., Nishizeki, T.: Secret sharing scheme realizing general access structure. In: Proceedings of IEEE Globecom, pp. 99–102 (1987)
13. Shamir, A.: How to share a secret. Commun. ACM **22**(11), 612–613 (1979)

Encryption

Round-Efficient Private Stable Matching from Additive Homomorphic Encryption

Tadanori Teruya[1]($\boxtimes$) and Jun Sakuma[2,3]

[1] Information Technology Research Institute,
National Institute of Advanced Industrial Science and Technology,
AIST Tokyo Waterfront Bio-IT Research Building,
2-4-7 Aomi, Koto-ku, Tokyo 135-0064, Japan
tadanori.teruya@aist.go.jp
[2] Graduate School of Systems and Information Engineering,
University of Tsukuba, 1-1-1 Ten-nohdai, Tsukuba, Ibaraki 305-8573, Japan
[3] JST CREST, Tokyo, Japan

Abstract. In the present paper, we propose private stable matching protocols to solve the stable marriage problem with the round complexity $O(n^2)$, where n is the problem size. In the multiparty setting, the round complexity of our protocol is better than all of the existing practical protocols. We also implement our protocol on a standard personal computer, smartphones, and tablet computers for experimental performance evaluation. Our protocols are constructed by using additive homomorphic encryption only, and this construction yields improved round complexity and implementation-friendliness. To the best of our knowledge, our experiment is the first implementation report of a private stable matching protocol that has a feasible running time.

1 Introduction

The stable marriage problem is defined as finding stable matches between two equal-sized sets of men and women. Given an equal number of men and women to be paired in marriage, each man and each woman ranks all of the women and men, respectively, in order of their preference. Matching is stable when there exists no alternative man and woman pair that prefer each other to their already matched partners [9,15].

The stable marriage problem has applications in the design of two-sided markets. For example, consider the matching of two groups, such as venture companies and investment companies. Each venture company possesses intellectual property and is searching for an investor to support their business. Each investment company wishes to invest in the best possible venture company. Each venture company ranks all investment companies based on their investment principles and conditions, whereas each investment company ranks all venture companies in the order of the potential yield that the intellectual property is expected to produce. A stable matching achieves pairing of venture companies and investment companies that neither company has an incentive to switch partners.

© Springer International Publishing Switzerland 2015
Y. Desmedt (Ed.): ISC 2013, LNCS 7807, pp. 69–86, 2015.
DOI: 10.1007/978-3-319-27659-5_5

Classical algorithms are known to solve the stable marriage problem in a reasonable computation time [9,15].

Golle first introduced the notion of privacy into the stable marriage problem in [12]. Intuitively, in the private stable marriage problem, each participant desires to find a stable match while keeping their preference list confidential from other participants. In the example of investment companies and venture companies, the potential yields of the investment companies should be kept private due to confidentiality agreements, while the venture companies desire to keep their preference lists private because such information might reveal future business plans. If both still wish to find a stable match, this situation is represented as the private stable matching problem.

1.1 Related Work

Gale and Shapley proved that, for any equal number of men and women, it is always possible to solve the stable marriage problem, and proposed an algorithm, referred to as the Gale–Shapley algorithm, to find such a stable match [9,15]. The number of necessary iterations of the Gale–Shapley algorithm to find a stable match is $n^2 - n + 1$ for the worst input case, where n is the size of two sets of the given stable marriage problem [15, pp. 14–15], referred to as the size of stable marriage problem.

Secure multiparty computation enables two or more parties to evaluate a prescribed function with distributed private inputs. Generic secure multiparty computation techniques [1] allow us to find a stable match without sharing private preference lists. However, implementation of the Gale–Shapley algorithm by means of generic secure multiparty computation techniques has not previously been a realistic solution because the number of the internal states of the Gale–Shapley algorithm can exponentially increase with the number of iterations, thus resulting in extremely high computational and communication costs.

Golle [12] proposed a specific protocol design based on the Gale–Shapley algorithm for the private stable marriage problem. The design of existing protocols are such that one iteration of the main loop in the protocol corresponds to one iteration of the Gale–Shapley algorithm, and the one iteration of the main loop in these protocols causes several rounds of execution.

Golle defined the private stable marriage problem and presented a protocol that solves this problem using the re-encryption mix network [13] and the private equality test protocol [16] as primitives. Although the protocol works correctly in most cases, Franklin et al. suggested that the protocol fails in one particular situation [7]. Specifically, they reported that the counter used in Golle's protocol cannot be set to a sufficiently large number and can cause overflow. Franklin et al. showed that this failure can be fixed by introducing protocols based on the secret sharing scheme [2]. In the fixed version of the protocol (referred to hereinafter as GFGM), two different cryptographic primitives, namely, threshold additive homomorphic encryption and secret sharing, are used alternatively, and the round complexity of GFGM is $\widetilde{O}(n^3)$, where $\widetilde{O}(f)$ denotes the asymptotic upper bound of $O(f)$ ignoring $\log f$ factors (line 2 in Table 1 from [7]).

Franklin et al. proposed two protocols for the private stable marriage problem in [7]. The first protocol, FGM1, is an improvement of GFGM. In FGM1, two novel techniques, the single free man technique and Stern's private information retrieval (PIR) protocol [21] along with a protocol based on a secret sharing scheme [2], are introduced. FGM1 is terminated after $O(n^2)$ iterations of the main loop, and PIR with $O\left(\sqrt{\log n}\right)$ round complexity is invoked for each iteration. Thus, the round complexity of FGM1 is reduced to $\widetilde{O}(n^2)$ and this complexity is larger than $O(n^2)$ (line 3 in Table 1 from [7]).

Franklin et al.'s second protocol, FGM2, is completely different from GFGM and FGM1. Here, FGM2 consists of two primitives. Yao's garbled circuit [22] is used to compute part of the operations of the Gale–Shapley algorithm, and the Naor–Nissim protocol is used to securely share the private inputs [17]. This protocol achieves the best communication complexity among the currently existing protocols. However, FGM2 is not secure if collusion occurs between the two parties (line 4 in Table 1 from [7]).

Franklin et al. made a suggestion about the multiparty extension of FGM2 in [8], in which the secure multiparty computation [1] and a multiparty version of the Naor–Nissim protocol [17] are used as primitives. This protocol, referred to as FGM3, is collusion-resistant if the number of colluding parties is less than the prescribed threshold (greater than two) specified by all of the underlying cryptographic protocols. Note that [8] describes only the concept of FGM3 and does not provide a formal complexity analysis of FGM3. Here, we will discuss the round complexity of FGM3, the multiparty extension of FGM2. Since the round complexity of the multiparty version of the Naor–Nissim protocol [8] is $O(\log n)$, which is invoked $O(n^2)$ times, the round complexity of FGM3 is $\widetilde{O}(n^2)$, which is also larger than $O(n^2)$ (line 5 in Table 1 from [8]).

Considering the necessity for all parties to wait for the slowest party to complete its tasks and communication, it is clear that round complexity has a dominant influence on the completion time of the protocol. Thus, the achievement of small round complexity significantly contributes to reducing the actual computation time.

1.2 Contribution

Our contributions are two-fold: first, we present the first $O(n^2)$ protocol for the private stable matching problem, and, second, we guarantee the security of the protocol by using additive homomorphic encryption only.

As mentioned earlier, the all of existing protocols are constructed using several primitives: these are non-constant round protocols, the PIR with secret sharing schemes [2,21] and the multiparty version of the Naor–Nissim protocol [8]. Our protocol is basically designed as FGM1 and GFGM, and we modified the protocol, which consists of constant-round primitives only: private equality test and re-encryption mix network. By doing so, we improved the number of rounds required for private stable matching. To the best of our knowledge, this is the first $O(n^2)$ round practical protocol designed for private stable matching in a multiparty setting.

Furthermore, since our protocol employs homomorphic encryption alone, the resulting protocol can be easily implemented. The security of our protocol relies solely on the underlying threshold additive homomorphic encryption. We implemented our protocol by using Paillier encryption [20] for our experimental program. Since our protocol uses a small space of plaintexts, Paillier encryption can be replaced with ElGamal encryption on an elliptic curve [5], which would be superior to in computation time.

In the present paper, we propose two private stable matching protocols: a collusion-resistant protocol and a non-collusion-resistant protocol. The former protocol employs threshold additive homomorphic encryption, which makes the protocol collusion-resistant against t' colluding semi-honest adversaries (line 6 in Table 1). The latter protocol is designed mainly for implementation purposes (line 7 in Table 1) and is not collusion-resistant. In our implementation version, we presume that parties do not collude with each other. Based on this assumption, we can eliminate distributed decryption from the protocol and simplify the mix network. This makes the entire protocol design much simpler and more implementation friendly.

The remainder of the present paper is organized as follows. Preliminaries are presented in Sect. 2. The definition and previous protocols of private stable matching are introduced in Sect. 3. A new stable matching protocol with threshold additive homomorphic encryption is described in Sect. 4. The experimental implementation is presented in Sect. 5.

Table 1. Summary of comparison, where n denotes the size of stable marriage problem, $\widetilde{O}(f)$ denotes the asymptotic upper bound $O(f)$ ignoring polynomial of $\log f$ factors, MA denotes matching authority (explained in Sect. 4.2), AHE denotes ordinary additive homomorphic encryption [5,20], TAHE denotes threshold additive homomorphic encryption [3,6,10], SS denotes secret sharing [2], PIRSS denotes Stern's private information retrieval [21] and secret sharing [2], Yao denotes Yao's garbled circuit [22], NN denotes the Naor–Nissim protocol [17], SMC denotes the Beaver et al.'s protocol [1], and FGM denotes the Franklin et al.'s protocol [8].

Proposals	Primitives	Collusion resistance	# of MAs	Total comput.	Total comm.	Round
Gale–Shapley [9,15]	–	–	–	–	–	$n^2 - n + 1$
GFGM [7,12]	TAHE, SS	Yes	t	$O(n^5)$	$O(tn^5)$	$\widetilde{O}(n^3)$
FGM1 [7]	TAHE, SS, PIRSS	Yes	t	$O\left(n^4\sqrt{\log n}\right)$	$O(tn^3)$	$\widetilde{O}(n^2)$
FGM2 [7]	Yao, NN	No	2	$O(n^4)$	$O(n^2)$	$\widetilde{O}(n^2)$
FGM3 [8]	SMC, FGM	Yes	t	$O(n^4)$	$O(tn^2)$	$\widetilde{O}(n^2)$
Proposal (Sect. 4.2)	**TAHE**	Yes	t	$O(n^4)$	$O(tn^4)$	$O(n^2)$
Implemented version (Sect. 5.1)	**AHE**	No	–	$O(n^4)$	$O(n^4)$	$O(n^2)$

2   Preliminaries

In this section, we introduce the building blocks and notation. Our protocol is constructed using four sub-protocols: re-encryption mix network, private equality test, private index search, and private comparison. Their round complexity is $O(1)$ for the number of input ciphertexts. Note that these protocols are based on additive homomorphic encryption only.

Ordinary and Threshold Additive Homomorphic Encryption. The security guarantee of the proposed protocols is based on semantically (or IND-CPA) secure [11] ordinary or threshold additive homomorphic public-key encryption schemes. Threshold additive homomorphic encryption is used to construct a collusion-resistant protocol. The ElGamal encryption scheme [5], the Paillier encryption scheme [20], and the threshold versions thereof [3,6,10] are known as additive homomorphic encryption schemes. We denote the encryption of a plaintext m by $E(m)$. The additive homomorphism of encryption is denoted by $E(a) \cdot E(b) = E(a+b)$. Multiple application of operation "$\cdot$" derives $E(c)^d = E(cd)$. Let $v = (v_0, v_1, \ldots, v_{n-1})$, then we define $E(v) = \big(E(v_0), E(v_1), \ldots, E(v_{n-1})\big)$.

Re-encryption Mix Network. Let a party hold a sequence of ciphertexts. If the party and *mix servers* jointly compute the re-encryption mix network (MIX), the party obtains a randomly permuted and re-randomized (re-encrypted) sequence of the ciphertexts after execution of the protocol [13]. The MIX is *private* if the party and the mix servers cannot learn any information about the plaintexts or the secret permutation. Note that the MIX can be collusion resistant if a threshold encryption scheme is used. The computational, communication, and round complexities of the MIX are $O(n)$, $O(tn)$, and $O(1)$ for n ciphertexts and t mix servers, respectively. Parallelization of the mix network was investigated in [13]. This parallelized version of the MIX is used for existing private stable matching algorithms and our proposal in Sect. 4 for computational efficiency.

Private Equality Test. Let $E(m_1)$ and $E(m_2)$ be two ciphertexts of an ordinary or threshold additive homomorphic encryption scheme. Let EQTEST $\big(E(m_1), E(m_2)\big) = b$ denote a private equality test in which $b = 1$ if $m_1 = m_2$ otherwise $b = 0$. Here, EQTEST does not leak information to any parties, except for the equality relation, as long as the underlying ordinary or threshold additive homomorphic encryption scheme is semantically secure. The round, computational, and communication complexities of this protocol are all constant [16].

Lipmaa's private equality test [16] can be performed in a parallelized manner. Let EQTEST $\left(\big(E(m_{1,i})\big)_{i=0}^{n-1}, \big(E(m_{2,i})\big)_{i=0}^{n-1}\right) = (b_i)_{i=0}^{n-1}$ denote n parallel or batch execution of a private equality test, where $b_i = 1$ if $m_{1,i} = m_{2,i}$, otherwise $b_i = 0$ for all $i = 0, 1, \ldots, n-1$. The n parallel or batch execution of the private equality test can be performed in a constant round, $O(n)$ computational, and $O(tn)$ communication complexities.

Private Index Search. Let $c = (c_0, c_1, \ldots, c_{n-1})$ be a vector of n ciphertexts $c_0, c_1, \ldots, c_{n-1}$ of a threshold additive homomorphic encryption scheme. Given the ciphertext of an arbitrary message c', the private index search computes $\mathrm{INDEX}(C, c') = b$ if there exists $0 \leq b < n$ such that the plaintexts of c_b and c' are equal, otherwise $b = \bot$ is returned. Golle instantiated this protocol by n parallel or batch execution of $\mathrm{EQTEST}(c_i, c')$ for $0 \leq i < n$ [12]. While we make use of batch execution of this protocol, the protocol is still completed within a constant round.

Private Comparison. Let m_1 and m_2 be two plaintexts of an ordinary or threshold additive homomorphic encryption scheme, where $0 \leq m_1, m_2 < n$. When two parties hold private m_1 and m_2, private comparison evaluates whether $m_1 < m_2$ holds without sharing private values. Let $\mathrm{COMPARE}\left(\mathrm{E}(m_1), \mathrm{E}(m_2)\right) = b$ denote the computation of private comparison, where $b = 1$ if $m_1 < m_2$, $b = 0$ otherwise. This protocol can be executed in a constant round through the MIX and parallel execution of EQTEST [12].

3 Private Stable Matching

In this section, we introduce the Gale–Shapley algorithm [9,15], the definition of private stable matching, Golle [12], and Franklin et al.'s protocols [7].

3.1 Gale–Shapley Algorithm

Gale and Shapley defined the stable marriage problem and proposed an algorithm that solves it by producing stable matching [9]. In the stable marriage problem, there are two equal-sized sets of participants consisting of men and women. A matching is a one-to-one mapping between the two sets. We refer to the number of men and women as the size of the stable marriage problem. The objective is to find a matching so that none of the men or women has any incentive to undermine any matched pairs.

The Gale–Shapley algorithm allows us to find a stable matching of this problem with $O(n^2)$ computational complexity, where n is the size of the given stable marriage problem. The outline of the algorithm is shown in Algorithm 1, which is reprinted and slightly modified from [15] for notational convenience. None of the participants is assigned to any matches in the initial phase. Participants that have not been paired are referred to as free men and women. Then, in the loop part (lines 2–8 of Algorithm 1), each free man proposes to the highest ranked woman (according to his preference) that he has never previously proposed to, regardless of her engagement status. The algorithm is terminated when all of the participants have been engaged. The resulting engaged pairs are guaranteed to be a stable matching. The Gale–Shapley algorithm is not designed to preserve input privacy. All of the participants send their own preference lists to a single matching authority, which performs stable matching using the Gale–Shapley algorithm.

Algorithm 1. Gale–Shapley algorithm [15]

1: Assign each person to be free.
2: **while** some man m is free **do**
3:     $w :=$ the first woman on m's preference list to whom m has not yet proposed.
4:     **if** w is free **then** assign m and w to be engaged.
5:     **else**
6:         **if** w prefers m to her fiancé m' **then** assign m and w to be engaged and m' to be free.
7:         **else** w reject m.
8: **end while**
9: **return** The stable matching consisting of n engaged pairs.

3.2 Golle and Franklin–Gondree–Mohassel Private Stable Matching

Golle defined the algorithm or protocol preserving input privacy as the *private stable matching* as follows [12, Definition 1].

Definition 1 (Private stable matching). *An algorithm for computing a stable match is private if it outputs a stable match and reveals no other information to the adversary than what the adversary can learn from that match and from the preferences of the participants it controls.*

Golle and Franklin et al. proposed practical private stable matching protocols in the sense of Definition 1. Our protocol presented in Sect. 4 has better round complexity than the all of the currently existing practical protocols and it is constructed via our proposed bid technique, where bid is a data structure firstly proposed by Golle.

Golle defined two data structures, the *bid* and the *engaged bid*, in order to construct a private stable matching protocol based on the Gale–Shapley algorithm [12]. Bids and engaged bids constructed via ciphertexts, and are used to represent and hide the preference lists and the internal state of the Gale–Shapley algorithm. The bids and the engaged bids represent the statuses of free men and engaged pairs of a man and woman (explained later), respectively.

Franklin et al. modified Golle's bid to construct FGM1. Franklin et al. used Stern's PIR [21] and several ciphertexts in bids are stored into a PIR server. The number of ciphertexts in resulting bids of FGM1 is smaller than Golle's bid. However, PIR cannot be executed in natural manner because query indexes are encrypted and the PIR client does not know its plaintext. Moreover, FGM1 needs the operation to compute $E(\min\{a+1, b\})$ for given $E(a)$, where $a = 0, 1, \ldots, b$, and b is a publicly known integer. These operations cannot be executed efficiently with additive homomorphic encryption only. Franklin et al. solved these problems by using the secret sharing scheme [2]. Consequently, the round complexity of FGM1 is $\widetilde{O}(n^2)$.

4   Main Proposal

In this section, we propose a new private stable matching protocol, which is improved in two ways; specifically, a new bid definition and a new protocol for the proposed bid. Here, the bid is a data structure that represents the internal states of the problem. In what follows, we first introduce our new bid design. Then we describe our new private stable matching protocol. The complexity analysis of the proposed protocol is also explained in Sect. 4.3. We refer the reader to Appendices B and C for the correctness and security proof of our proposal.

4.1   New Bid Design

Ciphertext Vector Representation of the Integer. In this section, we introduce a ciphertext vector representation of integers. Let $E(a)$ be a ciphertext, where $0 \leq a < n$, and let $E(\boldsymbol{b}) = \big(E(b_0), E(b_1), \ldots, E(b_{n-1}) \big)$ be a vector of n ciphertexts. We say that a vector $E(\boldsymbol{b})$ is a *ciphertext vector* of $E(a)$, if $b_a = 1$ and $b_i = 0$ for all $i \neq a$. We introduce two operations for the ciphertext vectors. Given vector $\boldsymbol{b} = (b_0, b_1, \ldots, b_{n-1})$ of n elements, the k-right-rotated vector of $\boldsymbol{b}$ is defined by:

$$\boldsymbol{b} \ggg k = \big(b_{(-k) \bmod n}, b_{(1-k) \bmod n}, \ldots, b_{(n-1-k) \bmod n} \big). \tag{1}$$

Given $\boldsymbol{c} = (c_0, c_1, \ldots, c_{n-1})$, where $c_0, c_1, \ldots, c_{n-1}$ are n integers, the inner product operation of $E(\boldsymbol{b})$ and $\boldsymbol{c}$ is defined by $E(\boldsymbol{b}) \cdot \boldsymbol{c} := \prod_{i=0}^{n-1} E(b_i)^{c_i}$. If $E(\boldsymbol{b})$ is the ciphertext vector of $E(a)$ and $\boldsymbol{c} = (0, 1, \ldots, n-1)$, then:

$$E(\boldsymbol{b}) \cdot \boldsymbol{c} = \prod_{i=0}^{n-1} E(b_i)^i = E(a), \tag{2}$$

i.e., $E(\boldsymbol{b})$ can be transformed to $E(a)$ without any additional information or decryption. Based on the above considerations, an important property, $\big(E(\boldsymbol{b}) \ggg k \big) \cdot \boldsymbol{c} = E\big((a + k) \bmod n \big)$, is derived. This technique readily enables us to increment encryption of $m \bmod n$, $c \leftarrow E\big((m + 1) \bmod n \big)$, by:

$$c \leftarrow E(\boldsymbol{m}) \ggg 1. \tag{3}$$

The key concept behind the proposed protocol is replacing the internal counter of Golle's protocol with the ciphertext vector and incrementing the counter using the 1-right rotation technique. This resolves the counter overflow problem.

Bid with Ciphertext Vector Representation. In this section, we introduce a new bid by modifying the bid defined for Golle's protocol. The proposed protocol uses bids and engaged bids to represent the internal state of the protocol. The bids and the engaged bids represent the statuses of free men and engaged man and women pairs, respectively. Note that all information related to the private preference lists are represented as ciphertexts to prevent any party from learning any private information by observing the bids and the engaged bids.

We apply the single free man technique proposed by Franklin et al. [7] to our protocol, and for a given stable marriage problem of size n, we add $n + 1$ fake men and n fake women to the problem, after which the preferences of n men and n women are transformed to those of $2n + 1$ men and $2n$ women. The details of preference setting derived by the single free man technique is explained in Appendix A.

Let $A_0, A_1, \ldots, A_{2n}$ be $2n + 1$ men, and let $B_0, B_1, \ldots, B_{2n-1}$ be $2n$ women. We regard $i \in \{0, 1, \ldots, 2n\}$ and $j \in \{0, 1, \ldots, 2n - 1\}$ as the identities of a man and woman, respectively. Let $r_{i,j} \in \{0, 1, \ldots, 2n - 1\}$ be the rank of woman B_j for man A_i, and let $s_{j,i} \in \{0, 1, \ldots, 2n\}$ be the rank of man A_i for woman B_j. Our convention is that the highest possible rank is 0, and the lowest is $2n - 1$ or $2n$. The encryptions of the men's and women's ranks are denoted by $p_{i,j} := \mathrm{E}(r_{i,j})$ and $q_{j,i} := \mathrm{E}(s_{j,i})$, respectively. The preferences are strict and complete lists of ranking of the participants belonging to the opposite set, *i.e.*, a preference is the permutation of $(0, 1, \ldots, n - 1)$, where n is the number of persons in the opposite set. The encrypted preferences of man A_i are denoted in the form of vector $\boldsymbol{a}_i = (p_{i,0}, p_{i,1}, \ldots, p_{i,2n-1})$.

Now, we define the *bid of a man* A_i, which consists of the following five elements:

1. $\mathrm{E}(i)$: i is the identity of A_i.
2. $\boldsymbol{a}_i = (p_{i,0}, p_{i,1}, \ldots, p_{i,2n-1})$: encrypted preference of A_i.
3. $\boldsymbol{v}_i = (\mathrm{E}(0), \mathrm{E}(1), \ldots, \mathrm{E}(2n - 1))$: vector of encrypted identities of each woman.
4. $\boldsymbol{q}_i = (q_{0,i}, q_{1,i}, \ldots, q_{2n-1,i})$: vector of the encrypted ranks of A_i for each woman.
5. $\mathrm{E}(\boldsymbol{\rho}_i)$: ciphertext vector of $\mathrm{E}(\rho)$, where ρ is the number of A_i's rejected proposals.

The bid W_i of man A_i is denoted using the five elements as follows: $W_i = \left[\mathrm{E}(i), \boldsymbol{a}_i, \boldsymbol{v}_i, \boldsymbol{q}_i, \mathrm{E}(\boldsymbol{\rho}_i)\right]$. All of the ciphertexts contained in the bids are given by the input and generated in the initialization step. The details of the initialization step are explained in Appendix A. Note that the difference between our bid and Golle's bid [12] is the 5th element in above.

Next, the *engaged bid of man* A_i *and woman* B_j is defined by $\overline{W}_{i,j} = \langle W_i, \mathrm{E}(j), q_{j,i} \rangle$, where W_i is the bid of man A_i, $\mathrm{E}(j)$ is the encrypted identity of woman B_j, and $q_{j,i}$ is the encrypted rank of A_i for woman B_j. This definition is same as Golle's protocol [12], and is used to represent the engagement of man A_i and woman B_j.

4.2   New Private Stable Matching

In this section, we describe a new private stable matching protocol using our proposed bid. As mentioned previously, Franklin et al. improved the computational, communication, and round complexities by introducing the *single free man* technique into Golle's protocol [7]. The single free man technique is also used in the initialization step in proposed protocol for the same purpose (explained in Appendix A).

In our protocol, there are *matching authorities* (MA) who jointly execute distributed protocols based on the threshold homomorphic encryption scheme in order to compute a stable matching. The numbers of matching authorities are specified in advance.

A brief overview of our protocol is shown in Algorithm 2. Our protocol consists of five major steps: setup, input submission, initialization, main loop (lines 2–15 in Algorithm 2), and decryption. The correspondences between Algorithms 1 and 2 are line 3 and lines 4–7, as well as lines 6–7 and lines 8–12, respectively. At lines 3, 11, 12, and 14, $\mathcal{F}_k$ denotes a set of free bids (actually, only one bid is free in each iteration) and $\mathcal{E}_k$ denotes a set of engaged bids at the kth iteration of the main loop. The setup, input submission, and decryption steps are very similar to Golle and Franklin et al.'s protocols. We refer the reader to [7,12] for these steps. Initialization of our protocol basically follows FGM1 [7] and is easily derived, even though the details are dissimilar because our proposed bid is different to them. We explain initialization in Appendix A.

The differences of main loop between our protocol and FGM1 [7] are as follows:

- At the lines 4–5, two ciphertexts $E(j)$ and $E(s_{j,i})$ are found by using the INDEX explained in Sect. 2 with inputs a_i and $E(\rho_i)$, where a_i is the 2nd element of W_i and $E(\rho_i)$ is recovered by an operation locally described in Eq. (2) applying to the 5th element $E(\rho_i)$ of W_i.
- At the line 11, the 4th element $E(\rho_h)$ of "loser's" bid W_h is incremented by using an operation described in Eq. (3).

Consequently, our algorithm is executed by additive homomorphic encryption only. At the line 6 in Algorithm 2, pairs of decrypted man and woman's identities form a stable matching, the details are explained in Appendix B. We note that the increment of the 5th element of our bid is computed locally, the number of rounds is improved because this new increment method eliminates the need for the secret sharing scheme. The security of our protocol is described in Appendix C.

4.3   Complexity Analysis

Our protocol uses the EQTEST [16] and the MIX [13] introduced in Sect. 2. This implies the following claim:

Claim 2. *Suppose that the EQTEST and the MIX explained in Sect. 2 can be used. The size of a given stable marriage problem is n and the number of matching authorities is t. The total computational, total communication, and round complexities are $O(n^4)$, $O(tn^4)$, and $O(n^2)$, respectively.*

Algorithm 2. Our proposed protocol

1: Input submission and Initialization.
2: **for** $k = 1$ to $2n^2$ **do**
3:    Select the single free bid W_i from $\mathcal{F}_k$.
4:    Open W_i to recover the index $\mathrm{E}(\rho_i)$ from $\mathrm{E}(\rho_i)$.
5:    Find $\mathrm{E}(j)$ and $\mathrm{E}(s_{j,i})$ by using $\mathrm{E}(\rho_i)$.   // Use INDEX
6:    Form the engaged bid, $\langle W_i, \mathrm{E}(j), \mathrm{E}(s_{j,i}) \rangle$.
7:    Find the conflicting engaged bid, $\langle W_{i'}, \mathrm{E}(j), \mathrm{E}(s_{j,i'}) \rangle$.   // Use INDEX
8:    Mix these two engaged bids.   // Use MIX with $O(n)$ input ciphertexts
9:    Resolve the conflict to find the "winner" and "loser."   // Use COMPARE
10:    Break the engagement for the loser to obtain loser's free bid W_h.
11:    Increment $\mathrm{E}(\rho_h)$ of W_h and add this free bid to $\mathcal{F}_{k+1}$.
12:    Add the winner to $\mathcal{E}_k$.
13:    Mix the engaged bids.   // Use MIX with $O(n^2)$ input ciphertexts
14:    Let $\mathcal{E}_{k+1} \leftarrow \mathcal{E}_k$.
15: **end for**
16: Decrypt pairs of man and woman's encrypted identities in $\mathcal{E}_{2n^2+1}$, and announce stable matching.

Proof. The proposed protocol in Sect. 4.2 uses the constant round building blocks introduced in Sect. 2, specifically, the MIX, EQTEST, INDEX, and COMPARE based on the threshold additive homomorphic encryption scheme. The number of ciphertexts is determined by n.

In one iteration of the main loop, implementation of the MIX in line 13 is the most costly component, and $O(n^2)$ ciphertexts are input. Hence, its computational, communication, and round complexities are $O(n^2)$, $O(tn^2)$, and $O(1)$.

The complexities are dominated by the MIX in line 13. The main loop is invoked $2n^2$ times, so the total computational, total communication, and round complexities of the proposed protocol are $O(n^4)$, $O(tn^4)$, and $O(n^2)$, respectively.

Finally, the round complexity of our protocol is the same as the computational complexity of the Gale–Shapley algorithm.

5   Experimental Implementation

In this section, we outline the implementation friendly version of our protocol, explained in Sect. 5.1, and describe an experimental implementation of this protocol. To the best of our knowledge, this is the first implementation of a private stable matching protocol.

5.1   Implemented Version of Our Protocol

The proposed protocol described in Sect. 4 achieves collusion resistance by using threshold encryption and the MIX. One drawback of the use of threshold encryption is the synchronization cost of the distributed decryption and rerandomization of the MIX. Considering the ease of implementation, we propose a new implementation-friendly protocol by weakening the security assumption.

The security of the protocol proposed in Sect. 4 is proven assuming the number of the matching authorities that collude with each other is less than a prescribed threshold, which is specified by the underlying threshold homomorphic encryption. For the relaxed version of the protocol, we further assume that the matching authorities never collude with each other. Although the security of the relaxed version of the protocol is obviously weaker than that in Sect. 4, in return for this relaxation, we provide a more implementation-friendly protocol for the private stable marriage problem.

This relaxation also allows the following protocol simplifications. First, the process of main loop is executed by a single party, called *controller*. The EQTEST and the simplified MIX are executed by a single private-key holder, called *decryptor* and a group of several parties, called *mix group*, respectively. Second, distributed threshold decryption can be replaced by ordinary decryption by the decryptor. Third, the MIX is simplified, with the number of re-encryption operations and secret shuffles are reduced to one. This means that, in one time mix network execution, it is not necessary for all of the mix servers to evaluate re-encryption and secret shuffle. Instead, only one member of the mix group evaluates those operations. To preserve security and privacy, the controller must send a request for the simplified MIX so that the same mix group members do not receive the request twice consecutively. Note that in order to guarantee security, decryption and the simplified MIX are executed by individual parties. These replacements do not change the computational, communication, and round complexities of the protocol in Sect. 4.

The simplified protocol is also private if the underlying ordinary additive homomorphic encryption scheme is semantically secure, the simplified MIX is private against semi-honest probabilistic polynomial-time adversaries, and the parties do not collude with each other. The details of the protocol, complexity analysis, and security proof are described in the full version of this paper.

Table 2. Android devices.

Model number	CPU name	CPU freq.	Memory	Android OS	# of devices	Does it join to size 3?
Nexsus 7	Tegra 3	1.3 GHz	1 GB	4.2.1	2	Yes
Galaxy Nexsus	OMAP 4460	1.2 GHz	1 GB	4.0.1	1	Yes
Galaxy SII	Exynos 4210 Orion	1.2 GHz	1 GB	2.3.5	3	Yes
Infobar A01	Snapdoragon S2 MSM8655T	1.4 GHz	512 MB	2.3.3	1	Yes
IS05	Snapdoragon S2 MSM8655	1 GHz	512 MB	2.2.1	1	No
Desire A8181	Snapdragon QSD8250	1 GHz	576 MB	2.2.2	1	No

5.2   Experimental Settings

Development Environment. Our experimental program is designed assuming implementation using a client-server system. In the experimental implementation, Android smartphones, tablet computers, and a personal computer (PC) were used as clients and the server, respectively. The server program acts as the controller; the program was built with Java SE 6 [19] and ran on the Linux operating system. The runtime environment is Java SE 7 [19]. The server PC CPU is a Core i7 970 (3.2 GHz) with 12 GB RAM. The client programs act as executors of the simplified MIX and ordinary decryption and were built with Android SDK Tools Revision 21.1 [14]. The specifications of Android smartphone and tablet devices are listed in Table 2. One Galaxy SII device acts as the decryptor while the others are the members of the mix group.

Implementation of Primitives. We implemented Paillier encryption [20] as an additive homomorphic encryption in the experimental implementation. For the secure channels, the transport layer security provided by the standard Java runtime environment [19] and the Android platforms [14] were used. We did not use other optimization techniques for implementation, including the CPU-specific efficient implementation.

Parameter Setting. The key length of Paillier encryption was set to 896 bits or 1,024 bits, and the size of the input was set to 3 or 4. The combinations of the two parameters were tested, and a total of four cases are compared. Note that a longer key length is needed if a security level of more than 80 bits is required [4,18].

Network. The Android devices are connected to a LAN using Wi-Fi equipment. The PC connects to the same LAN via the Ethernet cable. The experiment is implemented using this equipment. There were no factors that cause an extreme delay of the communication during the execution of the programs in our experiment.

5.3   Experimental Results

The experimental results are presented in this subsection. The computation time, the communication time of the main loop (lines 2–15 in Algorithm 2), and their ratio of our experiments are shown in Table 3. Note that the computation time (Comput. column in Table 3) includes the communication time (Comm. column in Table 3).

The total execution time of a line 13 in Algorithm 2 in the case of a 896-bit key length were 113.61 s for size 3 and 347.33 s for size 4. In the case of the 1,024-bit key length were 162.42 s for size 3 and 511.88 s for size 4. Note that these times include computation and communication times. Based on these results, it is clear that the (simplified) MIX was the most expensive component in terms of computation time. Therefore, we can conclude that this protocol is the bottleneck of the proposed protocol.

Table 3. Benchmarking of the proposed protocol, where Size denotes the size of given stable marriage problem, Comput. denotes the computation times, and Comm. denotes the communication times of the entire iterations of the main loop.

Key length [bits]	Size	# of Android devices	Comput. [s]	Comm. [s]	Comm./comput. ratio
896	3	7	250.50	84.64	0.34
896	4	9	581.47	101.64	0.17
1,024	3	7	305.17	64.90	0.21
1,024	4	9	827.80	125.34	0.15

Acknowledgements. The work is supported by FIRST program and Grant-in-Aid 12913388. The authors would like to thank Jacob Schuldt, Nuttapong Attrapadung, and Naoto Yanai for the valuable discussion and comments. We also thank the members of Shin-Akarui-Angou-Benkyou-Kai and the anonymous reviewers of ISC 2013 for their valuable discussion and comments.

A   Initialization of the Proposed Protocol

The initialization step is performed by the matching authorities after the input submission step. In order to reduce the complexities, the bids are initialized using the single free man technique, as introduced by Franklin et al. [7]. An explicit overview of the initialization step procedure for the proposed bid design is provided below.

The initialization step consists of (1) modification of input encrypted preferences, (2) generation of dummy encrypted preferences, and (3) initialization of the fifth element of bids. After the input submission step, if the numbers of men and women are not the same, the matching authorities then generate and insert random preferences into the set that has fewer participants. Next, the matching authorities modify the encrypted preferences and generate the encrypted preferences of $n + 1$ fake men and n fake women as follows:

$$a_i = \begin{cases} (\overbrace{p_{i,0}, p_{i,1}, \ldots, p_{i,n-1}}^{\text{The original preference of } A_i}, \overbrace{p_{i,n}, p_{i,n+1}, \ldots, p_{i,2n-1}}^{\text{Part 1}}) \\ \qquad \text{for } i \in \{0, 1, \ldots, n-1\}, \\ (\overbrace{p_{i,0}, p_{i,1}, \ldots, p_{i,n-1}}^{\text{Part 2}}, \overbrace{p_{i,n}, p_{i,n+1}, \ldots, p_{i,2n-2}}^{\text{Part 3}}, E(n-1)) \\ \qquad \text{for } i \in \{n, n+1, \ldots, 2n\}, \end{cases} \tag{4}$$

$$b_j = \begin{cases} (\overbrace{q_{j,0}, q_{j,1}, \ldots, q_{j,n-1}}^{\text{The original preference of } B_j}, \overbrace{q_{j,n}, q_{j,n+1}, \ldots, q_{j,2n}}^{\text{Part 4}}) \\ \qquad \text{for } j \in \{0, 1, \ldots, n-1\}, \\ (\overbrace{q_{j,0}, q_{j,1}, \ldots, q_{j,n-1}}^{\text{Part 5}}, \overbrace{q_{j,n}, q_{j,n+1}, \ldots, q_{j,2n-1}}^{\text{Part 6}}, E(n)) \\ \qquad \text{for } j \in \{n, n+1, \ldots, 2n-1\}, \end{cases} \tag{5}$$

where $\boldsymbol{a}_i$ and $\boldsymbol{b}_j$ are encrypted preferences of man A_i and woman B_j, respectively. The ciphertexts of Parts 1 through 6 in Eqs. (4) and (5) are permutation vectors defined in Table 4, and all of the elements in the permutation vectors are encrypted. Then, all of the preferences are ordered as follows. The first n men and women are the true participants of the stable marriage problem. The remaining $n + 1$ men and n women are fake men and women. After the above modification, there are $2n + 1$ men's encrypted preferences and $2n$ women's encrypted preferences.

Table 4. Range of plaintext at Parts 1–6 in Eqs. (4) and (5).

Part	1	2	3	4	5	6
Range of plaintext	n to $2n-1$	n to $2n-1$	0 to $n-2$	n to $2n$	$n+1$ to $2n$	0 to $n-1$

Then, the matching authorities form $2n + 1$ vectors $\boldsymbol{q}_0, \boldsymbol{q}_1, \ldots, \boldsymbol{q}_{2n}$ from $2n$ vectors $\boldsymbol{b}_0, \boldsymbol{b}_1, \ldots, \boldsymbol{b}_{2n-1}$, in the same manner as Golle and Franklin et al.'s protocol [7, 12].

Then, $2n+1$ bids are arranged as $W_i = \big[\, \mathrm{E}(i), \boldsymbol{a}_i, \boldsymbol{v}_i, \boldsymbol{q}_i, \mathrm{E}(\boldsymbol{\rho}_i) \,\big]$. The arrangement of the bids is the same as in [12], except that the counter is given as the ciphertext vector.

Next, the matching authorities generate two sets $\mathcal{F}_1$ and $\mathcal{E}_1$, where $\mathcal{F}_1$ denotes a set of free bids and is initialized as $\mathcal{F}_1 := \{\, W_0 \,\}$, where W_0 is a bid of A_0. The fifth value $\mathrm{E}(\boldsymbol{\rho}_0)$ of the free bid W_0 is updated to the ciphertext vector, which represents $\mathrm{E}(0)$. Here, $\mathcal{E}_1$ denotes a set of engaged bids and includes $2n$ engaged bids. The engaged bids in $\mathcal{E}_1$ are initialized as follows. True men $A_1, A_2, \ldots, A_{n-1}$ get engaged to fake women $B_n, B_{n+1}, \ldots, B_{2n-2}$, respectively, and fake men $A_n, A_{n+1}, \ldots, A_{2n-1}$ get engaged to true women $B_0, B_1, \ldots, B_{n-1}$, respectively. Moreover, fake man A_{2n} gets engaged to fake woman B_{2n-1}. In other words,

$$\mathcal{E}_1 := \big\{\, \overline{W}_{i,n-1+i} \mid i = 1, 2, \ldots, n-1 \,\big\} \cup \big\{\, \overline{W}_{n+i,i} \mid i = 0, 1, \ldots, n-1 \,\big\} \cup \big\{\, \overline{W}_{2n,2n-1} \,\big\}.$$

Then, the matching authorities jointly apply the MIX to $\mathcal{F}_1$ and $\mathcal{E}_1$ independently. Application of the MIX to the bids in $\mathcal{F}_1$ is performed as follows. First, a randomly generated secret permutation is applied to the set of bids and engaged bids. Next, for each bid, all ciphertexts included in the bids are re-randomized and $W_i \leftarrow \big[\, \mathrm{E}(i), \pi(\boldsymbol{a}_i), \pi(\boldsymbol{v}_i), \pi(\boldsymbol{q}_i), \mathrm{E}(\boldsymbol{\rho}_i) \,\big]$ is then computed, where π is a randomly generated secret permutation. For the engaged bids in $\mathcal{E}_1$, the operation for the bid contained in each engaged bid is the same in above, then the remaining two ciphertexts are re-randomized.

B   Correctness of the Proposed Protocol

The differences between our protocol and FGM1 [7] are in lines 4–5 and line 11. The remaining steps are equivalent to FGM1. We confirm the correctness of the proposed protocol by ensuring that these two changes do not change the protocol behavior.

In lines 4–5, the encryption of the counter ρ_i used in Golle's protocol is readily obtained by $E(\rho_i) = \prod_{\ell=0}^{n-1} E(\rho_{i,\ell})^\ell$. Thus, the change of the representation of the counter does not affect the behavior of the protocol.

Next, we consider the treatment of the increment of the counter (at line 11). Since the preferences are set by Eqs. (4) and (5), the true men (resp. fake men) prefer the true women (resp. fake women) to the fake women (resp. true women). Thus, the true men (resp. fake men) never propose to the fake women (resp. true women). None of the fake men prefer B_{2n-1}. Therefore, all of the fake men propose to B_{2n-1} as a last resort. No matter which fake man proposes to B_{2n-1}, the resulting engagement is stable, except for the case in which A_{2n} proposes. Thus, man A_{2n} always becomes single after $2n$ pairs are made. At the same time, no fake women proposed to by A_{2n} will agree with the engagement because A_{2n} is ranked as the worst by all of the women. Thus, for any input preferences, proposals by A_{2n} are declined at any time. Note that n is the largest number of rejected proposals for the stable marriage problem of size n. In the proposed protocol, the counter $E(\rho_{2n})$ is incremented by 1-right rotation $E(\rho_{2n}) \ggg 1$ for each engagement. This operation corresponds to incrementing with modulo n. Since 1-right rotation is not an arithmetic operation and the ciphertext vector representing the counter is made to be sufficiently long, the operation $E(\rho_{2n}) \ggg 1$ does not cause overflow.

Therefore, the behavior of the proposed protocol is equivalent to that of Golle and Franklin et al.'s protocol and outputs stable matching correctly after $2n^2$ iterations of the main loop of Algorithm 2 (lines 2–15) [7, 12].

C   Security of the Proposed Protocol

In the proposed protocol, the main building blocks are the EQTEST and the MIX. These are based on the threshold additive homomorphic encryption. The other building blocks are constructed using the main building blocks, as explained in Sect. 2. The security and input privacy of the proposed stable matching protocol are guaranteed by the underlying threshold additive homomorphic encryption and the MIX, which are shown by the following theorem.

Theorem 3. *Suppose that the threshold additive homomorphic encryption scheme is semantically secure, that the MIX is private against any probabilistic polynomial-time semi-honest adversaries, and that the number of adversaries that collude with each other is less than the threshold, which is specified by the underlying threshold additive homomorphic encryption scheme.*

The proposed protocol presented in Sect. 4.2 is private against any probabilistic polynomial-time semi-honest adversaries in the sense of Definition 1.

Proof (Sketch). We prove the security of the proposed protocol by showing that the modifications to GFGM and FGM1 do not affect the proof of [12, Proposition 3]. Since the difference of our protocol and Golle and Franklin et al.'s protocols is the 5th element of bid, we state the security proof of this part. Assume an adversary that can distinguish the 5th element of our bid. In such conditions, using this adversary can break the semantic security of the underlying additive homomorphic encryption. Hence, our protocol is private with the two primitives described in the sections above.

References

1. Beaver, D., Micali, S., Rogaway, P.: The round complexity of secure protocols (extended abstract). In: Ortiz, H. (ed.) STOC, pp. 503–513. ACM (1990)
2. Damgård, I.B., Fitzi, M., Kiltz, E., Nielsen, J.B., Toft, T.: Unconditionally secure constant-rounds multi-party computation for equality, comparison, bits and exponentiation. In: Halevi, S., Rabin, T. (eds.) TCC 2006. LNCS, vol. 3876, pp. 285–304. Springer, Heidelberg (2006)
3. Damgård, I., Jurik, M.: A generalisation, a simplification and some applications of Paillier's probabilistic public-key system. In: Kim, K. (ed.) PKC 2001. LNCS, vol. 1992, pp. 119–136. Springer, Heidelberg (2001)
4. ECRYPT II: Yearly report on algorithms and keysize (2011–2012), September 2012. http://www.ecrypt.eu.org/
5. El Gamal, T.: A public key cryptosystem and a signature scheme based on discrete logarithms. In: Blakely, G.R., Chaum, D. (eds.) CRYPTO 1984. LNCS, vol. 196, pp. 10–18. Springer, Heidelberg (1985)
6. Fouque, P.-A., Poupard, G., Stern, J.: Sharing decryption in the context of voting or lotteries. In: Frankel, Y. (ed.) FC 2000. LNCS, vol. 1962, pp. 90–104. Springer, Heidelberg (2001)
7. Franklin, M.K., Gondree, M., Mohassel, P.: Improved efficiency for private stable matching. In: Abe, M. (ed.) CT-RSA 2007. LNCS, vol. 4377, pp. 163–177. Springer, Heidelberg (2006)
8. Franklin, M.K., Gondree, M., Mohassel, P.: Multi-party indirect indexing and applications. In: Kurosawa, K. (ed.) ASIACRYPT 2007. LNCS, vol. 4833, pp. 283–297. Springer, Heidelberg (2007)
9. Gale, D., Shapley, L.S.: College admissions and the stability of marriage. Am. Math. Mon. **69**(1), 9–15 (1962)
10. Gennaro, R., Jarecki, S., Krawczyk, H., Rabin, T.: Secure distributed key generation for discrete-log based cryptosystems. J. Crypt. **20**(1), 51–83 (2007)
11. Goldwasser, S., Micali, S.: Probabilistic encryption. J. Comput. Syst. Sci. **28**(2), 270–299 (1984)
12. Golle, P.: A private stable matching algorithm. In: Di Crescenzo, G., Rubin, A. (eds.) FC 2006. LNCS, vol. 4107, pp. 65–80. Springer, Heidelberg (2006)
13. Golle, P., Juels, A.: Parallel mixing. In: Atluri, V., Pfitzmann, B., McDaniel, P.D. (eds.) ACM Conference on Computer and Communications Security, pp. 220–226. ACM (2004)
14. Google, Open Handset Alliance: Android developers. http://developer.android.com/
15. Gusfield, D., Irving, R.W.: The Stable Marriage Problem: Structure and Algorithms. The Foundations of Computing. MIT Press, Cambridge (1989)
16. Lipmaa, H.: Verifiable homomorphic oblivious transfer and private equality test. In: Laih, C.-S. (ed.) ASIACRYPT 2003. LNCS, vol. 2894, pp. 416–433. Springer, Heidelberg (2003)

17. Naor, M., Nissim, K.: Communication preserving protocols for secure function evaluation. In: Vitter, J.S., Spirakis, P.G., Yannakakis, M. (eds.) STOC, pp. 590–599. ACM (2001)
18. NIST: Special publication 800-57, recommendation for key management - part 1: General (revision 3), July 2012. http://csrc.nist.gov/publications/PubsSPs.html
19. Oracle: Java.com. http://java.com/
20. Paillier, P.: Public-key cryptosystems based on composite degree residuosity classes. In: Stern, J. (ed.) EUROCRYPT 1999. LNCS, vol. 1592, pp. 223–238. Springer, Heidelberg (1999)
21. Stern, J.P.: A new and efficient all-or-nothing disclosure of secrets protocol. In: Ohta, K., Pei, D. (eds.) ASIACRYPT 1998. LNCS, vol. 1514, pp. 357–371. Springer, Heidelberg (1998)
22. Yao, A.C.C.: How to generate and exchange secrets (extended abstract). In: FOCS, pp. 162–167. IEEE Computer Society (1986)

Efficient and Fully Secure Forward Secure Ciphertext-Policy Attribute-Based Encryption

Takashi Kitagawa[1]([✉]), Hiroki Kojima[2],
Nuttapong Attrapadung[3], and Hideki Imai[1]

[1] Chuo University, 1-13-27, Kasuga Bunkyo-ku, Tokyo 112-8551, Japan
t.kitagawa.73@gmail.com
[2] Internet Initiative Japan Inc., Tokyo, Japan
[3] National Institute of Advanced Industrial Science and Technology (AIST),
Tokyo, Japan

Abstract. Attribute-based encryption (ABE) schemes provide a fine-grained access control mechanism over encrypted data, and are useful for cloud online-storage services, or Pay-TV systems and so on. To apply ABE for such services, key exposure protection mechanisms are necessary. Unfortunately, standard security notions of ABE offer no protection against key exposure. One solution to this problem is to give forward security to ABE schemes. In forward secure cryptographic schemes, even if a secret key is exposed, messages encrypted during all time periods prior to the key leak remain secret. In this paper we propose an efficient *Forward Secure Ciphertext-Policy Attribute-Based Encryption* (FS-CP-ABE) which is efficient and fully secure. To construct efficient FS-CP-ABE, we first introduce a new cryptographic primitive called *Ciphertext-Policy Attribute-Based Encryption with Augmented Hierarchy* (CP-ABE-AH). Intuitively, CP-ABE-AH is an encryption scheme with both hierarchical identity based encryption and CP-ABE properties. Then we show that FS-CP-ABE can be constructed from CP-ABE-AH generically. We give the security definition of FS-CP-ABE, and security proofs based on three complexity assumptions. The size of public parameter is $O(\log T)$, and the secret key size is $O(\log^2 T)$ where T is the number of time slots.

1 Introduction

In cryptographic schemes, the standard notions of security offer no protection whatsoever once the secret key of the system has been compromised. Exposure of the secret key implies that all security guarantees are lost. In 2003, Canetti, Halevi, and Katz proposed forward secure public key encryption (FS-PKE) to solve the key exposure problem [7]. FS-PKE is a key-evolving public key encryption scheme and achieves forward security as follows: The lifetime of the system is divided into T time periods labeled $1, \ldots, T$, and the secret key evolves with time. The receiver generates a public key PK and an initial secret key SK_1. He/she then publishes the public key and stores secret key SK_1. On the first day, a sender encrypts message m with the public key PK and the current time

© Springer International Publishing Switzerland 2015
Y. Desmedt (Ed.): ISC 2013, LNCS 7807, pp. 87–99, 2015.
DOI: 10.1007/978-3-319-27659-5_6

1, and obtains ciphertext C_1. The receiver can decrypt the ciphertext C_1 with the secret key SK_1. On the next day, a sender encrypts message m' with PK and the current time 2 and obtains a ciphertext C_2. To decrypt C_2, the receiver updates SK_1 to SK_2, and then uses SK_2. Namely, at the beginning of a time period i, the receiver applies a key update function to the key SK_{i-1} to derive the new key SK_i. Moreover, the old key SK_{i-1} is then erased and SK_i is used for all secret cryptographic operations during period i. In forward secure encryption schemes, the key update function should be designed to be infeasible to invert. The public key remains fixed throughout the lifetime of the system. Due to inversion hardness of key update function, an FS-PKE scheme guarantees that even if an adversary learns SK_i (for some i), messages encrypted during all time periods prior to i remain secret.

Forward Secure Ciphertext-Policy Attribute Based Encryption. Attribute based encryption schemes provide a fine-grained access control mechanism over encrypted data. In ciphertext-policy attribute based encryption, data is encrypted with an access policies, and a decryption key is associated with a set of attribute. A decryption key can decrypt encrypted data if the set of attributes satisfies the access policy which is attached to the ciphertext. The access control mechanism of ABE is useful for cloud online-storage systems, Pay-TV systems and so on. However, to manage these systems with ABE scheme, countermeasures against key exposure are necessary. To overcome this issue, we propose an efficient and fully secure forward secure CP-ABE scheme.

Before introducing our contributions, we point out that one can easily make them to have forward security by representing time information as attributes. Here, we introduce two such schemes, and show that these schemes are impractical due to their huge key sizes.

Settings: Let T be the total number of time periods, and $\mathcal{U}$ be an attribute universe. The system prepares another attribute universe $\mathcal{T} = \{1, \ldots, T\}$ such that $\mathcal{U} \cap \mathcal{T} = \emptyset$, and generates a public parameter for attribute universe $\mathcal{U} \cup \mathcal{T}$.

Trivial Scheme 1: When a user requests a decryption key for a set of attribute ω, the key generation center (KGC) produces T decryption keys $\mathsf{sk}_{\omega,1}, \ldots, \mathsf{sk}_{\omega,T}$ where $\mathsf{sk}_{\omega,i}$ is a key for attribute set $\omega \cup \{i\}$ ($i \in \mathcal{T}$). A ciphertext $CT_{\mathbb{A},i}$ for an access structure $\mathbb{A}$ and time period i is generated as $\mathsf{Encryption}(\mathsf{pk}, \mathbb{A} \wedge i, m)$. The ciphertext $CT_{\mathbb{A},i}$ can be decrypted with $\mathsf{sk}_{\omega,i}$. At the end of each time period, the user removes the current decryption key. We call this scheme *"trivial FS-CP-ABE 1"*. The upper bound of the decryption key size is $O(T)$.

Trivial Scheme 2: In this construction, key derivation function is required for a CP-ABE scheme. On a key request for a set of attribute ω, the KGC produces a decryption key $\mathsf{sk}_{\omega,\{1,\ldots,T\}}$ for attribute set $\omega \cup \{1, \ldots, T\}$. A ciphertext for an access structure $\mathbb{A}$ and time period i is generated as $\mathsf{Encrypt}(\mathsf{pk}, (\mathbb{A} \wedge i \wedge \ldots \wedge T), m)$. To update a decryption key $\mathsf{sk}_{\omega,\{i,\ldots,T\}}$, the key owner uses the key derivation function of CP-ABE and obtain $\mathsf{sk}_{\omega,\{i+1,\ldots,T\}}$. We call this scheme *"trivial FS-CP-ABE 2"*. In many CP-ABE schemes, the decryption key size is linear in the size of attribute set. Thus, the key size of this scheme is also $O(T)$.

Our Contributions. In this paper, we propose an efficient *Forward Secure Ciphertext-Policy Attribute-Based Encryption* (FS-CP-ABE) scheme which is efficient and fully secure in the standard model. Toward constructing an efficient and fully secure FS-CP-ABE scheme, we introduce a new primitive called *Ciphertext-Policy Attribute-Based Encryption with Augmented Hierarchy* (CP-ABE-AH), and then show how to construct FS-CP-ABE from CP-ABE-AH generically. Roughly speaking, a CP-ABE-AH scheme has both CP-ABE and HIBE properties. The key generation algorithm of CP-ABE-AH takes as a set of attributes and an ID-tuple and outputs a decryption key. The encryption algorithm takes as input an ID-tuple and an access structure, and outputs a ciphertext. If the ID-tuples of the secret key and the ciphertext are the same, and the set of attributes of the secret key satisfies the access structure of the ciphertext, then the ciphertext can be decrypted with the secret key. Furthermore, CP-ABE-AH scheme has a key derivation function which is similar to the key derivation function of HIBE which creates a secret key for a child node. To construct fully secure FS-CP-ABE, CP-ABE-AH should have adaptive security. We define an adaptive security notion for CP-ABE-AH schemes, and give a concrete construction of the scheme based on two encryption schemes: HIBE of Lewko and Waters [10] and CP-ABE of Lewko et al. [9]. To prove security of our CP-ABE-AH system, we adapt the dual system encryption technique proposed by Waters [13]. The security of our CP-ABE-AH scheme is reduced to three complexity assumptions proposed in [9]. We then propose a generic conversion from CP-ABE-AH to FS-CP-ABE. The conversion uses the "time tree" technique of [7], which was used to construct a forward secure public key encryption scheme from a binary tree encryption scheme. Our conversion is essentially the same as that of [7] except that the attribute is introduced. Finally, we prove that the FS-CP-ABE scheme constructed from our CP-ABE-AH has full security.

Related Works. The first efficient forward secure public key encryption scheme was proposed by Canetti et al. based on a hierarchical identity-based encryption scheme [7]. Yao et al. then proposed the first forward secure HIBE and the first forward secure public key broadcast encryption scheme [15] which is selectively secure in the standard model. Boneh et al. [4] and Attrapadung et al. [1] subsequently proposed efficiency improvements over Yao et al.'s schemes. In this paper, we consider forward security for ciphertext-policy ABE; however, the dual notion called key-policy ABE (KP-ABE) can also be considered. Boneh and Hamburg [5] proposed the notion of spatial encryption and briefly suggested how to construct forward secure KP-ABE from it. However, the policy class for which spatial encryption can express seems more limited than general monotone access structures. Recently, Wang et al. proposed the first explicit (selectively secure) expressive forward secure KP-ABE [12]. They also pointed out that constructing forward secure ciphertext-policy scheme has been an open problem.

2 Preliminaries

2.1 Composite Order Bilinear Maps and Assumptions

In this subsection we review composite order bilinear maps and three complexity assumptions.

Composite Order Bilinear Maps. Let $\mathcal{G}$ be an group generator algorithm which takes as input a security parameter λ, and outputs a tuple $(p_1, p_2, p_3, G, G_T, e)$ where p_1, p_2, p_3 are distinct primes, G and G_T are two cyclic groups of order $N = p_1 p_2 p_3$, and e is a function $e : G^2 \to G_T$. The map is called a composite order bilinear map, and satisfies the following properties:

1. Bilinear: For any $g, h \in G$, $a, b \in \mathbb{Z}_N$, we have $e(g^a, h^b) = e(g, h)^{ab}$,
2. Non-degenerate: There exists an element $g \in G$ such that $e(g, g)$ has order N in G_T,
3. Computable: For any $g, h \in G$, there exists an efficient algorithm which computes $e(g, h)$.

We let G_{p_1}, G_{p_2}, and G_{p_3} denote the subgroups of order p_1, p_2 and p_3 in G respectively. We note that when $g \in G_{p_i}$ and $h \in G_{p_j}$ for $i \neq j$, $e(g, h) = 1_{G_T}$ (identity element of G_T).

Complexity Assumptions. Our FS-CP-ABE scheme is based on a ciphertext-policy attribute-based encryption scheme proposed by Lewko et al. [9], and security of our scheme is reduced to three complexity assumptions which were also proposed in [9]. Here, we present the three assumptions.

Assumption 1. *For a given group generator $\mathcal{G}$, we define the following distribution:*

$$\mathbb{G} = (N = p_1 p_2 p_3, G, G_T, e) \xleftarrow{R} \mathcal{G}, g \xleftarrow{R} G_{p_1}, X_3 \xleftarrow{R} G_{p_3},$$
$$D = (\mathbb{G}, g, X_3), T_1 \xleftarrow{R} G_{p_1 p_2}, T_2 \xleftarrow{R} G_{p_1}.$$

The advantage of an algorithm $\mathcal{A}$ in breaking Assumption 1 is defined as:

$$Adv1_{\mathcal{G}, \mathcal{A}}(\lambda) := |\Pr[\mathcal{A}(D, T_1) = 1] - \Pr[\mathcal{A}(D, T_2) = 1]|.$$

We say that Assumption 1 holds if $Adv1_{\mathcal{G}, \mathcal{A}}$ is negligible for any polynomial time algorithm $\mathcal{A}$.

Assumption 2. *For a given group generator $\mathcal{G}$, we define the following distribution:*

$$\mathbb{G} = (N = p_1 p_2 p_3, G, G_T, e) \xleftarrow{R} \mathcal{G}, \; g, X_1 \xleftarrow{R} G_{p_1}, \; X_2, Y_2 \xleftarrow{R} G_{p_2}, \; X_3, Y_3 \xleftarrow{R} G_{p_3},$$
$$D = (\mathbb{G}, g, X_1 X_2, X_3, Y_2 Y_3), T_1 \xleftarrow{R} G, T_2 \xleftarrow{R} G_{p_1 p_3}.$$

We define the advantage of an algorithm $\mathcal{A}$ in breaking Assumption 2 to be:

$$Adv2_{\mathcal{G},\ \mathcal{A}}(\lambda) := |\ \Pr[\mathcal{A}(D, T_1) = 1] - \Pr[\mathcal{A}(D, T_2) = 1]\ |.$$

We say that Assumption 2 holds if $Adv2_{\mathcal{G},\ \mathcal{A}}$ is negligible for any polynomial time algorithm $\mathcal{A}$.

Assumption 3. For a given group generator $\mathcal{G}$, we define the following distribution:

$$\mathbb{G} = (N = p_1 p_2 p_3, G, G_T, e) \xleftarrow{R} \mathcal{G},\ \alpha, s \xleftarrow{R} \mathbb{Z}_N,\ g \xleftarrow{R} G_{p_1},\ X_2, Y_2, Z_2 \xleftarrow{R} G_{p_2},\ X_3 \xleftarrow{R} G_{p_3},$$

$$D = (\mathbb{G}, g, g^\alpha X_2, X_3, g^s Y_2, Z_2),\ T_1 = e(g, g)^{\alpha s},\ T_2 \xleftarrow{R} G_T.$$

We define the advantage of an algorithm $\mathcal{A}$ in breaking Assumption 3 to be:

$$Adv3_{\mathcal{G},\mathcal{A}}(\lambda) := |\Pr[\mathcal{A}(D, T_1) = 1] - \Pr[\mathcal{A}(D, T_2) = 1]\ |.$$

We say that Assumption 3 holds if $Adv3_{\mathcal{G},\ \mathcal{A}}$ is negligible for any polynomial time algorithm $\mathcal{A}$.

2.2 Access Structures and Linear Secret Sharing Schemes

In this subsection, we introduce the notion of access structure and linear secret sharing scheme.

Definition 1 (Access Structures [3]). Let $\mathcal{P} = \{P_1, P_2, \ldots, P_n\}$ be a set of parties. A collection $\mathbb{A} \subseteq 2^{\mathcal{P}}$ is monotone if for all set B, C such that $B \in \mathbb{A}$ and $B \subseteq C$, we have $C \in \mathbb{A}$. An access structure (respectively, monotone access structure) is a collection (respectively, monotone collection) $\mathbb{A} \subseteq 2^{\mathcal{P}} \setminus \{\emptyset\}$.

Definition 2 (Linear Secret Sharing Scheme: LSSS [3]). A secret sharing scheme Π over a set of parties $\mathcal{P}$ is called linear (over $\mathbb{Z}_p$) if

1. The shares for each party form a vector over $\mathbb{Z}_p$.
2. There exists a matrix A of size $\ell \times d$ elements called the share-generating matrix for Π. For all $i = 1, \ldots, \ell$, the $i - th$ row of A is labeled by a party $\rho(i)$ (ρ is a function from $\{1, \ldots, \ell\}$ to $\mathcal{P}$). To share $s \in \mathbb{Z}_p$, we choose $y_2, y_3, \ldots, y_d$, and construct a column vector $(s, y_2, y_3, \ldots, y_d)$. The shares are elements of Ay. The share $\lambda_{\rho(i)} = A_i y$ belongs to party $\rho(i)$, where A_i is an i-th row of A.
3. There exists an efficient reconstruction algorithm which takes as input $\omega \in \mathbb{A}$. We define $I = \{i | \rho(i) \in \omega\}$. The algorithm outputs constants $\{\nu_i \in \mathbb{Z}_p\}_{i \in I}$ such that $\sum_{i \in I} \nu_i \lambda_{\rho(i)} = s$.

3   Fully Secure Forward Secure Ciphertext-Policy Attribute-Based Encryption

In this section, we define the notion of forward secure ciphertext-policy attribute-based encryption (FS-CP-ABE) and its full security definition. In an FS-CP-ABE scheme, a secret key is associated with a set of attributes ω and a time period τ. We denote this secret key by $\mathsf{sk}_{\omega,\tau}$. The ciphertext is associated with an access structure $\mathbb{A}$ and a time period τ'. If two conditions $\omega \in \mathbb{A}$ and $\tau = \tau'$ hold, then the secret key can decrypt the ciphertext. If the secret key is old one (i.e. $\tau < \tau'$), then the user can update the time period of the secret key without changing the set of attributes ω. The user can decrypt the ciphertext with the updated key.

3.1   The Model of FS-CP-ABE

Formally, a forward secure ciphertext-policy attribute-based encryption (FS-CP-ABE) scheme consists of five algorithms: Setup, KeyGen, Update, Encryption, and Decryption. Let $\mathcal{U}$ be the universe of attributes. Let $\mathcal{S}$ denote the universe of access structures over $\mathcal{U}$.

Setup($\lambda, \mathcal{U}, T$). This is a randomized algorithm that takes as input a security parameter λ, the attribute universe description $\mathcal{U}$, and the total number of time periods T. It outputs a public parameter pk and a master key mk.

KeyGen($\mathsf{pk}, \mathsf{mk}, \omega, \tau$). This is a randomized algorithm that takes as input the public parameter pk, the master key mk, a set of attributes ω, and an index $\tau \in \{1, \ldots T\}$ of the current time period. It outputs a secret key $\mathsf{sk}_{\omega,\tau}$.

Update($\mathsf{pk}, \omega, \tau, \mathsf{sk}_{\omega,\tau-1}$). This is a randomized algorithm that takes as input the public parameter pk, a set of attributes ω, an index τ of the current time period, and the secret key $\mathsf{sk}_{\omega,\tau-1}$ of time period $\tau - 1$. It outputs a secret key $\mathsf{sk}_{\omega,\tau}$.

Encryption($\mathsf{pk}, \mathbb{A}, \tau, m$). This is a randomized algorithm that takes as input the public parameter pk, an access structure $\mathbb{A} \in \mathcal{S}$, an index τ of the current time period, and a message m. It outputs a ciphertext CT.

Decryption($\mathsf{pk}, \mathsf{sk}_{\omega,\tau}, CT$). This is a deterministic algorithm that takes as input the system parameter pk, a secret key $\mathsf{sk}_{\omega,\tau}$ and a ciphertext CT associated with an access structure $\mathbb{A}$ and a time period τ'. If two conditions $\omega \in \mathbb{A}$ and $\tau = \tau'$ hold, then the secret key $\mathsf{sk}_{\omega,\tau}$ can decrypt the ciphertext CT. It outputs the message m.

3.2   Security Model for FS-CP-ABE

We give the full security model for FS-CP-ABE. The security notion is defined by the following game between a challenger and an adversary. The game has the following five phases:

Setup. The challenger runs the Setup algorithm with a security parameter λ, the attribute universe description $\mathcal{U}$, the total number of time period T, and obtains a public parameter pk and a master key mk. We assume that T is bounded some polynomial in λ. It gives pk to the adversary.

Phase 1. The adversary can adaptively issue key generation queries for $\langle \omega, \tau \rangle$ where ω is a set of attributes and τ is a time period. The challenger generates the decryption key by the KeyGen algorithm, and gives the secret key $\mathsf{sk}_{\omega,\tau}$ to the adversary.

Challenge. The adversary submits two equal length messages m_0 and m_1, and target access structure $\mathbb{A}^*$ and target index τ^* of the time period. The restriction is that for any key query $\langle \omega, \tau \rangle$ in Phase 1, if $\omega \in \mathbb{A}$ holds, then τ^* should be smaller than τ. The challenger flips a random bit $b \in \{0,1\}$ and computes the challenge ciphertext $CT^* = \mathsf{Encryption}(\mathsf{pk}, \mathbb{A}^*, \tau^*, m_b)$. It then gives CT^* to the adversary.

Phase 2. The adversary can issue key generation queries same as Phase 1. The adversary cannot ask key of $\langle \omega, \tau \rangle$ where $\omega \in \mathbb{A}$ and $\tau \leq \tau^*$ hold.

Guess. Finally, the adversary outputs a guess $b' \in \{0,1\}$ of b.

We define the advantage of the adversary in this game as

$$Adv_{\mathcal{A}}^{\text{FS-CP-ABE}}(\lambda) = \left| \Pr[\, b' = b \,] - \frac{1}{2} \right|.$$

Definition 3 (Full Security). *An FS-CP-ABE scheme is full secure, if all probabilistic polynomial time adversaries have at most a negligible advantage in the security game.*

4 Ciphertext-Policy Attribute-Based Encryption with Augmented Hierarchy (CP-ABE-AH)

Toward constructing an efficient and fully secure FS-CP-ABE, we introduce ciphertext-policy attribute-based encryption with augmented hierarchy (CP-ABE-AH). Roughly speaking, a CP-ABE-AH scheme has both CP-ABE and HIBE properties. The key generation algorithm of CP-ABE-AH takes a set of attributes and an ID-tuple, and produces a secret key which is associated with the pair of the set of attributes and the ID-tuple (ω, ID). The encryption algorithm takes an access structure and an ID-tuple, and produces a ciphertext. If the ID-tuples of the secret key and the ciphertext are the same, and the set of attributes of the secret key satisfies the access structure of the ciphertext, then the ciphertext can be decrypted with the secret key. Furthermore, CP-ABE-AH has a key derivation function which is similar to the key derivation function of HIBE which creates a secret key for a child node.

To construct CP-ABE-AH scheme, we combine two techniques from hierarchical identity based encryption of Lewko and Waters [10], and ciphertext-policy attribute based encryption of Lewko et al. [9]. We describe the concrete construction of CP-ABE-AH in Sect. 4.3. We denote the attribute universe by $\mathcal{U}$ and the identity space by $\mathcal{I}$. We also denote an ID-tuple of depth z by $\mathsf{ID}_z = (I_1, \ldots, I_z)$, a secret key by $\mathsf{sk}_{\omega,\,\mathsf{ID}_z}$ which is associated with the set of attributes ω and the ID-tuple ID_z.

4.1   The Model of CP-ABE-AH

Formally, CP-ABE-AH scheme consists of the following five algorithms Setup, KeyGen, Derive, Encryption, and Decryption.

Setup($\lambda, \mathcal{U}, L$): This is a randomized algorithm that takes a security parameter λ, the attribute universe $\mathcal{U}$, and the maximal hierarchy depth of the ID tuple L. It outputs a public parameter pk and a master key mk.

KeyGen(ID_z, ω, pk, mk): This is a randomized algorithm that takes as input an ID-tuple $\mathsf{ID}_z = (I_1, \ldots, I_z)$ at depth $z \leq L$, a set of attributes ω, the public parameter pk, and the master key mk. It outputs a secret key $\mathsf{sk}_{\omega,\,\mathsf{ID}_z}$.

Derive($\mathsf{ID}_z, \omega, \mathsf{sk}_{\omega,\,\mathsf{ID}_{z-1}}$, pk): This is a randomized algorithm that takes as input an ID-tuple $\mathsf{ID}_z = (I_1, \ldots, I_z)$ at depth $z \leq L$, a set of attributes ω, and a secret key $\mathsf{sk}_{\omega,\,\mathsf{ID}_{z-1}}$, and the public parameter pk. It outputs a secret key $\mathsf{sk}_{\omega,\,\mathsf{ID}_z}$ for depth z without changing the attribute set ω.

Encryption(pk, $\mathbb{A}$, ID_z, m): This is a randomized algorithm that takes as input the public parameter pk, an access structure $\mathbb{A}$, an ID-tuple ID_z, and a message m. It outputs a ciphertext CT.

Decryption(pk, $\mathsf{sk}_{\omega,\,\mathsf{ID}_z}$, CT): This is a deterministic algorithm that takes as input the public parameter pk, the decryption key $\mathsf{sk}_{\omega,\,\mathsf{ID}_z}$, and the ciphertext CT. If the ID-tuples of the secret key and the ciphertext are the same, and the set of attributes ω of the secret key satisfies the access structure $\mathbb{A}$ of the ciphertext, then the ciphertext can be decrypted with the secret key. It outputs the message m.

4.2   Security Model for CP-ABE-AH

We give the security definition of CP-ABE-AH. Our security definition captures adaptive security which means that an adversary declares the target access structure and the target identity tuple in the challenge phase. The security is defined by the following game between a challenger and an adversary.

Setup. The challenger runs the Setup algorithm of CP-ABE-AH to obtain a public parameter pk and a master key mk, and gives pk to the adversary.

Phase 1. The adversary can issue key generation queries for $\langle \omega,\ \mathsf{ID}_z \rangle$ adaptively. The challenger runs the KeyGen algorithm and sends the decryption key to the adversary.

Challenge. The adversary submits two equal length messages m_0 and m_1, and the target access structure $\mathbb{A}^*$ and the target identity tuple ID^*. The challenger flips a random bit $b \in \{0, 1\}$ and computes the challenge ciphertext $CT^* =$ Encryption $(\mathsf{pk}, \mathbb{A}^*, \mathsf{ID}^*, m_b)$. It then gives CT^* to the adversary.

Phase 2. The adversary can issue key generation queries for $\langle \omega, \mathsf{ID}_z \rangle$ same as Phase 1. The restriction is that if $\omega \in \mathbb{A}^*$ then ID_z must not be ID^* nor a prefix of ID^*.

Guess. Finally, the adversary outputs a guess $b' \in \{0, 1\}$ of b.

We define the advantage of the adversary in this game as $Adv_{\mathcal{A}}(\lambda) = \left| \Pr[\, b' = b \,] - \frac{1}{2} \right|$.

Definition 4. *We say that an CP-ABE-AH scheme is adaptively secure if for any polynomial time adversary $\mathcal{A}$, $Adv_{\mathcal{A}}(\lambda)$ is negligible in λ.*

4.3 CP-ABE-AH: Construction

In this subsection we present our CP-ABE-AH construction. The scheme is adaptively secure, and the security is reduced to three static complexity assumptions.

Setup(λ, n, L): This algorithm chooses a bilinear group G of order $N = p_1 p_2 p_3$ (3 distinct primes). We let G_{p_i} denote the subgroup of order p_i in G. It then randomly picks exponents $a, \alpha \in \mathbb{Z}_N$, and random group elements g, $h_1, \ldots, h_L, v \in G_{p_1}$. For each attribute $i \in \mathcal{U}$, it chooses a random value $s_i \in \mathbb{Z}_N$. The public parameter is $\mathsf{pk} = (N, g, e(g, g)^\alpha, g^a, T_i = g^{s_i}\ \forall i \in \mathcal{U}, h_1, \ldots, h_L, v)$. The master key is $\mathsf{mk} = (\alpha, g_3)$ where g_3 is a generator of G_{p_3}. It outputs $(\mathsf{pk}, \mathsf{mk})$.

KeyGen$(\mathsf{ID}_z, \omega, \mathsf{pk}, \mathsf{mk})$: The algorithm randomly chooses $\mu, r \in \mathbb{Z}_N$ and $R_0, R'_0, R_i\ (\forall i \in \omega) \in G_{p_3}$. It outputs the secret key $\mathsf{sk}_{\omega, \mathsf{ID}_z} = (\omega, D^{(1)}, D^{(2)}, \{D_i^{(3)}\}_{\forall i \in \omega}, K_0, K_{z+1}, \ldots, K_L)$ where

$$D^{(1)} = g^\alpha g^{a\mu}(h_1^{I_1} \cdots h_z^{I_z} v)^r R_0, \quad D^{(2)} = g^\mu R'_0, \quad D_i^{(3)} = T_i^\mu R_i\ \forall i \in \omega,$$
$$K_0 = g^r, \quad K_{z+1} = h_{z+1}^r, \ldots, K_L = h_L^r.$$

Derive$(\mathsf{ID}_z, \mathsf{sk}_{\omega, \mathsf{ID}_{z-1}}, \mathsf{pk})$: The algorithm generates a secret key $\mathsf{sk}_{\omega, \mathsf{ID}_z}$ from a given parent key $\mathsf{sk}_{\omega, \mathsf{ID}_{z-1}}$ in the ID hierarchy. Here, the parent key $\mathsf{sk}_{\omega, \mathsf{ID}_{z-1}}$ is of the following form,

$$\mathsf{sk}_{\omega, \mathsf{ID}_{z-1}} = (D^{(1)}, D^{(2)}, \{D_i^{(3)}\}_{\forall i \in \omega}, K_0, K_z, \ldots, K_L)$$
$$= (g^\alpha g^{a\mu}(h_1^{I_1} \cdots h_{z-1}^{I_{z-1}} v)^{r'} R_0, g^\mu R'_0, \{T_i^\mu R_i\}_{\forall i \in \omega}, g^{r'}, h_z^{r'}, \ldots, h_L^{r'}).$$

To generate a secret key $\mathsf{sk}_{\omega, \mathsf{ID}_z}$, Derive algorithm randomly chooses $\delta \in \mathbb{Z}_n$ and outputs

$$\mathsf{sk}_{\omega, \mathsf{ID}_z} = (D^{(1)} K_z^{I_z}(h_1^{I_1} \ldots h_z^{I_z} v)^\delta, D^{(2)}, \{D_i^{(3)}\}_{\forall i \in \omega}, K_0 g^\delta, K_{z+1} h_{z+1}^\delta, \ldots, K_L h_L^\delta).$$

The secret key is a properly distributed secret key for $\mathsf{ID}_z = (I_1, \ldots, I_z)$ for $r = r' + \delta$ because r', δ are chosen uniformly.

Encrypt(pk, (A, ρ), ID_z, m): Inputs to this algorithm are the public parameter pk, an LSSS access structure (A, ρ), an ID-tuple $\mathsf{ID}_z = (I_1, \ldots, I_z)$, and a plaintext m. Here, A is an $\ell \times d$ matrix and ρ is a map from each row A_x of A to an attribute $\rho(x)$. This algorithm first randomly chooses $s, y_2, \ldots, y_d \in \mathbb{Z}_N$ and sets vector $y = (s, y_2, \ldots, y_d) \in \mathbb{Z}_N^d$. For each row A_x of A, it randomly chooses $r_x \in \mathbb{Z}_N$. It outputs the ciphertext $CT = (C, C^{(1)}, \{C_x^{(2)}, C_x^{(3)}\}_{x \in \{1, \ell\}}, C^{(4)})$ where

$$C = m \cdot e(g, g)^{\alpha s}, \ C^{(1)} = g^s, \ C_x^{(2)} = g^{a \cdot A_x y} T_{\rho(x)}^{-r_x}, \ C_x^{(3)} = g^{r_x}, \ C^{(4)} = (h_1^{I_1} \cdots h_z^{I_z} v)^s.$$

Decrypt(pk, $\mathsf{sk}_{\omega, \ \mathsf{ID}_z}$, CT): This algorithm first computes constants $\nu_x \in \mathbb{Z}_N$ such that $\sum_{\rho(x) \in \omega} \nu_x A_x = (1, 0, \ldots, 0)$. Then it computes

$$K = e(C^{(1)}, D^{(1)}) / \prod_{\rho(x) \in \omega} \left(e(C_x^{(2)}, D^{(2)}) \cdot e(C_x^{(3)}, D_{\rho(x)}^{(3)}) \right)^{\nu_x} \cdot e(K_0, C^{(4)})$$

and obtains the plaintext $m = C/K$.

We can verify its correctness as

$$
\begin{aligned}
K &= \frac{e(g^s, g^\alpha g^{a\mu} \cdot (h_1^{I_1} \cdots h_z^{I_z} v)^r R_0)}{\prod_{\rho(x) \in \omega} \left(e(g^{a \cdot A_x \cdot y} \cdot T_{\rho(x)}^{-r_x}, g^\mu R_0') \cdot e(g^{r_x}, T_{\rho(x)}^\mu R_{\rho(x)}) \right)^{\nu_x}} \cdot \frac{1}{e(g^r, (h_1^{I_1} \cdots h_z^{I_z} v)^s)} \\
&= \frac{e(g^s, g^\alpha) \cdot e(g^s, g^{a\mu}) \cdot e(g^s, (h_1^{I_1} \cdots h_z^{I_z} v)^r)}{\prod_{\rho(x) \in \omega} \left(e(g^{a \cdot A_x y}, g^\mu) \right)^{\nu_x} \cdot e(g^r, (h_1^{I_1} \cdots h_z^{I_z} v)^s)} \\
&= e(g, g)^{\alpha s}.
\end{aligned}
$$

Theorem 1. *Our ciphertext-policy ABE with augmented hierarchy scheme is adaptively secure if Assumptions 1, 2 and 3 hold.*

Proof. The proof is postponed to the full version of this paper due to the lack of space. □

5   Construction of FS-CP-ABE from CP-ABE-AH

In this section, we propose a construction of FS-CP-ABE from CP-ABE-AH. Our construction uses the "time tree" technique of [7], which was used to construct a forward secure encryption from a binary tree encryption. Our conversion is essentially the same as that of [7] except that the attribute is introduced.

For an FS-CP-ABE with T time periods, we image a complete balance binary tree of depth $L = \log_2(T + 1) - 1$. Let each node be labeled with a string in $\{0, 1\}^{\leq L}$. We assign the root node with an empty string. The left and right children of a node $\Omega \in \{0,1\}^{\leq L}$ is assigned $\Omega \| 0$ and $\Omega \| 1$ respectively. Here, $\|$ means a concatenation of two strings.

From now, to distinguish the abstract "node" of an CP-ABE-AH system from nodes in the binary tree, we refer to the former as ah-node and the latter as usual. Following the notation in [7], we let Ω^τ to be the τ-th node in a pre-order traversal of the binary tree. Without loss of generality, we assume that $\{0,1\} \in \mathcal{I}$, the identity space. Hence, we can view a binary string of length $z \leq L$ as an ID-tuple of length z.

Encryption in time τ for an access structure $\mathbb{A}$ uses the encryption function of the CP-ABE-AH scheme to the multi-node $(\mathbb{A}, \Omega^\tau)$. At time τ the secret key also contains, beside the secret key of ah-node (ω, Ω^τ) of the CP-ABE-AH scheme, all the keys of ah-nodes (ω, y) where y is a right sibling of the nodes on the path from the root to Ω^τ in the binary tree. When updating the key to time $\tau + 1$, we compute the secret key of ah-node $(\omega, \Omega^{\tau+1})$ and erase the one of (ω, Ω^τ). Since $\Omega^{\tau+1}$ is a left child of Ω^τ or one of the nodes whose keys are stored as the additional keys at time τ, the derivation can be done, in particular, using at most one application of Derive. We denote this conversion as $\mathbf{C}(\cdot)$.

Theorem 2. *If a CP-ABE-AH scheme is adaptively secure then the converted FS-CP-ABE scheme $\mathbf{C}(CP\text{-}ABE\text{-}AH)$ is full secure.*

Proof. Suppose there exists an adversary $\mathcal{A}$ that has advantage ϵ against FS-CP-ABE ($\mathbf{C}$(CP-ABE-AH)). Then, we can construct an algorithm $\mathcal{B}$ that has advantage ϵ in breaking the CP-ABE-AH scheme. Below, we show how to construct $\mathcal{B}$.

Setup. $\mathcal{B}$ receives the public parameter pk from the challenger. $\mathcal{B}$ then runs $\mathcal{A}$ with public parameter pk.

Phase 1. In Phase 1, $\mathcal{A}$ issues KeyGen queries to $\mathcal{B}$, and $\mathcal{B}$ has to answer the queries. To answer a KeyGen query $\langle \omega, \tau \rangle$ for secret keys corresponding to a set of attributes ω and a time period τ, $\mathcal{B}$ first computes an identity tuple Ω^τ which represents the time period τ. $\mathcal{B}$ then sends $\langle \omega, \Omega^\tau \rangle$ query to the challenger and gets a decryption key. $\mathcal{B}$ passes the decryption key to $\mathcal{A}$.

Challenge. In the challenge phase, $\mathcal{A}$ issues $\langle m_0, m_1, \mathbb{A}^*, \tau^* \rangle$ to $\mathcal{B}$. $\mathcal{B}$ works as follows: $\mathcal{B}$ converts the time period τ^* to the identity tuple format, say Ω^{τ^*}. Then $\mathcal{B}$ issues the challenge query $\langle m_0, m_1, \mathbb{A}^*, \Omega^{\tau^*} \rangle$ to the challenger, and receives a challenge ciphertext CT^* from the challenger. $\mathcal{B}$ passes the challenge ciphertext to $\mathcal{A}$.

Phase 2. In Phase 2, $\mathcal{B}$ answers key queries from $\mathcal{A}$ same as Phase 1.

Guess. When $\mathcal{A}$ outputs a bit $b' \in \{0,1\}$, $\mathcal{B}$ outputs b' and halts.

In this game, if $\mathcal{A}$ wins the game, then $\mathcal{B}$ always wins the game. Thus, the advantage of $\mathcal{B}$ is the same as the advantage of $\mathcal{A}$. Therefore, the advantage of $\mathcal{B}$ is at most $\epsilon(\lambda)$. This concludes the proof of Theorem 2. $\square$

Table 1. Comparison among CP-ABE schemes

Scheme	Forward-sec.	$|pk|$	$|sk|$	$|CT|$
LOSTW [9]	No	$(2 + |\mathcal{U}|)|G| + |G_T|$	$(2 + |\omega|)|G|$	$(1 + 2\ell)|G| + |G_T|$
Trivial 1	Yes	$(2 + |\mathcal{U}| + T)|G| + |G_T|$	$T(3 + |\omega|)|G|$	$(3 + 2\ell)|G| + |G_T|$
Trivial 2	Yes	$(2 + |\mathcal{U}| + T)|G| + |G_T|$	$(2 + |\omega| + T)|G|$	$(3 + 2\ell)|G| + |G_T|$
Ours	Yes	$(3 + |\mathcal{U}| + \log T)|G| + |G_T|$	$(\log T)(3 + |\omega| + \log T)|G|$	$(2 + 2\ell)|G| + |G_T|$

6 Efficiency

In this section, we discuss efficiency of our FS-CP-ABE scheme. In Table 1, we compare sizes of public parameters $|pk|$, secret keys $|sk|$, and ciphertexts $|CT|$ among CP-ABE schemes: CP-ABE scheme by Lewko et al. [9], two trivial foward-secure CP-ABE schemes introduced in Sect. 1, and our FS-CP-ABE scheme. We denote the size of the attribute universe by $|\mathcal{U}|$, the number of all time slot by T, and the size of the set of attributes associated with the secret key by $|\omega|$, and the size of rows in the LSSS matrix by ℓ.

From this table, we can see that the key sizes of the trivial constructions are linear in the total number of time slot T, and will be very huge in real systems. In our scheme, the size of public parameter is $O(\log T)$, and the secret key size is $O(\log^2 T)$.

References

1. Attrapadung, N., Furukawa, J., Imai, H.: Forward-secure and searchable broadcast encryption with short ciphertexts and private keys. In: Lai, X., Chen, K. (eds.) ASIACRYPT 2006. LNCS, vol. 4284, pp. 161–177. Springer, Heidelberg (2006)
2. Attrapadung, N., Imai, H.: Conjunctive broadcast and attribute-based encryption. In: Shacham, H., Waters, B. (eds.) Pairing 2009. LNCS, vol. 5671, pp. 248–265. Springer, Heidelberg (2009)
3. Beimel, A.: Secure schemes for secret sharing and key distribution. Ph.D. thesis, Israel Institute of Technology, Haifa, Israel (1996)
4. Boneh, D., Boyen, X., Goh, E.: Hierarchical identity based encryption with constant size ciphertext. In: Cramer, R. (ed.) EUROCRYPT 2005. LNCS, vol. 3494, pp. 440–456. Springer, Heidelberg (2005)
5. Boneh, D., Hamburg, M.: Generalized identity based and broadcast encryption schemes. In: Pieprzyk, J. (ed.) ASIACRYPT 2008. LNCS, vol. 5350, pp. 455–470. Springer, Heidelberg (2008)
6. Bethencourt, J., Sahai, A., Waters, B.: Ciphertext-policy attribute-based encryption. In: Proceedings of IEEE Symposium on Security and Privacy 2007, pp. 321–334 (2007)
7. Canetti, R., Halevi, S., Katz, J.: A forward-secure public-key. In: Biham, E. (ed.) EUROCRYPT 2003. LNCS, vol. 2656, pp. 255–271. Springer, Heidelberg (2003)
8. Goyal, V., Pandey, O., Sahai, A., Waters, B.: Attribute-based encryption for fine-grained access control of encrypted data. In: Proceedings of the 13th ACM Conference on Computer and Communication Security (CCS 2006), pp. 89–98. ACM (2006)

9. Lewko, A., Okamoto, T., Sahai, A., Takashima, K., Waters, B.: Fully secure functional encryption: attribute-based encryption and (hierarchical) inner product encryption. In: Gilbert, H. (ed.) EUROCRYPT 2010. LNCS, vol. 6110, pp. 62–91. Springer, Heidelberg (2010)
10. Lewko, A., Waters, B.: New techniques for dual system encryption and fully secure HIBE with short ciphertexts. In: Micciancio, D. (ed.) TCC 2010. LNCS, vol. 5978, pp. 455–479. Springer, Heidelberg (2010)
11. Sahai, A., Waters, B.: Fuzzy identity-based encryption. In: Cramer, R. (ed.) EURO-CRYPT 2005. LNCS, vol. 3494, pp. 457–473. Springer, Heidelberg (2005)
12. Wang, Z., Yao D., Feng R.: Adaptive key protection in complex cryptosystems with attributes. In: IACR Cryptology ePrint Archive 2012/136, (2012)
13. Waters, B.: Dual system encryption: realizing fully secure IBE and HIBE under simple assumptions. In: Halevi, S. (ed.) CRYPTO 2009. LNCS, vol. 5677, pp. 619–636. Springer, Heidelberg (2009)
14. Waters, B.: Ciphertext-policy attribute-based encryption: an expressive, efficient, and provably secure realization. In: Catalano, D., Fazio, N., Gennaro, R., Nicolosi, A. (eds.) PKC 2011. LNCS, vol. 6571, pp. 53–70. Springer, Heidelberg (2011)
15. Yao, D., Fazio, N., Dodis, Y., Lysyanskaya, A.: ID-based encryption for complex hierarchies with applications to forward security and broadcast encryption. In: Proceedings of the 11th ACM Conference on Computer and Communications Security, pp. 354–363. ACM (2004)

Reducing Public Key Sizes in Bounded CCA-Secure KEMs with Optimal Ciphertext Length

Takashi Yamakawa[1,2]([✉]), Shota Yamada[1], Takahiro Matsuda[1], Goichiro Hanaoka[1], and Noboru Kunihiro[2]

[1] National Institute of Advanced Industrial Science and Technology (AIST), Tokyo, Japan
{yamada-shota,t-matsuda,hanaoka-goichiro}@aist.go.jp
[2] The University of Tokyo, Tokyo, Japan
yamakawa@it.k.u-tokyo.ac.jp, kunihiro@k.u-tokyo.ac.jp

Abstract. Currently, chosen-ciphertext (CCA) security is considered as the de facto standard security notion for public key encryption (PKE), and a number of CCA-secure schemes have been proposed thus far. However, CCA-secure PKE schemes are generally less efficient than schemes with weaker security, e.g., chosen-plaintext security, due to their strong security. Surprisingly, Cramer et al. (Asiacrypt 2007) demonstrated that it is possible to construct a PKE scheme from the *decisional Diffie-Hellman assumption* that yields (i) *bounded CCA* (BCCA) security which is only slightly weaker than CCA security, and (ii) *one group element of ciphertext overhead* which is optimal.

In this paper, we propose two novel BCCA-secure PKE schemes with optimal ciphertext length that are based on computational assumptions rather than decisional assumptions *and* that yield shorter (or at least comparable) public key sizes. Our first scheme is based on the computational bilinear Diffie-Hellman assumption and yields $O(\lambda q)$ group elements of public key length, and our second scheme is based on the factoring assumption and yields $O(\lambda q^2)$ group elements of public key length, while in Cramer et al.'s scheme, a public key consists of $O(\lambda q^2)$ group elements, where λ is the security parameter and q is the number of decryption queries. Moreover, our second scheme is the first PKE scheme which is BCCA-secure under the factoring assumption and yields optimal ciphertext overhead.

Keywords: Bounded CCA security · Factoring · CBDH assumption

1 Introduction

1.1 Background

Indistinguishability under chosen-ciphertext attack (IND-CCA) is now widely considered to be the standard notion of security in public-key encryption

---

The first and second authors are supported by a JSPS Fellowship for Young Scientists.

Y. Desmedt (Ed.): ISC 2013, LNCS 7807, pp. 100–109, 2015.
DOI: 10.1007/978-3-319-27659-5_7

(PKE) schemes. Currently, many practical IND-CCA secure PKE schemes in the standard model have been proposed thus far. However, IND-CCA secure PKE schemes are generally less efficient than schemes with weaker security, e.g., chosen-plaintext (CPA) security, due to their strong security. Especially, Hanaoka, Matsuda, and Schuldt [9] recently showed a negative result, which implies that it is hard to construct IND-CCA secure ElGamal-type PKE schemes (under any non-interactive assumptions) whose ciphertext length is as short as that of the ElGamal scheme. A feasible approach to overcoming this barrier and achieving shorter ciphertext length is to (reasonably) relax the notion of security from IND-CCA.

Surprisingly, Cramer et al. [3] demonstrated that it is possible to construct a PKE scheme from the *decisional Diffie-Hellman (DDH) assumption* that yields (i) *IND-bounded-CCA* (IND-BCCA) security which is only slightly weaker than CCA-security, and (ii) only *one group element of ciphertext overhead* (i.e., ciphertext length minus plaintext length), which is the same as that of the ElGamal scheme and thus considered to be optimal. The notion of IND-BCCA is identical to IND-CCA except that in this attack model, the number of decryption queries is a priori polynomially bounded.

However, in contrast to such a short ciphertext length, its public key consists of $O(\lambda q^2)$ group elements, where λ is the security parameter and q is the number of decryption queries, and it is thus considerably large. Furthermore, as previously described, Cramer et al.'s scheme is based on a decisional assumption, i.e., the DDH assumption. In general, decisional assumptions are a significantly stronger class of assumptions than computational assumptions, and therefore, schemes based on computational assumptions are generally preferred to those based on decisional assumptions. For example, the computational Diffie-Hellman (CDH) assumption is considered to be significantly weaker than the DDH assumption, and following [3], Pereira, Dowsley, Hanaoka and Nascimento [16] actually proposed an IND-BCCA secure scheme from the CDH assumption. However, its public key size become even larger than that of Cramer et al.'s scheme, and specifically, its public key consists of $O(\lambda^2 q^2)$ group elements.

1.2 Our Contribution

We propose two novel IND-BCCA secure PKE schemes with *optimal* ciphertext length under *computational* assumptions whose public keys are *shorter* than (or at least comparable to) that of Cramer et al.'s scheme [3]. More specifically, we construct the following two schemes:

- Our first scheme is IND-BCCA secure under the *computational bilinear Diffie-Hellman* (CBDH) assumption, where its ciphertext overhead is *optimal* (i.e., one group element of the underlying cyclic group), and its public key consists of $O(\lambda q)$ group elements.
- Our second scheme is IND-BCCA secure under the *factoring* assumption, where its ciphertext overhead is *optimal*, and its public key consists of $O(\lambda q^2)$ group elements. This is the *first* PKE scheme which is IND-BCCA secure under the factoring assumption and yields optimal ciphertext length.

Our first scheme is constructed by extending Pereira et al.'s scheme [16] in a non-trivial manner. Spefificically, we introduce the *two-dimensional representation of cover free families* [18] and the *two-dimensional representation of the key index* [10], and apply these two techniques to the Pereira et al.'s scheme for reducing the public key size. Note that applying these techniques simultaneously is totally non-trivial since both they are significantly complicated and thus may interfere with each other.

On the other hand, our second scheme is constructed by using the CDH assumption on $\mathbb{QR}_N$ and the Blum-Blum-Shub (BBS) pseudo-random number generator [1]. It is already known that the factoring assumption implies the CDH assumption on $\mathbb{QR}_N$ [17], and thus, it is possible to prove security of a cryptographic scheme under the factoring assumption by proving its security under the CDH assumption on $\mathbb{QR}_N$. We further show that the BBS generator works as a hard-core function of the CDH problem on $\mathbb{QR}_N$, and utilize this property for significantly reducing the size of a public key. To the best of our knowledge, such a property has not been explicitly mentioned in the literature.

In Table 1, a comparison among our proposed schemes and other existing IND-(B)CCA secure schemes is given. We see that in our first scheme (**Ours1**), the public-key size is considerably shorter than that of the Pereira et al.'s scheme (PDHN10) [16] without increasing the ciphertext length. Namely, our first scheme is also optimal in terms of the ciphertext length. Comparing with Haralambiev et al.'s scheme (HJKS10) [10], which is the currently best known CBDH-based IND-CCA secure scheme, ciphertext overhead of our first scheme is a half of that of HJKS10. We also see that our second scheme (**Ours2**) is the first optimal IND-BCCA secure scheme in terms of ciphertext length among factoring-based schemes, and its ciphertext overhead is a half of that of the best known factoring-based IND-CCA secure scheme, i.e., Hofheinz and Kiltz's scheme (HK09a) [12].

1.3   Related Works

There are generic conversions from IND-CPA secure PKE to IND-CCA secure PKE [5,15]. However, these conversions use NIZK proofs [2] and they are therefore not practical. Currently many practical constructions of IND-CCA secure schemes in the standard model have been proposed. In particular, Haralambiev et al. [10] and Yamada et al. [19] independently proposed efficient PKE schemes under the CBDH assumption and Hofheintz and Kiltz [12] proposed an efficient PKE scheme under the factoring assumption. Hohenberger, Lewko, and Waters [13] recently used an IND-BCCA secure PKE scheme as one of the building blocks to construct a (non-bounded) IND-CCA secure PKE scheme.

2   Preliminaries

2.1   Notation

We denote the set of all natural numbers by $\mathbb{N}$ and the set $\{1,\ldots n\}$ by $[n]$ for $n \in \mathbb{N}$. For prime order group $\mathbb{G}$, we denote $\mathbb{G} \setminus \{1\}$ by $\mathbb{G}^*$. We write $x \xleftarrow{\$} S$

Table 1. Comparison among IND-BCCA (or IND-CCA) secure KEMs with small ciphertext overhead, where λ is the security parameter, q is the number of queries, $|g|$ is size of an element of the underlying group, and $|MAC|$ is length of a message authentication code.

	Ciphertext overhead	Public key size	Computational assumption?	Security
PDHN10 [16]	$|g|$	$O(\lambda^2 q^2) \cdot |g|$	Yes(CDH)	IND-BCCA
Ours1 (Sect. 3)	$|g|$	$O(\lambda q) \cdot |g|$	Yes(CBDH)	IND-BCCA
HJKS10 [10]	$2 \cdot |g|$	$O(\lambda^{1/2}) \cdot |g|$	Yes(CBDH)	IND-CCA
CHH$^+$07 [3]	$|g|$	$O(\lambda q^2) \cdot |g|$	No(DDH)	IND-BCCA
YHK12 [18]	$|g|$	$O(\lambda^{1/2} q) \cdot |g|$	No(DBDH)	IND-BCCA
Ours2 (Sect. 4)	$|g|$	$O(\lambda q^2) \cdot |g|$	Yes(factoring)	IND-BCCA
HK09a [12]	$2 \cdot |g|$	$O(1) \cdot |g|$	Yes(factoring)	IND-CCA
HK09b [11]	$|g| + |MAC|$	$O(1) \cdot |g|$	No(HR)	IND-CCA

to mean that x is chosen uniformly at random from a finite set S, and write $x \leftarrow \mathcal{A}(y)$ to mean that x is output by an algorithm $\mathcal{A}$ with input y. A function $f(\cdot) : \mathbb{N} \to [0,1]$ is said to be *negligible* if for all positive polynomials $p(\cdot)$ and all sufficiently large $\lambda \in \mathbb{N}$, we have $f(\lambda) < 1/p(\lambda)$. We say that an algorithm $\mathcal{A}$ is *efficient* if there exists a polynomial p such that execution time of $\mathcal{A}$ is less than $p(\lambda)$ where λ is input size. For an integer k and $x_i \in \{0,1\}^k$ ($i \in [n]$), we denote the bitwise XOR of x_i for $i \in [n]$ by $\bigoplus_{i=1}^n x_i$ and the concatenation of x_i for $i \in [n]$ by $x_1||x_2||\ldots||x_n$. We consider the lexicographical order for pairs of integers. That is, we denote $(x_1, y_1) \leq (x_2, y_2)$ if $x_1 < x_2$ holds or $x_1 = x_2$ and $y_1 \leq y_2$ hold. We denote a security parameter by λ.

2.2 Syntax and Security Notions

Here, we review two basic definitions.

Key Encapsulation Mechanism and Its Security. Here, we review the definition of key encapsulation mechanism (KEM) and its security. It is known that an IND-CCA secure PKE scheme is obtained by combining an IND-CCA secure KEM and an IND-CCA secure symmetric cipher (DEM) [4]. Therefore we consider a KEM instead of PKE. A KEM consists of three algorithms (Gen, Enc, Dec). Gen takes a security parameter 1^λ as input and outputs (pk, sk), where pk is a public key and sk is a secret key. Enc takes a public key pk as input and outputs (C, K), where C is a ciphertext and K is a DEM key. Dec takes a public key pk, a secret key sk and a ciphertext C as input and outputs a DEM key K with length k or rejects. We require that for all (pk, sk) output by Gen and all (C, K) output by Enc(pk), we have Dec(pk, sk, C) = K. To define the IND-CCA security of a KEM, we consider the following game for an adversary $\mathcal{A}$ and a KEM Π. In the game, a public key and a secret key are generated as $(pk, sk) \leftarrow \mathsf{Gen}(1^\lambda)$, a challenge ciphertext and DEM key are generated as $(C^*, \bar{K}) \leftarrow \mathsf{Enc}(pk)$. Then, a random bit b is chosen as $b \xleftarrow{\$} \{0,1\}$. If $b = 1$, K^* is set as $K^* := \bar{K}$ and otherwise $K^* \xleftarrow{\$} \{0,1\}^k$. The adversary $\mathcal{A}$ is given (pk, C^*, K^*). At last, the adversary outputs b'. In the game, $\mathcal{A}$ has an access to an oracle $\mathcal{O}(sk, \cdot)$ that returns $\mathsf{Dec}(sk, C)$ given C. $\mathcal{A}$ is not allowed to query C^*. We call this phase a query phase. Let T be the event such that $b' = b$ holds in the above game. We define the IND-CCA advantage of $\mathcal{A}$ as $\mathsf{Adv}_{\Pi, \mathcal{A}}^{\text{ind-cca}}(\lambda) = |\Pr[T] - 1/2|$. We say that Π is IND-CCA secure if $\mathsf{Adv}_{\Pi, \mathcal{A}}^{\text{ind-cca}}(\lambda)$ is negligible for any efficient adversary $\mathcal{A}$. The IND-q-CCA advantage $\mathsf{Adv}_{\Pi, \mathcal{A}}^{\text{ind-}q\text{-cca}}(\lambda)$ and the IND-q-CCA security is defined in the same way except that $\mathcal{A}$ is allowed to access to $\mathcal{O}(sk, \cdot)$ at most q times. We say that the scheme is IND-BCCA secure if it is IND-q-CCA secure for some polynomially bounded q.

Target Collision Resistant Hash Function. For a function $H : X \to Y$ and an algorithm $\mathcal{A}$, we define $\mathsf{Adv}_{H, \mathcal{A}}^{\text{tcr}}(\lambda) := \Pr[x \xleftarrow{\$} X, x' \leftarrow \mathcal{A}(x, H) : x' \neq x \wedge H(x') = H(x)]$. We say that H is target collision resistant if for any efficient adversary $\mathcal{A}$, $\mathsf{Adv}_{H, \mathcal{A}}^{\text{tcr}}(\lambda)$ is negligible.

2.3   Number Theoretic Assumptions

Computational Bilinear Diffie-Hellman Assumption and Its Hard-Core Bit. Let $\mathbb{G}_1$, $\mathbb{G}_2$ and $\mathbb{G}_T$ be groups of prime order p with bilinear map $e : \mathbb{G}_1 \times \mathbb{G}_2 \to \mathbb{G}_T$. For any adversary $\mathcal{A}$, we define the CBDH advantage of $\mathcal{A}$ as $\mathsf{Adv}_{\mathcal{A}}^{cbdh}(\lambda) := \Pr[e(g_1, g_2)^{xyz} \leftarrow \mathcal{A}(g_1, g_1^x, g_1^y, g_2, g_2^y, g_2^z)]$ where $g_1 \xleftarrow{\$} \mathbb{G}_1^*$, $g_2 \xleftarrow{\$} \mathbb{G}_2^*$, $x, y, z \xleftarrow{\$} \mathbb{Z}_p$. We say that the CBDH assumption holds if $\mathsf{Adv}_{\mathcal{A}}^{cbdh}(\lambda)$ is negligible for any efficient adversary $\mathcal{A}$. Furthermore, we say that $h : \mathbb{G}_T \to \{0,1\}$ is a hard-core bit function of the CBDH problem if $\mathsf{Adv}_{\mathcal{A}}^{cbdh\text{-}hc}(\lambda) := |\Pr[1 \leftarrow \mathcal{A}(g_1, g_1^x, g_1^y, g_2, g_2^y, g_2^z, h(e(g_1, g_2)^{xyz}))] - \Pr[1 \leftarrow \mathcal{A}(g_1, g_1^x, g_1^y, g_2, g_2^y, g_2^z, T)]|$ where $g_1 \xleftarrow{\$} \mathbb{G}_1^*$, $g_2 \xleftarrow{\$} \mathbb{G}_2^*$, $T \xleftarrow{\$} \{0,1\}$, $x, y, z \xleftarrow{\$} \mathbb{Z}_p^*$ is negligible for any efficient adversary $\mathcal{A}$. Note that if the CBDH assumption holds, then there exists a hard-core bit function of the problem [8].

Factoring Assumption and Blum-Blum-Shub Pseudo-random Number Generator. Let RSAGen be an efficient algorithm which takes a security parameter 1^λ as input and outputs a set of integers (N, P, Q) with $N = PQ$, $P = 2P'+1$ and $Q = 2Q' + 1$ where P, Q, P', Q' are distinct odd primes. For an adversary $\mathcal{A}$, let $\mathsf{Adv}_{\mathcal{A}, \mathsf{RSAGen}}^{\text{fact}}(\lambda)$ be the probability that given N which is generated by RSAGen, $\mathcal{A}$ outputs a non-trivial factor of N. We say that the factoring assumption holds for RSAGen if $\mathsf{Adv}_{\mathcal{A}, \mathsf{RSAGen}}^{\text{fact}}(\lambda)$ is negligible for any efficient adversary $\mathcal{A}$. We define the group of quadratic residues $\mathbb{QR}_N := \{u^2 : u \in \mathbb{Z}_N^*\}$. This is a subgroup of $\mathbb{Z}_N^*$. Note that $\text{ord}(\mathbb{Z}_N^*) = 4P'Q'$ and $\text{ord}(\mathbb{QR}_N) = P'Q'$. The following is a useful proposition [12].

Proposition 1. *Let $N = PQ = (2P' + 1)(2Q' + 1)$ be an integer which is generated by RSAGen. Then the uniform distribution in $[P'Q']$ and the uniform* *distribution in* $\lfloor (N-1)/4 \rfloor$ *are negligibly close. In particular, the distribution of* g^x *where g is a random element of* $\mathbb{QR}_N$ *and* $x \xleftarrow{\$} \lfloor (N-1)/4 \rfloor$ *is negligibly close to the uniform distribution in* $\mathbb{QR}_N$.

This proposition claims that $\lfloor (N-1)/4 \rfloor$ is an approximation of the order of $\mathbb{QR}_N$. The remarkable point is that $\lfloor (N-1)/4 \rfloor$ can be computed efficiently without knowing P or Q.

We define the Blum-Blum-Shub (BBS) pseudo-random number generator [1,14] as follows. Let k be any integer which is polynomially bounded in the security parameter. For $u \in \mathbb{Z}_N^*$ and $r \in \{0,1\}^{\ell_N}$, we define $BBS_r(u) :=$ $(B_r(u), B_r(u^2), \ldots, B_r(u^{2^{k-1}}))$. Here, $B_r(u)$ is the Goldreich-Levin predicate. That is, $B_r(u) = \bigoplus u_i r_i$ where u_i and r_i are i-th bit of u and r respectively.

2.4 Cover Free Family and Its Two-Dimensional Representation

A cover free family is a family of sets which satisfies a certain combinatorial property. It is useful for designing IND-BCCA secure PKE [3]. The definition is as follows. Let $\mathcal{S} = (\mathcal{S}_i)_{i \in [v]}$ be a family of subsets of $[u]$ with $|\mathcal{S}_i| = \ell$ ($i \in [v]$). We say $\mathcal{S}$ is a (u, v, q)-ℓ-uniform cover free family (CFF) (or simply q-cover free family) if $\mathcal{S}_i \not\subset \bigcup_{j \in \mathcal{F}} \mathcal{S}_j$ for all $i \in [v]$ and for all $\mathcal{F} \subset [v] \setminus \{i\}$ such that $|\mathcal{F}| \leq q$. Given λ and q bounded by a polynomial of λ, an efficient construction of a cover free family is known for parameters $u(\lambda) = O(\lambda q^2), v(\lambda) = \Omega(2^\lambda), \ell(\lambda) = O(\lambda q)$ [6,7].

Here, we review the technique of two-dimensional representation of cover free families [18]. In the technique, we regard $[u]$ as $[u_1] \times [u_2]$, where u_1 and u_2 are integers satisfying $u_1 \geq u_2$ and $u_1 u_2 \geq u$. We regard $i \in [u]$ as an element of $[u_1] \times [u_2]$ by associating with $(\lceil i/u_2 \rceil, i - u_2(\lceil i/u_2 \rceil - 1))$. Then, all $\mathcal{S}_i$ can be seen as a subset of $[u_1] \times [u_2]$ in a natural way and $(\mathcal{S}_i)_{i \in [v]}$ can be seen as q-cover free family, over $[u_1] \times [u_2]$. We call such a cover free family $((u_1, u_2), v, q)$-ℓ-cover free family. Clearly, given λ and q bounded by a polynomial of λ, we can efficiently construct a $((u_1, u_2), v, q)$-ℓ-cover free family for parameters $u_1(\lambda), u_2(\lambda) = O(\lambda^{1/2} q), v(\lambda) = \Omega(2^\lambda), \ell(\lambda) = O(\lambda q)$.

3 Construction from the CBDH Assumption

This section discusses KEMs with optimal ciphertext overhead that are IND-BCCA secure under the CBDH assumption. We note that it is possible to construct such a scheme by modifying the KEM in [16] which is IND-BCCA secure under the CDH assumption. However, the scheme which is straightforwardly derived from [16] requires significantly large public keys, and more precisely, the public key size of this straightforward scheme is $O(\lambda^2 q^2)$ where q is the maximal number of decryption queries. In this section, we propose a new IND-BCCA secure KEM from the CBDH assumption whose public key size is only $O(\lambda q)$.

To achieve such shorter public key size, we use following two techniques: (1) *the two-dimensional representation of cover free families* [18] and (2) *the two-dimensional representation of the key index* [10]. The techniques (1) and (2) are used for reducing the public key size of the IND-(B)CCA KEMs in [3] and [10], respectively, by utilizing bilinear maps, and both these techniques are considered useful to construct an efficient IND-BCCA secure KEM under the CBDH assumption.

However, it is not easy to simultaneously handle these two techniques since both techniques require significantly complicated procedures, and therefore, they might interfere with each other. We demonstrate in the following that these techniques are compatible by a careful consideration. As a result, we obtain an IND-q-CCA secure KEM with optimal ciphertext overhead under the CBDH assumption whose public key consists of $O(\lambda q)$ elements.

3.1   Construction

Here, we present the construction of the proposed IND-BCCA secure KEM under the CBDH assumption. Our main idea is to apply both the technique of the two-dimensional representation of cover free families and the technique of two-dimensional representation of the key index to the scheme in [16] simultaneously. We then obtain an IND-q-CCA secure KEM under the CBDH assumption with public key size $O(\lambda q)$.

Let $\mathbb{G}_1$, $\mathbb{G}_2$ and $\mathbb{G}_T$ be groups of prime order p with bilinear map $e : \mathbb{G}_1 \times \mathbb{G}_2 \to \mathbb{G}_T$. Let S be a $((u_1, u_2), v, q)$-ℓ-uniform cover free family. Let $H : \mathbb{G}_1 \to [v]$ be a target collision resistant hash function and $h : \mathbb{G}_T \to \{0, 1\}$ be a hard-core bit function. Let $k = k_1 k_2$ be DEM key length of the KEM and for simplicity, we assume $k = \lambda$ in the following. In the following, $K_{1,1}||K_{1,2}||\ldots||K_{k_1,k_2}$ means that $K_{m,n}$ are put in lexicographical order in $[k_1] \times [k_2]$. We call the following scheme Ours1.

Gen(1^λ): This chooses $g_1 \in \mathbb{G}_1^*$, $g_2 \in \mathbb{G}_2^*$, $a_{m,i} \xleftarrow{\$} \mathbb{Z}_p$, $b_{n,j} \xleftarrow{\$} \mathbb{Z}_p$ and computes $A_{m,i} := g_1^{a_{m,i}}$ and $B_{n,j} := g_2^{b_{n,j}}$ ($m \in [k_1]$, $i \in [u_1]$, $n \in [k_2]$, $j \in [u_2]$). Then it returns public key $pk = (g_1, g_2, (A_{m,i})_{m \in [k_1], i \in [u_1]}, (B_{n,j})_{n \in [k_2], j \in [u_2]})$ and secret key $sk = ((a_{m,i})_{m \in [k_1], i \in [u_1]}, (b_{n,j})_{n \in [k_2], j \in [u_2]})$.

Enc(pk): This chooses $r \xleftarrow{\$} \mathbb{Z}_p$ and computes $C := g_1^r$ and $t := H(C)$. It sets $K := K_{1,1}||K_{1,2}||\ldots||K_{k_1,k_2}$ where $K_{m,n} := \bigoplus_{(i,j) \in S_t} h(e(A_{m,i}, B_{n,j})^r)$ ($m \in [k_1]$, $n \in [k_2]$). Then it returns ciphertext C and DEM key K.

Dec(pk, sk, C): This computes $t := H(C)$, $K_{m,n} := \bigoplus_{(i,j) \in S_t} h(e(C, g_2)^{a_{m,i} b_{n,j}})$ ($m \in [k_1]$, $n \in [k_2]$), $K := K_{1,1}||K_{1,2}||\ldots||K_{k_1,k_2}$. Then it returns DEM key K.

The above completes the description of scheme.

Public Key Size. Here, we discuss the public key size of the above scheme. We can set $u_1 = u_2 = O(\lambda^{1/2} q)$ (see Sect. 2.4) and $k_1 = k_2 = O(\lambda^{1/2})$. Then, public key of the scheme consists of $O(u_1 k_1 + u_2 k_2) = O(\lambda q)$ group elements. Note that we can further reduce the number of group elements of the public key to $1/\sqrt{2}$ of that in the above scheme if we use symmetric pairing as in [19].

3.2 Security

Here, we discuss the security of the scheme. We show that the above scheme is IND-q-CCA secure under the CBDH assumption.

Theorem 1. *If the CBDH assumption holds on $\mathbb{G}_1$, $\mathbb{G}_2$ and $\mathbb{G}_T$, h is a hardcore bit function of the CBDH assumption, and H is a target collision resistant hash function, then Ours1 is IND-q-CCA secure. Specifically, for any efficient adversary $\mathcal{A}$, there exist efficient adversaries $\mathcal{B}$ and $\mathcal{D}$ such that $\mathsf{Adv}_{\mathsf{Ours1},\mathcal{A}}^{\mathrm{ind}\text{-}q\text{-}\mathrm{cca}}(\lambda) \leq \mathsf{Adv}_{\mathcal{B},H}^{\mathrm{tcr}}(\lambda) + \ell k \mathsf{Adv}_{\mathcal{D}}^{\mathrm{cbdh}\text{-}\mathrm{hc}}(\lambda)$.*

The proof can be found in the full version.

4 Construction from the Factoring Assumption

This section presents another IND-BCCA secure KEM with optimal ciphertext overhead. Remarkably, this scheme is provably secure under the factoring assumption which is considered to be one of the most reliable assumptions in the area of cryptography. Our scheme is based on the fact that the factoring assumption implies the CDH assumption on $\mathbb{QR}_N$. By using this, we design an IND-BCCA secure KEM under the factoring assumption.

Moreover, we observe that the BBS generator is a hard-core function of the CDH assumption on $\mathbb{QR}_N$. Since the output length of the BBS generator can be any polynomial in the security parameter, we do not need to generate public keys for each bit of a DEM key as in [16]. Consequently, we can obtain an IND-q-CCA secure KEM under the factoring assumption whose public key consists of $O(\lambda q^2)$ group elements whereas that in the scheme in [16] based on the CDH assumption consists of $O(\lambda^2 q^2)$ group elements.

4.1 CDH Assumption on $\mathbb{QR}_N$ and BBS Pseudo-Random Number Generator

Here, let us recall that if the factoring assumption holds, then the CDH assumption holds on $\mathbb{QR}_N$ [17] and moreover, we show that the BBS generator is a hard-core function of the CDH problem. More formally, our claim is as follows.

Lemma 1. *For any adversary $\mathcal{A}$, we define the BBS hard-core advantage as $\mathsf{Adv}_{\mathcal{A},\mathsf{RSAGen}}^{\mathrm{bbs}\text{-}\mathrm{hc}} := |\Pr[1 \leftarrow \mathcal{A}(N, g, g^x, g^y, r, BBS_r(g^{xy}))] - \Pr[1 \leftarrow \mathcal{A}(N, g, g^x, g^y, r, T)]|$ where $(N, P, Q) \leftarrow \mathsf{RSAGen}(1^\lambda)$, $g \xleftarrow{\$} \mathbb{QR}_N{}^1$, $x, y \xleftarrow{\$} \mathbb{Z}_{\mathrm{ord}(\mathbb{QR}_N)}$, $r \xleftarrow{\$} \{0,1\}^{\ell_N}$, $T \xleftarrow{\$} \{0,1\}^k$. If the factoring assumption holds for $\mathsf{RSAGen}(1^\lambda)$, then $\mathsf{Adv}_{\mathcal{A},\mathsf{RSAGen}}^{\mathrm{bbs}\text{-}\mathrm{hc}}$ is negligible.*

To the best of our knowledge, this has not ever been explicitly shown. However, the (even CPA) security of the second scheme in [14] (ElGamal-like KEM under the factoring assumption) implies this. Note that the scheme is instantiated on a group called a semi-smooth subgroup, but we can instantiate the scheme on $\mathbb{QR}_N$ without adversely affecting the security.

---

[1] One may think that g should be sampled from generators of $\mathbb{QR}_N$, but since overwhelming fraction of elements of $\mathbb{QR}_N$ is a generator, it causes only negligible differences.

4.2   Construction

Here, we present the construction of the IND-BCCA secure KEM under the factoring assumption with optimal ciphertext length. Let $H : \mathbb{Z}_N^* \to [v]$ be a target collision resistant hash function and $\mathcal{S}$ be a (u, v, q)-ℓ-uniform cover free family. We call the following scheme Ours2.

Gen(1^λ): This generates $N \leftarrow \mathsf{RSAGen}(1^\lambda)$ and chooses $g \xleftarrow{\$} \mathbb{QR}_N$. Then it chooses $x_i \xleftarrow{\$} [(N-1)/4]$, $X_i := g^{x_i}$ $(i \in [u])$ and $r \leftarrow \{0,1\}^{\ell_N}$. Then it returns public key $pk = ((X_i)_{i \in [u]}, N, g, r)$, and secret key $sk = ((x_i)_{i \in [u]})$.

Enc(pk): This chooses $y \xleftarrow{\$} [(N-1)/4]$ and computes $C := g^y$, $t := H(C)$ and $K := \bigoplus_{i \in \mathcal{S}_t} BBS_r(X_i^y)$. Then it returns ciphertext C and DEM key K.

Dec(pk, sk, C): This computes $t := H(C)$ and $K := \bigoplus_{i \in \mathcal{S}_t} BBS_r(C^{x_i})$. Then it returns DEM key K.

The above completes the description of the scheme.

Public Key Size. Here, we discuss the public key size of the scheme. We can set $u = O(\lambda q^2)$ (see Sect. 2.4). Then public key of the scheme consists of $O(u) = O(\lambda q^2)$ group elements.

4.3   Security

Here, we show that the above scheme is IND-q-CCA secure under the factoring assumption.

Theorem 2. *If H is a target collision resistant hash functions and the factoring assumption holds for RSAGen, then Ours2 is IND-q-CCA secure. Specifically, for any efficient adversary $\mathcal{A}$, there exist efficient adversaries $\mathcal{B}$ and $\mathcal{D}$ such that*
$$\mathsf{Adv}^{\text{ind-}q\text{-cca}}_{\text{Ours2}, \mathcal{A}}(\lambda) \leq \mathsf{Adv}^{\text{tcr}}_{\mathcal{B}, H}(\lambda) + \ell \mathsf{Adv}^{\text{bbs-hc}}_{\mathcal{D}, \text{RSAGen}}(\lambda) + O(2^{-\lambda}).$$

The proof can be found in the full version.

Acknowledgement. The authors would like to thank the members of the study group "Shin-Akarui-Angou-Benkyou-Kai".

References

1. Blum, L., Blum, M., Shub, M.: A simple unpredictable pseudo-random number generator. SIAM J. Comput. **15**(2), 364–383 (1986)
2. Blum, M., Feldman, P., Micali, S.: Non-interactive zero-knowledge and its applications (extended abstract). In: STOC, pp. 103–112 (1988)
3. Cramer, R., Hanaoka, G., Hofheinz, D., Imai, H., Kiltz, E., Pass, R., Shelat, A., Vaikuntanathan, V.: Bounded CCA2-secure encryption. In: Kurosawa, K. (ed.) ASIACRYPT 2007. LNCS, vol. 4833, pp. 502–518. Springer, Heidelberg (2007)
4. Cramer, R., Shoup, V.: Design and analysis of practical public-key encryption schemes. SIAM J. Comput. **33**(1), 167–226 (2003)

5. Dolev, D., Dwork, C., Naor, M.: Non-malleable cryptography (extended abstract). In: STOC, pp. 542–552 (1991)

6. Erdös, P.L., Frankl, P., Füredi, Z.: Families of finite sets in which no set is covered by the union of two others. J. Comb. Theor. Ser. A **33**(2), 158–166 (1982)

7. Erdös, P.L., Frankl, P., Füredi, Z.: Families of finite sets in which no set is covered by the union of r others. Isr. J. Math. **51**, 79–89 (1985)

8. Galbraith, S.D., Hopkins, H.J., Shparlinski, I.E.: Secure bilinear Diffie-Hellman bits. In: Wang, H., Pieprzyk, J., Varadharajan, V. (eds.) ACISP 2004. LNCS, vol. 3108, pp. 370–378. Springer, Heidelberg (2004)

9. Hanaoka, G., Matsuda, T., Schuldt, J.C.N.: On the impossibility of constructing efficient key encapsulation and programmable hash functions in prime order groups. In: Safavi-Naini, R., Canetti, R. (eds.) CRYPTO 2012. LNCS, vol. 7417, pp. 812–831. Springer, Heidelberg (2012)

10. Haralambiev, K., Jager, T., Kiltz, E., Shoup, V.: Simple and efficient public-key encryption from computational Diffie-Hellman in the standard model. In: Nguyen, P.Q., Pointcheval, D. (eds.) PKC 2010. LNCS, vol. 6056, pp. 1–18. Springer, Heidelberg (2010)

11. Hofheinz, D., Kiltz, E.: The group of signed quadratic residues and applications. In: Halevi, S. (ed.) CRYPTO 2009. LNCS, vol. 5677, pp. 637–653. Springer, Heidelberg (2009)

12. Hofheinz, D., Kiltz, E.: Practical chosen ciphertext secure encryption from factoring. In: Joux, A. (ed.) EUROCRYPT 2009. LNCS, vol. 5479, pp. 313–332. Springer, Heidelberg (2009)

13. Hohenberger, S., Lewko, A., Waters, B.: Detecting dangerous queries: a new approach for chosen ciphertext security. In: Pointcheval, D., Johansson, T. (eds.) EUROCRYPT 2012. LNCS, vol. 7237, pp. 663–681. Springer, Heidelberg (2012)

14. Mei, Q., Li, B., Lu, X., Jia, D.: Chosen ciphertext secure encryption under factoring assumption revisited. In: Catalano, D., Fazio, N., Gennaro, R., Nicolosi, A. (eds.) PKC 2011. LNCS, vol. 6571, pp. 210–227. Springer, Heidelberg (2011)

15. Naor, M., Yung, M.: Public-key cryptosystems provably secure against chosen ciphertext attacks. In: STOC, pp. 427–437 (1990)

16. Pereira, M., Dowsley, R., Hanaoka, G., Nascimento, A.C.A.: Public key encryption schemes with bounded CCA security and optimal ciphertext length based on the CDH assumption. In: Burmester, M., Tsudik, G., Magliveras, S., Ilić, I. (eds.) ISC 2010. LNCS, vol. 6531, pp. 299–306. Springer, Heidelberg (2011)

17. Shmuely, Z.: Composite diffie-hellman public-key generating systems are hard to break. Technical report 356, Computer Science Department, Technion, Israel, (1985)

18. Yamada, S., Hanaoka, G., Kunihiro, N.: Two-dimensional representation of cover free families and its applications: short signatures and more. In: Dunkelman, O. (ed.) CT-RSA 2012. LNCS, vol. 7178, pp. 260–277. Springer, Heidelberg (2012)

19. Yamada, S., Kawai, Y., Hanaoka, G., Kunihiro, N.: Public key encryption schemes from the (b)cdh assumption with better efficiency. IEICE Trans. **93–A**(11), 1984–1993 (2010)

Malware and Critical Infrastructures

4GMOP: Mopping Malware Initiated SMS Traffic in Mobile Networks

Marián Kühnel[(✉)] and Ulrike Meyer

CS Department, RWTH Aachen University, Aachen, Germany
{kuehnel,meyer}@itsec.rwth-aachen.de

Abstract. Smartphones have become the most popular mobile devices. Due to their simplicity, portability and functionality comparable to recent computers users tend to store more and more sensitive information on mobile devices rendering them an attractive target for malware writers. As a consequence, mobile malware population is doubled every single year. Many approaches to detect mobile malware infections directly on mobile devices have been proposed. Detecting and blocking voice and SMS messages related to mobile malware in a mobile operator's network has, however, gained little attention so far. The 4GMOP proposed in this paper aims at closing this gap.

1 Introduction

In the past few years, the popularity of sophisticated mobile devices such as smartphones and tablets has continuously increased. This is due to the availability of increasingly diversified mobile applications for smartphones that complement the traditional call and SMS services offered by basic mobile phones. The mass adoption has, however, turned mobile devices into a new target for malware writers [21]. These are attracted by the ever increasing amount of sensitive data stored on the devices and the new opportunities to make money. Even more, due to the fact that most mobile devices are always-on, mobile malware writers can expect to be able to contact their victim devices at all times. At the same time, many end users believe that the mobile device itself or at least their mobile network operator (MNO) will protect them [14]. The most trivial forms of mobile malware just send premium SMS messages or make calls to premium numbers on behalf of their victims. More sophisticated mobile malware samples are also able to steal data (address books, mobile TANs, emails, SMS messages etc.) from mobile devices, reload malicious code, initiate in-app-purchases, or send out spam.

Some prior research on mobile malware focuses on providing an overview on current mobile malware (e.g. [15,32]) or a particular class of mobile malware samples [31]. Other works focus on analyzing a single form of mobile malware in detail [25,29]. Apart from these interesting descriptive works, many approaches to mitigate the mobile malware threat have been proposed (e.g. [5,8,10,11]). However, most of these proposals concentrate on detecting mobile malware on the mobile device itself. In cellular networks, the DNS traffic initiated by mobile

© Springer International Publishing Switzerland 2015
Y. Desmedt (Ed.): ISC 2013, LNCS 7807, pp. 113–129, 2015.
DOI: 10.1007/978-3-319-27659-5_8

devices has been investigated in [20] but little attention has been spent on monitoring other traffic initiated by mobile malware. This is particularly surprising as all mobile malware except ransomware requires some sort of communication over the network to fulfill its malicious goal [32]. Thus, filtering traffic initiated by mobile malware should stop the malicious intend of almost any mobile malware currently out in the wild. Note that netflow analysis [4] and intrusion detection and prevention systems [26] cannot directly be used to filter traffic initiated by mobile malware as these systems are typically designed for the TCP/IP protocol stack, which substantially differs from a 3G or 4G protocol stack and is in particular not able to filter SMS messages and voice traffic initiated by mobile malware. On the first glance, it may seem as if a mobile operator does not have an incentive to invest in such filtering although it would have several advantages. First, customers believe that it is the operator's job to protect them from infections [14] such that they risk loosing their reputation if they stay inactive. Second, MNOs may be able to sell the filtering as a service to their more concerned users. Finally, some proof of concepts (e.g. [9,12,27]) have shown that the infrastructure of MNOs can be targeted by DDOS attacks originating from malware-infected mobile devices.

In this paper, we introduce and evaluate the 4GMOP, a mobile malware detection system targeted to operator in a MNOs backbone network in order to detect SMS messages initiated by mobile malware. We concentrate on detecting SMS traffic as to the best of our knowledge there is no prior research work on this topic. The 4GMOP system consists of a first line of defense, which applies list-based, rule-based, and pattern-based filtering. This is complemented by a second line of defense in which more sophisticated classifiers using anomaly detection or machine learning techniques are applied. In particular, we implemented and evaluated a classifier for the detection of "malicious" SMS messages based on Support Vector Machines (SVMs). We evaluated this classifier on the SMS-MV1.0 corpus, a collection of malicious and benign SMS messages which we compiled and published alongside this paper. We show that our classifier is able to filter over 80 % of the malicious SMS messages with a false positive rate well below 0.1 %.

2   Mobile Malware Traffic

In this section we discuss what types of traffic initiated by mobile malware can be detected in a MNO's network. For this purpose we review prior work on analyzing mobile malware [15,22,25,29,31,32] as well as on proof-of-concept mobile malware [17,29,30]. We complement these prior findings with the results of our own analysis of 35 mobile malware samples targeting the Android platform. We divide our discussion into the infection and execution phase.

2.1   Traffic During Infection

Current mobile malware gain access to mobile devices using one of four infection techniques, namely repackaging [31], malicious updates, URI download, and drive-by download [32]. In the following we briefly discuss each of these techniques.

In repackaging, the malware author first identifies and downloads some popular benign app. He then disassembles the benign app and concatenates malicious payload. The original app complemented by some malicious functions is then resubmitted to the official or an alternative market where the user can download it in the belief that it is the original benign app. The malicious app typically claims the same functionality and package name as the original one. This common practice confuses users even more. In academic literature, the repackaging method is sometimes referred as piggybacking [15]. In malicious updates, a mobile malware writer conceals the malicious part by adding some sort of an update component to the app. This component then downloads the malicious payload later at runtime [32]. URI downloads use classical phishing techniques or cross-references in order to trick users into visiting and downloading malicious apps from websites that copy the layout and design of official markets or other popular sites.

A more advanced infection technique of mobile malware is a so-called drive-by download, i.e., a download without a person's knowledge while surfing the Internet. Drive-by downloads are typically triggered by opening a badly formatted web page. Here, malware writer exploits existing vulnerabilities in mobile browsers to download and install the mobile malware. Typically, the malware then connects to a predefined external site and downloads additional software which completes the installation and with the help of root privilege escalation exploits gains full access to the device.

Note that in our analysis of samples gained from the VirusTotal database [28], we encounter only repackaging, malicious updates and URI downloads but no drive-by downloads. This may indicate that either drive-by downloads are currently not used at all or that they are used only as a part of targeted attacks.

Detecting mobile malware during the infection phase in an MNO's network is difficult as the traffic related to repackaging, URI downloads, malicious updates, and drive-by downloads looks like regular IP traffic from the MNO's perspective. All an MNO could do here is to filter connections to suspicious alternative markets and servers known to be hosting malicious apps as part of their more general intrusion detection and prevention system. Note that the SMS service is not involved in the infection phase.

2.2 Traffic During Execution

After the infection phase in which mobile malware is downloaded and installed, the mobile malware remains undetectable for an MNO until it tries to contact some remote resources via some network. Note that the overwhelming majority of the 1260 mobile malware samples analyzed in [32] as well as the samples analyzed by us become active and initiate network traffic after a short period of time.

The most trivial mobile malware samples use only one single communication channel immediately after installation, e.g. send an SMS message or make a phone call to a premium number. Other mobile malware samples send out SMS messages to all contacts available on the infected mobile phone. Sometimes, SMS messages are used in the context of mobile spyware. In this case, the content of the SMS message carries the data harvested on the mobile phone. Most mobile spyware, however, sends out the data collected on the phone to a remote server via HTTP [32]. More evolved mobile malware create a network of infected mobile devices, a mobile botnet [29]. Such a mobile botnet is remotely controlled through a command and control (C&C) infrastructure. As known from botnets of desktop computers, the C&C infrastructure of a mobile botnet can be centralized with one or more central C&C servers or decentralized. In the latter case, commands are distributed to the infected devices in a peer-to-peer (P2P) fashion [17,29, 30]. Three types of command and control channels have been discussed and observed in the context of mobile botnets so far. The first one uses the HTTP protocol [32], the second one uses SMS messages [17], and the third one splits the communication into an SMS and an HTTP part [23]. Using the SMS service as (one of the) communication channels has the advantage that commands reach the infected mobile device even if it is currently switched off or out of network coverage: the MNO will store incoming messages and deliver them as soon as the mobile device is reachable again [17,30]. An advantage of using an SMS channel in addition to an HTTP-based C&C infrastructure is that it may add to the take-down resilience of the mobile botnet as a new C&C server can be announced via SMS after a successful take-down of an old C&C server. Finally, P2P botnets may be easier to implement with the help of SMS messages as IP-based communication directly between mobile devices is challenging as long as the majority of mobile devices do not use public IP addresses. In addition, SMS messages support transport of arbitrary binary data with the length limited to 140 octets (or 160 septets) each which is more than enough for a secure encrypted communication between the infected device and the botnet herder [22].

All of these activities generate traffic in the mobile operator's network. While it may be possible to reuse intrusion detection and prevention techniques developed in the context of desktop malware to cope with the IP-based part of the traffic initiated during the execution phase, to the best of our knowledge there is no prior work on filtering mobile malware initiated SMS traffic yet. In the rest of this paper we, therefore, focus on effectively detecting and filtering SMS messages initiated by mobile malware during the execution phase.

3   The 4GMOP Sensor

To enable filtering of mobile malware related traffic in a MNO's backbone network, we propose the 4G MObile malware Protection sensor (4GMOP). Our sensor is able to detect and filter SMS traffic originating from or terminating at mobile devices infected with mobile malware. It is extensible in the sense that it allows for the integration of new detection modules on top of the one we propose in this paper. In the following, we first provide an overview on the architecture of the 4GMOP (see also [16]) and then describe its components in more detail.

3.1 Architecture Overview

The 4GMOP is designed to reside in a MNO's backbone network and to monitor incoming and outgoing traffic. The core of the 4GMOP consists of three components: a filter, a checker, and a bridge as illustrated in Fig. 1.

Filter. The filter component is responsible for monitoring and filtering SMS-related incoming and outgoing traffic directly from the traffic flow in nearly real-time (users can not differentiate between filtered and unfiltered traffic). Filtering of SMS messages is particularly easy as both services are not immediate. In particular, it takes some time to deliver or receive new SMS messages [12]. Therefore, if the detection and prevention process requires only a few hundred milliseconds per SMS message sent, it will be unnoticeable to the user. When a new data flow is intercepted by the filter, the flow is replicated and sent to the checker and bridge component respectively. The idea behind the replication is to be able to run several detection modules in parallel. The checker provides highly efficient detection methods (list-based, content list-based and pattern-based filtering) to detect already known malicious traffic and thus acts as a first line of defense. The bridge forwards the traffic to one or more classifiers running directly in the network or are remotely operated. The classifiers built a second line of defense and provide more extensive but resource consuming anomaly detection algorithms [24] or machine learning techniques [13].

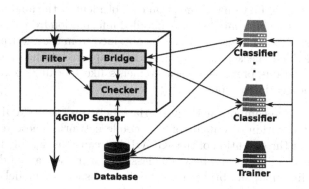

Fig. 1. The 4GMOP architecture and its interaction with other components.

Checker. The checker acts as a first line of detection and provides (content) list-based filtering of SMS messages and pattern-based filtering on SMS messages. In the following we describe these filtering techniques in more detail.

The list-based filtering mechanism checks the phone numbers involved in voice calls and SMS messages against a whitelist and a blacklist. The whitelist collects benign phone numbers set to be benign by the MNO. The blacklist gathers phone numbers that have been misused by mobile malware for malicious activities. In addition, SMS messages are filtered with the help of a so-called content blacklist where each substring of an SMS message is checked against a content blacklist. Note that all three types of lists need to be regularly updated. We propose to push a modified entry from a database each time a list has changed. Such updates may be triggered by external sources (e.g. new list entries provided by antivirus companies) or as the result of a MNO's own analysis of malware samples. Note that we currently do not expect that these lists will change on a daily basis, as different malware samples often reuse the same phone numbers. E.g. we found that the same short phone number 1161 is misused in the three mobile malware samples SmsSend.H, FakeInst.AH, and FakeNotify.A.

The last filtering method we use as part of the first line of defense in our 4GMOP is pattern-based filtering. It is also performed by the checker and filters SMS messages. Opposed to content blacklisting, pattern-based filtering uses a sliding window technique to match the current window content with regular expressions generated from patterns and strings used in already known mobile malware.

Matching known regular expression suffices as mobile malware send user or device specific sensitive information in SMS messages with fixed structure. For instance, an SMS message initiated by mobile malware (SIMM message) with content "IMEI:358967041111111" (NickySpy.A) would be detected by the content blacklist and by the patter-based filter. By the content blacklist because of the static string "IMEI" and by the patter-based filter because of the 15 digits starting with a valid[1] type allocation code [2].

In the 4GMOP, the checker component is always responsible for the final decisions. Only if the first line of detection cannot identify the analyzed data for certain, then the checker waits for more detailed information from the bridge and evaluates the situation based on the results obtained from the external classifiers via the bridge. The checker also decides what happens to the analyzed data. At this stage, various prevention measurements like blocking, partial content deletion or modification are possible.

Bridge. The bridge component is an interface between the 4GMOP and other resources located within or outside of the mobile network. These resources are not necessary for the execution of the 4GMOP but can considerably improve the detection rate. We differentiate between classifiers, a trainer, and a database. In the outgoing direction, the bridge parses data and specifies model parameters for classifiers. In the incoming direction, the bridge simply forwards results to the checker. If a response from classifiers does not reach the bridge in some predefined time, the bridge sends the delayed response to the database via the checker component for further manual processing. The same applies for ambiguous results.

Classifiers. Classifiers run more extensive computations and possess processing power exceeding that of the main sensor. Their detection algorithms are not bound to a specific service so that each classifier can handle many requests based on the model parameter. The model parameter specifies the trained model which should be used by the classifier. Models are requested either from the database

---

[1] http://www.mulliner.org/tacdb/feed/contrib/.

or are permanently stored in a local cache of the classifiers if the communication between the database and classifier should lead to notable decrease of performance. This might happen when trained models are larger and downloading of each model lasts longer than the classification process. In small mobile networks, the classifier can be a part of the checker. However, if the MNO has free resources then the classifier should be separated from the sensor to support more sophisticated methods and thus higher-quality detection. In addition, dedicated classifiers can be maintained more easily than dispersed sensors. Good choices for more extensive algorithms detecting classical malware in networks are support vectors machines (SVM) [6], random forests [7] or Bayesian additive regression trees [18]. These or their variants are often part of intrusion detection systems filtering classical malicious traffic directly in the network.

Trainer. In order to achieve good detection rates, each model should be frequently updated by a trainer. The trainer takes recent data from the database as input and generates new models reflecting the current state of the monitored traffic. Training a model typically consists of two steps. All gathered and analyzed data is divided into two set. One is used for training the model and one for testing. The trained model is then applied to a testing set to compute the detection rate. If the detection rate is sufficient, the trainer pushes the newly trained model to the respective classifier and maintains the classifier's cache based on the computed statistics and predictions. We separated the trainer from the classifiers because the training period for generating new models varies greatly based on the input data and type of the classifier. The classification itself needs a constant amount of time for classification.

Database. In the 4GMOP, the checker as well as all classifiers periodically inform the database about all occurred events. The database (or in larger mobile networks a set of databases) stores all relevant information indicating mobile malware initiated traffic such as whitelisted and blacklisted phone numbers, string patterns and data for training models. To optimize the time needed for classification, additional information indicating the state of the respective classifiers for load balancing may be also included in the database.

3.2   Sensor Placement

The 4G network architecture is highly complex and specifies many interfaces and planes. Nevertheless, all planes in a pure 4G architecture intersect in one central component called System Architecture Evolution GateWay (SAE-GW). The SAE-GW is responsible for IP address allocation, deep packet inspection, policy enforcement, and connectivity from mobile devices to external packet data networks (PDNs) important for SMS delivery and call transmission. We therefore propose to place the 4GMOP sensor in front of the SAE-GW. Note that possible sensor placements in the 2G and 3G architectures are also discussed in [16].

4   The SMS-Mv1.0 Corpus

In order to be able to evaluate our 4GMOP and in particular any newly proposed classifiers a data set of malicious and benign SMS messages is required.
Unfortunately, to date not such data set has been published. We close this gap
by introducing the SMS-Mv1.0 corpus which we published[2] alongside this paper.
We describe how we extracted the SMS messages sent and received by mobile
malware samples and built the malicious part of the SMS-Mv1.0 corpus. We
complemented these with benign SMS messages taken from the SMS Spam Collection v.1 corpus [3]. Note that spam messages differ greatly from SMS messages
sent by mobile malware. In particular, e.g. SMS messages used to distribute command and control information in a mobile botnet or SMS messages sent out to
premium numbers to generate profit will typically not have any similarity with
SMS spam messages.

4.1   SMS Usage in Mobile Malware Samples

The results of our analysis of 35 mobile malware samples obtained from [28]
are presented in Fig. 2. It shows how SMS messages are used in current mobile
malware samples. The first column of the figure gives the name of the analyzed
sample. The SHA-256 (32) value in the second column of the figure corresponds
to the first 32 bits of the SHA-256 hash value of the respective mobile malware
sample. In the *Premium* column we mark if the malware sample sends out SMS
messages to a premium (short) number with less than six digits. The column
Contacts marks if a malware sample sends out SMS messages to one or more
contacts stored in the infected phone's address book. The next four columns are
related to the content of SMS messages sent out by mobile malware samples.
The column *Hardcoded* indicates the number of SIMM messages sent or received
by mobile malware where the content of the SIMM message is hardcoded in
the source code of the malicious sample. If some parts of the content of the
SIMM messages are variable, then the number of SIMM messages is given in
the *Dynamic* column. The *IN* and *OUT* show whether the SIMM message is
sent to or from the infected mobile device. Finally, the last column *SMS* C&C
marks if the mobile malware sample uses an SMS based C&C channel. A check
mark denotes that we could indeed observe and state the behavior of the sample,
while an asterisk next to the name denotes that we were only able to determine
the behavior with the help of static analysis e.g. as the C&C server was already
down or we could not obtain files a mobile malware sample tries to open.

   As we can see in Fig. 2, the majority of the analyzed mobile malware samples
send fixed SIMM messages to fixed premium numbers. Note that all samples send
premium SMS messages in plaintext[3] such that once the content of these malicious messages is known to an operator, he can easily filter these messages with
content blacklisting. In the samples we analyzed, bidirectional SMS traffic is used

---

[2] https://itsec.rwth-aachen.de/smscorpus.
[3] Only the encoding differs from ASCII encoding.

Name	SHA-256(32)	Premium	Contacts	Hardcoded		Dynamic		SMS C&C
				IN	OUT	IN	OUT	
Arspam.A	1d22924b		✓		18			
DogWars.A	435bc70e	✓	✓		2			
FakeInst.AH	5760a43e	✓			3			
FakeInst.N	8a2554f6	✓			1			
Fakelogo.A	96b15c42	✓			2			
FakeNotify.A	7f3b99e6	✓			3			
FakePlayer.A	14ebc4e9	✓			3			
GppSpy.A	d221cf7a					17		✓
HippoSMS.A	02bd52e7				1			
Kmin.A	d2b6f618				1			
NickySpy.A	ccc38fe8						1	
NickySpy.C	e2752f49					17		✓
Opfake.A	16513df0	✓			2			
Opfake.A	f46ecaa3	✓			1			
Opfake.F	eeaf7972	✓			3			
Opfake.S	e03d393b	✓			1			
PremiumSms.AA	21f42e35	✓			2		2	
PremiumSms.B	708dd31e	✓			3			
Qicsomos.A	79a3bc6d	✓			4			
Raden.A	9ae7270c				1			
Raden.B	4742ec6a	✓			4			
RuFraud.A	7bb9b0b3	✓			2			
RuFraud.B	49d41f8d	✓			2			
SendSms.H	9734399b	✓			3			
SmsSend.Y	a9b11b91	✓			3			
SmsAgent.ES*	e32e9176				1			
SmsFoncy.A	98a402d8	✓			8			
SmsSpy.E	d56c8ef6	✓					1	
SmsZombie.A	741684cf						3	
Tcent.A	54ece852						1	
TigerBot.A*	db293fd1					10	3	✓
WalkSteal.A	c6eb43f2		✓		1			
ZertSecurity*	00ce460c					4		✓
Zitmo.A	40286c60			4	4	6	3	✓
Zsone.A	f533c7c1	✓			4			

Fig. 2. SMS Usage in Mobile Malware.

by only two mobile botnets (TigeerBot.A, Zitmo.A). The observed SIMM messages carrying mobile botnet commands differ from typical benign SMS messages as they contain a particularly high number of special characters and numerals used as separators. Other SIMM messages sent by samples we analyzed carry user-specific sensitive information like the International Mobile Station Equipment Identity (IMEI), phone numbers, contacts from the phone book, operator information and network information. Many mobile malware samples send sensitive information in SIMM messages in plaintext, such that it can potentially be detected and filtered by an MNO. In fact, only one of the samples we analyzed (ZertSecurity.A) communicates over an encrypted channel and two mobile malware botnets (NickySpy.C, GppSpy.A) utilize hashmaps to obfuscate their commands. I.e. they use a bilinear map of commands represented by numbers. Encrypted communication is obviously hard to filter in the MNO's network.

4.2   Building the SMS-Mv1.0 Corpus

Our SMS-Mv1.0 corpus contains 4539 benign SMS messages and 155 SIMM messages. We extracted the benign SMS messages from the SMS Spam Collection v.1 [3]. In particular, we extracted all single benign SMS messages (i.e., SMS messages containing at most 160 characters) in GSM 7-bit default alphabet encoding [1] written in the Latin alphabet. Some of the benign SMS messages from [3] were not correctly decoded. We processed wrongly decoded benign SMS messages by replacing all occurrences of "<", ">", "<#>", "0 × 94" and "0 × 96" by an empty string. We further replaced "0 × 92" by an apostrophe and "&"amp by an "&". Some benign SMS messages occurred more than three times in the extracted set of benign SMS messages. In these cases, we kept three of the identical messages and deleted any additional occurrences. This procedure removed 47 SMS messages from the extracted set and left us with the 4539 benign SMS messages in our SMS-Mv1.0 corpus.

We complement these benign messages with SIMM messages sent and received by the 35 mobile malware samples described above. The most common malware we found during our static and dynamic analyzes of the malware samples send constant SIMM messages in the sense that the whole content of the SMS message is statically set in the source code of the malware sample and does not change over time, see the Hardcoded column in Fig. 2. By adding such SIMM messages to our corpus, we applied the same rule. If we found that the mobile malware samples sends identical content of SIMM messages to more than just three numbers, we limited the number of accepted SIMM messages for the corpus to the first three entries. In addition, we decided to list at most two empty SIMM messages per mobile malware sample to prevent homogeneity in the SMS-Mv1.0 corpus due to too many empty SIMM messages.

Some of the samples we analyzed collect information about the infected device and/or subscriber, namely the International Mobile station Equipment Identity (IMEI) or the International Mobile Subscriber Identity (IMSI). Since each number is static regarding the entity, mobile malware samples send only one SIMM message per infected device and/or subscriber. However, these SIMM messages are not identical if sent from different entities. To overcome this issue with variable content in SIMM messages, we later describe feature selection in which using the same or variable IMSI and IMEI in each of these SIMM messages will not have any effect on the detection rate. Therefore, it suffices to randomly pick some valid values for IMSI and IMEI as shown in Table 1. Other mobile malware samples forward all incoming and outgoing benign SMS messages from the infected phone to a C&C server. In these cases, we added exactly three messages to our corpus where the benign SMS messages were taken from our SMS-Mv1.0 corpus. The content of the three SIMM messages as well as phone numbers, date and time is also indicated in Table 1. Command numbers occurring as text in command SIMM messages sent to mobile-botnet-infected devices change the phone number of the C&C server. During our mobile malware analysis, we found that phone command numbers of C&C servers are both regular and premium numbers. Respective commands are "secured" by a static key set by

Table 1. Strings used in SIMM messages.

Type of string	1st entry	2nd entry	3rd entry
IMSI	310111223344556		
IMEI	358967041111111		
Text	Sorry, I'll call later	I wonder if you'll get this text?	Tired. I haven't slept well the past few nights
Phone number	012367894500	02109876543	0506070809
Date and Time	2013-06-06 06:07:08	2012-05-05 01:22:33	2011-04-04 05:05:55
Command number	0666666660		
Premium number	5555		
Key	123456		
Random number	7156		
Process name	com.android.malicious		

initialization (NickySpy.C) or accompanied by a n-digit random number (TigerBot.A). Last entry in Table 1 refers to the TigerBot.A mobile malware sample which can manage processes.

To avoid any misunderstandings, let us assume the SmsZombie.A sample forwarding incoming legitimate SMS messages to the attacker. All SIMM messages sent by SmsZombie.A have a fixed structure:

- Date and Time: Phone number–Text

This tells the C&C server the date when the benign SMS message was received, the phone number of the sender and the content of the forwarded message. In this case we added the following three malicious SMS messages to our corpus:

- 2013-03-21 17:47:47:012367894500–Sorry, I'll call later
- 2012-05-05 01:22:33:02109876543–I wonder if you'll get this text?
- 2011-04-04 05:05:55:0506070809–Tired. I haven't slept well the past few nights.

In such manner we were able to obtain 155 malicious SMS messages from the 35 malware samples we analyzed. Altogether, our SMS-Mv1.0 corpus contains of 4737 SMS messages.

5   An Example Classifier

In this section we describe the design and evaluation of an example classifier that can be used in connection with the 4GMOP to detect and filter SMS messages initiated in the context of mobile malware. Virtually all classifiers can be used but we decided to use the Support Vector Machine algorithm (SVM) as it has been shown that the SVM classifier is one of the most accurate methods to classify ham and spam SMS messages [3]. Also SVMs have successfully been used for online traffic classification directly in the network [13]. The SVM itself represents a supervised learning technique suitable for solving classification problems where the number of available training data for one class is rather small. The later property is crucial for us. Although there are many captured samples of mobile malware every day, SIMM messages sent over the mobile network are quite similar. In many cases, they have identical structures leading to a relatively small space of SIMM messages compared to benign SMS messages. Another beneficial property of an SVM is that once a model has been generated, the time needed for classification of yet new SMS messages is negligible.

5.1 Feature Selection

The challenge task in using SVMs in the context of classifying SMS messages into benign and malicious messages is the design of the features used to train the SVM. In the following we describe which features we selected and why. We then show how using different combinations of these features to train an SVM influences the performance of the detection. In many jurisdiction systems it is illegal to process SMS messages on a semantic basis. We operate on the content of the SMS message in a non-semantic way. Note that we do not take any characteristics of the sending or receiving phone numbers into account as we do not have access to this information for the benign SMS messages. Also, characteristics such as the length of the premium numbers strongly vary between different countries and are therefore not a good source for the creation of universally usable features.

Overall we deduce eleven features based on the SIMM messages and benign messages in our corpus. Table 2 provides an overview on the features we considered. The first three features characterize SIMM messages. The content of the command messages used in the mobile botnets we analyzed consists of short strings with many special characters separating respective parameters. Compared to benign SMS messages, whitespace characters are very rare in the SIMM messages we observed. As a first feature (Feature 1) we use the absolute number of special characters in a message excluding the special characters that are frequently used in benign messages, namely whitespace, dot, comma, apostrophe, question and exclamation mark. While numerals occur in both benign SMS messages and SIMM messages, in benign SMS messages they are often accompanied by some text which has been represented by two additional features. Feature 2 counts the absolute number of numerals in a message, while Feature R2 denotes the ratio of the number of numerals to the overall number of characters in the SMS message. Feature 2R should be able to distinguish between a block of numerals accompanied by text and an SMS consisting of numerals only. Feature 0 denotes the length of the message in the number of characters and should detect empty SIMM messages sent to premium numbers by trivial mobile malware. Feature 3 counts whitespace characters. We observed that the ration of whitespace characters to the overall length of the message (Feature 3R) is around 0.2 for benign SMS messages. Finally, Feature 4 counts the absolute number of capital letters while Feature 5 counts the number of lowercase letters.

Table 2. List of features.

Feature	Description
0	Overall number of characters
1	Number of special characters except for . , '?!
2	Number of numerics
3	Number of whitespaces
4	Number of capital letters
5	Number of lowercase letters
xR	Ratio of Feature x to Feature 0

Feature 4R and Feature 5R denote again the ration of the capital and lower-case letters to the overall number of characters in the SMS message.

5.2 Evaluation

We empirically tested the SVM classifier using different combination of the features described above. All results were obtained from a light-weighted module of an SVM implementation called SVM^{light} [19]. We ran the SVM^{light} implementation with default parameters. We used a standard cross validation technique to estimate the detection rate of SIMM messages in the MNO network. In particular, we selected five-fold cross validation where the set of benign SMS messages as well as the set of SIMM messages in the SMS-Mv1.0 corpus were randomly divided into five sets of equal size each. Each set of benign SMS messages contained 900 randomly chosen messages and each set of SIMM messages contained the SIMM messages generated by seven randomly chosen mobile malware samples out of the 35 by us analyzed samples. Each round had five runs. In the first run, the first of each subsets was used for testing and the other subsets were used for training. In the second run, the second subset was used for testing and the remaining four subsets were used for training and so forth. The result of one round was then the averaged over the five runs. An example for a single round trained on features 1R, 2R and 3R is given in Table 3.

Table 3. A single round.

Set	SIMM messages	Benign messages	TP	FN	TN	FP	TPR	TNR
1.	48	900	47	1	900	0	0.979167	1
2.	31	900	27	4	899	1	0.870968	0.998889
3.	14	900	13	1	896	4	0.928571	0.995556
4.	20	900	13	7	900	0	0.650000	1
5.	42	900	28	14	900	0	0.666667	1
round							0.819075	0.998889

Table 4. Final results.

Features	MIN TPR	MAX TPR	TPR	TNR	ACC
1, 2, 3	0.646138	0.803078	**0.742781**	0.999107	**0.990470**
0, 1, 2, 3	0.403801	0.607739	**0.520294**	0.999980	**0.984036**
0, 1, 2, 3, 4, 5	0.397059	0.564518	**0.536214**	0.999982	**0.984708**
1R, 2R	0.660891	0.768364	**0.718388**	0.998838	**0.988761**
1R, 3R	0.666397	0.802566	**0.743966**	0.992128	**0.984023**
2R, 3R	0.734009	0.853231	**0.791920**	0.999377	**0.992118**
1R, 2R, 3R	**0.72058**	**0.855411**	**0.806840**	**0.999244**	0.992505
0, 1R, 2R, 3R	0.727168	0.845102	**0.791113**	0.999399	**0.992226**
1R, 2R, 3R, 4R	0.610152	0.765299	**0.69.076**	0.999769	**0.988475**
1R, 2R, 3R, 5R	0.663127	0.768443	**0.712789**	0.999475	**0.989409**

The true positives (TP) value in Table 3 is the number of correctly classified SIMM messages. The true negatives (TN) value is the number of benign messages correctly recognized as benign SMS messages. Complements to TP and TN are false negatives (FN) and false positives (FP) respectively. The true positive ratio (TPR) reflects the ability of the classifier to detect SIMM messages and can be computed as

$$TPR = \frac{TP}{TP + FN}. \tag{1}$$

In the wild, the number of sent benign messages exceeds malicious messages by far and users are more bothered by having benign SMS messages be blocked the MNO than by SIMM messages passing through the MNO's detection sensor. Thus, the MNO is interested in keeping the true negative ration (TNR), i.e., the ratio of benign messages incorrectly classified as SIMM messages as low as possible.

$$TNR = \frac{TN}{TN + FP} \tag{2}$$

In addition to the TPR and the TNR, the overall accuracy (ACC) of the system is represented as the total number of classifier's correct decisions divided by the overall number of messages classified in one round.

$$ACC = \frac{TP + TN}{TP + FN + TN + FP} \tag{3}$$

We empirically tested the various combinations of features listed in Table 2. To mitigated deviations, each test consisted of one hundred rounds.

The most interesting results we obtained are provided in Table 4. Here, the measured average values of the TPR and the TNR as well as the minimum and the maximum value of the TPR are provided in the first four columns. The last column shows the ACC. We found that features in absolute values (without R) tend to provide slightly better TNRs compared to features utilizing ratios, while the ratio features provide a considerably better TPR rate than the features counting absolute values. Next, we examined which features significantly improve the TPR. It turned out that the features counting special characters (Feature 1) and numerals (Feature 2) often occurring in SIMM messages and whitespace characters (Feature 3) occurring in the SMS messages are indeed essential. Surprisingly, ratio of numerals in an SMS message is more informative than the ratio of special characters. We analyzed this phenomenon and found out that emoticons in benign SMS messages are responsible for the slight increase of the TPR compared to 2R or 3R. Features 0, 4, 5 and their complements 4R and 5R were identified as essentially ineffective.

We obtained the best results with respect to the overall accuracy using the three features 1R, 2R and 3R. Here we obtained a TPR over 80 % and a TNR of over 99.9 %. In other words, 124 out of 155 SIMM messages would be correctly detected by our 4GMOP as SIMM messages and only 4 out of 4500 benign SMS messages were incorrectly classified as SIMM messages.

6 Conclusion

With the rise of mobile malware, more and more users are expecting mobile operators to protect them. Many of the negative effects of mobile malware can be mitigated by filtering malware-related traffic in a mobile operators network. We developed a novel sensor that monitors mobile initiated and mobile terminated SMS and voice traffic in order to detect and potentially block mobile malware-related traffic. This sensor supports two lines of defense, a first line that offers basic filtering techniques and a second line which allows for the integration of different classifiers, including the SVM-based classifier we propose in this paper. For the evaluation of this classifier we compiled the SMS-Mv1.0 corpus consisting of benign and malware-related SMS messages. The evaluation of our example classifier shows that our classifier alone is able to correctly classify 80 % of all SMS messages related to mobile malware and over 99.9 % of all benign SMS messages as benign.

Acknowledgments. Part of this work was funded by the German Federal Ministry of Education and Research under the references 01BY1010 - 01BY1015. The authors would like to thank Dominik Teubert for comments on ZertSecurity and the anonymous reviewers for their valuable suggestions and feedback.

References

1. 3GPP. Alphabets and Language-specific Information. TS 23.038, 3rd Generation Partnership Project (3GPP) (2008)
2. 3GPP. Numbering, Addressing and Identification. TS 23.003, 3rd Generation Part-nership Project (3GPP) (2008)
3. Almeida, T.A., Hidalgo, J.M.G., Yamakami, A.: Contributions to the study of sms spam filtering: new collection and results. In: Proceedings of the 11th ACM Symposium on Document Engineering, DocEng 2011, pp. 259–262. ACM (2011)

4. Bilge, L., Balzarotti, D., Robertson, W., Kirda, E., Kruegel, C.: Disclosure: detecting botnet command and control servers through large-scale netflow analysis. In: Proceedings of the 28th Annual Computer Security Applications Conference, ACSAC 2012, pp. 129–138. ACM (2012)
5. Blasing, T., Batyuk, L., Schmidt, A.-D., Camtepe, S.A., Albayrak, S.: An android application sandbox system for suspicious software detection. In: Malicious and Unwanted Software, MALWARE 2010, pp. 55–62. IEEE (2010)
6. Boser, B.E., Guyon, I.M., Vapnik, V.N.: A training algorithm for optimal margin classifiers. In: Proceedings of the 5th Annual Workshop on Computational Learning Theory, COLT 1992, pp. 144–152. ACM (1992)
7. Breiman, L.: Random Forests, vol. 45, pp. 5–32. Kluwer Academic organizations, Hingham (2001)
8. Burguera, I., Zurutuza, U., Nadjm-Tehrani, S.: Crowdroid: behavior-based malware detection system for android. In: Proceedings of the 1st ACM workshop on Security and Privacy in Smartphones and Mobile Devices, SPSM 2011, pp. 15–26. ACM (2011)
9. Chuanxiong Guo, H.J.W., Zhu, W.: Smart-phone attacks and defenses. In: Proceedings of the Third Workshop on Hot Topics in Networks, HotNets III. ACM (2004)
10. Elish, K.O., Yao, D., Ryder, B.G.: User-centric dependence analysis for identifying malicious mobile apps. In: Workshop on Mobile Security Technologies, IEEE (2012)
11. Enck, W., Gilbert, P., Chun, B.-G., Cox, L.P., Jung, J., McDaniel, P., Sheth, A.: Taintdroid: an information-flow tracking system for realtime privacy monitoring on smartphones. In: Proceedings of the 9th USENIX Conference on Operating Systems Design and Implementation, OSDI 2010, pp. 255–270. USENIX Association (2010)
12. Enck, W., Traynor, P., McDaniel, P., La Porta, T.: Exploiting open functionality in sms-capable cellular networks. In: Proceedings of the 12th ACM Conference on Computer and Communications Security, CCS 2005, pp. 393–404. ACM (2005)
13. Este, A., Gringoli, F., Salgarelli, L.: On-line svm traffic classification. In: 2011 7th International Wireless Communications and Mobile Computing Conference, IWCMC 2011, pp. 1778–1783. IEEE (2011)
14. Felt, A.P., Egelman, S., Wagner, D.: I've got 99 problems, but vibration ain't one: a survey of smartphone users' concerns. In: Proceedings of the 2nd ACM Workshop on Security and Privacy in Smartphones and Mobile Devices, SPSM 2012, pp. 33–44. ACM (2012)
15. Felt, A.P., Finifter, M., Chin, E., Hanna, S., Wagner, D.: A survey of mobile malware in the wild. In: Proceedings of the 1st ACM Workshop on Security and Privacy in Smartphones and Mobile Devices, SPSM 2011, pp. 3–14. ACM (2011)
16. Hoche, M., Kirsch, H., Kühnel, M.: Recommender system for security risk reduction - situational awareness for critical information infrastructures. Technical Report, ASMONIA project (2012)
17. Hua, J., Sakurai, K.: A SMS-based mobile botnet using flooding algorithm. In: Ardagna, C.A., Zhou, J. (eds.) WISTP 2011. LNCS, vol. 6633, pp. 264–279. Springer, Heidelberg (2011)
18. Hugh, E.I.G., Chipman, A., McCulloch, R.E.: BART: bayesian additive regression trees. Ann. Appl. Stat. 4, 266–298 (2010)
19. Joachims, T.: Making large scale SVM learning practical (1999)

20. Lever, C., Antonakakis, M., Reaves, B., Traynor, P., Lee, W.: The core of the matter: analyzing malicious traffic in cellular carriers. In: Proceedings of The 20th Annual Network and Distributed System Security Symposium, NDSS 2013, pp. 1–16. ISOC (2013)

21. Lookout.: Mobile security, state of mobile security. Technical report, Lookout (2012)

22. Mulliner, C., Miller, C.: Injecting sms messages into smart phones for security analysis. In: Proceedings of the 3rd USENIX Conference on Offensive Technologies, WOOT 2009, pp. 5–5. USENIX Association (2009)

23. Mulliner, C., Seifert, J.-P.: Rise of the ibots: owning a telco network. In: Malicious and Unwanted Software, MALWARE 2010, pp. 71–80. IEEE (2010)

24. Patcha, A., Park, J.-M.: An overview of anomaly detection techniques: existing solutions and latest technological trends. Comput. Netw. **51**(12), 3448–3470 (2007)

25. Porras, P., Saïdi, H., Yegneswaran, V.: An analysis of the iKee.B iPhone botnet. In: Schmidt, A.U., Russello, G., Lioy, A., Prasad, N.R., Lian, S. (eds.) MobiSec 2010. LNICST, vol. 47, pp. 141–152. Springer, Heidelberg (2010)

26. Scarfone, K.A., Mell, P.: Guide to intrusion detection and prevention systems (IDPS). Technical Report SP 800–94, (2012)

27. Traynor, P., Lin, M., Ongtang, M., Rao, V., Jaeger, T., McDaniel, P., La Porta, T.: On cellular botnets: measuring the impact of malicious devices on a cellular network core. In: Proceedings of the 16th ACM Conference on Computer and Communications Security, CCS 2009, pp. 223–234. ACM (2009)

28. VirusTotal.: Free online virus, malware and url scanner. https://www.virustotal.com

29. Xiang, C., Binxing, F., Lihua, Y., Xiaoyi, L., Tianning, Z.: Andbot: towards advanced mobile botnets. In: Proceedings of the 4th USENIX Conference on Large-scale Exploits and Emergent Threats, LEET 2011, pp. 11–18. USENIX Association (2011)

30. Zeng, Y., Shin, K.G., Hu, X.: Design of sms commanded-and-controlled and p2p-structured mobile botnets. In: Proceedings of the fifth ACM Conference on Security and Privacy in Wireless and Mobile Networks, WISEC 2012, pp. 137–148. ACM (2012)

31. Zhou, W., Zhou, Y., Jiang, X., Ning, P.: Detecting repackaged smartphone applications in third-party android marketplaces. In: Proceedings of the 2nd ACM Conference on Data and Application Security and Privacy, CODASPY 2012, pp. 317–326. ACM (2012)

32. Zhou, Y., Jiang, X.: Dissecting android malware: characterization and evolution. In: Proceedings of the 2012 IEEE Symposium on Security and Privacy, S&P 2012, pp. 95–109. IEEE (2012)

Design and Analysis of a Sophisticated Malware Attack Against Smart Grid

Byungho Min[⊠] and Vijay Varadharajan

Advanced Cyber Security Research Centre, Macquarie University,
Sydney, Australia
{byungho.min,vijay.varadharajan}@mq.edu.au

Abstract. In this paper, we propose a realistic malware attack against the smart grid. The paper first briefs the architecture of the smart grid in general. And then we explain our proposed attack that is specifically tailored for the smart grid infrastructures. The attack considers the characteristics of recent real malware attacks such as deceptive hardware attack and multi-stage operation. We believe this analysis will benefit the design and implementation of secure smart grid infrastructures by demonstrating how a sophisticated malware attack can damage the smart grid.

Keywords: Smart grid · Cyber-physical system · Cyber attack · Malware · Blackout · Security

1 Introduction

Smart grid is a modernised electricity infrastructure that consists of several subsystems and field devices such as supervisory control and data acquisition (SCADA), information systems, programmable logic controllers (PLCs) and smart meters. The infrastructure includes bulk generation, transmission, distribution, operations, markets, service provision and end-user clients. Because the smart grid is a huge integrated system consisting of various subsystems, i.e. a system of systems (SoS), it should be equipped for interoperability with present and future standards of components, devices, and systems that are cyber-secured against malicious attacks. For this reason, Federal Energy Regulatory Commission (FERC) has mandated the development of intersystem communications and cyber security specifications [1]. Many individual researchers and institutions have suggested smart grid security issues including two-way secure communications and increase in the number of paths from end-user clients to core subsystems and components because of increased connectivity [2–5].

Though there are various research works on smart grid security, most of them focus on the risks of individual subsystems or components such as smart meters and AMI [4,6,7]; only a few researchers have addressed security aspects of interplays among the smart grid subsystems and components [8]. Our main aim is to analyse the smart grid as a single integrated system to tackle as many

© Springer International Publishing Switzerland 2015
Y. Desmedt (Ed.): ISC 2013, LNCS 7807, pp. 130–139, 2015.
DOI: 10.1007/978-3-319-27659-5_9

security aspects as possible. In particular, attackers can cause serious damages to the smart grid by attacking more than one subsystem and component and overcoming the security features of the smart grid like self-healing [1].

When it comes to real attacks and offensive research on cyber-physical systems (CPS) including the smart grid, in 2010, Stuxnet has shown how a stealthy attack targeting both hardware and software is possible [9]. Since then, industry security experts have mainly focussed on either (1) demonstrating outright attacks that visually show how the field devices can be controlled using Human Machine Interface (HMI) software [10,11], or (2) disclosing traditional software vulnerabilities such as buffer overflow in SCADA software, which can be used to compromise the installed operating system, but cannot be used to compromise field devices [12]. However, two crucial aspects have been overlooked: (1) real attacks have to be stealthy and deceptive, hence it cannot be accomplished by controlling HMI machine via Graphical User Interface (GUI) connections; operators would notice it immediately. And (2) modern sophisticated malware like Stuxnet and Shamoon not only use traditional vulnerabilities to compromise target systems but also leverage some functionalities of benign software components installed on the victim systems to compromise field devices. To do so, attackers embed legitimate software modules inside malware (e.g. Shamoon) or develop a malicious component that uses those legal modules installed on target machines (e.g. Stuxnet).

Therefore, it is clear that attacks targeting CPS exploiting both hardware and software have unique characteristics and need to be investigated systematically to have an accurate view of such attacks and to build optimal defensive measures and protect the infrastructure from future cyber attacks. In this paper, to address these research issues, we have selected the smart grid infrastructure to be the CPS system.

The rest of this paper is organised as follows: an architecture of the smart grid are discussed in Sect. 2. A sophisticated smart grid blackout attack that reflects the characteristics of smart grid security and the malware attacks is presented in Sect. 3. We conclude the paper with conclusions and future work in Sect. 4.

2   Smart Grid Architecture

The smart grid can be divided into five domains: bulk generation, transmission, distribution, customer area, and operator/service provider (Fig. 1). Each domain has its own core subsystems and components, most of them will be infected, modified or damaged in the proposed blackout attack described in Sect. 3. Even though there is no unanimous definition of smart grid architecture, the following subsystems and components are treated as essential architectural constructs that are found in most smart grid architectures [1–3,6,13]. We give a brief outline of these subsystems and components; detailed descriptions can be found in [2,3].

Bulk Generation: Bulk generation plants have been the main source of power in traditional electric grid. This is still valid in the smart grid environment. Energy can be stored for later transmission and distribution.

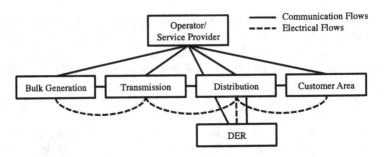

Fig. 1. Simplified smart grid architecture

Transmission: Bulk transfer of electrical energy, from power plants to distribution substations. Its components include transmission SCADA, phasor measurement unit (PMU), also known as synchrophasor, intelligent electronic devices (IED), remote terminal units (RTU) and energy storage.

Distribution: Local wiring between high-voltage substations and customers, distributing electricity to and from the customers. It manages and controls the smart meters and all intelligent field devices through a two-way wireless or wired communications network. Its components include distribution SCADA, distribution data collector, distribution automation field devices, RTUs and IEDs, field crew tools, sensors, distribution management system (DMS), smart switch, and storage. Also, distributed energy resources (DER) and energy sources of distributed generation (DG) may operate at the distribution level.

Customer Area: With smart grid, customers can generate electricity; so they can produce and store electricity, and manage the use of power as well as consuming the power. A customer can be at home or at a building, factory or other industrial facilities. Customer is connected to the distribution network through smart meters. Each customer has its own electricity premise and bi-directional networks connected to the smart grid. Its components include smart meter, customer energy management system (EMS), home area network (HAN) gateway, customer premise display, energy usage metering device (EUMD), plug-in hybrid electric vehicle (PHEV) and energy storage.

Operator/Service Provider: These provide power service to end-user clients, manage and operate the smart grid. They can be service providers, utility corporations, and/or independent system operator/regional transmission organisation (ISO/RTO). Their systems communicate with more than one subsystem to monitor, manage, and control electricity flows. Its components include advanced meter infrastructure (AMI) head end, energy management system (EMS), security/network/system management systems, wide area measurement system (WAMS), wide area control system (WACS), load management system/demand response management system (LMS/DRMS), meter data

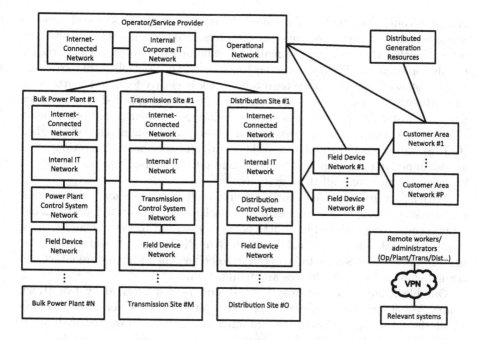

Fig. 2. Smart grid network architecture

management system (MDMS), outage management system (OMS), customer portal, customer information system (CIS), and back office.[1]

Smart grid network serves as a dynamic network for bi-directional energy flows [14]. For this, two-way end-to-end communication is required. This goes against the traditional control system networks because control system networks have been physically separated from corporate networks. This has necessitated subnetworks to be connected directly or indirectly, thus making air-gapping practically impossible [1,15,16]. As a result, all the subnetworks from operational network to customer area network are interconnected in smart grid as shown in Fig. 2.

3   Smart Grid Blackout Attack

In this section, we propose a new and concrete blackout attack against smart grid infrastructures. The attack reflects the characteristics of both smart grid security and recent CPS-related malware attacks. First of all, we found that attacks try to hide their physical impact, such as the stoppage of a motor, from operators. This is technically much harder than cyber-only attack because hardware malfunction or failure happens as soon as the attack is launched. As stated

---

[1] These operation systems logically belong to operator/service provider, and some of them may not be physically installed at operator/service provider premises.

in Sect. 1, controlling field devices using GUI is not enough. This type of attack is considered to be *deceptive* because the attackers need to ensure that operators do not notice that their systems are malfunctioning or stop working. This attack is possible since most CPS are "remotely" monitored and controlled. In particular, Stuxnet showed that deceptive hardware attack is clearly feasible for attackers. Next, these attacks are multi-stage attacks like most sophisticated cyber attacks. Because most cyber-physical systems, including power plants and other smart grid subsystems, are uniquely set up using customised commercial off-the-shelf (COTS) hardware and software solutions with site-specific configurations, it is almost impossible for attackers to implement one "universal" malware that can infect and compromise all these systems.

With smart grid, attackers have to nullify built-in security features and compromise subsystems in order to perform a blackout. For instance, for a black out attack, corrupting self-healing functionality is essential to prevent any form of recovery as well as infecting field devices such as PLCs at plants and substations. In addition, operators have to be deceived to believe their systems are intact and normal while actual field devices are malfunctioning.

Our black out attack against a smart grid is characterised by five attack phases. We assume that the attackers do not have any background information about the target smart grid configurations; so a specially targeted malware is deployed against the victim for information gathering prior to launching the deceptive attack. The first two phases are related to this cyber espionage aspect. The CPS-unique deceptive attack is illustrated in the latter three phases.

3.1   Phase 1: Initial Penetration

In the first phase, the attack involves the penetration of target subsystems using a range of attack vectors. On the server side, the targets include SCADA servers, IT servers, CIS, and customer portal; on the client-side, targets of the attack vectors are employees, contractors, and customers as well as field devices; on the network side, the attack involves network packet manipulation. After the penetration, the attack installs cyber espionage malware on the targeted systems and starts collecting information on the configuration of smart grid systems and networks.

3.2   Phase 2: Espionage

While penetration and malware propagation continue until the attack finds target field devices, the installed malware carries out typical cyber espionage tasks and collects information from the compromised systems. This information includes system and field device configuration data, network and system deployment map, etc. Internet-connected systems act as pivot points to relay data from isolated systems to the attackers. Similar to the analysed malware attacks, the malware uses benign protocols, such as HTTP(S) and RPC, and communications are encrypted; this makes it difficult for the commodity network and system security solutions to detect it. Furthermore, collected data stored on the infected systems is also encrypted to remain stealthy as well as making the forensic analysis difficult.

The fact that smart grid systems and field devices are not replaced frequently gives the attackers sufficient time to analyse the data, to understand proprietary protocols and data used in the components and subsystems, and to map the entire target smart grid. In example, Flame performed its malicious activities for years without being detected [17], and the oldest Stuxnet sample was submitted to a public scanning service in 2007, whereas it was only discovered in 2010 [18].

3.3   Phase 3: Development of Malware for the Deceptive Attack

Having gained and analysed enough information about the network, the system architecture and the configurations of the control systems, the next stage involves the development and testing of real attack payloads. To achieve this, a mirrored environment that includes field devices like PLCs, hardware modules, computer systems and other peripherals is required to determine how the physical components are actually affected by the malicious payloads. Then the malicious payloads are delivered to the infected targets for the deceptive attack.

The development of field device modification payloads can be totally different from that of traditional exploits that use vulnerabilities of the target software. In the smart grid world, it is impractical to find such vulnerabilities and develop zero-day exploits to compromise the field devices, as these devices are not well-known to public. For instance, finding a buffer overflow vulnerability and exploiting it on a PLC running a RTOS like V×Works is harder and more time consuming than discovering one from ×86 Windows application. Therefore, the attackers take a different strategy. First, they don't need to find such vulnerabilities on such field devices, as they already have access to the control software. In particular, Stuxnet infects, i.e. reprograms its target PLCs using the control system development tools (legitimate DLL of Siemens STEP7) [9]. Other research such as uploading ladder logic to Schneider PLCs using Modbus protocol [19] provides the evidence that this type of attack is possible and realistic. Second, the attackers can focus on finding hidden built-in passwords embedded in control software or field devices. Such passwords are usually hard-coded by the vendors to make debugging and other technical support easy [20]. These two strategies are a huge time saver and provide a reliable way for the attackers to implement their malware. Furthermore, the probability that the malware is detected by security tools such as anti-virus and network intrusion detection systems is low because the malware uses intended functionalities of the control system, e.g. field device reprogramming.

In this particular attack example, the attack involves the development of payloads for each component or subsystem. This is only one specific instance among many possible deceptive blackout scenarios.

1. Field devices: *PLCs on plants* are reprogrammed to over-run motors involved in power generation, which could lead to damages not only to PLCs but also to motors and other related field devices. The PLC payload is programmed to

report its rotational speed as normal so that all the SCADA specific IDS/IPS and HMI cannot detect such malfunction of the field devices. *Transmission IEDs and RTUs* are reprogrammed to transmit electricity at higher voltage and current in order to cause physical damages not only to the IEDs and RTUs but also to other transmission field devices such as Flexible AC Transmission Systems (FACTS) and transmission tower. *Distribution IEDs/RTUs* are reprogrammed in a similar way as the transmission IED/RTU. But for distribution IEDs/RTUs, the attackers develop the payload to just stop power distribution electricity.

2. *SCADA systems* on plants, transmission and distribution sites, and *operation systems* such as DMS, EMS, WAMS, WACS, OMS, and customer EMS: hooked so that these systems display normal values (projects, code, or configurations) on the HMI and on the development environment so that operators and developers cannot find the fact that the code on PLCs are modified by the malware. SCADA systems are used to reprogram the PLCs as well. In addition, any commands from the operator are intercepted and dropped by the hooked functions, while making them look normal to the operator. If the developers try to reprogram field devices in an attempt to recover, hooked functions prevent this by replacing the original code with the malicious one on the fly. In our example, the malware doesn't need to modify PLC monitoring routine nor intercept network packets, because PLCs report everything to be normal. However, intercepting network packets, and modifying or dropping them may be required depending on the specific implementation and configuration of the target system.

3. *Storage* at bulk generation, transmission, distribution and customer area: control code on either the control systems or on the controlling field devices of the storage modified to release all the stored electricity so that no power remains. Relevant control system will be modified so as to display the stored energy amount as expected.

4. *DERs and microgrids*: Similar payloads are also developed for control systems and field devices at these sites, as they are essentially same to the plants or the power grid. Even though the attackers hold all the information about DERs, e.g. geological locations (this information is centrally managed in the energy management systems or other IT systems of the operator/service provider), it may be impossible for the attackers to compromise all the DERs distributed through out the smart grid. Thus, some DER may remain uninfected.

5. *Smart switches*: modified to switch power improperly or not to switch, so that electricity from survived DERs cannot be provided to where it is needed.

6. *Smart meters & EUMD*: modified to stop providing any power to the customer premise, while reporting to the customer premise display that electricity provided is normal.

7. *Other IT systems* in smart grid sites: keeps monitoring employees' activities, e.g. keystrokes and screenshots, and report them to the attackers. This enables the attackers to keep their fingers on the pulse on the near-real-time situations of the target smart grid. The infected control and management systems report

their malicious situation to the attackers directly or indirectly depending on the connectivity.

8. *Utility back office*: modified in the same way as their original correspondents.

Network attacks such as packet interception, dropping, injection, and/or manipulation, are practical because the widely-used communication protocols in the smart grid control systems, e.g. DNP3 and Modbus, do not have encryption or authentication by default [5,8,15,19].

3.4 Phase 4: Deceptive Attack

After the development and testing, the payloads are introduced to the subsystems and components of the target smart grid. In most cases, this job is performed via the malware's C&C communications. The process of delivering the field device payloads is highly undetectable, because the malware reprograms the target devices using the legitimate control and development tools that are currently deployed in the target operation systems.

Now, the deceptive attack can be launched at any time. Once the attackers trigger it, all the payloads installed on IT systems and field devices cooperatively start the malicious actions developed in the previous phase. In this example, the attack begins at the bulk and distributed generation plants, because damaging motors at generators can take longer than damaging other field devices. This is why deception is important in CPS attack; in this case, SCADA systems keep reporting normal status, and operators who remotely monitor the plant cannot notice the attack. After infected systems at the plants report their attack has been started, other infected systems at the rest sites begin to malfunction. As the smart grid is all connected and communication is done in real-time, such malicious C&C communication can also be done.

3.5 Phase 5: Cleanup and Aftermath

In the last phase, the malware removes as many as possible of its traits, after launching the deceptive attack. It modifies and removes any history server logs, network and system access logs, and application logs. Furthermore, self-destruction of the malware is performed as a way of withdrawal on non-critical systems; malware instances infected on control systems are not destroyed, as they need to deceive operators and trouble-shooters.

However, once those instances on the control systems detect any changes in network connectivity so they cannot perform predefined malicious activities, e.g. packet interception and modification of PLC code block, self-destruction of the infected systems is executed to make digital forensics and recovery extremely hard; in the case of Wiper [21], no real malware sample has been found, because it was completely destructive. A recovery option for operators/service providers is to replace the IT systems with mirrored backup if they exist and if they are not infected with the malware. Setting-up new systems is another option, but this can take a long time.

The final action for the cleanup is the self-destruction of modified PLCs, RTUs, and IEDs; according to PLC and real-time OS programming guides from vendors such as V×Works (RTOS), Mitsubishi and Siemens (PLC), an inappropriately written PLC program can cause damages to CPU unit, which makes replacement of the unit unavoidable. This not only removes the malware's traits, but also makes recovery even harder.

After some physical outcome shows up, e.g. a generator's stoppage, the operators try to fix the problems, which they are not able to; the operation software is modified and control command packets are intercepted and dropped. They have to visit the actual places where the devices are installed, find out infected and destroyed field devices including PLCs, IEDs, RTUs and motors. Replacement is required, but this may take a long time, due to the availability of these devices. As the blackout proceeds through the entire smart grid, other operators at various sites and customers get to notice that something has gone wrong with their systems and field devices. But recovery is very hard due to the same reason.

Even when the operators/service providers ask DERs (which are intact) and energy storages to provide electricity to some critical regions, no power can be provided. First, electricity from intact DERs cannot be provided, as modified smart switches and distribution towers are not working. Second, all the storages are empty while they have been falsely reporting their status. The damages can be as big as or even bigger than a natural disaster. The blackout caused by the notorious Sandy in 2012 resulted blackouts for more than two weeks. The attack described above could cause a blackout for a similar period of time.

4   Concluding Remarks

Smart grid is the future power grid, and is one of the largest cyber-physical systems. In this paper, we have applied several recent malware techniques to the smart grid, and designed a stealthy and deceptive malware attack that targets both software systems and field devices. The proposed blackout attack is also considering the specifics of the smart grid so that it can be realistic. We are in the process of implementing a proof-of-concept smart grid testbed in order to evaluate the attack, and developing appropriate defensive techniques against such attacks.

References

1. Momoh, J.: Smart Grid: Fundamentals of Design and Analysis. Wiley, Hoboken (2012)
2. U.S. Government: NIST framework and roadmap for Smart Grid interoperability standards, release 1.0. NIST, January 2010
3. Cyber Security Working Group: Guidelines for Smart Grid Cyber Security: vol. 1, Smart Grid Cyber Security Strategy, Architecture, and High-Level Requirements. NIST, August 2010
4. McDaniel, P., McLaughlin, S.: Security and privacy challenges in the smart grid. IEEE Security & Privacy 7(3), 75–77 (2009)

5. Liu, J., Xiao, Y., Li, S., Liang, W., Philip Chen, C.L.: Cyber security and privacy issues in smart grids. IEEE Commun. Surv. Tutorials **14**(4), 981–997 (2012)
6. Fang, X., Misra, S., Xue, G., Yang, D.: Smart grid - the new and improved power grid: a survey. IEEE Commun. Surv. Tutorials **14**(4), 944–980 (2012)
7. Li, X., Liang, X., Rongxing, L., Shen, X., Lin, X., Zhu, H.: Securing smart grid: cyber attacks, countermeasures, and challenges. IEEE Commun. Mag. **50**(8), 38–45 (2012)
8. Sridhar, S., Hahn, A., Govindarasu, M.: Cyber-physical system security for the electric power grid. Proc. IEEE **100**(1), 210–224 (2012)
9. Falliere, N., Murchu, L.O., Chien, E.: W32.Stuxnet dossier. White paper, Symantec Corp., Security Response (2011)
10. Ganesalingam, M.: Type. In: Ganesalingam, M. (ed.) The Language of Mathematics. LNCS, vol. 7805, pp. 113–156. Springer, Heidelberg (2013)
11. Luigi Auriemma, Bugtraq: Vulnerabilities in some SCADA server softwares, March 2011. http://seclists.org/bugtraq/2011/Mar/187, Last Accessed on 15 May 2013
12. Secunia Vulnerability Review 2013, Secunia, March 2013
13. Gao, J., Xiao, Y., Liu, J., Liang, W., Philip Chen, C.L.: A survey of communication/networking in Smart Grids. Future Gener. Comput. Syst. **28**(2), 391–404 (2012)
14. Kolhe, M.: Smart grid: charting a new energy future: research, development and demonstration. Electricity J. **25**(2), 88–93 (2012)
15. Ernst & Young: Attacking the smart grid, December 2011
16. Byres, E.: Unicorns and Air Gaps - Do They Really Exist? Living with Reality in Critical Infrastructures, Tofino, July 2012
17. Symantec: The Symantec Intelligence Report: June 2012, June 2010
18. McDonald, G., O Murchu, L., Doherty, S., Chien, E.: Stuxnet 0.5: The Missing Link. White paper, Symantec Corp., Security Response, February 2013
19. Wightman, K.R.: Schneider Modicon Quantum, January 2012. http://www.digitalbond.com/tools/basecamp/schneider-modicon-quantum/, Last Accessed on 15 May 2013
20. Zetter, K.: SCADA System's Hard-Coded Password Circulated Online for Years, July 2010. http://www.wired.com/threatlevel/2010/07/siemens-scada/, Last Accessed on 15 May 2013
21. Global Research & Analysis Team, Kaspersky Lab: What was that Wiper thing? August 2012. https://www.securelist.com/en/blog/208193808/What_was_that_Wiper_thing, Last Accessed on 15 May 2013

Multi-round Attacks on Structural Controllability Properties for Non-complete Random Graphs

Cristina Alcaraz[1,4]([⊠]), Estefanía Etchevés Miciolino[2],
and Stephen Wolthusen[3,4]

[1] Computer Science Department, University of Málaga, Malaga, Spain
alcaraz@lcc.uma.es
[2] Complex Systems & Security Laboratory,
Universitá Campus Bio-Medico di Roma, Rome, Italy
e.etcheves@unicampus.it
[3] Norwegian Information Security Laboratory,
Gjøvik University College, Gjovik, Norway
stephen.wolthusen@rhul.ac.uk
[4] Information Security Group, Department of Mathematics, Royal Holloway,
University of London, Egham TW20 0EX, UK

Abstract. The notion of *controllability*, informally the ability to force a system into a desired state in a finite time or number of steps, is most closely associated with control systems such as those used to maintain power networks and other critical infrastructures, but has wider relevance in distributed systems. It is clearly highly desirable to understand under which conditions attackers may be able to disrupt legitimate control, or to force overriding controllability themselves. Following recent results by Liu *et al.* , there has been considerable interest also in graph-theoretical interpretation of Kalman controllability originally introduced by Lin, *structural controllability*. This permits the identification of sets of *driver nodes* with the desired state-forcing property, but determining such nodes is a $W[2]$-hard problem. To extract these nodes and represent the control relation, here we apply the POWER DOMINATING SET problem and investigate the effects of targeted *iterative* multiple-vertex removal. We report the impact that different attack strategies with multiple edge and vertex removal will have, based on underlying non-complete graphs, with an emphasis on power-law random graphs with different degree sequences.

Keywords: Structural controllability · Attack models · Complex networks

1 Introduction

Structural controllability was introduced by Lin's seminal work [1] as an alternative to the controllability, identifying a graph-theoretical model equivalent to

© Springer International Publishing Switzerland 2015
Y. Desmedt (Ed.): ISC 2013, LNCS 7807, pp. 140–151, 2015.
DOI: 10.1007/978-3-319-27659-5_10

Kalman's control [2] in order to reach a desired state from an arbitrary state in a finite number of steps. Although the Kalman's model enables the use of a general, rigorous, and well-understood framework for the design and analysis of not only control systems but also of networks in which a directed control relation between nodes is required, the model presents some restrictions for complex and large systems. A time-dependent linear dynamical system $\mathbf{A}$ is *controllable* if and only if $\text{rank}[\mathbf{B}, \mathbf{AB}, \mathbf{A}^2\mathbf{B}, \ldots, \mathbf{A}^{n-1}\mathbf{B}] = n$ (Kalman's rank criterion), where $\mathbf{A}$ is the $n \times n$ adjacency matrix identifying the interaction among nodes and the $n \times m$ *input* matrix $\mathbf{B}$ identifies the set of nodes controlled by the *input vector*, which forces the system to a desired state. Whilst straightforward, for large networks the exponential growth of input values as a function of nodes is problematic, giving importance to concept of structural controllability. In this context, the graph-theoretical interpretation would be $G(\mathbf{A}, \mathbf{B}) = (V, E)$ as a digraph where $V = V_{\mathbf{A}} \cup V_{\mathbf{B}}$ is the set of vertices and $E = E_{\mathbf{A}} \cup E_{\mathbf{B}}$ is the set of edges. In this representation, $V_{\mathbf{B}}$ comprises nodes able to inject control signals into the entire network.

Moreover, recent work by Liu *et al.* [3] has renewed interest in this approach as it allows the identification of *driver nodes* (n_d corresponding to $V_{\mathbf{B}}$) capable of observing the entire network (graph). This work is relied on a non-rigorous formulation of the maximum matching problem and has been expanded upon multiple times [4,5]. However, we here focus on the equivalent POWER DOMINATING SET (PDS) problem, originally introduced as an extension of DOMINATING SET by Haynes *et al.* [6], mainly motivated by the structure of electric power networks, and the need of offering efficient monitoring of such networks. A real world scenario related to this field is precisely the current control systems (e.g. SCADA systems) which deploy their elements following a mesh distribution to supervise other critical infrastructures (e.g. power systems), where $\mathscr{G} = (V, E)$ depicts the network distribution with V illustrating the elements (e.g. control terminal units, servers, etc.), and E representing the communication lines. In this context, PDS can be defined using the two following *observation rules* simplified by Kneis *et al.* [7]: **OR1**, a vertex in the power dominating set observes itself and all its neighbours; and **OR2**, if an observed vertex v of degree $d \geq 2$ is adjacent to $d - 1$ observed vertices, the remaining unobserved vertex becomes observed as well.

With the omission of **OR2**, this reverts to the DOMINATING SET problem already known to be $\mathscr{NP}$-complete with a polynomial-time approximation factor of $\Theta(\log n)$ as shown by Feige [8]. The approach relies on creating directed acyclic graphs $\mathscr{G} = (V, E)$ to find a sequence of driver nodes (denoted as $N_D/ \forall\, n_d \in N_D$) such that $N_D \subseteq V$ can observe all vertices in V satisfying **OR1** and **OR2**. Instances of driver nodes from a given $\mathscr{G} = (V, E)$ are not unique and clearly depend on the selection order of vertices $\in V$ to create DS using **OR1**. Here, we follow the three strategies defined in [9]: (1) Obtain the set of driver nodes with maximum out-degree satisfying **OR1** ($\mathbf{N}_D^{\max}$); (2) find the set of driver nodes with minimum out-degree satisfying **OR1** ($\mathbf{N}_D^{\min}$); and (3) obtain the set of random nodes satisfying **OR1** ($\mathbf{N}_D^{\text{rand}}$). Hence, each $\mathbf{N}_D^{strat}$ represents a partial order given by the out-degree ($\leq$ or $\geq$) in case of $\mathbf{N}_D^{\max}$ or

$\mathbf{N}_D^{\min}$, respectively; in case of $\mathbf{N}_D^{\mathrm{rand}}$, no such relation exists as its elements are randomly chosen.

These three strategies have already been analysed for non-interactive scenarios, in which a single vertex is exposed to a particular type of attack. Our contribution in this paper is therefore to expand the approach from [9] to multiple-round attacks, studying the robustness of controllability when multiple and combined attacks affect control in several different graph classes, namely random (Erdős-Renyi (ER)), small-world (Watts-Strogatz (WS)), and power-law (both (Barabási-Albert (BA)) and general power-law (PLOD) distributions)[1]. In addition, we also analyse here the interaction between different multi-round attack strategies and the underlying control graph topology on robustness, considering both the earlier work on single attacks [9] and new three multi-round attack scenarios. These scenarios are as follows: (1) Removal of some random edges $\in E$ from a single or several vertices, (2) isolation of some vertices $\in V$, and (3) removal of some random edges and vertices from a dense power-law subgraph.

The remainder of this paper is structured as follows: Sect. 2 describes the threat model based on three different multi-round attack scenarios and on a set of attack models characterised by the number of targets. Later, in Sect. 3 we proceed to evaluate the impact of exploiting strategic points of the mentioned topologies and its controllability ($\mathbf{N}_D^{\max}$, $\mathbf{N}_D^{\min}$, or $\mathbf{N}_D^{\mathrm{rand}}$), discussing the results obtained on connectivity and observability terms. Finally, conclusions together with our on-going work are given in Sect. 4.

2   Multi-round Threat Model

In order to study the robustness of the different types of network topologies, first we consider the different attack types (edge and vertex removal), which may disrupt controllability (e.g. denial of service attacks to communication lines in order to leave parts of a system uncontrolled, unprotected or isolated by n_d), and the resulting effects that such attacks may cause in the control, the network connectivity and observability (as the dual of controllability). The threats studied here are multi-round attacks with prior knowledge, but do not explicitly take mitigating responses of defenders into account.

These threats are based on the combination of five attack models (**AMs**), which have been grouped into three scenarios for the purposes of further analysis: **Scenario 1 (SCN-1)**, it focuses on removing a small number of random edges of one or several vertices, which may compromise controllability of dependent nodes or disconnect parts the of control graph and underlying network. The selection of target nodes depends on the **AM** described below, and the removal of edges avoids spurious node isolation. **Scenario 2 (SCN-2)** destined to isolate one or several vertices from the network by intentionally deleting all the links from these vertices. This threat may result in the isolation of vertices which depend on the compromised node or the partition of the network into several sub-graphs.

---

[1] For more detail on these distribution networks, please go to [9].

Scenario 3 (SCN-3) aims to attack one or several vertices of a sub-graph by randomly deleting part of their links **(SCN-1)**, or carry out the isolation of such nodes **(SCN-2)** so as to later assess the resulting effect of the threat with respect to the entire graph. For the extraction of the sub-graph, we consider the *Girvan-Newman* algorithm to detect and obtain specific communities within a complex graph [10]. A community structure refers to a subset of nodes with dense links within its community and with few connections to nodes belonging to less dense communities. For this, links between communities are sought by progressively calculating the betweenness of all existing edges and removing edges with the highest betweenness.

Algorithm 2.1. ATTACK MODELS ($\mathscr{G}(V, E), \mathbf{N}_D^{\text{strat}}, AM, Scenario$)

---

output (*Attack of one vertex for a given* $\mathscr{G}(V, E)$);
local $i, target$;

if $AM == \mathbf{AM}_1$ **(F)**
  then $\{target \leftarrow \mathbf{N}_D^{\text{strat}}[1]$;
       if $AM == \mathbf{AM}_2$ **(M)**
        then $\{target \leftarrow \mathbf{N}_D^{\text{strat}}[(\text{SIZE}(\mathbf{N}_D^{\text{strat}}))/2]$;
           if $AM == \mathbf{AM}_3$ **(L)**
           then
  else $\{target \leftarrow \mathbf{N}_D^{\text{strat}}[(\text{SIZE}(\mathbf{N}_D^{\text{strat}}))]$;
      else   if $AM == \mathbf{AM}_4$ **(BC)**
             then
        else $\{target \leftarrow \text{BETWEENNESS CENTRALITY}(\mathscr{G}(V, E))$;
              else $\{target \leftarrow \text{OUTSIDE } \mathbf{N}_D^{\text{strategy}}(\mathscr{G}(V, E), \mathbf{N}_D^{\text{strat}})$;
if $Scenario == \mathbf{SCN\text{-}1}$
  then REMOVE SELECTIVE EDGES($\mathscr{G}(V, E), target$);
if $Scenario == \mathbf{SCN\text{-}2}$
  then ISOLATE VERTEX($\mathscr{G}(V, E), target$);
return ($\mathscr{G}(V, E)$)

Algorithm 2.2. MULTI-ROUND ATTACKS($\mathscr{G}(V, E), \mathbf{N}_D^{\text{strat}}, \mathbf{TG\text{-}x}, Scenario$)

---

output (*Attack of one or several vertices for a given* $\mathscr{G}(V, E)$);
local $i, Combination\_AM, AM, SCN$;

if $Scenario == \mathbf{SCN\text{-}3}$
  then $\{\mathscr{G}_{sub}(V, E) \leftarrow \text{GIRVAN-NEWMAN}(\mathscr{G}(V, E))$;
       $\mathbf{N}_D^{\text{strat}} \leftarrow \text{EXTRACT DRIVER NODES FROM SUBGRAPH}(\mathscr{G}_{sub}(V, E), \mathbf{N}_D^{\text{strat}})$;
       $SCN \leftarrow \text{DETERMINE NEW } \mathbf{SCN\text{-}1\text{-}2}()$;
$Combination\_AM \leftarrow \text{COMBINE ATTACKS}(\mathbf{TG\text{-}x})$; **comment:** See table 1;
  for $i \leftarrow \text{SIZE}(Combination\_AM)$
       $AM \leftarrow Combination\_AM[i]$;
       if $Scenario == \mathbf{SCN\text{-}3}$
  do   **then** $\{\mathscr{G}(V, E) \leftarrow \text{ATTACK MODELSII}(\mathscr{G}(V, E), \mathscr{G}_{sub}(V, E), \mathbf{N}_D^{\text{strat}}, AM, SCN)$;
            comment: Algorithm analogous to 2.1, but considering $\mathscr{G}_{sub}(V, E)$
       else $\{\mathscr{G}(V, E) \leftarrow \text{ATTACK MODELS}(\mathscr{G}(V, E), \mathbf{N}_D^{\text{strat}}, AM, Scenario)$;
return ($\mathscr{G}(V, E)$;)

For each scenario, we select a set of attacks in which it is assumed that an attacker is able to know the distribution of the network and the power domination relation (control graph). In real scenarios, these attackers could be insiders

Table 1. Five attacks rounds with permuted AM

Targets	Combination of AM$-x$	Num. of attacks
TG-1	F, M, L, BC, O	5
TG-2	F-M, F-L, F-BC, F-O, M-L, M-BC, M-O, L-BC, L-O, BC-O	10
TG-3	F-M-L, F-M-BC, F-M-O, F-L-BC, F-L-O, F-BC-O, M-L-BC, M-L-O, M-BC-O, L-BC-O	10
TG-4	F-M-L-BC, F-M-L-O, F-M-BC-O, F-L-BC-O, M-L-BC-O	5
TG-5	F-M-L-BC-O	1

who belong to the system, such as human operators, who known the topology and its system itself; or outsiders who observe and learn from the topology to later damage the entire system or sub-parts. The mentioned attacks, summarised in Algorithm 2.1, are denoted as **AM-1** to **AM-5**. **AM-1** consists of attacking the first (**F**) driver node n_d in a given ordered set N_D^{strat}. Depending on the attack scenario, the attacker could randomly delete some edges or completely isolate the n_d from $\mathscr{G} = (V, E)$. In contrast, **AM-2** aims to attack or isolate a vertex n_d belonging to a given ordered N_D^{strat} positioned in the middle (**M**) of the set. **AM-3** attacks the last (**L**) driver node n_d in the ordered set given by N_D^{strat}. **AM-4** compromises the vertex $v \in V$ with the highest *betweenness centrality* (**BC**), whereas **AM-5** randomly chooses a vertex $v \in V$ and $\notin N_D^{strat}$ (outside (**O**)).

Combinations of **AM-x** (which are only representative of wider classes), such that $x \in \{1,2,3,4,5\}$, result in a set of rounds based on multi-target attacks, which are represented in Table 1 and described as follows: 1 **Target (TG-1)** illustrates a non-interactive scenario in which a single vertex $v \in V$ is attacked according to an **AM-x**, being v a driver node or an observed node. In contrast, **2 Targets (TG-2)** corresponds to a multi-round scenario based on two attacks **AM-x** and **AM-y** where $x, y \in \{1,2,3,4,5\}$ such that $x \neq y$, e.g. the attack **F-BC** identifies multiple attacks of type **AM-1** and **AM-4**, in which one or several attackers compromise two strategic nodes. Note that **3-5 Targets (TG-3-5)** is a multi-round scenario based on 3, 4 or 5 threats with analogous goals and similar features to **TG-2**. All objectives are summarised in Algorithm 2.2, which depends on the type of scenario and the number of targets to be attacked. For scenarios of type **SCN-3**, we first extract the sub-graph from $\mathscr{G}(V, E)$ using the Girvan-Newman algorithm and its driver nodes to be attacked. For the attack, we not only consider the sub-graph itself but also $\mathscr{G}(V, E)$ to study the effects that attacks on dense sub-graphs may have on the overall network.

3   Attack Scenarios on Structural Controllability

So as to evaluate the structural controllability strategies defined in [9] (N_D^{max}, N_D^{min}, N_D^{rand}) with respect to ER, WS, BA and PLOD distributions, scenarios **SCN-1**, **SCN-2** and **SCN-3** defined in Sect. 2 were studied through Matlab

Table 2. Nomenclature for analyses

Nomenclature	Definition
n_d	Driver node
AM-x	Attack model following a particular attack strategy x, such that $x \in$ {**AM-1**,..., **AM-5**}
TG-x	Number of target nodes such that $x \in$ {**TG-1**,..., **TG-5**}
N_D^{strat}	Set of driver nodes n_d following a particular controllability strategy such as $N_D^{max,min,rand}$
$N_D^{max,min,rand}$	An attack with minor impact on structural controllability $N_D^{max,min,rand}$
$N_D^{max\dagger,min\dagger,rand\dagger}$	An attack with intermediate impact on structural controllability, intensifying effect caused by $N_D^{max,min,rand}$
$N_D^{max\ddagger,min\ddagger,rand\ddagger}$	An attack with major impact on structural controllability, intensifying effect caused by $\dagger$
*	Symbol stating *for all* the cases
$N_{D_{s,l,*}}^{strat}$	Representation of small and large networks
*,{**AM-x**}	Influence of all attacks, but with a special vulnerability for **AM-x**
{**X-AM-x**}	Any X threat combined with **AM-x**
$x - y\%$	Minimum and maximum rate of observability

simulations. Several topologies and network sizes were generated, giving small (≤ 100) and large (≥ 100) networks with 100, 1000 and 2000 nodes, and with low connectivity probability so as to represent sparse networks.

Under these considerations, we assess here the robustness from two perspectives: First, the *degree of connectivity* using the diameter, the global density and the local density using the average clustering coefficient (CC). These statistical values should maintain small values in proportion to the growth and the average degree of links per node, and more specifically, after an attack. Second, the *degree of observability* by calculating the rate of unobserved nodes after a threat using **OR1** [9]. On the other hand, and given the number of simulations and results obtained[2], we have defined a language to summarize and interpret results shown in Table 2.

3.1   SCN-1 and SCN-2: Exploitation of Links and Vertices in Graphs

For **SCN-1** (see Table 3), we observe that ER topologies are sensitive in connectivity terms. The diameter for small networks is variable and, particularly, for networks under the control of $N_D^{max,min}$, with a special emphasis in scenarios **TG-3** where a complete break up of the network is verified and the observation rate is largely influenced, reaching null values. As for local and global density, it is also variable for all network distributions and for all **TG-x**, where the controllability $N_D^{min,rand}$ are mainly affected. For WS graphs, the diameter changes

---

[2] Full results and code is available from authors.

Table 3. SCN-1: Removal of a small number of edges $\in E$ from one or several vertices $\in V$

TGx	Network	Diameter	Density	CC	Attack	Observation	Attack	Rate
						Observability		
			Connectivity			Observation	Attack	Rate
TG-1	ER	$N_{D_s}^{max\dagger,min\dagger,rand\dagger}$	$N_{D_s}^{max,min\dagger,rand\dagger}$	$N_{D_s}^{max,min,rand}$	*	$N_{Dl}^{max,min,rand\dagger}$	*	96.8-100%
	WS	$N_{D_s}^{max\dagger,min\dagger,rand}$	-	$N_{D_s}^{max,min,rand}$	*,{BC}	$N_{D_s}^{max\dagger,min,rand}$	*	84-99%
	BA	$N_{D_s}^{max,min,rand}$	-	-	*,{BC}	$N_{D_s}^{max,min,rand}$	*,{F}	16-100%
	PLOD α≃0.1	$N_{D*}^{max\dagger,min,rand}$	-	$N_{D_s}^{max,min,rand\dagger}$	*,{BC}	-	-	≃100%
	PLOD α≃0.3	$N_{D*}^{max,rand}$	-	$N_{D_s}^{max,rand}$	*,{BC}	-	-	≃100%
	PLOD α≃0.5	$N_{D*}^{max,min,rand\ddagger}$	-	$N_{D_s}^{min,rand}$	*	-	-	≃100%
TG-2	ER	$N_{D*}^{max,min,rand}$	$N_{D*}^{max,min\dagger,rand\dagger}$	$N_{D*}^{max,min,rand\dagger}$	*, {X-BC}	$N_{Dl}^{max,rand\dagger}$	*	96.7-100%
	WS	$N_{D_s}^{max,min,rand}$	$N_{D_s}^{min,rand}$	$N_{D*}^{max,min,rand\dagger}$	*	$N_{D*}^{max\dagger,min,rand}$	*	88-97.85%
	BA	$N_{D*}^{max,min,rand}$	$N_{D_s}^{min,rand}$	$N_{D*}^{max,min,rand}$	*	$N_{D*}^{max\dagger,min,rand}$	*, {F-BC,L-BC}	4-100%
	PLOD α≃0.1	$N_{D*}^{max,min,rand\dagger}$	-	$N_{D*}^{max,min,rand}$	*, {F-BC, M-BC, BC-O}	-	-	≃100%
	PLOD α≃0.3	$N_{D*}^{max,min,rand\dagger}$	-	$N_{D*}^{max,min,rand}$	*, {M-BC, L-BC, BC-O}	-	-	≃100%
	PLOD α≃0.5	$N_{D*}^{max,min,rand\dagger}$	-	$N_{D_s}^{max,min,rand\dagger}$	*	-	-	≃100%
TG-3	ER	$N_{D_s}^{max\dagger,min\dagger,rand}$	$N_{D*}^{max,min\dagger,rand\dagger}$	$N_{D*}^{max,min,rand\dagger}$	*, {M-BC-O, L-BC-O}	$N_{D*}^{max\dagger,min,rand}$	*, {M-BC-O, L-BC-O}	0-100%
	WS	$N_{D*}^{max\dagger,min\dagger,rand}$	-	$N_{D*}^{max,min\dagger,rand\dagger}$	*, {M-BC-O, L-BC-O}	$N_{D*}^{max\dagger,min,rand}$	*, {M-BC-O, L-BC-O}	2-98%
	BA	$N_{D*}^{max\dagger,min\dagger,rand}$	$N_{D_s}^{rand}$	-	*, {M-BC-O, L-BC-O}	$N_{D*}^{max\dagger,min,rand}$	*, {F-M-L, M-BC-O, L-BC-O}	0-100%
	PLOD α≃0.1	$N_{D*}^{max\dagger,min,rand}$	-	$N_{D_s}^{max,min,rand}$	*, {M-BC-O, L-BC-O}	$N_{D*}^{max\dagger,min}$	*, {M-BC-O, L-BC-O}	0-100%
	PLOD α≃0.3	$N_{D*}^{max\dagger,min,rand}$	-	$N_{D_s}^{max,min,rand}$	*, {M-BC-O, L-BC-O}	$N_{D*}^{max\dagger,min}$	*, {M-BC-O, L-BC-O}	0-100%
	PLOD α≃0.5	$N_{D*}^{max\dagger,min,rand}$	-	$N_{D_s}^{max,min,rand\dagger}$	*, {M-BC-O, L-BC-O}	$N_{D*}^{max\dagger,min}$	*, {M-BC-O, L-BC-O}	0-100%
TG-4	ER	$N_{D_s}^{max,min,rand}$	$N_{D*}^{max,min\dagger,rand\dagger}$	$N_{D_s}^{max,min,rand\dagger}$	*	$N_{Dl}^{max,rand}$	*	96.4-100%
	WS	$N_{D_s}^{max,min,rand}$	-	$N_{D_s}^{max,min\dagger,rand\ddagger}$	*	$N_{D_s}^{max\dagger,min,rand\dagger}$	*	86-97.85%
	BA	$N_{D_s}^{max,min,rand}$	$N_{D_s}^{rand}$	-	*, {F-M-L-O}	$N_{D_s}^{max\dagger,min,rand}$	*, {F-M-L-O, F-M-BC-O}	4-100%
	PLOD α≃0.1	$N_{D*}^{max,min,rand}$	-	$N_{D_s}^{max\dagger,min,rand}$	*	-	-	≃100%
	PLOD α≃0.3	$N_{D_s}^{max,min,rand}$	-	$N_{D_s}^{max,min,rand}$	*	-	-	≃100%
	PLOD α≃0.5	$N_{D*}^{max,min,rand\dagger}$	-	$N_{D_s}^{max,min,rand}$	*	-	-	≃100%
TG-5	ER	$N_{D_s}^{rand}$	$N_{D*}^{max,min\dagger,rand\dagger}$	$N_{D_s}^{max,min\dagger,rand\dagger}$	*	N_{Dl}^{rand}	*	96.3-100%
	WS	$N_{D_s}^{max,min,rand}$	-	$N_{D_s}^{max,min,rand}$	*	$N_{D_s}^{max\dagger,min,rand\dagger}$	*	86-97.85%
	BA	$N_{D_s}^{max,min,rand}$	$N_{D_s}^{rand}$	-	*	$N_{D_s}^{max\dagger,min,rand}$	*	14-100%
	PLOD α≃0.1	$N_{D*}^{max,rand}$	-	$N_{D_s}^{min,rand}$	*	-	-	≃100%
	PLOD α≃0.3	$N_{D*}^{max,min,rand}$	-	$N_{D_s}^{max,min,rand}$	*	-	-	≃100%
	PLOD α≃0.5	$N_{D*}^{max,min,rand}$	-	$N_{D_s}^{max,min,rand}$	*	-	-	≃100%

for any distribution, but particularly for small networks, and the greatest effect is obtained when launching a **TG-3** attack. For this topology, the density of the network is slightly modified when performing a **TG-2** attack, whereas no relevant effect has been registered for the other cases. This does not, however, hold for local density, since the effects on the network become more and more evident as the number of targets increases, especially when the number of nodes that constitute the network is not high (as expected in small-world networks). The impact on the observability is not very accentuated for this topology, as the effect is more evident when performing an attack to the n_d with the maximum out-degree in small networks.

For BA graphs, the diameter shows a small variation for any N_D^{strat} and for both single and multiple targets. The difference is made by the **TG-3** strategy, for which the consequences on the network are remarkable both for small and large networks. The global density of the network is influenced mainly when a small network is considered and the links of a random n_d are damaged (N_D^{rand}).

Table 4. SCN-2: Isolation of one or several vertices $\in V$

TGs	Network	Diameter	Connectivity			Observability		
			Density	CC	Attack	Observation	Attack	Rate
TG-1	ER	$N_{D*}^{\max,\min,\text{rand}}$	$N_{Ds}^{\max\uparrow,\min\uparrow,\text{rand}\downarrow}$	$N_{Ds}^{\max\uparrow,\min\uparrow,\text{rand}\uparrow}$	*, {F, BC}	$N_{D*}^{\max\uparrow,\text{rand}\uparrow}$	*, {F,M}	86-100%
	WS	$N_{D*}^{\max,\min,\text{rand}}$	-	$N_{D*}^{\max\uparrow,\min\uparrow,\text{rand}\uparrow}$	*, {BC}	$N_{D*}^{\max,\min,\text{rand}}$	*	89-100%
	BA	-	-	-	-	$N_{D*}^{\max\uparrow,\text{rand}}$	*, {F, M, L, BC}	2-100%
	PLOD $\alpha \simeq 0.1$	$N_{D*}^{\max,\min,\text{rand}}$	-	$N_{D*}^{\max\uparrow,\min\uparrow,\text{rand}\uparrow}$	*, {BC}	$N_{D*}^{\max,\min,\text{rand}}$	*, {O}	99-100%
	PLOD $\alpha \simeq 0.3$	$N_{D*}^{\max,\min,\text{rand}}$	-	$N_{D*}^{\max\uparrow,\min\uparrow,\text{rand}\uparrow}$	*, {BC}	$N_{D*}^{\max,\min}$	*	98-100%
	PLOD $\alpha \simeq 0.5$	$N_{D*}^{\max,\min,\text{rand}}$	-	$N_{D*}^{\max\uparrow,\min\uparrow,\text{rand}\uparrow}$	*, {BC}	$N_{Ds}^{\max}$	*	97-100%
TG-2	ER	$N_{D*}^{\max,\min,\text{rand}}$	$N_{Ds}^{\max\uparrow,\min\uparrow,\text{rand}\downarrow}$	$N_{D*}^{\max\uparrow,\min\uparrow,\text{rand}\uparrow}$	*, {F, BC}	$N_{D*}^{\max\uparrow,\min\uparrow,\text{rand}\uparrow}$	*, {F-M, F-BC, F-O}	70-100%
	WS	$N_{D*}^{\max,\min,\text{rand}}$	$N_{Ds}^{\max,\min,\text{rand}}$	$N_{D*}^{\max\uparrow,\min\uparrow,\text{rand}\uparrow}$	*	$N_{D*}^{\max,\min,\text{rand}}$	*, {F-O}	84-98%
	BA	-	$N_{Ds}^{\min,\text{rand}}$	-	*	$N_{D*}^{\max,\min,\text{rand}}$	*	2-100%
	PLOD $\alpha \simeq 0.1$	$N_{D*}^{\max,\min,\text{rand}}$	-	$N_{Ds}^{\max,\min,\text{rand}}$	*, {F-BC, M-BC, L-BC, BC-O}	$N_{D*}^{\max,\min,\text{rand}}$	*	99-100%
	PLOD $\alpha \simeq 0.3$	$N_{D*}^{\max\uparrow,\min\uparrow,\text{rand}\uparrow}$	$N_{Ds}^{\max,\min,\text{rand}}$	$N_{D*}^{\max\uparrow,\min\uparrow,\text{rand}\uparrow}$	*, {L-BC, BC-O}	$N_{D*}^{\max,\min}$	*	98-100%
	PLOD $\alpha \simeq 0.5$	$N_{D*}^{\max,\min,\text{rand}}$	$N_{Ds}^{\max,\min,\text{rand}}$	$N_{D*}^{\max\uparrow,\min\uparrow,\text{rand}\uparrow}$	*, {F-BC, M-BC, L-BC, BC-O}	$N_{Ds}^{\max}$	*	97-100%
TG-3	ER	$N_{D*}^{\max\uparrow,\min\uparrow,\text{rand}}$	$N_{Ds}^{\max\uparrow,\min\uparrow,\text{rand}\uparrow}$	$N_{D*}^{\max\uparrow,\min\uparrow,\text{rand}\uparrow}$	*, {M-BC-O, L-BC-O}	$N_{D*}^{\max\uparrow,\min\uparrow,\text{rand}\uparrow}$	*, {M-BC-O, L-BC-O}	0.15-99.90%
	WS	$N_{D*}^{\max\uparrow,\min\uparrow,\text{rand}}$	$N_{D*}^{\max\uparrow,\min\uparrow,\text{rand}}$	$N_{D*}^{\max\uparrow,\min\uparrow,\text{rand}\uparrow}$	*, {M-BC-O, L-BC-O}	$N_{D*}^{\max\uparrow,\min\uparrow,\text{rand}}$	*, {M-BC-O, L-BC-O}	2-98%
	BA	$N_{D*}^{\max\uparrow,\min\uparrow,\text{rand}}$	$N_{Ds}^{\min,\text{rand}}$	-	*, {M-BC-O, L-BC-O}	$N_{D*}^{\max\uparrow,\min\uparrow,\text{rand}\uparrow}$	*, {M-BC-O, L-BC-O}	0-100%
	PLOD $\alpha \simeq 0.1$	$N_{D*}^{\max\uparrow,\min\uparrow,\text{rand}}$	$N_{Ds}^{\max,\min,\text{rand}}$	$N_{D*}^{\max,\min,\text{rand}}$	*, {M-BC-O, L-BC-O}	$N_{D*}^{\max\uparrow,\min\uparrow,\text{rand}}$	*, {M-BC-O, L-BC-O}	0.15-100%
	PLOD $\alpha \simeq 0.3$	$N_{D*}^{\max\uparrow,\min\uparrow,\text{rand}}$	$N_{D\uparrow}^{\max\uparrow,\min\uparrow,\text{rand}\uparrow}$	$N_{Ds}^{\max,\min,\text{rand}}$	*, {M-BC-O, L-BC-O}	$N_{D*}^{\max\uparrow,\min\uparrow}$	*, {M-BC-O, L-BC-O}	0-100%
	PLOD $\alpha \simeq 0.5$	$N_{D*}^{\max\uparrow,\min\uparrow,\text{rand}}$	$N_{D*}^{\max,\min,\text{rand}}$	$N_{Ds}^{\max,\min,\text{rand}}$	*, {M-L-O, L-BC-O, L-BC-O, M-BC-O}	$N_{D*}^{\max,\min,\text{rand}}$	*, {M-BC-O, L-BC-O}	0-100%
TG-4	ER	$N_{Ds}^{\max,\min,\text{rand}}$	$N_{D*}^{\max\uparrow,\min\uparrow,\text{rand}\uparrow}$	$N_{D*}^{\max\uparrow,\min\uparrow,\text{rand}\uparrow}$	*	$N_{D*}^{\max,\min,\text{rand}\uparrow}$	*	66-99.90%
	WS	$N_{Ds}^{\max,\min,\text{rand}}$	$N_{D*}^{\max\uparrow,\min\uparrow,\text{rand}\uparrow}$	$N_{D*}^{\max\uparrow,\min\uparrow,\text{rand}\uparrow}$	*	$N_{D*}^{\max\uparrow,\min\uparrow,\text{rand}\uparrow}$	*	82-97.85%
	BA	-	$N_{Ds}^{\max,\min,\text{rand}\uparrow}$	$N_{Ds}^{\min,\text{rand}}$	*	$N_{D*}^{\max,\min,\text{rand}\uparrow}$	*	2-100%
	PLOD $\alpha \simeq 0.1$	$N_{D*}^{\max,\min,\text{rand}}$	$N_{D*}^{\max,\min,\text{rand}}$	$N_{D*}^{\max,\min,\text{rand}}$	*	$N_{Ds}^{\max,\min,\text{rand}}$	*	99-100%
	PLOD $\alpha \simeq 0.3$	$N_{D*}^{\max,\min,\text{rand}}$	$N_{D*}^{\max,\min,\text{rand}}$	$N_{D*}^{\max,\min,\text{rand}}$	*	$N_{Ds}^{\max,\min}$	*	98-100%
	PLOD $\alpha \simeq 0.5$	$N_{D*}^{\max,\min,\text{rand}}$	$N_{Ds}^{\max,\min,\text{rand}}$	$N_{D*}^{\max,\min,\text{rand}\uparrow}$	*	$N_{Ds}^{\max}$	*	96-100%
TG-5	ER	$N_{Ds}^{\max,\min,\text{rand}}$	$N_{D*}^{\max\uparrow,\min\uparrow,\text{rand}\uparrow}$	$N_{D*}^{\max\uparrow,\min\uparrow,\text{rand}\uparrow}$	*	$N_{D*}^{\max\uparrow,\min\uparrow,\text{rand}\uparrow}$	*	68-99.85%
	WS	$N_{Ds}^{\max,\min,\text{rand}}$	$N_{D*}^{\max\uparrow,\min\uparrow,\text{rand}\uparrow}$	$N_{D*}^{\max\uparrow,\min\uparrow,\text{rand}\uparrow}$	*	$N_{D*}^{\max\uparrow,\min\uparrow,\text{rand}\uparrow}$	*	84-97.85%
	BA	-	$N_{Ds}^{\max,\min,\text{rand}\uparrow}$	$N_{Ds}^{\min,\text{rand}}$	*	$N_{D*}^{\max,\min,\text{rand}\uparrow}$	*	2-100%
	PLOD $\alpha \simeq 0.1$	$N_{D*}^{\max,\min,\text{rand}}$	$N_{D*}^{\max,\min,\text{rand}}$	$N_{D*}^{\max\uparrow,\min,\text{rand}\uparrow}$	*	$N_{Ds}^{\max,\min,\text{rand}}$	*	99-99.85%
	PLOD $\alpha \simeq 0.3$	$N_{D*}^{\max,\min,\text{rand}}$	$N_{D*}^{\max,\min,\text{rand}}$	$N_{Ds}^{\max,\min,\text{rand}}$	*	$N_{Ds}^{\max,\min}$	*	98-100%
	PLOD $\alpha \simeq 0.5$	$N_{D*}^{\max,\min,\text{rand}}$	$N_{D*}^{\max,\min,\text{rand}}$	$N_{D*}^{\max\uparrow,\min\uparrow,\text{rand}\uparrow}$	*	$N_{Ds}^{\max}$	*	96-100%

Unlike ER and WS, the CC of the BA does not significantly change, but its observability is heavily compromised for any **TG-x** where the control relies on $N_D^{\max}$. In contrast, power-law distributions with $\alpha = 0.1$, 0.3, 0.5 show a high robustness in connectivity and observability terms where observation rate reaches values $\simeq 100\,\%$. The global density is not affected even if CC mainly varies for small networks and the diameter specially impacts on both $N_D^{\min,\text{rand}}$ for dense distributions with $\alpha = 0.5$ and $N_D^{\max,\min}$ for different exponents in **TG-3** scenarios.

For **SCN-2** scenarios, we observe that ER topologies continues to be very sensitive in connection terms, and the global and local density drastically vary for any **TG-x**. The observation rate is moderately high, but it presents certain weaknesses to attack models containing **AM-1**, **AM-2**, **AM-4** and **AM-5** aiming to break down $N_D^{\max,\text{rand}}$. The diameter in WS networks slightly changes for any N_D^{strat} where the global density remains invariant for **TG-1** and its value notably decreases according to the number of isolated nodes, and specifically for small networks despite the drastic change for CC. The observation

Table 5. SCN-3: Removal of a few edges (SCN-1) of a given sugraph $\mathscr{G}_{sub} = (V, E)$

TGs	Network	Diameter	Density	CC	Attack	Observation	Rate	Attack
		Connectivity				**Observability**		
TG-1	PLOD α ≃ 0.1	$N_{D*}^{max,min,rand\dagger}$	-	$N_{Ds}^{max,min,rand}$	{M, L, BC}	$N_{Ds}^{max,rand}$	{F, M, L, BC}	99.70-100%
	PLOD α ≃ 0.2	N_{Dl}^{rand}	-	$N_{Ds}^{max,rand}$	{L}	-	-	≃ 100%
	PLOD α ≃ 0.3	$N_{Dl}^{max,min}$	-	$N_{Ds}^{max,min,rand}$	{L, BC}	-	-	≃ 100%
	PLOD α ≃ 0.4	$N_{D*}^{max,min,rand}$	-	$N_{Ds}^{max,min,rand}$	{M, L, BC}	N_{Ds}^{max}	*	98-100%
	PLOD α ≃ 0.5	$N_{Dl}^{max,min}$	-	$N_{Ds}^{max,min,rand}$	{L, BC}	N_{Ds}^{max}	*	98-100%
TG-2	PLOD α ≃ 0.1	$N_{D*}^{max,min\dagger,rand\dagger}$	-	$N_{Ds}^{max,min,rand}$	*,{X-BC}	$N_{Ds}^{max,rand}$	*	99.70-100%
	PLOD α ≃ 0.2	$N_{D*}^{max,min,rand}$	-	$N_{Ds}^{max,min,rand}$	{F-O, F-L, M-L, M-O}	-	-	≃100%
	PLOD α ≃ 0.3	$N_{Dl}^{max,min\dagger,rand\dagger}$	-	$N_{Ds}^{max,min\dagger,rand}$	*	-	-	≃100%
	PLOD α ≃ 0.4	$N_{D*}^{max,min\dagger,rand\dagger}$	-	$N_{Ds}^{max,min,rand}$	*	N_{Ds}^{max}	*	97-100%
	PLOD α ≃ 0.5	-	-	$N_{Ds}^{max,min,rand}$	{L, BC}	N_{Ds}^{max}	*	98-100%
TG-3	PLOD α ≃ 0.1	$N_{D*}^{max\dagger,min\dagger,rand\dagger}$	-	$N_{Ds}^{max,min,rand\dagger}$	*,{M-BC-O, L-BC-O}	$N_{D*}^{max\dagger,min\dagger,rand\dagger}$	*,{M-BC-O, L-BC-O}	0-100%
	PLOD α ≃ 0.2	$N_{D*}^{max\dagger,min\dagger,rand\dagger}$	-	$N_{Ds}^{max,min,rand}$	{M-L-O,M-BC-O} L-BC-0}	$N_{D*}^{max\dagger,min\dagger,rand\dagger}$	*,{M-BC-O, L-BC-0}	0-100%
	PLOD α ≃ 0.3	$N_{D*}^{max\dagger,min\dagger,rand\dagger}$	-	$N_{Ds}^{max\dagger,min\dagger,rand}$	*,{M-BC-O, L-BC-0}	$N_{D*}^{max\dagger,min\dagger,rand\dagger}$	*,{M-BC-O, L-BC-0}	0-100%
	PLOD α ≃ 0.4	$N_{D*}^{max\dagger,min\dagger,rand\dagger}$	-	$N_{Ds}^{max\dagger,min\dagger,rand}$	*,{M-BC-O, L-BC-0}	$N_{D*}^{max\dagger,min\dagger,rand\dagger}$	*,{M-BC-O, L-BC-0}	0-100%
	PLOD α ≃ 0.5	$N_{D*}^{max\dagger,min\dagger,rand\dagger}$	-	$N_{Ds}^{max\dagger,min\dagger,rand}$	*,{M-BC-O, L-BC-0}	$N_{D*}^{max\dagger,min\dagger,rand\dagger}$	*,{M-BC-O, L-BC-0}	0-100%
TG-4	PLOD α ≃ 0.1	$N_{D*}^{max\dagger,min\dagger,rand\dagger}$	-	$N_{Ds}^{max,min,rand\dagger}$	*	$N_{Ds}^{max,rand}$	*	99-100%
	PLOD α ≃ 0.2	$N_{D*}^{max,min,rand}$	-	$N_{Ds}^{max,min,rand}$	{F-L-BC-O,F-M-L-O} F-M-L-BC}	-	-	≃ 100%
	PLOD α ≃ 0.3	$N_{D*}^{max,min,rand}$	-	$N_{Ds}^{max\dagger,min\dagger,rand\dagger}$	*	-	-	≃ 100%
	PLOD α ≃ 0.4	$N_{D*}^{max\dagger,min\dagger,rand\dagger}$	-	N_{Ds}^{max}	*, {F-M-BC-O}	N_{Ds}^{max}	*, {F-M-BC-O}	97-100%
	PLOD α ≃ 0.5	N_{Ds}^{max}	-	$N_{Ds}^{max\dagger,min\dagger,rand}$	{M-L-BC-O}	N_{Ds}^{max}	*	98-100%
TG-5	PLOD α ≃ 0.1	$N_{Dl}^{max\dagger,min\dagger,rand\dagger}$	-	$N_{Ds}^{max,min,rand\dagger}$	*	$N_{Ds}^{max,rand}$	*	99-100%
	PLOD α ≃ 0.2	$N_{Dl}^{min,rand}$	-	N_{Ds}^{rand}	*	-	-	≃ 100%
	PLOD α ≃ 0.3	$N_{Dl}^{max,min,rand}$	-	$N_{Ds}^{max,min,rand}$	*	-	-	≃ 100%
	PLOD α ≃ 0.4	$N_{Dl}^{max,min,rand}$	-	-		N_{Ds}^{max}	*	97-100%
	PLOD α ≃ 0.5	-	-	$N_{Ds}^{max,min,rand}$		N_{Ds}^{max}	*	98-100%

rate remains high with exception to multi-interactive threat scenarios based on **TG-3**. As in **SCN-1**, the diameter, density and the CC of BA in **SCN-2** networks remains almost invariant what shows its robustness degree for all types of **AM-s**. Nonetheless, the densities can suffer some changes when three or more nodes are compromised and these nodes belong mainly to N_D^{rand}. Moreover, the rate reaches $\simeq 2\%$ of the observation when driver nodes primarily of the N_D^{max} are compromised (Table 4).

This does not occur with general power-law networks where the observability degree, except for **TG-3**, reaches the 90 % of the observation at all times, in addition to following similar behaviour pattern for any exponent value. While no effect is appreciated in diameter, the density decays only in small networks when two or more nodes are excluded from the graph. The consequences on the CC for small networks are not negligible, but the greatest consequences have been observed in observability when 3 nodes are removed. Lastly, common behaviours in **SCN-1** and **SCN-2** arise. The removal of random links in three vertices or the isolation of three vertices (**TG-3**) using the combination **M-BC-O** and **L-BC-O** can cause the breakdown of the entire graph. These two configurations seem to be the most menacing within the configuration given in Table 1, in which the observability is largely influenced for any distribution and the diameter is drastically decreased for $N_D^{max,min}$. In addition, threats of the type **AM-4** stand out from the rest, underlying the importance of protecting the node with the highest centrality.

3.2 SCN3: Exploitation of Links and Vertices in Power-Law Subgraphs

Tables 5 and 6 show results obtained for attacks on a small number of random edges (**SCN-1**) or isolation of one or several vertices (**SCN-2**) from power-law subgraphs. Varying the exponent, we observe that these types of networks have similar behavioural characteristics to those analysed in Sect. 3.1. Unfortunately, the observation degree decays extremely when the graph is subjected to attacks of type **M-BC-O** and **L-BC-O**, where two n_d of the sub-graph and a vertex of the sub-graph, but outside the N_D^{strat}, are attacked simultaneously. Moreover, these two attack combinations are also dangerous in connectivity terms. The diameter values radically vary for any N_D^{strat} and for any distribution, although the global density remains broadly constant. Obviously, when the sub-graph is subjected to massive attacks to isolate a single or multiple nodes, the diameter, density, and CC of the entire network vary. Table 6 shows this, where the diameter primarily changes for any large distribution, whereas the local and global

Table 6. SCN-3: Isolation of vertices (**SCN-2**) of a given sugraph $\mathcal{G}_{sub} = (V, E)$

TGs	Network	Connectivity				Observability		
		Diameter	Density	CC	Attack	Observation	Rate	Attack
TG-1	PLOD $\alpha \simeq 0.1$	$N_{D*}^{max_\uparrow,min_\uparrow,rand_\uparrow}$	-	$N_{D*}^{max,min,rand_\uparrow}$	{M, L, BC}	$N_{Ds}^{max,rand}$	•	99-100%
	PLOD $\alpha \simeq 0.2$	$N_{Dl}^{max,min,rand}$	$N_{Ds}^{max,min,rand}$	$N_{Ds}^{max,min,rand}$	*{L,BC}	-	-	$\simeq 100$
	PLOD $\alpha \simeq 0.3$	$N_{Dl}^{max_\uparrow,min_\uparrow,rand_\uparrow}$	-	$N_{Ds}^{max,min,rand}$	{L, BC}	-	-	$\simeq 100$
	PLOD $\alpha \simeq 0.4$	$N_{D*}^{max_\uparrow,min_\uparrow,rand_\uparrow}$	$N_{Ds}^{max,min,rand}$	$N_{Ds}^{max_\uparrow,min_\uparrow,rand_\uparrow}$	*{M, L, BC}	$N_{Ds}^{max_\uparrow,rand}$	•, {M, BC}	96-100%
	PLOD $\alpha \simeq 0.5$	$N_{D*}^{max,min,rand}$	-	$N_{Ds}^{max,min,rand}$	{M, L}	N_{Ds}^{max}	•	99.60-100%
TG-2	PLOD $\alpha \simeq 0.1$	$N_{D*}^{max_\uparrow,min_\uparrow,rand_\uparrow}$	$N_{Ds}^{max,min,rand}$	$N_{Ds}^{max,min,rand_\uparrow}$	{F-O, M-L, X-BC}	$N_{Ds}^{max,rand}$	•	98-100%
	PLOD $\alpha \simeq 0.2$	$N_{Dl}^{max,min,rand}$	$N_{Ds}^{max,min,rand}$	$N_{Ds}^{max,min,rand_\uparrow}$	*{F-O, M-L, L-O}	-	-	$\simeq 100\%$
	PLOD $\alpha \simeq 0.3$	$N_{Dl}^{max_\uparrow,min_\uparrow,rand_\uparrow}$	-	$N_{Ds}^{min_\uparrow,rand}$	{M-L, X-BC}	-	-	$\simeq 100\%$
	PLOD $\alpha \simeq 0.4$	$N_{D*}^{max_\uparrow,min_\uparrow,rand_\uparrow}$	$N_{D*}^{max_\uparrow,min_\uparrow,rand_\uparrow}$	$N_{Ds}^{max_\uparrow,min_\uparrow,rand_\uparrow}$	*{X-BC}	$N_{Ds}^{max_\uparrow,rand}$	•, {F-X, X-BC}	97-100%
	PLOD $\alpha \simeq 0.5$	$N_{D*}^{max_\uparrow,min,rand}$	-	$N_{Ds}^{max_\uparrow,min,rand}$	*,{F-L, M-L, X-BC}	N_{Ds}^{max}	•,{BC-O}	96-100%
TG-3	PLOD $\alpha \simeq 0.1$	$N_{D*}^{max_\uparrow,min_\uparrow,rand_\ddagger}$	$N_{Ds}^{max,min,rand}$	$N_{Ds}^{max,min,rand_\uparrow}$	*,{M-BC-O, L-BC-O}	$N_{Ds}^{max_\uparrow,min_\uparrow,rand_\ddagger}$	•	0-100%
	PLOD $\alpha \simeq 0.2$	$N_{D*}^{max_\uparrow,min_\uparrow,rand_\ddagger}$	$N_{Ds}^{max,min,rand}$	$N_{Ds}^{max_\uparrow,min_\uparrow,rand_\uparrow}$	*,{M-BC-O, L-BC-O}	$N_{Ds}^{max_\uparrow,min_\uparrow,rand_\ddagger}$	*,{M-BC-O, L-BC-O}	0-100%
	PLOD $\alpha \simeq 0.3$	$N_{D*}^{max_\uparrow,min_\uparrow,rand_\ddagger}$	$N_{Ds}^{max,min,rand}$	$N_{D*}^{max_\uparrow,min_\uparrow,rand}$	*,{M-BC-O, L-BC-O}	$N_{Ds}^{max_\uparrow,min_\uparrow,rand_\ddagger}$	*,{M-BC-O, L-BC-O}	0-100%
	PLOD $\alpha \simeq 0.4$	$N_{D*}^{max_\uparrow,min_\uparrow,rand_\ddagger}$	$N_{D*}^{max_\uparrow,min_\uparrow,rand_\ddagger}$	$N_{D*}^{max_\uparrow,min_\uparrow,rand_\uparrow}$	*,{M-BC-O, L-BC-O}	$N_{D*}^{max_\uparrow,min_\uparrow,rand_\ddagger}$	*,{M-BC-O, L-BC-O}	0-100%
	PLOD $\alpha \simeq 0.5$	$N_{D*}^{max_\uparrow,min_\uparrow,rand_\ddagger}$	$N_{Ds}^{max,min,rand}$	$N_{D*}^{max_\uparrow,min_\uparrow,rand_\ddagger}$	*,{M-BC-O, L-BC-O}	$N_{D*}^{max_\uparrow,min_\uparrow,rand_\ddagger}$	*,{M-BC-O, L-BC-O}	0-100%
TG-4	PLOD $\alpha \simeq 0.1$	$N_{D*}^{max_\uparrow,min_\uparrow,rand_\ddagger}$	$N_{Ds}^{max,min,rand}$	$N_{D*}^{max,min,rand_\uparrow}$	•	$N_{Ds}^{max,min,rand}$	•	99-100%
	PLOD $\alpha \simeq 0.2$	$N_{D*}^{max,min,rand}$	$N_{Ds}^{max,min,rand}$	$N_{Ds}^{max,min,rand}$	•	-	-	$\simeq 100\%$
	PLOD $\alpha \simeq 0.3$	$N_{Dl}^{max_\uparrow,min_\uparrow,rand_\uparrow}$	$N_{Ds}^{max,min,rand}$	$N_{D*}^{min_\uparrow}$	•	-	-	$\simeq 100\%$
	PLOD $\alpha \simeq 0.4$	$N_{D*}^{max_\ddagger,min_\uparrow,rand_\uparrow}$	$N_{D*}^{max_\uparrow,min_\uparrow,rand_\uparrow}$	$N_{D*}^{max_\uparrow,min_\uparrow,rand_\uparrow}$	•	$N_{D*}^{max_\uparrow,rand}$	•	96-100%
	PLOD $\alpha \simeq 0.5$	$N_{D*}^{max_\uparrow,min,rand}$	$N_{Ds}^{max,min,max}$	$N_{D*}^{max_\uparrow,min,rand}$	•	N_{Ds}^{max}	•	96-100%
TG-5	PLOD $\alpha \simeq 0.1$	$N_{D*}^{max_\uparrow,min_\uparrow,rand_\uparrow}$	$N_{Ds}^{max,min,rand}$	$N_{Ds}^{max,min,rand}$	•	$N_{Ds}^{max,min,rand}$	•	99-100%
	PLOD $\alpha \simeq 0.2$	$N_{Dl}^{max,min,rand}$	$N_{Ds}^{max,rand}$	$N_{Ds}^{max,rand}$	•	-	-	$\simeq 100\%$
	PLOD $\alpha \simeq 0.3$	$N_{Dl}^{max_\uparrow,min_\uparrow,rand_\uparrow}$	$N_{Ds}^{max,min,rand}$	$N_{Ds}^{min_\uparrow,rand}$	•	-	-	$\simeq 100\%$
	PLOD $\alpha \simeq 0.4$	$N_{D*}^{max_\uparrow,min,rand_\ddagger}$	$N_{D*}^{max_\uparrow,min_\uparrow,rand_\ddagger}$	$N_{D*}^{max,min_\uparrow,rand_\ddagger}$	•	$N_{D*}^{max_\uparrow,rand}$	•	96-100%
	PLOD $\alpha \simeq 0.5$	$N_{D*}^{max_\uparrow,min,rand}$	$N_{Ds}^{max,min,max}$	$N_{D*}^{max_\uparrow,min,rand}$	•	N_{Ds}^{max}	•	96-100%

densities impact on small networks. As in the previous case, the observability is high at all times, even if insignificant variations caused by attacks in N_D^{max} arise.

Given this, we conclude that both the connectivity and observation not only depend on the network topology and construction strategies of driver nodes (N_D^{strat}), but also on the nature of the perturbation [5], where degree-based attacks (e.g. **AM-1**) and attacks to centrality (**AM-4**) are primarily significant. On the other hand, BA (see Table 3) and power-law (PLOD) distributions present analogous behaviours with respect to observability. Both are mainly vulnerable to threats given in N_D^{max} for small networks, and they are no only sensitive to **TG-3** attacks, but also to **TG-4** based on a planned **F-M-BC-O** attack in **SCN-1**. This also means that an adversary with sufficient knowledge of the network distribution and its power domination can disconnect the entire network and leave it without observation at very low cost.

4   Conclusions

We have reported results of a robustness analysis on structural controllability through the POWER DOMINATING SET problem, extending the study given in [9] to consider multi-round attack scenarios. We have primarily focused on random (*Erdös-Renyi*), small-word (*Watts-Strogatz*), scale-free (*Barabási-Albert*) and power-law (*PLOD*) distributions, where we have observed that these networks are sensitive in connectivity and observability terms. These weaknesses are mainly notable when nodes with the highest degree distribution and with the maximum value of betweenness centrality are compromised. Moreover, we have shown that combined attacks based on three specific nodes (**M-BC-O** and **L-BC-O**) can become highly disruptive, even if the power-law network has proven to be robust with respect to the rest of topologies. Regarding future work, sub-optimal approximations to repair the controllability when the power dominance relationship might have been partially severed will be considered taking into account the handicap of the non-locality of the PDS and the $\mathcal{NP}$-hardness demonstrated in [6].

Acknowledgements. *Research of C. Alcaraz was funded by the Marie Curie COFUND programme "U-Mobility" co-financed by University of Málaga and the EU 7th FP (GA 246550), and Ministerio de Economía y Competitividad (COFUND2013-40259). Research by S. Wolthusen is based in part upon work supported by the EU 7th FP Joint Technology Initiatives Collaborative Project ARTEMIS (GA 269374).*

References

1. Lin, C.: Structual controllability. IEEE Trans. Autom. Control **19**(3), 201–208 (1974)
2. Kalman, R.: Mathematical description of linear dynamical systems. J. Soc. Ind. Appl. Math. Control Ser. A **1**, 152–192 (1963)

3. Liu, Y., Slotine, J., Barabási, A.: Controllability of complex networks. Nature **473**, 167–173 (2011)
4. Wang, W., Ni, X., Lai, Y., Grebogi, C.: Optimizing controllability of complex networks by minimum structural perturbations. Phys. Rev. E **85**(2), 026115 (2012)
5. Pu, C., Pei, W., Michaelson, A.: Robustness analysis of network controllability. Physica A **391**(18), 4420–4425 (2012)
6. Haynes, T., Hedetniemi, S., Hedetniemi, S., Henning, M.: Domination in graphs applied to electric power networks. SIAM J. Discrete Math. **15**(4), 519–529 (2002)
7. Kneis, J., Mölle, D., Richter, S., Rossmanith, P.: Parameterized power domination complexity. Inf. Process. Lett. **98**(4), 145–149 (2006)
8. Feige, U.: A threshold of $\ln n$ for approximating set cover. J. ACM **45**(4), 634–652 (1998)
9. Alcaraz, C., Miciolino, E.E., Wolthusen, S.: Structural controllability of networks for non-interactive adversarial vertex removal. In: Luiijf, E., Hartel, P. (eds.) CRITIS 2013. LNCS, vol. 8328, pp. 120–132. Springer, Heidelberg (2013)
10. Newman, M., Girvan, M.: Community structure in social and biological networks. In: Proceedings of the National Academy of Sciences of the United States of America, vol. 99(12), pp. 7821–7826 (2002)

Cryptanalysis

Improved Meet-in-the-Middle Attacks on Round-Reduced ARIA

Dongxia Bai and Hongbo Yu[✉]

Department of Computer Science and Technology, Tsinghua University,
Beijing 100084, China
baidx10@mails.tsinghua.edu.cn, yuhongbo@mail.tsinghua.edu.cn

Abstract. ARIA is a 128-bit SPN block cipher selected as a Korean standard. This paper processes meet-in-the-middle attacks on reduced-round ARIA. Some 4-round and 5-round significant distinguishing properties which involve much fewer bytes parameters are proposed. Based on these better distinguishers, attacks on 7-round ARIA-192/256 and 8-round ARIA-256 are mounted with much lower complexities than previous meet-in-the-middle attacks. Furthermore, we present 7-round attack on ARIA-128 and 9-round attack on ARIA-256, which are both the first results for ARIA in terms of the meet-in-the-middle attack.

Keywords: Meet-in-the-Middle Attack · Cryptanalysis · ARIA · Block cipher

1 Introduction

The block cipher ARIA was designed by Korean cryptographers Kwon *et al.* in 2003 [11,17]. The structure of ARIA is a SP-network structure with the same design idea of AES [3]. Its block size is 128 bits and it supports 128-, 192- and 256-bit key sizes with 12, 14 and 16 rounds, respectively. ARIA has been established as a Korean standard block cipher algorithm by the Ministry of Commerce, Industry and Energy [10] in 2004, and has been widely used in Korea, especially for government-to-public services.

The designers of ARIA algorithm gave several initial analyses of its security in [11]. Then Biryukov *et al.* [1] performed an evaluation of ARIA which focused on truncated differential and dedicated linear cryptanalysis, and were able to develop attacks on 7-round ARIA-128 and 10-round ARIA-192/256. In [19] Wu *et al.* firstly presented some 4-round non-trivial impossible differentials leading to a 6-round attack on ARIA. The cryptanalytic result was later improved respectively to 6-round attacks with lower complexities by Li *et al.* [13] and 7-round attack on ARIA-256 by Du *et al.* [7]. In [12] Li *et al.* presented some

Supported by 973 program (No. 2013CB834205), the National Natural Science Foundation of China (No. 61133013 and No. 61373142), the Tsinghua University Initiative Scientific Research Program (No. 20111080970).

© Springer International Publishing Switzerland 2015
Y. Desmedt (Ed.): ISC 2013, LNCS 7807, pp. 155–168, 2015.
DOI: 10.1007/978-3-319-27659-5_11

3-round integral distinguishers of ARIA which could be used to attack 4/5-round ARIA-128 and 6-round ARIA-192/256. Then by modifying the 3-round integral distinguishers, Li *et al.* [14] gave new 4-round integral distinguishers which resulted in improved integral attacks on 6-round ARIA-128 and 7-round ARIA-256. In [9] Fleischmann *et al.* proposed some boomerang attacks on 5/6-round ARIA-128 and 7-round ARIA-256. In [18], Tang *et al.* gave meet-in-the-middle attacks on 5/6-round ARIA-128, 7-round ARIA-192 and 8-round ARIA-256. Liu *et al.* [15] presented another linear cryptanalysis of ARIA including attacks on 7-round ARIA-128, 9-round ARIA-192/256 and 11-round ARIA-256. Besides, a biclique attack of the full ARIA-256 was given in [2] with almost exhaustive search complexity $2^{255.2}$.

The meet-in-the-middle attack was firstly introduced by Diffie and Hellman in the cryptanalysis of Two-DES [6], and its main idea is using the technique of the time-memory tradeoff. The meet-in-the-middle attack on block cipher AES was firstly given by Demirci and Selçuk in [4]. Later, Dunkelman *et al.* [8] presented the improved meet-in-the-middle attacks on AES by using some efficient techniques, which were recently improved by Derbez *et al.* in [5]. Inspired by their works, and due to the similarity to AES, we construct some new 4-round and 5-round distinguishers of ARIA and apply the meet-in-the-middle attacks against ARIA. By using the multisets and efficient truncated differential characteristics, we construct the new 4-round distinguisher and its variant respectively involving 16 and 15 bytes parameters instead of 31 bytes in previous work [18]. Based on these 4-round distinguishers, we can attack 7-round ARIA-128/192/256 and 8-round ARIA-256. Furthermore, we present a 5-round distinguisher for the first time which involves 31 byte parameters, and use it to attack 9-round ARIA-256. Although this kind of attack requires huge time and space in the precomputation, it only needs to compute and store once. In addition, though our results using the meet-in-the-middle attack do not reach more rounds than the known best attacks, in terms of the meet-in-the-middle attack, our attacks on 7-round ARIA-128 and 9-round ARIA-256 are both for the first time, and the other results in our paper also have much better complexities than previous work. Table 1 summaries all previous attacks and our results on ARIA. All these attacks do not contradict the security claims of ARIA.

The rest of the paper is organized as follows: Sect. 2 provides a brief description of ARIA and some notations used in the paper. We present the 4-round distinguisher of ARIA in Sect. 3, then give another 4/5-round distinguishers and meet-in-the-middle attacks on round-reduced ARIA in Sect. 4. Finally, we conclude our paper in Sect. 5.

2   Preliminary

2.1   A Short Description of ARIA

ARIA is an SP-network block cipher that supports key lengths of 128, 192 and 256 bits. A 128-bit plaintext is treated as a 4×4 byte matrix, where each byte represents a value in $GF(2^8)$. The number of rounds depends on the key

Table 1. Summary of attacks on ARIA

Attack type	Key size	Rounds	Data	Memory	Time	Source
IDC	all	5	$2^{71.3}$CP	2^{72b}	$2^{71.6}$	[13]
IDC	all	6	2^{121}CP	2^{121b}	2^{112}	[19]
IDC	all	6	$2^{120.5}$CP	2^{121b}	$2^{104.5}$	[13]
IDC	all	6	2^{113}CP	2^{113b}	$2^{121.6}$	[13]
IDC	256	7	2^{125}CP	a	2^{238}	[7]
TDC	all	7	2^{81}CP	2^{80}	2^{81}	[1]
TDC	all	7	2^{100}CP	2^{51}	2^{100}	[1]
LC	all	7	$2^{105.8}$KP	$2^{79.73}$	$2^{100.99}$	[15]
LC	128	7 (weak key)	2^{77}KP	2^{61}	2^{88}	[1]
LC	192/256	9	$2^{108.3}$KP	$2^{159.77}$	$2^{154.83}$	[15]
LC	192	10 (weak key)	2^{119}KP	2^{63}	2^{119}	[1]
LC	256	10 (weak key)	2^{119}KP	2^{63}	2^{119}	[1]
LC	256	11	$2^{110.3}$KP	$2^{239.8}$	$2^{218.54}$	[15]
Integral	all	5	$2^{27.5}$CP	$2^{27.5b}$	$2^{76.7}$	[12]
Integral	192/256	6	$2^{124.4}$CP	$2^{124.4b}$	$2^{172.4}$	[12]
Integral	all	6	$2^{99.2}$CP	a	$2^{71.4}$	[14]
Integral	256	7	$2^{100.6}$CP	a	$2^{225.8}$	[14]
Boomerang	all	5	2^{109}ACPC	2^{57}	2^{110}	[9]
Boomerang	all	6	2^{128}KP	2^{56}	2^{108}	[9]
Boomerang	256	7	2^{128}KP	2^{184}	2^{236}	[9]
Biclique	256	16 (full round)	2^{80}CP	a	$2^{255.2}$	[2]
MITM	all	5	25CP	2^{121}	$2^{122.5}$	[18]
MITM	all	6	2^{56}CP	2^{121}	$2^{122.5}$	[18]
MITM	**all**	**7**	2^{121}**CP**	2^{122}	$2^{125.7}$	**Sect. 4.3**
MITM	192/256	7	2^{96}CP	2^{185}	2^{187}	[18]
MITM	**192/256**	**7**	2^{113}**CP**	2^{130}	2^{132}	**Sect. 4.1**
MITM	256	8	2^{56}CP	2^{250}	2^{252}	[18]
MITM	**256**	**8**	2^{113}**CP**	2^{130}	$2^{244.61}$	**Sect. 4.2**
MITM	**256**	**9**	2^{121}**CP**	2^{250}	$2^{253.37}$	**Sect. 4.4**

IDC: Impossible Differential Cryptanalysis,
TDC: Truncated Differential Cryptanalysis,
LC: Linear Cryptanalysis, MITM: Meet-in-the-Middle Attack,
CP: Chosen Plaintexts, KP: Known Plaintexts,
ACPC: Adaptive Chosen Plaintexts and Ciphertexts,
a: Not given in the related paper, b: Estimated in [9].

size: 12 rounds for 128-bit key, 14 rounds for 192-bit key, and 16 rounds for 256-bit key. For sake of simplicity we denote ARIA with k-bit key by ARIA-k, e.g., ARIA with 128-bit key is denoted by ARIA-128. We use ARIA to mean all three variants of ARIA. An ARIA round applies three operations to the state matrix as follows:

Substitution Layer (SL): Based on four 8×8-bit S-boxes S_1, S_2 and their inverses S_1^{-1}, S_2^{-1}, ARIA has two types of substitution layers $SL1$ and $SL2$ that alternate between rounds. $SL1$ is used in the odd rounds, and $SL2$ is used in the even rounds.

$$SL1 = (S_1, S_2, S_1^{-1}, S_2^{-1}, S_1, S_2, S_1^{-1}, S_2^{-1}, S_1, S_2, S_1^{-1}, S_2^{-1}, S_1, S_2, S_1^{-1}, S_2^{-1}),$$
$$SL2 = (S_1^{-1}, S_2^{-1}, S_1, S_2, S_1^{-1}, S_2^{-1}, S_1, S_2, S_1^{-1}, S_2^{-1}, S_1, S_2, S_1^{-1}, S_2^{-1}, S_1, S_2).$$

Diffusion Layer (DL): The linear diffusion layer is a 16×16 involution binary matrix with branch number 8.

$$y_0 = x_3 \oplus x_4 \oplus x_6 \oplus x_8 \oplus x_9 \oplus x_{13} \oplus x_{14},$$
$$y_1 = x_2 \oplus x_5 \oplus x_7 \oplus x_8 \oplus x_9 \oplus x_{12} \oplus x_{15},$$
$$y_2 = x_1 \oplus x_4 \oplus x_6 \oplus x_{10} \oplus x_{11} \oplus x_{12} \oplus x_{15},$$
$$y_3 = x_0 \oplus x_5 \oplus x_7 \oplus x_{10} \oplus x_{11} \oplus x_{13} \oplus x_{14},$$
$$y_4 = x_0 \oplus x_2 \oplus x_5 \oplus x_8 \oplus x_{11} \oplus x_{14} \oplus x_{15},$$
$$y_5 = x_1 \oplus x_3 \oplus x_4 \oplus x_9 \oplus x_{10} \oplus x_{14} \oplus x_{15},$$
$$y_6 = x_0 \oplus x_2 \oplus x_7 \oplus x_9 \oplus x_{10} \oplus x_{12} \oplus x_{13},$$
$$y_7 = x_1 \oplus x_3 \oplus x_6 \oplus x_8 \oplus x_{11} \oplus x_{12} \oplus x_{13},$$
$$y_8 = x_0 \oplus x_1 \oplus x_4 \oplus x_7 \oplus x_{10} \oplus x_{13} \oplus x_{15},$$
$$y_9 = x_0 \oplus x_1 \oplus x_5 \oplus x_6 \oplus x_{11} \oplus x_{12} \oplus x_{14},$$
$$y_{10} = x_2 \oplus x_3 \oplus x_5 \oplus x_6 \oplus x_8 \oplus x_{13} \oplus x_{15},$$
$$y_{11} = x_2 \oplus x_3 \oplus x_4 \oplus x_7 \oplus x_9 \oplus x_{12} \oplus x_{14},$$
$$y_{12} = x_1 \oplus x_2 \oplus x_6 \oplus x_7 \oplus x_9 \oplus x_{11} \oplus x_{12},$$
$$y_{13} = x_0 \oplus x_3 \oplus x_6 \oplus x_7 \oplus x_8 \oplus x_{10} \oplus x_{13},$$
$$y_{14} = x_0 \oplus x_3 \oplus x_4 \oplus x_5 \oplus x_9 \oplus x_{11} \oplus x_{14},$$
$$y_{15} = x_1 \oplus x_2 \oplus x_4 \oplus x_5 \oplus x_8 \oplus x_{10} \oplus x_{15}.$$

Round Key Addition (RKA): This is done by XORing the 128-bit state with the 128-bit round key. The round keys are derived from master key through the key schedule which processes the key using a 3-round 256-bit Feistel cipher [11].

We outline an ARIA round in Fig. 1. In the first round an additional RKA operation is applied, and in the last round the DL operation is omitted.

2.2   Notations

The following notations are used to describe the attacks on ARIA in the next sections: We use x_i, y_i, z_i to respectively denote the state matrix after RKA, SL and DL of round i, and $x_{i,j}$ denotes the j-th byte of $x_i(j = 0, 1, \cdots, 15)$. Δx_i refers to the difference in the state x of round i.

The additional added subkey in the first round is denoted by k_0, and the regular one used in round i is denoted by k_i. Similar to AES block cipher, the order of DL operation and RKA operation of ARIA can be interchanged. As these operations are linear, they can be interchanged by first XORing the state

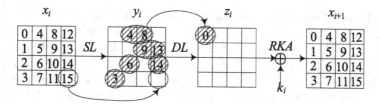

Fig. 1. An ARIA round

with an equivalent key and then applying the diffusion operation. We denote the equivalent subkey for the changed version by w_i, that is, $w_i = DL^{-1}(k_i) = DL(k_i)$[1].

We use the particular structure δ-set to denote the structured set of 256 ARIA-states that are all different in only one state byte (the active byte) which assumes each one of the 256 possible values, and all equal in the other 15 state bytes (the passive bytes).

We measure memory complexities of our attacks in units of 128-bit ARIA blocks and time complexities in terms of ARIA encryptions. Besides, to be completely fair, we count all operations carried out during our attacks, and in particular the time and memory required to prepare the various tables in the precomputation phase.

3 New 4-Round Meet-in-the-Middle Distinguisher of ARIA

In this section, we propose our new 4-round meet-in-the-middle distinguisher where we consider an un-ordered multiset instead of an ordered sequence.

Observation 1. *Consider the encryption of a δ-set $\{P^0, P^1, \cdots, P^{255}\}$ through four ARIA rounds, where P^0 belongs to a right pair with respect to the 4-round differential of Fig. 2 (i.e. both the input and output differences are nonzero in a single byte 0), the (un-ordered) multiset $\{x_{5,0}^0 \oplus x_{5,0}^0, x_{5,0}^0 \oplus x_{5,0}^1, \cdots, x_{5,0}^0 \oplus x_{5,0}^{255}\}$ is fully determined by the following 16 byte parameters:*

- $\Delta y_{1,0}$ *of the right pair,*
- $x_{2,i}^0 (i = 3, 4, 6, 8, 9, 13, 14)$,
- $\Delta z_{4,0}$ *of the right pair,*
- $y_{4,i}^0 (i = 3, 4, 6, 8, 9, 13, 14)$.

Hence, the multiset can assume only 2^{128} values out of the $\binom{510}{255} \approx 2^{505.2}$ theoretically possible values[2].

---

[1] The property $DL^{-1} = DL$ results from the fact that the matrix of diffusion layer is designed involutional.

[2] The calculation of the number of possible values is explained at the end of the proof.

Proof. The proof emphasizes the meet-in-the-middle nature of the observation.

Considering the "bottom side" of the four rounds first, we observe that if $\{x_3^0, x_3^1, \cdots, x_3^{255}\}$ and $k_{3,i}(i = 3, 4, 6, 8, 9, 13, 14)$ are known, the desired differences $\{x_{5,0}^0 \oplus x_{5,0}^0, x_{5,0}^0 \oplus x_{5,0}^1, \cdots, x_{5,0}^0 \oplus x_{5,0}^{255}\}$ are obtained after 256 encryptions of rounds 3 to 4 ($k_{4,0}$ is not needed to know as RKA operation preserves differences). To get the 256 values $\{x_3^0, x_3^1, \cdots, x_3^{255}\}$, it is sufficient to know one of them, e.g. x_3^0, and the differences $\{x_3^0 \oplus x_3^0, x_3^0 \oplus x_3^1, \cdots, x_3^0 \oplus x_3^{255}\}$.

Now for the "top side" of the four rounds, the differences $\{y_1^0 \oplus y_1^0, y_1^0 \oplus y_1^1, \cdots, y_1^0 \oplus y_1^{255}\}$ are known, which are exactly the 256 possible differences in byte 0 (the other fifteen bytes are equal). Since DL and RKA operations are linear, the differences $\{x_2^0 \oplus x_2^0, x_2^0 \oplus x_2^1, \cdots, x_2^0 \oplus x_2^{255}\}$ are also known. By the structure of the δ-set, these differences are active in bytes $3, 4, 6, 8, 9, 13, 14$ and passive in the other nine bytes. Since bytes $3, 4, 6, 8, 9, 13, 14$ of x_2^0 are given as part of the parameters, bytes $3, 4, 6, 8, 9, 13, 14$ of $\{x_2^1, \cdots, x_2^{255}\}$ are thus also known, and so are bytes $3, 4, 6, 8, 9, 13, 14$ of $\{y_2^0, y_2^1, \cdots, y_2^{255}\}$. Since the differences $y_2^0 \oplus y_2^i (i = 1, 2, \cdots, 255)$ in all the bytes except for $3, 4, 6, 8, 9, 13, 14$ are zero, the whole byte differences $\{y_2^0 \oplus y_2^0, y_2^0 \oplus y_2^1, \cdots, y_2^0 \oplus y_2^{255}\}$ are known. Since DL and RKA operations are linear, the differences $\{x_3^0 \oplus x_3^0, x_3^0 \oplus x_3^1, \cdots, x_3^0 \oplus x_3^{255}\}$ are also known, as required above.

Then we deduce the full 16-byte values of x_3^0 and seven bytes of subkey k_3 at $3, 4, 6, 8, 9, 13, 14$ by using the knowledge of the right pair, where the meet-in-the-middle idea is used again. We focus on the right pair satisfying the particular differential shown in Fig. 2 in the following part.

We start from the "top side" of the four rounds. Since DL and RKA operations are linear, the difference Δx_2 of the right pair is known from $\Delta y_{1,0}$, which is active in bytes $3, 4, 6, 8, 9, 13, 14$ and passive in the rest of the bytes. Together with the given bytes $x_{2,i}^0$ ($i = 3, 4, 6, 8, 9, 13, 14$), we can get the difference Δy_2 of the right pair, and the difference Δx_3 is also known due to the linear property of DL and RKA operations.

Then turn to the "bottom side" of the four rounds. Similarly, the byte difference $\Delta z_{4,0}$ of the right pair is given, so the difference Δy_4 can be easily deduced after the linear operation DL^{-1} (note that $DL^{-1}(X) = DL(X)$) which are active in bytes $3, 4, 6, 8, 9, 13, 14$ and passive in the rest of the bytes. Since bytes $y_{4,i}^0$ ($i = 3, 4, 6, 8, 9, 13, 14$) are known, the difference Δx_4 of the right pair is known, and then the difference Δy_3 is also known.

Now both the input and output differences of SBox in round 3 (i.e. Δx_3 and Δy_3) are already known. Meanwhile, it is well known that given the input and output differences of the SBox, there is one possibility on average for the actual pair of input/output values. Hence we can get in average one value of x_3^0, as required above.

Then for the solution of the required subkey k_3, the known values around the two RKA layers of round 3 and 4 suggest seven bytes of subkey k_3 and another seven bytes of the equivalent subkey $w_2 = DL(k_2)$ both at $3, 4, 6, 8, 9, 13, 14$, which are marked by • in Fig. 2.

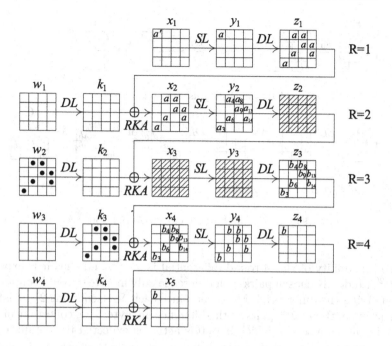

a', a, a_i, b, b_i : nonzero bytes;   ▨ : unknown bytes;

▣ : subkey bytes that can be deduced .

Fig. 2. The 4-round differential characteristic used in our attacks

Therefore, the multiset for difference $\Delta x_{5,0}$ is decided by the above 16 bytes parameters, and contains 2^{128} values which can be computed by first iterating on the 2^{128} possible values for the 16 byte parameters and for each of them deducing the possible values of 16 bytes of x_3^0 and 7 bytes of subkey k_3.

For the theoretically possible values of the multiset, we note that each entry $x_{5,0}^0 \oplus x_{5,i}^1$ (besides the entry $i = 0$ which is always 0) is distributed randomly. We focus on these 255 values which are chosen uniformly and independently from the set $\{0, 1, \cdots, 255\}$. For $i = 0, 1, \cdots, 255$, if c_i denotes the number of each value i encountered in the last 255 entries in the multiset (we disregard the first entry as it is always 0), we get $c_0 + c_1 + \cdots + c_{255} = 255$ $(c_i \geq 0)$. Let $c_i' = c_i + 1$, then $c_0' + c_1' + \cdots + c_{255}' = 511$ $(c_i' \geq 1)$. Then using the knowledge of combinatorics, it is easy to get that the number of possible multisets is $\binom{510}{255}$. □

Note that, in fact, not only for $l = 0$ but also for each $0 \leq l \leq 15$, the multiset $\{x_{5,l}^0 \oplus x_{5,l}^0, x_{5,l}^0 \oplus x_{5,l}^1, \cdots, x_{5,l}^0 \oplus x_{5,l}^{255}\}$ is fully determined by 16 byte parameters. For the sake of clarity, we use $l = 0$ in the following attacks, that is, the active byte of δ-set and the nonzero input/output differences of the particular differential are both taken to be byte 0.

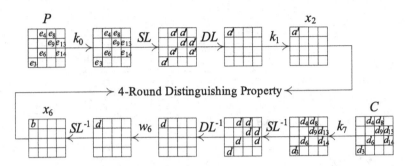

e_i, d, b, d, d_i : nonzero bytes.

Fig. 3. 7-Round attack on ARIA-192/256

The probability of this 4-round differential is 2^{-120}, and thus it is expected that 2^{120} randomly chosen pairs with difference only in byte 0 would contain one pair satisfying the differential. Moreover, since each δ-set contains 2^8 plaintexts which provide about 2^{15} pairs with difference in byte 0, a collection of 2^{105} randomly chosen δ-sets in which byte 0 is active is expected to contain a right pair with respect to the differential. That is, we have to consider as many as 2^{113} chosen plaintexts to exploit the particular differential.

4   Meet-in-the-Middle Attacks on Round-Reduced ARIA

In this section, we present 7/8/9 rounds meet-in-the-middle attacks on ARIA based on our new distinguishing properties.

4.1   7-Round Attack on ARIA-192/256

For the 7-round attack on ARIA-192/256, we add one round before the 4-round distinguisher and 2 rounds after, see Fig. 3. The procedure of the attack is depicted as follows:

Precomputation Phase. Compute the 2^{128} possible values of the multisets according to Observation 1 and store them in a hash table. The size of this table is 2^{130} 128-bit blocks by using the representation method introduced in [5, 8] which compresses such a 256-byte multiset into 512 bits of space from the point of view of information theory. The time complexity of constructing the table is 2^{128} partial encryptions on 256 messages, which is equivalent to 2^{132} encryptions.

Online Phase.

– **Phase A: Detecting the right pair**

1. Choose 2^{57} structures of plaintexts with the form that the bytes $3, 4, 6, 8, 9,$ 13, 14 assume 2^{56} possible values and the rest of the bytes are constants. Hence each structure contains 2^{56} plaintexts and we can collect about 2^{168} plaintext pairs with nonzero differences in bytes $3, 4, 6, 8, 9, 13, 14$. Encrypt the plaintexts in each structure and store the corresponding ciphertexts in a hash table, then keep the pairs with no difference in bytes $0, 1, 2, 5, 7, 10,$ 11, 12, 15. Since this is a 72-bit filtering, about 2^{96} pairs remain.

2. For each remaining pair, guess bytes $3, 4, 6, 8, 9, 13, 14$ of k_0 and check whether the difference in the state x_2 is nonzero only in byte 0. For each k_0 guess, there are about $2^{96-48} = 2^{48}$ pairs remaining. The time complexity of this step is about $(2 \cdot 2^{96} \cdot 2^8 \cdot \frac{1}{16} + 2 \cdot 2^{96} \cdot 2^8 \cdot 2^8 \cdot \frac{1}{16} \cdot 6)/7 = (2^{101} + 2^{109} \cdot 6)/7$ encryptions.

3. For each remaining pair, guess bytes $3, 4, 6, 8, 9, 13, 14$ of k_7 and check whether the difference in the state x_6 is nonzero only in byte 0. For each k_7 guess, about $2^{48-48} = 1$ pair is expected to remain. The operations carried in this step are about $(2 \cdot 2^{48} \cdot 2^{56} \cdot 2^8 \cdot \frac{1}{16} + 2 \cdot 2^{48} \cdot 2^{56+8} \cdot 2^8 \cdot \frac{1}{16} \cdot 6)/7 = (2^{109} + 2^{117} \cdot 6)/7$ encryptions.

- **Phase B: Constructing and checking the δ-set**
  1. Take one message of the right pair, denote it by P^0, and find its δ-set using the knowledge of bytes $3, 4, 6, 8, 9, 13, 14$ of k_0. This is done by taking $y^0_{1,i}(i = 3, 4, 6, 8, 9, 13, 14)$, XORing it with the 255 possible values $\{V^1, V^2, \cdots, V^{255}\}$ each of which has the same nonzero 8-bit value only in bytes $3, 4, 6, 8, 9, 13, 14$ (i.e. for each $1 \leqslant i \leqslant 255$, $V^i_3 = V^i_4 = V^i_6 = V^i_8 = V^i_9 = V^i_{13} = V^i_{14} \neq 0$ and $V^i_j = 0(0 \leqslant j \leqslant 15, j \neq 3, 4, 6, 8, 9, 13, 14)$, V^i_j denotes the j-th byte of V^i), and decrypting the 255 obtained values through round 1 using the known subkey bytes. Thus the resulting 255 plaintexts are the other members of the δ-set.
  2. $k_{7,i}(i = 3, 4, 6, 8, 9, 13, 14)$ are known, then we guess byte 0 of w_6 and partially decrypt the ciphertexts of δ-set to obtain the multiset $\{x^0_{6,0} \oplus x^0_{6,0}, x^0_{6,0} \oplus x^1_{6,0}, \cdots, x^0_{6,0} \oplus x^{255}_{6,0}\}$. Then check if the multiset exists in the hash table built in precomputation phase. If not, discard the subkey guess with certainty.

- **Phase C: Exhaustive search the rest of the key:** For each remaining subkey guess, find the remaining key bytes by exhaustive search.

From the description above, it is clear that the time complexity of the online phase is dominated by phase A which mainly includes: encrypting $2^{57+56} = 2^{113}$ chosen plaintexts needs 2^{113} encryptions, and guessing subkeys and detecting the right pair part processes about $(2^{101} + 2^{109} \cdot 6 + 2^{109} + 2^{117} \cdot 6)/7 = (2^{101} + 2^{109} \cdot 7 + 2^{117} \cdot 6)/7 \approx 2^{116.8}$ encryptions (Early abort technique [16] is applied to reduce the complexity in this part).

Besides, the time complexity of the precomputation phase is 2^{132} encryptions. Therefore, the data complexity of the attack is 2^{113} chosen plaintexts, the time complexity of the attack is about $2^{113} + 2^{116.8} + 2^{132} \approx 2^{132}$ encryptions, and the memory complexity is about 2^{130} 128-bit blocks dominated by storing the 2^{128} multisets in the precomputation phase.

4.2   Extension to 8-Round Attack on ARIA-256

Based on the same precomputation with the 7-round attack on ARIA-256 above, we add one more round at the bottom of the 7-round attack and mount a 8-round attack on ARIA-256. In this attack, we also collect 2^{113} plaintexts with the same form as the 7-round attack presented above. Then we need to guess the full k_8, and for each guess, decrypt all the ciphertexts through the last round and apply the 7-round attack. Consequently, the data complexity of the attack is 2^{113} chosen plaintexts, the memory requirement is 2^{130} 128-bit blocks (as in the 7-round attack above), and the time complexity is dominated by the detection of the right pair, which is mainly about $(2^{113} \cdot 2^{128} + 2 \cdot 2^{96} \cdot 2^{128} \cdot 2^8 \cdot \frac{1}{16} + 2 \cdot 2^{96} \cdot 2^{128+8} \cdot 2^8 \cdot \frac{1}{16} \cdot 7 + 2 \cdot 2^{48} \cdot 2^{128+56+8} \cdot 2^8 \cdot \frac{1}{16} \cdot 6)/8 = (2^{241} + 2^{229} + 2^{237} \cdot 7 + 2^{245} \cdot 6)/8 \approx 2^{244.61}$ encryptions.

4.3   Attack on 7-Round ARIA-128

Based on Observation 1, 16 bytes parameters generate 2^{128} possible multisets resulting in too huge complexities of the precomputation to attack ARIA-128. Hence, we slightly modify our Observation 1 by letting the differential satisfying $\Delta y_{1,0} = \Delta z_{4,0}$ so that one byte parameter is reduced. And the spacial variant of Observation 1 is described as follows:

Observation 2. *Consider the encryption of a δ-set $\{P^0, P^1, \cdots, P^{255}\}$ through four ARIA rounds, where P^0 belongs to a right pair with respect to the 4-round differential whose input and output differences are both nonzero in a single byte 0 and $\Delta y_{1,0} = \Delta z_{4,0}$, the (un-ordered) multiset $\{x_{5,0}^0 \oplus x_{5,0}^0, x_{5,0}^0 \oplus x_{5,0}^1, \cdots, x_{5,0}^0 \oplus x_{5,0}^{255}\}$ is fully determined by the following 15 byte parameters:*

- *$\Delta y_{1,0}$ of the right pair,*
- *$x_{2,i}^0 (i = 3, 4, 6, 8, 9, 13, 14)$,*
- *$y_{4,i}^0 (i = 3, 4, 6, 8, 9, 13, 14)$.*

Hence, the multiset can assume only 2^{120} values out of the $\binom{510}{255} \approx 2^{505.2}$ theoretically possible values.

Based on this observation, the attack on 7-round ARIA-128 becomes possible. The memory complexity of precomputation phase as the dominant part is 2^{122} 128-bit blocks to store the 2^{120} multisets. The time complexity of constructing the hash table in the precomputation phase is 2^{120} partial encryptions on 256 messages which is equivalent to 2^{124} encryptions. Since $\Delta z_{4,0} = \Delta y_{1,0}$, the probability of the particular differential is 2^{-128} that is lower than the previous one, and 2^{128} randomly chosen pairs with difference only in byte 0 are expected to contain one pair satisfying the differential. Thus 2^{113} randomly chosen δ-sets each of which contains 2^8 plaintexts and provide about 2^{15} pairs with difference in byte 0 are expected to contain a right pair with respect to the differential. As a result, 2^{121} chosen plaintexts are required to exploit the particular differential, so data complexity of the attack is 2^{121} chosen plaintexts which are provided by 2^{65} structures of 2^{56} plaintexts. During the online phase, we need guess 7 bytes of k_0, 7 bytes of k_7 and 1 byte of w_6 to detect the right pair, which contain one more subkey byte guess than the attacks above. The operations of this part mainly include: encrypting 2^{121} plaintexts needs 2^{121} encryptions, and guessing subkeys and detecting the right pair part processes about $(2 \cdot 2^{176-72} \cdot 2^8 \cdot \frac{1}{16} + 2 \cdot 2^{176-72} \cdot 2^8 \cdot 2^8 \cdot \frac{1}{16} \cdot 7 + 2 \cdot 2^{176-72-48} \cdot 2^{56+8} \cdot 2^8 \cdot \frac{1}{16} \cdot 7)/7 = (2^{109} + 2^{117} \cdot 7 + 2^{125} \cdot 7)/7 \approx 2^{125}$ encryptions. Taking into account the precomputation, the complexity of the attack on 7-round ARIA-128 is about $2^{121} + 2^{125} + 2^{124} \approx 2^{125.7}$ encryptions.

All in all, the data complexity of the 7-round attack on ARIA-128 is 2^{121} chosen plaintexts, the memory complexity is 2^{122} 128-bit blocks, and the time complexity is about $2^{125.7}$ encryptions. In terms of the meet-in-the-middle attack, our attack is the first 7-round attack on ARIA-128.

4.4   9-Round Attack on ARIA-256

Inspired by Observations 1 and 2, we present a 5-round meet-in-the-middle distinguisher on ARIA to attack 9-round ARIA-256.

Observation 3. *Consider the encryption of a δ-set $\{P^0, P^1, \cdots, P^{255}\}$ through five ARIA rounds, where P^0 belongs to a right pair with respect to the 5-round differential of Fig. 4 (i.e. both the input and output differences are nonzero in a single byte 0 and $\Delta y_{1,0} = \Delta z_{5,0}$), the (un-ordered) multiset $\{x^0_{6,0} \oplus x^0_{6,0}, x^0_{6,0} \oplus x^1_{6,0}, \cdots, x^0_{6,0} \oplus x^{255}_{6,0}\}$ is fully determined by the following 31 byte parameters:*

- *$\Delta y_{1,0}$ of the right pair,*
- *$x^0_{2,i}(i = 3, 4, 6, 8, 9, 13, 14)$,*
- *the full 16 bytes of x^0_3,*
- *$y^0_{5,i}(i = 3, 4, 6, 8, 9, 13, 14)$.*

Hence, the multiset can assume only 2^{248} values out of the $\binom{510}{255} \approx 2^{505.2}$ theoretically possible values.

The proof similar to Observation 1 using the meet-in-the-middle argument is omitted, and we directly discuss the attack on 9-round ARIA-256 based on this observation. We apply the 5-round distinguisher in rounds 2 to 6, and the attack is from round 1 to 9. After guessing the full k_9 and decrypting all the ciphertexts through the last round as 8-round attack, the attack procedure is almost the same as the 7-round attack on ARIA-128. The required data is 2^{121} chosen plaintexts (as in the 7-round attack on ARIA-128 due to the same probability of the two differentials), the memory complexity is 2^{250} 128-bit blocks to store the 2^{248} possible multisets, and the time complexity is about $2^{252}(pre) + (2^{121} \cdot 2^{128} + 2 \cdot 2^{176-72} \cdot 2^{128} \cdot 2^8 \cdot \frac{1}{16} + 2 \cdot 2^{176-72} \cdot 2^{128+8} \cdot 2^8 \cdot \frac{1}{16} \cdot 7 + 2 \cdot 2^{176-72-48} \cdot 2^{128+56+8} \cdot 2^8 \cdot \frac{1}{16} \cdot 7)/9(online) \approx 2^{252} + (2^{249} + 2^{237} + 2^{245} \cdot 7 + 2^{253} \cdot 7)/9 \approx 2^{253.37}$ encryptions. This attack is also the first 9-round attack on ARIA-256 in terms of the meet-in-the-middle attack.

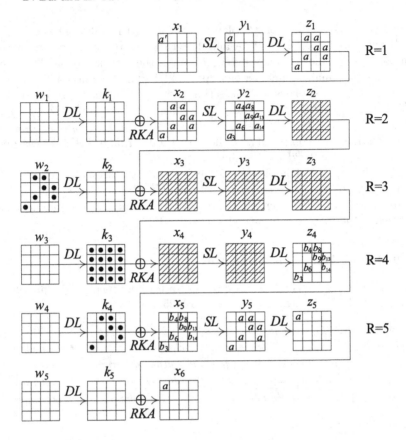

a', a, a_i, b_i : nonzero bytes ;   ▨ : unknown bytes ;

▣ : subkey bytes that can be deduced .

Fig. 4. The 5-Round differential characteristic used in our attacks

5   Conclusion

In this work, by using the ideas of multisets and truncated differential characteristics, we present some new and better 4-round and 5-round meet-in-the-middle distinguishing properties of ARIA which involve much fewer bytes parameters than previous work. Utilizing these distinguishers, we mount meet-in-the-middle attacks on 7-round ARIA-128/192/256 and 8/9-round ARIA-256, with time complexities $2^{125.7}$ encryptions for attack on 7-round ARIA-128, 2^{132} for 7-round ARIA-192/256, $2^{244.61}$ for 8-round ARIA-256 and $2^{253.37}$ for 9-round ARIA-256, respectively. All the above results are much better than previous meet-in-the-middle attacks. Although meet-in-the-middle attack do not break much more rounds of ARIA than other attack methods, such as truncated differential and linear cryptanalysis leading to the known best results, our attacks on 7-round ARIA-128 and 9-round ARIA-256 are both the first results for ARIA in the framework of meet-in-the-middle attack, and the other attacks are also mounted with much lower complexities than previous meet-in-the-middle attacks. The future work might focus on study of the key relations of ARIA which is significant for attacking ARIA block cipher, although its key schedule is complicated and there is few available result.

References

1. Biryukov, A., De Cannière, C., Lano, J., Ors, S.B., Preneel, B.: Security and Performance Analysis of ARIA, Version 1.2, 7 January 2004
2. Chen S., Xu T.: Biclique Attack of the Full ARIA-256. IACR eprint archive. https://eprint.iacr.org/2012/011.pdf
3. Daemen, J., Rijmen, V.: The Design of Rijndael: AES—The Advanced Encryption Standard. Springer, Heidelberg (2002)
4. Demirci, H., Selçuk, A.A.: A meet-in-the-middle attack on 8-round AES. In: Nyberg, K. (ed.) FSE 2008. LNCS, vol. 5086, pp. 116–126. Springer, Heidelberg (2008)
5. Derbez, P., Fouque, P.-A., Jean, J.: Improved key recovery attacks on reduced-round AES in the single-key setting. In: Johansson, T., Nguyen, P.Q. (eds.) EURO-CRYPT 2013. LNCS, vol. 7881, pp. 371–387. Springer, Heidelberg (2013)
6. Diffie, W., Hellman, M.: Special feature exhaustive cryptanalysis of the NBS data encryption standard. Computer 10, 74–84 (1977)
7. Du, C., Chen, J.: Impossible differential cryptanalysis of ARIA reduced to 7 rounds. In: Heng, S.-H., Wright, R.N., Goi, B.-M. (eds.) CANS 2010. LNCS, vol. 6467, pp. 20–30. Springer, Heidelberg (2010)
8. Dunkelman, O., Keller, N., Shamir, A.: Improved single-key attacks on 8-round AES-192 and AES-256. In: Abe, M. (ed.) ASIACRYPT 2010. LNCS, vol. 6477, pp. 158–176. Springer, Heidelberg (2010)
9. Fleischmann, E., Forler, C., Gorski, M., Lucks, S.: New boomerang attacks on ARIA. In: Gong, G., Gupta, K.C. (eds.) INDOCRYPT 2010. LNCS, vol. 6498, pp. 163–175. Springer, Heidelberg (2010)
10. Korean Agency for Technology and Standards (KATS): 128 bit block encryption algorithm ARIA, KS X 1213:2004, December 2004 (in Korean)
11. Kwon, D., Kim, J., Park, S., Sung, S.H., et al.: New block cipher: ARIA. In: Lim, J.-I., Lee, D.-H. (eds.) ICISC 2003. LNCS, vol. 2971, pp. 432–445. Springer, Heidelberg (2004)
12. Li, P., Sun, B., Li, C.: Integral cryptanalysis of ARIA. In: Bao, F., Yung, M., Lin, D., Jing, J. (eds.) Inscrypt 2009. LNCS, vol. 6151, pp. 1–14. Springer, Heidelberg (2010)
13. Li, R., Sun, B., Zhang, P., Li, C.: New Impossible Differential Cryptanalysis of ARIA. IACR eprint archive. https://eprint.iacr.org/2008/227.pdf
14. Li, Y., Wu, W., Zhang, L.: Integral attacks on reduced-round ARIA block cipher. In: Kwak, J., Deng, R.H., Won, Y., Wang, G. (eds.) ISPEC 2010. LNCS, vol. 6047, pp. 19–29. Springer, Heidelberg (2010)
15. Liu, Z., Gu, D., Liu, Y., Li, J., Li, W.: Linear cryptanalysis of ARIA block cipher. In: Qing, S., Susilo, W., Wang, G., Liu, D. (eds.) ICICS 2011. LNCS, vol. 7043, pp. 242–254. Springer, Heidelberg (2011)

16. Lu, J., Kim, J.-S., Keller, N., Dunkelman, O.: Improving the efficiency of impossible differential cryptanalysis of reduced camellia and MISTY1. In: Malkin, T. (ed.) CT-RSA 2008. LNCS, vol. 4964, pp. 370–386. Springer, Heidelberg (2008)
17. National Security Research Institute: Specification of ARIA, Version 1.0, January 2005. http://www.nsri.re.kr/ARIA/doc/ARIAspecification-e.pdf
18. Tang, X., Sun, B., Li, R., Li, C., Yin, J.: A meet-in-the-middle attack on reduced-round ARIA. J. Syst. Softw. **84**(10), 1685–1692 (2011)
19. Wu, W., Zhang, W., Feng, D.: Impossible differential cryptanalysis of reduced-round ARIA and Camellia. J. Comput. Sci. Technol. **22**(3), 449–456 (2007)

Establishing Equations: The Complexity of Algebraic and Fast Algebraic Attacks Revisited

Lin Jiao[1,2]([✉]), Bin Zhang[3], and Mingsheng Wang[3]

[1] TCA, Institute of Software, Chinese Academy of Sciences,
Beijing 100190, People's Republic of China
jiaolin@is.iscas.ac.cn
[2] Graduate University of Chinese Academy of Sciences,
Beijing 100049, People's Republic of China
[3] State Key Laboratory of Information Security,
Institute of Information Engineering, Chinese Academy of Sciences,
Beijing 100093, People's Republic of China

Abstract. Algebraic and fast algebraic attacks have posed serious threats to some deployed LFSR-based stream ciphers. Previous works on this topic focused on reducing the time complexity by lowering the degree of the equations, speeding up the substitution step by Fast Fourier Transform and analysis of Boolean functions exhibiting the optimal algebraic immunity. All of these works shared and overlooked a common base, i.e., establishing an adequate equation system first, which actually in some cases dominates the time or memory complexity if the direct methods are used, especially in fast algebraic attacks. In this paper, we present a complete analysis of the establishing equation procedure and show how the Frobenius form of the monomial state rewriting matrix can be applied to considerably reduce the complexity of this step.

Keywords: Algebraic attack · Stream cipher · Establishing equations · Coefficient sequence

1 Introduction

Algebraic and fast algebraic attacks [1,2,5,7] are powerful cryptanalytic methods for LFSR-based stream ciphers [3,4,8,11,13,16], which exploit some low degree algebraic relations between the generated keystream and the secret initial state of the underlying LFSRs. Usually, there are three steps in an algebraic attack, i.e., finding annihilators [12] of the involved function f or $f + 1$, deriving an algebraic equation system, and finally solving the resultant system to restore the secret initial state. The first step can be pre-computed off-line, while the other steps have to be executed online since the time instants of the keystream bits used to establish the equation system are unknown in advance.

In [5], fast algebraic attacks are proposed to substantially reduce the complexity by utilizing the consecutive keystream available to the adversary.

© Springer International Publishing Switzerland 2015
Y. Desmedt (Ed.): ISC 2013, LNCS 7807, pp. 169–184, 2015.
DOI: 10.1007/978-3-319-27659-5_12

The main idea is to eliminate the high degree parts of the localized equations, which have a recursive structure, by the well-known Berlekamp-Massey algorithm in the off-line phase. Several improvements are also possible, e.g., a parallelizable pre-computation algorithm was presented in [1] by Armknecht and in [6], Hawkes and Rose provided by far the most efficient pre-computation algorithm using Fast Fourier Transform (FFT). A fast algebraic attack also consists of three steps, i.e., finding localized equations, utilizing the pre-computation algorithm to eliminate the high degree parts and expanding the low degree relations; substituting the keystream bits into the low degree relations to obtain an algebraic system in the initial state variables; solving the algebraic equations. The second step was analyzed and optimized in [6]. Algebraic and fast algebraic attacks have given the best analyses of a series of primitives, e.g., Toyocrypt, LILI-128, WG-7, Sfinks, E0 and Sober-t32.

In this paper, we present a complete analysis of the establishing equation procedure in various algebraic and fast algebraic attacks and show how the Frobenius form of the monomial state rewriting matrix can be applied to considerably reduce the complexity of this step. Our method is adapted to the following attack categories: algebraic (AA) and fast algebraic attack (FAA), general algebraic and fast algebraic attack (GA-FAA) and the Rønjom-Helleseth attack (R-H), respectively. In each case, we make a comparison study of the methods and complexities. For the AA, we bring in the concept of matrix Frobenius form and show how the direct methods of normal polynomial multiplication can be replaced. For the FAA, we first show that the memory complexity required to store the low degree parts of localized equations is $O((D + E) \cdot E)$, instead of $O(E^2)$, i.e., the one used to estimate the memory complexity of the FAA, where E and D ($D \gg E$) are the attack parameters. Further, if we do this step online by the direct methods, the time complexity may exceed by a big margin those of solving equations and substituting keystream bits, i.e., the claimed total time complexity of the attacks. To resolve this problem, we combine the Frobenius form of the monomial state rewriting matrix with some time/memory tradeoff techniques. For the GA-FAA, we first investigate the features of the blocks in the Frobenius form of the monomial state rewriting matrix and point out that the maximum dimension of the blocks is determined by the length of the LFSR. Based on this finding, we present the method of establishing equations online with coefficients being polynomials of keystream bits and complexity analysis.

This paper is organized as follows. Some preliminaries of various algebraic attacks are introduced in Sect. 2. In Sects. 3 and 4, we describe the attack process, and discuss the direct and our new methods for establishing equations in the AA and FAA respectively. In Sect. 5, we further analyze the features of the blocks in the Frobenius form of the monomial state rewriting matrix and present the method for establishing equations in the GA-FAA. Finally, some conclusions are given in Sect. 6.

2   Preliminaries

The filter generator is an important building block in many stream ciphers and the basic/typical model in various algebraic attacks. It consists of an LFSR of n-bit length and a nonlinear filter function f. The state bit s_t of the LFSR is generated from the LFSR characteristic polynomial $r(x) = \sum_{i=0}^{n} a_i x^i$ ($a_n = a_0 = 1$) and the LFSR initial state $S_0 = (s_0, s_1, \ldots, s_{n-1})$ with the recursion $s_{t+n} = \sum_{i=0}^{n-1} a_i s_{t+i}$. The successor state S_{t+1} is derived from the predecessor state S_t according to an invertible linear mapping $L : GF(2)^n \to GF(2)^n$, called state update function deduced from $r(x)$, by $S_{t+1} = L(S_t)$. The function L can be represented by an $n \times n$ matrix $\mathbf{L}$ over $GF(2)$ as follows

$$
\mathbf{L} = \begin{pmatrix} 0 & 1 & \cdots & 0 \\ \vdots & \vdots & & \vdots \\ 0 & 0 & \cdots & 1 \\ a_0 & a_1 & \cdots & a_{n-1} \end{pmatrix},
$$

called state update matrix. Note that $S_t = L^t(S_0)$. The filter function f is assumed to have m input variables, corresponding to $m(m \leq n)$ cell positions of the LFSR chosen as taps. The keystream bit z_t is generated by applying the filter function to the current state as $z_t = f(S_t) = f(L^t(S_0))$.

The main idea of algebraic attacks is to derive a system of low degree multivariate equations from the underlying cryptosystem and then solve it to retrieve the secret information. At first, how to find an algebraic system for each cipher remains the most challenging part of the task. However, for the LFSR-based stream ciphers such as the filter generator, this is not a problem. The construction itself directly depicts such an algebraic system. Then there are several ways to solve the resultant system, e.g., linearization, XL and Gröbner basis. Usually, the methods of XL and Gröbner basis need fewer keystream bits, but the complexities are hard to evaluate, which can be quite huge in some cases. So far, most of the complexity results of algebraic attacks are based on linearization.

3   Algebraic Attacks

We first introduce two notations on algebraic attacks.

Definition 1. *The annihilator of a Boolean function f with m input variables is another Boolean function g with m input variables such that $f \cdot g = 0$.*

Definition 2. *For a given Boolean function f, the algebraic immunity $AI(f)$ is the minimum value d such that f or $f + 1$ has a nonzero annihilator of degree d.*

It was shown that $AI(f) \leq \min\{\lceil \frac{m}{2} \rceil, \deg(f)\}$ for any f with m inputs [12].

Now, let us describe the basic theory of algebraic attacks on a filter generator. In the off-line phase, the adversary first finds an annihilator g of the filter function

f (or $f + 1$), usually the one that admits a nonzero annihilator of degree AI^1. Assume d is the degree of g. Then given several keystream bits at different time instants with $z_t = 1$ (or $z_t = 0$), he obtains a system of low degree equations as:

$$0 = f(L^t(S_0)) \cdot g(L^t(S_0)) = z_t \cdot g(L^t(S_0)) = g(L^t(S_0)), \qquad \text{if } z_t = 1,$$
$$(\text{or } 0 = (f(L^t(S_0)) + 1) \cdot g(L^t(S_0)) = (z_t + 1) \cdot g(L^t(S_0)) = g(L^t(S_0)), \text{ if } z_t = 0).$$

This step has to be executed online, since the time instants of the keystream bits used to establish the equation system cannot be determined in advance. Then, the adversary converts the system into a linear one with $D = \sum_{i=0}^{d} \binom{n}{i}$ variables. Since there are D unknowns, around D linear equations, i.e., D keystream bits, are required to get a solvable system. Finally, the adversary solves the linear system and recovers S_0. The complete description is as follows.

Off-line phase
1: Find a nonzero annihilator g of the filter function f (or $f + 1$).
Online phase Given $z_t = 1$ and the corresponding time instants (or $z_t = 0$ and the corresponding time instants).
1: Establish equations like $g(L^t(S_0)) = 0$ and linearize them.
2: Solve the resultant system.

So far, algebraic attacks have been successfully applied to Toyocrypt, LILI-128, Sober-t32, WG-7 and Sfinks.

To date, the time complexity estimation of the attacks is confined to Step 2 online, which always exploits the Gaussian reduction, i.e., a linear system of D variables can be solved in time $O(D^w)$, where w is usually taken to be $\log_2 7$. The memory complexity of the attacks is $O(D^2)$, which is used to store the coefficient matrix of the linear system. Obviously, the time complexity of Step 1 has not been taken into consideration yet. Normally, there is a simple and straightforward method for establishing equations in this case.

3.1   Simple Method: Polynomial Multiplication

Let us take a closer look at the above diagram. At Step 1 in the online phase, we first use the recursion of S_0 to represent S_t as $S_t = L^t(S_0) = \mathbf{L}^t \cdot S_0^T$, where S_0^T denotes the transpose of S_0. Then we substitute it into the annihilator whose algebraic normal form (ANF) is $g = \sum_{A, 0 \leq wt(A) \leq d} c_A X^A$ with coefficients $c_A \in GF(2)$. There are n input binary variables $X = x_0, \ldots, x_{n-1}$ and for the multi-indices $A \in GF(2)^n$, denote the Hamming weight of A by $wt(A)$. Next, polynomial multiplication is used to expand $g(S_t)$, after which simplify the resultant system by merging similar terms. Finally, linearization is done.

---

[1] Even though more annihilators are taken into consideration, the complexity for the establishing equation step will not change for the total equation number of the system is fixed.

Now, let us analyze the complexity of this method. First, we give the complexity for representing S_t by S_0, which is based on the following theorem.

Theorem 1. *The complexity for computing $\mathbf{L}^{t+1}$ given $\mathbf{L}^t$ is $2n$.*

Thus for every state updating, the complexity for calculating $\mathbf{L}^t$, i.e., the representation of S_t is $2n$. Next, let us calculate the complexity for polynomial multiplication. For simplicity, we first consider the contribution from a single monomial in $g(S_t)$, say

$$S_t^A = s_{t+\alpha_1} s_{t+\alpha_2} \cdots s_{t+\alpha_{wt(A)}} = \left(\sum_{j=0}^{n-1} l_{\alpha_1,j}^t s_j \right) \left(\sum_{j=0}^{n-1} l_{\alpha_2,j}^t s_j \right) \cdots \left(\sum_{j=0}^{n-1} l_{\alpha_{wt(A)},j}^t s_j \right)$$

where $0 \le \alpha_i \le n-1$ $(1 \le i \le wt(A))$ are the positions of the components equal to 1 in A. Since each factor contains n terms, and there are $wt(A)$ factors, the complexity for expanding S_t^A is $n^{wt(A)}$, which can be realized by the data structure of linked list for polynomials in practice. In addition, it takes $n^i \cdot \binom{m}{i}$ computations for all the monomials of degree i within $g(X)$ due to the fact that the number of monomials with $wt(A) = i$ can be $\binom{m}{i}$, where m is the number of taps chosen by the filter function. Finally, taking all the monomials without the linear ones into consideration, the complexity for expanding $g(S_t)$ is $\sum_{i=2}^d n^i \binom{m}{i}$. The complexities for merging similar terms and linearization are ignored without further analysis. Note that here all the operations are not numerical, but symbolic. As stated above, we need to establish D equations. We can exploit $O(D)$ to estimate the domain of the given D keystream bits[2]. Thus the total complexity by direct substitution and polynomial multiplication is $C_1 = D \cdot \sum_{i=2}^d n^i \binom{m}{i} + 2n \cdot O(D)$.

3.2 Improved Method: Shift and Update from the Feedback Polynomial

We have another method here to establish equations, which is much faster than the simple one. We can compute $g(S_{t+1})$ by updating $g(S_t)$ from the feedback polynomial, more precisely, we can first derive all the factors in the monomials of $g(S_t)$ by a shift from s_i to s_{i+1} where $0 \le i \le n-1$, second substitute s_n into $\sum_{i=0}^{n-1} a_i s_i$, and then expand the monomials involving s_n, after which simplify the resultant system by merging similar terms. This method make the most of the result of the previous step. The main cost is for the substitution of s_n, calling for n operations for each, and there are at most nD operations for one equation. Thus it leads to an overall time complexity equal to $C_2 = nD^2$.

3.3 New Method: Frobenius Form of the Monomial State Rewriting Matrix

In order to further reduce the complexity, here we propose a new method using the Frobenius form of the monomial state rewriting matrix for establishing

---

[2] The range can be just a constant multiple of D, since 0 and 1 have around equal probability of occurrence for the randomness of the keystream bits.

equations. At first, we bring in the notations of matrix Frobenius form in [9] and the monomial state rewriting matrix mentioned in [6].

Definition 3. *A D-dimensional column vector with each component being a monomial of degree d or less in binary variables $x_0, \ldots, x_{n-1}$ is called a monomial vector.*

The ordering of the monomial components is arbitrary; for consistency we will enumerate using lower subscripts first. Substitute S_t into the monomial vector, and obtain the monomial state $M_d(t)$ at time t. There is a mapping from one monomial state to the successor as a matrix product, called monomial state rewriting matrix, as $M_d(t+1) = R_d \cdot M_d(t)$. Then $M_d(t) = R_d^t \cdot M_d$, where $M_d = M_d(0)$ is related to the initial state. Note that the monomial state rewriting matrix R_d only depends on the LFSR and the degree d. Each component of the next monomial state is just a linear function of the original monomial state components, whose coefficient vector constitutes one row of R_d. Moreover, R_d is invertible due to the invertibility of the LFSR. Any Boolean function can be represented as a product of its coefficient vector with the monomial vector. Let g' be the coefficient vector of g, then $g(S_t) = g' \cdot M_d(t)$. Combining these two relations, we get another expression of $g(S_t)$ as $g(S_t) = g' \cdot M_d(t) = g' \cdot R_d^t \cdot M_d$.

Theorem 2 (Linear Algebra). *Let K be a field and A be an $n \times n$ matrix over K. Then A is similar to a unique block diagonal matrix over K*

$$
A \sim \begin{pmatrix} P_1 & & & \\ & P_2 & & \\ & & \ddots & \\ & & & P_u \end{pmatrix}, \quad P_i = \begin{pmatrix} 0 & 1 & \cdots & 0 \\ \vdots & \vdots & & \vdots \\ 0 & 0 & \cdots & 1 \\ p_0 & p_1 & \cdots & p_{n_i-1} \end{pmatrix}_{n_i \times n_i}
$$

where P_i is the $n_i \times n_i$ companion matrix of the monic polynomial $\mathfrak{p}_i(x) = x^{n_i} + \sum_{j=0}^{n_i-1} p_j x^j \in K[x]$; in addition, the polynomials $\mathfrak{p}_1, \mathfrak{p}_2, \ldots, \mathfrak{p}_u$ are the invariant factors of A over K such that $\mathfrak{p}_{i+1}$ divides $\mathfrak{p}_i$ for $i = 1, \ldots, u$. The block diagonal matrix with these properties is called the Frobenius form of A, also called the rational canonical form.

Corollary 1 (Linear Algebra). *Just change $P_1, \ldots, P_u$ to the companion matrices of the elementary divisors of A over K and other notations remain the same as those in Theorem 2. Then the conclusion of Theorem 2 is still valid.*

Obviously, $\mathfrak{p}_i(x)$ is the characteristic polynomial of the companion matrix P_i. Hereafter, we take the notation in Corollary 1 as the definition of the matrix Frobenius form. It is known that the cost for computing the Frobenius form of a $D \times D$ matrix equals to the number of field operations required to multiply two $D \times D$ matrices [17,18]. In our context, the field is $GF(2)$ and the complexity can be estimated as $O(D^w)$ bit operations.

Now we use the method of matrix Frobenius form to establish equations. As will be shown, this can reduce the complexity of matrix multiplication. Recall the concrete steps of algebraic attacks. Here we add some procedures to the original process.

Off-line phase
1: Find a nonzero annihilator g of the filter function f (or $f + 1$).
2: Compute the monomial state rewriting matrix R_d depending on the LFSR and degree d of g.
3: Compute the Frobenius form of the monomial state rewriting matrix R_d, i.e., $R_d = Q \cdot \hat{R}_d \cdot Q^{-1}$, where $\hat{R}_d$ is the Frobenius form and Q is the $D \times D$ transform matrix.
4: Compute $\hat{g} = g' \cdot Q$, where g' is the coefficient vector of g.

Online phase Given $z_t = 1$ and the corresponding time instants (or $z_t = 0$ and the corresponding time instants).
1: Establish and meanwhile linearize the equations in $\hat{M}_d$ as follows: $g(L^t(S_0)) = \hat{g} \cdot \hat{R}_d^t \cdot \hat{M}_d = 0$, where $\hat{M}_d$ denotes $Q^{-1} \cdot M_d$ introduced as the new unknowns.
2: Solve the resultant system.
3: Compute $M_d = Q \cdot \hat{M}_d$.

Now, we present the justifications of the new method. Substituting $R_d = Q \cdot \hat{R}_d \cdot Q^{-1}$ into $g(S_t) = g' \cdot R_d^t \cdot M_d$, we have

$$g(S_t) = g' \cdot (Q \cdot \hat{R}_d \cdot Q^{-1})^t \cdot M_d = g' \cdot Q \cdot \hat{R}_d^t \cdot Q^{-1} \cdot M_d = \hat{g} \cdot \hat{R}_d^t \cdot \hat{M}_d = 0.$$

Assume we have the coefficient vector $\hat{g} \cdot \hat{R}_d^{t_1}$ for t_1. For the next time t_2 ($t_2 > t_1$), we need to multiply $\hat{g} \cdot \hat{R}_d^{t_1}$ with $\hat{R}_d$ by ($t_2 - t_1$) times more to establish the equation, as shown below

$$\hat{g} \cdot \hat{R}_d^{t_2} = (\hat{g} \cdot \hat{R}_d^{t_1}) \cdot \underbrace{\hat{R}_d \cdots \hat{R}_d}_{t_2 - t_1}.$$

Since there are at most two nonzero elements in each column of $\hat{R}_d$ and the positions of the nonzero elements are fixed as the form in Corollary 1, it takes only $2D$ operations to multiply a D-dimensional row vector with $\hat{R}_d$. We need to do the multiplication $O(D)$ times, which should cover the domain of the given keystream bits and it takes $2D \cdot O(D) = O(D^2)$ in total.

It is following that we have already solved the linear equations in $\hat{M}_d$; then we can obtain M_d and S_0 by $M_d = Q \cdot \hat{M}_d$. Moreover, we just need to calculate the first n components to recover S_0, and this step costs $n \cdot D$ computations for a multiplication of an $n \times D$ matrix with a D-dimensional column vector. Just like the time complexity estimation of algebraic attacks before, the cost for the off-line phase is not reckoned in here. Thus, the total complexity by using the Frobenius form of the monomial state rewriting matrix approximates $C_3 = O(D^2)$. Moreover, Step 2-4 added off-line cost D^2, D^w, and D^2 computations respectively, i.e., the pre-computation of our method is reasonable for the attack. Table 1 shows that our new method is significantly outstanding.

Table 1. Comparison of the complexities for establishing equations in algebraic attacks

	n	d	m	C_1	C_2	$\mathbf{C_3}$	Solving equations
Toyocrypt	128	3	128	2^{58}	2^{44}	$\mathbf{2^{37}}$	2^{52}
LILI-128	89	4	10	2^{55}	2^{48}	$\mathbf{2^{42}}$	2^{60}
Sober-t32	544	10	160	2^{211}	2^{147}	$\mathbf{2^{138}}$	2^{194}
WG-7	161	3	7	2^{47}	2^{46}	$\mathbf{2^{39}}$	2^{54}
Sfinks	256	6	17	2^{100}	2^{85}	$\mathbf{2^{77}}$	2^{108}

4   Fast Algebraic Attacks

Recall that in a fast algebraic attack, the first task is to find a relation $f \cdot g = h$ with small $e = \deg(g)$ and $d = \deg(h)$ not too large, called "localized" equations. The function sequence $h(L^i(x_1, \cdots, x_n)), i = 0, 1, \ldots$ can be synthesized by an LFSR with linear complexity $D = \sum_{i=0}^{d} \binom{n}{i}$. Here the Berlekamp-Massey algorithm is used to compute the characteristic polynomial and get the coefficients $\alpha_i, i = 0, \ldots, D - 1$. Then the adversary can eliminate the right side of these localized equations as

$$0 = \sum_{i=0}^{D-1} \alpha_i h \left(L^{i+t} (S_0) \right) = \sum_{i=0}^{D-1} \alpha_i z_{t+i} g \left(L^{t+i} (S_0) \right).$$

Thus, the adversary eventually only needs to solve a linear system of $E = \sum_{i=0}^{e} \binom{n}{i}$ unknowns by linearization, and finally recovers the initial state S_0. Since there are E unknowns, around E linear equations, each requiring D consecutive keystream bits, are required to obtain a solvable system. Hence, around $D + E$ consecutive keystream bits are needed by using them as sliding windows. Unlike algebraic attacks, fast algebraic attacks can pre-compute the low degree parts $g(L^t(S_0)), t = 1, \ldots, D + E$, since the keystream bits are consecutive. The value e is restricted with $e < d$ and it is easily to deduce $d \geq AI(f)$. Here comes the complete description of an FAA.

Off-line phase
1: Find a low degree function g such that the degree of $h = f \cdot g$ is not too large.
2: Synthesize the characteristic polynomial of the function sequence $h(L^i(x_1, \cdots, x_n)), i = 0, 1, \ldots$ and obtain the corresponding coefficients $\alpha_i, i = 0, \ldots, D - 1$.
3: Calculate and linearize $g(L^t(S_0))$ for $t = 1, \ldots, D + E$.

Online phase Given $z_t, t = 1, \ldots, D + E$
1: Substitute the keystream bits into the equations $\sum_{i=0}^{D-1} \alpha_i z_{t+i} g \left(L^{t+i} (S_0) \right) = 0$ using FFT.
2: Solve the system of linear equations.

So far, fast algebraic attacks have been successfully applied to Toyocrypt, LILI-128, E0, WG-7 and Sfinks.

Finally, let us look at the complexity analysis of fast algebraic attacks. The complexity of Step 2 in the online phase is about $O(E^w)$ by the Gaussian reduction. In 2004, it was pointed out in [6] that the previous complexity estimation of Step 1 in the online phase is incorrect and a method based on FFT was proposed to decrease the complexity of the substitution step, where the optimal complexity is $2DE \cdot \log_2 E$. Nevertheless, it was also pointed out that the substitution operation is based on the fact that $g(L^t(S_0)), t = 1, \ldots, D + E$ are known and the complexity for establishing these equations has been ignored. The memory complexity of the FAA is claimed as $O(E^2)$, for storing the coefficient matrix of the linear system. In addition, if we pre-compute $g(L^t(S_0)), t = 1, \ldots, D + E$, then some extra memory is needed to store the pre-computed result in the size of $M_1 = (D + E) \cdot E$, which is much larger than the estimated memory complexity $O(E^2)$, please see Table 2.

Table 2. Comparison of the claimed memory complexity of fast algebraic attacks and the actual complexity for storing the pre-computed result

	n	(d, e)	m	M_1	Claimed memory
Toyocrypt	128	(3, 1)	128	2^{25}	2^{15}
LILI-128	89	(4, 2)	10	2^{33}	2^{24}
WG-7	161	(3, 1)	7	2^{27}	2^{16}
Sfinks	256	(8, 2)	17	2^{63}	2^{30}
E0	128	(4, 3)	128	2^{45}	2^{37}

Now, we analyze the methods for pre-computing $g(L^t(S_0))$ in the off-line phase in an FAA, which are similar to those in the AA.

4.1   Simple Method: Polynomial Multiplication

Just substitute S_t using the recursion representation of S_0 into the ANF of function g, then make the polynomial multiplication to expand $g(S_t)$ and merge similar terms at Step 3 in the off-line phase. The complexity analysis is similar to that in Sect. 3.1. We just replace d with e in the complexity each time when calculating $g(S_t)$. It also neglects the complexity for merging similar terms and linearization. Here we need to calculate for $D + E$ consecutive times, and this method costs

$$CC_1 = \left(\sum_{i=2}^{e} n^i \binom{m}{i} + 2n \right) \cdot (D + E)$$

computations in total.

4.2 Improved Method: Shift and Update from the Feedback Polynomial

Compute $g(S_{t+1})$ by updating $g(S_t)$ from the feedback polynomial at Step 3 in the off-line phase. The complexity analysis is similar to that in Sect. 3.2. We just replace D with E in the complexity each time when calculating $g(S_t)$. Here we need to calculate for $D + E$ consecutive times, and the time complexity equals $CC_2 = nE(D + E)$.

4.3 New Method: Frobenius Form of the Monomial State Rewriting Matrix

The notations are the same as before. Here some procedures are added to the original process of an FAA, shown in the next page.

Off-line phase
1: Find a low degree function g such that the degree of $h = f \cdot g$ is not too large.
2: Synthesize the characteristic polynomial of the function sequence $h(L^i(x_1, \cdots, x_n)), i = 0, 1, \ldots$ and obtain the corresponding coefficients $\alpha_i, i = 0, \ldots, D - 1$.
3: Calculate the monomial state rewriting matrix R_e depending on the LFSR and degree e of g.
4: Calculate the Frobenius form of the monomial state rewriting matrix R_e, i.e., $R_e = Q \cdot \hat{R}_e \cdot Q^{-1}$, where $\hat{R}_e$ is the Frobenius form and Q is the $E \times E$ transform matrix.
5: Calculate $\hat{g} = g' \cdot Q$, where g' is the coefficient vector of g.
6: Calculate $g(L^t(S_0)) = \hat{g} \cdot \hat{R}_e^t \cdot \hat{M}_e, t = 1, \ldots, D + E$, where $\hat{M}_e$ denotes $Q^{-1} \cdot M_e$ the new unknowns, and linearize $g(L^t(S_0))$ for $t = 1, \ldots, D + E$.

Online phase Given z_t for $t = 1, \ldots, D + E$
1: Substitute the keystream bits into the equations of the form below using FFT

$$\sum_{i=0}^{D-1} \alpha_i z_{t+i} g\left(L^{t+i}(S_0)\right) = \sum_{i=0}^{D-1} \alpha_i z_{t+i}(\hat{g} \cdot \hat{R}_e^{t+i} \cdot \hat{M}_e) = \left(\sum_{i=0}^{D-1} \alpha_i z_{t+i}(\hat{g} \cdot \hat{R}_e^{t+i})\right) \cdot \hat{M}_e = 0.$$

2: Solve the system of linear equations.
3: Calculate $M_e = Q \cdot \hat{M}_e$.

The complexity analysis is similar to that in Sect. 3.3. But it is a little different that we should take into consideration the complexities of all the added steps here, since they work together as a method in the pre-computation. The cost of the new Step 3 in the off-line phase is about E^2. As stated above, the complexity for calculating the Frobenius form of an $E \times E$ matrix is about $O(E^w)$. The off-line Step 5 costs E^2 computations. The complexity analysis for the off-line step 6 is similar to that in Sect. 3.3. We just replace d with e in the complexity each time for calculating $g(L^t(S_0))$, which results in $2E$. We need to do the multiplication $D + E$ times here. Thus, the total complexity by this method is

$$CC_3 = E^2 + O(E^w) + E^2 + 2E \cdot (D + E) = O(DE + E^w + E^2).$$

Table 3 shows the complexity comparison of these three methods for calculating $g(L^t(S_0)), t = 1, \ldots, D + E$ in the off-line phase. But the operation in our method is numerical and bit-size, which may run easier and faster than the symbolic one of the simple and improved methods. In addition, we do not need extra computations for merging similar terms and linearization.

Table 3. Comparison of the complexities for pre-computing $g(L^t(S_0)), t = 1, \ldots, D+E$

	n	(d, e)	m	CC_1	CC_2	CC_3	Substitution	Solving equations
Toyocrypt	128	$(3, 1)$	128	2^{26}	2^{32}	$\mathbf{2^{25}}$	2^{29}	2^{20}
LILI-128	89	$(4, 2)$	10	2^{40}	2^{39}	$\mathbf{2^{35}}$	2^{38}	2^{35}
WG-7	161	$(3, 1)$	7	2^{28}	2^{34}	$\mathbf{2^{27}}$	2^{31}	2^{22}
Sfinks	256	$(8, 2)$	17	2^{72}	2^{71}	$\mathbf{2^{63}}$	2^{68}	2^{43}
E0	128	$(4, 3)$	128	2^{63}	2^{52}	$\mathbf{2^{54}}$	2^{47}	2^{54}

In addition, the memory complexity required for pre-computation can be reduced as well by a combination of our method with the time/memory trade-off techniques. According to [6], when substituting the keystream bits into the equations, $g(L^t(S_0))$ at P consecutive times are required to calculate per FFT, as below (the notations in the formula are the same as those in [6])

$$A_\phi = \frac{1}{P} \cdot \sum_{t=1}^{P} \overline{a}(t) \cdot \Lambda_\phi(-t).$$

In the optimal conditions, P is approximately equal to $2E$. Thus, we need the memory of $M = 2E^2$ to store the corresponding $g(L^t(S_0)$s for performing FFT once. To lower the requirement of memory, we can pre-compute $g(L^t(S_0))$ at the first $2E$ times off-line and store them. Next, we compute $g(L^t(S_0))$ once more and drop the first one by sliding, once an FFT is calculated, thus we need to compute $g(L^t(S_0))$ at $D+E-2E = D-E$ time instants online. The memory and online time complexities are shown in Table 4. The table also indicates that even using the time/memory tradeoff techniques, the simple and improved methods still cannot reach the claimed memory and time complexities of fast algebraic attacks on some ciphers.

Table 4. Comparison of the trade-offs of the memory and online time complexities

	M	Claimed memory	CC_1'	CC_2'	CC_3'	Substitution	Solving equations
Toyocrypt	$\mathbf{2^{16}}$	2^{15}	2^{26}	2^{32}	$\mathbf{2^{25}}$	2^{29}	2^{20}
LILI-128	$\mathbf{2^{25}}$	2^{24}	2^{40}	2^{39}	$\mathbf{2^{33}}$	2^{38}	2^{35}
WG-7	$\mathbf{2^{17}}$	2^{16}	2^{28}	2^{34}	$\mathbf{2^{27}}$	2^{31}	2^{22}
Sfinks	$\mathbf{2^{31}}$	2^{30}	2^{72}	2^{71}	$\mathbf{2^{63}}$	2^{68}	2^{43}
E0	$\mathbf{2^{41}}$	2^{37}	2^{63}	2^{52}	$\mathbf{2^{45}}$	2^{47}	2^{54}

5 General Algebraic and Fast Algebraic Attacks

General algebraic and fast algebraic attacks exploit functions like

$$g(X) = \sum_{A,0 \leq wt(A) \leq d} c_A X^A$$

whose coefficients c_A are derived from simple polynomials of the keystream bits in a small range $z_t, \ldots, z_{t+\theta}$. This is the main difference between the general and classic attacks, e.g., the "ad-hoc" equations mentioned in [5] are of the following form

$$\begin{cases} 0 = \beta + \sum \beta_i s_i + \sum \beta_j z_j + \sum \beta_{ij} z_j s_i + \sum \beta_{ijk} z_j z_k s_i + \cdots \\ \vdots \end{cases}$$

Thus the coefficient vector g' is no more a constant vector, but a vector dependent on the involved keystream bits. We denote it by g_t' and the corresponding Boolean function by $g_t(X)$, which have to be obtained online. Precisely, in general algebraic attacks, we establish the equations like $g_t(L^t(S_0)) = 0$; while in general fast algebraic attacks, the localized equations are of the form $h(L^t(S_0)) = g_t(L^t(S_0))$. Thus, the attacks run as eliminating the left side of the localized equations and deducing $0 = \sum_{i=0}^{D-1} \alpha_i h\left(L^{i+t}(S_0)\right) = \sum_{i=0}^{D-1} \alpha_i g_{t+i}\left(L^{t+i}(S_0)\right)$ [1,6]. Hence, we need to deal with the problem that how to efficiently compute $g_t(L^t(S_0))$ online.

5.1 Simple Method: Polynomial Multiplication

The simple method is applicable to the general attacks as well, even though the coefficients are changeable. The complexity issue is similar to that in the previous sections. Assume that the coefficients are relatively simple polynomials of the keystream (as stated in [6]), the only extra cost is to substitute the keystream bits into the coefficient vector g_t', which amounts to about $O(D^2)$ and $O(E \cdot (D+E))$ for general algebraic and fast algebraic attacks, respectively. Thus, the total complexities for establishing equations in general algebraic attacks and fast algebraic attacks are:

$$\widetilde{C}_1 = O(D) \cdot \left(\sum_{i=2}^{d} n^i \binom{m}{i} + 2n + D\right), \quad \widetilde{CC}_1 = O(D+E) \cdot \left(\sum_{i=2}^{e} n^i \binom{m}{i} + 2n + E\right).$$

5.2 Improved Method: Shift and Update from the Feedback Polynomial

The improved method cannot be used in this scenario since the coefficients of $g(x)$ are changeable and we can no more make use of the result of previous step.

5.3 New Method: Frobenius Form of the Monomial State Rewriting Matrix

Since g'_{t_1} is not necessarily equal to g'_{t_2}, we can no more recursively compute $g'_{t_2} \cdot Q \cdot \widehat{R}_d^{t_2}$ ($t_2 > t_1$) based on $g'_{t_1} \cdot Q \cdot \widehat{R}_d^{t_1}$ as done in the previous sections. Let us first take a closer look at the features of the blocks in the Frobenius form of the monomial state rewriting matrix. Suppose the characteristic polynomial $r(x)$ of the LFSR is primitive, which is always true in the current designs. Then based on a theorem by Key [10], we have our main theorem (Theorem 4) here.

Theorem 3 (Key [10]). *If $\gamma \in GF(2^n)$ is a root of the characteristic polynomial $r(x)$ of the LFSR, then the characteristic polynomial of R_d is $p^{(d)}(x) = \prod_{\psi:w(\psi)\leq d}(x-\gamma^\psi)$, where $w(\psi)$ is the number of 1's in the radix-2 representation of the integer ψ.*

Theorem 4. *If the LFSR of length n has a primitive characteristic polynomial $r(x)$ over $GF(2)$, then the Frobenius form of the monomial state rewriting matrix R_d determined by the LFSR and degree $d \leq \lceil n/2 \rceil$ is composed of blocks of which the dimensions are at most n. Moreover, the characteristic polynomials of the blocks are irreducible and are different from each other.*

Now, we present the method of calculating $g_t(L^t(S_0))$ online based on Theorem 4. For general algebraic attacks, we need to compute $\widehat{R}_d^t$, then $g'_t \cdot Q$, and finally $(g'_t \cdot Q) \cdot \widehat{R}_d^t$. The complexity for calculating $\widehat{R}_d^{t+1}$ given $\widehat{R}_d^t$ can be analyzed in the following way. The power of a block diagonal matrix equals to another block diagonal matrix, whose blocks are formed with the power of the blocks in the original block diagonal matrix. Since the blocks in $\widehat{R}_d$ are of the same form as Theorem 1, the cost for calculating the $(t+1)$-th power of such a block given the t-th power of the block is just the double of the block dimension. If there are u blocks in $\widehat{R}_d$, whose dimensions are $k_1, k_2, \ldots, k_u$ respectively, satisfying $k_1 + k_2 + \cdots + k_u = D$, ($k_i \leq n, 1 \leq i \leq u$), then the complexity for calculating $\widehat{R}_d^{t+1}$ given $\widehat{R}_d^t$ is $2k_1 + 2k_2 + \cdots + 2k_u = 2D$. Since we need to compute it for $O(D)$ times, the total cost of this step is $2D \cdot O(D)$. Next, we compute $g'_t \cdot Q$. It takes D^2 computations each time. We need to compute $g'_t \cdot Q$ for $O(D)$ times, and we can run this step all at once in the way $(g'_{t_1}, g'_{t_2}, \ldots, g'_{t_D})^T \cdot Q = (g'_{t_1} \cdot Q, g'_{t_2} \cdot Q, \ldots, g'_{t_D} \cdot Q)$, which takes $O(D^w)$ computations in total. Finally, since $\widehat{R}_d^t$ is still a block diagonal matrix, the number of nonzero elements in each column is at most the dimension of the block, i.e., it is not larger than n. Then the cost for calculating $(g'_t \cdot Q) \cdot \widehat{R}_d^t$ is $k_1^2 + k_2^2 + \cdots + k_u^2 \approx n^2 \cdot \frac{D}{n} = n \cdot D$. The total cost of this step for $O(D)$ times is

Table 5. Comparison of the complexities for computing $g_t(L^t(S_0)), t = 1, \ldots, D + E$ online

	n	(d, e)	m	$\widetilde{CC}_1$	$\widetilde{CC}_3$	Substitution	Solving equations
E0	128	(4,3)	128	2^{63}	$\mathbf{2^{57}}$	2^{47}	2^{54}

$nD \cdot O(D)$. Recall that we also need to add the complexity of substituting the keystream bits into g'_t. Thus, the complexity for computing $g_t(L^t(S_0))$ by this method in the general algebraic attack is about

$$\widetilde{C}_3 = 2D \cdot O(D) + O(D^w) + O(n \cdot D^2) + D^2 = O((D^w) + (n+3)D^2).$$

Similarly, the complexity for computing $g_t(L^t(S_0))$ in the general fast algebraic attack is about

$$\widetilde{CC}_3 = O((D + E)(E^{w-1} + (n+3)E)).$$

Let us take the general attack on the E0 keystream generator as an example. Here we expand g as one g_t rather than treat it as 10 subfunctions with constant coefficient vector. Then the complexities by these two methods are listed in Table 5.

Remark 1. Since the monomials containing $z_t, \ldots, z_{t+\theta}$ emerged in g'_t in the attack on E0 are in a small scale, just 10, it seems that turning g_t into several subfunctions with constant coefficient vector and calculating for each in the way stated in Sect. 4.2 costs smaller complexity. Moreover, when θ is small, the complexity to compute for 2^θ subfunctions of g is about $O((E + D) \cdot E \cdot 2^\theta)$.

6   Conclusion

In this paper, we have shown that previous works on algebraic and fast algebraic attacks against stream ciphers have overlooked a common base, i.e., establishing an adequate equation system first, which actually in some cases dominates the attack complexity if the direct methods are used. We have analyzed the complexity of this step in various algebraic attack scenarios and demonstrated a new method to fulfill this task based on the Frobenius form of the monomial state rewriting matrix. In each considered case, we make a comparison study and show that this technique has efficiently reduced the complexity of establishing equations. We think that the Frobenius form of the monomial state rewriting matrix and its properties may help the research of the equivalence of filter generators [14].

Acknowledgements. We would like to thank anonymous referees for their helpful comments and suggestions, especially a reviewer of Asiacrypt 2013. This work was supported by the National Grand Fundamental Research 973 Program of China (Grant No. 2013CB338002, No. 2013CB834203), the Strategic Priority Research Program of the Chinese Academy of Sciences (Grant No. XDA06010701), IIE's Research Project on Cryptography (Grant No. Y3Z0016102) and the programs of the National Natural Science Foundation of China (Grant Nos. 61379142, 60833008, 60603018, 61173134, 91118006, 61272476). Supported by the National Natural Science Foundation of China under Grant No. 91118006, the National Grand Fundamental Research 973 Program of China under Grant No. 2013CB338003.

References

1. Armknecht, F.: Improving fast algebraic attacks. In: Roy, B., Meier, W. (eds.) FSE 2004. LNCS, vol. 3017, pp. 65–82. Springer, Heidelberg (2004)
2. Armknecht, F., Krause, M.: Algebraic attacks on combiners with memory. In: Boneh, D. (ed.) CRYPTO 2003. LNCS, vol. 2729, pp. 162–175. Springer, Heidelberg (2003)
3. Bluetooth SIG. Specification of the Bluetooth system, version 1.1 (2001). http://www.bluetooth.com
4. Braeken, A., Lano, J., Mentens, N., Preneel, B., Verbauwhede, I.: Sfinks specification and source code, available on ecrypt stream cipher project page, April 2005. http://www.ecrypt.eu.org/stream/sfinks.html
5. Courtois, N.T.: Fast algebraic attacks on stream ciphers with linear feedback. In: Boneh, D. (ed.) CRYPTO 2003. LNCS, vol. 2729, pp. 176–194. Springer, Heidelberg (2003)
6. Hawkes, P., Rose, G.G.: Rewriting variables: the complexity of fast algebraic attacks on stream ciphers. In: Franklin, M. (ed.) CRYPTO 2004. LNCS, vol. 3152, pp. 390–406. Springer, Heidelberg (2004)
7. Courtois, N., Meier, W.: Algebraic attacks on stream ciphers with linear feedback. In: Biham, E. (ed.) Advances in Cryptology - EUROCRYPT 2003. Lecture Notes in Computer Science, vol. 2656, pp. 345–359. Springer, Berlin Heidelberg (2003)
8. Hawkes, P., Rose, G.: Primitive specification and supporting documentation for Sober-t32 submission to nessie. In: Proceedings of the First Open NESSIE Workshop, pp. 13–14 (2000)
9. Hoffman, K., Kunze, R.: Linear Algebra. Prentice-Hall, Englewood Cliffs (1971)
10. Key, E.: An analysis of the structure and complexity of nonlinear binary sequence generators. IEEE Trans. Inf. Theor. **22**(6), 732–736 (1976)
11. Luo, Y., Chai, Q., Gong, G., Lai, X.: A lightweight stream cipher WG-7 for RFID encryption and authentication. In: Global Telecommunications Conference (GLOBECOM 2010), pp. 1–6. IEEE (2010)
12. Meier, W., Pasalic, E., Carlet, C.: Algebraic attacks and decomposition of boolean functions. In: Cachin, C., Camenisch, J.L. (eds.) EUROCRYPT 2004. LNCS, vol. 3027, pp. 474–491. Springer, Heidelberg (2004)
13. Mihaljevic, M.J.: Cryptanalysis of Toyocrypt-HS1 stream cipher. IEICE Trans. Fundam. Electron. Commun. Comput. Sci. **85**(1), 66–73 (2002)
14. Rønjom, S., Cid, C.: Nonlinear equivalence of stream ciphers. In: Hong, S., Iwata, T. (eds.) FSE 2010. LNCS, vol. 6147, pp. 40–54. Springer, Heidelberg (2010)
15. Rønjom, S., Helleseth, T.: A new attack on the filter generator. IEEE Trans. Inf. Theor. **53**(5), 1752–1758 (2007)
16. Simpson, L.R., Dawson, E., Golić, J.D., Millan, W.L.: LILI keystream generator. In: Stinson, D.R., Tavares, S. (eds.) SAC 2000. LNCS, vol. 2012, pp. 248–261. Springer, Heidelberg (2001)

17. Storjohann, A.: An $O(n^3)$ algorithm for the Frobenius normal form. In: Proceedings of the 1998 International Symposium on Symbolic and Algebraic Computation, ISSAC 1998, pp. 101–105. ACM, New York (1998)
18. Storjohann, A., Villard, G.: Algorithms for similarity transforms. In: Seventh Rhine Workshop on Computer Algebra, Citeseer (2005)

Factoring a Multiprime Modulus
N with Random Bits

Routo Terada[✉] and Reynaldo Cáceres Villena

Department of Computer Science, University of São Paulo, São Paulo, Brazil
rt@ime.usp.br, reynaldo.cv@gmail.com

Abstract. In 2009, Heninger and Shacham presented an algorithm using the Hensel's lemma for reconstructing the prime factors of the modulus $N = r_1 r_2$. This algorithm computes the prime factors of N in polynomial time, with high probability, assuming that a fraction greater than or equal to 59 % random bits of its primes r_1 and r_2 is given. In this paper, we present the analysis of Hensel's lemma for a multiprime modulus $N = \prod_{i=1}^{u} r_i$ (for $u \geq 2$) and we generalise the Heninger and Shacham's algorithm to determine the minimum fraction of random bits of its prime factors that is sufficient to factor N in polynomial time with high probability.

Keywords: Factoring a multiprime modulus N · Random key bits leakage attack · Cold boot attack

1 Introduction

According to Skorobogatov [14], we know the recovery of information (bits) of the RAM can be done with a certain error due to the data remanent property of RAM and this error can be decreased by cooling techniques studied by Halderman [4]. This attack is known as cold boot attack [2] and it is able to make a copy of the DRAM used by the decryption process of an RSA cryptosystem with some private key identification techniques ([4,11,13]). Then, it may identify the set of correct bits of the secret key sk of the **Basic RSA cryptosystem.**[1] Inspired by this attack the underlying ideas are used to identify and recover the secret key bits of **a multiprime RSA cryptosystems**[2].

It's widely known that the main drawback of Basic RSA cryptosystem is the relatively expensive encryption and decryption operations. It is relevant to mention there is an advantage to use more than two primes in the RSA modulus N. The decryption process is faster when it is done partially with respect to each prime modulus and then combine them using the Chinese Remainder Theorem

---

R.C. Villena—Supported by CAPES, Brazil.

[1] Basic RSA is when the modulus N is product of two primes.

[2] Multi-prime RSA is a generalization of the Basic RSA where the modulus N is the product of two or more primes.

Y. Desmedt (Ed.): ISC 2013, LNCS 7807, pp. 185–196, 2015.
DOI: 10.1007/978-3-319-27659-5_13

(see [8, 12]). The more prime factors in the modulus N, the faster is the decryption process, providing a practical solution to the high cost of decryption. The advantages for performing these operations in parallel are that the number of bit operations is at most $\frac{3}{2u^3}n^3$ and the required space is only $\lg(r_i) = \frac{n}{u}$ where $n = \lg(N)$ (number of bits of modulus N) and u is the number of prime factors of N. The time and space used to perform the decryption process is lower for values u greater than 2 but the risk of the modulus N to be factored without extra information is increased [7].

As mentioned before, inspired by cold boot attacks, it was shown that if queries to an oracle for a relatively small number of bits of the secret key is given, it is possible to factor the Basic RSA modulus $N = pq$ in polynomial time with:

- $\frac{1}{4}n$ LSB (Least Significant Bits) or $\frac{1}{4}n$ MSB (Most Significant Bits) of p [3].
- a maximum of $\log\log(N)$ unknown blocks and $ln(2) \approx 0.70$ fraction of known bits of p [6].
- a fraction δ of random bits of p and q greater than or equal to $2 - 2^{\frac{1}{2}} \approx 0.59$ [5].

In comparison, for a multiprime modulus $N = r_1 r_2 ... r_u$, $\frac{i}{i+1}\frac{n}{u}$ LSB or $\frac{i}{i+1}\frac{n}{u}$ MSB of r_i, for $1 \le i \le u - 1$ is required [7].

An example: to factor a 3-prime modulus N ($u = 3$) the minimum requirement is:

- $\frac{n}{6}$ LSB or $\frac{n}{6}$ MSB of r_1, and $\frac{2n}{9}$ LSB or $\frac{2n}{9}$ MSB of r_2
- $0.38n$ fraction of bits of primes r_1 and r_2.

Hence more and more bits are required to factor a modulus N with u greater than 2.

The case that we analyzed is to factor a multiprime modulus N with a fraction δ of random bits of its primes, where δ was computed to factor N in polynomial time with high probability. Hence we show that a multiprime modulus N offers more security than a basic modulus N. Our main result is that:

- To factor the integer $N = \prod_{i=1}^{u} r_i$ in polynomial time, using Hensel's lemma, a fraction $\delta = 2 - 2^{\frac{1}{u}}$ of random bits of its primes is sufficient.

With this result, there is a need of $\delta \ge 2 - 2^{\frac{1}{3}} \approx 0.75$ fraction of random bits of prime factors to factor a 3-prime modulus N. Therefore 3-prime is better, adversarially, than $\delta \ge 2 - 2^{\frac{1}{2}} \approx 0.59$ for a basic modulus N.

Kogure et al. [9] proved a general theorem to factor a multi-power modulus $N = r_1^m r_2$ with random bits of its prime factors. The particular cases of Takagi's variant of RSA [15] and Paillier Cryptosystem [10] are addressed. The bounds for expected values in our cryptanalysis are derived directly, without applying their theorem.

2   Algorithm to Factor a Multiprime Modulus N

We consider an equation of integer $N = \prod_{i=1}^{u} r_i$ that can be expressed as a polynomial

$$f(x_1, x_2, ..., x_u) = N - \prod_{i=1}^{u} x_i$$

with solution (roots) $r = \langle r_1, r_2, ...r_u \rangle$. We applied the idea in Heninger and Shacham's algorithm, to rebuild the primes r_i beginning with their LSB and MSB. In others words, we can lift all roots of the polynomial $f(x_1, x_2, ..., x_u)$ (mod 2^{j+1}) from a root of the polynomial $f(x_1, x_2, ..., x_u)$ (mod 2^j). Applying this scheme, we can lift from one root of polynomial $f(x_1, x_2, ..., x_u)$ (mod 2) to obtain all roots of $f(x_1, x_2, ..., x_u)$ (mod 2^2). Then, from these roots, lift all roots of $f(x_1, x_2, ..., x_u)$ (mod 2^3) and so on, up to all roots for $f(x_1, x_2, ..., x_u)$ (mod $2^{\frac{n}{u}}$). One of these roots is the solution for $\langle r_1, r_2, .., r_u \rangle$, because we assume N is balanced[3] hence the length of its primes is of $\frac{n}{u}$ bits.

$$\langle r_1, r_2, .., r_u \rangle \in \text{ roots of } f(x_1, x_2, .., x_u) \pmod{2^{\frac{n}{u}}}$$

To understand the relation between a root of $f(x_1, x_2, .., x_u)$ (mod 2^j) and the roots of $f(x_1, x_2, .., x_u)$ (mod 2^{j+1}) we introduce below the Hensel's lemma for multivariate polynomials.

Lemma 1 (Multivariate Hensel's Lemma [5]). *Let $f(x_1, x_2, ..., x_n) \in \mathbb{Z}[x_1, x_2, ..., x_n]$ be a multivariate polynomial with integer coefficients. Let π be a positive integer and $r = (r_1, r_2, ..., r_n) \in \mathbb{Z}^n$ be a solution for $f(x_1, x_2, ..., x_n) \equiv 0 \pmod{\pi^j}$. Then r can be lifted to a root $r + b$ (mod π^{j+1}), if $b = (b_1 \pi^j, b_2 \pi^j, ..., b_n \pi^j)$, $0 \le b_i \le \pi - 1$, satisfies*

$$f(r + b) = f(r) + \sum_{i=1}^{n} b_i \pi^j f_{x_i}(r) \equiv 0 \pmod{\pi^{j+1}}$$

where f_{x_i} is the partial derivative of f with respect to x_i, or equivalently

$$\frac{f(r)}{\pi^j} + \sum_{i=1}^{n} b_i f_{x_i}(r) \equiv 0 \pmod{\pi}$$

Analyzing the polynomial $f(x_1, x_2, ..., x_u) = N - \prod_{i=1}^{u} x_i$ with the Hensel's lemma we obtained the following results. Let $r = (r'_1, r'_2, ..., r'_u)$ be a solution for $f(x_1, x_2, ..., x_u) \equiv 0 \pmod{2^j}$ where a root for $f(x_1, x_2, ..., x_u) \equiv 0 \pmod{2^{j+1}}$ is defined as $r = (r'_1 + 2^j b_1, r'_2 + 2^j b_2, ..., r'_u + 2^j b_u)$ where b_i represents a bit $r_i[j]$ such that

$$\left(N - \prod_{i=1}^{u} r'_i \right)[j] \equiv \sum_{i=1}^{u} r_i[j] \pmod{2}. \tag{1}$$

---

[3] N is the product of u primes with the same bit length, as in the Basic RSA.

It is an equation modulus 2. If all values $r_i[j]$ are considered as unknowns, it is an equation modulus $\pi = 2$ with u variables. An equation with u variables has a total number of solutions equal to $\pi^{u-1} = 2^{u-1}$. In other words, we get a maximum of 2^{u-1} roots for $f(x_1, x_2, .., x_u)$ (mod 2^{j+1}) from a root of $f(x_1, x_2, .., x_u)$ (mod 2^j). Furthermore, if a fraction of random bits are known, this number of roots decreases, as we show below.

Let $root[j]$ be a set of all possible roots of the polynomial $f(x_1, x_2, .., x_u)$ (mod 2^{j+1}). $root[0]$ is a set of single elements because the r_i's are primes hence the single root of $f(x_1, x_2, .., x_u)$ (mod 2) is $\langle 1_1, 1_2, .., 1_u \rangle$. With the definition of $root[j]$ we developed the following algorithm to factor a multiprime modulus N. In Algorithm 1 there are the following inputs: a big integer N, an integer u that is the number of prime factors of N. A fraction δ of random bits of the primes is known and given as $\tilde{r_1}, \tilde{r_2}...\tilde{r_n}$

Algorithm 1. Factoring N

    Input: $N, u, \langle \tilde{r_1}, \tilde{r_2}, ..., \tilde{r_u} \rangle$
    Output: $root[\frac{n}{u}]$ where $\langle r_1, r_2, ..., r_u \rangle$ is in $root[\frac{n}{u}]$
1 $root[0] = [\langle 1_1, 1_2, ..., 1_u \rangle];$
2 $j = 1;$
3 **for each** $\langle r'_1, r'_2, ..., r'_u \rangle$ in $root[j-1]$ **do**
4   **for all possible** *(as explained below (*))* $\langle r_1[j], r_2[j], ..., r_u[j] \rangle$ **do**
5   **if** $(N - \prod_{i=1}^{u} r'_i)[j] \equiv \sum_{i=1}^{u} r_i[j]$ (mod 2) **then**
6          $root[j].add(\langle r'_1 + 2^j r_1[j], r'_2 + 2^j r_2[j], ..., r'_u + 2^j r_u[j] \rangle)$

7 **if** $j < \frac{n}{u}$ **then**
8      $j := j + 1;$
9   go to step 3;
10 **return** $root[\frac{n}{u}];$

The algorithm begins with a set $root[0]$ of single roots $\langle 1_1, 1_2, ..., 1_u \rangle$. (*) In Line 4 for each root $\langle r'_1, r'_2, ..., r'_u \rangle \in root[j-1]$ we generate all permutations for bits $\langle r_1[j], r_2[j], ..., r_u[j] \rangle$. The number of values of $r_i[j]$ is one only if this bit is known in $\tilde{r_i}$, otherwise there are two values, 0 or 1. Each result $\langle r_1[j], r_2[j], ..., r_u[j] \rangle$ of this permutation is analyzed in Line 5 by the Hensel's Eq. (1); it is added to the set $root[j]$ if the equivalence is true. This procedure is done until the set $root[\frac{n}{u}]$ obtained contains the prime factors of N.

3   Behavior and Complexity of the Algorithm to Factor N

We developed a brute-force search algorithm lifting all possible roots for the polynomial $f(x_1, x_2, ..., x_u)$ (mod 2^j) for $1 \leq j \leq \frac{n}{u}$. This behavior is shown in Fig. 1 where we can see the root $r = \langle r_1, r_2, ..., r_u \rangle$ as a gray double circle. It was lifted in each level $j \in [1, \frac{n}{u}]$ from one root in $root[0]$. These roots are defined as good roots and are shown as no-color double circle. One good root in each level j always lifts the good root for the next level $j + 1$. Each incorrect root is represented as a single line circle.

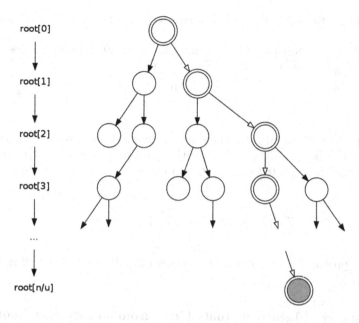

Fig. 1. (Factoring N) Behavior of Algorithm 1 to factor N

We know we have a number of $\frac{n}{u} + 1$ good roots in all executions of Algorithm 1, but the behavior of the algorithm is determined by the number of the lifted incorrect roots. Therefore the analysis was done with respect to incorrect roots, and to do this analysis, we defined the following random variables:

- Let G be the random variable for the number of incorrect roots lifted from a good root.
- Let B be the random variable for the number of incorrect roots lifted from an incorrect root.
- Let X_j be the random variable for the number of incorrect roots lifted at level j.

3.1 Number of Incorrect Roots Lifted from a Good Root (G)

All cases that may occur are described in the following Table where we have one good root $\langle r_1', r_2', ..., r_u' \rangle$ of $root[j-1]$ and let's define h as the number of unknown bits in $\langle r_1[j], r_2[j], ..., r_u[j] \rangle$.

There are h cases ($1 \leq h \leq u$ in Eq. (1)). It is an equation modulus 2 with h variables where the number of solutions is 2^{h-1}. Hence we get a total of 2^{h-1} roots for $root[j]$. In the case $h = 0$ we obtain a single root and it is the good root of $root[j]$ because it is built from the good root of $root[j-1]$ and all known bits are of the correct root. But we do not have the number of incorrect roots that were lifted. The number of incorrect roots lifted are in the third column

Table 1. (Factoring N) Number of incorrect roots lifted from a good root.

Cases	Number of lifted roots	Number of lifted incorrect roots
$1 \le h \le u$	2^{h-1}	$2^{h-1} - 1$
$h = 0$	1	0

of Table 1 and are the values of the second column decreased by 1 (because the good root in $root[j]$ is always lifted by the good root in $root[j-1]$). Therefore we can define the expected value of G as follows:

$$\mathbb{E}[G] = \sum_{h=1}^{u} (2^{h-1} - 1) \binom{u}{h} (1 - \delta)^h \delta^{u-h} \tag{2}$$

where the probability of occuring h unknown bits in a set of u bits is $\binom{u}{h}(1 - \delta)^h \delta^{u-h}$.

3.2   Number of Incorrect Roots Lifted from an Incorrect Root (B)

Before computing the number of incorrect roots lifted from an incorrect root let's define c_1 as the computed value of

$$c_1 = \left(N - \prod_{i=1}^{u} r_i' \right)[j]$$

from the good root in $root[j-1]$. With this definition, we can observe two kinds of incorrect roots in $root[j-1]$: either the computed value of $(N - \prod_{i=1}^{u} r_i')[j]$ is equal to c_1 or is different from c_1 (denoted by $\overline{c_1}$). Considering all this, we analyzed all cases for computing the number of incorrect roots lifted from an incorrect root in the next Table.

The cases where $1 \le h \le u$, the values c_1 and $\overline{c_1}$ are not important because in Hensel's Eq. (1) there is a modular equation of h variables, and a total of 2^{h-1} incorrect roots. For the case of c_1, the incorrect root is going to act like a good root, hence for $h = 0$ the incorrect root lifts an incorrect root. But in the case of $\overline{c_1}$ the incorrect root is dropped because we have a contradiction.

The computed value of $(N - \prod_{i=1}^{u} r_i')[j]$ in an incorrect root can be 0 or 1 with probability $\frac{1}{2}$. The probabilities are $P((N - \prod_{i=1}^{u} r_i')[j] = 1) = \frac{1}{2}$ and

Table 2. (Factoring N) Number of incorrect roots lifted from an incorrect root.

Cases	$(N - \prod_{i=1}^{u} r_i')[j] = c_1$	$(N - \prod_{i=1}^{u} r_i')[j] = \overline{c_1}$
$1 \le h \le u$	2^{h-1}	2^{h-1}
$h = 0$	1	0

$P((N - \prod_{i=1}^{u} r_i')[j] = 0) = \frac{1}{2}$. In other words, the probabilities are the same because c_1 and $\overline{c_1}$ represent the value of one bit. Hence we have $P((N - \prod_{i=1}^{u} r_i')[j] = c_1) = \frac{1}{2}$ and $P(N - \prod_{i=1}^{u} r_i')[j] = \overline{c_1}) = \frac{1}{2}$.

Analyzing Table 2 and with the probabilities defined above, we can determine the expected value of B.

$$\mathbb{E}[B] = \sum_{h=1}^{u} 2^{h-1} \binom{u}{h}(1-\delta)^h \delta^{u-h} \frac{1}{2} + \sum_{h=1}^{u} 2^{h-1} \binom{u}{h}(1-\delta)^h \delta^{u-h} \frac{1}{2} + \binom{u}{0}(1-\delta)^0 \delta^{u-0} \frac{1}{2}$$

$$\tag{3}$$

$$= \frac{(2-\delta)^u}{2}$$

3.3   Number of Incorrect Roots Lifted at Level j (X_j)

The expected value of the discrete random variable X_j is defined in the following recursion:

$$\mathbb{E}[X_j] = \mathbb{E}[X_{j-1}]\mathbb{E}[B] + \mathbb{E}[G]$$

because the number of incorrect roots at level j is equal to the number of incorrect roots lifted from the incorrect roots at level $j-1$ plus the number of incorrect roots lifted from the only one good root at level $j-1$. And we have $\mathbb{E}[X_1] = \mathbb{E}[G]$ because at level 0 there is no incorrect root, hence we can compute the closed form as follows:

$$\mathbb{E}[X_j] = \mathbb{E}[G]\frac{1 - \mathbb{E}[B]^j}{1 - \mathbb{E}[B]}. \tag{4}$$

3.4   Complexity of the Algorithm to Factor

The algorithm to factor N should run up to level $\frac{n}{u}$ and return the prime factors of N, thus the expected value of the number of incorrect roots analyzed by Algorithm 1 is defined as:

$$\mathbb{E}\left[\sum_{j=1}^{\frac{n}{u}} X_j\right] = \sum_{j=1}^{\frac{n}{u}} \mathbb{E}[X_j] \qquad \text{Property of expected value}$$

$$= \sum_{j=1}^{\frac{n}{u}} \mathbb{E}[G]\frac{1 - \mathbb{E}[B]^j}{1 - \mathbb{E}[B]} \qquad \text{Definition (4)}$$

$$= \frac{\mathbb{E}[G]}{1 - \mathbb{E}[B]} \sum_{j=1}^{\frac{n}{u}} 1 + \frac{\mathbb{E}[G]}{\mathbb{E}[B] - 1} \sum_{j=1}^{\frac{n}{u}} \mathbb{E}[B]^j$$

$$= \frac{\mathbb{E}[G]}{1 - \mathbb{E}[B]}\frac{n}{u} + \frac{\mathbb{E}[G]\mathbb{E}[B](\mathbb{E}[B]^{n/u} - 1)}{(\mathbb{E}[B] - 1)^2}.$$

The equation above is exponential on n and on $\mathbb{E}[B]$ but it can be bounded as follows. For values of $\mathbb{E}[B] > 1$ this function is actually exponential

($\lim_{n\to\infty} \mathbb{E}[B]^{n/u} = \infty$) but for values $\mathbb{E}[B] < 1$ we get $\lim_{n\to\infty} \mathbb{E}[B]^{n/u} < 1$. Therefore the expected number of analyzed incorrect roots is bounded by a linear equation on n for values $\mathbb{E}[B] < 1$.

$$\mathbb{E}\left[\sum_{j=1}^{\frac{n}{u}} X_j\right] = \frac{\mathbb{E}[G]}{1-\mathbb{E}[B]}\frac{n}{u} + \frac{\mathbb{E}[B]\mathbb{E}[G](\mathbb{E}[B]^{n/u}-1)}{(\mathbb{E}[B]-1)^2} \leq \frac{\mathbb{E}[G]}{1-\mathbb{E}[B]}\frac{n}{u} \text{ for } \mathbb{E}[B] < 1$$

In summary, we can factor the modulus $N = \prod_{i=1}^{u} r_i$ in polynomial time, given a δ fraction of random bits of its prime factors greater than $2 - 2^{\frac{1}{u}}$ (by Definition (3) $\mathbb{E}[B] = \frac{(2-\delta)^u}{2} < 1$) because the expected number of analyzed incorrect roots is $O(n)$.

$$\mathbb{E}[B] = \frac{(2-\delta)^u}{2} < 1$$
$$(2-\delta)^u < 2$$
$$2 - \delta < 2^{\frac{1}{u}}$$
$$\delta > 2 - 2^{\frac{1}{u}}$$

Some results from this analysis are, to factor in polynomial time an integer:

- $N = \prod_{i=1}^{2} r_i$, $\delta \geq 0.59(2-2^{\frac{1}{2}} \approx 0.5858)$ fraction of the bits of its prime factors is needed.
- $N = \prod_{i=1}^{3} r_i$, $\delta \geq 0.75(2-2^{\frac{1}{3}} \approx 0.7401)$ fraction of the bits of its prime factors is needed.
- $N = \prod_{i=1}^{4} r_i$, $\delta \geq 0.82(2-2^{\frac{1}{4}} \approx 0.8108)$ fraction of the bits of its prime factors is needed.

4   Implementation and Performance

The algorithm to factor N was implemented in 300 lines of code using the program language C with the library Relic-toolkit [1] that is focused for the implementation of cryptosystems, and was executed on a processor Intel Core I3 2.4 Ghz with 3 Mb of cache and 4 Gb of DDR3 Memory.

The experiments were executed for integers N ($n = 2048$ bits) and they were the product of u primes, $2 \leq u \leq 4$. For each value δ a total of 100 integers N were generated, and for each integer N 100 inputs with a fraction δ of bits of its primes were generated. The results of the total of 550000 experimental runs are shown in Tables 3, 4, 5 and Fig. 2.

With the results obtained by Heninger and Shacham in [5] we can say that the number of analyzed incorrect roots in an experiment has a low probability to surpass 1 million. In our experiments we did the same to avoid trashing, hence we canceled all experiments that surpassed one million analyzed incorrect roots.

In Tables 3, 4 and 5 we have in the second and third column the minimum and maximum analyzed incorrect roots, respectively. The fourth and sixth column

Table 3. Results of total examined roots by the algorithm to factor $N = \prod_{i=1}^{2} r_i$, 2048 bits.

δ	Number of analyzed roots			# Exp ($> 1M$)	Average time (s)
	Minimum	Maximum	Average		
0.61	1983	945728	4949	0	0.115277
0.60	2233	789608	6344	0	0.119484
0.59	2411	928829	8953	2	0.187600
0.58	2631	987577	14736	7	0.250224
0.57	3436	994640	24281	29	0.531079
0.56	4012	998414	42231	134	0.722388

Table 4. Results of total examined roots by the algorithm to factor $N = \prod_{i=1}^{3} r_i$, 2048 bits.

δ	Number of analyzed roots			# Exp ($> 1M$)	Average time (s)
	Minimum	Maximum	Average		
0.77	1128	171142	2022	0	0.033884
0.76	1205	323228	2777	0	0.049238
0.75	1380	177293	3723	1	0.099373
0.74	1607	571189	5941	1	0.197553
0.73	1681	999766	11470	11	0.281414
0.72	2087	983404	23826	50	0.995017

Table 5. Results of total examined roots by the algorithm to factor $N = \prod_{i=1}^{4} r_i$, 2048 bits.

δ	Number of analyzed roots			# Exp ($> 1M$)	Average time (s)
	Minimum	Maximum	Average		
0.84	716	31447	1245	0	0.024748
0.83	823	67456	1649	0	0.040714
0.82	931	217391	2424	0	0.063754
0.81	1044	558521	4408	1	0.111688
0.80	1249	994386	9571	14	0.236320
0.79	1632	972196	24085	58	0.609435

contain the average number and the average time of analyzed incorrect roots in all experiments that did not surpassed one million of incorrect roots. The fifth column contains the number in all experiments that were canceled because it surpassed one million incorrect roots.

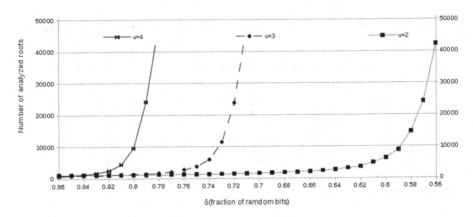

Fig. 2. (Factoring N) Average number of analyzed roots by the algorithm to factor $N = \prod_{i=1}^{u} r_i$ where $2 \leq u \leq 4$

Table 6. Comparison of basic, 2-power and 3-primes modulus N.

Cases			
	Basic Modulus N	2-power Modulus N	3-primes Modulus N
	$N = r_1 r_2$	$N = r_1^2 r_2$	$N = \prod_{i=1}^{3} r_i$
Random bits	$\delta \geq 0.59$	$\delta \geq 0.59$	$\delta \geq 0.75$

For all experiments, we obtained an average time less than 1 second to factor N. And only 305 experiments were canceled because they had over one million of analyzed incorrect roots. For the rest of experiments, the algorithm always returned the prime factors of N.

Figure 2 shows the average number of analyzed roots of our experiments to factor N with $n = 2048$ bits. We observe the exponential growth of $\mathbb{E}\left[\sum_{j=1}^{\frac{n}{u}} X_j\right]$ for values of δ lower than $2 - 2^{\frac{1}{u}}$ ($\mathbb{E}[B] > 1$) for u in $[2, 4]$.

5   Concluding Remarks

We designed an algorithm to factor a multiprime integer N based on Hensel's lemma.

The statistical analysis shows that factoring a multiprime modulus N for u greater than 2 offers more security (adversarially thinking) than for $u = 2$, assuming a fraction of random bits of its primes is given. Table 6 shows a comparison done for Basic, 2-power and 3 multiprime modulus N.

Using a multi-power $N = r_1^m r_2$ allows a faster decryption process than using a basic $N = r_1^1 r_2$. There is no advantage to factor a multi-power modulus N with random bits because for any value of $m \geq 1$ we always need a fraction $\delta \geq 0.59$ of random bits. Due to page number restrictions, our analysis and implementation results to factor a general multipower modulus $N = r_1^m r_2$ (for the cases even and odd m) with random bits of its prime factors are given in the extended version of this paper to be published elsewhere.

The advantages of using a multiprime modulus N are: the decryption is faster, and with respect to cold boot attacks, the attacker needs more than $2^{\frac{1}{u}} - 2^{\frac{1}{2}}$ fraction of random bits if a basic modulus N is used. Therefore if $u > 2$, to factor N is harder but there is a limit for the value u. When u is large the modulus N can be factored without extra information using the algorithm called Number Field Sieve (NFS)[4] or by an elliptic curve method (ECM)[5].

Acknowledgment. We thank anonymous referees who pointed out the work by Kogure et al. [9].

References

1. Aranha, D.F., Gouvêa, C.P.L.: RELIC is an Efficient Library for Cryptography. http://code.google.com/p/relic-toolkit/
2. Bar-El, H.: Introduction to side channel attacks. White Paper, Discretix Technologies Ltd. (2003)
3. Boneh, D.: Twenty years of attacks on the RSA cryptosystem. Not. AMS **46**(2), 203–213 (1999)
4. Halderman, J.A., Schoen, S.D., Heninger, N., Clarkson, W., Paul, W., Calandrino, J.A., Feldman, A.J., Appelbaum, J., Felten, E.W.: Lest we remember: cold-boot attacks on encryption keys. Commun. ACM **52**(5), 91–98 (2009)
5. Heninger, N., Shacham, H.: Reconstructing RSA private keys from random key bits. In: Halevi, S. (ed.) CRYPTO 2009. LNCS, vol. 5677, pp. 1–17. Springer, Heidelberg (2009)
6. Herrmann, M., May, A.: Solving linear equations modulo divisors: on factoring given any bits. In: Pieprzyk, J. (ed.) ASIACRYPT 2008. LNCS, vol. 5350, pp. 406–424. Springer, Heidelberg (2008)
7. Hinek, M.J.: On the security of multi-prime RSA. J. Math. Cryptol. **2**(2), 117–147 (2008)
8. Jonsson, J., Kaliski, B.: Public-key cryptography standards (PKCS)# 1: Rsa cryptography specifications version 2.1. Technical report, RFC 3447, February 2003
9. Kogure, J., Kunihiro, N., Yamamoto, H.: Generalized security analysis of the random key bits leakage attack. In: Yung, M., Jung, S. (eds.) WISA 2011. LNCS, vol. 7115, pp. 13–27. Springer, Heidelberg (2012)
10. Paillier, P.: Public-key cryptosystems based on composite degree residuosity classes. In: Stern, J. (ed.) EUROCRYPT 1999. LNCS, vol. 1592, pp. 223–238. Springer, Heidelberg (1999)
11. Ptacek, T. : Recover a private key from process memory (2006). http://chargen.matasano.com/chargen/2006/1/25/recover-a-private-key-from-process-memory.html
12. Quisquater, J.J., Couvreur, C.: Fast decipherment algorithm for RSA public-key cryptosystem. Electron. Lett. **18**(21), 905–907 (1982)

---

[4] It is an algorithm to factor an integer N with a very good performance.

[5] It is an algorithm to compute a non-trivial factor of N.

13. Shamir, A., van Someren, N.: Playing 'Hide and Seek' with stored keys. In: Franklin, M.K. (ed.) FC 1999. LNCS, vol. 1648, pp. 118–124. Springer, Heidelberg (1999)
14. Skorobogatov, S.: Low temperature data remanence in static ram. University of Cambridge Computer Laborary Technical Report 536 (2002)
15. Takagi, T.: Fast RSA-type cryptosystem modulo $p^k q$. In: Krawczyk, H. (ed.) CRYPTO 1998. LNCS, vol. 1462, pp. 318–326. Springer, Heidelberg (1998)

Block Ciphers and Stream Ciphers

Faster 128-EEA3 and 128-EIA3 Software

Roberto Avanzi[1]([✉]) and Billy Bob Brumley[2]

[1] Qualcomm Product Research Germany, Munich, Germany
mocenigo@qti.qualcomm.com, roberto.avanzi@gmail.com
[2] Department of Pervasive Computing, Tampere University of Technology,
Tampere, Finland
billy.brumley@tut.fi

Abstract. The 3GPP Task Force recently supplemented mobile LTE network security with an additional set of confidentiality and integrity algorithms, namely 128-EEA3 and 128-EIA3 built on top of ZUC, a new keystream generator. We contribute two techniques to improve the software performance of these algorithms. We show how delayed modular reduction increases the efficiency of the LFSR feedback function, yielding performance gains for ZUC and thus both 128-EEA3 and 128-EIA3. We also show how to leverage carryless multiplication to evaluate the universal hash function making up the core of 128-EIA3. Our software implementation results on Qualcomm's Hexagon DSP architecture indicate significant performance gains when employing these techniques: up to roughly a 2.4-fold and a 4-fold throughput improvement for 128-EEA3 and 128-EIA3, respectively.

Keywords: Stream ciphers · Universal hash functions · ZUC · 128-EEA3 · 128-EIA3 · Carryless multiplication · LTE

1 Preliminaries

In 2009, Chinese regulators mandated augmenting mobile LTE security algorithms with a new set of algorithms. Standardized in 2012, new LTE confidentiality and integrity algorithms 128-EEA3 and 128-EIA3 [1] (hereafter EEA3 and EIA3) rely on the new stream cipher ZUC [2]. In contrast to existing literature [3–6] focused on hardware implementation aspects of these algorithms, this work focuses exclusively on efficient software implementation.

Keystream Generator: ZUC. As Fig. 1 illustrates, ZUC utilizes a 16-stage Linear Feedback Shift Register (LFSR) defined over $\mathbb{F}_p$ for $p = 2^{31} - 1$. ZUC produces one 32-bit keystream word per clock by combining LFSR and Finite State Machine (FSM) outputs. Let $\mathbb{F}_p = \{1, 2, \ldots, p-1, p\}$, the canonical representation with the exception of representing 0 by p. The LFSR feedback function $F_1 : \mathbb{F}_p^5 \to \mathbb{F}_p$ is defined as follows.

$$F_1 : (s_0, s_4, s_{10}, s_{13}, s_{15}) \mapsto (1 + 2^8)s_0 + 2^{20}s_4 + 2^{21}s_{10} + 2^{17}s_{13} + 2^{15}s_{15} \quad (1)$$

Full version: http://eprint.iacr.org/2013/428/.

© Springer International Publishing Switzerland 2015
Y. Desmedt (Ed.): ISC 2013, LNCS 7807, pp. 199–208, 2015.
DOI: 10.1007/978-3-319-27659-5_14

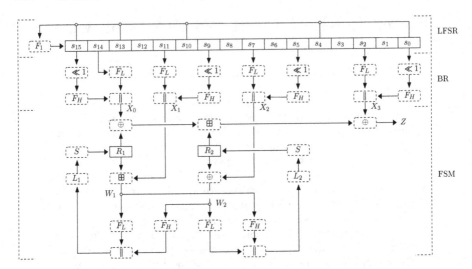

Fig. 1. The ZUC keystream generator. Solid boxes are registers. Dashed boxes are functions. The specification describes the process of extracting and concatenating partial LFSR cells for input to the FSM as the *bit reorganization* (BR) layer. Denote $\oplus$, $\boxplus$, $\ll$, and $\|$ addition in $\mathbb{F}_2^{32}$ (i.e., XOR), addition in $\mathbb{Z}_{2^{32}}$, logical left shift, and concatenation (resp.). Let $F_L, F_H : \mathbb{F}_2^{32} \to \mathbb{F}_2^{16}$ be $F_L : x \mapsto (x_0, \ldots, x_{15})$ and $F_H : x \mapsto (x_{16}, \ldots, x_{31})$. Denote $L_1, L_2 : \mathbb{F}_2^{32} \to \mathbb{F}_2^{32}$ linear transformations and $S : \mathbb{F}_{2^8}^4 \to \mathbb{F}_{2^8}^4$ a nonlinear function implemented by four parallel 8 to 8-bit S-boxes.

Confidentiality Algorithm: EEA3. Built on top of ZUC, EEA3 is a binary additive stream cipher utilizing ZUC keystream words in the obvious way: Ciphertext bits are message bits XOR-summed with ZUC keystream word bits. Keystream bits z_0 to z_{31} are the MSB to LSB of keystream word Z_0, bits z_{32} to z_{63} of Z_1, and so on. A noteworthy restriction is that EEA3 and EIA3 limit message lengths from 1 to 65504 bits (i.e., 4 bytes shy of 8kB).

Integrity Algorithm: EIA3. Built on top of ZUC, EIA3 is a Message Authentication Algorithm (MAA) utilizing ZUC keystream words to produce a 32-bit Message Authentication Code (MAC) for a message. At a high level, the keystream bits z_i and message bits m_i are inputs to an $\mathbb{F}_2$-linear universal hash function (UHF). A dedicated keystream word serves as a one-time pad (OTP), encrypting this 32-bit UHF output. Briefly, the steps are (1) Append a one followed by 31 zeroes to m; (2) Append zeroes to m until the length is a multiple of 32, i.e. from 0 to 31 zeroes; (3) Append a one to m. Denoting n the resulting length of m, EIA3 MACs are the output of $H : \mathbb{F}_2^n \times \mathbb{F}_2^{n+31} \to \mathbb{F}_2^{32}$ computed as

$$H : (m, z) \mapsto \sum_{i=0}^{n-1} m_i \cdot (z_{i+31}, \ldots, z_i) \tag{2}$$

In this light, the construction is similar to the formalization by Krawczyk [7, Sec. 3.2].

2   Software Optimizations

This section describes many techniques to increase the performance of ZUC, EEA3, and EIA3 software. Our main contributions are the application of delayed modular reduction in the ZUC LFSR feedback function and carryless multiplication in the EIA3 UHF. While these techniques can potentially apply to a wide range of architectures, we concentrate on one particular architecture where all of these optimizations apply: Qualcomm's Hexagon digital signal processor (DSP).

Delayed Modular Reduction. The standard exploits the fact that reduction modulo $p = 2^{31} - 1$ is fast by specifying first reduced computation of each summand in (1). Each multiplication by a power of two is a 31-bit rotation in this field: free in hardware but rather awkward in software. The computation then successively reduces each sum. The following formula reduces a 32-bit positive value $k \leq 2^{32} - 2$ e.g. the sum of two reduced quantities to the range $1 \leq k' \leq p$, i.e. consistent with the definition of $\mathbb{F}_p$ in the specification.

$$k' = (k \mathbin{\&} \texttt{0x7FFFFFFF}) + (k \gg 31) \tag{3}$$

The same formula applies, suitably repeated, to reduce any integer: any input that is at least 62 bits long shortens by 30 bits or more. The only 32-bit value that requires (3) to be applied twice is $2^{32} - 1$. In the context of Elliptic Curve Cryptography (ECC), accumulating the results of several additions before reduction can be effective: using sufficiently small prime moduli and accumulating without increasing the precision [8,9]. Furthermore, the lesson of [10,11] is that increasing the unreduced accumulator precision can be acceptable to reduce the number of reductions, even if this requires extending the reduction routine: the latter can take a performance hit but the net effect can still be a significant overall speedup. Along these lines, our approach is to use 64-bit registers (or pairs of 32-bit registers) and compute the unreduced sum of *integer values*

$$k = s_0 + 2^8 s_0 + 2^{20} s_4 + 2^{21} s_{10} + 2^{17} s_{13} + 2^{15} s_{15} \ .$$

This positive integer is clearly smaller than $2^{31} \cdot 2^{22} = 2^{53}$. Now we proceed to reduce it, first by computing

$$k' = (k \mathbin{\&} \texttt{0x7FFFFFFF}) + (k \gg 31) \leq (2^{31} - 1) + (2^{22} - 1) < 2^{32} - 2$$

and then to further reduce k' to the range $1 \leq k' \leq p$ requires only one additional application of (3) to a 32-bit value. Even on a 32-bit architecture, this is faster than the straightforward approach in the specification, as the savings from the fewer reductions vastly offset the more expensive double precision additions. This is our most significant optimization to ZUC in this work.

Carryless Multiplication. Integrating carryless multiplication (i.e. multiplication of words as polynomials in $\mathbb{F}_2[x]$) into an instruction set architecture (ISA) is a budding trend in commodity microprocessors due to its applications to signal processing, finite fields, error correcting codes, and cryptography.

In the latter case, previous results show how to leverage the instruction for efficient implementation of many cryptosystems, e.g. GHASH in AES-GCM [12] and ECC on curves over binary fields [13–15]. Similar to integer multiplication, the instruction first computes shifted partial products, yet the final summation in carryless multiplication is an XOR sum, discarding carries (Hexagon features such an instruction). We aim to leverage this to compute (2) a word at a time rather than a bit at a time. Define polynomials $a, b, c, d, e \in \mathbb{F}_2[x]$ as follows.

$$a = \sum_{i=0}^{31} z_{31-i} x^i, \quad b = \sum_{i=0}^{31} z_{63-i} x^i, \quad c = ax^{32} + b$$

$$d = \sum_{i=0}^{31} m_i x^i \tag{4}$$

$$e = cd = e_2 x^{64} + e_1 x^{32} + e_0 \tag{5}$$

That is, a is the first 32-bit keystream word as a 31-degree polynomial in $\mathbb{F}_2[x]$, b the next 32-bit keystream word, c the 63-degree polynomial in two 32-bit words. Note the bit ordering of keystream bits to words to polynomials (a, b) is consistent with the standard, yet the ordering in d differs, reversing the message word bits m_i. The three e_i are the 32-bit words of the product of c and d. Given these equations, e_1 in (5) is the output of 32 consecutive iterations of the summation in (2). To see why this is so, consider the following matrix.

$$U_0 = \begin{bmatrix} z_{31} & z_{32} & \cdots & z_{62} \\ z_{30} & z_{31} & \cdots & z_{61} \\ \vdots & \vdots & \ddots & \vdots \\ z_0 & z_1 & \cdots & z_{31} \end{bmatrix}$$

Denote $v = (m_0, m_1, \ldots, m_{31})^T$, i.e., d as a column vector, and observe $U_0 v$ computes the first 32 iterations of (2). The low and high words of the products ad and bd in (5) are $U_1 v$ and $U_2 v$ (resp.) where U_1 and U_2 are the following matrices.

$$U_1 = \begin{bmatrix} a_0 & 0 & \cdots & 0 \\ a_1 & a_0 & \cdots & 0 \\ \vdots & \vdots & \ddots & \vdots \\ a_{31} & a_{30} & \cdots & a_0 \end{bmatrix} = \begin{bmatrix} z_{31} & 0 & \cdots & 0 \\ z_{30} & z_{31} & \cdots & 0 \\ \vdots & \vdots & \ddots & \vdots \\ z_0 & z_1 & \cdots & z_{31} \end{bmatrix}, \quad U_2 = \begin{bmatrix} 0 & b_{31} & \cdots & b_1 \\ 0 & 0 & \cdots & \vdots \\ \vdots & \vdots & \ddots & b_{31} \\ 0 & 0 & \cdots & 0 \end{bmatrix} = \begin{bmatrix} 0 & z_{32} & \cdots & z_{62} \\ 0 & 0 & \cdots & \vdots \\ \vdots & \vdots & \ddots & z_{32} \\ 0 & 0 & \cdots & 0 \end{bmatrix}$$

The important equality is $U_0 = U_1 + U_2$ hence $U_1 v + U_2 v = U_0 v = e_1$. Repeating these steps for subsequent message words allows us to calculate (2) a message word at a time instead of a message bit at a time, and furthermore using no branch instructions. Considering software implementation aspects, forming variables a, b, and c have no software implications; they are simply keystream words. In contrast, (4) and (5) must be implemented. Reversing the bits of a message word in (4) requires either a dedicated bit reverse instruction (Hexagon features such an instruction) or a sequence of logic implementing a manual bit reverse (bit twiddling, table lookups, etc.). Two instances of a 32 by 32 to 64-bit carry-less multiplication instruction (ad, bd) followed by a single 32-bit XOR implement (5) producing e_1 (e_0 and e_2 are discarded). Finally, an additional 32-bit XOR accumulates to the tag.

Optimizing the S-box. S-boxes S_0 and S_1 (8 to 8 bits) implement the nonlinear function S of ZUC. These must be applied to each byte of a 32 bit word as follows. Let $w = w_0 \| w_1 \| w_2 \| w_3$ be a 32-bit input where each w_i is 8-bit. Its nonlinear transform is $S(w) = S_0(w_0) \| S_1(w_1) \| S_0(w_2) \| S_1(w_3)$, requiring bit shifts and masking for both extracting each w_i and assembling the final result. On the target architecture the ratio of the memory subsystem clock to the CPU clock is relatively small, so we reduce the amount of shifts by keeping two 32-bit tables for each S-box where $S_0' = S_0 \ll 24$, $S_0'' = S_0 \ll 8$, $S_1' = S_1 \ll 16$, and $S_1'' = S_1$ and computing $S(w)$ as $S(w) = S_0'(w_0) \oplus S_1'(w_1) \oplus S_0''(w_2) \oplus S_1''(w_3)$.

Optimizing the Keystream Generator. One important step in the keystream generator is the concatenation of two 16-bit halfwords extracted from 32-bit values into a third 32-bit value, e.g. to compute F_L and F_H followed by $\|$ in Fig. 1. There are six such calculations in the keystream generator. The Hexagon architecture includes a `combine` instruction that performs such an operation.

Classical Techniques. We implement the LFSR state as a circular buffer with a sliding window [16, Sec. 2.2] to avoid unnecessary data movement and simplified indexing. In order to improve code path execution locality, the EIA3 implementation keeps a buffer of ZUC keystream words, up to 64 words, generated all together on demand. Similarly, we unroll EEA3 up to 16 times and always invokes the ZUC keystream generator to provide the necessary amount of keystream words. Other than this, all optimizations are standard software tuning optimizations, e.g. explicit loop unrolling with overlapping and interleaving of loop body boundaries.

3 Results

Our target architecture is Qualcomm's Hexagon DSP, the global unit market leading architecture for DSP silicon shipments [17]. Qualcomm's recent MSM-8960 and MSM8974 Snapdragon system on chips (SoCs) aimed at mobile markets both feature multiple instances of Hexagon DSPs. Since the Hexagon architecture is not widely known, we briefly summarize its salient aspects before presenting and discussing performance results.

3.1 Hexagon Architecture

Hexagon is an unusual type of DSP because it inherits several features from general purpose CPUs and Very Long Instruction Word (VLIW) machines, enabling programming with standard development tools (toolchains based on gcc and clang/llvm are available) and running generic operating systems with virtualization support. It natively supports a complete RISC instructions set working on integer and floating point types, and vector operations. It features 32 32-bit general purpose registers, optionally paired to form 64-bit registers.

VLIW Architecture. Up to four instructions group together (at compile time) in variable length packets. The packets execute *in order*. The absence of a complex instruction scheduler reduces area and power consumption. Most arithmetic and logic operations can be accumulated: Hexagon does not only offer DSP-typical multiply-and-accumulate operations, but combinations such as and-then-add or add-then-xor as well. It features zero overhead hardware loops and various types of operations can be executed conditionally on four different sets of predicates.

A Barrel Processor Design. Three or four hardware threads can execute in a round robin fashion with single cycle granularity. For instance, a 600 MHz Hexagon (typical frequency of the DSP inside a recent Qualcomm modem) can present itself as a three-core CPU clocked at 200 MHz. This feature reduces the visible latency per thread to, usually, a single cycle.

Memory Management. Hexagon has a unified memory model similar to that of a general purpose CPU. It addresses a linear memory space with memory mapped I/O, integrating an ARM compliant MMU with two stages of translation, has separate L1 data and instruction caches and a large L2 unified cache.

Relevant Instructions. Table 1 highlights instructions that are vital to implementing our optimizations for the Hexagon architecture. The intrinsics can be used as if they were C functions and are directly translated by the compiler into machine instructions. The ZUC specification mandates big endian byte ordering on keystream words: Hexagon features a dedicated endianness swap instruction.

Table 1. Noteworthy Hexagon instructions

Mnemonic	Intrinsic	Description
swiz	Q6_R_swiz_R	4-byte word endianness swap
brev	Q6_R_brev_R	32-bit word bit reverse
pmpyw	Q6_P_pmpyw_RR	carryless multiplication of 32-bit operands
combine	Q6_R_combine_R[hl]R[hl]	combine two halfwords into a word

3.2 Performance

We compare the performance of two versions of our code. The first version is a clean room implementation of the standard, presenting none of the optimizations described in this work, with essentially the same performance as the standard's reference implementation. The second version implements all the optimizations described in this work. We built the code with Qualcomm's Hexagon development tools (v6.2). It includes two C compilers based on gcc 4.6.2 and clang 3.2: We used the clang compiler since it performs consistently better than gcc on our code base.

Throughput. Tables 2, 3, and 4 present the performance results as throughput, the unit being *processed bits per hardware thread cycle*, initialization phase inclusive. We include the timings on small buffers to underline the impact of initialization, but note that large buffers are most common since LTE chiefly carries large amounts of data at high speed. For EIA3 we also compare the performance of the optimized code but without our carryless multiplication optimization, in order to highlight its impact.

Comments. The keystream generator approaches an 82 % throughput increase and comes mostly from the improvements in the LFSR, i.e. the delayed modular

Table 2. ZUC keystream generator performance on Hexagon

Length (bytes)	Throughput (bits/cycle)		Throughput increase
	Unoptimized	Optimized	
128	0.2775	0.4406	59 %
256	0.3758	0.6236	66 %
512	0.4566	0.7871	72 %
1024	0.5117	0.9058	77 %
1500	0.5322	0.9513	79 %
2048	0.5445	0.9797	80 %
4096	0.5625	1.0213	82 %
8188	0.5721	1.0435	82 %

Table 3. EEA3 confidentiality algorithm performance on Hexagon

Length (bytes)	Throughput (bits/cycle)		Throughput increase
	Unoptimized	Optimized	
128	0.2213	0.4180	89 %
256	0.2824	0.5819	106 %
512	0.3277	0.7237	121 %
1024	0.3562	0.8242	131 %
1500	0.3665	0.8599	125 %
2048	0.3725	0.8856	138 %
4096	0.3812	0.9199	141 %
8188	0.3856	0.9375	143 %

Table 4. EIA3 integrity algorithm performance on Hexagon

Length (bytes)	Throughput (bits/cycle)			Throughput increase		
	a: Unoptimized	b: No clmul	c: Optimized	b over a	c over b	c over a
128	0.1497	0.2239	0.3705	50 %	65 %	147 %
256	0.1776	0.2871	0.5119	62 %	78 %	188 %
512	0.1960	0.3343	0.6715	71 %	101 %	243 %
1024	0.2065	0.3566	0.7676	73 %	115 %	272 %
1500	0.2103	0.3663	0.8084	74 %	121 %	284 %
2048	0.2126	0.3729	0.8426	75 %	126 %	296 %
4096	0.2157	0.3817	0.8771	77 %	130 %	307 %
8188	0.2168	0.3861	0.8995	78 %	133 %	315 %

reduction and the use of a sliding window circular buffer, but also to a lesser extent the use of the `combine` instruction. Loop unrolling and standard optimizations are the main reason the optimized implementation of EEA3 reduces the gap between the unoptimized implementations of the keystream generator and EEA3: for large packets throughput more than doubles. In the case of EIA3, the mathematical improvements implemented via the carryless multiplication instruction more than double the throughput, bringing it much closer to the performance of the keystream generator alone: the optimized integrity algorithm performs about four times faster than the standard implementation.

LTE Performance. In theory, a single hardware thread on a 600 MHz Hexagon is capable of processing 182 Mbps for integrity and 175 Mbps for confidentiality: two threads can meet the LTE CAT 4 150 Mbps requirements. The actual performance is lower since a lightweight operating system is also running on the chip to manage the baseband. However, LTE data streams are split into relatively short segments (of up to 8188 bytes) which can be processed in parallel, so the effective throughput triples with respect of that of a single operation on a single thread. This means that in practice, Hexagon is comfortably capable of handling LTE CAT 4 150/50 data streams even at lower clock speeds. This performance would not be attainable without the improvements presented in this work.

Other Architectures. The full version of this paper contains benchmarks for an Intel Core i7-2760QM CPU. The results are similar, with the gain for EIA3 being smaller and the Intel chip processing significantly less bits per cycle in most cases.

4   Conclusion

Being not only new algorithms but also standardized and widely-deployed, ZUC, EEA3, and EIA3 are ideal candidates to consider performance optimizations. To this end, the software techniques presented in this work prove highly effective on a particularly relevant platform for these algorithms. Delayed modular reduction for ZUC and carryless multiplication for EIA3 yield up to roughly a 2.4-fold and 4-fold throughput improvement for EEA3 and EIA3, respectively, demonstrated on Qualcomm's Hexagon DSP architecture.

Our proposed use of delayed modular reduction in ZUC stems from public key cryptography optimization techniques and applies them, for the first time to our knowledge, to a stream cipher. This shows that the linear part of LFSR based stream ciphers, traditionally accomplished with an LFSR over a binary field, can indeed be efficiently realized in other algebraic structures providing similar provable theoretic properties.

Our proposed use of carryless multiplication to evaluate the UHF in EIA3 shows yet another application of this increasingly important microprocessor instruction to standardized symmetric cryptography. In 1999, Nevelsteen and Preneel wrote that Krawczyk's UHF construction "is more suited for hardware, and is not very fast in software" [18, Sec. 3.4]. Unquestionably true at the time, this work exemplifies ways cryptography engineering has evolved to make mutually exclusive design concepts more compatible. On one hand, the throughput improvement shows our proposed technique is dramatically effective. On the other hand, the bit ordering mandated by the specification implies an obtuse bit reversal on message words: fortunately, Hexagon is equipped to handle this natively, but this is not the case for all architectures. Cryptographically speaking, this bit ordering is irrelevant and this oversight in the specification highlights the importance of careful consideration and close collaboration between cryptologists, standardization bodies, and cryptography engineers.

Acknowledgments. We thank Alex Dent for his input on EIA3 performance optimizations.

References

1. ETSI/SAGE: Specification of the 3GPP confidentiality and integrity algorithms 128-EEA3 & 128-EIA3: 128-EEA3 & 128-EIA3 specification. Document 1, Version 1.7 (2011)
2. ETSI/SAGE: Specification of the 3GPP confidentiality and integrity algorithms 128-EEA3 & 128-EIA3: ZUC specification. Document 2, Version 1.6 (2011)
3. Kitsos, P., Sklavos, N., Skodras, A.N.: An FPGA implementation of the ZUC stream cipher. In: DSD, pp. 814–817. IEEE (2011)
4. Wang, L., Jing, J., Liu, Z., Zhang, L., Pan, W.: Evaluating optimized implementations of stream cipher ZUC algorithm on FPGA. In: Qing, S., Susilo, W., Wang, G., Liu, D. (eds.) ICICS 2011. LNCS, vol. 7043, pp. 202–215. Springer, Heidelberg (2011)
5. Traboulsi, S., Pohl, N., Hausner, J., Bilgic, A., Frascolla, V.: Power analysis and optimization of the ZUC stream cipher for LTE-advanced mobile terminals. In: Proceedings of the 3rd IEEE Latin American Symposium on Circuits and Systems (LASCAS 2012), pp. 1–4, Playa del Carmen, Mexico (2012)

6. Kitsos, P., Sklavos, N., Provelengios, G., Skodras, A.N.: FPGA-based performance analysis of stream ciphers ZUC, SNOW3G, Grain V1, Mickey V2, Trivium and E0. Microprocess. Microsyst. Embed. Hardware Des. **37**, 235–245 (2013)
7. Krawczyk, H.: LFSR-based hashing and authentication. In: Desmedt, Y.G. (ed.) CRYPTO 1994. LNCS, vol. 839, pp. 129–139. Springer, Heidelberg (1994)
8. Lim, C.H., Hwang, H.S.: Fast implementation of elliptic curve arithmetic in GF(p). In: Imai, H., Zheng, Y. (eds.) PKC 2000. LNCS, vol. 1751, pp. 405–421. Springer, Heidelberg (2000)
9. Gonda, M., Matsuo, K., Aoki, K., Chao, J., Tsujii, S.: Improvements of addition algorithm on genus 3 hyperelliptic curves and their implementation. IEICE Trans. **88-A**, 89–96 (2005)
10. Avanzi, R., Mihailescu, P.: Generic efficient arithmetic algorithms for PAFFs (Processor Adequate Finite Fields) and related algebraic structures(extended abstract). In: Matsui, M., Zuccherato, R.J. (eds.) SAC 2003. LNCS, vol. 3006, pp. 320–334. Springer, Heidelberg (2004)
11. Avanzi, R.M.: Aspects of hyperelliptic curves over large prime fields in software implementations. In: Joye, M., Quisquater, J.-J. (eds.) CHES 2004. LNCS, vol. 3156, pp. 148–162. Springer, Heidelberg (2004)
12. Gueron, S., Kounavis, M.E.: Efficient implementation of the Galois counter mode using a carry-less multiplier and a fast reduction algorithm. Inf. Process. Lett. **110**, 549–553 (2010)
13. Taverne, J., Faz-Hernández, A., Aranha, D.F., Rodríguez-Henríquez, F., Hankerson, D., López, J.: Software implementation of binary elliptic curves: impact of the carry-less multiplier on scalar multiplication. In: Preneel, B., Takagi, T. (eds.) CHES 2011. LNCS, vol. 6917, pp. 108–123. Springer, Heidelberg (2011)
14. Aranha, D.F., Faz-Hernández, A., López, J., Rodríguez-Henríquez, F.: Faster implementation of scalar multiplication on Koblitz curves. In: Hevia, A., Neven, G. (eds.) LatinCrypt 2012. LNCS, vol. 7533, pp. 177–193. Springer, Heidelberg (2012)
15. Oliveira, T., López, J., Aranha, D.F., Rodríguez-Henríquez, F.: Two is the fastest prime. Cryptology ePrint Archive, report 2013/131 (2013). http://eprint.iacr.org/2013/131/
16. Rose, G.G.: A stream cipher based on linear feedback over $GF(2^8)$. In: Dawson, E., Boyd, C. (eds.) ACISP 1998. LNCS, vol. 1438, pp. 135–146. Springer, Heidelberg (1998)
17. Forward Concepts: Qualcomm Leads in Global DSP Silicon Shipments (2012). http://www.fwdconcepts.com/dsp111212.htm
18. Nevelsteen, W., Preneel, B.: Software performance of universal hash functions. In: Stern, J. (ed.) EUROCRYPT 1999. LNCS, vol. 1592, pp. 24–41. Springer, Heidelberg (1999)

Merging the Camellia, SMS4 and AES S-Boxes in a Single S-Box with Composite Bases

Alberto F. Martínez-Herrera[⊠], Carlos Mex-Perera, and Juan Nolazco-Flores

Tecnológico de Monterrey, 2501, Garza Sada Sur, Tecnológico, Monterrey, Mexico
{a00798620,carlosmex,jnolazco}@itesm.mx

Abstract. For some block ciphers such as AES, substitution box (S-box) based on multiplicative inversion is the most complex operation. Efficient constructions should be found for optimizing features like the area, the amount of memory, etc. Composite representations in finite fields are the prominent ways to represent the multiplicative inverse operation in a compact way. In this manuscript, different constructions based on composite fields are shown to represent the AES, Camellia and SMS4 S-boxes. Mainly, this manuscript describes representations in $GF((2^4)^2)$. From these representations, an evaluation is performed to choose those feasible solutions that help to merge the AES, Camellia and SMS4 S-boxes into a single one. For instance, by using merged matrices and the same composite polynomial basis, it is possible to reduce from 172 XOR gates (independent matrices) to 146 XOR gates (merged matrices).

Keywords: Block ciphers · S-boxes · Composite fields · Multiplicative inverse · Merging

1 Introduction

Currently, information protection is an important task that must be applied to every existing communication environment. However, some environments have restrictive requirements on area, data storage, power consumption or processing time, thus compelling to hardware designers to look for ways to adapt existing cryptographic primitives to obtain compacts representations, either individually or merging two or more cryptographic primitives [17,18]. Furthermore, it is important to provide the users with different alternatives to protect their information and not only to limit them in the use of a given cryptographic primitive. Then, it is interesting to apply an approach of "Swiss Army knife" concept in Cryptography for merging common operations among different cryptographic primitives, consequently, saving footprint and allowing the users to perform different security tasks (encryption, hashing, etc.) by using the same hardware resources. An example is given by Beuchat et al. [3] where the current USA standard block cipher AES is merged with the hash function Echo. An additional example is given by Rogawski et al. [16], where AES is merged with the

A.F. Martínez-Herrera—Project partially supported by CONACyT Mexico.

© Springer International Publishing Switzerland 2015
Y. Desmedt (Ed.): ISC 2013, LNCS 7807, pp. 209–217, 2015.
DOI: 10.1007/978-3-319-27659-5_15

hash function Grøstl. The previous mentioned hash functions participated in the NIST SHA-3 contest[1].

In this work, different constructions based on composite fields in $GF((2^4)^2)$ are shown to represent the AES, Camellia and SMS4 S-boxes. From these constructions, different ways of merging the S-boxes are described, hence, obtaining merged S-box representations like AES-Camellia, AES-SMS4, Camellia-SMS4 and AES-Camellia-SMS4. In this way, only one multiplicative inverse operation is used instead of different Look Up Tables (LUTs).

This manuscript is formed by the following sections. In Sect. 2, composite bases are described. In Sect. 3, a brief description of the Camellia, AES and SMS4 S-boxes is given [2]. In Sect. 4, results and comparison tables that show the number of gates used to implement the AES, Camellia and SMS4 S-boxes are presented. In Sect. 5, the conclusions of this work are summarized.

2   Notation and Mathematical Representations

An octet can be represented as a vector of bits $\mathbf{b} = [b_0 \; b_1 \; b_2 \; b_3 \; b_4 \; b_5 \; b_6 \; b_7]$ (more details in [4,12,23]). Vector $\mathbf{b}$ can also be represented in $GF((2^4)^2)$, where the fields used are the bases $Y^8 + Y^4 + Y^2 + Y$, $y^4 + y^3 + y + 1$, $X^{16} + X$, $x + 1$. For instance, $\mathbf{b}$ can be represented as Normal-Normal (NN) with $b(X, Y) = [b_0 Y + b_1 Y^2 + b_2 Y^4 + b_3 Y^8] X + [b_4 Y + b_5 Y^2 + b_6 Y^4 + b_7 Y^8] X^{16}$. Expressed in binary notation and considering 1 as an example, let NN $1 = [1 \; 1 \; 1 \; 1 \; 1 \; 1 \; 1 \; 1]$, taking into account that 1 is equivalent to have all-ones for $\mathbf{b}$ in normal bases. It is also possible to find similar equivalences for PP, NP and PN representations. On the other hand, being the irreducible polynomial $f(z)$ defined in $GF(2^8)$, a Boolean matrix of dimension 8×8 is generated by a root $\beta = \mathbf{b}$ that nulls $f(z)$. Thus, $\mathbf{M} = [\mathbf{b}_0^T \; \mathbf{b}_1^T \; \mathbf{b}_2^T \; \mathbf{b}_3^T \; \mathbf{b}_4^T \; \mathbf{b}_5^T \; \mathbf{b}_6^T \; \mathbf{b}_7^T]$, where each sub-index indicates the power that β was raised. Besides, there are eight different Boolean matrix transformations derived from the conjugates of β that nulls $f(z)$ [12,13,15]. Regarding the use of composite fields, let h and l the subindexes that indicate the most significant and the least significant component of the composite field, respectively, $\tau, \nu, \Delta, \alpha_h, \alpha_l, b_h, b_l \in GF(2^4)$, where τ, ν are constants. According to Canright [4], the multiplicative inverse operation can be computed as

Normal basis		Polynomial basis	
$\Delta = \alpha_h \alpha_l \tau^2 + (\alpha_h + \alpha_l)^2 \nu$	(1)	$\Delta = (\alpha_h)^2 \nu + (\alpha_h \tau + \alpha_l)\alpha_l$	(4)
$\gamma_l = \alpha_h \Delta^{-1}$	(2)	$\gamma_l = (\alpha_h \tau + \alpha_l)\Delta^{-1}$	(5)
$\gamma_h = \alpha_l \Delta^{-1}$	(3)	$\gamma_h = \alpha_h \Delta^{-1}$	(6)

---

[1] The winner of the contest was Keccak, as shown in the NIST webpage http://csrc. nist.gov/groups/ST/hash/sha-3/winner_sha-3.html.

Then, the complete operation can be represented as

$$\alpha = \mathbf{Ma} \tag{7}$$

$$\gamma = [\gamma_l \; \gamma_h] \tag{8}$$

$$\mathbf{b} = \mathbf{M}^{-1}\gamma \tag{9}$$

3 Mathematical Representation of the Camellia, AES and SMS4 S-Boxes

Camellia S-Box. Camellia is a Japanese cipher designed by NTT DoCoMo and Mitsubishi Corporation [2]. Its construction is based on a Feistel Network. Four S-boxes are used as the non-linear stage of the cipher, but the last three S-boxes are derived from the first S-box. Letting $\mathbf{a}$ and $\mathbf{b}$ the input and output of the Camellia S-box, then $\mathbf{b} = S_1(\mathbf{a})$, $S_2(\mathbf{a}) = [b_7 \; b_0 \; b_1 \; b_2 \; b_3 \; b_4 \; b_5 \; b_6]$, $S_3(\mathbf{a}) = [b_1 \; b_2 \; b_3 \; b_4 \; b_5 \; b_6 \; b_7 \; b_0]$, $S_4(\mathbf{a}) = S_1([a_7 \; a_0 \; a_1 \; a_2 \; a_3 \; a_4 \; a_5 \; a_6])$, Camellia primitive polynomial is $f(z) = z^8 + z^6 + z^5 + z^3 + 1$ and the composite polynomial is $q(w) = w^4 + w + 1$ [2]. Satoh et al. specified the composite polynomial $p(x) = x^2 + \tau w + \nu$ with $\tau = 1 = [1\ 0\ 0\ 0]$ and $\nu = 1 + w^3 = [1\ 0\ 0\ 1]$ under $GF(2^4)$ [18]. The equations that describe Camellia are shown as

$$\mathbf{b} = S_{CAM}(\mathbf{a}) = \mathbf{H}[Z(\mathbf{F}(\mathbf{a} + \mathbf{c}_{i1}))] + \mathbf{c}_{o1} \in GF((2^4)^2) \tag{10}$$

$$\mathbf{b} = S_{CAMA}(\mathbf{a}) = \mathbf{H}_o(\mathbf{F}_o(\mathbf{a} + \mathbf{c}_{i1}))^{-1} + \mathbf{c}_{o1} \in GF(2^8) \tag{11}$$

where $S_1(\mathbf{a}) = S_{CAM}(\mathbf{a}) = S_{CAMA}(\mathbf{a})$, $\mathbf{F}$ and $\mathbf{H}$ are Boolean matrices, $\mathbf{c}_{i1} = [1\ 0\ 1\ 0\ 0\ 0\ 1\ 1]^T$ and $\mathbf{c}_{o1} = [0\ 1\ 1\ 1\ 0\ 1\ 1\ 0]^T$ are Boolean vectors, and Z is treated as the composite operation in $GF((2^4)^2)$. Additionally, $\mathbf{F} = \mathbf{MF}_o$ and $\mathbf{H} = \mathbf{H}_o\mathbf{M}^{-1}$. Thus, $\mathbf{H}_o$ and $\mathbf{F}_o$ can be computed as $\mathbf{F}_o = \mathbf{M}^{-1}\mathbf{F}$ and $\mathbf{H}_o = \mathbf{HM}$, respectively [12]. The name of each equation is used to distinguish the representation of the operation, being $S_{CAM}(\mathbf{a})$ for the original equation based on the composite inverse operation and $S_{CAMA}(\mathbf{a})$ based on the raw multiplicative inverse.

AES S-Box. AES is currently the USA block cipher standard. Based on Rijndael, it was designed by Rijmen and Daemen as a Substitution Permutation Network [5]. AES is divided in 4 stages denoted as SubBytes, ShiftRows, MixColumns and AddRoundKey. SubBytes is the non-linear stage of this cipher and it is formed by two S-boxes. $S_{AES}(\mathbf{a})$ is used for encryption and $S_{AESinv}(\mathbf{a})$ is used for decryption. AES irreducible polynomial is $f(z) = z^8 + z^4 + z^3 + z + 1$. Letting $\mathbf{a}$ and $\mathbf{b}$ the input and output of the AES S-box, then

$$\mathbf{b} = S_{AES}(\mathbf{a}) = \mathbf{A}(\mathbf{a})^{-1} + \mathbf{c} \in GF(2^8) \tag{12}$$

$$\mathbf{b}_{inv} = S_{AESinv}(\mathbf{a}) = \mathbf{A}^{-1}(\mathbf{a} + \mathbf{c})^{-1} \in GF(2^8) \tag{13}$$

where $\mathbf{c} = [1\ 1\ 0\ 0\ 0\ 1\ 1\ 0]^T$ is a Boolean vector and $\mathbf{A}$, $\mathbf{A}^{-1}$ are Boolean matrices.

SMS4 S-Box. SMS4 is a Feistel block cipher designed by Chinese researchers [20]. SMS4 uses one S-box as non-linear stage. The way of obtaining the SMS4 S-box are given by description is given by Liu et al. by inferring the most accurate representation of the S-box from the published tables [11], and Erickson et al. [6] . According to them, the irreducible polynomial is $f(z) = z^8 + z^7 + z^6 + z^5 + z^4 + z^2 + 1$. Letting $\mathbf{a}$ and $\mathbf{b}$ the input and output of the SMS4 S-box, the mathematical description is given as

$$\mathbf{b} = S_{SMS4}(\mathbf{a}) = [(\mathbf{a}\mathbf{A}_1 + \mathbf{c}_{i2})^{-1}]\mathbf{A}_2 + \mathbf{c}_{o2} \in GF(2^8) \tag{14}$$

$$\mathbf{b} = S_{SMS4A}(\mathbf{a}) = \mathbf{A}_2[(\mathbf{A}_1\mathbf{a} + \mathbf{c}_{i2})^{-1}] + \mathbf{c}_{o2} \in GF(2^8) \tag{15}$$

where $c_{i2} = c_{o2} = [1\ 1\ 0\ 0\ 1\ 0\ 1\ 1]$ is a Boolean vector, $\mathbf{A}_1$ is a Boolean matrix and $\mathbf{A}_1 = \mathbf{A}_2$ in the case of Eq. 14 ([11]). For Eq. 15, $\mathbf{c}_{i2} = [1\ 1\ 0\ 1\ 0\ 0\ 1\ 1]^T$, $\mathbf{c}_{o2} = [1\ 1\ 0\ 0\ 1\ 0\ 1\ 1]^T$ are Boolean vectors, $\mathbf{A}_1$ and $\mathbf{A}_1$ are Boolean matrices, where $\mathbf{A}_1 \neq \mathbf{A}_2$ ([6]). In this manuscript, Eq. 15 is used. Nevertheless, the input, constants and the final output should be reversed for maintaining consistency before and after using the multiplicative inverse, while the matrix set is the same as shown by Erickson et al.[2].

3.1   Merging the Camellia, AES and SMS4 S-Boxes by Using Composite Fields

From previous descriptions of the Camellia, AES and SMS4 S-boxes, all the S-boxes can share the same Z operation (composite inverse). Equations (16–19) are the composite field versions of the Camellia, SMS4, AES and AES inverse S-boxes where $\mathbf{F} = \mathbf{M}\mathbf{F}_o$, $\mathbf{H} = \mathbf{H}_o\mathbf{M}^{-1}$, $\tilde{\mathbf{A}}_1 = \mathbf{M}\mathbf{A}_1$, $\tilde{\mathbf{A}}_2 = \mathbf{A}_2\mathbf{M}^{-1}$, $\tilde{\mathbf{c}}_{i2} = \mathbf{M}c_{i2}$, $\tilde{\mathbf{A}} = \mathbf{A}\mathbf{M}^{-1}$, $\tilde{\mathbf{B}} = \mathbf{M}\mathbf{A}^{-1}$. Then, the identities are listed as follows

$$S_{CAM}(\mathbf{a}) = \mathbf{H}[Z(\mathbf{F}(\mathbf{a} + \mathbf{c}_{i1}))] + \mathbf{c}_{o1} \tag{16}$$

$$S_{SMS4Ac}(\mathbf{a}) = \tilde{\mathbf{A}}_2[Z(\tilde{\mathbf{A}}_1\mathbf{a} + \tilde{\mathbf{c}}_{i2})] + \mathbf{c}_{o2} \tag{17}$$

$$S_{AESc}(\mathbf{a}) = \tilde{\mathbf{A}}[Z(\mathbf{M}\mathbf{a})] + \mathbf{c} \tag{18}$$

$$S_{AESinvc}(\mathbf{a}) = \mathbf{M}^{-1}[Z(\tilde{\mathbf{B}}(\mathbf{a} + \mathbf{c}))] \tag{19}$$

Note that $\tilde{\mathbf{c}}_{i2}$ will change because of the matrix transformation that is used. By using $\mathbf{F}$, $\mathbf{H}$, $\tilde{\mathbf{A}}_1$, $\tilde{\mathbf{A}}_2$, $\mathbf{M}$, $\tilde{\mathbf{A}}$, $\tilde{\mathbf{B}}$ and $\mathbf{M}^{-1}$, we are able to determine the number of minimal XOR gates that represent such matrix transformations. For description purposes, let $\mathbf{U} = \mathbf{F}$, $\mathbf{V} = \mathbf{H}$ for the matrix representations of the Camellia S-box, $\mathbf{U} = \tilde{\mathbf{A}}_1$, $\mathbf{V} = \tilde{\mathbf{A}}_2$ for the SMS4 S-box, $\mathbf{U} = \mathbf{M}$, $\mathbf{V} = \tilde{\mathbf{A}}$ for the AES S-box and $\mathbf{U} = \tilde{\mathbf{B}}$, $\mathbf{V} = \mathbf{M}^{-1}$ for the AES inverse S-box.

4   Results and Comparisons

Paar's matrix generation algorithm [15] was applied to compute the set of matrices of the Camellia S-box. A similar analysis was performed to the set of matrices

---

[2] The same observation applies on Eq. 17 when computing $\tilde{\mathbf{c}_{i2}} = \mathbf{M}c_{i2}$.

of the AES and SMS4 S-boxes by using Zhang et al.'s algorithm [24]. That means, the way to compute $\mathbf{M}$ (or equivalent matrix representations such as $\mathbf{U}$ and $\mathbf{V}$). For the optimization of these matrices, Boyar et al.'s LDG technique helps to compute the number of XOR gates and the critical path for each obtained matrix [10]. In similar ways to previous works available in the literature, identity $\tau = 1$ was considered for all the representations. An additional analysis with respect to Martinez et al.'s work is the inclusion of normal bases in $GF(2^4)$. Tables 1 and 2 include the number of gates (NG) and critical path (CP) in terms of XOR, AND and NOT gates because the results include the non-linear term γ. By adopting Martinez et al.'s notation [12], X means XOR, No means NOT, A means AND, while N means Normal and P means polynomial basis representation. Additionally, XOR means to have two-input XOR gate, AND means to have two-input AND gate.

Performing an extensive search for the given composite bases, there are feasible solutions to implement the Camellia, AES and SMS4 S-boxes at the same time with PP and PN representations. That means, the three S-boxes use the same composite field representation. Condensed results are shown in Table 1, which includes those results that are feasible to be merged. Those cases reported by Xu et al. [22] and Abbasi et al. [1] were considered as described in those references. The same criterion was applied to include the Camellia S-box reported by Martinez et al., where $(\tau = 2, \nu = 2)$ (marked in Table 1 as %). To complement the reported results, the given S-boxes were synthesized by using XILINX ISE Design Suite 14.4 with the FPGA Virtex 6 Kit ML605, thus obtaining the corresponding number of used LUTs and slices in a simulated way. The estimated path delay is also reported (in nano-seconds).

The results shown in Table 2 are summarized from the data showed in Table 1, by adding the corresponding AND/XOR/NOT gates and merging the Z operation. Cases marked as "M Set" were obtained by concatenating the corresponding

Table 1. Number of gates (NG) and critical path (CP) for the Camellia, SMS4 and AES S-boxes (D=delay).

Field	Cipher	NG (U,γ,V)	CP (U,γ,V)	LUTs/Slices/D(ns)
PP	Camellia % [12]	91 X /58 A/9 No	15 X/4 A/2 No	
PPP	SMS4 [22]	157 X /63 A		
NNN	SMS4 [1]	134 X /36 A		
PP	Camellia [18]	89 X/58 A/9 No	15 X/4 A/1 No	40/16/5.796
	SMS4	102 X/58 A/9 No	17 X/4 A/2 No	66/28/7.341
	AES [18]	127 X/ 58 A/8 No/2 MUX	17 X/4 A/1 No/2 MUX	80/34/8.998
NP	Camellia [12]	94 X/58 A/9 No	14 X/4 A/2 No	37/15/5.158
	SMS4	99 X/58 A/11 No	16 X/4 A/2 No	65/33/6.837
PN	Camellia	98 X/58 A/9 No	17 X/4 A/2 No	50/20/7.945
	SMS4	102 X/58 A/7 No	17 X/4 A/2 No	52/21/7.801
	AES	129 X/58 A/8 No/2 MUX	17 X/4 A/1 No/2 MUX	60/21/9.892
NN	Camellia	100 X/58 A/9 No	16 X/4 A/2 No	54/23/8.392
	SMS4	101 X/58 A/8 No	15 X/4 A/2 No	54/23/8.048

Table 2. Merged cases of the Camellia, SMS4 and AES S-boxes (D=delay).

Field	Cipher	NG (U,γ,V)	CP (**U**,γ,**V**)	LUTs/Slices/D(ns)
PP	AES/Cam [18]	143 X/ 58 A/17 No/2 MUX	17 X/4 A/1 No/2 MUX	89/34/7.810
	AES/SMS4	156 X/ 58 A/17 No/2 MUX	17 X/4 A/1 No/2 MUX	71/28/9.459
	Cam/SMS4	118 X/ 58 A/18 No/2 MUX	17 X/4 A/2 No/2 MUX	74/27/8.839
	Set	172 X/ 58 A/26 No/2 MUX	17 X/4 A/2 No/2 MUX	78/31/8.878
	M Set	146 X/ 58 A/26 No/2 MUX	17 X/4 A/2 No/2 MUX	81/28/8.878
NP	Cam/SMS4	120 X/ 58 A/20 No/2 MUX	16 X/4 A/2 No/2 MUX	60/24/7.064
PN	AES/Cam	153 X/58 A/17 No/2 MUX	17 X/4 A/2 No/2 MUX	76/33/10.204
	AES/SMS4	157 X/58 A/15 No/2 MUX	17 X/4 A/2 No/2 MUX	71/27/9.650
	Cam/SMS4	126 X/58 A/16 No/2 MUX	17 X/4 A/2 No/2 MUX	66/26/9.580
	Set	181 X/58 A/24 No/2 MUX	17 X/4 A/2 No/2 MUX	87/37/12.504
	M Set	161 X/58 A/24 No/2 MUX	17 X/4 A/2 No/2 MUX	81/32/10.817
NN	Cam/SMS4	127 X/58 A/17 No/2 MUX	16 X/4 A/2 No/2 MUX	60/25/8.867

matrices as $\mathbf{G}_I = [\mathbf{F}\ \tilde{\mathbf{A}}_1\ \mathbf{M}\ \tilde{\mathbf{B}}]^T$ and $\mathbf{G}_O = [\mathbf{H}\ \tilde{\mathbf{A}}_2\ \tilde{\mathbf{A}}\ \mathbf{M}^{-1}]^T$, each one with dimensions 32×8. For PP representation $\mathbf{G}_I$ has 35 XOR gates and $\mathbf{G}_O$ has 38 XOR gates. For PN representation $\mathbf{G}_I$ has 44 XOR gates and $\mathbf{G}_O$ has 43 XOR gates. It is needed to add two multiplexers to choose the corresponding S-box and it is important to consider that these components can add extra delay at the critical path.

For calculating the number of gates in Δ^{-1}, identities provided by Wolkerstorfer et al. [21] and Nikova et al. [14] were applied to compute the corresponding outputs. For the sake of simplicity, only cases for P with $p_1(y) = y^4 + y + 1$ and N with $p_2(y) = y^4 + y^3 + y^2 + y + 1$ were considered. For P there are 18 X/10 A gates with 3 X/2 A gates as the critical path. For N there are 17 X/10 A gates with 3 X/2 A gates as the critical path. Nikova et al.'s suggest to use outputs A and H (Table 2 of [14]) as the suitable ones. Nevertheless, it is possible that outputs D and G can also be suitable. This claim is supported by using the Little-Fermat-Theorem version of the multiplicative inverse published in the IEEE P-1363 standard documents (see [7,8]) and additional sources (see [9,19]) where D and G are obtained for normal and optimal normal bases, respectively. For G, we obtain

$$a_0^{-1} = x_0x_1 + x_2 + x_0x_2 + x_0x_1x_2 + x_1x_3 + x_0x_2x_3 + x_1x_2x_3 \tag{20}$$

$$a_1^{-1} = x_0x_2 + x_1x_2 + x_3 + x_1x_3 + x_0x_1x_3 + x_0x_2x_3 + x_1x_2x_3 \tag{21}$$

$$a_2^{-1} = x_0 + x_0x_2 + x_0x_1x_2 + x_1x_3 + x_0x_1x_3 + x_2x_3 + x_0x_2x_3 \tag{22}$$

$$a_3^{-1} = x_1 + x_0x_2 + x_0x_1x_2 + x_0x_3 + x_1x_3 + x_0x_1x_3 + x_1x_2x_3 \tag{23}$$

Here, identities of Eqs. 20–23 were used.

5   Conclusions

With respect to SMS4 under composite field implementations, the cases reported in this manuscript are shorter in number of XOR gates than previous cases given by Abbasi et al. and Xu et al. Nevertheless, the number of AND gates shown in this manuscript is worse than Abbasi et al.'s normal basis case. Nonetheless, it is needed to have more accurate parameters to be able to compare the SMS4 S-box in $GF(((2^2)^2)^2)$ and such task is left as future work. Unfortunately, there is not a straightforward way to compare the theoretical critical path among the Abbassi et al.'s and Xu et al.'s cases and the cases shown in this manuscript. If the AES and Camellia S-boxes are combined, Satoh et al.'s case remains as the best one. Nevertheless, there are additional ways to merge the Camellia and SMS4 S-boxes, AES and SMS4 S-boxes, and the complete set of S-boxes. A new way to construct S-boxes by using normal bases is also provided with PN representation. It is interesting to see that merging the transformation matrices in a unique matrix, the number of XOR gates can be reduced in a significant way. For PP representation, 172-146= 26 XOR gates are saved, while for PN representation, 181-161=20 XOR gates are saved. There is a penalty by merging the complete set of S-boxes, which is the use of two multiplexers. Even so, this impact is minimal if we consider that each S-box implemented individually spends more hardware resources than in merged way i.e. a multiplexer is less complex than implementing a complete S-box as Satoh et al. demonstrated in their work [18]. By using FPGA platforms, the extended matrix merged Satoh's case remains as the best one because it works with 78 LUTs/31 slices/8.878 ns for non-merged matrix set and 81 LUTs/28 slices/8.878 ns for merged matrix set. As future work, the authors will implement the given constructions with appropriate standard CMOS libraries in order to obtain more accurate results for ASIC cases.

Acknowledgments. Alberto F. Martinez is very grateful with CONACyT and "Biometrics and Secure Protocols Chair" for supporting his PhD studies at Tecnológico de Monterrey.

References

1. Abbasi, I., Afzal, M.: A compact S-Box design for SMS4 block cipher. In: Park, J.J., Arabnia, H., Chang, H.-B., Shon, T. (eds.) IT Convergence and Services. Lecture Notes in Electrical Engineering, pp. 641–658. Springer, Netherlands (2011)
2. Aoki, K., Ichikawa, T., Kanda, M., Matsui, M., Moriai, S., Nakajima, J., Tokita, T.: Specifications of Camellia, a 128 bits block cipher. Technical report 1, Mitsubishi and NTT DoCoMo, Tokio, Japan, August (2001)
3. Beuchat, J.-L., Okamoto, E., Yamazaki, T.: A low-area unified hardware architecture for the AES and the cryptographic hash function ECHO. J. Crypt. Eng. 1(2), 101–121 (2011)
4. Canright, D.: A very compact Rijndael S-box. Technical report, Naval Postgraduate School, Monterey, CA, USA (2005)
5. Daemen, J., Rijmen, V.: The design of Rijndael: AES-the advanced encryption standard. Information Security and Cryptography. Springer, Heidelberg (2002)
6. Erickson, J., Ding, J., Christensen, C.: Algebraic cryptanalysis of SMS4: Gröbner basis attack and SAT attack compared. In: Lee, D., Hong, S. (eds.) ICISC 2009. LNCS, vol. 5984, pp. 73–86. Springer, Heidelberg (2010)

7. IEEE: IEEE Std 1363–2000 IEEE Standard Specifications for Public-Key Cryptography (2000)
8. IEEE: IEEE Standard Specifications for Public-Key Cryptography- Amendment 1: Additional Techniques. IEEE Std 1363a–2004 (Amendment to IEEE Std 1363–2000), pp. 1–159 (2004)
9. Deschamps, J.-P., Luis, I.J., Gustavo, D.S.: Hardware Implementation of Finite-Field Arithmetic, vol. 2009. McGraw Hill, New York (2009)
10. Boyar, J., Peralta, R.: A depth-16 circuit for the AES S-box. Cryptology ePrint Archive, Report 2011/332 (2011). http://eprint.iacr.org/
11. Liu, F., Ji, W., Hu, L., Ding, J., Lv, S., Pyshkin, A., Weinmann, R.-P.: Analysis of the SMS4 block cipher. In: Pieprzyk, J., Ghodosi, H., Dawson, E. (eds.) ACISP 2007. LNCS, vol. 4586, pp. 158–170. Springer, Heidelberg (2007)
12. Martínez-Herrera, A.F., Mex-Perera, J.C., Nolazco-Flores, J.A.: Some representations of the S-Box of Camellia in $GF(((2^2)^2)^2)$. In: Pieprzyk, J., Sadeghi, A.-R., Manulis, M. (eds.) CANS 2012. LNCS, vol. 7712, pp. 296–309. Springer, Heidelberg (2012)
13. Mentens, N., Batina, L., Preneel, B., Verbauwhede, I.: A systematic evaluation of compact hardware implementations for the Rijndael S-Box. In: Menezes, A. (ed.) CT-RSA 2005. LNCS, vol. 3376, pp. 323–333. Springer, Heidelberg (2005)
14. Nikova, S., Rijmen, V., Schläffer, M.: Using normal bases for compact hardware implementations of the AES S-Box. In: Ostrovsky, R., De Prisco, R., Visconti, I. (eds.) SCN 2008. LNCS, vol. 5229, pp. 236–245. Springer, Heidelberg (2008)
15. Paar, C.: Efficient VLSI architectures for bit-parallel computation in Galois fields. Dissertation, Institute for Experimental Mathematics, Universitt Essen, Essen (1994)
16. Rogawski, M., Gaj, K.: A high-speed unified hardware architecture for AES and the SHA-3 candidate Grøstl. In: 2012 15th Euromicro Conference on Digital System Design (DSD), pp. 568–575 (2012)
17. Satoh, A., Morioka, S.: Hardware-focused performance comparison for the standard block ciphers AES, Camellia, and triple-DES. In: Boyd, C., Mao, W. (eds.) ISC 2003. LNCS, vol. 2851, pp. 252–266. Springer, Heidelberg (2003)
18. Satoh, A., Morioka, S.: Unified hardware architecture for 128-bit block ciphers AES and Camellia. In: Walter, C.D., Koç, Ç.K., Paar, C. (eds.) CHES 2003. LNCS, vol. 2779, pp. 304–318. Springer, Heidelberg (2003)
19. Itoh, T., Tsujii, S.: A fast algorithm for computing multiplicative inverses in $GF(2^m)$ using normal bases. Inf. Comput. **78**(3), 171–177 (1988)
20. Diffie, W., Ledin, G. (translators): SMS4 encryption algorithm for wireless networks. Cryptology ePrint Archive, Report 2008/329, Translation version of the original document in Chinese (2008). http://www.oscca.gov.cn/UpFile/200621016423197990.pdf
21. Wolkerstorfer, J., Oswald, E., Lamberger, M.: An ASIC implementation of the AES SBoxes. In: Preneel, B. (ed.) CT-RSA 2002. LNCS, vol. 2271, p. 67. Springer, Heidelberg (2002)

22. Xu, Y., Bai, X., Guo, L.: An efficient implementation of SMS4 cipher with multiplicative masking resistant to differential power analysis attack. In: WRI International Conference on Communications and Mobile Computing, CMC 2009, vol. 3, pp. 364–369 (2009)
23. Yasuyuki, N., Kenta, N., Tetsumi, T., Naoto, H., Yoshitaka, M.: Mixed bases for efficient inversion in $F((2^2)^2)^2$ and conversion matrices of subbytes of AES. IEICE Trans. Fundam. Electron. Commun. Comput. Sci. **94**(6), 1318–1327 (2011)
24. Zhang, X., Parhi, K.: High-speed VLSI architectures for the AES algorithm. IEEE Trans. Very Large Scale Integr. VLSI Syst. **12**(9), 957–967 (2004)

Entity Authentication

Offline Dictionary Attack on Password Authentication Schemes Using Smart Cards

Ding Wang[1,2(✉)] and Ping Wang[2,3]

[1] School of EECS, Peking University, Beijing 100871, China
`wangdingg@mail.nankai.edu.cn`
[2] National Engineering Research Center for Software Engineering,
Beijing 100871, China
[3] School of Software and Microelectronics, Peking University, Beijing 100260, China
`pwang@pku.edu.cn`

Abstract. The design of secure and efficient smart-card-based password authentication schemes remains a challenging problem today despite two decades of intensive research in the security community, and the current crux lies in how to achieve truly two-factor security even if the smart cards can be tampered. In this paper, we analyze two recent proposals, namely, Hsieh-Leu's scheme and Wang's PSCAV scheme. We show that, under their non-tamper-resistance assumption of the smart cards, both schemes are still prone to offline dictionary attack, in which an attacker can obtain the victim's password when getting temporary access to the victim's smart card. This indicates that compromising a single factor (i.e., the smart card) of these two schemes leads to the downfall of both factors (i.e., both the smart card and the password), thereby invalidating their claim of preserving two-factor security. Remarkably, our attack on the latter protocol, which is not captured in Wang's original protocol security model, *reveals a new attacking scenario* and gives rise to the strongest adversary model so far. In addition, we make the first attempt to explain why smart cards, instead of common cheap storage devices (e.g., USB sticks), are preferred in most two-factor authentication schemes for security-critical applications.

Keywords: Password authentication · Offline dictionary attack · Smart card · Common memory device · Non-tamper resistant

1 Introduction

Back in 1992, Bellovin and Merritt [3] demonstrated how two parties, who only share a low-entropy password and communicate over a public network, can authenticate each other and agree on a cryptographically strong session key to secure their subsequent communications. Their work, known as encrypted key exchange, is a great success in protecting poorly-chosen passwords from the notorious offline dictionary attacks and thus confirms the feasibility of using password-only protocols to establish virtually secure channels over public networks, which is one of the main practical applications of cryptography. Due to the

© Springer International Publishing Switzerland 2015
Y. Desmedt (Ed.): ISC 2013, LNCS 7807, pp. 221–237, 2015.
DOI: 10.1007/978-3-319-27659-5_16

practical significance of password-based authentication, Bellovin-Merritt's seminal work has been followed by a number of remarkable proposals (e.g., [6,7,27]) with various levels of security and complexity.

While password authentication protocols are well suited to applications with moderate security demands, they are inadequate for use in security-critical applications such as e-banking, e-health and e-government [8]. Since password-based protocols generally require the server to store and manage a sensitive password-related file, a compromise of this file will lead to an exposure of the passwords of all the registered users, resulting in the downfall of the entire system. With the prevalence of zero-day attacks [4], these days it is no news to see the headlines about catastrophic leakages of tens of millions of passwords [13,16]. It is due to this inherent limitation that two-factor authentication schemes[1] are introduced to enhance the systems' security and privacy. Owing to its portability, simplicity and cryptographic capability, smart-card-based password authentication has become one of the most effective, prevalent and promising two-factor authentication mechanisms.

Since Chang and Wu [9] developed the first smart-card-based password authentication scheme in 1991, there have been ample (in the hundreds) of this type of schemes proposed [15,20,23,26,28,31,48,53,57,58]. Unfortunately, as stated in [34,45], although there has been no lack of literature, it remains an immature area – all existing schemes are far from ideal and each has been shown to be either insecure or short of important features. For an intuitive grasp, we summarize the "break-fix-break-fix" history of this area in Fig. 1. Note that many other important schemes cannot be included here only due to space constraints.

Motivations. The past thirty years of research on password-only protocols have proved that it is incredibly difficult to get a single-factor protocol right [43,60], while the past twenty years of "break-fix-break-fix" cycle of smart-card-based password protocols have manifested designing a two-factor scheme can only be harder [33,34,40]. It remains an open problem to construct an efficient and secure two-factor protocol that can meet all the security goals (see Sect. 2 of [54]) and preserve all the desirable features such as user anonymity and repairability (see [34] for a comprehensive list of desirable features).

We have analyzed more than one hundred and fifty smart-card-based password protocols and observe that, as with the domain of password-based single-factor authentication, offline dictionary attack is still the most prominent issue in two-factor authentication. This attack against many of previous protocols has emphasized the need for rigorous proofs of security in a formal, well-defined model. On the other hand, the practicality of a formal model largely depends on whether it "accurately captures the realistic capabilities of the adversary" [17]. As stated by Alfred Menezes [36,37], although many formal security definitions "have an appealing logical elegance and nicely reflect certain notions of security, they fail to take into account many types of attacks and do not provide a comprehensive model of adversarial behavior", and "the old-fashioned cryptanalysis continues to play an important role in establishing confidence in the security of a

---

[1] Note that the terms "protocol" and "scheme" will be used interchangeably thereafter.

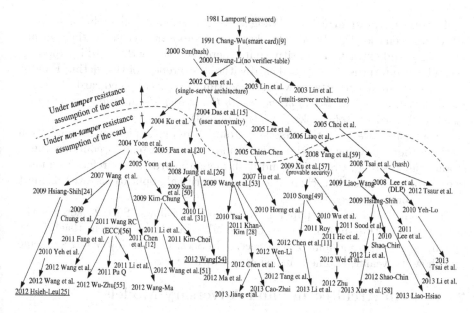

Fig. 1. A brief history of smart-card-based password authentication

cryptographic system". All this and the continuous failures in designing a practical two-factor scheme outline the need for exploring the adversarial behaviors and for revealing the underlying subtleties by cryptanalysis.

Recent studies have pointed out that the secret parameters stored in common smart cards can be extracted by side-channel attacks such as power analysis [29,38,39] or reverse engineering techniques [35,42]. Even though the card manufacturers may have considered the risks of side-channel attacks and provided countermeasures to cope with the problem, how much confidence can one have that these countermeasures residing in the card are still effective after three years of the card production and circulation? Considering this, since 2004 most schemes have preferred to use a non-tamper-resistant smart card (see the arcuate dash line of Fig. 1). This brings forth a question: While non-tamper resistance assumption has been made about smart cards (which means the core feature of the smart cards is lost), why not just use cheap memory devices (e.g., USB sticks) instead? As far as we know, little attention has been paid to this interesting (and fundamental) question.

Our Contributions. This paper examines the security of two recently proposed schemes, namely Hsieh-Leu's scheme [25] and Wang's PSCAV scheme [54]. These two schemes are the foremost ones and claimed to be secure against various known attacks. However, this work invalidates their claims by demonstrating that, under their assumption of the capabilities of the adversary, both schemes are vulnerable to the offline dictionary attack. This indicates that none of them can achieve the "precious" two-factor security.

Interestingly, our attack on Wang's PSCAV scheme [54] highlights a new attacking scenario: Firstly, an attacker gets temporary access to the victim's smart card and extracts its sensitive data (hereafter we say this card is exposed); Secondly, she returns the exposed card without awareness of the victim; Finally, she performs malicious attacks when the victim uses this exposed card. *This new attacking scenario has already given rise to the strongest adversary model so far* (see the "Returned stolen token" Section of [61]).

In addition, we take the first step toward giving a plausible explanation to the rather confusing question – why smart cards, instead of common cheap storage devices (e.g., USB sticks and flash-memory cards), are preferred in most two-factor authentication schemes for security-critical applications, even if smart cards can be tampered?

The remainder of this paper is organized as follows: Sect. 2 sketches the system architecture and elaborates on the adversary model; Then, Hsieh-Leu's scheme is reviewed and analyzed in Sect. 3; In Sect. 4, we review Wang's scheme and show its weakness; The conclusion is drawn in Sect. 5.

2   System Architecture and Adversary Models

2.1   System Architecture of Two-Factor Authentication

In this paper, we mainly focus on the most general case of two-factor authentication where the communication parties only involve a single server and a set of users, i.e. the traditional client/server architecture. It is not difficult to see that our results in this paper can be applied to more complex architectures where more than one server are involved, such as the multi-server authentication environments [58], the mobile network roaming environments [48] and the hierarchical wireless sensor networks [14].

In this sort of schemes, firstly the user chooses an identity (often as well as a password) and registers at the server; The server returns the user a smart card storing some security parameters. After registration, whenever the user wants to login to the server, she inserts the card into a terminal and enters her password. Then the card constructs a login request and sends it to the server. Upon receiving the request, the server checks its validity and will offer the requested service if the verification holds. Generally, a session key is established for securing the subsequent data communications. More sophisticated schemes also achieves mutual authentication, i.e. the client is also convinced that the server on the other end is authentic. What a truly two-factor protocol can guarantee is that, only the user who is in possession of both the smart card and the corresponding password can pass the verification of the server. This implies that a compromise of either factor will pose no danger to the security of a truly two-factor protocol.

2.2   Adversary Models for Smart-card-based Authentication and for Common-memory-based Authentication

In this section, we attempt to take the initial step to justify the use of smart cards rather than common memory devices in security-critical applications. Firstly, we explicitly define the practical capabilities that an attacker may have in the smart-card-based authentication environment and in the memory-device-based authentication environment, respectively. Then, we investigate into the advantages and disadvantages of these two kinds of authentication.

Two Kinds of Mobile Devices. A smart card is an integrated circuit card with a processor for executing applications and a memory, coupled to the processor, for storing multiple applications. This kind of device has been widely used for various security-critical applications ranging from online-banking over digital rights management (DRM) to stream media (e.g., Pay-TV). For example, a HiPerSmart-P9SC648 smart card [47] from the 32-bit HiPerSmart^{TM} family is of the RISC MIPS32 architecture, with a maximum clock speed of 36 MHz, a 512 Kbyte Flash, a 142 Kbyte EEPROM and a 16 Kbyte RAM. In the current market, such a smart card is priced at $3.0 \sim 3.5$. In contrast, a common USB memory stick is a data storage device that includes the flash memory with an integrated Universal Serial Bus (USB) interface, and the typical cost of an 1 GB USB stick is $1.3 \sim 1.5$ [21]. Since USB memory sticks[2] are not equipped with micro-processors, they cannot execute cryptographic operations as opposed to smart cards, and thus the operations have to be performed on the user terminal (e.g., PCs and PDAs).

As discussed in the previous section, it is prudent and reasonable to take into consideration the side-channel attacks [29,38,39,42] when designing a smart-card-based two-factor authentication scheme. In other words, the secret data stored in the card memory are assumed to be extractable when the smart card is in the hands of an attacker. On the other hand, in the past it was just the tamper-resistant feature that makes smart cards prevail over other cheap (but non-tamper-resistant) memory devices. *Now that smart cards can be tampered, why we do not choose cheap USB memory sticks instead of expensive smart cards?* Or equally, what's the rationale under these propositions [20,25,31,50,51,55,57,59] that endeavor to construct two-factor authentication schemes using non-tamper resistant smart cards rather than memory sticks? To the best of our knowledge, until now, little attention has been given to this question.

Two Kinds of Adversary Models. To identify the differences in security provisions offered by two-factor authentication schemes using these two different devices, we need to discuss the realistic capabilities that an attacker may have under these two different authentication environments. On the basis of the studies [50,54,57,59], the following assumptions are made on the capabilities of the adversary $\mathcal{M}$ in the smart-card-based environment:

S(i) $\mathcal{M}$ can fully control the communication channel between the user and the server. In other words, she can inject, modify, block, and delete messages exchanged in the channel at will. This assumption is consistent with the Dolev-Yao model;

---

[2] Hereafter, we use "USB sticks" and "common memory devices" interchangeably. In this work, we do not consider hybrid devices like Trust Extension Devices [1].

S(ii) $\mathcal{M}$ is able to get access to the smart card and may compromise the user's smart card through side-channel attacks (only) when getting access to the smart card for a relatively long period of time(e.g., a few hours) [54,59];

S(iii) $\mathcal{M}$ may comprise the user's password (e.g., by shoulder-surfing or malicious card reader [19,32]).

S(iv) $\mathcal{M}$ is *not able to* extract the sensitive information on the smart card while intercepting the victim's password by using a malicious card reader, since the user is on the scene and the time is not sufficient for launching a side-channel attack [2,54];

S(v) $\mathcal{M}$ is not allowed to first compromise the user's password (e.g., by shoulder-surfing) and then compromise the smart card [51,54,57]. Otherwise, no scheme can prevent $\mathcal{M}$ from succeeding. More specifically, if $\mathcal{M}$ has compromised both factors, there is no way to prevent $\mathcal{M}$ from impersonating the user, since it is these two factors together that precisely identifies the user. This is a trivial case.

The above Assumptions $S(i) \sim S(v)$ have been made in most recent schemes and their reasonableness is quite evident. For a detailed justification, readers are referred to [52]. It is worth noting that, Assumptions $S(ii)$ and $S(iv)$ together imply that the common non-tamper-resistance assumption made about the smart cards is *conditional*. In particular, it is Assumption $S(iv)$ that makes it possible for the smart-card-based schemes to be adopted in completely hostile environments, yet most studies [11,20,25,28,51,57–59] (except few ones [52,54]) do not make this assumption clear and just implicitly rely on it. Failing to catch this subtlety may cause great misconceptions and lead to curious situations as it did in the works [10,44,45,59], which will be discussed later in this section.

Regarding USB-stick-based schemes, Assumption $S(iv)$ will not be valid, because it is not difficult for a malware to copy all the contents in the USB memory stick within only seconds, even if the user appears on the scene. Nevertheless, the other four assumptions do roughly hold for common-memory-based environment:

M(i) $\mathcal{M}$ can fully control the communication channel between the user and the server. In other words, she can inject, modify, block, and delete messages exchanged in the channel at will. This assumption is consistent with the Dolev-Yao model;

M(ii) $\mathcal{M}$ is able to compromise the user's memory device through malware within a short time period (e.g., in a few seconds);

M(iii) $\mathcal{M}$ may comprise the user's password (e.g., by shoulder-surfing or social engineering);

M(iv) $\mathcal{M}$ is *able to* extract the sensitive data on the memory device while intercepting the password that the user input by using malwares;

M(v) $\mathcal{M}$ is not allowed to first compromise the user's password and then compromise the user's memory device. Clearly, if $\mathcal{M}$ compromises both factors, there is no way to prevent $\mathcal{M}$ from impersonating the user, since these two factors together precisely identify the user. It is a trivial case.

Justification for Using Smart Cards. Having examining the differences of adversary models between the smart card scenario and the common memory device scenario, we proceed to look into the rationales underlying the wide use of smart cards rather than common memory devices in two-factor authentication.

Recently, with the popularity of mobile devices, a few studies [10, 44] advocated the use of common memory devices instead of smart cards to construct two-factor schemes, and claimed that their schemes can "enjoy all the advantages of authentication schemes using smart cards" [44]. However, such a claim is a bit optimistic. According to the above adversary model for common-memory-device environment, such a claim holds only when the scheme is adopted in a trusted user terminal (otherwise, the malicious terminal could just intercept the password and copy the content of the memory device, and with no doubt the attacker is able to impersonate the victim in future). Smart-card-based schemes, in contrast, do not subject to this restriction. For example, under the five assumptions $S(i) \sim S(v)$, Wang et al. [52] manage to construct a smart-card-based scheme with provable security, and this scheme can well operate in a hostile user terminal.

In contrast to the optimistic view of [10, 44], the work in [45] pessimistically stated that, if the smart card are assumed to be non-tamper-resistant, then "it is no better than a passive token". Consequently, smart cards are abandoned in their choice and static clonable tokens are in place, and a software-only two-factor scheme is proposed. Obviously, according to our above analysis, such a software-only scheme can never achieve the same level of security as compared to smart-card-based schemes. Nevertheless, this scheme may be suitable for applications where costs gain more concerns than security. The authors in [59] also explicitly advocate that they "do not make assumption on the existence of any special security features supported by the smart-cards" and "simply consider a smart-card to be a memory card with an embedded micro-processor for performing required operations specified in a scheme." It is not difficult to see that, in the light of their statements, their proposed smart-card-based scheme [59] can never achieve the claimed two-factor security.

In security-critical applications, user terminals are often the targets of attackers and may be infected with viruses, trojans and malwares, only two-factor authentication schemes using smart cards (which is though only conditionally tamper-proof) are suitable for such environments, common-memory-device-based two-factor schemes *cannot* "enjoy all the advantages of authentication schemes using smart cards". This explicates why most studies adhere to use smart cards rather than common memory devices when designing two-factor schemes (which is made for security-critical applications), even if it is supposed that the data stored in the card memory can be extracted.

3 Cryptanalysis of Hsieh-Leu's Scheme

In 2012, Hsieh and Leu [25] demonstrated several attacks against Hsiang-Shih's [24] smart-card-based password authentication scheme. To remedy the identified security flaws, they proposed an enhanced version over Hsiang-Shih's scheme [24] by "exploiting hash functions", and claimed that their improved scheme can withstand offline dictionary attack even if the sensitive parameters are extracted by the adversary. However, as we will show in the following, under their non-tamper-resistance assumption of the smart cards, Hsieh-Leu's scheme is still vulnerable to offline dictionary attack, which is similar to the one that Hsiang-Shih's scheme suffers.

3.1 A Brief Review of Hsieh-Leu's Scheme

For ease of presentation, we employ some intuitive notations as listed in Table 1 and will follow the descriptions in Hsieh-Leu's scheme [25] as closely as possible. This scheme is composed of four phases: registration, login, verification and password change.

Table 1. Notations and abbreviations

Symbol	Description
U_i	i^{th} user
S	remote server
$\mathcal{M}$	malicious attacker
ID_i	identity of user U_i
PW_i	password of user U_i
x	the secret key of remote server S
$\oplus$	the bitwise XOR operation
$\parallel$	the string concatenation operation
$h(\cdot)$	collision free one-way hash function
$A \rightarrow B : C$	message C is transferred through a common channel from A to B
$A \Rightarrow B : C$	message C is transferred through a secure channel from A to B

Registration Phase. In this phase, the initial registration is different from the re-registration. Since the re-registration process has little relevance with our discussions, it is omitted here. The initial registration is depicted as follows.

(1) U_i chooses a random number b and computes $h(b \oplus PW_i)$.

(2) $U_i \Rightarrow S : ID_i, h(PW_i), h(b \oplus PW_i)$.

(3) On receiving the login request, in the account database, server S creates an entry for U_i and stores $n = 0$ in this entry.

(4) S computes $EID = (h(ID_i)\|n)$, $P = h(EID \oplus x)$, $R = P \oplus h(b \oplus PW_i)$ and $V = h(h(PW_i) \oplus h(x))$, and stores V in the entry corresponding to U_i.

(5) $S \Rightarrow U_i$: a smart card containing R and $h(\cdot)$.

(6) On receiving the smart card, U_i inputs b into his smart card and does not need to remember b since then.

Login Phase. When user U_i wants to login to S, she inserts her smart card into the card reader and keys her ID_i with PW_i. The smart card performs the following steps:

(1) The smart card computes $C_1 = R \oplus h(b \oplus PW_i)$ and $C_2 = h(C_1 \oplus T_i)$, where T_i denotes U_i's current timestamp.

(2) $U_i \rightarrow S : \{ID_i, T_i, C_2\}$.

Verification Phase. On receiving the login request from U_i, the remote server S and U_i's smart card perform the following steps:

(1) If either ID_i or T_i is invalid or $T_s - T_i \leq 0$, S rejects U_i's login request. Otherwise, S computes $C_2' = h(h(EID \oplus x) \oplus T_i)$, and compares C_2' with the received C_2. If they are equal, S accepts U_i's login request and proceeds to compute $C_3 = h(h(EID \oplus x) \oplus h(T_s))$, where T_s denotes S's current timestamp. Otherwise, U_i's login request is rejected.

(2) $S \rightarrow U : \{T_s, C_3\}$.

(3) If either T_s is invalid or $T_s = T_i$, U_i terminates the session. Otherwise, U_i computes $C_3' = h(C_1 \oplus h(T_s))$, and compares the computed C_3' with the received C_3. If they are equal, U_i authenticates S successfully.

Password Change Phase. When U_i wants to update her password, this phase is employed. Since this phase has little relevance with our discussions, it is omitted.

3.2 Offline Dictionary Attack

Offline dictionary attack is the most damaging threat that a practical password-based protocol must be able to guard against [3,27]. Hsieh and Leu showed that Hsiang-Shih's scheme [24] is vulnerable to offline dictionary attack once the secret parameters stored in the victim's smart card are revealed by the adversary "by monitoring the power consumption or by analyzing the leaked information".

Now let's see how exactly the same attack could be successfully launched with Hsieh-Leu's own scheme in place. Suppose user U_i's smart card is somehow (stolen or picked up) in the possession of an adversary $\mathcal{M}$, and the parameters R and b can be revealed using side-channel attacks [35,38]. With the previously intercepted authentication transcripts $\{ID_i, C_2, T_i\}$ from the public channel, $\mathcal{M}$ can obtain U_i's password PW_i as follows:

Step 1. Guesses the value of PW_i to be PW_i^* from the dictionary space $\mathcal{D}_{pw}$.

Step 2. Computes $C_1^* = R \oplus h(b \oplus PW_i)$, where R, b is extracted from U_i's smart card.

Step 3. Computes $C_2^* = h(C_1^* \oplus T_i)$, where T_i is previously intercepted from the public channel.

Step 4. Verifies the correctness of PW_i^* by checking if the computed C_2^* is equal to the intercepted C_2.

Step 5. Repeats Step 1 $\sim$ 4 of this procedure until the correct value of PW_i is found.

Our attack shows that once the smart-card factor is compromised, the corresponding password factor can be offline guessed and hence the entire system collapses. This indicates that Hsieh-Leu's scheme is intrinsically not a two-factor scheme and is as insecure as the original scheme (i.e., Hsiang-Shih's scheme [24]). This also corroborates the "public-key principle" [33] that, under the non-tamper resistance assumption of the smart cards, only symmetric-key techniques (such as Hash, block cipher) are inherently unable to resist offline dictionary attack.

Let $|\mathcal{D}_{pw}|$ denote the number of passwords in $\mathcal{D}_{pw}$. The time complexity of the above attack procedure is $\mathcal{O}(|\mathcal{D}_{pw}| * (2T_H + 3T_X))$, where T_H is the running time for Hash function and T_X the running time for bitwise XOR operation. It is easy to see that, the time for $\mathcal{M}$ to recover U_i's password is a linear function of the number of passwords in the password space. And hence our attack is quite effective. For an intuitive grasp of the effectiveness of this attack (and the following attack on PSCAV), we further obtain the running time (see Table 2) for the related operations on common Laptop PCs by using the publicly-available, multi-precision integer and rational arithmetic C/C++ library MIRACL [46]. In practice, the password space is very limited, e.g., $|\mathcal{D}_{pw}| \leq 10^6$ [5,18,56], and it follows that the above attack can be completed in seconds on a common PC.

Table 2. Computation evaluation of related operations on common Laptop PCs

Experimental platform (common PCs)	Exponentiation T_E ($|n|$=1024)	Symmetric encryption T_S (AES-128)	Hash operation T_H (SHA-1)	Other lightweight operations(e.g.,XOR)
Intel T5870 2.00 GHz	10.526 ms	2.012 μs	2.437 μs	0.011 μs
Intel E5500 2.80 GHz	7.716 ms	0.530 μs	0.756 μs	0.009 μs
Intel i5-3210 2.50 GHz	4.390 ms	0.415 μs	1.132 μs	0.008 μs

The above attack can be generalized as follows: with the security parameters extracted from the smart card and the transcripts intercepted during the previous login session(s), the attacker can repeatedly guess the victim's password via an offline automated program. This attack strategy is not new. Actually, it is the common "Waterloo" of many broken schemes [11,12,24,28,49]. This attack scenario (adversary behavior) has been captured in several two-factor security models [54,55,57]. Yet, the following attacker is still at large.

4   Cryptanalysis of PSCAV from SEC 2012

In SEC'12, Wang [54] observed that the previous papers in this area present attacks on protocols in earlier works and put forward new proposals without proper security justification (let alone a security model to fully identify the practical threats), which constitutes the main cause of the long-standing failure. Accordingly, Wang presented three kinds of security models, namely Type I, II and III. In the Type III model, which is the harshest model, mainly three assumptions are made:

(1) an adversary $\mathcal{M}$ is allowed to have full control of the communication channel between the user and the server;
(2) the smart card is assumed to be non-tamper resistant and the user's password may be intercepted by $\mathcal{M}$ using a malicious smart card reader, but not both;
(3) there is no counter protection in the smart card, i.e. $\mathcal{M}$ can issue a large amount of queries to the smart card using a malicious card reader to learn some useful information.

Note that, the above Assumption 1 accords with $\mathbf{S(i)}$, and Assumption 2 is consistent with $\mathbf{S(ii)} \sim \mathbf{S(v)}$ (see Sect. 2.2). As for Assumption 3, its opposite is implicitly made in most of previous schemes as well as the model introduced in Sect. 2.2. Apparently, a scheme which is secure in Type III shall also be secure in a model only with Assumptions 1 and 2. To the best of our knowledge, the Type III model is the strongest model that has ever been proposed for smart-card-based password authentication so far.

Wang [54] further proposed four schemes, only two of which, i.e. PSCAb and PSCAV, are claimed to be secure under the Type III model. However, PSCAb requires Weil or Tate pairing operations to defend against offline dictionary attack and may not be suitable for systems where pairing operations are considered to be too expensive or infeasible to implement. Moreover, PSCAb suffers from the well-known key escrow problem and lacks some desirable features such as repairability, user anonymity and local password update. As for PSCAV, in this paper, we will show that it is susceptible to offline dictionary attack under Assumptions 1 and 2 (or equally, $\mathbf{S(ii)} \sim \mathbf{S(v)}$) plus a new (but realistic) assumption – the attacker can return a victim's exposed card without detection.

4.1   A Brief Review of PSCAV

In this section, we firstly give a brief review of PSCAV and then present the attack. Here we just follow the original notations in [54] as closely as possible. Assume that the server has a master secret β (β could be user specific also). For each user (or called client) C with identity $\mathcal{C}$ and password α, let the user specific generator be $g_C = \mathcal{H}(\mathcal{C}, \alpha, \beta)$, the value $g_C^{\mathcal{H}_2(\alpha)} (= \mathcal{E}_{\mathcal{H}_2(\alpha)}(g_C)$, and thus $g_C = \mathcal{D}_{\mathcal{H}_2(\alpha)}(g_C^{\mathcal{H}_2(\alpha)}))$ is stored in the smart card, where $\mathcal{H}$ and $\mathcal{H}_2$ are two independent hash functions, and $\mathcal{E}/\mathcal{D}$ stand for symmetric encryption/decryption (see Sect. 3.2 of [54]). The value $g_C = \mathcal{H}(\mathcal{C}, \alpha, \beta)$ will be stored in the server's database for this user. The remaining of the protocol runs as follows:

(1) The card selects random x, computes $g_C = \mathcal{D}_{\mathcal{H}_2(\alpha)}(g_C^{\mathcal{H}_2(\alpha)})$ and sends $R_A = g_C^x$ to the server;
(2) Server selects random y and sends $R_A = g_C^y$ to the card;
(3) The card computes $u = \mathcal{H}(\mathcal{C}, \mathcal{S}, R_A, R_B)$ and $sk = g_C^{y(x+u)}$, where S is identity string of the server;

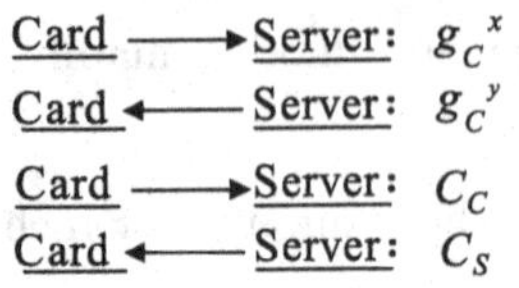

$$\begin{array}{ll}
\text{Card} \longrightarrow \text{Server:} & g_C{}^x \\
\text{Card} \longleftarrow \text{Server:} & g_C{}^y \\
\text{Card} \longrightarrow \text{Server:} & C_C \\
\text{Card} \longleftarrow \text{Server:} & C_S
\end{array}$$

$$\begin{array}{ll}
\text{Card} \longrightarrow \text{Server}(\mathcal{A}) : & g_C{}^x \\
\text{Card} \longleftarrow \text{Server}(\mathcal{A}) : & \boxed{g_C{}^{\mathcal{H}(\alpha)}} \\
\text{Card} \longrightarrow \text{Server}(\mathcal{A}) : & C_C
\end{array}$$

Fig. 2. Message flows of PSCAV 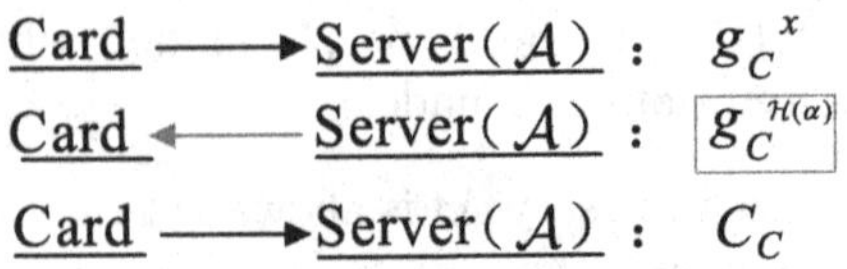   **Fig. 3.** Our attack

(4) The card sends $C_C = \mathcal{H}(sk, \mathcal{C}, \mathcal{S}, R_A, R_B, 1)$ to the server;

(5) After verifying that C_C is correct, the server computes $u = \mathcal{H}(\mathcal{C}, \mathcal{S}, R_A, R_B)$, $sk = g_C^{y(x+u\alpha)} = (g_C^x)^y \cdot g_C^{yu\alpha} = (R_A)^y \cdot g_C^{yu\alpha}$, and sends $C_S = \mathcal{H}(sk, \mathcal{S}, \mathcal{C}, R_B, R_A, 2)$ to the card.

The message flows of PSCAV are shown in the Fig. 2. Since the session key sk is computed with the contribution of the password α by server S in the above Step 5, the password α (or the parameter g_C^α) is needed to be known by S. However, the original specification in [54] does not explicitly explain how can the server obtain the user's password α to compute sk in the above Step 5. We assume (suggest) g_C^α is also stored in the server's database, i.e. an entry $(\mathcal{C}, g_C, g_C^\alpha)$ corresponding to user $\mathcal{C}$ is stored in the server's database.[3] This ambiguity does not affect our security analysis however.

4.2 Offline Dictionary Attack

Suppose an adversary $\mathcal{M}$ has got temporary access to the client C's smart card and obtained the stored secret $g_C^{\mathcal{H}_2(\alpha)}$. Then $\mathcal{M}$ sends back the card without awareness of the victim C. Once C uses the exposed smart card, the attacker can impersonate as the server to interact with C and to learn C's password. The attack, as summarized in Fig. 3, can be carried out by $\mathcal{M}$ as follows:

Step 1. On intercepting $R_A = g_C^x$ from client C, $\mathcal{M}$ blocks it and sends $R_B = g_C^{\mathcal{H}_2(\alpha)}$ to the client on behalf of the server, where $g_C^{\mathcal{H}_2(\alpha)}$ is extracted from C's card;

Step 2. On receiving the response C_C, $\mathcal{M}$ computes $u = \mathcal{H}(\mathcal{C}, \mathcal{S}, R_A, R_B)$.

Step 3. Guesses the value of password α to be α^* from dictionary $\mathcal{D}_{pw}$.

Step 4. Computes $g_C^* = \mathscr{D}_{\mathcal{H}_2(\alpha^*)}(g_C^{\mathcal{H}_2(\alpha)})$;

Step 5. Computes $sk^* = g_C^{x\mathcal{H}_2(\alpha^*)} \cdot (g_C^*)^{u\alpha^* \mathcal{H}_2(\alpha^*)}$
$= (R_A)^{\mathcal{H}_2(\alpha^*)} \cdot (g_C^*)^{u \cdot \alpha^* \cdot \mathcal{H}_2(\alpha^*)}$;

Step 6. $\mathcal{M}$ computes $C_C^* = \mathcal{H}(sk^*, \mathcal{C}, \mathcal{S}, R_A, R_B, 1)$;

Step 7. Verifies the correctness of α^* by checking if the computed C_C^* is equal to the received C_C;

Step 8. Repeats the above Steps 3–8 until the correct value of α is found.

The time complexity of the above attack is $\mathcal{O}(|\mathcal{D}_{pw}| * (3T_E + T_S + 3T_H))$. As the size of the password dictionary, i.e. $|\mathcal{D}_{pw}|$, is very limited in practice

---

[3] This ambiguity and our suggested remedy have been confirmed by the author of [54], and he earns our deep respect for his frankly and quickly acknowledgement.

[5,18,56], e.g. $|\mathcal{D}_{pw}| \leq 10^6$, the above attack can be completed in polynomial time. Further considering the experimental timings listed in Table 2, $\mathcal{M}$ may recover the password in minutes on a PC by a single run of PSCAV.

Interestingly, our attack on Wang's PSCAV scheme [54] highlights *a new attacking scenario*: Firstly, an attacker gets temporary access to the victim's card and extracts its security parameters; Secondly, she sends back the exposed card without awareness of the victim; Finally, she performs malicious attacks when the victim uses this exposed card. Note that this attacking scenario is quite realistic. For example, an employee accidentally leaves her bank card on her desk after work, the attacker picks this card and performs the side-channel attacks herself (or with recourse to professional labs) in the evening and puts it back before the victim comes to work the next morning. The victim will find no abnormality and use this card as usual. Unfortunately, once this card is put to use, the corresponding password may be leaked, while the above procedure well serves to illustrate how the password can be leaked to an attacker. As reported in [41], "agencies are interested in quickly accessing someone's room, install some bug in the her mobile device and then return it without detection". This also confirms the practicality of our attack.

Wang's PSCAV scheme is secure in their security model yet vulnerable to our new attacking strategy. Since the identified attacking scenario is realistically oriented towards a serious threat, it deserves special attention when defining the underlying security model for smart-card-based password authentication. This once again suggests that, a good security model is not one that denies the capabilities of the attacker but rather one designed to capture the attacker's practical abilities as comprehensively as possible, and the powers not allowed to the attacker are those that would allow her to trivially break any of this type of schemes [22,30]. Fortunately, *our observation has already given rise to the strongest adversary model so far*: Just two weeks ago, a new security model named Type III-r was developed in [61].

5   Conclusion

Understanding security pitfalls of cryptographic protocols is the key to both patching existing protocols and designing future schemes. In this paper, we have demonstrated that Hsieh-Leu's scheme and Wang's PSCAV scheme suffer from the offline dictionary attack under two different attacking strategies, which reveals the challenges in constructing a practical authentication scheme with truly two-factor security. Remarkably, our attack on Wang's PSCAV scheme highlights a new realistic attack scenario and thus uncovers a new behavior of the attacker – returning the exposed smart card without awareness of the victim. As for future work, we are considering designing a practical scheme that can survive in the Type III-r model.

Acknowledgment. The corresponding author is Ping Wang. We are grateful to Prof. Yongge Wang from UNC Charlotte, USA, for the constructive discussions and Prof.

David Naccache for referring us to [41]. This research was partially supported by the National Natural Science Foundation of China under No. 61472016.

References

1. Asokan, N., Ekberg, J.-E., Kostiainen, K.: The untapped potential of trusted execution environments on mobile devices. In: Sadeghi, A.-R. (ed.) FC 2013. LNCS, vol. 7859, pp. 293–294. Springer, Heidelberg (2013)

2. Barenghi, A., Breveglieri, L., Koren, I., Naccache, D.: Fault injection attacks on cryptographic devices: theory, practice, and countermeasures. Proc. IEEE **100**(11), 3056–3076 (2012)

3. Bellovin, S.M., Merritt, M.: Encrypted key exchange: password-based protocols secure against dictionary attacks. In: Proceedings of IEEE S&P 1992, pp. 72–84. IEEE (1992)

4. Bilge, L., Dumitras, T.: Before we knew it: an empirical study of zero-day attacks in the real world. In: Proceedings of ACM CCS 2012, pp. 833–844. ACM (2012)

5. Bonneau, J.: The science of guessing: analyzing an anonymized corpus of 70 million passwords. In: Proceedings of IEEE S&P 2012, pp. 538–552. IEEE Computer Society (2012)

6. Boyd, C., Montague, P., Nguyen, K.: Elliptic curve based password authenticated key exchange protocols. In: Varadharajan, V., Mu, Y. (eds.) ACISP 2001. LNCS, vol. 2119, p. 487. Springer, Heidelberg (2001)

7. Bresson, E., Chevassut, O., Pointcheval, D.: New security results on encrypted key exchange. In: Bao, F., Deng, R., Zhou, J. (eds.) PKC 2004. LNCS, vol. 2947, pp. 145–158. Springer, Heidelberg (2004)

8. Burr, W., Dodson, D., Perlner, R., Polk, W., Gupta, S., Nabbus, E.: NIST Special Publication 800-63-1: Electronic Authentication Guideline. National Institute of Standards and Technology, Gaithersburg (2011)

9. Chang, C.C., Wu, T.C.: Remote password authentication with smart cards. IEE Proc. Comput. Digital Tech. **138**(3), 165–168 (1991)

10. Chen, B.L., Kuo, W.C., Wuu, L.C.: A secure password-based remote user authentication scheme without smart cards. Inf. Technol. Control **41**(1), 53–59 (2012)

11. Chen, B.L., Kuo, W.C., Wuu, L.C.: Robust smart-card-based remote user password authentication scheme. Int. J. Commun. Syst. **27**(2), 377–389 (2014)

12. Chen, T.H., Hsiang, H.C., Shih, W.K.: Security enhancement on an improvement on two remote user authentication schemes using smart cards. Future Gener. Comput. Syst. **27**(4), 377–380 (2011)

13. Constantin, L.: Sony stresses that PSN passwords were hashed. Online news (2011). http://news.softpedia.com/news/Sony-Stresses-PSN-Passwords-Were-Hashed-198218.shtml

14. Das, M.L.: Two-factor user authentication in wireless sensor networks. IEEE Trans. Wirel. Commun. **8**(3), 1086–1090 (2009)

15. Das, M., Saxena, A., Gulati, V.: A dynamic id-based remote user authentication scheme. IEEE Trans. Consum. Electron. **50**(2), 629–631 (2004)

16. Dazzlepod Inc.: CSDN cleartext passwords. Online news (2013). http://dazzlepod.com/csdn/

17. Degabriele, J.P., Paterson, K., Watson, G.: Provable security in the real world. IEEE Secur. Priv. **9**(3), 33–41 (2011)

18. Dell'Amico, M., Michiardi, P., Roudier, Y.: Password strength: an empirical analysis. In: Proceedings of INFOCOM 2010, pp. 1–9. IEEE (2010)

19. Drimer, S., Murdoch, S.J., Anderson, R.: Thinking inside the box: system-level failures of tamper proofing. In: Proceedings IEEE S&P 2008, pp. 281–295. IEEE (2008)
20. Fan, C., Chan, Y., Zhang, Z.: Robust remote authentication scheme with smart cards. Comput. Secur. **24**(8), 619–628 (2005)
21. Focus Technology Co., Ltd: Prices for 1GB Usb Flash Drive (2013). http://www. made-in-china.com/products-search/hot-china-products/1gb_Usb_Flash_Drive. html
22. Hao, F.: On robust key agreement based on public key authentication. In: Sion, R. (ed.) FC 2010. LNCS, vol. 6052, pp. 383–390. Springer, Heidelberg (2010)
23. He, D., Ma, M., Zhang, Y., Chen, C., Bu, J.: A strong user authentication scheme with smart cards for wireless communications. Comput. Commun. **34**(3), 367–374 (2011)
24. Hsiang, H., Shih, W.: Weaknesses and improvements of the yoon-ryu-yoo remote user authentication scheme using smart cards. Comput. Commun. **32**(4), 649–652 (2009)
25. Hsieh, W., Leu, J.: Exploiting hash functions to intensify the remote user authentication scheme. Comput. Secur. **31**(6), 791–798 (2012)
26. Juang, W.S., Chen, S.T., Liaw, H.T.: Robust and efficient password-authenticated key agreement using smart cards. IEEE Trans. Industr. Electron. **55**(6), 2551–2556 (2008)
27. Katz, J., Ostrovsky, R., Yung, M.: Efficient and secure authenticated key exchange using weak passwords. J. ACM **57**(1), 1–41 (2009)
28. Khan, M., Kim, S.: Cryptanalysis and security enhancement of a more efficient & secure dynamic id-based remote user authentication scheme. Comput. Commun. **34**(3), 305–309 (2011)
29. Kim, T.H., Kim, C., Park, I.: Side channel analysis attacks using am demodulation on commercial smart cards with seed. J. Syst. Soft. **85**(12), 2899–2908 (2012)
30. Krawczyk, H.: HMQV: A high-performance secure Diffie-Hellman protocol. In: Shoup, V. (ed.) CRYPTO 2005. LNCS, vol. 3621, pp. 546–566. Springer, Heidelberg (2005)
31. Li, X., Qiu, W., Zheng, D., Chen, K., Li, J.: Anonymity enhancement on robust and efficient password-authenticated key agreement using smart cards. IEEE Trans. Ind. Electron. **57**(2), 793–800 (2010)
32. Long, J.: No Tech Hacking: A Guide to Social Engineering, Dumpster Diving, and Shoulder Surfing. Syngress, Burlington (2011)
33. Ma, C.G., Wang, D., Zhao, S.: Security flaws in two improved remote user authentication schemes using smart cards. Int. J. Commun. Syst. **27**(10), 2215–2227 (2014)
34. Madhusudhan, R., Mittal, R.: Dynamic id-based remote user password authentication schemes using smart cards: a review. J. Netw. Comput. Appl. **35**(4), 1235–1248 (2012)
35. Mangard, S., Oswald, E., Popp, T.: Power Analysis Attacks: Revealing the Secrets of Smart Cards. Springer, Heidelberg (2007)
36. Menezes, A.: Another look at HMQV. J. Math. Cryptol. **1**(1), 47–64 (2007)
37. Menezes, A.: Another look at provable security. In: Pointcheval, D., Johansson, T. (eds.) EUROCRYPT 2012. LNCS, vol. 7237, pp. 8–8. Springer, Heidelberg (2012)
38. Messerges, T.S., Dabbish, E.A., Sloan, R.H.: Examining smart-card security under the threat of power analysis attacks. IEEE Trans. Comput. **51**(5), 541–552 (2002)
39. Moradi, A., Barenghi, A., Kasper, T., Paar, C.: On the vulnerability of FPGA bitstream encryption against power analysis attacks: extracting keys from xilinx Virtex-II FPGAs. In: Proceedings of ACM CCS 2011, pp. 111–124. ACM (2011)

40. Murdoch, S.J., Drimer, S., Anderson, R., Bond, M.: Chip and pin is broken. In: Proceedings of IEEE Security & Privacy 2010, pp. 433–446. IEEE Computer Society (2010)

41. Naccache, D.: National security, forensics and mobile communications. In: Won, D.H., Kim, S. (eds.) ICISC 2005. LNCS, vol. 3935, pp. 1–1. Springer, Heidelberg (2006)

42. Nohl, K., Evans, D., Starbug, S., Plötz, H.: Reverse-engineering a cryptographic rfid tag. In: Proceedings of USENIX Security 2008, pp. 185–193. USENIX Association (2008)

43. Pointcheval, D.: Password-based authenticated key exchange. In: Fischlin, M., Buchmann, J., Manulis, M. (eds.) PKC 2012. LNCS, vol. 7293, pp. 390–397. Springer, Heidelberg (2012)

44. Rhee, H.S., Kwon, J.O., Lee, D.H.: A remote user authentication scheme without using smart cards. Comput. Stan. Interfaces 31(1), 6–13 (2009)

45. Scott, M.: Replacing username/password with software-only two-factor authentication. Technical report, Cryptology ePrint Archive, Report 2012/148 (2012). http://eprint.iacr.org/2012/148.pdf

46. Shamus Software Ltd.: Miracl library (2013). http://www.shamus.ie/index.php?page=home

47. Smart Card Alliance: Philips Advances Smart Card Security for Mobile Applications (2013). http://www.ceic-cn.org/files/NXP2006zcard.pdf

48. Son, K., Han, D., Won, D.: A privacy-protecting authentication scheme for roaming services with smart cards. IEICE Trans. Commun. 95(5), 1819–1821 (2012)

49. Song, R.: Advanced smart card based password authentication protocol. Comput. Stand. Interfaces 32(5), 321–325 (2010)

50. Sun, D.Z., Huai, J.P., Sun, J.Z.: Improvements of juang et al'.s password-authenticated key agreement scheme using smart cards. IEEE Trans. Industr. Electron. 56(6), 2284–2291 (2009)

51. Wang, D., Ma, C., Wu, P.: Secure password-based remote user authentication scheme with non-tamper resistant smart cards. In: Cuppens-Boulahia, N., Cuppens, F., Garcia-Alfaro, J. (eds.) DBSec 2012. LNCS, vol. 7371, pp. 114–121. Springer, Heidelberg (2012)

52. Wang, D., Ma, C., Wang, P., Chen, Z.: Robust smart card based password authentication scheme against smart card security breach. In: Cryptology ePrint Archive, Report 2012/439 (2012). http://eprint.iacr.org/2012/439.pdf

53. Wang, Y., Liu, J., Xiao, F., Dan, J.: A more efficient and secure dynamic id-based remote user authentication scheme. Comput. Commun. 32(4), 583–585 (2009)

54. Wang, Y.: Password protected smart card and memory stick authentication against off-line dictionary attacks. In: Gritzalis, D., Furnell, S., Theoharidou, M. (eds.) SEC 2012. IFIP AICT, vol. 376, pp. 489–500. Springer, Heidelberg (2012)

55. Wu, S.H., Zhu, Y.F., Pu, Q.: Robust smart-cards-based user authentication scheme with user anonymity. Secur. Commun. Netw. 5(2), 236–248 (2012)

56. Wu, T.: A real-world analysis of kerberos password security. In: Proceedings of NDSS 1999, pp. 13–22. Internet Society (1999)

57. Xu, J., Zhu, W., Feng, D.: An improved smart card based password authentication scheme with provable security. Comput. Stand. Inter. 31(4), 723–728 (2009)

58. Xue, K., Hong, P., Ma, C.: A lightweight dynamic pseudonym identity based authentication and key agreement protocol without verification tables for multi-server architecture. J. Comput. Syst. Sci, 80(1), 195–206 (2014)

59. Yang, G., Wong, D., Wang, H., Deng, X.: Two-factor mutual authentication based on smart cards and passwords. J. Comput. Syst. Sci. 74(7), 1160–1172 (2008)

60. Zhao, Z., Dong, Z., Wang, Y.G.: Security analysis of a password-based authentication protocol proposed to IEEE 1363. Theoret. Comput. Sci. **352**(1), 280–287 (2006)
61. Zhao, Z., Wang, Y.G.: Secure communication and authentication against offline dictionary attacks in smart grid systems (2013). http://coitweb.uncc.edu/yonwang/papers/smartgridfull.pdf

Self-blindable Credential: Towards Anonymous Entity Authentication Upon Resource Constrained Devices

Yanjiang Yang[1]([✉]), Xuhua Ding[2], Haibing Lu[3],
Jian Weng[4], and Jianying Zhou[1]

[1] Institute for Infocomm Research, Singapore, Singapore
{yyang,jyzhou}@i2r.a-star.edu.sg
[2] School of Information Systems, Singapore Management University,
Singapore, Singapore
xhding@smu.edu.sg
[3] The Leavey School of Business, Santa Clara University, Santa Clara, USA
hlu@scu.edu
[4] Department of Computer Science, Jinan University, Guangzhou, China
cryptjweng@gmail.com

Abstract. We are witnessing the rapid expansion of smart devices in our daily life. The need for individual privacy protection calls for anonymous entity authentication techniques with affordable efficiency upon the resource-constrained smart devices. Towards this objective, in this paper we propose *self-blindable credential*, a lightweight anonymous entity authentication primitive. We provide a formulation of the primitive and present two concrete instantiations.

1 Introduction

The recent advances of hardware technology such as mobile phones, embedded devices, and sensors, coupled with modern networking technology, set off an explosive growth of applications using digital credentials for entity authentication upon resource-constrained smart devices. For instance, vehicles can be embedded with smart sensors carrying an electronic plate number issued from the DMV (Department of Motor Vehicles), such that, they can communicate with road-side devices for the road condition or traffic alerts. A mobile phone can carry its owner's personal credential, e.g., an electronic driver license, such that the owner can use the mobile phone to prove his identity or certain capabilities.

Two security related issues emerge from these applications. One is personal privacy protection. Unlike a physical credential such as a plastic driver license card which is presented by the user herself, digital credentials are often automatically applied, without the user's notice or explicit approval. This implies that digital credentials residing on smart devices may backfire on the user's personal privacy, despite its easiness of use. The other issue is credential revocation,

© Springer International Publishing Switzerland 2015
Y. Desmedt (Ed.): ISC 2013, LNCS 7807, pp. 238–247, 2015.
DOI: 10.1007/978-3-319-27659-5_17

which becomes even harder if the credentials are used in a privacy-preserving manner where the verifier cannot link credentials with user identities. Worse yet, these two issues are aggravated by the limited computation and communication capabilities of smart devices. The resource constraints of smart devices dictate that the solution for privacy preservation and revocation support should have lightweight computation and communication in order to minimize the time delay and energy consumption.

Anonymous credentials [3,9–12] address user privacy in entity authentication where credentials are used anonymously such that two authentication transactions using the same credential cannot be linked by the verifier. Nonetheless, existing anonymous credential schemes are *not* suitable for smart devices due to high communication or computation overhead, just as observed in [7]. The RSA-based schemes (e.g., [10,11]) normally involve costly zero-knowledge range proofs, which entail tens of kilobits in communication and tens of modular exponentiation operations in an RSA algebraic group. Although the IDEMIX anonymous credential and the DAA (both are RSA-based) have been implemented on JAVA card, e.g., [2,5,9,14], the implementations either are not practically efficient enough or do not well address credential revocation. The state-of-the-art bilinear map-based schemes such as [3,4,12] rely on bilinear pairing operations or computations over large bilinear groups.

Self-blindable certificate in [15] is another primitive that can be used for anonymous entity authentication. The notion of self-blindable certificate considers a privacy-preserving variant of the conventional public key certificate: the certificate holder can *blind* the public key in the certificate by herself, such that multiple uses of the same certificate cannot be linked, while the validity of the CA signature is preserved. When used for entity authentication, a self-blindable certificate essentially functions as an anonymous credential, but with lighter computation. The high efficiency comes from the fact that the certificate holder only needs to perform computation in G_1 of an asymmetric bilinear map $e : G_1 \times G_2 \to G_T$. Nonetheless, despite its high performance for smart devices [6], it does not provide a satisfactory credential revocation mechanism.

To address this issue, we propose a lightweight anonymous credential scheme, *self-blindable credential*. It follows the same working mechanism of self-blindable certificate: the computation at the user side works entirely in G_1, and the resulting authentication data only consist of group elements of G_1. As G_1 is much more compact than G_2 and G_T, and the computation in G_1 is much faster than in G_2, G_T and pairing operation, self-blindable credential achieves better performance than existing anonymous credential schemes.

2 Modeling of Self-blindable Credential

We consider a credential system that enables smart devices to authenticate themselves to a *device reader* anonymously, such that repeated uses of a credential cannot be linked by the reader. The primary issue to be addressed is that smart devices and the reader are asymmetric in terms of resources: smart devices are restraint with limited computation capability and energy resources, while the reader is relatively powerful and has no resource constraints. In the rest, "user" and "device" are used interchangeably. We propose the concept of *self-blindable credential* as the solution to this asymmetric scenario.

A self-blindable credential system comprises a set of users, each obtaining a special credential called *self-blindable credential* from a credential issuer. These credentials are used for anonymous authentication to the verifier, e.g., a service provider, who trusts the credential issuer. To use her self-blindable credential, a user generates a *blinded credential* by blinding it with random factors. The verifier checks the blinded credential to determine its validity. It is mandated that blinded credentials produced from the same self-blindable credential cannot be linked by the verifier. Credential revocation is supported, such that the blinded credentials resulting from a revoked credential cannot be accepted. Formally, a revocable self-blindable credential scheme is defined below.

Definition 1 (Revocable Self-blindable Credential). *Let $\mathcal{C}$ denote the domain of the self-blindable credentials, and $\mathcal{BC}$ denote the collection of all blinded credentials. A revocable self-blindable credential scheme is composed of five algorithms* Setup, CredIssue, Blind, Revoke, CredVerify *as follows.*

- *Setup$(1^\kappa) \to (params, msk)$: The setup algorithm takes as input a security parameter 1^κ, and outputs a set of public system parameters params, and a master secret key msk. Below we assume that params is implicitly included as input to the rest four algorithms.*
- *CredIssue$(msk, u) \to c$: The credential issuance algorithm takes as input msk and user identity u, and outputs a self-blindable credential $c \in \mathcal{C}$ for u.*
- *Blind$(c) \to bc$: The blinding algorithm takes as input a self-blindable credential $c \in \mathcal{C}$ produced by CredIssue(), and outputs a blinded credential $bc \in \mathcal{BC}$. This is normally an interactive algorithm between a user and a verifier who inputs a challenge message to ensure freshness. For the sake of convenience, we omit the verifier's challenge which should be clear from the context.*
- *Revoke$(\lceil msk \rfloor, c) \to CRL \cup \{c\}$: The credential revocation algorithm takes as input a self-blindable credential $c \in \mathcal{C}$ and optionally master secret key msk, and outputs the updated Credential Revocation List (CRL), which is initially empty.*
- *CredVerify$(bc, CRL) \to \{0, 1\}$: The credential verification algorithm takes as input a blinded credential bc and CRL, and outputs either 1 (accept) or 0 (reject).*

Correctness. For all $c \leftarrow$ CredIssue(msk, u), where $(params, sk) \leftarrow$ Setup(1^κ), it holds that CredVerify(Blind$(c), CRL) = 1$ on the condition that $c \notin CRL$.

Security Notions. We formulate and impose the following security requirements upon the revocable self-blindable credential scheme.

Unforgeability. For the self-blindable credential scheme, it mandates that an adversary cannot forge either self-blindable credentials or blinded credentials.

Definition 2 (Unforgeability). *A revocable self-blindable credential scheme satisfies unforgeability if for any PPT adversary $\mathcal{A}$, the probability of the following "unforgeability game" returning 1 is negligible in κ.*

1. $(params, msk) \leftarrow Setup(1^\kappa)$;
2. $bc \leftarrow \mathcal{A}^{CredIssue(msk,\cdot)}(params)$;
3. *if* $CredVerify(bc, CRL) = 1 \wedge Origin(bc) \notin \{c_1, c_2 \ldots c_\ell\}$ *then return 1; and returns 0 otherwise, whereby* $\{c_i\}_{i=1}^{\ell}$ *are the set of credentials returned by the* $CredIssue(msk, \cdot)$ *oracle, and* $Origin : \mathcal{BC} \rightarrow \mathcal{C}$ *is a function taking as input a blinded credential and outputting the original credential from which the former is generated.*

Unlinkability. For privacy protection, it should not possible for the adversary to determine whether two blinded credentials are produced from the same self-blindable credential.

Definition 3 (Unlinkability). *A revocable self-blindable credential scheme satisfies unlinkability if for any PPT adversary $\mathcal{A}$, the probability of the following "unlinkability game" returns 1 is $1/2 + \nu(\kappa)$, where $\nu(.)$ is a negligible function.*

1. $(params, msk) \leftarrow Setup(1^\kappa)$;
   $c_0 \leftarrow CredIssue(msk, u_0)$;
   $c_1 \leftarrow CredIssue(msk, u_1)$
2. $\sigma \xleftarrow{R} \{0, 1\}$;
3. $bc \leftarrow Blind(c_\sigma)$;
4. $\sigma^* \leftarrow \mathcal{A}(params, c_0, c_1, bc)$;
5. *if* $\sigma = \sigma^*$ *then return 1 else return 0;*

A weaker notion of unlinkability would be such that, the adversary $\mathcal{A}$ in the above game is not given the original credentials c_0, c_1, but two blinded credentials (one is generated from c_0, and the other from c_1), prior to being challenged with bc. We refer to this notion as *non-forward unlinkability*, which models the level of anonymity attained by the verifier-local revocation mechanism.

Another security property is *revocability*, which mandates that once a self-blindable credential is revoked, any resulting blinded credential must be rejected by the verifier. In addition, possession of a credential represents the holder's access rights. Thus, sharing of a credential with other users who do not have the access rights should be disallowed. Ideally, a self-blindable credential scheme should deter a credential holder from sharing her credential with others. We call this property as *non-shareability*.

3   Self-blindable Credential with Verifier-Local Revocation

Our constructions of self-blindable credential will be based on the BBS+ signature scheme [1]. The BBS+ scheme, together with [3,4,12], represents the state of the art of bilinear map-based anonymous credentials. We start with a brief review of the BBS+ signature scheme. The BBS+ signature scheme works over a bilinear map $e : G_1 \times G_2 \to G_T$, where G_1, G_2, G_T are multiplicative cyclic groups of prime order q. A signer's public key is $(Z = h^z, h \in G_2, a, b, d \in G_1)$ and the private key is $z \in Z_q^*$. A BBS+ signature upon message m is defined as (M, k, s) where $k, s \in_R Z_q^*$, and $M = (a^m b^s d)^{\frac{1}{k+z}} \in G_1$. The resulting signature can be verified by testing $e(M, Z \cdot h^k) \stackrel{?}{=} e(A, h)$ where $A = a^m b^s d$.

More interestingly, the signature verification can also be conducted in a zero-knowledge proof of knowledge protocol that enables the holder of the signature to prove the possession of (M, k, s, m) to a verifier, without revealing any information on the signature. Specifically, it works as follows: let $g_1, g_2 \in G_1$ be two additional public parameters; first compute and publishes $M_1 = M \cdot g_1^{r_1}, M_2 = g_1^{r_2} g_2^{r_1}$, where $r_1, r_2 \in_R Z_q$; and then compute a standard zero-knowledge proof of knowledge protocol (ZKPoK), denoted as $PoK\{(k, m, s, r_1, r_2, \delta_1, \delta_2) : M_2 = g_1^{r_2} g_2^{r_1} \wedge M_2^k = g_1^{\delta_2} g_2^{\delta_1} \wedge \frac{e(M_1, Z)}{e(d, h)} = e(M_1, h)^{-k} \cdot e(a, h)^m \cdot e(b, h)^s \cdot e(g_1, h)^{r_1} \cdot e(g_1, h)^{\delta_1}\}$, where $\delta_1 = k \cdot r_1, \delta_2 = k \cdot r_2$. It can be seen that the computation of this ZKPoK protocol works mostly in G_T, which is actually a much larger group than G_1.

3.1 Design Rationale

The basic approach of our design is to use the BBS+ signature scheme as the self-blindable credential issuance algorithm. In other words, a self-blindable credential c is a BBS+ signature on the credential holder's attribute. We then design a blinding algorithm, such that the credential holder can randomize her BBS+ signature into a blinded credential bc. To convince the verifier that her bc is valid, the credential holder proves that bc is well formed in the sense that it is derived from a valid c. Our key innovation is the design of a highly efficient blinding algorithm, replacing the above zero-knowledge signature verification protocol of the BBS+ scheme.

Given a BBS+ signature $\sigma = (M, k, s)$ on message m, we observe that it can be blinded as follows. Select a blinding factor $f \in_R Z_q^*$ and compute $M' = M^f$. Namely, $M' = (a^{mf} b^{sf} d^f)^{\frac{1}{k+z}}$. Thus, M' and $A' = (a^m b^s d)^f$ can be verified by

$$e(M', Z \cdot h^k) = e(A', h) \tag{1}$$

To fully hide the original signature σ, we need to hide k as well. From (1), we get

$$\begin{aligned} e(M', Z \cdot h^k) &= e(A', h) \\ \Leftrightarrow e(M', Z)e(M', h^k) &= e(A', h) \\ \Leftrightarrow e(M', Z)e(M'^k, h) &= e(A', h) \end{aligned} \tag{2}$$

Let $M'' = M'^k = M^{f \cdot k}$, then k is blinded by f. As such, we get a blinded credential $bc = (M', M'', A')$. To show its validity, a proof of knowledge protocol is needed to attest that M', M'' and A' are in a correct form. At this point of time, an important observation is that this procedure only involves computation in G_1, accounting for higher efficiency.

3.2   Construction Details

We proceed to present the details of our construction of a self-blindable credential scheme with verifier-local revocation, whereby the verifier checks the revocation status of blinded credentials against the revoked items in the CRL. The verifier-local revocation approach has been widely used in the literature, e.g., [8,9].

- Setup(1^κ): Given a system parameter 1^κ, determine a bilinear map $e : G_1 \times G_2 \to G_T$. Select $a, b, d \in G_1$, $h \in G_2$. Compute $Z = h^z$, where $z \in_R Z_q^*$. Note that (a, b, d, h, Z) are the parameters of the BBS+ signature scheme. Set the public parameters $params = (e, a, b, d, Z, CRL = \emptyset)$ and master secret key $msk = (z)$.
- CredIssue($msk = (z), u$): The credential issuer computes a BBS+ signature (M, k, s) on a user's identity u, where $M = (a^u b^s d)^{\frac{1}{k+z}} \in G_1$, and $k, s \in_R Z_q^*$. Set $c = (M, k, s, u)$.
- Blind($c = (M, k, s, u)$): User u computes a blinded credential as follows.
    1. Select $f \in_R Z_q$, and compute $M' = M^f, M'' = M'^k, A' = (a^u b^s d)^f$.
    2. Construct a standard ZKPoK protocol (based upon the challenge from the verifier), denoted as PoK, as follows.

$$PoK\{(k, \mu, \varsigma, f) : M'' = M'^k \wedge A' = a^\mu b^\varsigma d^f\}$$

       where $\mu = u \cdot f, \varsigma = s \cdot f$.
    3. Set $bc = (M', M'', A', PoK)$.
- Revoke($\lceil msk \rfloor, c = (M, k, s, u)$): To revoke credential c, the credential issuer updates CRL with k such that $CRL = CRL \cup \{k\}$. Similar to a CRL in the traditional PKI, CRL is signed by the credential issuer.
- CredVerify(bc, CRL): Given the CRL and a blinded credential $bc = (M', M'', A', PoK)$, the verifier outputs 1 if *all* of the following are *true*; otherwise outputs 0.

$$\begin{cases} M' \neq 1 \in G_1 \\ PoK \text{ is valid} \\ e(M', Z)e(M'', h) \stackrel{?}{=} e(A', h) \\ \forall k \in CRL : M'' \neq M'^k \end{cases}$$

<u>Remark.</u> The reason why M' is not allowed to be the unity in G_1 is the following: if $M' = 1$, then $f = 0 \pmod q$ and any value of k would trivially satisfy the proof PoK. The check actually provides a guarantee that $f \neq 0 \pmod q$.

3.3   Security Analysis

Correctness of the scheme is easily verified, and we next analyze its security with respect to the requirements set out in Sect. 2.

Theorem 1. *The proposed construction achieves unforgeability, given that the BBS+ signature scheme [1] is existentially unforgeable.*

Proof. We show that the unforgeability of our scheme is based on that of the BBS+ signature scheme. Given an adversary $\mathcal{A}$ against the unforgeability of our scheme, the forger $\mathcal{F}_{BBS}$ for the BBS+ signature scheme is constructed as follow. $\mathcal{F}_{BBS}$ invokes $\mathcal{A}$, and answers the latter's CredIssue oracle using its own signature signing oracle. Upon the output of $\mathcal{A}$, $\mathcal{F}_{BBS}$ executes the knowledge extractor of the ZKPoK protocol to get (k, u', s', f), and outputs $(M'^{\frac{1}{f}}, k, \frac{s'}{f}, \frac{u'}{f})$ as the forgery for the BBS+ signature.   □

For unlinkability, we need the DDH assumption to hold in G_1. Let $g_1, g_2 \in G_1$. The DDH assumption states that it is computationally infeasible to distinguish between (g_1, g_2, g_1^x, g_2^x) and (g_1, g_2, g_1^x, g_2^y), where $x, y \in_R Z_q^*$. In the context of bilinear map, the DDH assumption is commonly referred to as XDH (external Diffie-Hellman) assumption.

Theorem 2. *Our construction achieves non-forward unlinkability under the XDH assumption.*

Proof. We construct a distinguisher $\mathcal{D}$ for distinguishing a DDH tuple, from an adversary $\mathcal{A}$ which links blinded credentials in our scheme. Specifically, $\mathcal{D}(g_1, g_2, g_1^x, C \in G_1)$ works as follows.

(1) Execute Setup;

(2) Generate a credential c with CredIssue first, and then generate a blinded credential bc_0 from c;

(3) Generate another blinded credential bc_1 from g_1, g_1^x as follows. Set $M' = g_1, M'' = g_1^x$, compute $A' = M'^z M''$, where z is the master key. It can be checked that (M', M'', A') satisfies $e(M', h^z)e(M'', h) = e(A', h)$. Next, invoke the zero-knowledge proof simulator to produce a simulated proof PoK accordingly. Then set $bc_1 = (M', M'', A', PoK)$. Clearly bc_1 is a valid blinded credential;

(4) Generate the challenge blinded credential bc from (g_2, C) as in 3);

(5) Challenge $\mathcal{A}$ with bc_0, bc_1, and bc ;

(6) if $\mathcal{A}$ outputs 1, then return 1; else return 0;

Analysis. When $C = g_2^y$ with $y \neq x$, then bc and bc_1 are not from the same credential; on the other hand, the probability that bc and bc_0 are from the same credential is clearly negligible. Consequently, $\mathcal{A}$ would output 0 and 1 with an equal probability, except for a negligible difference. That is $\Pr[\mathcal{D}(g_1, g_2, g_1^x, g_2^y) = 1] = 1/2 + \nu_0$, where ν_0 is a negligible function.

When $C = g_2^x$, then bc and bc_1 are from the same credential. Then $\mathcal{A}$ outputs 1 (i.e., $\sigma^* = \sigma$ in the indistinguishability game) with a probability $1/2 + Adv$, where Adv is the advantage of $\mathcal{A}$ in linking blinded credentials. That is $\Pr[\mathcal{D}(g_1, g_2, g_1^x, g_2^x) = 1] = 1/2 + Adv$. We thus have $|\Pr[\mathcal{D}(g_1, g_2, g_1^x, g_2^x) = 1] - \Pr[\mathcal{D}(g_1, g_2, g_1^x, g_2^y) = 1]| = Adv - \nu_0$. This completes the proof.   □

Revocability is straightforward. For non-shareability, the above scheme in its current form does not provide this feature, but it is easy to implement the so called all-or-nothing approach, where the user identity u encoded in a credential is replaced by, e.g., the user's long term signing key.

4 Self-blindable Credential with Forward Unlinkability and Scalable Revocation

The above construction suffers from two weaknesses. (1) It lacks *forward unlinkability* – once a credential is revoked and the corresponding k is published in the CRL, those blinded credentials generated prior to revocation become linkable. (2) The verifier's computation is linear to the total number of revoked credentials, which grows over the time. Even though the verifier does not have resource constraints, the unscalable revocation cost may hinder the practical deployment of the scheme. We next propose another construction to address these issues.

4.1 Forward Unlinkable Self-blindable Credential

We continue to use the BBS+ signature scheme for credential issuance. But to achieve forward unlinkability, we cannot simply use $M'' = M^{f \cdot k}$ to hide k since k can be exposed in the CRL. We can further blind k as $M'' = M^{f \cdot k} t^r$, together with $h^r \in G_2$ (which is used to cancel out the randomness t^r in credential verification), where $t \in_R G_1, r \in_R Z_q$. However, this requires h^r to be an element in G_2, contradicting our efforts in making user side computation work entirely over G_1. It appears to us a challenge to solve this problem, without modifying the BBS+ signature scheme.

We get over this issue by introducing one more pair of public parameters $(t, T = t^z,)$ into the BBS+ signature setting, where $t \in G_1$. Specifically, the new public key of the credential system becomes $(Z = h^z, h, a, b, d, t, T)$ and the private key remains $z \in Z_q^*$. The signature generation and verification algorithm remain the same. The newly introduced (t, T) are used for blinding purposes only.

Specifically, a blinded credential is generated from (M, k, s, u) as follows (based upon the challenge from the verifier), where $f, r_1, r_2 \in_R Z_q^*$:

$$M' = M^f \cdot t^{r_1} \in G_1$$
$$M'' = M^{f \cdot k} \cdot T^{r_2} \in G_1$$
$$A' = (a^u b^s d)^f \in G_1 \qquad (3)$$
$$T'_1 = T^{r_1} \in G_1$$
$$T'_2 = t^{r_2} \in G_1.$$

together with a standard $PoK\{(k, \mu, \varsigma, f, \gamma, r_1, r_2) : M'' = M'^k t^{-\gamma} T^{r_2} \wedge A' = a^\mu b^\varsigma d^f \wedge T'_1 = T^{r_1} \wedge T'_2 = t^{r_2}\}$, where $\gamma = k \cdot r_1$. The blinded credential $(M', M'', A', T'_1, T'_2, PoK)$ can be verified by checking:

$$\begin{cases} A' \neq 1 \in G_1 \\ PoK \text{ is valid} \\ e(M', Z)e(M'', h) \overset{?}{=} e(A', h)e(T'_1, h)e(T'_2, Z) \end{cases}$$

Security. For the security of this construction (especially that the introduction of (t, T) does not affect unforgeability of credentials), we have the following theorem, and the proof will be provided in the full version of the paper.

Theorem 3. *If the BBS+ signature is existentially unforgeable, then the above forward unlinkable self-blindable credential scheme achieves unforgeability. The scheme also achieves unlinkability if the XDH assumption holds.*

4.2   Scalable Revocation

To avoid the linear computation at the verifier side, we take advantage of the dynamic accumulator in [1,13], a revocation technique widely used in anonymous credentials and group signatures. An accumulator scheme allows a large set of values to be accumulated into a single value called the *accumulator*. For each accumulated value, there exists a *witness*, which is the evidence attesting that the accumulated value is indeed contained in the accumulator. Such a membership proof can be carried out in a zero-knowledge fashion such that no information is exposed about the witness and the value.

Nguyen's dynamic accumulator [1,13] works over a bilinear map $e : G_1 \times G_2 \to G_T$. Let h be generators of G_2. The public parameters include $(Z = h^z, h)$, and the private key is $z \in Z_q^*$. Let Λ be the present accumulator, the witness for a value k accumulated in Λ is $W = \Lambda^{\frac{1}{k+z}}$. As such, (W, k) can be verified by $e(W, Z \cdot h^k) = e(\Lambda, h)$. At this point of time, it can be seen that Nguyen's dynamic accumulator quite resembles the BBS+ signature in structure. As a result, our blinding technique for the above forward unlinkable self-blindable credential scheme can be directly applied to blinding (W, k, Λ) in Nguyen's dynamic accumulator.

The complete construction is a combination of the above forward unlinkable credential scheme and Nguyen's dynamic accumulator scheme. The basic idea is that the "k" element of each credential is accumulated into an accumulator, so that if a credential is revoked, then the corresponding "k" element is removed from the accumulator. To make the combination seamless and also for better efficiency consideration, the two primitives would share system parameters — the master secret key z and the public parameter $Z = h^z$. We omit the details as they are a bit straightforward.

Outsourcing of Witness Update. One more issue to discuss is that Nguyen's dynamic accumulator requires all users to update their witnesses in the event of credential revocation. To get her witness updated, a user should either keep connected to the revocation server around the clock or do a batch update after a period of time. For resource-constrained devices, batch update seems the only likely choice. In a large-scale system where credential revocations are frequent, a batch update consists of a plethora of witness update events. Then, the out-of-the-band witness update may become the bottleneck. Fortunately, in our scheme the credential component corresponding to the accumulator (i.e., W, k) can be public, as its role is simply a testimony that the credential is not revoked. This suggests that a user can outsource the witness update task to an *untrusted* third party, who helps update her witness. The user simply needs retrieving her witness back at the time of authentication.

Acknowledgments. The fourth author was supported by the National Science Foundation of China under Grant No. 61373158, and the Fok Ying Tung Education Foundation under Grant No. 131066.

References

1. Au, M.H., Susilo, W., Mu, Y.: Constant-size dynamic k-TAA. In: Prisco, R., Yung, M. (eds.) SCN 2006. LNCS, vol. 4116, pp. 111–125. Springer, Heidelberg (2006)
2. Balasch, J.: Smart Card Implementation of Anonymous Credentials, Master thesis. K.U, Leuven (2008)
3. Boneh, D., Boyen, X.: Short signatures without random oracles. In: Cachin, C., Camenisch, J.L. (eds.) EUROCRYPT 2004. LNCS, vol. 3027, pp. 56–73. Springer, Heidelberg (2004)
4. Boneh, D., Boyen, X., Shacham, H.: Short group signatures. In: Franklin, M. (ed.) CRYPTO 2004. LNCS, vol. 3152, pp. 41–55. Springer, Heidelberg (2004)
5. Bichsel, P., Camenisch, J., Groß, T., Shoup, V.: Anonymous credentials on a standard java card. In: Proceedings of the ACM Conference on Computer and Communication Security, CCS 2009, pp. 600–610 (2009)
6. Batina, L., Hoepman, J.-H., Jacobs, B., Mostowski, W., Vullers, P.: Developing efficient blinded attribute certificates on smart cards via pairings. In: Gollmann, D., Lanet, J.-L., Iguchi-Cartigny, J. (eds.) CARDIS 2010. LNCS, vol. 6035, pp. 209–222. Springer, Heidelberg (2010)
7. Baldimtsi, F., Lysyanskaya, A.: Anonymous Credentials Light. http://eprint.iacr.org/2012/298.pdf
8. Boneh, D., Shacham, H.: Group signatures with verifier-local revocation. In: Proceedings of the ACM conference on Computer and Communications Security, CCS 2004, pp. 168–177 (2004)
9. Camenisch, J., Herreweghen, E.V.: Design and implementation of the idemix anonymous credential system. In: Proceedings of the ACM Conference on Computer and Communication Security, CCS 2002 (2002)
10. Camenisch, J., Lysyanskaya, A.: An efficient sysem for non-transferable anonymous credentials with optional anonymity revocation. In: Proceedings of the Advances in Cryptology, Eurocrypt 2001, pp. 93–118 (2001)
11. Camenisch, J.L., Lysyanskaya, A.: A signature scheme with efficient protocols. In: Cimato, S., Galdi, C., Persiano, G. (eds.) SCN 2002. LNCS, vol. 2576, pp. 268–289. Springer, Heidelberg (2003)
12. Camenisch, J., Kohlweiss, M., Soriente, C.: An accumulator based on bilinear maps and efficient revocation for anonymous credentials. In: Jarecki, S., Tsudik, G. (eds.) PKC 2009. LNCS, vol. 5443, pp. 481–500. Springer, Heidelberg (2009)
13. Nguyen, L.: Accumulators from bilinear pairings and applications. In: Menezes, A. (ed.) CT-RSA 2005. LNCS, vol. 3376, pp. 275–292. Springer, Heidelberg (2005)
14. Sterckx, M., Gierlichs, B., Preneel, B., Verbauwhede, T.: Efficient implementation of anonymous credentials on java card smart cards. In: Proceedings of the Information Forensics and Security, WIFS 2009, pp. 106–110. IEEE (2009)
15. Verheul, E.R.: Self-blindable credential certificates from the weil pairing. In: Boyd, C. (ed.) ASIACRYPT 2001. LNCS, vol. 2248, p. 533. Springer, Heidelberg (2001)

Practical and Provably Secure Distance-Bounding

Ioana Boureanu[1,2], Aikaterini Mitrokotsa[3], and Serge Vaudenay[4(✉)]

[1] University of Applied Sciences Western Switzerland, Delémont, Switzerland
[2] HEIG-VD, Yverdon-les-bains, Switzerland
ioana.carlson@heig-vd.ch
[3] Chalmers University of Technology, Gothenburg, Sweden
aikaterini.mitrokotsa@chalmers.se
[4] Ecole Polytechnique Fédérale de Lausanne (EPFL), Lausanne, Switzerland
serge.vaudenay@epfl.ch

Abstract. From contactless payments to remote car unlocking, many applications are vulnerable to relay attacks. Distance bounding protocols are the main practical countermeasure against these attacks. At FSE 2013, we presented **SKI** as the *first* family of *provably secure* distance bounding protocols. At LIGHTSEC 2013, we presented the best attacks against **SKI**. In this paper, we present the security proofs. More precisely, we explicate a general formalism for distance-bounding protocols. Then, we prove that **SKI** and its variants is provably secure, even under the real-life setting of noisy communications, against the main types of relay attacks: distance-fraud and generalised versions of mafia- and terrorist-fraud. For this, we reinforce the idea of using secret sharing, combined with the new notion of a *leakage scheme*. In view of resistance to mafia-frauds and terrorist-frauds, we present the notion of *circular-keying* for pseudorandom functions (PRFs); this notion models the employment of a PRF, with possible *linear reuse* of the key. We also use *PRF masking* to fix common mistakes in existing security proofs/claims.

1 Introduction

Recently, we proposed the **SKI** [6–8] family of distance-bounding (DB) protocols.[1] In this paper, we present a formalism for distance-bounding, which includes a sound communication and adversarial model. We incorporate the notion of time-of-flight for distance-based communication. We further formalise security against distance-fraud, man-in-the-middle (MiM) generalising mafia-frauds, and an enhanced version of terrorist-fraud that we call *collusion-fraud*. Our formalisations take noisy communications into account.

Mainly in the context of security against generalised mafia-frauds (when TF-resistance is also enforced), we introduce the concept of *circular-keying security*

The full version of this paper is available as [8].

[1] Due to space constraints, we refer to these papers for an overview of DB protocols.

© Springer International Publishing Switzerland 2015
Y. Desmedt (Ed.): ISC 2013, LNCS 7807, pp. 248–258, 2015.
DOI: 10.1007/978-3-319-27659-5_18

to extend the security of a pseudorandom function (PRF) f to its possible uses in maps of the form $y \mapsto L(x) + f_x(y)$, for a secret key x and a transformation L. We also introduce a *leakage scheme*, to resist to collusion frauds, and adopt the *PRF masking* technique from [4,5] to address distance-fraud issues. These formal mechanisms come to counteract mistakes like those in proofs based on PRF-constructions, errors of the kind exposed by Boureanu *et al.* [4] and Hancke [13].

We analyse and propose variants of **SKI** [6,7] and conclude that **SKI is historically the first practical class of distance-bounding protocols enjoying full provable security**.[2] On the way to this, we formalise the DB-driven requirements of the **SKI** protocols' components.

2   Model for Distance-Bounding Protocols

We consider a multiparty setting where each participant U is modelled by a probabilistic polynomial-time (PPT) interactive Turing machine (ITM), has a location loc_U, and where communication messages from a location to another take some time, depending on the distance to travel.

Consider two honest participants P and V, each running a predefined *algorithm*. Along standard lines, a general communication is formalised via an *experiment*, generically denoted $exp = (P(x; r_P) \longleftrightarrow V(y; r_V))$, where $r_{(.)}$ are the random coins of the participants. The experiment above can be "enlarged" with an adversary $\mathcal{A}$ which interferes in the communication, up to the transmitting-time constraints. This is denoted by $(P(x; r_P) \longleftrightarrow \mathcal{A}(r_\mathcal{A}) \longleftrightarrow V(y; r_V))$. At the end of each experiment, the participant V has an output bit Out_V denoting acceptance or rejection. The *view* of a participant on an experiment is the collection of all its initial inputs (including coins) and his incoming messages. We may group several participants under the same symbolic name.

The constant $\mathbb{B}$ denotes a bound defining what it means to be "close-enough".

The crux of proving security of DB protocols lies in Lemma 1: if V sends a challenge c, the answer r in a time-critical challenge-response round is locally computed by a close participant $\mathcal{A}$ from its own view and incoming messages from far-away participants $\mathcal{B}$ which are independent from c. Clearly, it also captures the case where the adversary collects information during the previous rounds. On the one hand, we could just introduce a full model in which such a lemma holds. We do so in our full version [8]. On the other hand, we could also just state the text of the lemma and take it axiomatically.

Lemma 1. *Consider an experiment $\mathcal{B}(z; r_\mathcal{B}) \leftrightarrow \mathcal{A}(u; r_\mathcal{A}) \leftrightarrow V(y; r_V)$ in which the verifier V broadcasts a message c, then waits for a response r, and accepts if r took at most time $2\mathbb{B}$ to arrive. In the experiment, $\mathcal{A}$ is the set of all participants which are within a distance up to $\mathbb{B}$ to V, and $\mathcal{B}$ is the set of all other participants. For each user U, we consider his view $View_U$ just before the time when U can*

---

[2] As far as we know, there exists only one other protocol with full provable security. It was presented at ACNS 2013 [12] and compared with **SKI** at PROVSEC 2013 [17]. All other protocols fail against at least one threat model. (See [7, Section 2].).

see the broadcast message c. We say that a message by U is independent from c if it is the result of applying U on $View_U$, or a prefix of it. There exists an algorithm $\mathcal{A}$ and a list w of messages independent from c such that if V accepts, then $r = \mathcal{A}(View_\mathcal{A}, c, w)$, where $View_\mathcal{A}$ is the list of all $View_A$, $A \in \mathcal{A}$.

When modelling distance-bounding protocols, we consider provers P and verifiers V. $\mathcal{A}$ denotes the adversary and P^* denotes a dishonest prover.

Definition 2 (DB Protocols). *A **distance-bounding protocol** is a tuple $(Gen, P, V, \mathbb{B})$, where Gen is a randomised, key-generation algorithm such that (x, y) is the output[3] of $Gen(1^s; r_k)$, where r_k are the coins and s is a security parameter; $P(x; r_P)$ and $V(y; r_V)$ are PPT ITM running the algorithm of the prover and the verifier with their own coins, respectively; and $\mathbb{B}$ is a distance-bound. They must be such that the following two facts hold:*

- ***Termination:** $(\forall s)(\forall R)(\forall r_k, r_V)(\forall loc_V)$ when doing $(\cdot, y) \leftarrow Gen(1^s; r_k)$ and $(R \longleftrightarrow V(y; r_V))$, it is the case that V halts in $Poly(s)$ computational steps, where R is any set of (unbounded) algorithms;*
- *p-**Completeness:** $(\forall s)$ $(\forall loc_V, loc_P$ such that $d(loc_V, loc_P) \leq \mathbb{B})$ we have*

$$\Pr_{r_k, r_P, r_V}\left[\mathsf{Out}_V = 1 : \begin{matrix} (x, y) \leftarrow Gen(1^s; r_k) \\ P(x; r_P) \longleftrightarrow V(y; r_V) \end{matrix}\right] \geq p.$$

Our model <u>implicitly</u> assumes *concurrency*.

Definition 3 (α-resistance to distance-fraud). *$(\forall s)$ $(\forall P^*)$ $(\forall loc_V$ such that $d(loc_V, loc_{P^*}) > \mathbb{B})$ $(\forall r_k)$, we have*

$$\Pr_{r_V}\left[\mathsf{Out}_V = 1 : \begin{matrix} (x, y) \leftarrow Gen(1^s; r_k) \\ P^*(x) \longleftrightarrow V(y; r_V) \end{matrix}\right] \leq \alpha$$

where P^* is any (unbounded) dishonest prover. In a concurrent setting, we implicitly allow a polynomially bounded number of honest $P(x')$ and $V(y')$ close to $V(y)$ with independent (x', y').[4]

We now formalise resistance to MiM attacks. During a learning phase, the attacker $\mathcal{A}$ interacts with m provers and z verifiers. In the attack phase, $\mathcal{A}$ tries to win in an experiment in front of a verifier which is far-away from $\ell - m$ provers.

Definition 4 (β -resistance to MiM). *$(\forall s)(\forall m, \ell, z)$ polynomially bounded, $(\forall \mathcal{A}_1, \mathcal{A}_2)$ polynomially bounded, for all locations such that $d(loc_{P_j}, loc_V) > \mathbb{B}$, where $j \in \{m+1, \ldots, \ell\}$, we have*

$$\Pr\left[\mathsf{Out}_V = 1 : \begin{matrix} (x, y) \leftarrow Gen(1^s) \\ P_1(x), \ldots, P_m(x) \longleftrightarrow \mathcal{A}_1 \longleftrightarrow V_1(y), \ldots, V_z(y) \\ P_{m+1}(x), \ldots, P_\ell(x) \longleftrightarrow \mathcal{A}_2(View_{\mathcal{A}_1}) \longleftrightarrow V(y) \end{matrix}\right] \leq \beta$$

---

[3] In this paper, there is just one common input, i.e., we assume $x = y$.
[4] This is to capture distance hijacking [10]. (See [8].).

over all random coins, where $View_{\mathcal{A}_1}$ is the final view of $\mathcal{A}_1$. In a concurrent setting, we implicitly allow a polynomially bounded number of $P(x')$, $P^*(x')$, and $V(y')$ with independent (x', y'), anywhere.

The classical notion of mafia-fraud [1] corresponds to $m = z = 0$ and $\ell = 1$. The classical notion of impersonation corresponds to $\ell = m$.

We now formalise the terrorist-fraud by [6,8].

Definition 5 $((\gamma, \gamma')$-resistance to collusion-fraud). $(\forall s)(\forall P^*)$ $(\forall loc_{V_0}$ s.t. $d(loc_{V_0}, loc_{P^*}) > \mathbb{B})$ $(\forall \mathcal{A}^{\mathsf{CF}}$ PPT) such that

$$\Pr\left[\mathsf{Out}_{V_0} = 1 : \begin{array}{c} (x, y) \leftarrow Gen(1^s) \\ P^*(x) \longleftrightarrow \mathcal{A}^{\mathsf{CF}} \longleftrightarrow V_0(y) \end{array}\right] \geq \gamma$$

over all random coins, there exists a (kind of)[5] MiM attack with some parameters $m, \ell, z, \mathcal{A}_1, \mathcal{A}_2, P_i, P_j, V_{i'}$ using P and P^* in the learning phase, such that

$$\Pr\left[\mathsf{Out}_V = 1 : \begin{array}{c} (x, y) \leftarrow Gen(1^s) \\ P_1^{(*)}(x), \ldots, P_m^{(*)}(x) \longleftrightarrow \mathcal{A}_1 \longleftrightarrow V_1(y), \ldots, V_z(y) \\ P_{m+1}(x), \ldots, P_\ell(x) \longleftrightarrow \mathcal{A}_2(View_{\mathcal{A}_1}) \longleftrightarrow V(y) \end{array}\right] \geq \gamma'$$

where P^* is any (unbounded) dishonest prover and $P^{(*)} \in \{P, P^*\}$. Following the MiM requirements, $d(loc_{P_j}, loc_V) > \mathbb{B}$, for all $j \in \{m+1, \ell\}$. In a concurrent setting, we implicitly allow a polynomially bounded number of $P(x')$, $P^*(x')$, $V(y')$ with independent (x', y'), but no honest participant close to V_0.

Definition 5 expresses the following. If a prover P^*, situated far-away from V_0, can help an adversary $\mathcal{A}^{\mathsf{CF}}$ to pass, then a malicious $(\mathcal{A}_1, \mathcal{A}_2)$ could run a rather successful MiM attack playing with possibly multiple instances of $P^*(x)$ in the learning phase. In other words, a dishonest prover P^* cannot successfully collude with $\mathcal{A}^{\mathsf{CF}}$ without leaking some private information. We can find in [17] a discussion on the relation with other forms of terrorist frauds, including SimTF [11,12].

3 Practical and Secure Distance-Bounding Protocols

The protocol **SKI** [6,7] follows a long dynasty originated from [14]. It is sketched in Fig. 1. We use the parameters $(s, q, n, k, t, t', \tau)$, where s is the security parameter. The **SKI** protocols are built using a function family $(f_x)_{x \in GF(q)^s}$, with q being a small power of prime. In the DB phase, n rounds are used, with $n \in \Omega(s)$. Then, **SKI** uses the value $f_x(N_P, N_V, L) \in GF(q)^{t'n}$, with nonces $N_P, N_V \in \{0,1\}^k$ and a mask $M \in GF(q)^{t'n}$, where $k \in \Omega(s)$. The element $a = (a_1, \ldots, a_n)$ is established by V in the initialisation phase, and it is sent encrypted as $M := a \oplus f_x(N_P, N_V, L)$, with $M \in GF(q)^{t'n}$. Similarly, V selects a

---

[5] Here, we deviate from Definition 4 a bit by introducing $P^*(x)$ in the MiM attack.

random linear transformation L from a set $\mathcal{L}$ (the *leakage scheme*), which is specified by the **SKI** protocol instance, and the parties compute $x' = L(x)$. The purpose of $\mathcal{L}$ is to leak $L(x)$ in the case of a collusion-fraud. Further, $c = (c_1, \ldots, c_n)$ is the challenge-vector with $c_i \in \{1, \ldots, t\}$, $r_i := F(c_i, a_i, x'_i) \in GF(q)$ is the response to the challenge c_i, $i \in \{1, \ldots, n\}$, with F (the *F-scheme*) as specified below. The protocol ends with a message Out_V denoting acceptance or rejection.

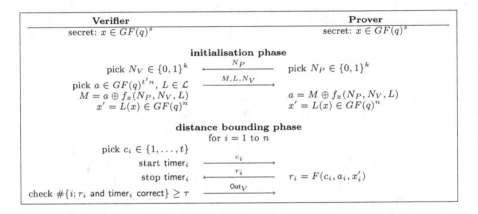

Fig. 1. The **SKI** schema of distance-bounding protocols

In [6,7], several variants of **SKI** were proposed. We concentrate on two of them using $q = 2$, $t' = 2$, and the response-function

$$F(1, a_i, x'_i) = (a_i)_1 \qquad F(2, a_i, x'_i) = (a_i)_2 \qquad F(3, a_i, x'_i) = x'_i + (a_i)_1 + (a_i)_2,$$

where $(a_i)_j$ denotes the jth bit of a_i. In the **SKI**$_\mathbf{pro}$ variant, we have $t = 3$ and $\mathcal{L} = \mathcal{L}_{\mathsf{bit}}$, consisting of all L_μ transforms defined by $L_\mu(x) = (\mu \cdot x, \ldots, \mu \cdot x)$ for each vector $\mu \in GF(q)^s$. I.e., n repetitions of the same bit $\mu \cdot x$, the dot product of μ and x. In the **SKI**$_\mathbf{lite}$ variant, we have $t = 2$ with the transform-set $\mathcal{L} = \{\emptyset\}$. Namely, **SKI**$_\mathbf{lite}$ never uses the $c_i = 3$ challenge or the leakage scheme.

We note that both instances are efficient. Indeed, we could precompute the table of $F(\cdot, a_i, x'_i)$ and just do a table lookup to compute r_i from c_i. For **SKI**$_\mathbf{pro}$, this can be done with a circuit of only 7 NAND gates and depth 4. For **SKI**$_\mathbf{lite}$, 3 NAND gates and a depth of 2 are enough. The heavy computation lies in the f_x evaluation, which occurs in a non time-critical phase.

In [8], we also consider other variants with different F-schemes.

SKI *Completeness (in Noisy Communications).* Each (c_i, r_i) exchange is time-critical, so it is subject to errors. To address this, we introduce the probability p_{noise} of one response being erroneous. In practice, we take p_{noise} as a constant. Then, our protocol specifies that the verifier accepts only if the number of correct answers is at least a linear threshold τ. The probability that at least τ responses out of n are correct is given by:

$$B(n, \tau, 1 - p_{noise}) = \sum_{i=\tau}^{n} \binom{n}{i} (1 - p_{noise})^i p_{noise}^{n-i}$$

Thanks to the Chernoff-Hoeffding bound [9,15], $\tau \leq (1 - p_{\text{noise}} - \varepsilon)n$ implies $B(n, \tau, 1 - p_{noise}) \geq 1 - e^{-2\varepsilon^2 n}$. So, we obtain the following result.

Lemma 6. *For $\varepsilon > 0$ and $\frac{\tau}{n} \leq 1 - p_{\text{noise}} - \varepsilon$, **SKI** is $(1 - e^{-2\varepsilon^2 n})$-complete.*

PRF Masking. Importantly, **SKI** applies a random mask M on the output of f_x to thwart weaknesses against PRF programming [4]. This was called *PRF masking* in [4,5]. So, the malicious prover cannot influence the distribution of a.

F-scheme. Related to the response-function F, we advance the concept of *F-scheme*. This will take the response-function based on secret sharing by Avoine *et al.* [2] further, beyond protection against terrorist-fraud *only*, offering formalised sufficient conditions to protect against *all* three possible frauds.[6] Thus, we stress that using a secret sharing scheme in computing the responses may be too strong and/or insufficient to characterise the protection against frauds mounted onto DB protocols, and we amend this with Definitions 7 and 11.

Definition 7 *(F -scheme).* *Let $t, t' \geq 2$. An F -**scheme** is a function $F :$ $\{1, \ldots, t\} \times GF(q)^{t'} \times GF(q) \rightarrow GF(q)$ characterised as follows.*

*We say that the F-scheme is **linear** if for all challenges c_i in their domain, the $F(c_i, \cdot, \cdot)$ function is a linear form over the $GF(q)$-vector space $GF(q)^{t'} \times GF(q)$ which is non-degenerate in the a_i component.*

*We say the F-scheme is **pairwise uniform** if*

$$(\forall I \subsetneq \{1, \ldots, n\}, \#I \leq 2)(H(x'_i | F(c_i, a_i, x'_i)_{c_i \in I}) = H(x'_i)),$$

where $(a_i, x'_i) \in_U GF(q)^{t'} \times GF(q)$, $\#S$ denotes the cardinality of a set S, and H denotes the Shannon entropy.

*We say the F-scheme is t -**leaking** if there exists a polynomial time algorithm E such that for all $(a_i, x'_i) \in GF(q)^{t'} \times GF(q)$, we have*

$$E\big(F(1, a_i, x'_i), \ldots, F(t, a_i, x'_i)\big) = x'_i.$$

*Let F_{a_i, x'_i} denote $F(\cdot, a_i, x'_i)$. We say that the F-scheme is σ -**bounded** if for any $x'_i \in GF(q)$, we have*

$$\mathbb{E}_{a_i}\left(\max_y \left(\#(F_{a_i, x'_i}^{-1}(y))\right)\right) \leq \sigma,$$

where $x'_i \in GF(q)$ and the expected-value is $\mathbb{E}$ taken over $a_i \in GF(q)^{t'}$.

---

[6] Secret sharing is used to defeat an attack from [16] which is further discussed in [3].

The pairwise uniformity and the t-leaking property of the F-scheme say that knowing the complete table of the response-function F for a given c_i leaks x_i', yet knowing only up to 2 entries challenge-response in this table discloses no information about x_i'. The σ-boundedness of the schemes says that the expected value (taken on the choice of the subsecrets a_i) of the largest preimage of the map $c_i \mapsto F(c_i, a_i, x_i')$ is bounded by a constant σ. We have $\frac{t}{q} \leq \sigma \leq t$ due to the pigeonhole principle, since $\sum_y \#(F_{a_i,x_i'}^{-1}(y)) = t$. Furthermore, $\sigma \geq 1$.

Lemma 8. *The F-scheme of* $\mathbf{SKI_{pro}}$ *is linear, pairwise uniform, $\frac{9}{4}$-bounded, and t-leaking. The F-scheme of* $\mathbf{SKI_{lite}}$ *is linear, pairwise uniform, $\frac{3}{2}$-bounded, but not t-leaking.*

The proof is available in [8].

Leakage Scheme. We can consider several sets $\mathcal{L}$ of transformations to be used in the PRF-instance, of the **SKI** initialisation phase. The idea of the set $\mathcal{L}$ is that, when leaking some noisy versions of $L(x)$ for some random $L \in \mathcal{L}$, the adversary can reconstruct x without noise to defeat the terrorist fraud by Hancke [13].

Definition 9 (Leakage scheme). *Let $\mathcal{L}$ be a set of linear functions from $GF(q)^s$ to $GF(q)^n$. Given $x \in GF(q)^s$ and a PPT algorithm $e(x, L; r)$, we define an oracle $\mathcal{O}_{\mathcal{L},x,e}$ producing a random pair $(L, e(x, L))$ with $L \in_U \mathcal{L}$. $\mathcal{L}$ is a (T, r)-leakage scheme if there exists an oracle PPT algorithm $\mathcal{A}^{(\cdot)}$ such that for all $x \in GF(q)^s$, for all PPT e, $\Pr[\mathcal{A}^{\mathcal{O}_{\mathcal{L},x,e}} = x] \geq \Pr_r[d_H(e(x, L), L(x)) < T]^r$, where d_H denotes the Hamming distance.*

Lemma 10. *$\mathcal{L}_{\mathsf{bit}}$ is a $(\frac{n}{2}, s)$-leakage scheme.*

Proof. $\mathcal{A}$ calls the oracle s times, then —by computing the majority— $\mathcal{A}$ deduces $\mu \cdot x$ with probability p, for each of the obtained μ. We run $\mathcal{O}_{\mathcal{L},x,e}$ until we collect s linearly independent μ values. All the s obtained $\mu \cdot x$ are correct with probability p^s. Then, we deduce x by solving a linear system. $\square$

Circular-Keying Security. We introduce the notion of *security against circular-keying*, which is needed to prove security in the context in which the key x is used not only in the f_x computation.

Definition 11 (Circular-Keying). *Let s be some security parameter, let b be a bit, let $q \geq 2$, let $m \in Poly(s)$, and let $x, \overline{x} \in GF(q)^s$ be two row-vectors. Let $(f_x)_{x \in GF(q)^s}$ be a family of (keyed) functions, e.g., $f_x : \{0,1\}^* \to GF(q)^m$. For an input y, the output $f_x(y)$ can be represented as a row-vector in $GF(q)^m$.*
We define an oracle $\mathcal{O}_{f_x,\overline{x}}$, which upon a query of form (y_i, A_i, B_i), $A_i \in GF(q)^s$, $B_i \in GF(q)^m$, answers $(A_i \cdot \overline{x}) + (B_i \cdot f_x(y_i))$. The game $Circ_{f_x,\overline{x}}$ of circular-keying with an adversary $\mathcal{A}$ is described as follows: we set $b_{f_x,\overline{x}} := \mathcal{A}^{\mathcal{O}_{f_x,\overline{x}}}$, where the queries (y_i, A_i, B_i) from $\mathcal{A}$ must follow the restriction that

$$(\forall c_1, \ldots, c_k \in GF(q)) \left(\#\{y_i; c_i \neq 0\} = 1, \sum_{j=1}^k c_j B_j = 0 \Longrightarrow \sum_{j=1}^k c_j A_j = 0 \right).$$

We say that the family of functions $(f_x)_{x \in GF(q)^s}$ is an (ε, C, Q)-circular-PRF if for any PPT adversary $\mathcal{A}$ making Q queries and having complexity C, it is the case that $\Pr[b_{f_x,x} = b_{f^*,\overline{x}}] \leq \frac{1}{2} + \varepsilon$, where the probability is taken over the random coins of $\mathcal{A}$ and over the random selection of $x, \overline{x} \in GF(q)^s$ and f^*.

The condition on the queries means that for any set of queries with the same value y_i, any linear combination making B_j vanish makes A_j vanish at the same time. (Otherwise, linear combinations would extract some information about $\overline{x}$.)

We note that it is possible to create secure circular-keying in the random oracle model. Indeed, any "reasonable" PRF should satisfy this constraint. Special constructions (e.g., the ones based on PRF programming from [4]) would not.

Lemma 12. *Let $f_x(y) = H(x, y)$, where H is a random oracle, $x \in \{0, 1\}^s$, and $y \in \{0, 1\}^*$. Then, f is a $(T2^{-s}, T, Q)$-circular PRF for any T and Q.*

The proof is available in [8].

We now state the security of **SKI**.

Theorem 13. *The **SKI** protocols are secure distance-bounding protocols, i.e.,:*

- *A. If the F-scheme is linear and σ-bounded, if $(f_x)_{x \in GF(q)^n}$ is a (ε, nN, C)-circular PRF, then the **SKI** protocols offer α-resistance to distance-fraud, with $\alpha = B(n, \tau, \frac{\sigma}{t}) + \varepsilon$, for attacks limited to complexity C and N participants. So, we need $\frac{\tau}{n} > \frac{\sigma}{t}$ for security.*
- *B. If the F-scheme is linear and pairwise uniform, if $(f_x)_{x \in GF(q)^n}$ is a $(\varepsilon, n(\ell + z + 1), C)$-circular PRF, if $\mathcal{L}$ is a set of linear mappings, the **SKI** protocols are β-resilient against MiM attackers with parameters ℓ and z and a complexity bounded by C,*

$$\beta = B\left(n, \tau, \frac{1}{t} + \frac{t-1}{t} \times \frac{1}{q}\right) + 2^{-k}\left(\frac{\ell(\ell-1)}{2} + \frac{z(z+1)}{2}\right) + \varepsilon.$$

  So, we need $\frac{\tau}{n} > \frac{1}{t} + \frac{t-1}{t} \times \frac{1}{q}$ for security.
- *B'. If the F-scheme is linear and pairwise uniform, if $(f_x)_{x \in GF(q)^n}$ is a $(\varepsilon, n(\ell + z + 1), C)$-PRF, if the function $F(c_i, a_i, \cdot)$ is constant for each c_i, a_i, the **SKI** protocols are β-resilient against MiM attackers as above.*
- *C. If the F-scheme is t-leaking, if $\mathcal{L}$ is a (T, r)-leakage scheme, for all $\theta \in]0, 1[$, the **SKI** protocols offer (γ, γ')-resistance to collusion-fraud, for γ^{-1} polynomially bounded, and*

$$\gamma \geq B(T, T + \tau - n, \frac{t-1}{t})^{1-\theta}, \quad \gamma' = \left(1 - B\left(T, T + \tau - n, \frac{t-1}{t}\right)^{\theta}\right)^r.$$

  So, we need $\frac{\tau}{n} > 1 - \frac{T}{tn}$ for security.

Theorem 13 is tight for **SKI**$_{\text{pro}}$ and **SKI**$_{\text{lite}}$, due to the attacks shown in [6,7]. Following Lemma 8 and Theorem 13, we deduce the following security parameters:

$$
\begin{array}{c|ccc}
 & \alpha & \beta & \gamma \\
\hline
\mathbf{SKI_{pro}} & B(n,\tau,\tfrac{3}{4}) & B(n,\tau,\tfrac{2}{3}) & B(\tfrac{n}{2},\tau-\tfrac{n}{2},\tfrac{2}{3}) \\
\mathbf{SKI_{lite}} & B(n,\tau,\tfrac{3}{4}) & B(n,\tau,\tfrac{3}{4}) & 1
\end{array}
$$

According to the data in the table above, we must take $1 - p_{\mathsf{noise}} - \varepsilon \geq \frac{\tau}{n} \geq \frac{3}{4} + \varepsilon$ to make the above instances of **SKI** secure, with a failure probability bounded by $e^{-2\varepsilon^2 n}$ (by the Chernoff-Hoeffding bound [9,15]). If we require TF-resistance (as per Theorem 13.C), we also get a constraint of $\frac{\tau}{n} > \frac{5}{6} + \frac{\varepsilon}{2}$, similarly.

The proof of Theorem 13.B$'$ is similar (and simplified) as the one of Theorem 13.B. So, we prove below the A, B, and C parts only.

Proof. (Theorem 13.A) For each key $x' \neq x$ for which there is a $P(x')$ close to V, we apply the circular-PRF reduction and loose some probability ε. (Details as for why we can apply this reduction will appear in the proof of Theorem 13.B.)

If r_i comes form $P(x')$, due to the F-scheme being linear, r_i is correct with probability $\frac{1}{t}$. If r_i now comes from P^*, due to Lemma 1, r_i must be a function independent from c_i. So, for any secret x and a, the probability to get one response right is given by $p_i = \Pr_{c_i \in \{1,\dots,t\}}[r_i = F(c_i, a_i, x'_i)]$. Thanks to PRF masking, the distribution of the a_i's is uniform.

Consider the partitions I_j, $j \in \{1,\dots,t\}$ as follows: I_j is the set of all i's such that $\max_y \left(\#(F^{-1}_{a_i,x'_i}(y)) \right) = j$. Then, we are looking at the probability

$$
P_j(x'_i) := \Pr_{a_i}\left[\max_y \left(\#(F^{-1}_{a_i,x'_i}(y)) \right) = j \right],
$$

Given x' fixed, each iteration has a probability to succeed equal to $\sum_j \frac{jP_j}{t} = \frac{\sigma}{t}$. So, the probability to win the experiment is bounded by $p = B(n, \tau, \frac{\sigma}{t})$. □

Proof. (Theorem 13.B) Let $Game_0$ be the MiM attack-game described in Definition 4. Below we consider a prover P_j and a verifier V_k in an experiment, $j \in \{1,\dots,\ell\}, k \in \{1,\dots,z+1\}$. Let $(N_{P,j}, \overline{M}_j, \overline{L}_j, \overline{N}_{V,j})$ be the values of the nonces (N_P, N_V), of the mask M, and of the transformation L that the prover P_j generates or sees respectively, and $(\overline{N}_{P,k}, M_k, L_k, N_{V,k})$ be the values of the nonces (N_P, N_V), mask M, and transformation L that a verifier V_k generates or sees at his turn, $j \in \{1,\dots,\ell\}, k \in \{1,\dots,z+1\}$.

Using a reduction by failure-event F, the game $Game_0$ is indistinguishable to game $Game_1$ where no repetitions on $N_{P,j}$ or on $N_{V,k}$ happen, $j \in \{1,\dots,\ell\}$, $k \in \{1,\dots,z+1\}$ based on $\Pr[F] \leq 2^{-k}\left(\frac{\ell(\ell-1)}{2} + \frac{z(z+1)}{2}\right)$.

Since the F-scheme is linear, we can write $F(c_i, a_i, x'_i) = u_i(c_i)x'_i + (v_i(c_i) \cdot a_i)$ where $u_i(c_i) \in GF(q), v_i(c_i) \in GF(q)^{t'}$. Note that, in terms of i, the vectors $(v_i(1),\dots,v_i(t))$ span independent linear spaces. In $Game_1$, each (N_P, N_V, L, i) tuple can be invoked only twice (with a prover and a verifier) by the adversary. The pairwise uniformity of the F-scheme implies that $yv_i(c_i) + y'v_i(c'_i) = 0$ implies $yu_i(c_i) + y'u_i(c'_i) = 0$ for all $c_i, c'_i \in \{1,\dots,t\}$ and all $y, y' \in GF(q)$. So, we deduce that the condition to apply the circular-keying reduction is fulfilled. We can thus apply the circular-PRF reduction and reduce to $Game_2$, where

$F(c_i, f_x(N_P, N_V, L)_i, x_i')$ is replaced by $u_i(c_i)\tilde{x}_i + (v_i(c_i) \cdot f^*(N_P, N_V, L)_i)$, where f^* is a random function. This reduction has a probability loss of up to ε.

From here, we use a simple bridging step to say that the adversary $\mathcal{A}$ has virtually no advantage over $Game_2$ and a game $Game_3$, where the vector $a = f^*(N_P, N_V, L)$ is selected at random. So, the probability p of $\mathcal{A}$ of succeeding in $Game_3$ is the probability that at least τ rounds have a correct r_i. Due to Lemma 1, r_i must be computed by $\mathcal{A}$ (and not P_j). Getting r_i correct for c_i can thus be attained in two distinct ways: 1. in the event $e1$ of guessing $c_i' = c_i$ and sending it beforehand to P_j and getting the correct response r_i, or 2. in the event $e2$ of simply guessing the correct answer r_i (for a challenge $c_i' \neq c_i$). So, $p = B(n, \tau, \Pr[e1] + \Pr[e2]) = B(n, \tau, \frac{1}{t} + \frac{t-1}{t} \times \frac{1}{q})$. $\qquad\square$

Proof. (Theorem 13.C) Assume as per the requirement for resistance to collusion-fraud that there is an experiment $exp^{\mathsf{CF}} = (P^*(x) \longleftrightarrow \mathcal{A}^{\mathsf{CF}}(r_{\mathsf{CF}}) \longleftrightarrow V_0(y; r_{V_0}))$, with P^* a coerced prover who is far away from V_0 and that $\Pr_{r_{V_0}, r_{\mathsf{CF}}}[\mathsf{Out}_{V_0} = 1] = \gamma$. Given some random $c_1, \ldots, c_n$ from V_0, we define $View_i$ as being the view of $\mathcal{A}^{\mathsf{CF}}$ before receiving c_i from V, and w_i as being all the information that $\mathcal{A}^{\mathsf{CF}}$ has received from P^* before it would be too late to send r_i on to V_0. This answer r_i done by $\mathcal{A}^{\mathsf{CF}}$ is formalised in Lemma 1. So, $r_i := \mathcal{A}^{\mathsf{CF}}(View_i \| c_i \| w_i)$.

Let C_i be the set of all possible c_i's on which the functions $\mathcal{A}^{\mathsf{CF}}(View_i \| \cdot \| w_i)$ and $F(., a_i, x_i')$ match. Let $C_i = \{c \in \{1, \ldots, t\} \,|\, \mathcal{A}^{\mathsf{CF}}(View_i \| c \| w_i) = F(c, a_i, x_i')\}$, $S = \{i \in \{1, \ldots, n\} \,|\, c_i \in C_i\}$, and $R = \{i \in \{1, \ldots, n\} \,|\, \#C_i = t\}$. The adversary $\mathcal{A}$ succeeds in exp^{CF} if $\#S \geq \tau$.

If we were to pick a set of challenges such that $\#S \geq \tau$ and $\#R \leq n - T$, we should select a good challenge (from no more than $t - 1$ existing out of t), for at least $T + \tau - n$ rounds out of T. In other words, $\Pr[\#S \geq \tau, \#R \leq n - T] \leq B(T, T + \tau - n, \frac{t-1}{t})$. But, by the hypothesis, $\Pr[\#S \geq \tau] \geq \gamma$. So, we deduce immediately that $\Pr[\#R \leq n - T | \#S \geq \tau] \leq \gamma^{-1} B(T, T + \tau - n, \frac{t-1}{t})$. Therefore, $\Pr[\#R > n - T | \#S \geq \tau] \geq 1 - \gamma^{-1} B(T, T + \tau - n, \frac{t-1}{t})$.

We use $m = \ell = z = \mathcal{O}(\gamma^{-1} r)$ (i.e., $\mathcal{A}_2$ will directly impersonate P to V after $\mathcal{A}_1$ ran m times the collusion fraud, with P^* and V). We define $\mathcal{A}_2$ such that, for each execution of the collusion fraud with P^* and V, it gets $View_i$, w_i. For each i, $\mathcal{A}_2$ computes the table $c \mapsto \mathcal{A}^{\mathsf{CF}}(View_i \| c \| w_i)$ and apply the t-leaking function E of the F-scheme on this table to obtain $y_i = E(c \mapsto \mathcal{A}^{\mathsf{CF}}(View_i \| c \| w_i))$. For each $i \in R$, the table matches the one of $c \mapsto F(c, a_i, x_i')$ with $x' = L(x)$, and we have $y_i = x_i'$. So, $\mathcal{A}_2$ computes a vector y. If V accepts the proof, then y coincides with $L(x)$ on at least $n - T + 1$ positions, with a probability of at least $p := 1 - \gamma^{-1} B(T, T + \tau - n, \frac{t-1}{t})$. That is, after $\mathcal{O}(\gamma^{-1})$ runs, $\mathcal{A}_2$ produces a random $L \in \mathcal{L}$ and a y which has a Hamming distance to $L(x)$ up to $T - 1$.

By applying the leakage scheme decoder e on this oracle, with r samples, it can fully recover x, with probability at least p^r. Then, by taking $\gamma = B(T, T + \tau - n, \frac{t-1}{t})^{1-\theta}$ and $\gamma' = \left(1 - B(T, T + \tau - n, \frac{t-1}{t})^\theta\right)^s$, we obtain our result. $\qquad\square$

References

1. Avoine, G., Bingöl, M., Kardas, S., Lauradoux, C., Martin, B.: A framework for analyzing RFID distance bounding protocols. J. Comput. Secur. **19**(2), 289–317 (2011)
2. Avoine, G., Lauradoux, C., Martin, B.: How secret-sharing can defeat terrorist fraud. In: ACM Conference on Wireless Network Security, WISEC 2011, Hamburg, Germany, pp. 145–156. ACM (2011)
3. Bay, A., Boureanu, I., Mitrokotsa, A., Spulber, I., Vaudenay, S.: The bussard-bagga and other distance-bounding protocols under attacks. In: Kutyłowski, M., Yung, M. (eds.) Inscrypt 2012. LNCS, vol. 7763, pp. 371–391. Springer, Heidelberg (2013)
4. Boureanu, I., Mitrokotsa, A., Vaudenay, S.: On the pseudorandom function assumption in (secure) distance-bounding protocols. In: Hevia, A., Neven, G. (eds.) LatinCrypt 2012. LNCS, vol. 7533, pp. 100–120. Springer, Heidelberg (2012)
5. Boureanu, I., Mitrokotsa, A., Vaudenay,S.: On the need for secure distance-bounding. In: Early Symmetric Crypto, ESC 2013, Mondorf-les-Bains, Luxembourg, pp. 52–60. University of Luxembourg (2013)
6. Boureanu, I., Mitrokotsa, A., Vaudenay, S.: Towards secure distance bounding. In: Moriai, S. (ed.) FSE 2013. LNCS, vol. 8424, pp. 55–68. Springer, Heidelberg (2014). http://eprint.iacr.org/2015/208.pdf
7. Boureanu, I., Mitrokotsa, A., Vaudenay, S.: Secure and lightweight distance-bounding. In: Avoine, G., Kara, O. (eds.) LightSec 2013. LNCS, vol. 8162, pp. 97–113. Springer, Heidelberg (2013)
8. Boureanu, I., Mitrokotsa, K., Vaudenay, S.: Practical and provably secure distance-bounding. To appear in the Journal of Computer Security (JCS). IOS Press, Eprint 2013/465. http://eprint.iacr.org/2013/465.pdf
9. Chernoff, H.: A measure of asymptotic efficiency for tests of a hypothesis based on the sum of observations. Ann. Math. Stat. **23**(4), 493–507 (1952)
10. Cremers, C.J.F., Rasmussen, K.B., Schmidt, B., Čapkun, S.: Distance hijacking attacks on distance bounding protocols. In: IEEE Symposium on Security and Privacy, S&P 2012, San Francisco, California, USA, pp. 113-127. IEEE Computer Society (2012)
11. Dürholz, U., Fischlin, M., Kasper, M., Onete, C.: A formal approach to distance-bounding RFID protocols. In: Zhou, J., Li, H., Lai, X. (eds.) ISC 2011. LNCS, vol. 7001, pp. 47–62. Springer, Heidelberg (2011)
12. Fischlin, M., Onete, C.: Terrorism in distance bounding: modeling terrorist-fraud resistance. In: Jacobson, M., Locasto, M., Mohassel, P., Safavi-Naini, R. (eds.) ACNS 2013. LNCS, vol. 7954, pp. 414–431. Springer, Heidelberg (2013)
13. Hancke, G.P: Distance bounding for RFID: effectiveness of terrorist fraud. In: Conference on RFID-Technologies and Applications, RFID-TA 2012, Nice, France, pp. 91–96. IEEE (2012)
14. Hancke, G.P., Kuhn, M.G.: An RFID distance bounding protocol. In: Conference on Security and Privacy for Emerging Areas in Communications Networks, SecureComm 2005, Athens, Greece, pp. 67-73. IEEE (2005)
15. Hoeffding, W.: Probability inequalities for sums of bounded random variables. J. Am. Stat. Assoc. **58**, 13–30 (1963)
16. Kim, C.H., Avoine, G., Koeune, F., Standaert, F.-X., Pereira, O.: The swiss-knife RFID distance bounding protocol. In: Lee, P.J., Cheon, J.H. (eds.) ICISC 2008. LNCS, vol. 5461, pp. 98–115. Springer, Heidelberg (2009)
17. Vaudenay, S.: On modeling terrorist frauds. In: Susilo, W., Reyhanitabar, R. (eds.) ProvSec 2013. LNCS, vol. 8209, pp. 1–20. Springer, Heidelberg (2013)

Usability and Risk Perception

On the Viability of CAPTCHAs for use in Telephony Systems: A Usability Field Study

Niharika Sachdeva[1]($\boxtimes$), Nitesh Saxena[2], and Ponnurangam Kumaraguru[1]

[1] IIIT-Delhi, New Delhi, India
{niharikas,pk}@iiitd.ac.in
[2] University of Alabama at Birmingham, Birmingham, USA
saxena@cis.uab.edu

Abstract. Telephony systems are imperative for information exchange offering low cost services and reachability to millions of customers. They have not only benefited legitimate users but have also opened up a convenient communication medium for spammers. Voice spam is often encountered on telephony systems in various forms, such as by means of an automated telemarketing call asking to call a number to win a reward. A large percentage of voice spam is generated through auto-mated system which introduces the classical challenge of distinguishing machines from humans on telephony systems. CAPTCHA is a conventional solution deployed on the web to address this problem. Audio-based CAPTCHAs have been proposed as a solution to curb voice spam. In this paper, we conducted a field study with 90 participants in order to answer two primary research questions: quantifying the amount of inconvenience telephony-based CAPTCHA may cause to users, and how various features of the CAPTCHA, such as duration and size, influence usability of telephony-based CAPTCHA. Our results suggest that currently proposed CAPTCHAs are far from usable, with very low solving accuracies, high solving times and poor overall user experience. We provide certain guidelines that may help improve existing CAPTCHAs for use in telephony systems.

1 Introduction

Telephony is a vital medium for information exchange as it offers services to more than 6 billion mobile users in the world today [19]. In the last decade, telephony systems migrated from Public Switched Telephone Networks (PSTN) to Internet Telephony for communication. Internet telephony also known as Voice over Internet Protocol (VoIP) offers low-cost, and instant communication facilities, e.g., distant calling and video conferencing anywhere around the world. However, VoIP is vulnerable to many attacks such as interception and modification of the transmitting voice packets, and cyber criminal activities, e.g., phishing, and malware [23]. Voice spam, also referred to as Spam over Internet Telephony (SPIT), is an emerging threat to telephony systems causing direct

---

The total length of this paper, when put in LNCS format, is at most 16 pages.

© Springer International Publishing Switzerland 2015
Y. Desmedt (Ed.): ISC 2013, LNCS 7807, pp. 261–279, 2015.
DOI: 10.1007/978-3-319-27659-5_19

or indirect loss to users. For instance, during the Canadian spring 2011 federal election, thousands of voters complained about receiving false automated calls, misleading voters about polling locations and discouraging to cast votes [11]. SPIT might originate from the Internet but also affects both PSTN and wireless users. Internet telephony attracts spammers, as SPIT is convenient to generate by reusing the existing botnet infrastructure used for email spam, and can impact masses by sending bulk calls to many users [29]. The prime stakeholders interested in producing SPIT include telemarketers, and malicious bodies intending to fool people forcing them to call expensive numbers (*voice phishing*). The threat raised by SPIT is real and worrisome; for instance, the Telecom Regulatory Authority of India (TRAI) stated that 36,156 subscribers were issued notices, 22,769 subscribers were disconnected, and 94 telemarketers were penalized for spreading spam. Similarly, the Federal Trade Commission (FTC) received more than 200,000 complaints every month in 2012, about automated calls even though 200 million phone users had registered for the "Do-Not-Call" facility. Some of these calls scammed users by offering convenient solutions to save money from their credit card investments [15]. Recent reports show criminals have targeted telephony systems of financial institutions such as banks and emergency helplines, using automated dialing programs and multiple accounts to overwhelm the phone lines [27,34].

CAPTCHA (Completely Automated Public Turing test to tell Computers and Humans Apart) is a mechanism that can differentiate machines (bots) from human users and has successfully reduced the abuse of the Internet resources, particularly reducing spam [36]. Given the success of CAPTCHA (hereafter denoted "captcha" for simplicity) on the Internet, the systems that use *audio captcha* over telephony have been prototyped [24]. FTC also announced a challenge in October 2012 to fight automated calls, asking innovators to propose solutions for stopping robocalls. FTC offered $50,000 to the winners. Many of the solutions proposed during the challenge offered protection through captcha on telephony, e.g., Baton, Telephone Captcha, Call Captcha, and Captcha Calls [2]. The two co-winners of the challenge proposed to filter out unapproved automated calls using a captcha. The winners proposed routing calls to a secondary line, and hung-up the pre-recorded / automated calls using captcha even before the phone rang. This allowed only real callers to connect. However, white lists could be used if a user would like to get genuine automated calls from authenticated sources. Captcha is a classic case for the "human-in-the-loop" paradigm [13] therefore, it is very important to assess how the humans fare with captcha in telephony systems. Telephony communication is lossy in nature, and audio quality is poor in comparison to the Internet which changes the experience of audio captcha on telephony. Audio captcha, like any other captcha, is intended to be easy for humans and hard for machines. However, recent research on telephony captcha largely concentrates on making it hard for machines than making it usable for humans. In the context of the Internet, there has been some recent work on the usability of different types of captcha [7,10]. Bursztein et al. found that 0.77 % (N = 14,000,000) of the time users preferred to answer eBay's audio captcha rather than image captcha on the web [10]. They found this number to be significantly large and felt essential to improve audio captcha on the web [10]. To the best of our knowledge, there has been no comprehensive analysis of the usability of different audio captcha over the phone / mobile through a full-fledged field study. The scope and impact of such an analysis would be quite broad, given that audio captcha will affect every user of the telephony system.

Contributions: In this paper, we analyze the usage pattern and human perspective when faced with captcha on telephony via a comprehensive usability field study. Although captcha could be potentially applied to multiple scenarios, we draw on a banking scenario to transfer money as an initial case study given that users have been affected due to telephony scams [27,34]. We make the following contributions related to the use of audio captcha in telephony systems:

1. We conducted a field study of various captchas with 90 participants evaluating their performance in the real world telephony environment. Participants remotely dialed our study set-up from 5 cities in India (Delhi, Mumbai, Chennai, Noida, and Vellore).
2. We evaluated and compared the tradeoff among users' accuracy, time spent and keystrokes while solving audio captcha on telephony. We found that the accuracy of captcha decreased multifold on telephony in comparison to web. Also, time taken to solve captcha increased for popular captcha schemes e.g. Recaptcha and slashdot.
3. We propose guiding principles for designing and improving telephony captcha.

Organization: Sect. 2 elaborates the previous captcha usability studies and telephony captcha studies. Sections 3 and 4 present various hypotheses formulated and the types of captcha used in our study. The implementation and design details, and study methodology are discussed in Sect. 5. Section 6 elaborates main findings regarding the captcha usage and current user practices. Sections 7 and 8 present the discussion, guidelines proposed from the study and future work.

2 Related Work

SPIT, broadcasting unsolicited bulk calls through VoIP, is one of the emerging threats to the telephony. Various techniques have been suggested to deal with SPIT e.g. device fingerprinting, use of the White, Grey, or Black lists, heuristics, and captcha [3]. Most of the proposed system use combination of one or more above mentioned techniques, to fight SPIT. Captcha is commonly used as a final check for the user. Captcha on the web has been subject to a broad range of research, including design, study of guiding principles, comparative evaluation of different captcha, and attack / threat models. Different types of captcha have been designed for protecting various Internet resources like online accounts, and emails. A few notable design examples include, asking users to identify garbled string of words or characters, identify objects in an image rather than characters [14], identify videos [25], and identify textual captcha that involves clicking on the images rather than typing the response [30]. Other variants include sketcha, which is based on object orientation [31], and Asirra, which uses pictures of cats and dogs [20]. Yan et al. found that contrary to the usual opinion, text based captcha was difficult for foreigners. They showed that the length of captcha interestingly influenced usability and security [21]. Audio captcha, another type of captcha, was especially designed for the visually impaired users on the web [16]. Lazar et al. conducted a study with 40 participants, sighted and blind, to evaluate the radio-clip based captcha. They showed various usability issues related with this captcha and also, proved it to improve the task success rate for sighted users whereas, it was still difficult for blind users [26]. Bursztein et al. showed that captcha especially audio captcha was remarkably difficult for users to solve. They also found that non-native speakers felt English captcha difficult and were slow in solving captcha [10].

Captcha's effectiveness in controlling machine attacks on the web encouraged its use over telephony. Telephony for years has largely supported verbal / voice based communication. We found that systems proposed for curbing SPIT used the existing web-based audio captcha setup. Tsiakis et al. proposed the principles for understanding the spam economic models, and their analogies to SPIT, which could help evaluate the benefits of audio captcha protection against the costs involved [35]. Polakis et al. developed different attacks, threat models, and solutions for phone captcha [28]. Soupionis et al. proposed and assessed various attributes of an audio captcha, which make it effective against automated test. They also evaluated audio captcha against open source bot implementation [33]. Zhang et al. used out-of-band communication such as the Short Message Service (SMS) to send the captcha text to differentiate bots from humans [37]. In addition to these research efforts, some patents have been developed around audio captcha. These include captcha based on contextual degradation [4] and random personal codes [5]. Johansen et al., developed a VoIP anti-SPIT framework using open source PBX system [24]. A few commercial products aimed at reducing SPIT have also been designed by NEC and Microsoft [1,18]. However, the usability of audio captcha on telephony in the real world has not been tested. Some preliminary work has been done on evaluating telephony captcha [28]. Soupionis et al. also conceptually evaluated the existing audio captcha solutions [32]. They discouraged use of alphabetic captcha on telephony and suggested a new algorithm for telephony audio captcha. They used soft phones,[1] which were different from real world implementation of telephony captcha. On the contrary, in our work, we conducted our experiment on a real-world system that users could call-in from anywhere in the world.

The study presented in this paper is different from the existing studies in important aspects. Prior studies were geared for the web, using traditional computing devices or for telephony using soft phones, whereas, the target platform for our work is telephony system and the terminal with which the user interacts within our setting is a phone. Furthermore, previous studies were performed in a controlled environment; in contrast, our study is a field evaluation, which

---

[1] Softphone is an application that allows a desktop, laptop or workstation computer to work as a telephone via Voice over IP technology e.g. Skype.

involves users interacting with the system in a real world environment. It is also the first study where 90 users participated in evaluating different kind of captchas (web-based and the explicitly designed telephone captcha) in the real world.

3 Hypotheses

We now discuss our hypotheses related to captcha usage and viability on telephony.

H1: Users might be close to the expected / correct answers even though the overall captcha solving accuracy on telephony may be low.

Captcha comprises of a simple challenge not involving much human intelligence, e.g., the addition of 2 numbers. However, the existing literature suggests that users' accuracy to solve audio captcha is low. We hypothesize that the accuracy will be higher, if 1 or 2 mistakes in the user's response are discounted. We calculate the edit distance between the user's response and the correct answer to evaluate response's closeness to the correct answer.

H2: Users' accuracy of answering the captcha correctly on telephony will decrease as the number of key presses required increases.

Audio captcha presents various cognitive challenges to the user. Human brain sequentially processes speech and "short-term" memory handles only $7(+/-2)$ chunks of information [8]. For audio captcha, cognitive load increases with the increase in the size of the captcha, i.e., the number of digits / characters to remember or recognize. This increases the chances of errors. We hypothesize accuracy of users decrease as the size increases. We measure the size (number of digits / characters) input by recording the key presses for each captcha. The key presses are recorded in our study setup through the number of DTMF received by the server (as discussed in Sect. 5).

H3: Users will take more time responding to a captcha that requires more key presses than to the one requiring less key presses.

Size of the captcha, i.e., the number of digits / characters a user has to press also affects the amount of time the user spends on the captcha. We hypothesize that the user will spend more time on a captcha which requires more number of key presses than on a captcha which requires less number of key presses. Analyzing the amount of time a user spends on solving captcha on the telephony is important because more is the time spent, more is the inconvenience caused.

4 Studied Audio CAPTCHAs

In this section, we describe various audio captchas (web and telephony) used in our study and the associated challenges posed to participants. Existing studies proposed to make use of distortions and noise in the existing telephony captcha

Table 1. Studied audio captchas with their features. Char. set represents the character set. Duration presents average playtime of captcha in seconds. RPC represents Random Personal Code Captcha

Category	Char. Set	Word	Repeat	Duration	Noise	Voice	Beep	Min length	Max length
Google	0-9	No	Yes	34.4	Yes	Male	yes	5	15
Ebay	0-9	No	No	3.7	Yes	Various	No	6	6
Yahoo	0-9	No	No	18.0	Yes	Child	No	6	8
Recaptcha	a-z	Yes	No	10.6	Yes	Female	No	6	6
Slashdot	a-z	Yes	No	2.9	No	Male	No	1	1
CD	1-5	No	No	14	Yes	Male	No	1	1
Math-function	0-9	No	No	6.0	No	Male	No	4	3
RPC	0-9	No	No	20.0	No	Male	No	3	2
C+CD	0-9	No	No	14.0	No	Male	No	4	3

to improve the security. We found that existing audio captchas on the web offered these features and, therefore, were also included for evaluation. We summarize various features of the web and the telephony audio captchas in Table 1.

Captchas from the Web: We deployed various web based captchas comprising of numeric or alphabetical challenges on telephony in our study. **Yahoo!** offered audio captcha as an alternative to the text captcha on the "create account page"[2] of its e-mail account service. The audio test started with 3 beeps, followed by 6 to 8 digits in various voices (children and females). **Google** captchas obtained from the "Google Account" page were shown when a user requested for an audio captcha. They started with 3 beeps followed by 5 to 15 digits in male voice and offered assistance by repeating the captcha test following the phrase "once again." It took longest to annotate Google captchas (annotation process is discussed in Sect. 5), as it was difficult to make decisions between noise, e.g. "Oh," "it," and "now," and digits, like "zero," and "eight." **eBay** audio captchas were obtained from the eBay website; these were offered as an alternative to the text captcha. These consisted of the same six digits as shown on the website. The tests were consistently 6 digits long in various voices (male and female). The frequency at which digits occurred in the eBay audio was reported to be faster than the other schemes e.g. Google and Yahoo!. **Recaptcha** audios were collected from the "Gmail's login page," and comprised of 6 words in female voice, for example "white, wednesday, two, chef, coach, napkin." **Slashdot** captchas were collected from the "login and join page" of Slashdot website.[3] Each audio presented a word in a male voice. They also offered assistance by spelling the word contained in every test for e.g. "Wrapping w r a p p i n g" where first the complete word was said and then each letter was spelled out.

Captchas for Telephony: We deployed following telephony captchas in our study. **Random Personal Code (RPC)** used random numbers as a menu

---

option instead of a standard menu [5]. For evaluating the scheme, we implemented a 3-digit random menu number using the age details of the participant (discussed in Sect. 5) e.g. the audio content included, "Press 182, if your age is less than 18." **Contextual Degradation (CD)** [4] suggested adding background noise depending on the context of the call and the individuals associated with the call; this assumes contextual noise is less interfering. For evaluating the scheme, a voice menu was implemented based on the education details of the participant (collected during the pre-study) with mild music from an instrument in the background as contextual noise. **Math-function** captcha [17], recommended using mathematical function, e.g. adding 2 numbers as a test. We implemented this variant requiring participants to add two, 2 or 3 digit numbers chosen randomly, for e.g. "Solve the following, and enter your response; 48 plus 45 to continue." **Math-function with Contextual Degradation (C + CD)** required participants to solve a simple math function with some contextual music playing in the background, e.g. "Solve the following and enter your response; 48 plus 45 to continue". The assumption is that the simple usage of Math function would not offer sufficient security.

5 Usability Evaluation

In this section, we present details of our usability field study, including the experimental setup, study methodology, participant recruitment and demographics.

Experimental Setup: Fig. 1 presents the 3 phases of our study: pre-study, participants calling up our setup (the actual study), and post-study. First, participants registered for our study and were provided with a scenario of credit card transaction. They were asked to imagine making a transaction worth 10,000 INR (200 USD) using a bank telephony service. At this time the captcha was shown to the participants. We provided participants with a telephone number where they could call to participate in our study, an application ID, and a PIN / password using which participants to access our setup. In the second phase, participants called up the given phone number and authenticated to the system, after which a series of 9 audio captchas (discussed in Sect. 4) were presented to them. We developed a counterbalancing schedule [9] to reduce learning effect and avoid the influence of natural responses of participants on captcha solving ability. Participants were divided randomly and equally into groups of 9 each. Every participant in the group was assigned a captcha using Latin Squares of 9 X 9 [9]. In the last phase, an email was sent to participants requesting for their feedback about captchas used in our study. We used System Usability Scale (SUS) in addition to few other questions on the user's preference to evaluate system performance.

System Design and Implementation: Participants were required to call our system to provide their responses. Our implementation emulated a captcha shield between the Source (caller, which may have malicious intent) and the service being offered (such as making a credit card transaction or checking balance of a bank account). The shield required the caller to correctly answer the presented

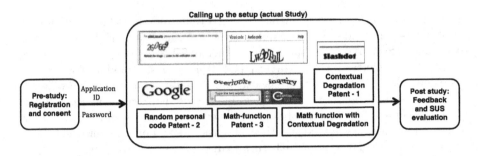

Fig. 1. Three phases of the study: pre-study, calling up the setup, and post-study.

challenge for accessing the intended service. Participants could call our implementation at anytime and the call could originate from any of the telephony networks, such as PSTN, Cellular Network or VoIP. The input to the captcha shield was DTMFs (Dual-Tone-Multi-Frequency) sent through the key press on the phone. Figure 2 shows the system components included a Linksys gateway SPA 3102 and a Linux Server supporting FreeSWITCH[4]. In order to support calls through FreeSWITCH, we used a Linksys SPA 3102 device as a gateway, which allowed connection to the PSTN network as depicted in Fig. 2. The gateway converted analog signals into compatible SIP (Session Initiation Protocol) format, which were then forwarded to FreeSWITCH on the server. We implemented a simple authentication login (using a pre-registered ID and a PIN) for users to participate in the study. For maintaining the privacy of participants, calls were not recorded; only DTMF input to the setup was captured.

Annotators: As a prerequisite to our study, it was essential to create a corpus of audio captchas (discussed in Sect. 4), and their respective true positive answers. We built the corpus by manual annotation of each captcha; this methodology has been used in the prior studies [32]. Each annotator annotated 50 correct captcha of the assigned service, e.g. eBay, and Google. They entered their response for the captcha challenge presented to them through the respective web service. Once the answer was accepted as correct answer by captcha server of the website, it was added to correct captcha corpus. Annotators were recruited through the mailing list of our institute. They were from Computer Science background; some were undergraduate but the majority were postgraduate students, pursuing Masters or Ph.D degrees at the IIITD, India, e.g. Slashdot annotator visiting Slashdot new user page.[5]

Participants: We recruited participants for evaluating captcha through word of mouth. Participants from different cities of India, Mumbai, Chennai, Delhi, Vellore, and Noida took part in the study. A monetary reward of 75 INR (1.5 USD)

---

[4] FreeSWITCH is one of the open source telephony platforms which has enabled easy access to telephony often required by various businesses. http://www.freeswitch.org//.

[5] https://slashdot.org/my/newuser.

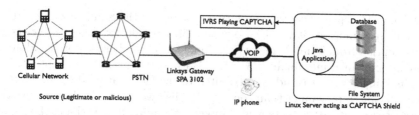

Fig. 2. The IVR system setup. The user dials the IVR on phone from any network. The call is received by Gateway, which forwards it to FreeSWITCH. An application written in Java answers the call by playing appropriate voice prompts. The Java application accesses database, file-system for storing and retrieving information.

was offered to every participant for contributing to the study. One hundred and forty participants registered for the study; of these 90 participants called up our system and completed the study. We were not required to go through an Institutional Review Board (IRB) approval process before conducting the study. However, the authors of this paper have previously been involved in studies with U.S. IRB approvals, and have applied similar practices in this study. Participants were shown "consent information" on the registration page, which they agreed to participate in our study. Participants belonged to different age groups, ranging from 18 years to 65 years. Participants' profession varied with 45.56 % from Computer Science, 8.89 % from Designing in various fields, 10 % from Finance, and 35.55 % were Lawyers, Journalists, and Homemakers. As reported, 25.56 % participants had used IVR for 2 to 3 years, 24.44 % had used IVR for 3 to 5 years and another 25.56 % for 5 years also, and 24.44 % users had used IVR for 0 to 2 years. Participants could call in from any type of a phone, may use a headphone or a paper and pen during the call.

6   Study Results

We now discuss the two primary research questions of our study: how much inconvenience does the captcha causes to the users, and how different features of captcha, e.g. duration, size and character set influence captcha's usability.

6.1   Captcha Inconvenience

In this section, we discuss the first question, i.e., the inconvenience caused to the users in terms of time spent, accuracy and experience with the different audio captchas.

Accuracy: Captchas are meant to be easy for humans to solve however, captchas which can't be guessed correctly cause considerable inconvenience to the users [10]. We calculate accuracy defined as the percentage of all the captchas solved correctly in each category to measure captcha inconvenience. Table 2 shows that the maximum average accuracy was only 13.71 % for telephony captcha. CD telephony captcha performed the best with 18.71 % accuracy. It was easier to remember as it involved one time instruction for users like select the correct option from a simple menu [12]. Among the web-based captcha, alphabet captcha performed marginally ($\Delta = 0.97\,\%$) better than number captcha. This marginal improvement could be attributed to the fact that random numbers are more difficult to remember than common English words [12]. Table 2 shows that the percentage of participants who skipped responding to captcha challenge was maximum (46.07 %) for Recaptcha. High Skip rate and low accuracy for most captchas show the difficulty caused in solving audio captcha on telephony. We found significant difference (Chi-sq = 81.42, p-value < 0.001) between Accuracy and Error showing considerable inconvenience caused to users while solving audio captcha.

Further comparing the accuracy of audio captcha on the web and telephony, we analyzed our results with existing studies on the web. Bursztein et al. found that Google's audio captchas were hardest to solve, with only 35 % *optimistic accuracy* [10], while Slashdot and Yahoo! performed the best with 68 % accuracy followed by eBay yielding 63 % accuracy on the web. Participants achieved 47 % accuracy for Recaptcha on the web. However, in our experiment the accuracy was nil for Google captcha. Slashdot performed the best on telephony as well, but accuracy dropped to 13.73 %. eBay performed marginally (1.01 %) better than Yahoo! on telephony. We understand that these comparisons may not give an exact picture of the differences between the web and telephony as the two experiments were conducted in different environments and with participants of different ethnicity. However, the large difference in accuracy on the two media, shows the significant increase in the inconvenience caused to participants when shown audio captcha on telephony.

Solving Time: Time is another important aspect which helps in measuring the inconvenience caused to users while solving an audio captcha on telephony. It has been found on the web that a captcha which takes more than 20 s causes inconvenience to the users [10]. We found that users took much longer to solve a captcha on telephony than on the web through our study. We measured solving time per captcha as the time elapsed from the instance when the user is presented with a captcha to the instance when the user moves to the next captcha type. Table 2 shows the average time taken to solve different captcha types. Users took the least of 80.25 s to solve eBay captcha. There was no significant difference in time taken by users for solving web-based captcha to telephony-based captcha. We found that the most time consuming captcha on telephony was RPC captcha with an average solving time of 147.44 s. Among the web-based captcha, Google, ReCaptcha and Slashdot were the most time consuming with mean greater than 120 s (min: 120.64 s and max: 123.49 s). On analyzing the existing studies on the web, we found that Google and ReCaptcha were the most time consuming with a mean value greater than 25 s. However, users took on an average 12 s to solve Slashdot captcha on the web [10] in comparison to 122.57 s on telephony. The increase in the solving time shows that the inconvenience caused to users is more for solving audio captcha on telephony than that on the web.

Table 2. Aggregate of error, accuracy values for each of the voice captcha in percentage. Skip gives the percentage of participants who skipped the Captcha. N represents the total number of Captcha presented in each category.

Captcha	Category	Time (s)	Accuracy (%)	Skip (%)	Total (N)
CD	Telephony	96.11	18.71	35.67	171
Math-function	Telephony	90.23	17.47	26.51	166
RPC	Telephony	147.44	15.47	40.33	181
C + CD	Telephony	109.59	4.57	40.10	197
Total	**Telephony**	**85.03**	**13.71**	**35.94**	**715**
Ebay	Web-Number	80.25	8.75	13.13	160
Google	Web-Number	123.49	0.00	43.83	162
Yahoo	Web-Number	95.88	7.74	20.24	168
Total	**Web-Number**	**99.87**	**5.51**	**25.71**	**490**
ReCaptcha	Web-Alphabet	120.64	0.00	46.07	171
Slashdot	Web-Alphabet	122.57	13.73	30.06	153
Total	**Web-Alphabet**	**121.60**	**6.48**	**39.51**	**324**

User Experience: As the ultimate assessment metric to understand the inconvenience caused, we study the feedback provided by the participants for different captcha types. Figure 3(a) shows 50 % of the participants found the system (on which users called to answer captcha in our study) extremely complex to use. We found statistical difference (Chi-sq = 12.77, p-value < 0.001) in user's preference for different captcha (numeric, alphabetic or math function). Users' feedback suggests that they did not like alphabet audio captcha as only 14.44 % of users preferred alphabet audio captcha. Most participants (52.22 %) preferred numeric captcha (Contextual Degradation, Random menu captcha and numeric web based captcha) and 33.33 % of the users favored captcha involving math functions (math-function and math-function with contextual degradation). We also analyzed if age has any effect on captcha preference of the participants. Figure 3(b) shows participants in the age group of 36 to 50 did not prefer to use the alphabet audio captcha at all, where as numeric captcha was appreciated among all age groups.

Next, we wanted to analyze if participants felt that using speakerphones or headphones would help them solve the captcha better. We did not find significant difference between participants who agreed / disagreed that use of speakerphones would help (Chi-sq = 0.3846, p-value = 0.5351) but headphones were felt to be helpful by significant number of participants (Chi-sq = 22.70, p-value <0.001). We found that 30 % of the users disagreed and 8.89 % strongly disagreed, feeling that speakerphones will be of no use. A participant mentioned *"the voice recording was not clear, therefore, any audio accessory would not have helped"* disagreeing with the use of speakerphones. We also asked the participants if they felt the use of headphones would help them solve the captcha better.

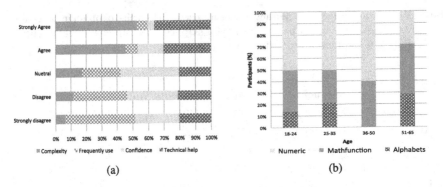

Fig. 3. (a) Users reported the system to be complex, not usable, suggesting the need for technical help for using captcha over telephony. (b) Participants in various age groups found the numeric captcha to be most usable whereas alphabet captcha was least preferred by the participants.

The results show that 15.56 % of the users strongly agreed and 70 % agreed; using headphones would help them respond better to the challenge.

In order to understand the user perspective about the mode of input, we asked users if they would prefer to respond verbally to the captcha challenge. We found that statistically significant (Chi-sq = 24.8205, p-value < 0.001) number of participants felt that the verbal input would be helpful; 36.67 % of the users agreed with the statement and 28.89 % strongly agreed. This suggests that entering responses using a keypad is difficult and causes trouble for respondents; this might be one of the primary reasons for errors in the captcha responses leading to low solving accuracy in the study [22]. We suggest the need for further research to investigate what makes an audio captcha easier to answer – verbal response or keypad touch. We calculated the SUS score for the telephony captcha as 38.42, which is extremely low.[6] Participants (35.71 %) also complained about voice being not clear, a participant commented *"It sounded like ghost voices. I was not able to understand almost any utterance."* Around 8.92 % explicitly complained about the accent in the voice captcha stating, *"at least the accent should be better."* Participants (17.85 %) also complained about the noise in the audio being very disturbing. A participant commented, *"too many disturbances and the accent was bad and 80 % of time I couldn't understand."*

6.2 Hypotheses Validation

The inconvenience parameters discussed above are important for evaluating the usability of captcha. However, these do not provide much guidance on how different captchas feature like duration, and length of captcha (as discussed in Table 2) influence the users' accuracy. In this section, we test the various hypotheses

---

[6] Given that SUS is 68 for average usable system.http://www.measuringusability.com/sus.php.

(discussed in Sect. 3) to study the influence of some of these features on audio captcha usability.

H1– Accuracy vs. Closeness: Sect. 6.1 shows that accuracy of solving captcha on telephony was low as maximum accuracy achieved was only 13.71 % for telephony captcha. However, we found that the users were close to the actual answer of the captcha presented. To analyze closeness, we calculated the most frequent edit distance (also known as Levenshtein distance) between the user's response and the expected answer. Figure 4 shows that the edit distance was 2 for most of the captcha types, followed by 1 ($\mu = 3.22$ and $\sigma^2 = 3.40$), implying that users committed 2 errors per captcha response frequently. As an example, for the audio challenge, "824388" (eBay), the user responded "624386". Users were required to remember and input many words for Recaptcha resulting in exceptionally high edit distance. This supports our Hypothesis H1. This also suggests the need for further research on developing fault tolerant captcha, which could distinguish between human natural behavior error variance, and machine attacks on audio captcha. Analyzing human behavior when solving captcha has already been proposed for image based captcha, which can help decrease the inconvenience caused to users.[7]

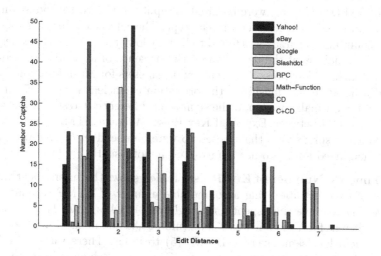

Fig. 4. The relation between edit distance and number of captcha for each captcha type.

H2 – Expected Key Press vs. Accuracy: We found that the length of the answer i.e. size of captcha did not influence the accuracy of the user's response. The accuracy decreased from 18.71 % (CD) to 4.57 % (C + CD) irrespective of the fact that users were required to solve the captcha comprising of similar tasks

---

[7] Are you human Captcha. Secure from All Angles, http://areyouahuman.com/security/.

Table 3. The Average DTMF expected for captcha (Avg. DTMF), accuracy, time and Average DTMF input by users (Avg. User DTMF) of each captcha. N represents the total number of Captcha presented in each category.

Scheme	Category	Avg. DTMF	Accuracy	Time	Avg. User DTMF	Total (N)
CD	Telephony	1.00	18.71	96.11	1.76	171
Math-function	Telephony	2.05	17.47	90.23	2.71	166
RPC	Telephony	3.00	15.47	147.44	3.92	181
C + CD	Telephony	2.06	4.57	109.59	2.65	197
Ebay	Web	6.00	8.75	80.25	3.85	160
Google	Web	6.36	0.00	123.49	4.68	162
Yahoo	Web	7.09	7.74	95.88	4.99	168
Slashdot	Web	15.34	13.73	120.64	6.02	153
ReCaptcha	Web	64.93	0.00	122.57	10.97	171

and comparable expected DTMF count. Similar trends were noticed for the web captcha, where users were expected to identify a similar number of spoken digits (eBay, Google, Yahoo) but the accuracy varied from 0 % to 8.75 %. Table 3 shows the expected DTMF users were required to input for a correct response and the corresponding accuracy for each captcha type. The correlation between expected DTMF count and accuracy was found to be very low (r = −0.52) with a negative fit. Further analysis of the data showed the presence of a positive relationship between Expected key press and accuracy parameters for Math function, but we noticed a negative relationship with correlation coefficient r = −0.47 for web-based captcha. Finally, we found the significant difference (t-test, t-value = 5.30 p-value < 0.001) between Expected Key Press (Average DTMF) and accuracy in statistical results shows that these two were independent of each other. The results mentioned above do not approve our hypothesis H2.

H3 – Time vs. Number of Key Press: Table 3 shows that users spent varying amount of time in submitting a comparable number of DTMF responses. For example, the average time spent for Google was 123.49 s (min: 17.15 and max: 341.21) whereas for Yahoo, it was 95.88 s (min: 25.88 and max: 278.00), although both of them had same average DTMF (5) to input. There was a significant difference between the time taken to solve Google vs. Yahoo! (t-Test, t-value = −12.39, p-value < 0.01). Further, we found a correlation (r =0.85) between time spent and DTMF input for Math-function captcha, suggesting an increase in the time was proportionate to DTMF input. However, this correlation dropped to r = 0.56 for web-based captcha, implying an absence of any strong relativity between time and DTMF input. The results from our study suggest lack of any strong relationship between the time spent by the participants in solving a captcha and the number of DTMF input from them. We found that the correlation between the time spent to answer the captcha and DTMF response from the users was 0.36 for all the captcha used in our study. We found the significant difference (t-test, t-value = 4.33, p-value < 0.0001) between number of key press

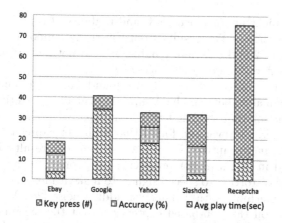

Fig. 5. Figure shows Aggregate accuracy (%), Number of DTMF and Average play time (seconds) of web-based captcha. Exposing users longer to Captcha does not help improve accuracy.

(Average User DTMF) and accuracy in statistical results suggesting that these two were independent of each other. We further tested, if the duration for which a captcha is played influences the accuracy but found that exposing users longer to a captcha did not help improve solving accuracy. Figure 5 shows the average playtime of the number web-based captcha (eBay, Yahoo, Google) varied from as low as 3.7 to 34.4 s where all these required a similar number of DTMFs to be recognized. Google captcha provided a feature to repeat the challenge in each attempt, without users asking for it explicitly, irrespective of these; the correct response was 0 % for Google and 8.75 % for eBay.

7   Discussion

In this paper, we explored user's experiences and views on telephony captcha through a real world study. We concentrated on two primary research questions: how much inconvenience does captcha causes to the user, and how different features of the captcha, e.g. duration, size and character set influence captcha's usability. We measured the level of inconvenience caused to users in terms of time spent, accuracy, and perceived difficulty / satisfaction of using various captchas schemes. We found that the accuracy of captcha decreased multifold on telephony in comparison to web, and the time taken to solve captcha increased to as high as 122.57 and 120.64 s for popular captcha schemes, e.g. Recaptcha and Slashdot, respectively. However, we found that users were relatively close to the expected correct answers (discussed in Hypotheses Validation of H1), which may suggest the possibility of deploying captcha on telephony platforms in the future. We found that the captcha could be a viable solution for telephony with improved features, such as fault tolerance, better voice and accent as most participants suggested in their feedback. Next, to study the influence of different features, which might improve accuracy, and usability of captcha on telephony, we tested 3 hypotheses. The results from the study supported hypotheses 1, whereas hypothesis 2 and 3 remain tenable. We did not find strong influence of captcha size and duration on solving accuracy.

Contrary to the existing work [28]; we found Math-function captcha performed better than alphabet captcha. Soupionis et al. discarded the use of alphabet captcha assuming that sending letters to answer a captcha could be difficult for an average user. However, we found that alphabet captcha's accuracy was comparable to numeric captcha. Finally, we present our results for recommendations proposed in literature for improving telephony captcha. Polakis et al. suggested adding distortion to speech signals to make it more usable for humans and difficult for machines rather than just adding noise [28]. We used the distortions available on the web-based captchas to test the recommendation. We understand that these distortions might not be the best but as these have been able to provide sufficient security on the web, therefore, for initial testing we used distortions available in web-based captcha. Contrary to the recommendations, we found that it was still difficult for participants to solve these captchas. We found that both forms of noise, intermediate and background, caused inconvenience for the users and captcha solving accuracy was low in the presence of both of them.

We suspect instances during the study, when the DTMF sent by the users may not have completely reached the captcha server. In our setup, the receiver used a PSTN network, which helped in minimizing such errors but in certain real world scenario, where both receiver and caller are wireless users, the lossy nature may lead to total failure of the captcha test [6]. The telephony captcha would probably need to be more loss-tolerant, but this would demand a trade-off between accuracy of captchas and security (i.e., resistance to automated attacks). Telephony network consists of inherent noise, which effects the audio quality. As also observed by the annotators during our annotation phase, the quality of the audio being played through the laptop speaker (often used in the studies so far with soft phones) was much more audible and clear than the one from speakers of the telephone / mobile phone. It would be interesting to study the influence of these factors on the captcha solving performance.

8   Guidelines

Based on our overall results and analysis, we recommend following design conventions for improved telephony captchas.

1. *One time instruction:* All telephony captchas and slashdot captcha in our study presented one time instruction to the users whereas most web-based captchas had random numbers or strings. We found that the accuracy of the telephony captcha, and Slashdot was comparatively better than random strings. This indicates that the captcha involving one time instruction or challenge are appropriate for telephony interfaces (e.g., one word challenge or logic questions) as speech competes with verbal processing [8].

2. *Loss/error tolerant:* The captcha should be error / loss tolerant since the telephony network might drop DTMF carrying user response. The telephone network itself introduces its own noise causing the audio to degrade [6]; hence external noise has to be calibrated accordingly.
3. *Feedback:* Visual/audio feedback for the response should be made available to the users for the response they input, especially required on voice medium because of its inherent lossy nature. We suggest presenting the characters of the captcha for a fraction of a second while the user is solving it (e.g. as in the some of the latest handheld devices for entering the passwords).
4. *Verbal responses:* Users are better trained and prefer voice as input modality instead of keypad touch as telephony networks are primarily voice based. It is advisable to use captcha based on secure verbal inputs (voice recognition) instead of key press. This can help reduce the manual errors in keying in the responses and improve usability.

Finally, we note that our study has some limitations. As the study was conducted in the real world, we had no control on the environmental conditions and assume that all participants had the similar environment. Participants could opt to finish the study in multiple sessions, some participants who called in multiple times to the system were exposed more to the captchas and experienced varied cognitive load.

In the future, we envisage applying other techniques such as illusion effects, earcons to build a captcha system and to evaluate the effectiveness of such new approaches. We plan to conduct a detailed study of the cognitive loads and psychology of the auditory system with captchas to help us design a better mechanism to differentiate between machines and human beings.

Acknowledgements. The research of the first author is supported by TCS (Tata Consultancy Service) Research Scholarship. We would like to thank Dr. Iulia Ion and Paridhi Jain for their input on the study. The authors would also like to thank International Development Research Centre (IRDC) and all members of PreCog research group at IIIT-Delhi. We would like to thank Siddhartha Asthana for helping in deployment of the system and all participants in the study.

References

1. The Dark Side of Voice. http://content.yudu.com/A1qlhz/CommsDealerJan11/resources/38.htm
2. FTC Robocalls Challenge (2012). http://robocall.challenge.gov/submissions/
3. Andreas, N.K., Schmidt, U., Khayari, R.E.: Spam over internet telephony and how to deal with it. arXiv preprint arXiv:0806.1610 (2008)
4. Baird, H., Bentley, J., Lopresti, D., Wang, S.-Y.: Methods and Apparatus for Defending Against Telephone-Based Robotic Attacks Using Contextual-Based Degradation. United States Patent (2011)
5. Baird, H., Bentley, J., Lopresti, D., Wang, S.-Y.: Methods and Apparatus for Defending against Telephone-Based Robotic Attacks using Random Rersonal Codes. United States Patent (2011)

6. Balasubramaniyan, V.A., Poonawalla, A., Ahamad, M., Hunter, M.T., Traynor, P.: PinDr0p: using single-ended audio features to determine call provenance. In: Proceedings of the 17th ACM Conference on Computer and Communications Security. ACM (2010)

7. Bigham, J.P., Cavender, A.C.: Evaluating existing audio CAPTCHAs and an interface optimized for non-visual use. In: Proceedings of the SIGCHI Conference on Human Factors in Computing Systems. ACM (2009)

8. Bonneau, D.G., Blanchard, H.E.: Human Factors and Voice Interactive Systems. Signals and Communication Technology. Springer, New York (2008)

9. Bradley, J.: Complete counterbalancing of immediate sequential effects in a latin square design. J. Am. Stat. Assoc. **53**(282), 525–528 (1958)

10. Bursztein, E., Bethard, S., Fabry, C., J. Mitchell, C., Jurafsky, D.: How good are humans at solving CAPTCHAs? a large scale evaluation. In: IEEE Symposium on Security and Privacy (SP) (2010)

11. Canadian election robocall scan. http://news.nationalpost.com/2012/03/05/robocalls-scandal-likely-the-fault-of-elections-canada-tory-mp/

12. Cooper, G.: Research into cognitive load theory and instructional design at UNSW. http://webmedia.unmc.edu/leis/birk/CooperCogLoad.pdf (1998)

13. Cranor, L.F.: A framework for reasoning about the human in the loop. In: Usability, Psychology, and Security (2008)

14. Datta, R., Li, J., Wang, J.Z.: Imagination: a robust image-based captcha generation system. In: MULTIMEDIA 2005, pp. 331–334 (2005)

15. Federal Trade Commission. Robocalls: All the rage, an FTC summit. http://www.ftc.gov/bcp/workshops/robocalls/docs/RobocallSummitTranscript.pdf (2012)

16. Sauer, G., Hochheiser, H., Feng, J., Lazar, J.: Towards a universally usable CAPTCHA. In: Symposium On Usable Privacy and Security (2008)

17. Gross, J.N.: Captcha Using Challenges Optimized for distinguishing between humans and machines. U.S. Patent Application (2009)

18. Hoffstadt, D., Sorge, C., Rebahi, Y.: Spam over internet telephony. http://www.tu-chemnitz.de/etit/kn/Zukunft_der_Netze/presentation_hoffstadt.pdf

19. International Telecommunication Union. Measuring the information Society. http://www.itu.int/ITU-D/ict/publications/idi/material/2012/MIS2012_without_Annex_4.pdf

20. Elson, J., Douceur, J., Howell, J., Saul, J.: Asirra: a CAPTCHA that exploits interest-aligned manual image categorization. In: ACM Conference on Computer and Communications Security (2007)

21. Yan, J., Ahmad, A.: Usability of CAPTCHAs or usability issues in CAPTCHA design. In: Symposium on Usable Privacy and Security (2008)

22. Jakobsson, M., Akavipat, R.: Rethinking passwords to adapt to constrained keyboards. In: MoST (2012)

23. Jakobsson, M., Ramzan, Z.: Crimeware: Understanding New Attacks and Defenses. Symantec Press, Cupertino (2008)

24. Johansen, A.J.: Improvement of spit prevention technique based on turing test. Master's thesis. Mahanakorn University of Technology (2010)

25. Kluever, K., Zanibbi, R.: Balancing usability and security in a video CAPTCHA. In: Symposium On Usable Privacy and Security, pp. 1–11 (2009)

26. Lazar et al. POSTER: Assessing the Usability of the new Radio Clip Based Human Interaction Proofs. Symposium On Usable Privacy and Security (2010)

27. Martin, S.: Hold the Phone-Will TDoS Be Your Next Big Threat? http://bankinnovation.net/2013/07/hold-the-phone-will-tdos-be-your-next-big-threat/, July 2013

28. Polakis, I., Kontaxis, G., Ioannidis, S.: CAPTCHuring automated (smart) phone attacks. In: SysSec Workshop (SysSec), 2011 First. IEEE (2011)
29. Quittek, J., Niccolini, S., Tartarelli, S., Stiemerling, M., Brunner, M., Ewald, T.: Detecting spit calls by checking human communication patterns. In: IEEE International Conference on Communications, ICC 2007. IEEE (2007)
30. Chow, R., Golle, P., Jakobsson, M., Wang, L., Wang, X.: Making CAPTCHAs clickable. In: HotMobile (2008)
31. Ross, S., Halderman, J., Finkelstein, A.: Sketcha: a CAPTCHA based on line drawings of 3D models. In: Conference on World Wide Web (WWW) (2010)
32. Soupionis, Y., Gritzalis, D.: Audio CAPTCHA: existing solutions assessment and a new implementation for VoIP telephony. Comput. Secur. **29**, 603–618 (2010)
33. Soupionis, Y., Tountas, G., Gritzalis, D.: Audio CAPTCHA for SIP-based VoIP. In: Gritzalis, D., Lopez, J. (eds.) SEC 2009. IFIP AICT, vol. 297, pp. 25–38. Springer, Heidelberg (2009)
34. The Federal Bureau of Investigation. The Latest Phone Scam Targets Your Bank Account. http://www.fbi.gov/news/stories/2010/june/phone-scam, June 2010
35. Tsiakis, T., Katsaros, P., Gritzalis, D.: Economic evaluation of interactive audio media for securing internet services. In: ICGS3/e-Democracy, pp. 46–53 (2011)
36. von Ahn, L., Blum, M., Langford, J.: Telling Humans and Computers Apart (Automatically) or How Lazy Cryptographers Do AI. Computer Science Department 149 (2002)
37. Zhang, H., Wen, X., He, P., Zheng, W.: Dealing with telephone fraud using captcha. In: ICIS (2009)

Cars, Condoms, and Facebook

Vaibhav Garg[1](✉) and L. Jean Camp[1,2]

[1] Drexel University, Philadelphia, USA
me@vaibhavgarg.net
[2] Indiana University, Bloomington, USA

Abstract. Participation on Online Social Networks (OSNs) inherently requires information sharing and thus exposes individuals to privacy risks. Risk mitigation then has been encouraged through adoption of usable privacy controls. Apparently stronger privacy enhancing technologies (PETs) decrease both risk and perceptions of risk. As a result individuals feel safer and may respond by in fact accepting more risk. Such perverse results have been observed offline. Risk perception offline has been understood to be a function of characteristics of the risks involved rather than as a calculus grounded only in the probability of the risk and the magnitude of harm. In this work we use nine characteristics of risk from a classic and proven offline model of perceived risk to conduct a survey based evaluation of perceptions of privacy risks on Facebook. We find that these dimensions of risk provide a statistically significant explanation of perceived risk of information sharing on Facebook.

Keywords: Privacy · Facebook · Risk perception · Control

1 Introduction

Information sharing on Online Social Networks (OSNs), e.g. Facebook, exposes individuals to privacy risks. These risks often manifest as tractable losses, e.g. Facebook fired. Yet participation in Facebook is continent upon sharing information. It is then not surprising that although individuals express privacy concerns, they willingly post potentially harmful information online. This disconnect between the expressed preference for privacy and observed behavior of willful disclosure has been called the privacy paradox [3]. To alleviate the harm from this information sharing, the foremost proposal has been that of Privacy Enhancing Technologies (PETs); for Facebook specifically these manifest as privacy controls. These controls have been bemoaned for the lack of usability [15]. However, assuming that usable controls are available corresponding reduction in harm is not given. As in the case of cars and seat belts, individuals may compensate for better privacy controls with risk seeking behavior [2]. Even when individual perceive a higher control in the publication of information they tend to share more [4]. Thus, similar to case of automobile safety the protection provided by stronger PETs may be mitigated by increase in information sharing.

© Springer International Publishing Switzerland 2015
Y. Desmedt (Ed.): ISC 2013, LNCS 7807, pp. 280–289, 2015.
DOI: 10.1007/978-3-319-27659-5_20

The presence of strong technical solutions that are usable is necessary to enable privacy online. However, it is not sufficient as individuals do not engage a economically rational calculus, optimizing the cost-benefit tradeoff, when sharing/protecting information [12]. Instead privacy behaviors, akin to behaviors offline, are boundedly rational [1]. Thus, the acceptability of (privacy) risks is driven by the perceived risk vs. the perceived benefit of an activity. Previous research indicates that perceived risk offline is driven by nine characteristics of the hazard [9]: (1) voluntariness, (2) immediacy, (3) knowledge to the exposed, (4) knowledge to experts, (5) control, (6) newness, (7) common-dread, (8) chronic-catastrophic, and (9) severity. Online, this framework has been used to explain perceptions of technical security risks [10] and insider threats [8].

In this paper, we will conduct a first examination of this framework for privacy risks on Facebook using the psychometric paradigm of expressed preferences. In the process we adapt and translate Fischhoff's canonical nine dimensional model for privacy risks on Facebook. By grounding our analysis in a framework that has been used to examine perceived risk across domains and cultures we allow for a systematic comparative across risk perception studies, both online and offline. We detail the related work in Sect. 2. Section 3 outlines the methodology including the survey instrument design and deployment procedure. We present our findings in Sect. 4. Section 5 discusses the implications of our findings. We conclude in Sect. 6 with a description of future work.

2   Background and Related Work

Information disclosure on Facebook is to a large extent voluntary. Individuals, however, share more information when disclosure is voluntary [21]. Thus, individuals who perceive information sharing on Facebook to be voluntary should share more than others. Similarly, higher perceived control over publication can increase information sharing [4]. Perceived risk of an activity appears lower when the consequences are delayed. Smoking, for example, in the immediate term provides stress-relief, but the long term may lead to cancer. Regret on Facebook is similarly delayed and felt only after the information has been shared [25].

As individuals better understand the underpinnings of an activity their perceptions of risk are similarly informed. When privacy risks are communicated in an effective manner, individuals share information in a manner aligned with their preferences [5]. Counterintuitively, informed individuals may feel empowered and share more. The perceived knowledge to experts, or in this case the effectiveness of expert systems also informs risk perceptions and therefore behaviors. For example, non-experts assume comprehensive anonymous communication when running Tor, even though the protection is only available selectively [19].

The newness of a risk impinges the individual ability for objective evaluation. New risks would be poorly understood and thus likely to be exaggerated or underestimated. For example, offline information sharing is likely one to one. Online, information shared on different platforms, at various times, with distinct entities can be aggregated and thus the potential for privacy violations is exponentially higher. Such privacy risks are both intractable for the end-users, as humans are better at averages than aggregation [24], and not acceptable [17]. Perceptions of risks that are commonly encountered are typically lower than those rarely encountered. The evolutionary rationale for such perceptions is intuitive. If individuals constantly worried about the risk of crossing the street if would lead to a functional paralysis. Simultaneously, the data on rare risks would be sparse; thus, it would be difficult to ex-ante approximate a strategy for risk mitigation. Information sharing is a risk that is commonly encountered and is commonly beneficial as it increases market efficiency; however the data on privacy risks is difficult to obtain. Even when information is shared willingly, it is difficult (in fact impossible) for an individual to identify how often the information was accessed, by whom, and for how long [20].

Catastrophic risks, where many people are impacted in a single incidence of an event, may appear more scary than those in which only an individual is impacted. For example, terrorist attacks often impact multiple individuals and thus can be overestimated. Food poisoning appears to impinge solitary individuals and thus appears relatively benign. However, in most countries more individuals die of food poisoning than of terrorist attacks. The perceived severity of the consequences of information sharing also impinges the perceived privacy risk. For example, acknowledging affinity for an unconventional book may simply lead to teasing the peer group; however, sharing sexual orientation can lead to social discrimination, denial of employment, and even physical violence for traditionally vulnerable communities.

While perceptions of risks are driven by the characteristics of the risk, individual demographic considerations are equally important. Factors such as income, age, and gender are equally relevant. Individuals with lower incomes are less concerned about privacy [1]. Older adults may share less information than younger cohorts [7]. Women are more risk averse than men both online and offline [11] and thus should share less information [14]. Finally, the perceived risk of an activity is also influenced by its perceived benefit. Previous research indicates that for most activities there exists a negative correlation between the respective perceived risk and perceived benefit [9]. Thus, activities that are considered to be less risky are seen as more beneficial and vice versa.

H_{0_1} : There is no correlation between the perceived risk of sharing an information item and its perceived voluntariness.

H_{0_2} : There is no correlation between the perceived risk of sharing an information item and the perceived immediacy of consequences.

H_{0_3} : There is no correlation between the perceived risk of sharing an information item and perceived knowledge to exposed.

H_{0_4} : There is no correlation between the perceived risk of sharing an information item and perceived knowledge to experts.

H_{0_5} : There is no correlation between the perceived risk of sharing an information item and perceived control over consequences.

H_{0_6} : There is no correlation between the perceived risk of sharing an information item and its perceived newness.

H_{0_7} : There is no correlation between the perceived risk of sharing an information item and its perceived rarity.

H_{0_8} : There is no correlation between the perceived risk of sharing an information item and catastrophic nature of its impact.

H_{0_9} : There is no correlation between the perceived risk of sharing an information item and perceived severity of impact.

$H_{0_{10}}$: There is no correlation between perceived risk of sharing and individual privacy preferences.

$H_{0_{11}}$: There is no correlation between perceived risk of sharing and income.

$H_{0_{12}}$: There is no correlation between perceived risk of sharing and age.

$H_{0_{13}}$: There is no correlation between perceived risk of sharing and gender.

$H_{0_{14}}$: There is no correlation between perceived risk of sharing an information item and the corresponding perceived benefit.

3 Methodology

In this research we are concerned with the underlying determinants of perceived risk, as well as the relationship between perceived risk and perceived benefit, as they pertain to sharing information on Facebook. To the extent that information sharing on Facebook is a risk, we posit that perceived risk would be informed by nine characteristics of risk [9]: (1) voluntariness, (2) immediacy, (3) knowledge to the exposed, (4) knowledge to experts, (5) control, (6) newness, (7) common-dread, (8) chronic-catastrophic, and (9) severity.

We use the psychometric paradigm of expressed preferences, which surveys individuals to elicit perceived risk. Previous research has identified, acknowledged, and addressed the limitations of this methodology [22]. However, given that privacy decisions are situated in the context of praxis [18], a survey based approach is additionally limited as it may not illuminate deeper specific factors that can be discovered from an in-situ study. To reduce the impact of divergent contexts, we focus our study on information sharing on Facebook and target a relatively self similar demographic in terms of age, education etc. by selectively recruiting participants from an undergraduate computer science class.

The design of the survey was kept similar to the original instrument used by Fischhoff et al. for consistency. Participants provided general demographic information: (1) gender, (2) age, (3) household income, (4) frequency of Facebook accesses, (5) frequency of status message updates on Facebook, and (6) frequency of location sharing on Facebook. Individual privacy preferences were enumerated by using a subset of the Internet Users' Information Privacy Concerns (IUIPC) scale [16]. The subset measures global privacy concerns rather than concerns about specific contexts such as consumer privacy.

A typical Facebook profile consists of twenty-two information items: real name, DoB (without year) or DoB (with year), current address, telephone, email id, personal website, music, movies, books, television, personal interests, photographs, political affiliation, religious affiliation, sexual orientation, friends list, education, work experience, current employment, and hometown. All participants were asked to identify which of these information items they shared on Facebook and with whom, i.e. friends, friends of friends, or everyone. (No sharing was coded as 0, sharing with friends, friends of friends, and everyone was coded as 1, 2, and 3 respectively).

Participants then rated the risk (or benefit) of sharing individual information item on Facebook. Participants were not given a definition of what is implied by either risk or benefit. Participants rated the least risk (or beneficial) item '10'. Thus, if sharing your DoB with the year gave you the least risk (or benefit), then that would be rated '10'. Each subsequent item was to be evaluated in comparison with this item. Thus, an item that was rated '20' would be twice as risky (or beneficial) as the least risky (or beneficial) item.

All participants rated the risk of each of the 22 items on the nine dimensions of perceived risk [9]. The nine dimensions were defined as:

1. Voluntariness: Do you share this information voluntarily? Or is this information demanded by external entities such as Facebook, friends, etc.? (1 = Voluntary; 7 = Involuntary)
2. Immediacy: Is the impact of sharing this information immediate or does it happen at a later point in time? (1 = immediate; 7 = delayed)
3. Knowledge to exposed: To what extent are you aware of the consequences of sharing this information? (1 = known precisely; 7 = unknown)
4. Knowledge to experts: To what extent do you think experts are aware of the consequences of sharing the information? (1 = known precisely; 7 = unknown)
5. Control: Do you think you have control of the consequences of sharing the information? (1 = uncontrollable; 7 = controllable)
6. Newness: Do you think the implications generated from sharing this information are new? (1 = new; 7 = old)
7. Chronic-catastrophic: Does sharing this information affect only you (chronic) or several people (catastrophic)? (1 = chronic; 7 = catastrophic)
8. Common-Dread: Is sharing this information so common that you don't think about it? Or is it so unique that it fills you with dread? (1 = common; 7 = dread)
9. Severity: How severe do you think are the consequences of sharing this information? (1 = certain to not have adverse consequences; 7 = certain to have adverse consequences)

The study was conducted using paper surveys. The order of presentation of the 22 information items was static and consistent across all survey instruments. Participants were recruited from a convenience sample of college undergraduates. Students were allowed a two-course-credit bonus to incentivize participation, contingent on their having used Facebook. The alternative was to opt out and write a short essay, on Facebook or privacy, (≈500 words) instead. Participants blindly selected one of two survey instruments. The study was approved by the Institutional Review Board (IRB) at Indiana University, Bloomington.

4   Results

Of the 200 students who took the survey, 74 were returned. Thus, the response rate was approximately 37 %. One of the surveys was discarded as it was completely empty. Two survey instruments were discarded as participants did not follow the instructions. Specifically, participants were asked to rank the nine dimensions on a scale of 1 through 7. However, one of the participants provided ratings higher than 7. Participants were also asked to give the item with the lowest perceived risk a rating of 10. A second participant provided risk ratings less than 10. Thus, there were 71 correctly completed survey instruments returned.

40 participants completed the perceived benefit survey. Of these, 30 were men and 10 were women. 38 participants were between the ages of 18–25 while 2 participants were between the ages 26–30. 31 participants completed the perceived risk survey. Of these, 24 were men and 7 were women. 30 participants were ages 18–25, and 1 participant was 26–30.

We acknowledge that this is a convenience sample. Participants consisted of individuals in an undergraduate computer science class. Therefore, they are likely to be more informed. The average privacy rating for participants completing the benefit survey was 26.81579, while that for risk was 26.03571. A one-sided T-test did not indicate a statistically significant difference with p-value = 0.7935. The correlation for the mean values of perceived benefit and perceived risk was not statistically significant with a p-value = 0.6321. The correlation for the respective median values was similarly not significant statistically with a p-value = 0.9367. Participants were also asked to rate the 22 risk items on Fischhoff's nine dimensions. We computed the (Spearman) correlation (ρ) between the nine dimensions of perceived risk as shown in Table 1. We also constructed two Ordinary Least Squared (OLS) linear regression model with perceived risk as the dependent variable; independent variables were limited to Fischhoff's nine dimensions in the first model, while the second included demographic variables as well as item order, information shared, and privacy preferences; Table 1[1].

5   Discussion

In this paper, we examine the perceived benefit of information sharing on Facebook, compared to the perceived risk. There are several limitations to our study, i.e. small sample size, convenience sample, ordering effects. Thus, our findings are not generalizable. We also can not compare the relative sensitivity of different information items. Our analysis of the relative importance of Fischhoff's nine dimensions and the framework itself is appropriate. As noted in the regression model in Table 1, information order is not statistically significant. Despite these limitations this study allows us to test a set of falsifiable hypotheses.

Table 1 indicates that hypotheses $H_{0_1}, H_{0_3}, H_{0_5}, H_{0_7}, H_{0_8}$, and H_{0_9} can be rejected; however, there is limited evidence to reject to H_{0_2}, H_{0_4}, and H_{0_6}. Thus,

---

[1] Age is not considered as the standard deviation for this variable is ≈0.

Table 1. Linear regression analyses and correlations

Dimension	OLS Nine Dim.		OLS With Dem.Var		Correlation
	Estimate	Std. Error	Estimate	Std. Error	ρ
(Intercept)	1.080	0.0342***	0.532	0.1352***	
Voluntariness	0.008	0.0042	0.003	0.0059	0.194***
Immediacy	-0.006	0.0039	-0.007	0.0052	-0.085
Knowledge to Exposed	-0.015	0.0038***	-0.015	0.0048**	-0.197***
Knowledge to Expert	0.003	0.0052	0.004	0.0068	-0.086
Control	0.006	0.0040	0.004	0.0051	-0.106*
Newness	-0.007	0.0037	0.003	0.0050	-0.070
Common-Dread	0.005	0.0034	0.008	0.0042	0.114*
Chronic-Catastrophic	0.004	0.0051	0.011	0.0071	0.163***
Severity	0.016	0.0047***	0.007	0.0058	0.167***
Gender			0.035	0.0294	0.031
Income			0.011	0.0052*	0.034
Facebook Access			0.010	0.0158	-0.007
Status Update			-0.007	0.0188	-0.049
Location Update			-0.004	0.0395	-0.018
Privacy			0.0123	0.0027***	0.150***
Info Order			-0.0002	0.0016	-0.1222***
Info Shared			0.029	0.0137*	0.073
p-value: $0 < {*}{*}{*} < 0.001 < {*}{*} < 0.01 < {*} < 0.05$					
Multiple R-squared	0.1498		0.2084		
Adjusted R-squared	0.1317		0.1634		
F-statistic:	$8.282_{9,423}$***		$4.63_{17,299}$***		

perceptions of privacy risks are lower when information sharing appears voluntary, individuals know more about the risk, the consequences of sharing appear controllable, the information is commonly shared, information sharing impacts only individuals, and the severity of consequences appears low.

The rejection of H_{0_1}, H_{0_3} indicate a counterintuitive insight for the providers of Online Social Networks, specifically Facebook. If individuals perceive higher control on consequences of sharing and sharing appears voluntary, they share more. Thus, if OSN should provide better PETs and empower their users.

The rejection of H_{0_3} is also counterintuitive. We agree that there is need to educate end-users about the consequences of sharing information. However, educated individuals may feel a false sense of safety as awareness lowers perceptions of risk. Thus, OSN providers should invest in privacy education as it lowers the inhibitions of their users. The impact of such educational input is made salient by Table 1, as knowledge to the exposed is a statistically significant determinant of perceived risk.

Intuitively, information that is commonly shared is perceived to be less risky. However, often commonly shared attributes such as real name can lead to privacy violations. For example, using real name on OSNs can make it easier for an adversary to search and locate an individual's profile. (Note that while individuals do not consider Real Name to be a commonly shared attributed (mean $= 3.0$); it is a required information item on Facebook). Items marked as commonly shared by the participants, such as sexual orientation or political affiliation, can clearly have a real life impact. (In fact many of the participants report sharing such sensitive information online. For example, in our sample 54 participants report sharing their sexual orientation on Facebook).

Information that impacts fewer individuals is perceived to be less risky. This is not problematic when individuals correctly assess whether the information is catastrophic in nature or not. However, often this assessment may be incorrect; for example, individuals may consider that Friends List is not a catastrophic risk. Arguably, sharing the friends list would not only impinge the individual sharing but also all their friends.

Sharing information when the severity of consequences is lower is also perceived to be less risky. Offline severity is the most important determinant of perceived risk [9]. There is evidence that severity is very important even for perceptions of privacy risks. Severity is significantly correlated with perceived risk (Table 1) and also statistically significant in the regression model (Table 1).

The nine-dimensional framework provided a statistically significant explanation (p-value $\ll 0.001$) of the (13.17 %) variance in perceived risk of information sharing on Facebook (Table 1). Perceptions of privacy risks on Facebook may then be similar to those offline and may be addressed by translating offline strategies online. For example, public awareness campaigns have successfully addressed drunken driving [13]. Our results indicate that it is in the interest of OSN providers to facilitate similar campaigns online and simultaneously provide (subsidized/usable) technical solutions for privacy. Investment in such awareness may be additionally justified by the costs of self-regulated behavior under a perceived panopticon that may hamper information sharing [23].

Individual privacy preferences were strongly and positively correlated with the perceived risk of information sharing, rejecting $H_{0_{10}}$. Thus, while privacy decisions are often contextual, general risk attitudes towards information sharing significantly impinge on an individual's decision to divulge information on social networking sites as well. Given that contextual user education about information sharing may be expensive and less tractable, general awareness about privacy, if leveraged, would still improve outcomes.

$H_{0_{11}}, H_{0_{12}}$, and $H_{0_{13}}$ could not be rejected. $H_{0_{11}}$ was difficult to test. About one-third of the sample, i.e. 22 participants did not report their household income, while another third, i.e. 24 participants, had a income higher than \$75,000. $H_{0_{12}}$ could not be tested as most participants were of the same age. $H_{0_{13}}$ similarly could not be tested appropriately as the sample was heavily gender skewed with more than three-fourths of the participants being male.

Finally, $H_{0_{14}}$ could not be rejected. In similar offline studies, perceived risk has been negatively correlated with perceived benefit for most activities, e.g. smoking. The lack of correlation suggests that certain information items are not perceived as beneficial, but are shared due to the design of the website, the need to fill in blanks, etc. [21].

6   Conclusion and Future Work

Condoms alone do not limit the spread of Sexually Transmitted Diseases (STDs) as individuals compensate by have multiple partners or more risky sexual encounters [6]. The effective strategy has been addressing behaviors, for example in Uganda, rather than a singular reliance on technology. Similarly, it is imperative to address non-expert behaviors and lower the individual risk budget for security and privacy risks online.

In this paper we used the psychometric paradigm of expressed preferences to survey individuals regarding the perceived risk of sharing information on Facebook. The results starkly resemble previous research on offline risks, despite the lack of physical harm online. This has the promise of translating existing literature in risk communication and public policy for security and privacy risks online. We validated prior results based in revealed preferences. Voluntary disclosure and greater control may encourage more information sharing. Simultaneously, more informed users have lower perceptions of risk and thus may share more. Thus, there is a perverse incentive for OSN providers, like Facebook, to empower their users to protect privacy. Educated users may demonstrate behaviors that reduce harm for a single incidence of information disclosure. However, as perceived risk of information sharing decreases they may share information more frequently. Thus, the overall privacy risk remains the constant, i.e. the risk thermostat is not impinged as individuals compensate [2].

Finally, while the acceptability of privacy risks manifests contextually, our results indicate that baseline privacy preferences may significantly inform individual perceptions. Thus, risk communication through generalized privacy campaigns is needed and can be potentially effective. Risk communication designers should focus on the relevant determinants of perceived risk on Facebook, i.e. severity and knowledge to the exposed. Future work should validate these findings with a larger representative participant pool.

References

1. Acquisti, A., Grossklags, J.: Privacy and rationality in individual decision making. IEEE Secur. Priv. 3(1), 26–33 (2005)
2. Adams, J.: Cars, cholera, and cows, vol. 335, pp. 1–49. CATO Institute (1999)
3. Barnes, S.B.: A privacy paradox: Social networking in the united states. First Monday 11(9) (2006)
4. Brandimarte, L., Acquisti, A., Loewenstein, G.: Misplaced confidences: privacy and the control paradox. Soc. Psychol. Pers. Sci. 4, 340–347 (2012)
5. Caine, K., Kisselburgh, L.G., Lareau, L.: Audience visualization influences disclosures in online social networks. In: Extended Abstracts on Human Factors in Computing Systems, CHI 2011, pp. 1663–1668. ACM (2011)
6. Cassell, M., Halperin, D., Shelton, J., Stanton, D.: Risk compensation: the achilles' heel of innovations in HIV prevention? Br. Med. J. 332(7541), 605–607 (2006)
7. Christofides, E., Muise, A., Desmarais, S.: Hey mom, whats on your facebook? Comparing facebook disclosure and privacy in adolescents and adults. Soc. Psychol. Pers. Sci. 3(1), 48–54 (2012)

Cars, Condoms, and Facebook   289

8. Farahmand, F., Spafford, E.H.: Understanding insiders: an analysis of risk-taking behavior. Inf. Syst. Front. **15**, 5–15 (2013)
9. Fischhoff, B., Slovic, P., Lichtenstein, S., Read, S., Combs, B.: How is safe enough? A psychometric study of attitudes towards technological risks and benefits. Policy Sci. **9**(2), 127–152 (1978)
10. Garg, V., Camp, L.J.: End user perception of online risk under uncertainty. In: 45th Hawaii International Conference on System Science, pp. 3278–3287. IEEE (2012)
11. Garg, V., Nilizadeh, S.: Craigslist scams and community composition: investigating online fraud victimization. In: International Workshop on Cyber Crime. IEEE (2013)
12. Grossklags, J., Acquisti, A.: When 25 cents is too much: an experiment on willingness-to-sell and willingness-to-protect personal information. In: Workshop on the Economics of Information Security (2007)
13. Hingson, R., McGovern, T., Howland, J., Heeren, T., Winter, M., Zakocs, R.: Reducing alcohol-impaired driving in Massachusetts: the saving lives program. Am. J. Public Health **86**(6), 791–797 (1996)
14. Hoy, M.G., Milne, G.: Gender differences in privacy-related measures for young adult facebook users. J. Interact. Advertising **10**(2), 28–45 (2010)
15. Lipford, H.R., Besmer, A., Watson, J.: Understanding privacy settings in facebook with an audience view. In: Proceedings of the 1st Conference on Usability, Psychology, and Security, UPSEC 2008, pp. 2:1–2:8. USENIX Association, Berkeley (2008)
16. Malhotra, N.K., Kim, S.S., Agarwal, J.: Internet Users' Information Privacy Concerns (IUIPC): the construct, the scale, and a causal model. Info. Sys. Res. **15**, 336–355 (2004)
17. Malin, B., Sweeney, L.: Re-identification of dna through an automated linkage process. In: Proceedings of the AMIA Symposium, p. 423. American Medical Informatics Association (2001)
18. Nissenbaum, H.: Privacy in Context: Technology, Policy, and the Integrity of Social Life. Stanford Law & Politics, Stanford (2010)
19. Norcie, G., Caine, K., Camp, L.J.: Eliminating stop-points in the installation and use of anonymity systems: a usability evaluation of the tor browser bundle. In: HotPETS (2012)
20. Patil, S., Kapadia, A.: Are you exposed?: Conveying information exposure. In: Proceedings of the ACM 2012 Conference on Computer Supported Cooperative Work Companion, pp. 191–194. ACM (2012)
21. Preibusch, S., Krol, K., Beresford, A.: The privacy economics of voluntary over-disclosure in web forms. In: 11th Annual Workshop on the Economics of Information Security, WEIS (2012)
22. Slovic, P., Fischhoff, B., Lichtenstein, S.: Why study risk perception. Risk Anal. **2**(2), 83–93 (1982)
23. Solove, D.: Nothing to Hide: The False Tradeoff Between Privacy and Security. Yale University Press, New Haven (2011)
24. Tversky, A., Kahneman, D.: Judgment under uncertainty: heuristics and biases. Science **185**(4157), 1124 (1974)
25. Wang, Y., Norcie, G., Komanduri, S., Acquisti, A., Leon, P., Cranor, L.: I regretted the minute i pressed share: a qualitative study of regrets on facebook. In: Proceedings of the Seventh Symposium on Usable Privacy and Security, p. 10. ACM (2011)

Access Control

Achieving Revocable Fine-Grained Cryptographic Access Control over Cloud Data

Yanjiang Yang[1]([✉]), Xuhua Ding[2], Haibing Lu[3],
Zhiguo Wan[4], and Jianying Zhou[1]

[1] Institute for Infocomm Research, Singapore, Singapore
{yyang,jyzhou}@i2r.a-star.edu.sg
[2] School of Information Systems, Singapore Management University,
Singapore, Singapore
xhding@smu.edu.sg
[3] The Leavey School of Business, Santa Clara University, Santa Clara, USA
hlu@scu.edu
[4] School of Software, Tsinghua University, Beijing, China
wanzhiguo@tsinghua.edu.cn

Abstract. Attribute-based encryption (ABE) is well suited for fine-grained access control for data residing on a cloud server. However, existing approaches for user revocation are not satisfactory. In this work, we propose a new approach which works by splitting an authorized user's decryption capability between the cloud and the user herself. User revocation is attained by simply nullifying the decryption ability at the cloud, requiring neither key update nor re-generation of cloud data. We propose a concrete scheme instantiating the approach, which features lightweight computation at the user side. This makes it possible for users to use resource-constrained devices such as mobile phones to access cloud data. We implement our scheme, and also empirically evaluate its performance.

1 Introduction

Data residing on a cloud storage need to be encrypted in order to safeguard their secrecy against the untrusted cloud provider [8–10], and to serve as an access control mechanism where a user's decryption capability is assigned according to the access control policy. For instance, a hospital encrypts its medical data outsourced to a cloud storage such that a patient's medical records are only allowed to be decrypted by her doctors and nurses. Attribute-based encryption (ABE) [6,12,18], has been hailed as the solution to cloud data encryption because it enforces fine-grained access control over the decryption capabilities. Informally, as an one-to-many encryption mechanism, ABE allows data to be encrypted with certain policy/attributes while each decryption key is associated with certain attributes/policy. Only when the attributes satisfy the policy can the ciphertext be deciphered correctly by the key.

Nonetheless, *user revocation* remains a thorny problem in the setting of cloud data encryption without a satisfactory solution. In the following, we review

© Springer International Publishing Switzerland 2015
Y. Desmedt (Ed.): ISC 2013, LNCS 7807, pp. 293–308, 2015.
DOI: 10.1007/978-3-319-27659-5_21

several possible approaches to user revocation. Firstly, authentication-based revocation used in conventional access control systems are expensive for the cloud setting. This approach requires an extra authentication mechanism at the user-cloud interface. It costs the user to possess extra secrets and the cloud server is burdened with the authentication task. The second approach is key-update based revocation as proposed in [1,19,20]. This method suffers from poor scalability as all data must be re-encrypted and all remaining legitimate user keys are to be updated or re-distributed, whose cost is tremendously high when the data volume or the number of users scales up.

The third approach is to retrofit ABE schemes with revocation support by assigning revocation related attributes. The ABE schemes in [6,12] propose to include an "expiry time" attribute in the attribute set such that each decryption key is effective only for a period of time. The shortcoming of this method is that it does not allow for immediate revocation due to the time gap. In [16], Ostrovsky et. al. propose *negative* constrains in the access policy, such that a revocation of certain attributes amounts to negating these attributes. This mechanism is not scalable in revoking individual users, as each encryption has to involve information of all revoked users each of which is treated as a distinctive attribute.

The fourth approach is key splitting [4], where an untrusted security mediator holds one part of a decryption key. Once a user is revoked the mediator immediately refuses to participate in her decryption. Although this paradigm is suitable for the cloud setting where the cloud server plays the role as a security mediator, it requires the underlying decryption algorithm to be homomorphic. However, existing homomorphic encryption schemes do not allow for fine-grained access control policies. Another downside of this approach is that it requires a TTP (Trusted Third Party) to perform key splitting which is not suitable for certain cloud storage applications.

In short, cloud storage applications desire an encryption mechanism with the following two properties: (a) fine-grained access control with strong expressiveness to describe complex access policies; (b) scalable and efficient revocation to instantly nullify a user's decryption privilege without affecting legitimate users and inflicting high cost on the cloud server. This paper presents such an encryption system for cloud storage. We first envision a general approach solving the user revocation problem in encryption of cloud storage, with the basic idea of splitting a user's decryption capability between the cloud server and the user herself, such that a full decryption requires the cloud server's assistance. User revocation is achieved by instructing the cloud server not to offer the needed assistance. We then propose a concrete scheme realizing the approach, which achieves the same level of fine-grained access control as ABE. Different from key splitting, decryption-capability splitting does not require a TTP to know all users' secrets. Another feature of our scheme is the lightweight computation at the user end, such that a user only performs power exponentiations in a regular algebraic group, though the scheme is based on bilinear mapping. We have implemented our scheme, and empirically tested on a smartphone where the decryption at the user side only takes 12 ms.

Organization. In Sect. 2, we elaborate our decryption-capability splitting approach for user revocation, and formulate a system model. A concrete instantiation is presented in Sect. 3. Experimental results are given in Sect. 4, and Sect. 5 introduces related work. Section 6 concludes the paper.

2   Synopsis

2.1   System Setting

A data owner (denoted as Owner) uploads her data records to a cloud storage server (denoted by Server). Without fully trusting the Server, the Owner encrypts her cloud data such that data privacy is protected against the Server. This encrypted cloud data storage is to be accessed by a group of users authorized by the Owner. Data encryption enforces fine-grained access control, such that different users have different decryption capabilities matching their respective functional roles. In particular, a user's decryption capability is delineated by a set of attributes according to her role. Each data encryption is associated with an access control policy such that a user can successfully decipher the encrypted record only if her attributes satisfy the record's policy. Under certain circumstances, the Owner may need to revoke a user, in the sense that the revoked user is not allowed to decipher any record in the cloud. We consider the Server as an honest-but-curious adversary, which honestly runs the algorithms or tasks assigned to it while attempting to attack data privacy. Figure 1 depicts an overview of the system.

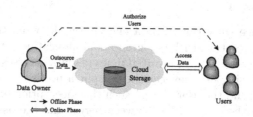

Fig. 1. An overview of the cloud storage system

2.2   Fine-Grained Access Control

To facilitate fine-grained decryption capabilities, we use "attribute" and "access structure" utilized in [18] to describe our access control model.

Attributes. Let Λ denote the dictionary of attributes used in the system. Each user u of the cloud storage is assigned with a set of attributes $S_u \subseteq \Lambda$. The attribute assignment procedure is application specific which is beyond the scope of this paper.

Policy and Access Structure. In our system, an access control policy is expressed by a monotonic access structure which is a subset of 2^Λ. In particular, a collection $\mathbb{A} \subset 2^\Lambda$ is monotone if $\forall B, C$: if $B \in \mathbb{A}$ and $B \subseteq C$, then $C \in \mathbb{A}$. An access structure (respectively, monotone access structure) is a collection (respectively, monotone collection) $\mathbb{A}$ of non-empty subsets of Λ. The sets in $\mathbb{A}$ are called the authorized sets, and the sets not in $\mathbb{A}$ are called the unauthorized sets. We restrict our attention to monotone access structures in this work.

Linear Secret-Sharing Schemes. Linear secret-sharing schemes will be used to establish access structures. A secret-sharing scheme Π over a set S of attributes is linear if (1) the shares for each attribute form a vector over Z_p; (2) there exists a matrix M (with ℓ rows and n columns) called the share-generating matrix for Π. For the ith row of M, i = 1, ..., ℓ, we let the function ρ define the attribute labeling row i as $\rho(i)$. When we consider the column vector $v = (x, y_2, \cdots, y_n)$, where $x \in Z_p$ is the secret to be shared, and $y_2, \cdots, y_n \in Z_p$ are random, then $M \cdot v$ is the vector of ℓ shares of the secret x according to Π. The share $(M \cdot v)_i$ belongs to attribute $\rho(i)$.

It is shown in [2] that every linear secret-sharing scheme as above also enjoys the linear reconstruction property: Suppose that Π is a linear secret-sharing scheme for the access structure $\mathbb{A}$. Let $S \in \mathbb{A}$ be any authorized set, and let $I = \{i : \rho(i) \in S\} \subset \{1, 2, ..., \ell\}$. Then, there exist a set of constants $\{\omega_i\}_{i \in I}$ such that if $\{\lambda_i\}_{i \in I}$ are valid shares of any secret x according to Π, then $\sum_{i \in I} \omega_i \lambda_i = x$. Furthermore, these constants $\{\omega_i\}_{i \in I}$ can be found in time polynomial in the size of the share-generating matrix M.

2.3 Our Approach

A notable difference (in terms of data encryption) between the cloud storage setting and the conventional PKI or group communication settings is that the untrusted cloud server is always involved in users' data accesses. To leverage this fact towards addressing user revocation, we split a user's decryption capability between the Server and the user herself, such that decryption of encrypted cloud record depends on the cooperation between Server and the user. Specifically, a user's decryption capability is rendered by a *server-side key* and a *user-side key*, where the former is held by the Server and the latter is possessed by the user. To manage users' server-side keys, the Server maintains a Server-side Key list, with each entry containing a user's identity and her server-side key. When the user requests a data record from cloud, the Server executes a *server decryption* operation over the data with the user's server-side key, generating an intermediate value. The intermediate value is then returned to the user, who gets the plaintext data by a *user decryption* operation using her user-side key. We remark that the pair of server-side key and user-side key are not the result of key splitting. Therefore, our approach does not require a trusted party (i.e., the Owner in our case) to compute the user-side key on behalf of the user.

In line with our approach, a secure cloud storage system involves three types of entities, the Owner, a set of users, and the Server. These entities interact with one another in the following algorithms.

Definition 1. *A secure cloud storage system (SCSS) is defined as a collection of the following seven algorithms.*

Setup$(1^\kappa) \rightarrow (params, msk)$: *Taking as input a security parameter 1^κ, the Owner executes this algorithm to set up public parameters params and a master secret key msk. Below we assume that params is implicit in the input of the rest algorithms, unless stated explicitly.*

UsKGen$(u) \rightarrow (Upk_u, Usk_u)$: *The user-side key generation algorithm takes as input the public parameters and a user identity u, and outputs a pair of user-side public/private keys (Upk_u, Usk_u) for u.*
Each user executes this algorithm to generate a key pair for herself.

SsKGen$(msk, Upk_u, S) \rightarrow SsK_u$: *The server-side key generation algorithm takes as input master secret key msk, user-side public key Upk_u, and a set $S \subset \Lambda$ of attributes, and outputs a server-side key SsK_u for u.*
The Owner executes this algorithm to authorize a user, based on her attributes. The server-side key SsK_u will be secretly given to the Server who then adds a new entry in the Server-side Key list $\mathcal{L}_{SsK}$, i.e., $\mathcal{L}_{SsK} = \mathcal{L}_{SsK} \cup \{u, SsK_u\}$.

Encrypt$(m, \mathbb{A}) \rightarrow c$: *The encryption algorithm takes as input a message m and an access structure $\mathbb{A}$, and outputs a ciphertext c by encrypting data m under the access structure.*
The Owner executes this algorithm to encrypt a data record to be uploaded to the Server.

SDecrypt$(SsK_u, c) \rightarrow v$: *The server decryption algorithm takes as input a server-side key SsK_u and a ciphertext c, and outputs an intermediate value v.*
The Server executes this algorithm to help a user decrypt a scrambled data record requested by the user u with her server-side key.

UDecrypt$(Usk_u, v) \rightarrow m$: *The user decryption algorithm takes as input a user-side private key Usk_u and an intermediate value v, and outputs a plaintext m.*
An authorized users executes this algorithm to obtain the desired data from the intermediate value returned by the Server.

Revoke$(u, \mathcal{L}_{SsK}) \rightarrow \mathcal{L}_{SsK} \setminus \{u, SsK_u\}$: *Taking as input a user identity u and the Server-side Key list $\mathcal{L}_{SsK}$, the algorithm revokes u's decryption capability by removing her entry from $\mathcal{L}_{SsK}$, and outputs the updated $\mathcal{L}_{SsK} = \mathcal{L}_{SsK} - \{u, SsK_u\}$.*

Correctness of the system requires that $\texttt{UDecrypt}(Usk_u, \texttt{SDecrypt}(SsK_u, c)) = m$ if S satisfies $\mathbb{A}$, for all $(Upk_u, Usk_u) \leftarrow \texttt{UsKGen}(u), SsK_u \leftarrow \texttt{SsKGen}(msk, Upk_u, S)$ and $c \leftarrow \texttt{Encrypt}(m, \mathbb{A})$, where $(params, msk) \leftarrow \texttt{Setup}(1^\kappa)$.

Caveat. To highlight the distinction between decryption-capability splitting and key splitting syntactically, we point out that for the latter, the UsKGen algorithm and the SsKGen algorithm above could be combined into a single algorithm which is to be executed by the same entity (i.e., the Owner in our case).

Security Requirements. Below we explain the intuitions of three security requirements imposed upon the system, while the formulations are deferred to Appendix A.

Data Privacy Against Cloud. In our adversarial model, the Server is an honest-but-curious adversary. It stores the Owner's data and performs server decryptions to serve users' accesses by applying the corresponding server-side keys. It mandates that the Server cannot learn any semantic information about the data in the storage, but it should behave honestly in terms of managing cloud data, processing user access requests, and other administrative activities.

Data Privacy Against Users. It mandates that a user cannot obtain data beyond the authorized access rights stipulated by the Owner. In particular, the collusion between a set of malicious users does not yield new decryption capabilities beyond those privileges assigned to those users.

User Revocation Support. When a user's decryption capability is revoked, she is no long able to decipher the encrypted data on the storage. In other words, without the assistance of the Server, no user can decipher the encrypted data by herself, even when her attributes satisfy the policy attached to the ciphertext.

3   A Concrete Instantiation

In this section, we present a concrete instantiation of the above approach and algorithms. Of particular interest of our scheme is the computation efficiency at the user side, i.e., the user decryption algorithm UDecrypt only involves exponentiation operations in regular algebraic groups, while the scheme itself is based on bilinear mapping. This makes possible for users to use resource-constrained device such as mobile phone to access the cloud data. This is one of the features that distinguish our scheme from all other proposals on using ABE for encryption of cloud data, e.g., those reviewed in Sect. 5.

3.1   Construction Details

Our construction is based on the scheme in [18], which is proved secure under the decisional q-BDHE assumption. The main trick we have rests with the generation of a user's server-side key, such that an ABE ciphertext can be transformed into one under the user's (standard) public key.

Let $s \in_R S$ denote an element s randomly drawn from a set S. The details of our scheme are as follows.

Setup(1^κ) $\rightarrow$ ($params, msk$)**:** On input a security parameter 1^κ, the setup algorithm

- determines a bilinear map $e : G_0 \times G_0 \rightarrow G_1$, where G_0 and G_1 are cyclic multiplicative groups of κ-bit prime order p.
- selects random exponents $z, a \in Z_p$, and a generator g of G_0.
- chooses a cryptographic hash function $H : \{0,1\}^* \rightarrow G_0$.
- decides a standard public key encryption scheme. Below we use $\mathsf{Enc}(\cdot, \cdot)$ to denote both the description of the scheme and its encryption function.
- sets $params = (g, e(g,g)^z, g^a, H, \mathsf{Enc})$, and $msk = g^z$.

UsKGen$(u) \rightarrow (Upk_u, Usk_u)$: On input a user identity u, the user-side key generation algorithm outputs a public/private key pair (Upk_u, Usk_u) for Enc.

SsKGen$(msk, Upk_u, S) \rightarrow SsK_u$: On input master secret key $msk = g^z$, a user public key Upk_u, and a set of attributes S, the server-side key generation algorithm picks $\alpha, t \in_R Z_p$, and sets the server-side key SsK_u for u as

$$SsK_u = \Big(K = g^{z\alpha} g^{at}, K' = \mathsf{Enc}(Upk_u, \alpha), L = g^t,$$

$$\{\forall s \in S : K_s = H(s)^t\} \Big),$$

where $\mathsf{Enc}(Upk_u, \alpha)$ denotes encryption of α by Enc under Upk_u.

Encrypt$(m, \mathbb{A}) \rightarrow c$: Taking as input a message m, and an access structure $\mathbb{A} = (M, \rho)$, and implicitly $params$, the encryption algorithm proceeds as follows.

We limit ρ to be injective function, i.e., an attribute is associated with at most one row of M. Let M be an $\ell \times n$ matrix. It first selects a random column vector $\boldsymbol{v} = (x, y_2, \ldots, y_n) \in Z_p^n$, which will be used to secret-share the exponent x. Calculates $\lambda_i = M_i \cdot \boldsymbol{v}, i = 1$ to ℓ, where M_i denotes the ith row of M. Sets the ciphertext c as

$$c = (C = m \cdot e(g,g)^{zx}, C' = g^x, \{\forall i \in [1 \cdot \cdot l] : C_i = g^{a\lambda_i} H(\rho(i))^{-x}\}, (M, \rho))$$

SDecrypt$(SsK_u, c) \rightarrow v$: On input a server-side key SsK_u associating with a set of attributes S, and a ciphertext c under access structure (M, ρ), the server decryption algorithm outputs an intermediate value v if S satisfies the access structure, or $\perp$ otherwise. Suppose S satisfies the access structure and $I = \{i : \rho(i) \in S\} \subset \{1, 2, \cdots, \ell\}$. Then, let $\{\omega_i\}_{i \in I}$ be a set of constants such that if $\{\lambda_i\}$ are valid shares of a secret x according to M, then $\sum_{i \in I} \omega_i \lambda_i = x$. Note that it suffices to determine $\{\omega_i\}_{i \in I}$ based on M and I. The algorithm first computes

$$\frac{e(C', K)}{\prod_{i \in I}(e(C_i, L)e(C', K_{\rho(i)}))^{\omega_i}}$$

$$= \frac{e(g^x, g^{z\alpha} g^{at})}{\prod_{i \in I}(e(g^{a\lambda_i} H(\rho(i))^{-x}, g^t)e(g^x, H(\rho(i))^t))^{\omega_i}}$$

$$= \frac{e(g,g)^{xz\alpha} e(g,g)^{xat}}{\prod_{i \in I}(e(g,g)^{a\lambda_i t} e(H(\rho(i)), g)^{-xt} e(g, H(\rho(i)))^t)^{\omega_i}}$$

$$= \frac{e(g,g)^{xz\alpha} e(g,g)^{xat}}{\prod_{i \in I} e(g,g)^{a\lambda_i t\omega_i}}$$

$$= e(g,g)^{xz\alpha}.$$

Then, sets v as

$$v = (V_1, V_2, V_3)$$
$$= (C = m \cdot e(g,g)^{zx}, e(g,g)^{xz\alpha}, K' = \mathsf{Enc}(Upk_u, \alpha))$$

UDecrypt$(Usk_u, v) \to m$: On input a user-side private key Usk_u and an intermediate value v resulting from the server decryption algorithm with u's server-side key, the user decryption algorithm works as follows. Recall that $v = (V_1 = m \cdot e(g,g)^{zx}, V_2 = e(g,g)^{xz\alpha}, v_3 = \mathsf{Enc}(Upk_u, \alpha))$. Decryption is straightforward, by decrypting V_3 using Usk_u to get α, and then computing $e(g,g)^{xz} = (V_2)^{1/\alpha}$ and finally getting $m = V_1/e(g,g)^{xz}$.

Revoke$(u, \mathcal{L}_{SsK}) \to \mathcal{L}_{SsK} \setminus \{u, SsK_u\}$: On input of a user identity u and the Server-side Key list $\mathcal{L}_{SsK}$, the entry corresponding to u is removed from $\mathcal{L}_{SsK}$. Depending on applications, either the Server updates $\mathcal{L}_{SsK}$ instructed by the Owner, or an interface is provided to the Owner so that he does the deletion.

Correctness. Correctness of the construction is easily verified, so we do not elaborate.

Performance. The bit length of the intermediate value v returned by the SDecrypt algorithm is $2|G_1| + |\mathsf{Enc}(\cdot)|$, independent of the complexity of the encryption access policy (represented by the total number of rows of the share-generating matrix). So is the computation overhead of the UDecrypt algorithm, which consists mainly of a decryption operation of a standard public key encryption scheme and a power exponentiation in G_1. This means that no pairing operation is involved at the user side, although the scheme bases itself on bilinear mapping and enjoys the fine grained encryption/decryption capabilities comparable to the ABE schemes in [6,18].

3.2   Security Analysis

Security of our scheme is reduced to the decisional q-Bilinear Diffie-Hellman Exponnet (q-BDHE) assumption defined in [18].

Assumption 1 *[Decisional q-BDHE Assumption].* Let G_0 be a group of prime order p. Let $a, x \in Z_p$ be randomly chosen, and g be a generator of G_0. Let
$$\boldsymbol{v} = (g, g^x, g^a, g^{a^2}, g^{a^3}, \cdots, g^{a^q}, g^{a^{q+2}}, \cdots, g^{a^{2q}}).$$ The decisional q-BDHE assumption holds if for any PPT adversary $\mathcal{A}$ and $Z \in_R G_0$,

$$|\Pr[\mathcal{A}(\boldsymbol{v}, g^{a^{x(q+1)}}) = 1] - \Pr[\mathcal{A}(\boldsymbol{v}, Z) = 1]| < \nu$$

where ν is a negligible function, and the the probability is taken over the random choice of $a, x \in Z_p$, $Z \in G_1$, and of the random coins of $\mathcal{A}$.

We have the following theorem, regarding data privacy and user revocation support of our scheme, and the security proof can be found in Appendix B.

Theorem 1. *The above scheme achieves data privacy and user revocation support (specified in Definitions 2 and 3), if the decisional q-BDHE assumption holds, the standard public key encryption* Enc *is semantically secure, and* $H(\cdot)$ *is a random oracle.*

4   Experimental Results

To gauge its performance, we have implemented and experimented with our proposed scheme. The implementation is coded in Java, and the cryptographic algorithms are implemented based on the Bouncy Castle Java Crypto Library[1]. We instantiated the bilinear map in the scheme with a 512-bit supersingular curve with embedding degree 2.

4.1   Experimental Results

Cost in Cloud and Owner. In our scheme, the computation costs of both Encrypt and SDecrypt are dependent on the complexity of the access control policy, linear to the number of rows of the share-generating matrix. These costs constitute the most demanding part of our construction.

To empirically evaluate the computational costs of the Encrypt and SDecrypt algorithms (while avoiding compounding factors such as network latency, instability of on-demand computing, etc.), we run these algorithms on a PC with 2.66 GHz Intel Core2Duo and 3.25 GB RAM. We experiment them with a set of access structures, whose share-generating matrixes are of ℓ rows and ℓ columns. Access structures in such a form ensure that all involved attributes are used in the SDecrypt algorithm, thus imposing the heaviest workload. We repeat each experiment for 100 times and calculate the average. The experimental results are shown in Fig. 2, which displays the time of the two algorithms with respect to the number of attributes (i.e., the number of rows of the share-generating matrix).

As evident from the figure, the results corroborate the fact that both algorithms perform linear computations with the number of attributes. Note that the cost of SDecrypt with 60 attributes is about 1.7 s. This performance should be acceptable for practical applications, since 50–60 attributes should suffice for specifying access control policies based on functional roles.

Cost in User End. We have also implemented and tested the UDecrypt algorithm of our scheme on an HTC HD2 smartphone, which is configured with a 1 GHz Scorpion CPU and 448 MB RAM. We instantiate the standard public-key encryption scheme Enc associated with the user-side public/private key pair by the ElGamal-type encryption in G_0, i.e., $(Upk_u, Usk_u) = (g^{x_u}, x_u \in Z_p^*)$. The experimental results indicate that on average, it takes about 12 ms to decrypt a ciphertext of the form $(m \cdot e(g,g)^{zx}, e(g,g)^{xz\alpha}, Enc(Upk_u, \alpha))$. On the other hand, the communication overhead for the user is $2|G_1| + 2|G_0|$, about 1.5 Kbits in our implementation. These results suggest that it is affordable for a user to access the cloud storage using a low-end device like a smartphone.

---

[1] http://www.bouncycastle.org/java.html.

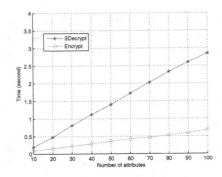

Fig. 2. Experimental results

5 Related Work

This section provides an overview of the related work on encryption of cloud data and user revocation, respectively.

Encryption of Cloud Data with ABE. Among many proposals on enforcement of cryptographic access control upon cloud data with encryption, we focus on those using ABE and PRE. The proposal by Yu *et al.* applies KP-ABE for encryption of cloud data to achieve fine-grained data sharing [20]. For user revocation support, they suggest adopting the specific technique of PRE scheme [3] to update users' decryption keys. The advantage is that the cloud is entrusted to taking the majority of the workload for re-generation of cloud data and re-distribution of new keys. While their scheme improves considerably over the trivial solution, i.e., the Owner is fully responsible for data re-generation and key re-distribution, it is always preferable not to burden the cloud if possible. In addition, their scheme requires the cloud to maintain user revocation information for legitimate users to gradually complete key update. Our decryption-capability splitting approach avoids these problems and the overhead incurred due to user revocation is minor.

Wang *et al.* achieve hierarchical attribute-based encryption for cloud storage, by augmenting CP-ABE with hierarchical identity-based encryption [19]. Hierarchical attribute-based encryption could cope with more complicated application requirements, but for user revocation, their scheme is similar to [20]. The proposal by Liu *et al.* also aims at hierarchical attribute-set-based encryption for cloud storage [15], and its approach for user revocation is the "expiry time" mechanism.

As a final note, our proposed scheme distinguishes itself from all the above work because the computation at the user side is lightweight, independent of the complexity of the access control policy of the underlying ABE scheme.

Key-Split Cryptography. We realize that the idea of splitting key for revocation of cryptographic capabilities is not new. Boneh *et al.* propose "mediated RSA" to split the private key of RSA into two shares, such that one share is delegated to an online "mediator" and the other is given to the user [4]. As RSA decryption and signing require the engagement of both parties, the user's cryptographic capabilities are immediately revoked if the mediator does not cooperate. Our approach for user revocation follows a similar rationale, but it is more precisely split of decryption capability (rather than simply split of key). A technical difference resulting from this distinction is that the party responsible for key split knows both shares, but the party in charge of capability split does not necessarily know both shares, i.e. in our scheme, the Owner does not learn users' private keys.

A broader class of cryptographic primitives related to key split is threshold cryptography, e.g., [13,17]. A threshold cryptosystem works by splitting a private key among n parties, in a way that any t out of n parties together can decrypt or sign. Threshold cryptography is by no means designed for user revocation purposes; rather, it is intended to work in a distributed environment where individual parties are restricted from abusing cryptographic capabilities.

The recent work by Green et al. [11] proposes delegating the bulk of decryption overhead of ABE to a powerful proxy server in order to mitigate the burden at the user side. As a result, the user only performs a standard ElGamal decryption operation (similar to ours). While their constructions are not intended for user revocation, they can be directly used to instantiate our approach, but resulting in a scheme of key splitting. In contrast, our scheme implements decryption-capability splitting with the advantage that users do not need to disclose their secret keys to the Owner.

6   Conclusions

A main issue to be addressed when using ABE for encryption of cloud storage is user revocation. In this work we proposed a decryption-capability splitting approach for user revocation, which is advantageous over existing solutions. A user's decryption capability is split between the cloud and the user herself, such that user revocation is achieved by simply invalidating the cloud's decryption ability. As a result, neither key update nor re-generation of cloud data is required. We further proposed a concrete scheme instantiating the approach, which is featured with lightweight computation at the user side such that users can use resource-constrained devices to access cloud data.

Acknowledgments. This work is supported in part by A*STAR funded project SecDC-112172014 (Singapore), and the second author is funded by the Singapore Management University through the research grant MSS12C004 from the Ministry of Education Academic Research Fund Tier 1.

A   Formulation of Security Notions

The definitional model for data privacy against cloud is captured in the following game between a challenger managing a SCSS system and an adversary who wants to break the system.

Definition 2 *[Data Privacy Against Cloud]. A secure cloud storage system (SCSS) satisfies data privacy against cloud if for any PPT adversary, the probability of the following game returns 1 is $1/2 + \nu(\kappa)$, where $\nu(.)$ is a negligible function.*

Setup. *The challenger runs the Setup algorithm and gives the public parameters params to the adversary.*

Phase 1. *The adversary makes repeated queries to the server-side key generation oracle by submitting sets of attributes $S_1, ..., S_{q_1}$. For each query, the challenger first runs the UsKGen algorithm to get a user-side public/private key pair; with the user-side public key and the attribute set S_i, the challenger then runs the SsKGen algorithm to get a server-side key; the challenger returns the server-side key together with the user-side public key to the adversary.*

Challenge. *The adversary submits two equal length messages m_0 and m_1, together with a challenge access structure $\mathbb{A}^*$. The challenger flips a random coin b, runs the Encrypt algorithm on m_b and $\mathbb{A}^*$, and returns the ciphertext c^* to the adversary.*

Phase 2. *Phase 1 is repeated.*

Guess. *The adversary outputs a guess b' on b. If $b' = b$, then the challenger returns 1; otherwise returns 0.*

The formulation of data privacy against authorized users and of user revocation support bases on the same fact that without an appropriate server-side key, a user cannot decrypt even with her user private key. Following is the formal security model.

Definition 3 *[Data Privacy against Users & Revocation Support]. A secure cloud storage system (SCSS) satisfies data privacy against users and user revocation support if for any PPT adversary, the probability of the following game returns 1 is $1/2 + \nu(\kappa)$, where $\nu(.)$ is a negligible function.*

Init. *The adversary declares the access structure $\mathbb{A}^*$ he wants to be challenged upon.*

Setup. *The challenger runs the Setup algorithm and returns the public parameters params to the adversary.*

Phase 1. *The adversary makes repeated queries to the user-side key generation oracle (UsKGen), and the server-side key generation oracle (SsKGen). For the former, the challenger returns the resulting user-side key (both public and private) to the adversary; for the latter, the adversary submits sets of attributes $S_1, ..., S_{q_1}$ with the restriction that each S_i does not satisfy $\mathbb{A}^*$, and the challenger returns the resulting server-side key to the adversary.*

Challenge. *The adversary submits two equal length messages m_0 and m_1, together with the challenge access structure $\mathbb{A}^*$. The challenger flips a random* *coin b, runs the Encrypt algorithm on m_b and $\mathbb{A}^*$, and returns the ciphertext c^* to the adversary.*

Phase 2. *Phase 1 is repeated.*

Guess. *The adversary outputs a guess b' on b. If $b' = b$, then the challenger returns 1; otherwise returns 0.*

We stress that giving the server-side keys to the adversary models authorized users's ability to get intermediate values from the Server (who uses the server-side keys). Intuitively, user revocation support (in which case the adversary does not have any server-side key) is implied by the fact the adversary even cannot decrypt the challenge ciphertext without *appropriate* server-side keys.

B   Security Proof for Theorem 1

Proof. We prove that our scheme satisfies Definitions 2 and 3, respectively.

Satisfying Definition 2. The proof is much simpler than in [18], due to the use of semantically secure public-key encryption Enc, and the fact that the adversary does not have the private key. Satisfaction of Definition 2 is actually based on the DBDH (Decisional Bilinear Hiffie-Hellman) assumption, which states that it is infeasible to distinguish between $(g \in G_0, g^c, g^d, g^x, e(g,g)^{cdx} \in G_1)$ and $(g, g^c, g^d, g^x, Z \in_R G_1)$. The DBDH assumption clearly is weaker than the decisional q-BDHE assumption.

Suppose we have an adversary $\mathcal{A}$ with non-negligible advantage $\mathsf{Adv}_{\mathcal{A}}$ in the game of Definition 2 against our scheme. We build a challenger $\mathcal{C}$ breaking the DBDH assumption. Details follow.

Setup. The challenger takes in the DBDH challenge (g, g^c, g^d, g^x, Z). The challenger implicitly sets $z = cd$ by setting $e(g,g)^z = e(g^c, g^d)$, and selects a random number in G_0 as g^a. In addition, the challenger programs the random oracle H by building a table as follows. Consider a call to $H(s)$. If $H(s)$ was already defined in the table, then simply return the same answer as before; otherwise, select a random value $\tau_s \in Z_p$ and define $H(s) = g^{\tau_s}$.

Phase 1. The challenger answers server-side key generation queries from the adversary. For a query, the challenger first generates a public/private key pair for Enc by executing UsKGen; then chooses $z', t \in_R Z_p$ and a random K' from the range of Enc, and computes $K = g^{z'} g^{at}, L = g^t, \forall s \in S : K_s = g^{\tau_s t}$. We argue that the distribution of the simulated key $(K, K', L, \{K_s\})$ so generated is computationally indistinguishable from the actual server-side key. First, due to the semantic security of Enc, the randomly chosen K' is indistinguishable from Enc(α) in the actual key. Second, conditioned on the random K' replacing Enc(α), the $g^{z\alpha}$ in the actual K is no different from $g^{z'}$ for a random z'. Our argument thus holds.

Challenge. The challenger builds the challenge ciphertext. The challenger flips a coin b. Then it computes $C = m_b Z$, and sets $C' = g^x$. Suppose the challenge access structure is $\mathbb{A}^* = (M^*, \rho^*)$, where the share-generating matrix M^* has ℓ^* rows. The challenger computes the shares $\{\lambda_i\}$ as usual according to M^*, and then computes $\forall i = 1, \cdots, \ell^*, C_i = g^{a\lambda_i}(g^x)^{\tau_{\rho^*(i)}}$.

Phase 2. Same as Phase 1.

Guess. The adversary outputs a guess b' of b. If $b = b'$ then the challenger outputs 1 to indicate that $Z = e(g,g)^{cdx}$; otherwise, it outputs 0 to indicate that Z is a random element in G_1.

When $Z = e(g,g)^{cdx}$, then the above simulation by the challenger $\mathcal{C}$ for the challenge ciphertext is perfect. Thus we have $\Pr[\mathcal{C}(g, g^c, g^d, g^x, g^{cdx}) = 1] = \Pr[b' = b] = 1/2 + \mathsf{Adv}_\mathcal{A}$. On the other hand, if Z is random number in G_1, then m_b in the challenge ciphertext of the above simulation is completely hidden from the adversary. Thus we have $\Pr[\mathcal{C}(g, g^c, g^d, g^x, T) = 1] = \Pr[b' = b] = 1/2$. Combined, we get $|\Pr[\mathcal{C}(g, g^c, g^d, g^x, g^{cdx}) = 1] - \Pr[\mathcal{C}(g, g^c, g^d, g^x, T) = 1]| = \mathsf{Adv}_\mathcal{A}$. This completes the proof.

Satisfying Definition 3. We prove this by presenting a reduction from Waters' scheme which is proved secure under the decisional q-BDHE assumption in [18] to ours. To this end, we first point out that the main differences between our scheme and Waters' that are relevant to the proof here are the format of the server-side key in our scheme and of the private key in Waters' scheme. In Waters' scheme, the format of a private key is $(K = g^z g^{at}, L = g^t, \{\forall s \in S : K_s = H(s)^t\})$. Bearing this difference in mind, we build an adversary $\mathcal{B}$ against Waters' scheme, given an adversary $\mathcal{A}$ of our scheme. Details follow.

$\mathcal{B}$ acts as the challenger in the game in Definition 3.

Init. $\mathcal{A}$ declares a challenge access structure $\mathbb{A}^*$ to $\mathcal{B}$, who then declares $\mathbb{A}^*$ to the challenger of Waters' scheme.

Setup. $\mathcal{B}$ takes in the public parameters of a Waters' scheme, and gives them to $\mathcal{A}$. $\mathcal{B}$ also determines a standard public-key encryption scheme Enc and gives the description to $\mathcal{A}$.

Phase 1. $\mathcal{B}$ answers user-side key generation and server-side key generation queries from $\mathcal{A}$. To answer a user-side key generation query, $\mathcal{B}$ simply generates a public/private key pair according to Enc. To answer a server-side key generation query on a set S of attributes and a user public key Upk, $\mathcal{B}$ submits a key generation (KeyGen) query to the challenger of Waters' scheme with S (if S does not satisfy $\mathbb{A}^*$), and as a response $\mathcal{B}$ is returned a key of the form $(K = g^z g^{at}, L = g^t, \{\forall s \in S : K_s = H(s)^t\})$. Then $\mathcal{B}$ selects $\alpha \in_R Z_p$, and computes $\mathsf{Enc}(Upk, \alpha)$ and sets the server-side key as $(K^\alpha, \mathsf{Enc}(Upk, \alpha), L^\alpha, \{\forall s \in S : K_s^\alpha\})$. It can easily see that the resulting server-side key is valid with respect to our scheme.

Challenge. $\mathcal{B}$ builds a challenge ciphertext under $\mathbb{A}^*$, given m_0, m_1 from $\mathcal{A}$. To this end, $\mathcal{B}$ submits m_0 and m_1 to the challenger of Waters' scheme as a challenge, and gets back a challenge ciphertext c^*. $\mathcal{B}$ returns c^* as the challenge ciphertext to $\mathcal{A}$.

Phase 2. Same as Phase 1.

Guess. $\mathcal{A}$ outputs a guess b', which is also used by $\mathcal{B}$ as the guess to the challenger of Waters' scheme. It is easily seen that the simulation by $\mathcal{B}$ is perfect, and the advantage of $\mathcal{B}$ is at least that of $\mathcal{A}$. This completes the proof.   □

References

1. Attrapadung, N., Imai, H.: Attribute-based encryption supporting direct/indirect revocation modes. In: Proceedings IMA International Conference on Cryptography and Coding, pp. 278–300 (2009)
2. Beimel, A.: Secure schemes for secret sharing and key distribution, Ph.D. thesis, Israel Institute of Technology, Technion, Haifa, Israel (1996)
3. Blaze, M., Bleumer, G., Strauss, M.J.: Divertible protocols and atomic proxy cryptography. In: Nyberg, K. (ed.) EUROCRYPT 1998. LNCS, vol. 1403, pp. 127–144. Springer, Heidelberg (1998)
4. Boneh, D., Ding, X., Tsudik, G., Wong, C.M.: A method for fast revocation of public key certificates and security capabilities. In: Proceedings USENIX Security (2001)
5. Bobba, R., Khurana, H., Prabhakaran, M.: A pracitically motivated enhancement to attribute-based encryption. In: Proceedings ESORICs (2009)
6. Bethencourt, J., Sahai, A., Waters, B.: Ciphertext-policy attribute-based encryption. In: Proceedings IEEE S&P (2007)
7. Dodis, Y., Yampolskiy, A.: A verifiable random function with short proofs and keys. In: Vaudenay, S. (ed.) PKC 2005. LNCS, vol. 3386, pp. 416–431. Springer, Heidelberg (2005)
8. Cloud security alliance: security guidance for critical areas of focus in cloud computing (2009). http://www.cloudsecurityalliance.org
9. European network and information security agency: cloud computing risk assessment (2009). http://www.enisa.europa.eu/act/rm/_les/deliverables/cloud-computing-risk-assessment
10. Gartner: don't trust cloud provider to protect your corporate assets, 28 May 2012. http://www.mis-asia.com/resource/cloud-computing/gartner-dont-trust-cloud-provider-to-protect-your-corporate-assets
11. Green, M., Hohenberger, S., Waters, B.: Outsourcing the decryption of ABE ciphertexts. In: Proceedings USENIX Security (2011)
12. Goyal, V., Pandy, O., Sahai, A., Waters, B.: Attribute-based encryption for fine-grained access control of encrypted data. In: Proceedings ACM CCS 2006 (2006)
13. Gennaro, R., Jarecki, S., Krawczyk, H., Rabin, T.: Robust threshold DSS signatures. In: Maurer, U.M. (ed.) EUROCRYPT 1996. LNCS, vol. 1070, pp. 354–371. Springer, Heidelberg (1996)
14. Liang, X., Cao, Z., Lin, H., Shao, J.: Attribute-based proxy re-encrytpion with delegating capabilities. In: Proceedings ACM ASIACCS 2009, pp. 276–286 (2009)
15. Liu, J., Wan, Z., Gu, M.: Hierarchical attribute-set based encryption for scalable, flexible and fine-grained access control in cloud computing. In: Proceedings 7th Information Security Practice and Experience Conference, ISPEC 2011 (2011)
16. Ostrovsky, R., Sahai, A., Waters, B.: Attribute-based encryption with non-monotonic access structures. In: Proceedings ACM CCS 2007, pp. 195–203 (2007)
17. Shoup, V., Gennaro, R.: Securing threshold cryptosystems against chosen ciphertext attack. J. Cryptol. 15(2), 75–96 (2002)

18. Waters, B.: Ciphertext-policy attribute-Based encryption: an expressive, efficient, and provably aecure realization. In: Proceedings Practice and Theory in Public Key Cryptography, PKC 2011, pp. 53–70 (2011)
19. Wang, G., Liu, Q., Wu, J.: Hierarhical attribute-based encryption for fine-grained access control in cloud storage services. In: Proceedings ACM CCS 2010 (2010)
20. Yu, S., Wang, C., Ren, K., Lou, W.: Achieving secure, scalable, and fine-grained data access control in cloud computing. In: Proceedings IEEE INFOCOM 2010 (2010)

Fine-Grained Access Control for HTML5-Based Mobile Applications in Android

Xing Jin[✉], Lusha Wang, Tongbo Luo, and Wenliang Du

Syracuse University, Syracuse, NY, USA
xjin05@syr.edu

Abstract. HTML5-based mobile applications are becoming more and more popular because they can run on different platforms. Several newly introduced mobile OS natively support HTML5-based applications. For those that do not provide native support, such as Android, iOS, and Windows Phone, developers can develop HTML5-based applications using middlewares, such as PhoneGap. In these platforms, programs are loaded into a web component, called WebView, which can render HTML5 pages and execute JavaScript code. In order for the program to access the system resources, which are isolated from the content inside WebView due to its sandbox, bridges need to be built between JavaScript and the native code (e.g. Java code in Android). Unfortunately, such bridges break the existing protection that was originally built into WebView. In this paper, we study the potential risks of HTML5-based applications, and investigate how the existing mobile systems' access control supports these applications. We focus on Android and the PhoneGap middleware. However, our ideas can be applied to other platforms. Our studies indicate that Android does not provide an adequate access control for this kind of applications. We propose a fine-grained access control mechanism for the bridge in Android system. We have implemented our scheme in Android and have evaluated its effectiveness and performance.

1 Introduction

With the increasing support for HTML5, HTML5-based mobile applications are becoming more and more popular [2,6]. These applications are built on standard technologies such as HTML5, CSS and JavaScript, with HTML5 and CSS being used for building the graphical user interface, and JavaScript being used for the programming logic. Because these technologies are the basis of the Web, they are universally supported by all mainstream mobile systems. Porting such apps from one platform to another is much more simplified; of course, if they use platform-specific APIs, they need to be modified to run on a different platform, but this job is much easier than porting the native mobile applications [3].

The advantages of HTML5-based applications have attracted people to use the same technology to develop applications for existing popular mobile platforms such as Android and iOS, so developers only need to develop one version of applications that can run on multiple platforms. Because the OS cannot natively

© Springer International Publishing Switzerland 2015
Y. Desmedt (Ed.): ISC 2013, LNCS 7807, pp. 309–318, 2015.
DOI: 10.1007/978-3-319-27659-5_22

support HTML5-based applications, middleware is needed for such applications to run on these platforms. Several such middlewares have been developed, including PhoneGap, RhoMobile, Appcelerator, WidgetPad, MoSync, etc. Because PhoneGap is the most popular one [5], in the rest of this paper, we use PhoneGap to represent this entire class of middlewares.

For HTML5-based applications, bridges need to be built, allowing JavaScript code inside to access the mobile system resources. However, at the same time, the bridges bring in risks into the mobile systems. We did a study on the PhoneGap framework for Android. In the application that we used in this study, there are two regions: one is called the main frame, and the other is called subframe (achieved using `iframe`). The main frame contains the code from the developers and the subframe contains the code from a third-party. The application is given a set of permissions, which are meant to be given to the code running in the main frame. However, our investigation shows that the JavaScript code inside the subframe can use exactly the same permissions.

Contribution of this Paper. In this paper, we make the following contributions: (1) We systematically study the "bridges" that expose mobile resources to JavaScript in order to support HTML5-based mobile apps. Based on the emerging threats that we have identified, we point out that most mobile systems' access controls support for HTML5-based mobile applications is not sufficient, because the assumptions that are true for native mobile applications may not be true anymore for HTML5-based applications. (2) We propose a fine-grained access control model for Android, which can provide a solid trusted computing base for HTML5-based applications. We have implemented it in Android.

In the rest of this paper, we first conduct an in-depth analysis of the access control for HTML5-based applications (Sect. 2). Then we present the design of a fine-grained access control system (Sect. 3). We have implemented our design in Android, which involves the modification of the operating system code and the WebKit engine. We use a comprehensive evaluation to demonstrate the effectiveness and the efficiency of our design (Sect. 4).

2   The Problem

To support HTML5-based mobile applications, bridges need to be provided, so JavaScript code inside web container can access the system resources, which were originally blocked by the sandbox of web container. There are two typical approaches. One is used by Firefox OS and Tizen OS, which natively supports HTML5-based applications; we call it the *Native-API approach*. The second approach is used by the PhoneGap middleware and alike in Android and iOS; we call it the *Middleware approach*. (More details can be found in full version [10] for these two approaches.)

2.1   Security Problems

Android does not provide a system-level access control to protect the invocation from JavaScript to Java, whether the invocation is indirect or direct. It is application's or middleware's responsibility to enforce the access control. For the indirect approach, the job is easier, as there is a single entry point, i.e., the event handler; this place can be used for access control. Unfortunately, for the direct approach using addJavascriptInterface, implementing access control inside applications and middleware is problematic due to the following reasons.

First, when applications attach a Java object to WebView, it can perform access control based on the origin of the page inside WebView (typically using a whitelist, like what PhoneGap does), but once the object is attached, there is no more access control when the object's APIs are invoked, unlike the onJsPrompt() approach, which can conduct access control on every invocation. This is not a problem if the contents inside WebView all come from the same origin. Unfortunately, when a Java object is attached to WebView, it is attached to all the frames inside WebView, such as iframes. These frames are not subject to the whitelist checking at the attaching time (only the main frame is subject to that access control); namely, even if their URLs are not on the whitelist, they can still be loaded into iframes. The assumption behind this decision is that if we trust a web page, we should trust all the frames it contains; this is a wrong assumption.

Second, once a Java object is attached to WebView, there is no further restriction on what permissions an invocation can have. Currently, the invocation has all the application's permissions, even though it is potentially triggered by untrusted code. Clearly, there is a lack of granularity. There is no easy way for applications to restrict what permissions an invocation can have, because the permissions used by an invocation are not clear during the invocation time. For example, when a Java API is invoked by JavaScript, it is not easy to know whether the API will lead to the use of camera or not.

2.2 Our Approach

We believe that the current access control systems for Android and PhoneGap are not appropriate for supporting HTML5-based mobile applications. If the situation is not improved, the problem will get worse, because more and more developers are going to switch to developing HTML5-based applications. This calls for a research to study what kind of access control system is adequate for this emerging type of mobile applications. The solution should have the following properties:

- The solution should be built into Android, not PhoneGap. This is because PhoneGap is not the only framework that supports HTML5-based mobile application development. There are several other frameworks, including Rho-Mobile, Appcelerator, MoSync, WidgetPad, etc. A solution at the OS level can benefit all these frameworks.
- We should not give all the application's permissions to every frame inside WebView. Because the page in WebView can embed pages from different origins, it is important for the system to distinguish between the accesses initiated by untrusted origins from those by trusted ones, and give them different permissions.

3   Design

3.1   Access Control Model

The fundamental problem of WebView is that when JavaScript code invokes Java code through the bridge on the web container, there is no isolation of privileges, so all the invocations from the bridge have the same privileges. In Android, this means all the invocations have the same permissions that are assigned to the application. A good access control system should be able to grant different permissions to different invocations, depending on where the invocations are initiated. Inside WebView, contents from multiple origins can co-exist, because each page inside WebView can have frames (such as iframes), which can contain pages from different URLs, some are more trustworthy than the others. Thus, different frames should be granted with different permissions.

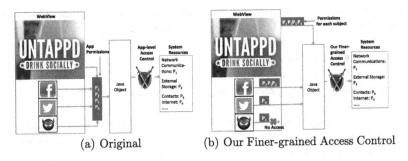

(a) Original   (b) Our Finer-grained Access Control

Fig. 1. Access control in the original Android and our proposed model

We propose an access control model that allows developers to assign different permissions to different frames. We use an example to illustrate our model. Figure 1(a) illustrates the original access control model in Android, and our model is illustrated in Fig. 1(b). In both figures, The main frame is called "UNTAPPD", and it has three iframe pages: Facebook, Twitter, and a page from an untrusted origin. The application has four permissions, $P_1, \ldots, P_4$. In Fig. 1(a), we can see that all the iframes have these four permissions. In Fig. 1(b), through the configuration provided by the developer, different sets of permissions are given to different frames, based on the requirement of the web pages and how much developers trust them. We can even prohibit an untrusted page from invoking any Java API from its frame.

3.2   Policy Configuration

We provide two ways for developers to assign permissions. First, developers can assign permissions directly to each frame (in the HTML file), and this kind of permissions is called *frame permissions* (denoted by P_{frame}). Second, developers can also assign permissions to origins (in the manifest file), and these permissions are called *origin permissions* (denoted by P_{origin}). We also use P_{app} to represent the permission assigned to the entire application. The effective permissions ($P_{effective}$) for each frame is the intersection of these three types of permissions:

$$P_{effective} = P_{app} \bigcap P_{frame} \bigcap P_{origin} \qquad (1)$$

It should be noted that P_{origin} can change, so every time the origin inside a frame changes, a new $P_{effective}$ will be calculated for this frame. The definition of "origin" in our model is the same as the "origin" in the Same-Origin Policy, i.e., it is the unique combinations of three elements: port, scheme, and domain. Developers can specify frame permissions using the permissions attribute for frames in HTML code:

```
<iframe permissions="READ_CONTACTS" src="http://www.untappd.com"/>
```

Or developers can configure origin permissions in the manifest file:

```
<access origin=http://*.untappd.com>
    <origin-permission android:name="ACCESS_NETWORK_STATE"/>
    <origin-permission android:name="READ_EXTERNAL_STORAGE"/>
    <origin-permission android:name="WRITE_EXTERNAL_STORAGE"/>
    <origin-permission android:name="READ_CONTACTS"/>
</access>
```

(More details of permission assignment can be found in full version [10].)

3.3   Assigning Effective Permission to Frame

As we have discussed above, our security policies are specified in two places: in HTML pages (for frame permissions) and in the manifest file (for origin permissions). To read the permission information, we extend the existing manifest file parser and the HTML parser (in Webkit) to retrieve the permission information from these two places. The origin permissions will be stored in the same place where Android stores permissions for each application. The frame permission is stored as an attribute of the frame object in the DOM tree. Using Eq. (1), we can calculate the effective permission of a frame.

Every time a page is loaded into a frame, an object called SecurityOrigin is created, and this object is used by browsers to enforce the same-origin policy, so JavaScript code from one origin cannot access the resources belonging to other origins. There is one SecurityOrigin object per frame. We store the frame's effective permission in this object. Every time a new page is loaded into a frame, the effective permissions will be recalculated, and the corresponding values in SecurityOrigin will be updated accordingly.

3.4   Setting Effective Permission at Invocation

Setting the effective permissions for each frame is not enough, we need to ensure that when JavaScript inside a frame invokes a Java API through the bridge, the

API is executed only with the frame's effective permissions, not the application's permissions. To achieve this goal, we need to understand how JavaScript invokes a Java API in Android; we need to intercept this invocation, and set the effective permissions before the API code starts running.

As we have discussed before, there are two ways for JavaScript in WebView to invoke Java code: indirect invocation and direct invocation. The indirect invocation is quite straightforward, and easy to be intercepted. The direct invocation, i.e., through the APIs attached by addJavascriptInterface(), is quite complicated. In the following, we only focus on the direct invocation method.

How JavaScript Invokes Java code. In browsers, it is often necessary to allow JavaScript to interact with browser plugins, such as Flash, PDF reader, Java Applet, etc. A de facto standard for such an interaction was initially developed for Netscape, but was subsequently implemented by many other browsers [4]. It is called Netscape Plugin Application Programming Interface (NPAPI) [4], which provides a cross-platform plugin architecture for browsers. It allows JavaScript within a browser to access the APIs of plugins, and vice versa. In Android, from the WebView's perspective, Java is treated just as a plugin, and invocation of Java code from JavaScript follows the NPAPI standard.

To explain how NPAPI works, we use an example, which is depicted in Fig. 2(a). In this example, there is a Java class called ClassFoo, and an instance of this class called javaFoo. This instance is bound to WebView through addJavascriptInterface(), resulting in a new JavaScript object called jsFoo in WebView. When the JavaScript code in WebView invokes jsFoo.bar(), a series of actions will be performed, leading to the eventual invocation of the bar method of the Java object javaFoo.

Figure 2(b) shows how the APIs of plugins (Java object, C# object, etc.) are provided to JavaScript. (More detail explanation is provided in full version [10].)

From Fig. 2(b), we can see that there are several places where we can intercept the invocation. We choose the place between V8Object and NPObject, because at this point, it is easier to get the frame information. Moreover, this design does not depend on the types of plugins, so it also works if the plugins are not Java, but C# or Flash, etc.

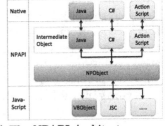

(a) How JavaScript invokes a Java API   (b) The NPAPI Architecture

Fig. 2. JavaScript-Java Communication

3.5   Checking Effective Permissions

We extend Android's existing *Reference Monitor* to check the effective permissions when an application tries to access protected resources, such as external storage, camera, contact, etc. (More details can be found in full version [10])

4   Evaluation

In this section, we evaluate our work on two aspects: effectiveness and performance. First, we use different cases to show how our work can be effectively used to isolate the privilege of web components at the frame level. Then, we evaluate the overhead caused by our work.

4.1   Restrict Permissions of Untrusted Frames

In this experiment, we show how our work can achieve privilege isolation for frames. In all our experiments, we assume that the INTERNET permission is granted. We use a PhoneGap application called HealthTap, which is a very popular app with more than one million downloads. We added several contact entries into the phone, one of which is Alice, with phone number and email address. We will use this information in our demonstration. HealthTap requires 13 permissions. Several permissions are related to mobile system resources. Once granted, all the frames in this app can access the corresponding mobile system resources, using the app's full privilege, through the bridge attached by PhoneGap. With our work, we can easily limit the privileges of the frames without affecting the original application. We achieve that by setting the origin permissions and/or frame permissions.

To show how our work can limit the privileges of frames, we need to slightly change the app. We first use Apktool to disassemble the application APK file; then we add an iframe into the original app's webpage; finally we repackage the APK file with the modified manifest file and sign it with our key. Now we can demonstrate how to limit the privileges of iframes.

Social Network Plugin. Developers often include social network plugins, such as the Facebook "Like" button, in their applications to attract more users, and iframes is widely used to load social network plugins. In this evaluation, we load a Facebook "Like" button into an iframe of the HealthTap app (see Fig. 3(a)). Since we know that these kinds of social network plugins do not need to require mobile system resources, we should not give this iframe any permission. We can give this frame an empty permission list:

```
<iframe src="http://www.facebook.com/plugins/like.php?href=https
%3A%2F%2Fwww.facebook.com%2FHealthTap&amp;&amp;" permissions="">
</iframe>
```

From Fig. 3(b), we can see that in the mainframe we can still get Alice's email address. But if attackers try to get the contacts in the iframe, a "Permission Denial" exception will be thrown (see Fig. 3(c)). This is because the frame

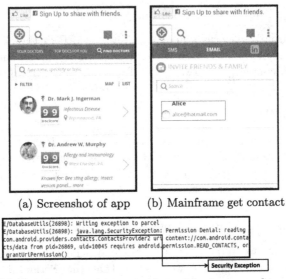

(a) Screenshot of app   (b) Mainframe get contact

(c) Security exception caused by not having enough permission to read contact

(d) Cannot find Java object

Fig. 3. App with Social Network Plugin

permission of this iframe is empty, i.e., it can invoke Java APIs, but will not be able to have any permission during the execution. In this situation, we can see that although the app has the READ_CONTACTS permission, the iframe that loads the Facebook plugin does not have the permission.

Sometimes, if the social network plugin is a faked one, not from Facebook, it will fail if it tries to invoke Java APIs. As Fig. 3(d) shows, the API cannot be found. This is because the origin is not in the origin permissions list, which means this origin is not trusted, and the JavaScript code from this origin cannot invoke any Java API through the WebView bridges. (More evaluation experiments are provided in full version [10].)

4.2   Performance Evaluation

Our environment is set up as the following: we use Jelly Bean (*android-4.2.1_r2*), and we run our modified Android in Unbuntu 11.04 using an emulator. The configuration for the emulator is the following: Nexus One (3.7, 480*720: hdpi), RAM (2 GB), VM Heap (32 MB), Internal Storage (200 MB), and No SDCard. The hosting machine is Intel Core i7–3540 M @ 3.00 GHZ, with 8 GB memory.

For system overhead, all overheads are below 1 %. For application overhead, loading overhead is about is about 5.6 % to 8.2 %, depending on the number of URLs in the list; invocation overhead is about 4.9 % to 8.2 %. (See full version [10] for details of performance evaluation results.)

5 Related Work

The problems with the `addJavascriptInterface` in WebView were initially identified by Luo et al. [12].

Privilege Separation and Isolation in Web. A large number of works have been proposed to limit the privilege of JavaScript in web applications: The sandbox attribute of iframe [7] allows developers to decide whether to allow JavaScript to execute or not. Maffeis et al. [13,14] propose a language-based approach to filter and rewrite untrusted JavaScript. Similarly, Caja [1] and ADsafe [8] use a safe subset of JavaScript, and they eliminate dangerous DOM APIs such as `eval` and `document.write`, which could allow advertisements to take control of the entire webpage. A representative work of the holistic approach is the Escudo work [9]: Escudo proposes a ring-based access control model for web browsers.

Privilege Separation and Isolation in Android. Advertisements are critical third-party components of mobile applications, and they have the same privileges as the hosting app. Several works attempt to address this problem by separating advertisements' privileges from the apps: AdSplit [16] isolates the advertisement into a separate process so that ads will have a separate set of permissions; Leontiadis et al. [11] also use a separate application to host the advertisement with IPC to support communications with the app. AdDroid [15] provides its own advertisement SDK and ads-specific permissions aiming at protecting user privacy.

6 Summary

In this paper, we study the potential security problems of the HTML5-based applications in mobile systems. We have identified the insufficiency of the access control in the existing platforms. We propose a fine-grained access control mechanism to support HTML5-based applications in Android platform. In our access control, we define a frame-based and origin-based policy to separate subjects within the same application. We enforce our access control in the operating system, so developers of the HTML5-based applications only need to configure their security policies, without worrying about implementing the enforcement by themselves. Our implementation only requires light-weight code modification of the original Android system, and poses only small overhead. The evaluation demonstrates that our access control prototype can effectively separate privileges for different principles within the same app.

References

1. Caja. http://code.google.com/p/google-caja/
2. The future of mobile development: Html5 vs. native apps. http://www.businessinsider.com/html5-vs-native-apps-for-mobile-2013-4?op=1/
3. Html5 vs native: The mobile app debate. http://www.html5rocks.com/en/mobile/nativedebate/
4. Npapi. http://en.wikipedia.org/wiki/NPAPI/
5. Phonegap best and free cross-platform mobile app framework. http://crossplatformappmart.blogspot.com/2013/03/phonegap-best-free-cross-platform.html
6. The shared future of html5 and native apps. http://itbusinessedge.com/blogs/data-and-telecom/the-shared-future-of-html5-and-native-apps.html/
7. Html5 sandbox attribute. http://www.whatwg.org/specs/web-apps/current-work/#attr-iframe-sandbox, 2010
8. Crockford, D.: ADSafe. http://www.adsafe.org
9. Jayaraman, K., Du, W., Rajagopalan, B., Chapin, S.J.: Escudo: a fine-grained protection model for web browsers. In: Proceedings of the 2010 IEEE 30th International Conference on Distributed Computing Systems, ICDCS 2010, pp. 231–240. IEEE Computer Society, Washington, DC (2010)
10. Jin, X., Wang, L., Luo, T., Du, W.: Fine-grained access control for html5-based mobile applications in android. http://www.cis.syr.edu/wedu/Research/paper/phonegap_isc2013.pdf
11. Leontiadis, I., Efstratiou, C., Picone, M., Mascolo, C.: Don't kill my ads!: balancing privacy in an ad-supported mobile application market. In: Proceedings of the Twelfth Workshop on Mobile Computing Systems and Applications, HotMobile 2012, pp. 2:1–2:6. ACM, New York (2012)
12. Luo, T., Hao Hao, Du, W., Wang, Y., Yin, H.: Attacks on webview in the android system. In: Proceedings of the 27th Annual Computer Security Applications Conference, ACSAC 2011, pp. 343–352. ACM, New York (2011)
13. Maffeis, S., Mitchell, J.C., Taly, A.: Isolating JavaScript with Filters, Rewriting, and Wrappers. In: Backes, M., Ning, P. (eds.) ESORICS 2009. LNCS, vol. 5789, pp. 505–522. Springer, Heidelberg (2009)
14. Maffeis, S., Taly, A.: Language-based isolation of untrusted javascript. In: Proceedings of the 2009 22nd IEEE Computer Security Foundations Symposium, CSF 2009, pp. 77–91. IEEE Computer Society, Washington, DC (2009)
15. Paul, P., Adrienne, P.F., Nunez, G., Wagner, D.: AdDroid: Privilege separation for applications and advertisers in android. In: Proceedings of the 7th ACM Symposium on Information, Computer and Communications Security, AsiaCCS 2012 (2012)
16. Shekhar, S., Dietz, M., Wallach, D.S.: AdSplit: separating smartphone advertising from applications. In: Proceedings of the 21st USENIX conference on Security symposium, USENIX Security 2012, p. 28. USENIX Association, Berkeley (2012)

Computer Security

CrowdFlow: Efficient Information Flow Security

Christoph Kerschbaumer[✉], Éric Hennigan, Per Larsen, Stefan Brunthaler,
and Michael Franz

University of California, Irvine, USA
{ckerschb,eric.hennigan,perl,s.brunthaler,franz}@uci.edu

Abstract. The widespread use of JavaScript (JS) as the dominant web programming language opens the door to attacks such as Cross Site Scripting that steal sensitive information from users. Information flow tracking successfully addresses current browser security shortcomings, but current implementations incur a significant runtime overhead cost that prevents adoption.

We present a novel approach to information flow security that distributes the tracking workload across all page visitors by probabilistically switching between two JavaScript execution modes. Our framework reports attempts to steal information from a user's browser to a third party that maintains a blacklist of malicious URLs. Participating users can then benefit from receiving warnings about blacklisted URLs, similar to anti-phishing filters.

Our measurements indicate that our approach is both *efficient* and *effective*. First, our technique is efficient because it reduces performance impact by an order of magnitude. Second, our system is effective, i.e., it detects 99.45 % of all information flow violations on the Alexa Top 500 pages using a conservative 5 % sampling rate. Most sites need fewer samples in practice; and will therefore incur even less overhead.

1 Motivation

Modern web pages have become complex web applications that mash up scripts from different origins inside a single execution context in a user's browser. Unfortunately, this execution scheme opens the door for attackers, too. Vulnerability studies consistently rank Cross Site Scripting (XSS) highest in the list of the most prevalent type of attacks on web applications [1–3]. Attackers use XSS to gain access to confidential user information. A recent study on privacy violating flows confirms the ubiquity of user data theft when browsing the web [4].

Previous work on browser security shows that information flow tracking can counter such attacks [5–9]. Even though information flow tracking prevents misappropriation of sensitive data, all known approaches introduce runtime overheads that make execution of JS code at least two to three times slower. We believe that industry will never adopt the information flow approach without a substantial reduction in this overhead.

Taint tracking is a more efficiently implementable subset of information flow tracking; for example, TaintDroid [10] reports an overhead of just 14 %. Information flow tracking increases security by tracking both data and control flow,

© Springer International Publishing Switzerland 2015
Y. Desmedt (Ed.): ISC 2013, LNCS 7807, pp. 321–337, 2015.
DOI: 10.1007/978-3-319-27659-5_23

but unfortunately no efficient implementation is known for dynamically typed languages such as JS.

Our solution distributes the tracking overhead among a crowd of visitors, leveraging the same property that attackers target: site popularity. The more visitors a site has, the less tracking effort is required by an individual client. To balance precision and performance, our system, CrowdFlow, primarily executes code in a partial taint tracking interpreter and probabilistically switches to a slower information flow tracking interpreter at decision points such as function boundaries.

The probabilistic switching between the two JS interpreters allows individual clients to execute web applications much faster than traditional approaches where every client always performs the costly information flow tracking. Even though the CrowdFlow approach permits individuals to miss detection of specific information flow violations, we show that a crowd of users, in aggregate, detects the majority of information flow violations. Clients report policy violating flows to a trusted third party that collects suspicious information flow reports, similar to commercial blacklisting initiatives like Google's *Safe Browsing* [11] or Microsoft's *Smartscreen-Filter* [12].

Currently, corporations hosting URL blacklist services populate the database at their own expense, through automated scanning that tends to miss real-world use of web applications by logged-in users. These services also provide a form through which end-users can submit a malicious URL for investigation, but this collection mechanism tends to catch code that causes user-level annoyance rather than surreptitious and silent data theft. Additionally, website operators in adversarial competition submit false allegations in an attempt to put competing websites on the blacklist.

We believe that automating the reporting process on the client side and basing it on privacy-violating information flow results in three benefits. First, automated reporting increases the amount of data that these systems have, enabling them to improve report validation. Second, automated reporting reduces the number of false allegations by raising the bar on the level of detail a report contains. Third, automated reporting tracks into the deep web, inspecting application behavior after a user has logged in. CrowdFlow, with its low per-user overhead, is a perfect front-end for these systems.

We provide background information on JS security (Sect. 2) that motivates the development of CrowdFlow, define the threat model our system defends against (Sect. 3) and make the following contributions:

- We introduce CrowdFlow (Sect. 4), a novel approach to information flow tracking that switches between two JS interpreters to balance performance and security. This architecture distributes the tracking costs across a crowd of visitors to a page.
- We present a comprehensive information flow tracking browser (Sect. 5) based on WebKit [13] and provide implementation details for both partial taint tracking and information flow tracking modes.

- We evaluate our system on a variety of real-world websites. In particular, we demonstrate the practicality of our framework (Sect. 6) by showing that our system satisfies the following important properties:
  - **Efficiency:** CrowdFlow executes JS an order of magnitude faster than traditional approaches for information flow tracking, with an average runtime overhead of 27.84 % for SunSpider [14] and 32.05 % for V8 [15] benchmarks. To compare, execution overhead of traditional information flow implementations ranges between 200 % and 300 %.
  - **Effectiveness:** Our approach finds almost all (99.45 %) information flow violations on the Alexa Top 500 [16] web sites compared to a traditional information flow tracking system. We achieve this detection rate with a crowd of only five users, and a conservative function invocation sampling rate of 5 %.

2   Background on JS Security

XSS is a code injection attack that allows an adversary to execute code without the user's knowledge and consent. For example, XSS allows attackers to harvest sensitive information such as keystrokes, authentication credentials and credit card numbers. A malicious script can even traverse the Document Object Model (DOM) [17] and steal all visible data on a compromised web page [18].

Web developers often include third-party functionality such as jQuery, Google Analytics, and Facebook APIs to enrich a user's browsing experience. Recent work by Nikiforakis et al. [19] highlights the problematic situation of granting third-party scripts access to application internals and shows the potential of included code to perform malicious actions without attracting attention from either developers or end users.

Currently, browsers rely on the Same Origin Policy (SOP) [20], and the Content Security Policy (CSP) [21] to limit a script's access to information. The CSP allows page authors to whitelist trusted sources and the SOP prevents access for scripts of different origins when properly isolated with `iframe`-tags. However, neither policy can prevent JS from stealing information on a page when developers include multiple libraries in the same execution context, as currently practiced [19].

3   Threat Model

Throughout this paper we assume that attackers have the following abilities: (i) attackers can operate their own hosts, and (ii) can inject code into other web pages. Code injection into other pages relies either on exploiting a XSS vulnerability of a page, or the ability to provide content for mashups, advertisements, libraries, etc., that victim sites include. The attacker's capabilities, however, are limited to JS and the attacker can neither intercept nor control network traffic.

Phishing Campaigns vs. Targeted Attacks: In contrast to common information flow tracking systems, the architecture of CrowdFlow does not attempt to prevent information theft attacks from within the user's browser. Rather, it reports detected information flow violations to a trusted third-party aggregator, such as Google's *Safebrowsing* initiative or Microsoft's *Smartscreen-Filter*. CrowdFlow is not designed to defend against a targeted attack, in which the attacker tries to steal information of one particular person. The architecture of CrowdFlow aims to protect the majority of users against phishing campaigns, where the attacker distributes exploit code to high-traffic web pages to gather as much information as possible.

Threat Examples CrowdFlow Defends Against: To steal information from a browser, malicious code must surreptitiously communicate it to an attacker-controlled server. For example, by placing an image on the page, the attacker can steal sensitive information through the target URL of an image request:

```
1 elem.src = "evil.com/p.png?v=" + creditcard_number;
```

The GET request for the image p.png acts as a channel through which the attacker steals the user's credit card number as a query parameter of the target URL. The attacker-controlled server records the image request, including the stolen data, in its logs.

4   CrowdFlow

The design of traditional JS information flow tracking systems requires every client to track all information flows [5–9]. In contrast, CrowdFlow implements a probabilistic approach, where each user only spends a fraction of the execution time in the slower information flow tracking interpreter, thus paying only a fraction of the performance cost. Following the distributed system design of the Internet itself, CrowdFlow distributes the security analysis across a crowd of visitors, aggregates the flow reports at a trusted third party, and shares findings back to users, warning them of potentially malicious pages.

4.1   Probabilistic Tracking

The CrowdFlow browser primarily executes in a partial taint tracking interpreter (state PTT in Fig. 1) that propagates labels only across direct assignments (a = b;).

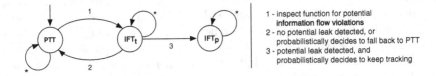

Fig. 1. Execution states in CrowdFlow. PTT - Partial Taint Tracking, IFT$_t$ - Information Flow Tracking (trial), IFT$_p$ - Information Flow Tracking (permanent).

CrowdFlow has a configurable *sampling rate*, that controls the switch from state PTT to the *trial* information flow tracking interpreter (state IFT) at every function invocation. Both IFT modes propagate every operation's dependence on control-flow predicates (see Sect. 5.2), preventing malicious code from using inference of control-flow branches to circumvent the partial taint tracking. When executing in IFT$_t$ mode, CrowdFlow watches for operations that involve the mixing of data from multiple domains, as this occurrence indicates a potential information flow violation.

Definition of a Potential Information Flow Violation: *We define a potential information flow violation as the result of two domains influencing a value.*

For example, assume variable a originates from domain A and variable b originates from domain B, then b += a; constitutes a potential information flow violation because data from both domains A and B influence the resulting value of variable b. When malicious code attempts to steal data from a page, the copy or encoding operations involved follow this definition and CrowdFlow detects the confluence of values from multiple domains.

When no potential violation occurs in the *trial* information flow tracking mode (IFT$_t$ state), the browser returns to the PTT state at the end of the function invocation. But if the CrowdFlow browser detects a potential violation while operating in IFT$_t$, it probabilistically switches to the *permanent* information flow tracking interpreter (state IFT$_p$). The probability of transferring to state IFT$_p$ and continue tracking the potential information flow violation is also configurable. From here on, information flow tracking occurs not only intra-procedurally but also inter-procedurally, preventing malicious code from gaming the system by splitting the information theft attack across several functions.

4.2 Tracking Multiple Domains

Our system tracks the flow of information throughout program execution by applying a label to every program value. These labels take the form of a bit-vector that encodes information about a program's origin (Sect. 5.4). CrowdFlow maintains a registry of all domains represented on a page, mapping a unique bit to each page. When running in information flow tracking mode, CrowdFlow labels each value resulting from an operation with the set union of all domains of all inputs, including implicit inputs such as the predicates of any currently executing branches and the origin of the code itself.

4.3 Reporting Information Flows

CrowdFlow tracks flows of information not only in the JS engine, but also across scripting-exposed browser subsystems, including the DOM and user-generated events. During execution, CrowdFlow monitors network traffic for information leaks.

Definition of an Information Leak: We define an information leak as the inequality of domains between a network data payload and the target.

When the label of the payload indicates that the data has been influenced by any origin other than the destination domain, the network request represents a communication to a foreign party, possibly an attacker-controlled server. Crowd-Flow detects the attempt and reports the source domains involved in the leak and the target URL to a commercial blacklisting initiative. We use the defined *Example Threat* from our Threat Model, as the running example to explain how CrowdFlow detects such an information leak.

```
1 var url = "http://evil.com/p.png?v=" + creditcard_number;
2 img_elem.src = url;
```

Using a XSS vulnerability the attacker injects the example code on a page from host bank.com. When loading the page, the CrowdFlow browser maps the host URL bank.com to a unique label bit, say 0001. Because this snippet appears within the page, it has access to all the host page's application content.

To steal information, the malicious code appends the sensitive information stored in host variable creditcard_number as part of the target query-string for an image request (line 1). Setting the source attribute of an image element on the host page causes the browser to issue a GET request to evil.com. CrowdFlow registers the new domain with another unique label bit, 0010. Before emitting the request on the network, CrowdFlow inspects the label on the payload (0001) and finds that it differs from the target (0010), triggering an information flow violation report.

Note that the same code, even when dynamically loaded from evil.com, also triggers a flow report. In this case, the malicious code carries label of evil.com while the host variable creditcard_number still carries the label of bank.com. As a result of CrowdFlow's label propagation rules, the computed url payload carries the join of these domains (0011), which differs from the target domain (0010).

5   Implementation

A single web page can incorporate data from several different domains. Within the JS engine, data and objects originating from different domains (security principals) may interact, creating values that derive from more than one domain. To model this behavior, we take inspiration from Myers' decentralized label model [22] and represent security labels as a lattice join over domains. Internally, the CrowdFlow browser associates each domain with a unique marker and implements joins as a set union over domains.

5.1   Partial Taint Tracking Interpreter

We implement the CrowdFlow browser by modifying WebKit, which ships with a register-based direct-threaded JS interpreter (JavaScriptCore), so that all values carry a label indicating the domains that influenced its construction.

The partial taint tracking interpreter operates on tainted data and efficiently propagates labels for direct assignments due to our label encoding: Because the label resides in the virtual machine level representation of a JS value, a direct assignment from one variable to another also carries that label, without additional computation logic.

```
1  var pub = secret;
```

This assignment shows that the content of **pub** depends directly on the value of the secret variable **secret**. If the variable **pub** is publicly observable, then the secret variable **secret** explicitly leaks through this flow of information. After the assignment, variable **pub** not only has the value of variable **secret**, but it also carries the label of variable **secret**, since the assignment is a full copy of the variable contents. Again, the partial taint tracking interpreter propagates labels only for direct assignments.

5.2   Information Flow Tracking Interpreter

Conventional static analysis techniques for information flow, such as those developed for the Java-based Jif [23], are not directly applicable to dynamically typed languages, such as JS. However, we adapt these techniques by introducing a *control-flow stack* that manages labels for different regions of a running program, which is a common technique for securing programs [5,9]. At runtime, CrowdFlow updates the label on top of this stack at every control-flow branch and join within a program, to model entry and exit points for secure regions of a program. The top of the control-flow stack always contains the current security label of the current *program counter*, which carries the set join of predicates in all enclosing branches.

Tracking Data Flow: The following accumulation operator shows the content of variable **secret** adding or concatenating with the public variable **pub**.

```
1  pub += secret;
```

This code snippet illustrates how CrowdFlow can stop a specific data theft attempt. An attacker gathers sensitive information on a web page, but before the attacker can steal that information by sending it back to a server under his control, he needs to concatenate the sensitive payload to the query-string of the request. The information flow tracking interpreter tracks the operation by joining the labels of the operands of the addition/concatenation together with the label of the current program counter.

Tracking Control Flow: The following code snippet shows an implicit *direct* information flow [24] which occurs when a control-flow branch predicate influences a value.

```
1  var pub = undefined;
2  if (secret)
3      pub = true;
```

As illustrated, the script code steals a secret variable `secret` using such an implicit direct information flow. An attacker can gain information about the secret variable by inspecting the value of the variable `pub` after execution of the `if` statement. The handling of implicit direct information flows therefore requires joining the label of the variable `pub` with the label of the current program region. The CrowdFlow information flow tracking interpreter propagates implicit direct information flows by updating the label of the current program counter to reflect its dependence on the variable `secret`. At the assignment (line 3), the variable `pub` becomes tainted with the label of `secret` by virtue of joining with the current program counter.

The efficient handling of implicit *indirect* information flows [24], where information can be inferred by inspecting values in the non-executed path, still remains an open research question. Our implementation can not track such implicit indirect information flows. The browser information flow system presented by Vogt et al. [5] for example, jumps to a conservative secure mode if their static analysis detects a function call or use `eval` in the non-executed branch. CrowdFlow does not implement this technique because it steadily elevates labels on all values and objects, leading to a phenomenon known as *label creep* [25].

5.3   Switching Interpreters

The naive way to implement our technique adds a condition to each interpreter instruction checking whether to perform the operation in partial taint tracking or information flow tracking mode. Our modifications to WebKit achieve the same effect more efficiently by duplicating the set of interpreter instructions to obtain an information flow tracking instruction set in addition to the existing instruction set. We make efficient use of WebKit's direct-threaded JS interpreter by duplicating opcodes and providing an information flow tracking equivalent implementation of every opcode.

For example, the opcode `op_add` now also has an information flow tracking equivalent `op_ift_add`. Our framework uses abstract interpretation to lazily replace opcodes with information flow tracking opcodes the first time a function is chosen to be executed using the information flow tracking interpreter. Having two instruction streams allows fast and easy switching between the partial taint tracking and the information flow tracking interpreter by directing the interpreter's instruction pointer to either the original or our modified information flow tracking instruction stream at function entry.

5.4   Multi-domain Label Encoding

We implement security labeling by repurposing the memory layout of `JSValues`, the virtual machine level representation of a JS value in WebKit. This modification of bits inside `JSValues` allows for low overhead encoding of a 16-bit label within the 64-bit word size indicating the origin.

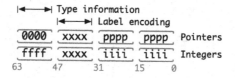

Fig. 2. Label encoding using bits 32–47 in JSValues.

Pointers/Immediates: JSValues starting with the highest 16 bits all set to zero (see Fig. 2), indicate a pointer or immediate type. Pointers have alignment that forces the lowest four bits to be zero. This encoding allows WebKit to efficiently distinguish real pointers from immediate values which are all encoded in the lowest four bits: null:0x02, false:0x06, true:0x07, undefined:0x0a.

The actual address of a pointer in WebKit uses 48 bits (bits 0–47). This design unfortunately does not leave any space to directly encode a label for pointers within JSValues. To encode a label, we repurpose bits and change the current encoding of pointers. We use mmap with the 32_BIT flag, to force memory allocations to be within the 32 bit address space, freeing up 16 bits (bits 32–47) in the pointer address space. Using these 16 bits allows us to encode up to 16 different domains in a label (marked as xxxx).

Kerschbaumer et al. [9] show that web pages, on average, include content from 12 different domains. They also provide a technique for overcoming the space limitation for encoding domains in values by reserving the highest bit as an overflow flag, indicating that the page includes content from more domains than the available encoding space, where the lower bits become an index into an array. Furthermore, this design of encoding labels allows us to use efficient bit arithmetic for label join operations that propagate labels within the browser and equality operations that detect information leaks at network requests.

Integers/Doubles: Values starting with the highest 16 bits all set to one indicate an integer type. The ECMAScript specification [26] defines JS integers to be 31-bit. To encode security labels in integers we can also make use of the bits 32–47, which are unused, even in the original WebKit encoding of JSValues.

WebKit's encoding reserves all other values (highest 16 bits between 0x0001 and 0xfffe) for doubles. Since doubles in JS follow the double-precision 64 bit format, there are no bits left for tagging JSValue doubles. Therefore we conservatively label doubles by using the highest currently available security label in the lattice (i.e., the join of all registered domains).

6 Evaluation

6.1 Security (Effectiveness)

To measure how well CrowdFlow matches the capabilities of a traditional information flow tracking system, we simulate a crowd of users with a web crawler that automatically visits the Alexa Top 500 web pages and stays on each web

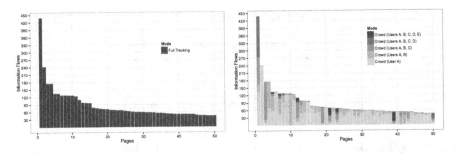

Fig. 3. Reported information flow violations for the 50 pages that trigger the most warnings when visiting the Alexa Top 500 pages. One user executing the information flow tracking interpreter vs. a crowd of up to 5 users using CrowdFlow.

page for 60 s. The crawler simulates user interaction by filling out and submitting the first available HTML-form on each visited page.

Full (Baseline) Information Flow Tracking: To establish a baseline against which to compare CrowdFlow we arrange for the crawler to run in permanent information flow tracking mode (state IFT_p in Fig. 1). This experiment detected information flows across domain boundaries on 433 of the Alexa Top 500 pages. The crawler detected a total of 8,764 such flows which are sent to a total of 1,384 distinct domains on the Internet. Together, the Alexa Top 500 pages use a total of 391,930 different JS functions (as of 2012/12/24) which are invoked 13.5 million times in total.

CrowdFlow: To show that the detection rate provided by CrowdFlow converges with that of traditional information flow tracking systems, we revisit the Alexa Top 500 pages using CrowdFlow and compare the results against the baseline. To evaluate this claim we set CrowdFlow's sampling rate at 5 %. For popular sites, this setting "oversamples" given the number of visitors seen in practice. However, we chose this rate because it allows evaluation of CrowdFlow with a small, crawler-simulated crowd of five users.

Figure 3 (left) shows the 50 pages that have the most information flow violations, reported by one browser using a traditional information flow tracking system. We sort and normalize pages based on the number of detected information flow violations. For illustration purposes, we only show 50 pages in the plot, but discuss our findings for all of the Alexa Top 500 pages. Figure 3 (left) shows a total of 4,359 detected information flow violations as reported by our baseline. On all of the Alexa Top 500 pages combined, our framework detects a total of 8,764 information flows.

Figure 3 (right) shows the detected information flows by five CrowdFlow clients when revisiting the 50 pages having the most information flows on the Alexa Top 500 pages. Due to randomized sampling, user A does not detect all information flow violations present in the baseline. User A detects and reports a total of 5,480 (58,77 % in Fig. 3) information flow violations when browsing the Alexa Top 500 pages. In addition to the flows found and reported by User A,

User B reports 1,957 (23.49 % in Fig. 3) new information flow violations. User C finds an additional 903 (13.81 %) information flows and User D finds a further 173 (1.33 %) information flows. Finally, User E detects 203 (2.54 %) information flows not previously discovered by either User A, B, C, or D.

In total, the crawler-simulated crowd of five visitors found 8,716 information flows out of 8,764 (4,357 out of 4,359 in Fig. 3) reported by a traditional information flow tracking system, which represents a detection rate of 99.45 %.

6.2 Performance (Efficiency)

To evaluate how CrowdFlow reduces the performance penalty of information flow tracking within browsers, we modified WebKit version 1.4.2. We execute all benchmarks on a dual Quad Core Intel Xeon E5462 2.80 GHz with 9.8 GB RAM running Ubuntu 11.10 (kernel 3.2.0) where we use `nice -n -20` to minimize operating system scheduler effects. For evaluating the performance impact of our framework, we measure performance using the SunSpider [14] and the V8 [15] benchmark suites. Both are frequently used to evaluate JS security and therefore facilitate comparison to related work.

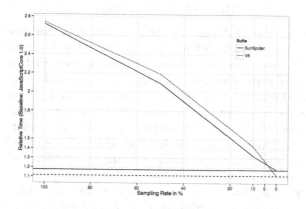

Fig. 4. Performance impact of CrowdFlow.

Figure 4 shows that CrowdFlow's performance is directly proportional to the sampling rate it uses. With a 100 % sampling rate, CrowdFlow performs similar to other information flow tracking systems, i.e., showing a slowdown by about 2.7×, or 170 % when normalized to WebKit's original JS interpreter, `JavaScriptCore`.

Using our conservative setting of five percent sampling rate reduces this overhead by 5×, down to about 30 % overhead compared to `JavaScriptCore`. The lower, horizontal lines show the measured performance of both benchmark suites using only our partial taint tracking interpreter. Interestingly, it shows that for SunSpider we are already close to the lower bound, which is slightly below 20 % overhead. CrowdFlow's performance on V8 shows different results: even though our sampling rate converges to zero percent, using only the partial taint tracking results in almost ten percent further performance improvement.

6.3   Discussion and Limitations

Currently browsers do not support any kind of information flow tracking and provide little security against information theft attacks. Previous information flow tracking systems support only full tracking which severely affects a user's browsing experience. CrowdFlow provides a balanced, flexible approach that trades the guarantee of 100 % information flow tracking in return for improved performance. In aggregate, the CrowdFlow approach captures almost all of the information flows found by the full tracking system, but at a much lower per-user performance cost.

Approach Limitations: Our multi-domain labeling strategy allows our system to clearly identify Content Distribution Networks (CDNs) which modern web pages use for performance reasons to serve content to their users. Before our approach can be adopted, we need a policy that allows web site authors to express allowed information flows, for example, flows within their own CDNs (cf. [27]). For example, a declaration of such a policy in the HTTP header, similar to the approach of Jim et al. [28], is feasible. At the moment, we also leave statistical analysis of the information flow reports up to a third-party aggregator (commercial URL blacklisting service).

Implementation Limitations: Dynamic information flow tracking systems are susceptible to timing channel attacks, and ours is no exception. At this time we are primarily concerned with passive adversaries, those that are not actively trying to subvert our countermeasures. Therefore, we consider this problem out-of-scope and are focused on improving the speed of tracking. Should our system be widely adopted, we expect that attackers will begin to craft code that exploits the randomization mechanism, only leaking data when not running in information flow tracking mode. We can modify CrowdFlow to label results of accesses to the JS built-in Date class, effectively tainting the system clock as proposed by Myers [29] and Zdancewic [30].

A privacy-violating flow report may reveal information about the user who reported it. In the current implementation, CrowdFlow elides all information about the state of the web application and restricts the report contents to contain only the set of source domains and the target domain involved in the privacy-violating flow. To hide information from the URL blacklisting service about who visited what site, we can also incorporate a traffic anonymizing service such as TOR [31].

7   Related Work

Distributed Dataflow Analysis: In 2011, Greathouse et al. [32,33] demonstrate that sampling is a promising approach to optimize the performance of dynamic data flow analysis. They show that a large population, in aggregate, can analyze larger portions of a program than any single user individually running the full analysis of a program.

Information Flow Systems: The survey paper of Sabelfeld and Myers [25] puts the related work in the area of language-based information flow up until 2003 into perspective.

In 2007, Vogt et al. [5] present their implementation of information flow control in the Firefox browser. In 2010, Russo et al. [34] provide a mechanism for tracking information flow within dynamic tree structures. In 2011, Just et al. [7] present their information flow system, improving upon results made by Vogt et al. Finally, in 2012 De Groef et al. [6] describe their implementation of secure-multi-execution [35] in the Firefox browser to give strong information flow security guarantees.

CrowdFlow shares similarities and takes inspirations from all of these systems, e.g., support for multi-domain labeling, comprehensive DOM coverage, and a combination of taint and information flow tracking. However, these past approaches universally follow the all-or-nothing paradigm, forcing every client to perform full information flow tracking. CrowdFlow distinguishes itself by performing full tracking on randomized program subsets, increasing execution speed at the expense of information flow coverage.

There exist many other approaches to secure JavaScript, such as previous work by Hedin and Sabelfeld [36], Austin and Flanagan [8,34,37], Chugh et al. [38], and Nadji et al. [39]. The key differentiator between these approaches and CrowdFlow is practicality. Our system has an efficient implementation and does not require invasive changes to the existing web architecture.

Third-Party Security Systems: In 2011, Canali et al. present a system called Prophiler [40] and Thomas et al. present a system called Monarch [41]. Both approaches describe details of machine learning techniques used to classify malware on the web.

For CrowdFlow, both of these projects (and the commercial blacklisting initiatives mentioned previously) are complimentary because our approach adds efficient and effective information flow tracking as another source of input. For example, the analysis performed by Prophiler or the rich honey-clients used in Monarch can prioritize URLs better with data from CrowdFlow reports.

8   Conclusion

We have presented a modified browser that probabilistically switches between a fast partial taint tracking interpreter and a slower information flow tracking interpreter. The probabilistic approach enables both performant code execution by participating clients and prevention of attacker code from deterministically evading the information flow tracking mechanism. Switching interpreters during execution of a program allows different users to track the flow of information in different subsets of an application, enabling the distribution of tracking costs across the crowd of visitors to a web page.

CrowdFlow can report privacy-violating information flows to a blacklisting URL service. Users benefit from their participation in information flow tracking by receiving warnings about malicious code on a page.

Our results demonstrate that the CrowdFlow system is both: *efficient*, we report slowdowns of around 30 % on two popular JS benchmark suites, and *effective*, finding 99.45 % of information flow violations on the Alexa Top 500 pages using a conservative 5 % function invocation sampling rate (Table 1).

Acknowledgements. This material is based upon work partially supported by the Defense Advanced Research Projects Agency (DARPA) under contract No. D11PC20024, by the National Science Foundation (NSF) under grant No. CCF-1117162, and by a gift from Google.

Any opinions, findings, and conclusions or recommendations expressed in this material are those of the authors and do not necessarily reflect the views of the Defense Advanced Research Projects Agency (DARPA) or its Contracting Agent, the U.S. Department of the Interior, National Business Center, Acquisition Services Directorate, Sierra Vista Branch, the National Science Foundation, or any other agency of the U.S. Government.

Thanks to Michael Bebenita, Stephen Crane, Andrei Homescu, Christopher Horn, Mark Murphy, Mathias Payer, Codrut Stancu, Gregor Wagner, Christian Wimmer, and Wei Zhang for their feedback and insightful comments.

A Detailed Benchmark Results

Table 1. Detailed performance numbers for V8 and Sunspider benchmarks normalized by the JavaScriptCore interpreter.

Benchmark	JSCore (%)	PTT (%)	IFT (%)	Crowd (%)
V8-Total	6691.5 (0.0)	7466.8 (11.59)	18362.1 (174.41)	8835.9 (32.05)
crypto	1846.3 (0.0)	1896.9 (2.74)	5541.4 (200.14)	2133.8 (15.57)
deltablue	1317.7 (0.0)	1504.7 (14.19)	4255.4 (222.94)	1925.9 (46.16)
earley-boyer	425.8 (0.0)	532.2 (24.99)	1467.7 (244.69)	667.6 (56.79)
raytrace	246.7 (0.0)	269.1 (9.08)	513.8 (108.27)	332.6 (34.82)
regexp	901.5 (0.0)	917.3 (1.75)	913.7 (1.35)	904.2 (0.3)
richards	1644.8 (0.0)	2003.0 (21.78)	5088.7 (209.38)	2505.0 (52.3)
splay	308.7 (0.0)	343.6 (11.31)	581.4 (88.34)	366.8 (18.82)
Sunspider-Total	807.6 (0.0)	950.2 (17.66)	2198.0 (172.16)	1032.4 (27.84)
cube	27.8 (0.0)	34.0 (22.3)	90.0 (223.74)	37.5 (34.89)
morph	32.0 (0.0)	36.6 (14.38)	123.0 (284.38)	38.4 (20.0)
raytrace	34.7 (0.0)	38.9 (12.1)	79.7 (129.68)	46.1 (32.85)
binary-trees	10.0 (0.0)	13.2 (32.0)	38.9 (289.0)	16.0 (60.0)
fannkuch	63.8 (0.0)	89.7 (40.6)	225.7 (253.76)	106.3 (66.61)
nbody	28.5 (0.0)	30.7 (7.72)	84.9 (197.89)	33.3 (16.84)
nsieve	14.1 (0.0)	20.0 (41.84)	73.0 (417.73)	23.4 (65.96)

(Continued)

Table 1. (Continued)

Benchmark	JSCore (%)	PTT (%)	IFT (%)	Crowd (%)
3bit-bits-in-byte	22.0 (0.0)	26.9 (22.27)	86.5 (293.18)	30.1 (36.82)
bits-in-byte	22.1 (0.0)	34.1 (54.3)	124.1 (461.54)	40.9 (85.07)
bitwise-and	23.9 (0.0)	36.2 (51.46)	115.7 (384.1)	34.2 (43.1)
nsieve-bits	31.0 (0.0)	38.0 (22.58)	141.2 (355.48)	38.0 (22.58)
recursive	12.0 (0.0)	17.0 (41.67)	70.2 (485.0)	21.6 (80.0)
aes	25.0 (0.0)	29.2 (16.8)	61.0 (144.0)	31.3 (25.2)
md5	15.2 (0.0)	19.1 (25.66)	54.6 (259.21)	22.0 (44.74)
sha1	15.0 (0.0)	18.2 (21.33)	57.3 (282.0)	20.7 (38.0)
format-tofte	21.0 (0.0)	26.0 (23.81)	51.0 (142.86)	28.2 (34.29)
format-xparb	16.5 (0.0)	21.9 (32.73)	33.2 (101.21)	24.7 (49.7)
cordic	32.4 (0.0)	40.6 (25.31)	137.5 (324.38)	48.6 (50.0)
partial-sums	38.6 (0.0)	40.6 (5.18)	74.3 (92.49)	41.2 (6.74)
spectral-norm	21.1 (0.0)	23.9 (13.27)	78.7 (272.99)	27.5 (30.33)
dna	159.5 (0.0)	158.2 (−0.82)	159.5 (0.0)	159.9 (0.25)
base64	20.3 (0.0)	22.8 (12.32)	43.2 (112.81)	23.9 (17.73)
fasta	21.6 (0.0)	28.1 (30.09)	63.7 (194.91)	30.0 (38.89)
tagcloud	33.0 (0.0)	35.0 (6.06)	42.9 (30.0)	35.1 (6.36)
unpack-code	47.4 (0.0)	50.2 (5.91)	54.1 (14.14)	52.0 (9.7)
validate-input	19.1 (0.0)	21.1 (10.47)	34.1 (78.53)	21.5 (12.57)

References

1. OWASP: The open web application security project (2012). https://www.owasp. org/. Accessed April 2013
2. The MITRE Corporation: Common weakness enumeration: A community-developed dictionary of software weakness types (2012). http://cwe.mitre.org/top25/. Accessed April 2013
3. Microsoft: Microsoft Security Intelligence Report, vol. 13, January–June 2012 (2012). http://www.microsoft.com/security/sir/default.aspx. Accessed April 2013
4. Jang, D., Jhala, R., Lerner, S., Shacham, H.: An empirical study of privacy-violating information flows in JavaScript web applications. In: Proceedings of the ACM Conference on Computer and Communications Security, pp. 270–283. ACM (2010)
5. Vogt, P., Nentwich, F., Jovanovic, N., Kruegel, C., Kirda, E., Vigna, G.: Cross site scripting prevention with dynamic data tainting and static analysis. In: Proceedings of the Annual Network and Distributed System Security Symposium. The Internet Society (2007)
6. Groef, W.D., Devriese, D., Nikiforakis, N., Piessens, F.: FlowFox: a web browser with flexible and precise information flow control. In: Proceedings of the ACM Conference on Computer and Communications Security, pp. 748–759. ACM (2012)

7. Just, S., Cleary, A., Shirley, B., Hammer, C.: Information flow analysis for JavaScript. In: Proceedings of the ACM SIGPLAN International Workshop on Programming Language and Systems Technologies for Internet Clients, pp. 9–18. ACM (2011)

8. Austin, T.H., Flanagan, C.: Multiple facets for dynamic information flow. In: Proceedings of the ACM SIGPLAN-SIGACT Symposium on Principals of Programming Languages, pp. 165–178. ACM (2012)

9. Kerschbaumer, C., Hennigan, E., Larsen, P., Brunthaler, S., Franz, M.: Towards precise and efficient information flow control in web browsers. In: [42]

10. Enck, W., Gilbert, P., Chun, B.G., Cox, L.P., Jung, J., McDaniel, P., Sheth, A.N.: TaintDroid: an information-flow tracking system for realtime privacy monitoring on smartphones. In: Proceedings of the USENIX Symposium on Operating Systems Design and Implementation, pp. 393–407 (2010)

11. Provos, N.: Safe browsing - protecting web users for 5 years and counting (2012). http://googleonlinesecurity.blogspot.com/2012/06/safe-browsing-protecting-web-users-for.html. Accessed April 2013

12. Microsoft: SmartScreen Filter (2012). http://windows.microsoft.com/en-US/internet-explorer/products/ie-9/features/smartscreen-filter. Accessed April 2013

13. WebKit: The webkit open source project (2012). http://www.webkit.org. Accessed April 2013

14. SunSpider: SunSpider JavaScript benchmark (2012). http://www2.webkit.org/perf/sunspider-0.9/sunspider.html. Accessed April 2013

15. Google: V8 Benchmark Suite (2013). https://developers.google.com/v8/benchmarks. Accessed April 2013

16. Alexa: Alexa Global Top Sites. http://www.alexa.com/topsites. Accessed April 2013

17. W3C - World Wide Web Consortium: Document object model (DOM) level 3 core specification (2004). http://www.w3.org/TR/2004/REC-DOM-Level-3-Core-20040407/DOM3-Core.pdf. Accessed April 2013

18. Russo, A., Sabelfeld, A., Chudnov, A.: Tracking information flow in dynamic tree structures. In: Backes, M., Ning, P. (eds.) ESORICS 2009. LNCS, vol. 5789, pp. 86–103. Springer, Heidelberg (2009)

19. Nikiforakis, N., Invernizzi, L., Kapravelos, A., Acker, S.V., Joosen, W., Kruegel, C., Piessens, F., Vigna, G.: You are what you include: large-scale evaluation of remote javascript inclusions. In: Proceedings of the ACM Conference on Computer and Communications Security, pp. 736–747. ACM (2012)

20. Mozilla Foundation: Same origin policy for JavaScript (2008). https://developer.mozilla.org/En/Same_origin_policy_for_JavaScript. Accessed April 2013

21. W3C: Content security policy 1.0 (2013). http://www.w3.org/TR/CSP/. Accessed July 2013

22. Myers, A.C., Liskov, B.: Protecting privacy using the decentralized label model. ACM Trans. Softw. Eng. Methodol. 9, 410–442 (2000)

23. Myers, A.C., Zheng, L., Zdancewic, S., Chong, S., Nystrom, N.: Jif: Java information flow (2001). http://www.cs.cornell.edu/jif. Accessed April 2013

24. Hennigan, E., Kerschbaumer, C., Larsen, P., Brunthaler, S., Franz, M.: First-class labels: using information flow to debug security holes. In: [42]

25. Sabelfeld, A., Myers, A.C.: Language-based information-flow security. IEEE J. Sel. Areas Commun. 21, 5–19 (2003)

26. Ecma International: Standard ECMA-262. The ECMAScript language specification (2009). http://www.ecma-international.org/publications/standards/Ecma-262.htm. Accessed April 2013

27. Anonymous: Web statistics when crawling the alexa top 500 web pages. Technical report, Anonymous (2013)
28. Jim, T., Swamy, N., Hicks, M.: Defeating script injection attacks with browser-enforced embedded policies. In: Proceedings of the ACM International Conference on World Wide Web. ACM (2007)
29. Myers, A.C.: Jflow: practical mostly-static information flow control. In: Proceedings of the ACM SIGPLAN-SIGACT Symposium on Principals of Programming Languages, pp. 228–241. ACM (1999)
30. Zdancewic, S.A.: Programming Languages for information security. Ph.D. thesis, Cornell University (2002)
31. The Tor Project: Tor: Anonymity Online (2013). https://www.torproject.org/. Accessed April 2013
32. Greathouse, J.L., LeBlanc, C., Austin, T., Bertacco, V.: Highly scalable distributed dataflow analysis. In: Proceedings of the IEEE/ACM International Symposium on Code Generation and Optimization, pp. 277–288. IEEE (2011)
33. Greathouse, J.L., Austin, T.: The potential of sampling for dynamic analysis. In: Proceedings of the ACM SIGPLAN Workshop on Programming Languages and Analysis for Security, pp. 3.1–3.6. ACM (2011)
34. Austin, T.H., Flanagan, C.: Permissive dynamic information flow analysis. In: Proceedings of the ACM SIGPLAN Workshop on Programming Languages and Analysis for Security, pp. 1–12. ACM (2010)
35. Devriese, D., Peissens, F.: Noninterference through secure multi-execution. In: Proceedings of the IEEE Symposium on Security and Privacy, pp. 109–124. IEEE (2010)
36. Hedin, D., Sabelfeld, A.: Information-flow security for a core of JavaScript. In: Proceedings of the IEEE Computer Security Foundations Symposium, pp. 3–18. IEEE (2012)
37. Austin, T.H., Flanagan, C.: Efficient purely-dynamic information flow analysis. In: Proceedings of the ACM SIGPLAN Workshop on Programming Languages and Analysis for Security, pp. 113–124. ACM (2009)
38. Chugh, R., Meister, J.A., Jhala, R., Lerner, S.: Staged information flow for JavaScript. In: Proceedings of the ACM SIGPLAN Conference on Programming Language Design and Implementation, pp. 50–62. ACM (2009)
39. Nadji, Y., Saxena, P., Song, D.: Document structure integrity: a robust basis for cross-site scripting defense. In: Proceedings of the Annual Network and Distributed System Security Symposium. The Internet Society (2009)
40. Canali, D., Cova, M., Vigna, G., Kruegel, C.: Prophiler: a fast filter for the large-scale detection of malicious web pages. In: Proceedings of the ACM International Conference on World Wide Web, pp. 197–206. ACM (2011)
41. Thomas, K., Grie, C., Ma, J., Paxson, V., Song, D.: Design and evaluation of a real-time url spam filtering service. In: Proceedings of the IEEE Symposium on Security and Privacy, pp. 447–462. IEEE (2011)
42. Proceedings of the 6th International Conference on Trust and Trustworthy Computing, TRUST 2013, London, UK, June 17–19. Springer (2013)

Privacy Attacks

DroidTest: Testing Android Applications for Leakage of Private Information

Sarker T. Ahmed Rumee$^{(\boxtimes)}$ and Donggang Liu

Department of Computer Science and Engineering,
University of Texas at Arlington, Arlington 76019, USA
sarker.ahmedrumee@mavs.uta.edu, dliu@uta.edu

Abstract. Smartphones have become a basic necessity in recent years, and a large portion of users are using them for storing private data such as personal contacts and performing sensitive operations such as financial transactions. As a result, there is a high incentive for attackers to compromise these devices. Researchers have also found that there are indeed many malicious applications on official or unofficial Android markets, and a large fraction of them steal private user data once they are installed on smartphones. In this paper, we propose a novel method to test Android applications for the leakage of private data. Our method reuses existing test cases, produced either manually or automatically, and converts each of them into a set of new *correlated* test cases. The property of these correlated test cases is such that- they will trigger the same result in our system if there is no leakage of private data. As a result, the leakage of information can be detected if we observe different outputs from executions under correlated inputs. We have evaluated our system on an Android malware dataset and the top 50 free applications on official Android market. The result shows that our tool can effectively and efficiently detect leakage of private data.

1 Introduction

The use of smartphones are increasing day by day. According to a recent survey [7], over 50 percent of the US mobile users own smartphones. Nowadays, a smartphone can be used for almost all the purposes a normal user can think of, such as web browsing, online chatting, email, social networking, gaming, audio and video conferences.

To meet the wide range of users' need, millions of applications have been developed and available in various online application stores, such as - Apple Appstore, Google Playstore for Android etc. While these online markets make it convenient for users to customize their smartphone systems for their needs, attackers have also become interested in them for compromising users' systems. Attackers may upload malicious applications and then compromise the systems that download and install those applications. For example, these malicious applications may steal private data or send SMS messages to premium numbers without user's knowledge. In addition, pirated versions of popular smartphone applications are commonly available at unofficial market places too. Attackers often

© Springer International Publishing Switzerland 2015
Y. Desmedt (Ed.): ISC 2013, LNCS 7807, pp. 341–353, 2015.
DOI: 10.1007/978-3-319-27659-5_24

embed malicious code in these pirated versions and can compromise a device when installed.

The above information leakage problem has already been studied in the literature. Here we restrict our study to Android platform. Existing solutions include static analysis [16] and dynamic monitoring [10]. Static analysis scans byte code or source code to find paths that may leak information. However, it does not execute the program and lacks program dynamic information. As a result, it suffers from high false positive rate. On the other hand, dynamic analysis monitors the execution of an application on a modified Android platform. However, the modification of Android system is not always practical from the end user perspective. In addition, dynamic monitoring often increases the overhead at the user side significantly.

In this paper, we propose to test Android applications before placing them on the market. The testing can be done by the market owner or a third party other than application developers by uploading the applications to a offline server running the proposed system. Conceptually, the first step of testing is to generate test cases to explore different program paths, and the second step is to examine each program path to see if it is possible to leak any sensitive information. The first step can be done by using GUI-based test case generation [19] or concolic testing like DART and CUTE [17,21] as long as they are ported to Android platform. Here, we assume that there exists a set of test cases produced either manually or automatically by various existing methods, and our focus is on the second step, i.e., to test if the execution under a given test input is leaking sensitive information. One method is to monitor the outgoing packet of an application and check the content to see if it is leaking something similar to a phone number, a credit card number, etc. However, when the attacker obfuscates the packet, e.g., by encryption, then this method will fail. Another natural way to solve this problem is to use taint analysis, e.g., if the outgoing packet is tainted by private data, then we can say that this application is leaking information. For example, TaintDroid [10] is built on this simple idea. However, the problem with such idea is that, the application needs to be instrumented and monitored, which requires access to the source code. While the source code can be obtained by reverse engineering, a common trend right now is that many application developers obfuscate their code to make it difficult for source code-based program analysis.

To remove the need for program source code and relieve user side from expensive monitoring, in this paper we propose *DroidTest*, a server side black-box testing method; we only work on the input and the output of the application under test. In our system, each existing test case is used to produce a set of correlated test inputs. These correlated inputs are crafted in such a way that, the output will stay the same if there is no leakage of private information. In fact, the only difference between two correlated test cases is the input that includes sensitive information, e.g., current location, personal pictures, etc. As a result, if we observe different outputs generated by a set of correlated test cases, then we can say that the difference is due to the difference in the sensitive inputs.

The benefit of DroidTest are as follows. First, it does not require access to the source code. As a result, obfuscating source code does not stop us from detecting the leakage of information. Second, it can detect both explicit and implicit data leakage.

We have evaluated our technique on two datasets. The first dataset includes applications that are known to contain malicious code leaking information; the second dataset includes the top 50 free applications from Android market. The result shows that we can successfully detect the information leakage of the applications in the first dataset. In addition, we have also found a good number of applications in the second dataset that are also leaking some private information without user's knowledge.

The remainder of the paper is organized as follows. Section 3 provides a necessary background on the Android security mechanism along with the assumptions made. Section 2 reviews related work on Android security. Section 4 describes the high level overview of the proposed approach. Section 5 provides detailed description of the proposed method. Section 6 contains the experimental results and findings. The last section concludes the paper and discusses some possible future directions.

2   Related Work

Security and privacy of smartphone applications is a field of active research in the recent years. Among them, stealing sensitive information from smartphones is one of the major threats [12].

Static and dynamic analysis techniques have been applied to track the suspicious behavior of applications. PiOS [9] applies static analysis on iOS apps to detect possible privacy leak. In particular, it first constructs the control flow graph of an iOS application, then checks whether there is an execution path from the nodes that access privacy source to the nodes corresponding to network operations. If such a path exists, it is considered a potential for information leakage. SCANDAL [20] also employs similar techniques to find the path between the sensitive sources of data and the network write operations in Android applications. However, as we mentioned, static analysis tools often suffer from high false positive rate.

TaintDroid [10] uses dynamic taint analysis to track data flow inside the Android operating system. It taints data from private information sources, and then checks the data leaving the system via network interface. It raises an alert when the outgoing data include tainted information. A major limitation of this system is it only looks for explicit information flow; thus cannot detect data leakage through implicit flow of information.

ScanDroid [15] extracts security specifications from the manifests that accompany Android applications, and then checks whether the information flow is consistent with those specifications. However, the analysis results in [14] and [11] show that such specification may not be always sufficient. Malicious applications can easily bypass them and still leak data.

TISSA [23] gives users detailed control over an application's access to a few selected private data (phone identity, location, contacts, and the call log) by letting the user decide whether the application can see the true data or some mock data. MockDroid [8] allows users to mock the access from an untrusted application to particular resources at runtime. AppFence [18] replaces sensitive information with shadow data. While these methods stop the leakage of data, they also impact legitimate applications that are allowed to access these data.

3   Background and Assumptions

3.1   Android Permission Scheme

Android governs the access to resources such as internet, SMS, Contacts etc. through its permission mechanism. At the install time, each application declares its required permissions such as - internet access, GPS data access, read phone state etc. There is no way to selectively accept or reject these permission requests. A user must accept all of those to install the application, otherwise abort the procedure. This was done with a view to informing users about which specific resources are accessed by each application.

But in practice, users pay little attention to these permission requests [13] and unnecessary permissions are often granted to applications. For example, an email application needs to send and receive emails. In Android, such an application must acquire the full internet access permission, which is more than necessary and can be exploited.

3.2   Sensitive Information Source and Sink

To detect the leakage of sensitive data, the first task is to define the set of private or sensitive information sources. Some commonly regarded source of private data are: Device id (IMEI), Subscriber Id (IMSI), Phone Number, Location and Contact information, User account information, SMS/MMS messages etc. However, the nature of application and context information are also important to decide whether a particular piece of data is sensitive or not. For example, location information sent by the popular Android application *Gasbuddy* cannot be termed as an instance of privacy violation, as it is the part of the its task and user is also aware of that.

Information sink means the ways data can leave the device, which includes - Network access, Outgoing SMS, MMS etc. Here, we check whether the information going through the sink contains some private data.

3.3   Adversary Model

In this paper, we assume that the attacker fully controls the development of the application under test. In other words, he can embed any code he wants. We assume that the application has the permission to read some of the sensitive information sources and access Internet. The question for us is to see if such sensitive data is leaked through Internet. During the test, we also assume that except the application under test, all other system components, e.g., the Android OS and the Dalvik VM, are secure. If they are compromised, then the adversary can easily bypass our monitoring. This assumption is reasonable since the testing system is built specifically for the purpose of detecting information leakage. On the other hand, we cannot make such assumption if the detection is done at the user end. Finally, we also assume that the malicious application does not compromise the Dalvik VM or Android OS during the execution.

4 DroidTest Overview

The objective of DroidTest is to detect malicious activity in Android smartphone applications that send out privacy-sensitive information out through network interfaces. A straightforward idea to solve this problem is to use static analysis techniques. Basically, we scan the program source code or binary to see if the data write operation is reachable from the read operation performed on sensitive data. However, as we mentioned, these techniques suffer from high false positive rate. Dynamic analysis does not suffer from the abundance of false positives. However, they involve significant modification of the Android operating system and also require user devices to do the expensive monitoring.

DroidTest is a black-box testing method; the system only works on the input and the output of the application under test. As mentioned, DroidTest uses existing test cases. Given a test case, it will examine the path triggered by such test case to see if there is any information leakage. The main idea of DroidTest is based on the following observation: given a deterministic function $f(x)$ $(x \in \mathcal{X})$, the result of this function does not leak any information about x if for all x_1 and x_2 we have $f(x_1) = f(x_2)$. In other words, given $f(x)$, the probability distribution of x is a uniform distribution over $\mathcal{X}$. As a result, if we test $f(\cdot)$ using two inputs $\{x_1, x_2\}$ and find that $f(x_1) \neq f(x_2)$, then it is for sure that function $f(x)$ is leaking some information about the input x. This basically means that if we fix all inputs to an application except those that are considered as sensitive, then the content of outgoing traffic should not change if there is no leakage of sensitive data.

In the high level, DroidTest works as follows. For each existing test case, we convert it into multiple correlated test cases. We consider these test cases as correlated since they only differ in the inputs from sensitive sources, e.g., current location, personal pictures, etc. In this paper, we only produce two correlated test cases from each of the existing test cases since we found that two is often enough for tracking the information leakage as long as the private data part is randomly mutated. Once we have the two correlated test cases, we run the application twice and monitor the outgoing traffic. If we see any difference in the outgoing traffic, then we can say that such difference is due to the difference in the sensitive data. This basically means, some private information is leaked by this application.

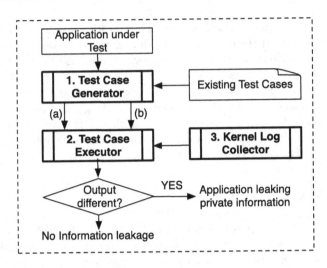

Fig. 1. High-level view of the proposed system. (a) and (b) are a pair of correlated test cases produced from an existing test case.

5   Implementation

Figure 1 depicts a conceptual view of the DroidTest system. DroidTest has three major components: *test case generator, test case executor* and *kernel log collector.* The test case generator converts each existing test case into a pair of correlated test cases that only differ in the private data part; the test case executor runs the application once for each of the two correlated test cases and analyze if any private information is leaked through network interfaces; the kernel log collector basically monitors the network interface and collects the outgoing packet data. In the rest of this section, we first describe the necessary settings made in the Android operating system and then discuss the three major components of the proposed system in detail.

5.1   Test Environment Setup

DroidTest systm is a modified Android Operating system based on version 2.2, popularly known as Froyo. Applications are loaded and run in the emulator built from this modified Android system.

At first, We locate all APIs that are required to read phone specific information, find location data, contact lists and read incoming SMS contents etc. Then custom source code is inserted in these methods to change the return values with randomly generated values. As a result, different invocation of these methods will return different values. This setting helps us to create co-related test cases with variations in the sensitive data.

For example, to get the *Device ID* or *IMEI number*, one has to call the *getDeviceId()* method of the *Android.telephony.TelePhonyManager* class.

It internally uses the *getDeviceId()* method of the class *PhoneSubInfo* under the package *com.Android.internal.telephony*. We modified the *getDeviceId()* of *PhoneSubInfo* class to read a mock IMEI number (randomly generated) and return it to the application.

In addition to the modification at the information sources, we also try to fix program inputs such as system time, random number generators, and environment variables to constant values. In the current implementation, we only modified the *java.util.Random* and *java.lang.System* classes. It aids to offset variation in program output for multiple runs due to the factors other than the user provided inputs.

5.2   Test Case Generator

As said earlier, we have manually generated test cases for the applications under test. Each application is run for some time (around 5 min) in the emulator. We manually exercise its basic features, e.g., try to navigate to all the screens, click the available buttons and links etc. For each such activity, we check whether the application has performed any sort of network activity or sent any text message. If so, the sequence of events that led up to this point from the application home screen(entry point) is taken as one candidate test case for this application. Test cases not resulting in any outgoing data are dropped.

5.3   Test Case Executor

This component will take a pair of correlated test cases and execute the application once for each of them. The executor takes two command line arguments to run - *the application name, the name of the file containing the test cases*. It then converts these test cases to Junit [3] test scripts. Within the Junit framework, individual test methods are written using the APIs of Robotium [6], which automatically passes the GUI events (actions in the test case) to the Android emulator.

Once the execution is done for each of the correlated test cases, we retrieve and compare the monitoring results from the kernel logs. If they are different, then we report an alarm since some sensitive information is leaked through the internet by the application under test.

5.4   Kernel Log Collector

The last key component of our system is a simple Loadable Kernel Module, that intercepts the outgoing network packets. To do that, we hook the System Call Table of the Android operating system. This is done by placing a custom system call table in the same address as the original system call table.

Android operating system uses system call - *sys_sendto* to send data to network. We intercept this system call and log its parameters(packet data) to the kernel logs.

6   Experiment and Results

6.1   Scope of Sensitive Information Source and Sink

We have discussed about the sensitive information sources earlier. For this study, we only consider the ones listed in Table 1. As the sink of sensitive information, we consider the *network interfaces*. However, Our system can be easily extended to work with additional sources and sinks of private data.

Table 1. Information sources considered private

IMEI number, IMSI number, Android OS Version,
Phone Number, Phone Model, Contacts,
Location information, Incoming SMS contents

6.2   Datasets

We consider two datasets. The first dataset [4] includes the Android applications that are known to contain malwares. The second data set includes applications from the Official Android Marketplace [5]. Whether these applications leak private data or not is unknown beforehand.

Data Set 1: Malicious Applications. The malware database [4] has total 1260 samples under 45 different malware families. Among them, 28 were found to leak users private data by [2,22]. So, we also restrict our study to these malware samples.

From these samples, we further discarded any application having one or more of the following properties. Because, in that case an application do not have the capability to send data outside through internet. This further reduces our malware data set to *222 samples from 20 malware families.*

1. Perform no internet activity during its execution.
2. Conditions to activate or complete the malicious activity is no longer present. For example, the web server where the stolen information is sent is down, or the emulator has to send SMS to premium rate number, which is not possible in an emulated environment etc.

Data Set 2: Android Marketplace Applications. From the Android market place, We select top 50 (as of March 2013) free applications to perfrom the testing. While collecting applications, we check whether they require certain permissions: *Full Internet access* and at least one of - *Read phone specific information, Contact data, and Location information.* Applications not having such permissions are discarded from further analysis. Table 3 lists the name of these applications along with their leaked information.

Table 2. Android malwares and types of leaked information

Malware samples		
Malware family	Number of samples	Leaked information
BeanBot	4	IMEI, IMSI, Phone Number
		Android OS Version
BgServ	4	IMEI, Phone Number, Android OS Version
DroidDelux	1	IMSI, Phone Model, Android OS version
DroidDreamLight	30	IMEI, IMSI
DroidKungFu1	16	IMEI, Android OS version,Phone model
DroidKungFu2	8	IMEI, Android OS version,Phone model
DroidKungFuSapp	3	IMEI, Android OS version,Phone model
DroidKungFuUpdate	1	IMEI, Phone Number, Android OS Version
GoldFream	34	Incoming SMS, IMEI
Gone60	9	Contacts, SMS
LoveTrap	1	IMSI, GeoLocation
Plankton	11	IMEI
PjApps	47	IMEI, Phone Number
RougeSP Push	9	IMEI, Phone Number, Android OS version
SMSReplicator	1	Incoming SMS
SndApps	10	IMEI, Phone Number
WalkinWat	1	IMEI, Phone Number,
		Phone Model and Android OS Version
YZHC	22	IMEI, Incoming SMS
zHash	11	IMEI, IMSI
Zitmo	1	IMEI, Incoming SMS
Total	222	

6.3 Results

Experiment Results of Malware Dataset. Table 2 shows the result of experiment, that includes - the name of the malware family, number of samples in the test suite and the leaked information type. For each of these samples, we could successfully detect its known data leaking behavior. Hence, the detection rate for the proposed tool was found to be 100 %.

Experiment Results of Android Market Place Applications. Next, we apply the proposed method to test the *top 50 free applications* from the Android market place [5]. Table 3 lists the name of these applications alongside the type of information leaked. The value *Nil* indicates that we didn't find any leakage of information during the testing.

From the experiment, we see that some highly rated applications can also leak private data without user's consent. The permission requests presented by these

Table 3. Top 50 free applications from Android market and leaked information

Application names	Leaked information
TuneInRadio	Location
Crackle Movie	IMEI, IMSI, Android OS version
Brightest LED FlashLight	Location Android OS version, Phone model, Build Version
Tiny Flashlight, Zillo, Instagram, JetPack Joyride, AskFM, FruitNinja, Lines, Simpson, Drag Racing, Vector, PicsArt, Ant Smasher, Google Translate	Nil
Scramble Free, iHeartRadio, HelloKitty	IMEI, Android OS version, Phone model, Build Version
Craiglist Mobile, Inkpad, MeetMe, Tagged, Shoot Bubble, AccuWeather	Android OS version, Phone model, Build version
Logo quiz, Cut the Rope, Amazon MP3	Android OS version Phone model, Build version
Speed Test	Current Location, IMEI Build version
Sound Hound	IMSI
Sudoku	Current Location, Phone model Build version
Alarm Clock Extreme	Phone Model
DH Texas Poker, Words with Friends, ESPN score center, Restaurant Story Angry Gran Run, Castle Defence, Zombie Frontier, Mind Game	IMEI, Android OS version, Phone model
Imdb, iFunny, GoWeatherEX, Texas HoldEm Poker, My Mixtapez Fashion Story, 4 Pics 1 Word, Tetris,	Android OS version, Phone model
Hulu plus	Android OS version

applications had no direct mention about their sending of private information to third party. We found that, *36 out of 50 applications (72 %)* send one or more sensitive data to outside, mostly to advertising servers. This number is quite disturbing taking into the fact that, these applications are very much popular and widely used [5].

6.4   Discussions and Findings

We tested the applications by creating co-related pair of test cases for the program paths explored manually. So, it may miss some instances of true positives, as the set of test cases is not comprehensive. Detection rates of malicious applications reported above are also based on the generated test cases only. DroidTest

Table 4. DroidTest vs Google App verfication service

Malware samples and Detection results		
Malware family	Detected samples	
	DroidTest	App verification service
BeanBot	4	0
BgServ	4	0
DroidDelux	1	0
DroidDreamLight	30	18
DroidKungFu1	16	8
DroidKungFu2	8	9
DroidKungFuSapp	3	0
DroidKungFuUpdate	1	0
GoldFream	34	6
Gone60	9	0
LoveTrap	1	0
Plankton	11	2
PjApps	47	8
RougeSP Push	9	0
SMSReplicator	1	0
SndApps	10	0
WalkinWat	1	0
YZHC	22	3
zHash	9	1
Zitmo	1	0
Total	222	56

can theoretically produce false positives, because we fixed only random numbers and system time to constant, and there may be other factors that can change program output without changing the sensitive input. But for the applications we tested, every instances of variation in output could be traced back to change in sensitive input sources, thus no false positives were produced.

From Tables 2 and 3, we can see the type of information leaked by various applications. The most commonly leaked information is the unique device id or the IMEI number by both type of applications. If we closely observe the results of analysis of these applications, we can easily see that, applications from the malware data set leaks IMEI, IMSI, Phone number more than the other sensitive data. On the other hand, the mostly leaked information by the Android market place applications include Android operating system version, Phone model which are definitely not as sensitive as the device id (IMEI), subscriber id (IMSI) and the phone number. So, user must avoid downloading applications from the untrusted third party market places. The chance of leaking sensitive data are much higher in case of the unofficial market place applications, because unofficial market places apply hardly any security check of the applications.

Recently, with the release of latest Android 4.2 (JellyBean), google announced a new and exciting security feature called the *"Application Verification Service"*.Performance of this service in detecting malicious applications has been studied in [1]. Based on that, Table 4 shows the comparison of the results found by *DroidTest* and *Application Verfication Service*. It clearly shows that, the proposed system performed way better than App Verification Service.

7 Conclusion

The growing popularity of smartphones has led to the rising threats from malicious mobile applications. In this paper, we have demonstrated the need for testing Android applications before they are put into the market place. It comes from the fact that, many popular applications found in the official and unofficial Android market places leak private data to some third parties without proper user consent. To test mobile applications for data stealing behavior, we have proposed the DroidTest system and described its architecture, operation and evaluation through the testing of two datasets. The experiment results shows its effectiveness in detecting private information leakage.

Currently our system is an offline testing tool. In future, we plan to move the monitoring to the device to notify user about information leakage dynamically. We also plan to include more information sources in the sensitive input list. This will make DroidTest better equipped to detect zero day smartphone malwares. Currently, we manually generate the test cases for the applications under test. To make our system more robust, we also plan to generate meaningful test cases for Android applications automatically in future.

Acknowledgments. The authors would like to thank Professor Xuxian Jiang and his research group from North Carolina State University for sharing us with the android malware data set.

References

1. Analysis of appverification tool from google. http://www.csc.ncsu.edu/faculty/jiang/appverify/
2. Contagio mobile malware mini dump. http://contagiominidump.blogspot.com/
3. Junit. http://junit.sourceforge.net/
4. Malware data set. http://www.malgenomeproject.org/policy.html
5. Official android marketplace: Google play. https://play.google.com/
6. Robotium. http://code.google.com/p/robotium/
7. Survey on smartphone users. http://www.engadget.com/2012/05/07/nielsen-smartphone-share-march-2012/

8. Beresford, A., Rice, A., Skehin, N., Sohan, R.: Mockdroid: trading privacy for application functionality on smartphones. In: Proceedings of the 12th Workshop on Mobile Computing Systems and Applications, pp. 49–54. ACM (2011)

9. Egele, M., Kruegel, C., Kirda, E., Vigna, G.: Pios: detecting privacy leaks in ios applications. In: Proceedings of the Network and Distributed System Security Symposium (2011)

10. Enck, W., Gilbert, P., Chun, B., Cox, L., Jung, J., McDaniel, P., Sheth, A.: Taintdroid: an information-flow tracking system for realtime privacy monitoring on smartphones. In: Proceedings of the 9th USENIX Conference on Operating Systems Design and Implementation, pp. 1–6 (2010)

11. Felt, A., Chin, E., Hanna, S., Song, D., Wagner, D.: Android permissions demystified. In: Proceedings of the 18th ACM Conference on Computer and Communications Security, pp. 627–638. ACM (2011)

12. Felt, A., Finifter, M., Chin, E., Hanna, S., Wagner, D.: A survey of mobile malware in the wild. In: Proceedings of the 1st ACM Workshop on Security and Privacy in Smartphones and Mobile Devices, pp. 3–14. ACM (2011)

13. Felt, A., Ha, E., Egelman, S., Haney, A., Chin, E., Wagner, D.: Android permissions: user attention, comprehension, and behavior. In: Proceedings of the Eighth Symposium on Usable Privacy and Security, p. 3. ACM (2012)

14. Felt, A.P., Greenwood, K., Wagner, D.: The effectiveness of application permissions. In: Procedings of the USENIX Conference on Web Application Development (2011)

15. Fuchs, A., Chaudhuri, A., Foster, J.: Scandroid: automated security certification of android applications. Manuscript, Univ. of Maryland (2009). http://www.cs.umd. edu/~avik/projects/scandroidascaa

16. Gibler, C., Crussell, J., Erickson, J., Chen, H.: AndroidLeaks: automatically detecting potential privacy leaks in android applications on a large scale. In: Katzenbeisser, S., Weippl, E., Camp, L.J., Volkamer, M., Reiter, M., Zhang, X. (eds.) Trust 2012. LNCS, vol. 7344, pp. 291–307. Springer, Heidelberg (2012)

17. Godefroid, P., Klarlund, N., Sen, K.: Dart: directed automated random testing. In: ACM Sigplan Notices, vol. 40, pp. 213–223. ACM (2005)

18. Hornyack, P., Han, S., Jung, J., Schechter, S., Wetherall, D.: These aren't the droids you're looking for: retrofitting android to protect data from imperious applications. In: Proceedings of the 18th ACM Conference on Computer and Communications Security, pp. 639–652. ACM (2011)

19. Hu, C., Neamtiu, I.: Automating gui testing for android applications. In: Proceedings of the 6th International Workshop on Automation of Software Test, pp. 77–83. ACM (2011)

20. Kim, J., Yoon, Y., Yi, K., Shin, J., Center, S.: Scandal: static analyzer for detecting privacy leaks in android applications. In Proc. of the MoST (2012)

21. K. Sen, D. Marinov, G. Agha.: CUTE: a concolic unit testing engine for C. In: Proceedings of the 10th European Software Engineering Conference Held Jointly with 13th ACM SIGSOFT International Symposium on Foundations of Software Engineering, vol. 30, pp. 263-272 (2005)

22. Zhou, Y., Jiang, X.: Dissecting android malware: characterization and evolution. In: 2012 IEEE Symposium on Security and Privacy (SP), pp. 95–109. IEEE (2012)

23. Zhou, Y., Zhang, X., Jiang, X., Freeh, V.W.: Taming information-stealing smartphone applications (on Android). In: McCune, J.M., Balacheff, B., Perrig, A., Sadeghi, A.-R., Sasse, A., Beres, Y. (eds.) Trust 2011. LNCS, vol. 6740, pp. 93–107. Springer, Heidelberg (2011)

A Dangerous Mix: Large-Scale Analysis of Mixed-Content Websites

Ping Chen$^{(\boxtimes)}$, Nick Nikiforakis, Christophe Huygens, and Lieven Desmet

iMinds-DistriNet, KU Leuven, 3001 Leuven, Belgium
{ping.chen,nick.nikiforakis,christophe.huygens,
lieven.desmet}@cs.kuleuven.be

Abstract. In this paper, we investigate the current state of practice about mixed-content websites, websites that are accessed using the HTTPS protocol, yet include some additional resources using HTTP. Through a large-scale experiment, we show that about half of the Internet's most popular websites are currently using this practice and are thus vulnerable to a wide range of attacks, including the stealing of cookies and the injection of malicious JavaScript in the context of the vulnerable websites. Additionally, we investigate the default behavior of browsers on mobile devices and show that most of them, by default, allow the rendering of mixed content, which demonstrates that hundreds of thousands of mobile users are currently vulnerable to MITM attacks.

1 Introduction

Internet users today rely on HTTPS (HTTP over SSL/TLS) for secure communication of sensitive data. While websites are migrating to HTTPS, attackers are also shifting efforts to break the TLS communication. Complementary to protocol and infrastructure vulnerabilities in TLS and HTTPS, as illustrated by recent attacks such as CRIME [19] and Lucky 13 [10], attackers can also exploit mixed-content vulnerabilities to compromise TLS-protected websites.

In mixed-content websites, the webpage is delivered to the browser over TLS, but some of the additional content, such as images and scripts, are delivered over a non-secured HTTP connection. These non-secured communications can be exploited by network attackers to gain access to wide set of capabilities ranging from access to cookies and the forging of arbitrary requests, to the execution of arbitrary JavaScript code in the security context of the TLS-protected website.

Desktop browsers are recently catching up to mitigate this vulnerability, but the large majority of browsers on mobile devices, such as smartphones and tablets, leave the end-user unprotected against this type of attack. This is worsened by the fact that it is typically pretty straightforward to launch an active network attack against a mobile user (e.g. via setting up a fake wireless hotspot).

In this paper, we report on an in-depth assessment of the state-of-practice with respect to mixed-content vulnerabilities. In particular, the main contributions of this paper are the following: (1) We study the different types of mixed-content inclusions, and assess their security impact. (2) We present a detailed

© Springer International Publishing Switzerland 2015
Y. Desmedt (Ed.): ISC 2013, LNCS 7807, pp. 354–363, 2015.
DOI: 10.1007/978-3-319-27659-5_25

analysis of mixed-content inclusions over the Alexa top 100,000 Internet domains, showing that 43 % of the Internet's most popular websites suffer from mixed-content vulnerabilities. (3) We document the behavior of mobile browsers in the face of mixed-content inclusions. (4) We enumerate the best practices as well as novel mitigation techniques against mixed-content inclusions for browsers, website owners and content providers.

2 Problem Statement

It is well-known that HTTP is vulnerable to eavesdropping and man-in-the-middle (MITM) attacks, and HTTPS is designed to precisely prevent these attacks by adding the security capabilities of SSL/TLS to HTTP. SSL/TSL enables authentication of the web server, and provides bidirectional encryption of the communication channel between the client and server. Apart from the attacks against the SSL/TLS protocol, we show that attackers can also exploit mixed-content vulnerabilities to compromise TLS-protected websites.

The attacker model used in this paper, is the *active network attacker*. The active network attacker positions himself on a network between the web browser and the web server, and is able to intercept and tamper with the network traffic passing by. The attacker can read, modify, delete, and inject HTTP requests and responses, but he is not able to decipher encrypted information, nor impersonate an HTTPS endpoint without a valid TLS certificate.

In mixed content (also known as non-secure/insecure content) websites, the web page is delivered to the browser over TLS, but some of the additional content, such as images and scripts, are directly delivered over a non-secured HTTP connection from the content provider towards the web browser. Although the active network attacker can not attack the web page delivery over HTTPS, he can still compromise the TLS-enabled website by compromising any of the additional resources that are loaded over HTTP.

3 Impact of Mixed Content Attacks

Five specific types of mixed content are studied in this paper: Image, iframe, CSS, JavaScript and Flash. The impact of different types of mixed content attack can be categorized as follows:

- **Cookie stealing:** When a browser requests mixed content, it may include cookies associated with the content provider, which allows the attacker to obtain the cookies. Moreover, if the content provider and the TLS-protected website using mixed content happen to be on the same domain, sensitive cookies used over HTTPS can get exposed to the attacker via a HTTP request, unless the cookie is protected by the "secure" flag.
- **Request forgery:** As mixed content is requested over HTTP, the attacker can manipulate the HTTP requests and responses and use them to trigger or forge arbitrary HTTP requests, which may lead to certain variants of SSL-Stripping [16] and Cross-Site Request Forgery (CSRF) [12] attacks.

Table 1. Impact of mixed content attacks

Type	Cookie stealing	Request forgery	DOM data leakage	JavaScript execution
Image	x	x		
iframe	x	x		
CSS	x	x	x	
JavaScript	x	x	x	x
Flash	x	x	x	x

- **DOM data leakage:** Mixed content may leak confidential data that is displayed as part of the HTTPS webpage. For example, mixed-CSS content can be used to obtain sensitive data in the DOM via scriptless attacks [14]: CSS selectors can match against particular content in the DOM, and leak the result of the test by fetching a web resource (e.g. image) monitored by the attacker.
- **JavaScript execution:** For mixed-JavaScript and mixed-Flash content, the attacker can inject arbitrary JavaScript code that will be executed in the context of the HTTPS website using the mixed content. This allows the attacker to run arbitrary JavaScript code as if it was originating from the TLS-protected site, and access a variety of security-sensitive JavaScript APIs. Moreover, the attacker can inject malicious payloads, such as the BeEF framework [2], to take over the user's browser and launch various attacks.

The various types of mixed content and their impact are summarized in Table 1.

4   Data Collection

In this section, we describe the setup and results of our large-scale data collection experiment.

4.1   Crawling Experiment

Starting with Alexa's list of 100,000 most popular domains, we first filter out the domains that are not available over TLS. Next, we use the Bing Search API [3] to automatically query for a set of 200 HTTPS page URLs for each website.

To discover mixed-content inclusions on TLS-enabled websites, we apply the approach as described in [18]: the headless HtmlUnit browser is used to visit the page URLs, and the HTTPS pages are analyzed to locate mixed-content inclusions. HtmlUnit is able to execute the JavaScript code similar to a real browser, and as such, it can detect dynamically-included mixed content.

4.2   Data Collection Results

With the aforementioned approach, we extracted 18,526 HTTPS websites from Alexa top 100,000 Internet domains, and in total 481,656 HTTPS pages are crawled, with an average of 26 HTTPS pages per website.

Table 2. Overview of distribution of mixed-content inclusions

	# Inclusions	% remote inclusions	# Files	# Webpages	% Websites
Image	406,932	38 %	138,959	45,417	30 %
iframe	25,362	90 %	15,227	15,419	14 %
CSS	35,957	44 %	6,680	15,911	12 %
JavaScript	150,179	72 %	29,952	45,059	26 %
Flash	1,721	62 %	638	1,474	2 %
Total	620,151	47 %	191,456	74,946	43 %

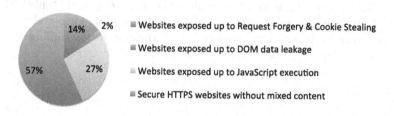

14% 2% ▪ Websites exposed up to Request Forgery & Cookie Stealing

▪ Websites exposed up to DOM data leakage

57% 27% ▪ Websites exposed up to JavaScript execution

▪ Secure HTTPS websites without mixed content

Fig. 1. Percentage of TLS-enabled websites vulnerable to different attacks

From the crawled HTTPS websites, 7,980 (43 %) were found to have at least one type of mixed content. This means that almost half of the HTTPS protected websites, are vulnerable to one or more of the attacks mentioned in the previous sections. In total, 620,151 mixed-content inclusions were found through our experiment, which maps to 191,456 mixed-content files and 74,946 HTTPS webpages. Table 2 gives an overview of the distribution of mixed-content inclusions. Image and JavaScript are the most included mixed content types, with 30 % and 26 % of the HTTPS websites using them respectively, while mixed-Flash content is much less used. As for the distribution over remote and local inclusions for each mixed content type, mixed iframe, JavaScript, and Flash content is mostly served by remote providers, while the majority of mixed Image and CSS inclusions are locally included.

To better understand the risks associated with websites using different types of mixed content, we calculate the percentage of websites that are exposed to different levels of attacks as shown in Fig. 1. The calculation is based on the impact analysis for each mixed content type (Table 1), which groups different types of mixed-content inclusions according to the associated attacks. Figure 1 shows that 27 % websites are exposed to attacks up to "JavaScript execution", by including mixed JavaScript or Flash content.

5 Discussion

In this section, we discuss some characteristics of mixed content and the websites including them, as discovered in our experiment. First, we identify the distribution of websites having mixed content over different categories, and then present some examples of important websites having mixed-JavaScript content. Second, we investigate the availability of mixed content files over HTTPS.

5.1   Websites Having Mixed Content

To better understand the websites having mixed content, we categorize the websites based on McAfee's TrustedSource Web Database [17]. Most of the visited HTTPS websites are categorized into 88 categories, with 1,181 websites remaining uncategorized. The majority of visited websites (66 %) can be categorized into 10 popular categories. As shown in Fig. 2, The 'Government/Military' websites are doing better than websites in all other categories, with "only" 31 % of them websites having mixed content. 38 % of 'Finance/Banking' websites having mixed content, which is worrisome, since these websites contain valuable information and are typically the targets of attackers.

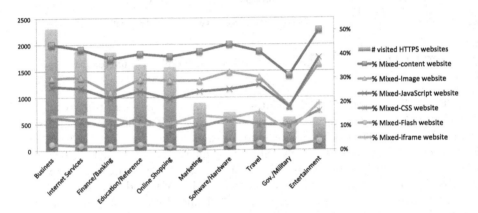

Fig. 2. Distribution of websites having mixed content over top 10 categories

For the 74,946 HTTPS pages having mixed content, we check whether these pages have an equivalent HTTP version of the same content. While most of them do have an HTTP version, 9,792 (11 %) pages are only served over HTTPS, and these "HTTPS-Only" pages map to 1,678 (9 %) HTTPS websites. We consider it likely that these "HTTPS-Only" pages contain more sensitive data and should be more secure, compared to those pages having the same content served over HTTP. Thus, mixed-content inclusions on "HTTPS-Only" pages can have more severe consequences when successfully exploited.

Table 3 lists ten examples of "HTTPS-Only" pages (selected from Alexa's top 1,000 websites) having mixed-JavaScript content. These pages provide important functionalities like "Account Signup", "Account Login", and "Password Recovery", all of which process sensitive user information and thus can lead to user-data leakage if the mixed-JavaScript content is intercepted by an attacker.

Of the 1,678 HTTPS websites that have "HTTPS-Only" pages, we found 97 websites that are using HTTP Strict Transport Security (HSTS) policy [15],

Table 3. Ten example "HTTPS-Only" pages having mixed-JavaScript content

HTTPS-Only pages	Functionality
http://www.aweber.com/signup.htm	Account Signup
http://www36.verizon.com/callassistant/signin.aspx	Account Login
http://secure.pornhublive.com/forgot-password/	Password Recovery
http://euw.leagueoflegends.com/account/recovery/password	Password Recovery
http://ww15.itau.com.br/privatebank/contatoprivate/en/index.aspx	Contact Form
http://dv.secure.force.com/applyonline/Page1?brand=ccn	Application Form
http://www.tribalfusion.com/adapp/forms/contactForm.jsp	Contact Form
http://support.makemytrip.com/ForgotPassword.aspx	Password Recovery
http://jdagccc.custhelp.com/app/utils/create_account/red/1	Account Signup
http://ssl6.ovh.net/~pasfacil/boutiquemedievale/login.php	Account Login

which indicates that these websites are making use of the latest protection technology for ensuring the use of SSL, but they still fail to achieve their goal by including mixed content from insecure channels.

5.2   Providers of Mixed-Content Files

For the total of 191,456 mixed-content files, we check whether the providers serve these files over a secure HTTPS channel next to their insecure HTTP versions. While the majority of mixed JavaScript, iframe and CSS content files are available over HTTPS, the percentage of mixed Image content files available over HTTPS is significantly less, as shown in Table 4. Though website owners should be responsible for the mixed content issue, the data in Table 4 indicates that blaming them is too simplistic, since it ignores the fact that approximately half of the mixed content files are only available over HTTP.

6   Mixed Content Mitigation Techniques

In this section, we investigate and enumerate protection techniques that can be used for browsers, TLS-protected websites, and content providers, to mitigate the issue of insecure inclusion of content.

Table 4. Percentage of "HTTPS-Available" files, per mixed content type

Type	# Files	% HTTPS-Available	Type	# Files	% HTTPS-Available
Image	138,959	40 %	JavaScript	29,952	58 %
iframe	15,227	77 %	Flash	638	46 %
CSS	6,680	60 %	Total	191,456	47 %

6.1   Browser Vendors

Blocking mixed content at the browser-level, is the most straightforward way to mitigate the mixed content issue. While most desktop browsers have developed a mixed-content blocker to protect users against insecure content, mobile browsers strongly lag behind on this, despite the fact that mobile browsing is becoming increasingly important to users. According to recent statistics from StatCounter, the market share of mobile browsing has almost tripled in the last two years, having reached 16.08 % in June 2013.

As part of our study, we investigated how all the major mobile browsers for Android, iOS, Windows Phone and Windows RT platform handle mixed content – shown in Table 5. We unfortunately discovered that most of them do not have a mixed-content blocker, with the exception of Chrome for Android and IE 10 Mobile which protect the user against mixed content. Firefox for Android plans to have a mixed-content blocker in a future release [1].

Table 5. Mobile browsers' behavior towards mixed content

Platform	Mobile browser	Blocked?	Secure padlock shown?
Google Android 4.2	Chrome 28	Yes	with a yellow triangle
	Firefox 23	No	No
	Android browser	No	open padlock
	Opera Mobile 12	No	No
Apple iOS 6.1	Safari 6	No	No
	Chrome 28	No	with a yellow triangle
	Opera Mini 7	No	No
Windows Phone/RT 8	IE 10 Mobile	Yes	No

With respect to desktop browsers, Internet Explorer (IE) is the first browser that detected and blocked mixed content with IE 7, released in 2006. When mixed content is detected, the browser warns the user and allows her to choose whether insecure content should be loaded [7]. Many users, however, would probably click "Yes", rendering the mixed-content blocker useless [21]. An elegant way to handle mixed content would be to silently block mixed content without prompting the users. This approach has been chosen in Chrome (version 21+) [8], Internet Explorer (version 9+) [4], and the recently released Firefox 23 [9]. Safari and Opera browsers do not currently have a mixed-content blocker, which means that about 10 % of desktop users are still exposed to the dangers of mixed content.[1]

Chrome, IE, and Firefox all have a mixed-content blocker, but they only block mixed iframe, CSS, JavaScript and Flash content, and mixed Image content is

---

[1] Safari and Opera each owns 8.39 % and 1.03 % market share respectively, according to the statistics of usage share of desktop browsers for June 2013 from StatCounter [6].

left out. An interesting fact is that mixed-Image content is blocked in IE 7 and IE 8, but it is not blocked in IE 9 and IE 10. Since mixed Image and iframe content technically have the same impact which may lead to attacks "Request forgery" and "Cookie stealing", we recommend all browsers vendors to block all types of mixed content, thus completely eliminating the mixed content issue from the browser side. While this move would likely break some insecurely-coded websites, the security benefits of mixed-content-blocking definitely outweigh the temporary frustration of users when they encounter some websites that do not properly work.

6.2   Website Owners

TLS-protected websites can explicitly opt-in to only include content from secure channels. As shown in Table 4, 47 % of the mixed-content files are not correctly included, since the secure version of the resources exist and could thus be used. For the remaining set of mixed-content files that do not have a secure version, the resources can be cached locally, or proxied using their own SSL server.

To provide better security, a website using HTTPS can use a combination of the HTTP Strict Transport Security (HSTS) and Content Security Policy (CSP) [20] protocols, as illustrated in Listing 1.1.

Listing 1.1. Protecting TLS-protected sites via HSTS and CSP

```
1  Strict-Transport-Security: max-age=86400; includeSubDomains
2  Content-Security-Policy: default-src https:; \
3  script-src https: 'unsafe-inline'; \
4  style-src https: 'unsafe-inline'
```

First, HSTS can be used to guarantee that webpages are only served over HTTPS by forcing a compliant browser to only issue HTTPS requests for that website (line 1). By enforcing the HSTS policy, it can prevent SSL-stripping attacks [16]. Second, CSP can be used to detect mixed content violations (in report-only mode), and to actively block mixed content by specifying that only secure resources are allowed to be included (line 2). Notice that in this example the *unsafe-inline* directives are added to preserve temporary compatibility (lines 3–4), but website owners are encouraged to fully embrace the CSP technology so that they achieve full protection and no longer need these unsafe directives.

6.3   Resource Providers

Resource providers can also mitigate the mixed content issue by offering content over HTTPS (even only over HTTPS). Moreover, resource provider can also use HSTS to migrate non-HTTPS resources automatically and secure to HTTPS version. Notice, however, that not all browsers have support for HSTS policies (e.g., IE 10 and Safari 6), and that HSTS inherently has a bootstrapping problem during a browser's very first visit to an HSTS website. During this first request, an active network attacker can strip the HSTS header and circumvent this protection technique.

7 Related Work

To the best of our knowledge, this paper is the first that attempts to systematically discover the current state of practice of mixed content and uncover the various types of mixed-content inclusions and how they could be used to attack users and services.

While HTTPS is widely used for securing web communications, many attacks on HTTPS have been reported over the years [13]. Apart from the exploit of cryptographic weaknesses and design flaws in the SSL and TLS protocols, e.g., CRIME [19] and Lucky 13 [10], the incorrect adoption and configuration of HTTPS by websites, may also allow attackers to bypass HTTPS. For example, websites not using an HSTS policy are vulnerable to SSL-Stripping attacks [16]. According to the latest surveys of August 2013, about 76 % of HTTPS websites have security issues with their SSL implementations [5].

Web browsers also play an important role in web security, since they can automatically handle many sensitive, HTTPS security decisions, and provide security indicators through their user interfaces. While, in the last few years, desktop browsers, in response to various attacks like XSS and CSRF, have been substantially hardened, mobile browsers have unfortunately not caught up. Mobile browsers, when compared to desktop browsers, have less support for displaying HTTPS connection details, and for the warning about mixed content [11].

8 Conclusion

When migrating to HTTPS, many websites fail to fully update their applications, resulting in mixed-content inclusion, which can render the HTTPS protection useless. In this paper, we show that there is a considerable number of TLS-protected websites that currently have mixed content. We also observed that, while the desktop browsers are catching up to mitigate this issue, most mobile browsers do not have protections against mixed content yet, despite the increasing popularity of mobile devices. Since users are entering into the "Post-PC era", i.e., prefering mobile devices for regular Internet browsing and even for sensitive online transactions, it is important for mobile browsers to develop a mixed-content blocker, as several desktop browsers have already done. To handle this transitory phase, we investigated and reported the best practices for websites owners and content providers which can be used to counter the issue and protect their users against MITM attacks.

Acknowledgements. This research is partially funded by the Research Fund KU Leuven, iMinds, IWT, and by the EU FP7 projects WebSand, NESSoS and STREWS. With the financial support from the Prevention of and Fight against Crime Programme of the European Union (B-CCENTRE).

References

1. Add support for Mixed Content Blocking - Android. https://bugzilla.mozilla.org/show_bug.cgi?id=860581
2. BeEF - The Browser Exploitation Framework Project. http://beefproject.com/
3. Bing Search API. http://datamarket.azure.com/dataset/bing/search
4. "Only secure content is displayed" notification in internet explorer 9 or later. http://support.microsoft.com/kb/2625928
5. SSL Pulse. https://www.trustworthyinternet.org/ssl-pulse/
6. StatCounter. http://statcounter.com/
7. Internet Explorer 8 Mixed Content Handling (2009). http://msdn.microsoft.com/en-us/library/ee264315(v=vs.85).aspx
8. Ending mixed scripting vulnerabilities (2012). http://blog.chromium.org/2012/08/ending-mixed-scripting-vulnerabilities.html
9. Mixed content blocking enabled in firefox 23! (2013). https://blog.mozilla.org/tanvi/2013/04/10/mixed-content-blocking-enabled-in-firefox-23/
10. Al Fardan, N.J., Paterson, K.G.: Lucky Thirteen: breaking the TLS and DTLS record protocols. In: IEEE Symposium on Security and Privacy, SP 2013, pp. 526–540 (2013)
11. Amrutkar, C., Traynor, P., van Oorschot, P.C.: Measuring SSL indicators on mobile browsers: extended life, or end of the road? In: Gollmann, D., Freiling, F.C. (eds.) ISC 2012. LNCS, vol. 7483, pp. 86–103. Springer, Heidelberg (2012)
12. Barth, A., Jackson, C., Mitchell, J.C.: Robust defenses for cross-site request forgery. In: Proceedings of the 15th ACM Conference on Computer and Communications Security, CCS 2008, pp. 75–88. ACM, New York, NY, USA (2008)
13. Clark, J., van Oorschot, P.C.: SoK: SSL and HTTPS: revisiting past challenges and evaluating certificate trust model enhancements. In: IEEE Symposium on Security and Privacy, SP 2013, pp. 511–525 (2013)
14. Heiderich, M., Niemietz, M., Schuster, F., Holz, T., Schwenk, J.: Scriptless attacks: stealing the pie without touching the sill. In: Proceedings of the 2012 ACM Conference on Computer and Communications Security, CCS 2012, pp. 760–771. ACM, New York, NY, USA (2012)
15. Hodges, J., Jackson, C., Barth, A.: HTTP strict transport security (HSTS), IETF RFC (2012)
16. Marlinspike, M.: New Tricks for Defeating SSL in Practice, Blackhat (2009)
17. McAfee. TrustedSource Web Database. https://www.trustedsource.org/en/feedback/url
18. Nikiforakis, N., Invernizzi, L., Kapravelos, A., van Acker, S., Joosen, W., Kruegel, C., Piessens, F., Vigna, G.: You are what you include: large-scale evaluation of remote javascript inclusions. In: Proceedings of the 2012 ACM Conference on Computer and Communications Security, CCS 2012, pp. 736–747. ACM, New York, NY, USA (2012)
19. Rizzo, J., Duong, T.: Crime: Compression ratio info-leak made easy. In: ekoparty Security Conference (2012)
20. Stamm, S., Sterne, B., Markham, G.: Reining in the web with content security policy. In: Proceedings of the 19th International Conference on World Wide Web, WWW 2010, pp. 921–930. ACM, New York, NY, USA (2010)
21. Sunshine, J., Egelman, S., Almuhimedi, H., Atri, N., Cranor, L.F.: Crying Wolf: an empirical study of SSL warning effectiveness. In: Proceedings of the 18th Usenix Security Symposium, pp. 399–416 (2009)

Cryptography

An Ordered Multisignature Scheme Under the CDH Assumption Without Random Oracles

Naoto Yanai[1]([✉]), Masahiro Mambo[2], and Eiji Okamoto[1]

[1] Graduate School of System and Information Engineering,
University of Tsukuba, Tsukuba, Japan
yanai@cipher.risk.tsukuba.ac.jp, okamoto@risk.tsukuba.ac.jp
[2] Institute of Science and Engineering, Kanazawa University, Kanazawa, Japan
mambo@ec.t.kanazawa-u.ac.jp

Abstract. Ordered multisignatures are digital signatures which allow multiple signers to guarantee the signing order as well as the validity of a message, and thus are useful for constructing secure routing protocols. Although one of approaches to constructing the ordered multisignatures is to utilize aggregate signatures, there is no known scheme which is provably secure without using aggregate signatures under a reasonable complexity assumption in the standard model. In this paper we propose a provably secure ordered multisignature scheme under the CDH assumption in the standard model from scratch. Our proposed scheme has a positive property that the data size of signatures and the number of computations of bilinear maps are fixed with respect to the number of signers and the message length.

1 Introduction

1.1 Motivation

The current Internet design aims to provide high security for routing protocols without decreasing availability. A main approach to providing such a capability is to apply cryptography to the routing protocols. For instance, secure-border gateway protocol (S-BGP) [11] and border gateway protocol security (BGPSEC) [13] are inter-domain routing protocols with digital signatures where each autonomous system (AS) signs its own path information. These protocols can prevent route hijacking by virtue of the digital signatures, and is currently under consideration for standardization by IETF. Whereas cryptographic tools are expected to drastically improve security of network systems, they increase processing costs of the systems. Indeed, there are 36,000 ASes in the Internet [5], and in such a large scale network the cryptographic tools often cause a large amount of loads to AS routers. In fact, the deployment of the above technologies have been prevented due to the cost of ballooning memory of the routers [18]. A cryptographic primitive to overcome such an overloading problem is a multisignature scheme [9] where n signers sign a message and generate a single short signature instead of n individual signatures. This primitive is suitable for devices with low computational power and small storage such as routers.

© Springer International Publishing Switzerland 2015
Y. Desmedt (Ed.): ISC 2013, LNCS 7807, pp. 367–377, 2015.
DOI: 10.1007/978-3-319-27659-5_26

Table 1. Evaluation of the schemes: We denote by n the number of signers, by ℓ the message length, by $\mathcal{P}$ the computational cost of one bilinear map, by $\mathcal{E}$ the computational cost of one exponentiation, by $\mathcal{H}$ the computational cost of one map-to-point, by $\mathcal{L}(p)$ the binary length of p, by k the security parameter, and by ROM the random oracle model. Typical values for these parameters are $\mathcal{L}(p) = 176$ on a symmetric pairing for 80-bit security, $\ell = 176$, and $n = 20$. With Type A curve in PBC library [15], the cost per one $\mathcal{P}$ is 2.2078 msec, the cost per one $\mathcal{E}$ is 2.5591 msec and the cost per one $\mathcal{H}$ is 5.8960 msec.

Schemes	Computational cost for i-th Signer	Computational cost for verifier	Signature size	Public key size	Proof model
BGOY07 [3]	$(i+4)\mathcal{E} + \mathcal{H}$	$3\mathcal{P} + n\mathcal{E} + \mathcal{H}$	$2\mathcal{L}(p)$	$3\mathcal{L}(p)$	ROM
LOSSW06 [14]	$5\mathcal{E}$	$3\mathcal{P}$	$2\mathcal{L}(p)$	$(\ell+2)\mathcal{L}(p)$	Standard
AGH10 [1]	$(\ell+5)\mathcal{E}$	$(\ell+3)\mathcal{P} + 2\mathcal{E}$	$2\mathcal{L}(p) + k$	$\mathcal{L}(p)$	Standard
Our scheme	$(i+4)\mathcal{E}$	$4\mathcal{P} + n\mathcal{E}$	$3\mathcal{L}(p)$	$3\mathcal{L}(p)$	Standard

Ordered multisignatures [6] enjoy such efficiency improvement of multisignatures [9] and also guarantee the signing order. They are suitable for the border gateway protocol with data-plane security [7], which guarantees not only the validity of path information but also packet forwardings through the path. The existing provably secure ordered multisignature schemes [1,14] require a large memory and there is no practical scheme whose security is proven under only standard assumptions.

1.2 Our Contribution

We propose an efficient and provably secure ordered multisignature scheme under only the standard assumptions, i.e., under the CDH assumption and without the random oracles. Our scheme is more efficient than the existing schemes in the sense that the number of elements of public keys and the number of computations of bilinear maps, whose cost is heavy, are independent of the message length. Although several parts of the computations depend on the number of signers, it is quite less than the message length in a practical scenario. According to Kanaoka et al. [10], a distance between any two ASes can be fully covered by 20 hops. Thus, the number of signers of ordered multisignatures for routing security is at most 20 while the message length is at least 160 for 80-bit security. Hence, our scheme is efficient in the practical scenario: more specifically, the computational time of the proposed scheme is always less than one-tenth of that of the AGH10 scheme, and the memory size of routers is one percent of that of the LOSSW06 scheme.

The efficiency of our proposed scheme is achieved by eliminating the use of aggregate signatures [4], which are generalized multisignatures allowing each signer to sign an individual document. While any aggregate signature scheme gives rise to an ordered multisignature scheme [3], the existing aggregate signature schemes [1,14] under the CDH assumption in the standard model are inefficient. In this work, we construct an ordered multisignature scheme from scratch, i.e., without the aggregate signatures.

As described in Sect. 3, according to Boldyreva et al. [3], the BGOY07 scheme [3] based on the random oracle cannot be proven secure in the standard model even by introducing the Waters hash function [19]. In order to overcome this problem, we utilize two techniques, i.e., *dual re-randomization* and *full aggregation*. Intuitively, these techniques allow one to assign individual random numbers to each component of ordered multisignatures and re-ranzomize them. They do not contradict the claim by Boldyreva et al., and we can prove the security in an improved approach.

1.3   Related Work

The first multisignature scheme was proposed by Itakura and Nakamura [9], and the security was formalized by Ohta and Okamoto [17] and Micali et al. [16]. The first ordered multisignature scheme was proposed by Doi et al. [6] and, to the best of our knowledge, the existing scheme with provable security is given in [3], called the BGOY07 scheme. As described in Sect. 1, the BGOY07 scheme has been proposed in the random oracle model. Meanwhile, a provably secure ordered multisignature scheme can be derived from an aggregate signature scheme in a straightforward way as follows. Each signer signs a concatenation of a common message and a signing list from the first signer to the current signer. To the best of our knowledge, there are two aggregate-signature-based schemes, i.e., the AGH10 scheme [1] and the LOSSW06 scheme [14], based on the CDH problem without the random oracles. However, as shown in Table 1, the number of computations of the bilinear maps in the AGH10 scheme [1] and the number of elements of the public key in the LOSSW06 scheme [14] are linear in the message length, more precisely, the length of a hash digest of a message, which is quite large. Thus, these schemes are impractical for routers.

As the latest results, Lee et al. [12] proposed a sequential aggregate signature scheme under a reasonable assumption without the random oracles via the dual system methodology [20]. Hohemberger et al. [8] proposed full-domain hash signatures. Ordered multisignatures in the standard model can be obtained via these results. These constructions are elegant in the standpoint of cryptographic theory, but are impractical due to the use of multilinear maps or a stronger security assumption. In contrast, our goal is to construct a practical scheme under the CDH assumption in the standard model.

2   Preliminaries

Notations: Let the number of signers be n. We denote by m a message to be signed, by m_i the ith bit of the message m, by σ_i a signature generated by an ith signer, by pk_i a public key of the ith signer and by sk_i its corresponding secret key, by $\bot$ an error symbol, and by $a \parallel b$ a concatenation of any elements a and b, where the concatenation can be divided into the original elements a and *b.* We define $\psi_i := pk_1 \parallel \cdots \parallel pk_i$ to be the signing order from the first signer to ith signer where $\psi_0 := \emptyset$, and denote by $|\psi_i|$ the number of signers in ψ_i.

Security Assumption: Let $\mathbb{G}$ and $\mathbb{G}_T$ be groups with the same prime order p. We then define bilinear maps, bilinear groups and the CDH assumption in a bilinear group as follows:

Definition 1 (Bilinear Maps). A bilinear map $e : \mathbb{G} \times \mathbb{G} \to \mathbb{G}_T$ is a map such that the following conditions hold, where g is a generator of $\mathbb{G}$: (Bilinearity) For all $u, v \in \mathbb{G}$ and $a, b \in \mathbb{Z}_p^*$, $e(u^a, v^b) = e(u, v)^{ab}$; (Non-degeneracy) For any generator $g \in \mathbb{G}$, $e(g, g) \neq 1_{\mathbb{G}_T}$, $1_{\mathbb{G}_T}$ is an identity element over $\mathbb{G}_T$; (Computable) There is an efficient algorithm to compute $e(u, v)$ for any $u, v \in \mathbb{G}$.

In this paper, we say that $\mathbb{G}$ is a bilinear group if all these conditions hold, and we assume that the discrete logarithm problem (DLP) in the bilinear groups is hard. We call the parameter $(p, \mathbb{G}, \mathbb{G}_T, e)$ *pairing parameter*.

Definition 2 ((t, ϵ)-CDH Assumption in $\mathbb{G}$). We define the CDH problem in a bilinear group $\mathbb{G}$ with a security parameter 1^k as follows: for a given $(g, g^a, g^b) \in \mathbb{G}$ with uniformly random $(a, b) \in \mathbb{Z}_p$ and a pairing parameter $(p, \mathbb{G}, \mathbb{G}_T, e)$ as input, compute $g^{ab} \in \mathbb{G}$. We say the (t, ϵ)-CDH assumption holds in $\mathbb{G}$ if there is no probabilistic polynomial-time algorithm which can solve the CDH problem in $\mathbb{G}$ with an execution time t with a probability greater than ϵ.

3   Ordered Multisignatures

In this section, we define a syntax of an ordered multisignature scheme and its security. Ordered multisignatures are a natural extension of multisignatures where signatures guarantee not only messages but also the signing order. Its signing procedure is not interactive but sequential among a group of signers. A case that multiple signers sign in parallel is out of the scope of this primitive.

3.1   The Syntax

An ordered multisignature scheme consists of the following algorithms.

Setup: Given security parameter 1^k, generate a public parameter *para*.

Key Generation: Given *para*, generate a secret key sk_i and its corresponding public key pk_i.

Signing: Given sk_i, pk_i, a message m, a signing order ψ_{i-1} and a multisignature σ', generate a signature σ. If any problem occur, output an error symbol $\perp$. Otherwise, output σ.

Verification: Given m, σ, ψ_n and $\{pk_i\}_{i=1}^n$, output *accept* or *reject*.

(Correctness). The correctness of the ordered multisignature scheme is defined as follows. In an ordered multisignature scheme, we say that the scheme is correct if, for all *para*, sk_i and pk_i given by **Setup** and **Key Generation**, Verification(m, **Signing** $(sk_i, pk_i, m, \sigma', \psi_{i-1}), \psi_i, \{pk_j\}_{j=1}^i$) outputs *accept*.

3.2 Security Model

A security model in this paper deals with a more generic forgery in comparison with the security model in [21]. In the model, there exist an adversary $\mathcal{A}$ and a challenger $\mathcal{C}$. Our model is a variant of the certified key model [2]. The certified key model assumes that each signer knows a secret key corresponding to its own public key. $\mathcal{C}$ has a list $\mathcal{L}$ of certified keys that is used to certify users' own public keys. $\mathcal{A}$ can know all secret keys corresponding to public keys included in $\mathcal{L}$ except for the one given by $\mathcal{C}$ to a target signer. $\mathcal{A}$'s advantage is defined as a probability that $\mathcal{C}$ outputs *accept* in the following game. Similarly as the existing model of ordered multisignatures [3], our security model guarantees authenticity of a message signed by an honest signer and its position i in a signing group, but not which signers signed before or will sign after the i-th signer. Namely, we do not consider switching of the positions among colluding malicious signers. According to [3], this setting seems to be acceptable in the application described in [7]. Hereinafter, we denote by $x^{(i)}$ the value of the ith query for all x. $\mathcal{C}$ interacts with $\mathcal{A}$ as follows:

Initial Phase: Generate a public parameter *para* by **Setup** and a pair of challenger keys (sk^*, pk^*) by using **Key Generation**. Then, register pk^* in $\mathcal{L}$, and run $\mathcal{A}$ with *para* and pk^* as input.

Certification Query: Given (sk_i, pk_i) by $\mathcal{A}$, check if sk_i is a secret key corresponding to pk_i, and then register pk_i in $\mathcal{L}$ if so. Otherwise, return $\bot$.

Signing Query: Given a signing query $(m^{(h)}, \sigma', pk^*, \psi_{i^{(h)}-1})$ by $\mathcal{A}$ of the challenge key for all $i \in [1, n]$, check if the following conditions hold: **Verification** algorithm outputs *accept*; $\psi_{i^{(h)}-1}$ does not include pk^*; for $j = [1, i-1]$, pk_j in $\psi_{i^{(h)}-1}$ is registered in $\mathcal{L}$; $|\psi_{i^{(h)}-1}| < n$. If all the conditions hold, via **Signing** $(sk^*, pk^*, m^{(h)}, \sigma', \psi_{i^{(h)}})$, return σ. Otherwise, return $\bot$.

Output: After iterating over the above steps, $\mathcal{A}$ outputs a forgery $(m^*, \sigma^*, \psi_n^*)$, where let the signer with pk^* be the i^*th signer in ψ_n^* and n be the number of signers. Check if the following conditions hold for the given forgery: **Verification**$(m^*, \sigma^*, \psi_n^*, \{pk_i\}_{i=1}^n)$ outputs *accept*; $(m^*, i^*) \notin \{(m^{(h)}, i^{(h)})\}_{h=1}^{q_s}$ holds; ψ_n^* includes pk^*; for $j = [1, n]$, pk_j in ψ_n^* is included in $\mathcal{L}$. If all these conditions hold, then output *accept*. Otherwise, output *reject*.

Definition 3. We say that an adversary $\mathcal{A}$ breaks an ordered multisignature scheme with $(t, q_c, q_s, \ell, n, \epsilon)$ if a challenger $\mathcal{C}$ outputs *accept* in the security game described above within an execution time t and with a probability greater than ϵ. Here, $\mathcal{A}$ can generate at most q_c certification queries and at most q_s signing queries, ℓ is the length of a message, and n is the number of signers.

3.3 Technical Problem

Boldyreva et al. [3] proposed the CDH-based ordered multisignature scheme in the random oracle model, and one might think that an ordered multisignature scheme without random oracles can be constructed from their scheme. However, according to [3], if the Waters multisignature scheme [14] is substituted for a part of the random oracle in their ordered multisignature scheme, the approach to proving the security no longer seems to work. More specifically, a reduction algorithm without the random oracles requires a new component including random numbers in order to simulate the signing oracle while a reduction algorithm with the random oracles does not require it. Here, we note that ordered multisignatures contains two components, i.e., a message and the signing order. If a random number included in a signature is re-utilized in the other component in order to reduce the signature size, then the reduction algorithm has to compute with the random number, which is unknown for the algorithm. Namely, the simulation becomes unworkable due to interference by the unknown random number. An approach to overcoming this problem is to compress a signature component into a single one by utilizing aggregate signatures. Intuitively, the approach allows the reduction algorithm to avoid the interference of the random number. However, the aggregate signatures bring a degradation of the efficiency. Thus, we have to solve the problem without the aggregate signatures.

4   Proposed Scheme

We propose an ordered multisignature scheme. First, we describe our approach to overcoming the problem in Sect. 3.3, and then describe a construction. We assume that there exists a trusted center to generate a public parameter.

4.1   Our Strategy

Our main strategy is to utilize two properties, called *dual re-randomization* and *full aggregation*. The proofs in [3,21] are based on the re-randomization technique. Our idea is to separate an algebraic structure of the signatures into three components, i.e., secret keys, a message and the signing order, and to give an individual secret value to each component in order to dually execute the re-randomization. We call this technique the dual re-randomization. The schemes in [3,21] deal with only two secret values, and so the interference occurs. In contrast, our scheme deals with three components, and the re-randomization for each component is executed individually. In this strategy, while the signing oracle can be simulated as long as either of the components is re-randomizable, the other random number is not affected by the random number simulating the oracle. In other words, our proof can be considered as simulations of standard signatures in a dual way, and we can avoid the interference.

Meanwhile, another important property, the full aggregation (of random numbers), is a property such that the size of random parts in the signatures is independent of the number of signers. The full aggregation provides the efficiency and also makes reduction cost smaller. In particular, even if the dual re-randomization is executable, the reduction algorithm has to execute its reduction mechanism for each random number unless achieving the full aggregation.

This implies that the efficiency of the security reduction is degraded by the exponential order with respect to the number of the signers. In other words, by compressing the random numbers as small as possible, a perspective of the proof with multiple signers comes closer to a proof of standard signatures for a single signer, and thus the security can be proven.

4.2 The Construction

A message m will be dealt with a bit-string $\{0,1\}^\ell$ for all ℓ. We can let the ℓ-bit string be the output of a collision-resistant hash functions $H : \{0,1\}^* \to \{0,1\}^\ell$.

Setup: Given 1^k, generate a pairing parameter $(p, \mathbb{G}, \mathbb{G}_T, e)$, random generators $g_1, g_2 \in \mathbb{G}$ and $\ell + 1$ generators $(u', u_1, \cdots, u_\ell) \in \mathbb{G}^{\ell+1}$. Output $(p, \mathbb{G}, \mathbb{G}_T, e, g_1, g_2, u', u_1, \cdots, u_\ell)$ as a public parameter *para*.

Key Generation: Given $(p, \mathbb{G}, \mathbb{G}_T, e, g, u', u_1, \cdots, u_\ell)$, choose random numbers $\alpha_i, t_i, v_i \leftarrow \mathbb{Z}_p^*$, and set $A_i = g_1^{\alpha_i}, T_i = g_1^{t_i}$ and $V_i = g_1^{v_i}$. Output $(g_2^{\alpha_i}, t_i, v_i)$ as a secret key sk_i and (A_i, T_i, V_i) as its corresponding public key pk_i.

Signing: Given $(sk_i, pk_i, m, \sigma', \psi_{i-1})$, parse m as ℓ-bit strings $(m_1, \cdots, m_\ell) \in \{0,1\}^\ell$, σ' as $(S_{i-1}, R_{i-1}, W_{i-1})$ and ψ_{i-1} as a set $\{pk_j\}_{j \in [1, i-1]}$ of public keys, where $pk_i = (A_i, T_i, V_i)$ for all i. If $i = 1$, i.e., for the first signer in the signing group, then set $(S_{i-1}, R_{i-1}, W_{i-1}) = (1, 1, 1)$ and $\{pk_j\}_{j \in [1, i-1]} = \emptyset$ and the following verification step is skipped. Next, check that ψ_{i-1} includes pk_i. If so, output $\bot$. Otherwise, verify that the received signature σ' is accepted on m in ψ_{i-1} by using **Verification** for $n = i - 1$. If **Verification** outputs *reject*, abort the process and output $\bot$. Otherwise, generate random numbers $(r_i, w_i) \leftarrow \mathbb{Z}_p^*$ and compute as follows: $R_i = R_{i-1} \cdot g_1^{r_i}, W_i = W_{i-1} \cdot g_1^{w_i}$, and $S_i = S_{i-1} \cdot g_2^{\alpha_i} \left(u' \prod_{j=1}^\ell u_j^{m_j} \right)^{r_i} W_i^{it_i + v_i} \left(\prod_{l \in [1, i-1]} T_l^l V_l \right)^{w_i}$. Finally, output m, $\sigma = (S_i, R_i, W_i)$.

Verification: Given $(m, \sigma, \psi_n, \{pk_i\}_{i=1}^n)$, parse m as an ℓ-bit string $(m_1, \cdots, m_\ell) \in \{0,1\}^\ell$, σ as (S_n, R_n, W_n), and extract each signer's public key (A_i, T_i, V_i) from $\{pk_i\}_{i=1}^n$. Then, check that all of $\{pk_i\}_{i=1}^n$ are distinct, and output *reject* if not. Otherwise, verify that the following equation holds:

$$e(S_n, g_1) \stackrel{?}{=} e\left(g_2, \prod_{i=1}^n A_i\right) e\left(R_n, u' \prod_{j=1}^\ell u_j^{m_j}\right) e\left(W_n, \prod_{i=1}^n T_i^i V_i\right).$$

If not, output *reject*. Otherwise, output *accept*.

4.3 Security Analysis

Theorem 4. The proposed scheme is the $(t, q_c, q_s, \ell, n, \epsilon)$-secure if (t', ϵ')-CDH assumption in $\mathbb{G}$ holds, where $t' = t + (2q_c + nq_s + n)t_e$, $\epsilon' = \frac{\epsilon}{16e(\ell+1)q_s(q_s+1)}$, t_e is the computational cost for one exponentiation and e is base of natural logarithm.

Proof. We assume that there exists an adversary $\mathcal{A}$ who breaks the proposed scheme with $(t, q_c, q_s, \ell, n, \epsilon)$. Then, we build an algorithm $\mathcal{B}$ that solves the CDH problem. In this proof, without the loss of generality, there exists exactly one signer, the target signer, who corresponds to a challenge key. $\mathcal{B}$ has the list $\mathcal{L}$ of certified-keys. $\mathcal{B}$ interacts with $\mathcal{A}$ as follows:

Initial Phase: Given a CDH challenge value (g, g^a, g^b) and a pairing parameter $(p, \mathbb{G}, \mathbb{G}_T, e)$, $\mathcal{B}$ sets $\mathcal{L} = \emptyset$, $d = 4q_s$, $g_1 = g$ and $g_2 = g^b$. Then, $\mathcal{B}$ chooses $s \leftarrow \{0, \cdots, \ell\}$, ℓ-length vectors $x_i \leftarrow \mathbb{Z}_d^\ell$ and $y_i \leftarrow \mathbb{Z}_p^\ell$, $x' \leftarrow \mathbb{Z}_d$, and $y' \leftarrow \mathbb{Z}_p$. Here, we define polynomials $F(m) = (p - ds) + x' + \sum_{i=1}^\ell x_i m_i$ and $J(m) = y' + \sum_{i=1}^\ell y_i m_i$. $\mathcal{B}$ also sets $u' = g_2^{\prime p - ds + x'} g_1^{y'}$ and $u_i = g_2^{\prime x_i} g_1^{y_i}$ as the public parameter, i.e., $u' \prod_{j=1}^\ell u_j^{m_j} = g_2^{F(m)} g^{J(m)}$. Then, $\mathcal{B}$ generates a random number $k^* \leftarrow [1, n]$ where n is the number of signers for $\mathcal{A}$'s capability, and $(t^*, v^*) \leftarrow \mathbb{Z}_p$. Finally, $\mathcal{B}$ sets $T^* = (g^a)^{t^*}$, $V^* = (g^a)^{-t^* k^*} g^{v^*}$, and $A^* = g^a$ as the public key of the target signer. This means that $\mathcal{B}$ implicitly sets ab as the target signer's secret key. Then, $\mathcal{B}$ runs $\mathcal{A}$ with $(p, \mathbb{G}, \mathbb{G}_T, e, g_1, g_2, u', u_1, \cdots, u_\ell, A_i, T_i, V_i)$.

Certification Query: For any signer, given $sk_i = (g_2^{\alpha_i}, t_i, v_i)$ and $pk = (A_i, T_i, V_i)$ by $\mathcal{A}$, $\mathcal{B}$ checks if $e(g_2^{\alpha_i}, g_1) = e(g_2, A_i)$, $V_i = g_1^{v_i}$, and $T_i = g_1^{t_i}$ hold. If these equations hold, pk_i is registered in $\mathcal{L}$. Otherwise, the output is $\perp$.

Signing Query: Given a signing query $(pk^*, m^{(h)}, \psi_{i^{(h)}-1}, \sigma')$, $\mathcal{B}$ checks if $F(m^{(h)}) \neq 0 \vee i^{(h)} \neq k^*$ holds where $i^{(h)}$ is a position of the target signer for hth query, and aborts the process if the condition does not hold. Otherwise, $\mathcal{B}$ generates $(r, w) \leftarrow \mathbb{Z}_p$ and computes either one of the following cases:

(Case 1). $F(m^{(h)}) \neq 0$: Compute $R_{i^{(h)}} = g^r (g^a)^{-\frac{1}{F(m^{(h)})}}$, $W_{i^{(h)}} = g^w$, and
$$S_{i^{(h)}} = (g^a)^{-\frac{J(m^{(h)})}{F(m^{(h)})}} \left(u' \prod_{j=1}^\ell u_j^{m_j} \right)^r \left(\prod_{l=1}^{i^{(h)}} (T_l^l V_l) \right)^w g_2^{\sum_{l \in [1, i^{(h)}-1]} \alpha_l}.$$
From **Initial Phase**, this (S_i, R_i, W_i) is accepted as follows:

$$S_{i^{(h)}} = g^{ab} \left((g^b)^{F(m^{(h)})} g^{J(m^{(h)})} \right)^{-\frac{a}{F(m^{(h)})}} \left(u' \prod_{j=1}^\ell u_j^{m_j} \right)^r \left(\prod_{l=1}^{i^{(h)}} T_l^l V_l \right)^w g_2^{\sum_{l \in [1, i^{(h)}-1]} \alpha_l}$$

$$= g_2^{a + \sum_{l \in [1, i^{(h)}-1]} \alpha_l} \left(u' \prod_{j=1}^\ell u_j^{m_j} \right)^{r - \frac{a}{F(m^{(h)})}} \left(\prod_{l=1}^{i^{(h)}} T_l^l V_l \right)^w.$$

(Case 2). $F(m^{(h)}) = 0 \wedge i^{(h)} \neq k^*$: Compute $R_{i^{(h)}} = g^r$, $W_{i^{(h)}} = g^w$, $(g^b)^{-\frac{1}{t^*(i^{(h)}-k^*)}}$,

$$S_{i^{(h)}} = (g^b)^{-\frac{v^*}{t^*(i^{(h)}-k^*)}} \left((g^a)^{i^{(h)} t^*} (g^a)^{-t^* k^*} g^{v^*} \right)^w \left(u' \prod_{j=1}^\ell u_j^{m_j} \right)^r$$

$$\times (W_{i^{(h)}})^{\sum_{l \in [1, i^{(h)}-1]} (l t_l + v_l)} g_2^{\sum_{l \in [1, i^{(h)}-1]} \alpha_l}.$$

From **Initial Phase**, this (S_i, R_i, W_i) is accepted as follows:

$$S_{i^{(h)}} = g^{ab} g^{-ab\frac{t^*(i^{(h)}-k^*)}{t^*(i^{(h)}-k^*)}} (g^b)^{-\frac{v^*}{t^*(i^{(h)}-k^*)}} \left((g^a)^{i^{(h)} t^*} (g^a)^{-t^* k^*} g^{v^*} \right)^w$$

$$\times \left(u' \prod_{j=1}^{\ell} u_j^{m_j} \right)^r (W_{i^{(h)}})^{\sum_{l \in [1, i^{(h)}-1]} l t_l + v_l} g_2^{\sum_{l \in [1, i^{(h)}-1]} \alpha_l}$$

$$= g_2^{a + \sum_{l \in [1, i^{(h)}-1]} \alpha_l} \left(u' \prod_{j=1}^{\ell} u_j^{m_j} \right)^r \left(\prod_{l=1}^{i^{(h)}} T_l^l V_l \right)^{w - \frac{b}{t^*(i^{(h)}-k^*)}}.$$

Output: After iterating over the steps described above, $\mathcal{A}$ outputs a forgery $\sigma^* = (S_n^*, R_n^*, W_n^*)$ on a message m^* in the signing order ψ_n^*. If $F(m^*) \neq 0 \vee i^* \neq k^*$ holds in the forgery output by $\mathcal{A}$ where i^* is the position of the target signer, then $\mathcal{B}$ aborts. Otherwise, $\mathcal{B}$ can solve the CDH problem as follows. If the verification equation holds holds, then S^* can be written as follows:

$$S^* = g_2^{a + \sum_{i=1 \wedge i \neq i^*}^n \alpha_i} \left((g^b)^{F(m^*)} g^{J(m^*)} \right)^r \left((g^a)^{t^*(i^* - k^*)} g^{v^*} \prod_{i=1 \wedge i \neq i^*}^n T_i^i V_i \right)^w$$

$$= g_2^{a + \sum_{i=1 \wedge i \neq i^*}^n \alpha_i} \left(g^{J(m^*)} \right)^r \left(g^{v^*} \prod_{i=1 \wedge i \neq i^*}^n T_i^i V_i \right)^w.$$

$$\therefore g^{ab} = \frac{S^*}{g_2^{\sum_{j=1 \wedge j \neq i^*}^n \alpha_j} (R^*)^{J(m^*)} (W^*)^{v^* + \sum_{i=1 \wedge i \neq i^*}^n (i t_i + v_i)}}.$$

$\mathcal{B}$ knows all the secret values except for ab and so can compute the above values. If $\mathcal{B}$'s guess is correct, $\mathcal{B}$ can solve the CDH problem. Therefore, the probability is given as $\epsilon' \geq \epsilon \cdot \Pr[E_1] \Pr[E_2]$, where $E_1 = \left[(\bigwedge_{h=1}^{q_s} F(m^{(h)}) \neq 0) \wedge F(m^*) = 0 \right]$, $E_2 = \left[\bigwedge_{h=1}^{q_s} (i^{(h)} \neq k^*) \wedge i^* = k^* \right]$ and $i^{(h)}$ is the position of the target signer for the signing queries. E_1 is analyzed in a manner similar to the proof in [19], and E_2 is analyzed in a manner similar to the proof in [3]. Therefore, $\Pr[E_1] = \frac{1}{16 q_s (\ell+1)}$ and $\Pr[E_2] = \frac{1}{e(q_s+1)}$. Thus, the probability is $\epsilon' = \frac{\epsilon}{16 e(\ell+1) q_s (q_s+1)}$. Additionally, the execution time of $\mathcal{B}$ is that of $\mathcal{A}$ plus two exponentiation computations for **Certification Query**, n exponentiation computations for **Signing Query** for q_s times, and n exponentiations for the final step. Therefore, $t' = t + (2 q_c + n q_s + n) t_e$ holds, where t_e is the computational time for one exponentiation. $\square$

Acknowledgement. A part of this research is supported by JSPS A3 Foresight Program, and Support Center for Advanced Telecommunications Technology Research. We would like to appreciate their supports. We would also like to appreciate Shin-Akarui-Angou-Benkyou-Kai for their valuable comments.

References

1. Ahn, J.H., Green, M., Hohenberger, S.: Synchronized aggregate signatures: new definitions, constructions and applications. In: Proceedings of the ACM CCS 2011, pp. 473–484. ACM (2010)
2. Boldyreva, A.: Threshold signatures, multisignatures and blind signatures based on the gap-diffie-hellman-group signature scheme. In: Desmedt, Y.G. (ed.) PKC 2003. LNCS, vol. 2567, pp. 31–46. Springer, Heidelberg (2002)
3. Boldyreva, A., Gentry, C., O'Neill, A., Yum, D.H.: Ordered multisignatures and identity-based sequential aggregate signatures, with applications to secure routing (extended abstract). In: Proceedings of ACM CCS 2007, pp. 276–285. ACM (2007)
4. Boneh, D., Gentry, C., Lynn, B.: Aggregate and verifiably encrypted signatures from bilinear maps. In: Biham, E. (ed.) EUROCRYPT 2003. LNCS, vol. 2656, pp. 416–432. Springer, Heidelberg (2003)
5. Chi, Y.-J., Oliveira, R., Zhang, L.: Cyclops: the as-level connectivity observatory. ACM Sigcomm Comput. Commun. Rev. **38**(4), 5–16 (2008)
6. Doi, H., Mambo, M., Okamoto, E.: Multisignature schemes using structured group id. Tech. Rep. IEICE **98**, 43–48 (1998). IEICE
7. Feamster, N., Balakrishnan, H., Rexford, J.: Some foundational problems in inter-domain routing. In: Proceedings of HotNets-3 2004. ACM (2004)
8. Hohenberger, S., Sahai, A., Waters, B.: Full domain hash from (leveled) multilinear maps and identity-based aggregate signatures. In: Canetti, R., Garay, J.A. (eds.) CRYPTO 2013, Part I. LNCS, vol. 8042, pp. 494–512. Springer, Heidelberg (2013)
9. Itakura, K., Nakamura, K.: A public-key cryptosystem suitable for digital multi-signatures. NEC Res. Dev. **71**, 1–8 (1983)
10. Kanaoka, A., Okada, M., Katsuno, Y., Okamoto, E.: Probabilistic packet marking method considering topology property for efficiency re-building dos attack paths. TIPSJ **52**(3), 929–939 (2011)
11. Kent, S., Lynn, C., Seo, K.: Secure border gateway protocol. IEEE J. Sel. Areas Commun. **18**(4), 582–592 (2000)
12. Lee, K., Lee, D.H., Yung, M.: Sequential aggregate signatures with short public keys: design, analysis and implementation studies. In: Kurosawa, K., Hanaoka, G. (eds.) PKC 2013. LNCS, vol. 7778, pp. 423–442. Springer, Heidelberg (2013)
13. Lepinski, M., Turner, S.L: An overview of bgpsec. Internet Draft (2011). http://tools.ietf.org/html/draft-ietf-sidr-bgpsec-overview-01
14. Lu, S., Ostrovsky, R., Sahai, A., Shacham, H., Waters, B.: Sequential aggregate signatures and multisignatures without random oracles. In: Vaudenay, S. (ed.) EUROCRYPT 2006. LNCS, vol. 4004, pp. 465–485. Springer, Heidelberg (2006)
15. Lynn, B.: Pbc library (2013). http://crypto.stanford.edu/pbc/
16. Micali, S., Ohta, K., Reyzin, L.: Accountable-subgroup multisignatures: extended abstract. In: Proceedings of ACM CCS 2001, pp. 245–254. ACM (2001)
17. Ohta, K., Okamoto, T.: Multi-signature schemes secure against active insider attacks. IEICE Trans. Fundam. Electron. Commun. Comput. Sci. **E82**(A(1)), 21–31 (1999)
18. Sriram, K., Borchert, O., Kim, O., Cooper, D., Montgomery, D.: Rib size estimation for bgpsec. IETF SIDR WG Meeting, IETF 81 (2011). http://www.antd.nist.gov/ksriram/BGPSEC_RIB_Estimation.pdf
19. Waters, B.: Efficient identity-based encryption without random oracles. In: Cramer, R. (ed.) EUROCRYPT 2005. LNCS, vol. 3494, pp. 114–127. Springer, Heidelberg (2005)

20. Waters, B.: Dual system encryption: realizing fully secure IBE and HIBE under simple assumptions. In: Halevi, S. (ed.) CRYPTO 2009. LNCS, vol. 5677, pp. 619–636. Springer, Heidelberg (2009)
21. Yanai, N., Chida, E., Mambo, M., Okamoto, E.: A cdh-based ordered multisignature scheme provably secure without random oracles. JIP **55**(2), 366–375 (2014)

Human Assisted Randomness Generation Using Video Games

Mohsen Alimomeni[(⊠)] and Reihaneh Safavi-Naini

Department of Computer Science, University of Calgary, Calgary, Canada
{malimome,rei}@ucalgary.ca

Abstract. Random number generators have direct applications in information security, online gaming, gambling, and computer science in general. True random number generators need an entropy source which is a physical source with inherent uncertainty, to ensure unpredictability of the output. In this paper we propose a new indirect approach to collecting entropy using human errors in the game play of a user against a computer. We argue that these errors are due to a large set of factors and provide a good source of randomness. To show the viability of this proposal, we design and implement a game, conduct a user study in which we collect user input in the game, and extract randomness from it. We measure the rate and the quality of the resulting randomness that clearly show effectiveness of the approach. Our work opens a new direction for construction of entropy sources that can be incorporated into a large class of video games.

1 Introduction

Randomness has a central role in computer science and in particular information security. Security of cryptographic algorithms and protocols relies on keys that must be random. Random coins used in randomized encryption and authentication algorithms and values such as nonces in protocols, must be unpredictable. In all these cases, unpredictability of random values is crucial for security proofs. There are also applications such as online games, gambling applications and lotteries in which unpredictability is a critical requirement.

Poor choices of randomness in the past have resulted in complete breakdown of security and expected functionality of the system. Early reported examples of bad choices of randomness resulting in security failure include attack on Netscape implementation of the SSL protocol [GW96] and weakness of entropy collection in Linux Pseudo-Random Generator [GPR06]. A more recent high profile reported case was the discovery of collisions among secret (and public) keys generated by individuals around the world [LHA+12, HDWH12]. Further studies attributed the phenomenon partly due to the flaw in Linux kernel randomness generation subsystem.

In computer systems, true randomness is commonly generated by sampling a complex external source such as disk accesses or time intervals between system

© Springer International Publishing Switzerland 2015
Y. Desmedt (Ed.): ISC 2013, LNCS 7807, pp. 378–390, 2015.
DOI: 10.1007/978-3-319-27659-5_27

interrupts, or is from users' inputs. Importance of true randomness in computer systems has been well recognized and operating systems such as Linux and Windows have dedicated subsystems for entropy collection and randomness generation. These subsystems use internal system interrupts as well as user generated events as entropy source. High demand on entropy pools, for example when a computer runs multiple processes and algorithms that require randomness at the same time, can result in either pseudorandom values instead of truly random values, or stopping the execution until sufficient randomness become available.

The rate of randomness generation can be increased by including new sources of randomness which in many cased requires new hardware. An attractive alternative that does not require additional hardware is to use human assistance in randomness generation. This can be by directly asking human to input random numbers or move the mouse randomly [ZLwW+09]. The process is unintuitive and experiments in psychology have shown that the resulting randomness has bias [Wag72].

In this paper, we propose a novel indirect approach to entropy collection from human input in game play that uses games as a targeted activity that the human engages in, and as a by product generates random values. Video games are one of the most widely used computer applications and embedding entropy collection in a large class of such games provides a rich source of entropy for computer systems.

1.1   Our Work

Our main observation is that human, even if highly skilled, would not be able to have perfect game play in video games because of a large set of factors related to human cognitive processes and motor skill and coordination, limitations of computer interface including display, keyboard and mouse, and unpredictability elements in the game. The combination of these factors in well designed games results in the player "missing" the target in the game where although the goal may appear simple, achieving it is not always possible.

We propose to use the error resulting from the confluence of the complex factors outlined above, as an entropy source. The unpredictability in the output of this source is inherent in the game design: that is a game that always results in win or loose is not "interesting" and will not be designed. In contrast games in which the user can "loose" a good portion of rounds are considered interesting. In a human game play randomness can be collected from different variables in the game, including the timing of different actions, the size of the "miss" as well as variables recording aspects of the human input such as angle of a shot, and so in each round, even when the user wins, a good amount of entropy can be generated.

Related Work. Halprin et al. [HN09] proposed to use human input in a game played against a computer as an entropy source. Their work was inspired by

Rapport et al.'s [RB92] experiments in psychology that showed a human playing a competitive zero-sum game with uniform optimal strategy, generates better randomness compared to the case that they are directly instructed to supply random inputs. Halprin et al. used an expanded version (larger input set) of the game and replaced one of the users by the computer. The underlying assumption in this approach is that the human sequence of actions, when engaged in a game with uniform optimal strategy, simulates the game optimal strategy and so can be used as a uniform source of randomness. For the choices of human to be close to random, Psychological results require that human is presented with few choices, otherwise the human will tend to select certain choices with more probability. So Alimomeni et al. [ASNS14] proposed a game design along the above game-theoretic approach in which human had only 3 choices and the randomness extraction was done as part of the game design with no need for seed. They showed that this design still keep the rate of min-entropy high because of the added extractor in the game that needs no randomness.

The above approaches are fundamentally different from the approach in this paper that uses the complexity of the process of generation of human input in the game, as the entropy source. Our approach is more in the spirit of sampling a complex process such as disk access, now using human and computer interaction as the complex process.

To use Halrin et al.'s approach in practice, one needs to design a two-party game with the supporting game-theoretic analysis to show the optimal strategy is uniform. The next step is to convert the game into an interesting game between the human and computer and validate that human would play as expected (is able to simulate the optimal strategy). In contrast our approach can be easily incorporated into video games such as target shooting games and does not need new game designs.

Implementation. As a proof of concept we designed and implemented a multi-level archery game, collected user inputs in the game and extracted randomness from the collected inputs.

Our results clearly show that error variables, for example the distance between the target and the trajectory of the arrow, provides a very good source of entropy. The experiments show that the game can generate 15 to 21.5 bits of min-entropy per user shot using only the error variable. The variation in the amount of min-entropy is due to the variations in the game level and also varying levels of skill and learnability of users. Our experiments demonstrate that although entropy decreases as players become more experienced, but the entropy of the error variable will stay non-zero and even for the most experienced player at the lowest level of the game, 15 bits entropy per shot can be expected.

1.2   Applications

Game Consoles and Smart Phones. Game consoles require true randomness for secure communication with the game servers, checking the digitally signed games and firmware updates from the server and to provide randomness to the games that is played. Lack of good random generation subsystems in these consoles may result in attacks such as reported in [Hot10]. Incorporating our approach into the video games played in such consoles would provide a method of generating randomness with high rate and verifiable properties. Our approach also provides an ideal entropy source for small devices such as smart phones that are used for gaming and have limited source of entropy.

On-demand RNG in OS. An immediate application of our proposal is to provide on-demand entropy source for OS random number generation module. In softwares such as PGP, Openssl, and GnuPG that need generation of cryptographic keys, using true randomness is critical. Such applications rely on the random number generation of the OS which may not have true randomness available at the time of the request. Our proposed entropy source can be used for entropy collection from users by asking them to play a simple game. Our experiments showed that producing 100 bits of entropy required 6 runs of the game, making the approach an effective solution in these situations.

Contributory Random Number Generation. In virtualized environments, multiple users share the same hardware (including CPU and RAM) and so the entropy pools of different users share a substantial amount of entropy produced by the system's shared hardware, resulting in the risk of dependence between entropy pools of different users. This is an important concern if the resulting randomness is used for key generation, potentially leading to attacks such as those reported in [HDWH12]. Using users' game play provides a source of randomness that is independent from the underlying hardware and other users' randomness.

2   Preliminaries

We will use the following notations. Random variables are denoted by capital letters, such as X. A random variable X is defined over a set $\mathcal{X}$ with a probability distribution $\Pr_X$, meaning that X takes the value $x \in \mathcal{X}$ with probability $\Pr_X(x) = \Pr[X = x]$. Uniform distribution over a set $\mathcal{X}$ is denoted by $U_\mathcal{X}$. Min-entropy of a source is a worst case measure and represents the best chance of the adversary in predicting the output of an entropy source. The *min-entropy* $H_\infty(X)$ of a random variable X is given by, $H_\infty(X) = -\log_2 \max_x \Pr_X(x)$. *Statistical distance* measures closeness of distributions and is used to measure closeness of the output of an entropy source to that of a perfect entropy source. The *statistical distance* $\Delta(X, Y)$ between two random variables X and Y over the same range $\mathcal{A}$, is given by $\Delta(X, Y) = \frac{1}{2} \sum_{a \in \mathcal{A}} |\Pr_X(a) - \Pr_Y(a)|$. If $\Delta(X, U_\mathcal{X}) \leq \epsilon$, then we say X is ϵ-biased or ϵ-close to uniform. We say X is *almost truly random* if X is ϵ-biased for a sufficiently small ϵ. A sequence of random variables $\{X_i\}_{i=1}^n$ is called an almost truly random sequence, if $\{X_i | X_{i-1} = x_{i-1}, \ldots, X_1 = x_1\}_{i=1}^n$ is ϵ-biased. An entropy source is a generator of sequences of symbols $\{x_i\}_{i=1}^n$ each sampled from a random variable X_i, where all X_i are defined over a finite set $\mathcal{X}$. It is important to note that output symbols of an entropy source may be correlated and not necessarily have the same distribution.

2.1   True Random Number Generators (TRNG)

A TRNG has two components: (1) An *entropy source* that generates possibly biased and dependent sequence of random numbers. This in practice is by reading the output of a physical source such as a lava lamp [C71], sampling a complex process such as disk access in a computer system, or sampling user's input. This sequence can be further sampled and quantized; and (2) A function that is applied to the output of the first step, resulting in an almost truly random sequence that removes the biases and dependencies among symbols of the input. The aim of a TRNG is to generate an *almost truly random sequence*. The closeness to a true random sequence is measured using *statistical distance*. The *rate of a TRNG* that uses human as the entropy source is the number of random output bits per user action. A commonly used functions in the last step of a TRNG are *extractors*, briefly recalled below.

Randomness Extractor. A randomness extractor [NZ96] is a function that transforms an entropy source X with non-uniform distribution to an almost truly random source Y, i.e. $\Delta(\text{ext}(X), U_Y) \leq \epsilon$ However, there exists no deterministic extractor that can extract from more general sources, i.e. sources with min-entropy k. But by adding a random seed of logarithmic length, there exists extractor that can extract from sources with min-entropy k. The extractor seed needs a source of true randomness that may not be available in practice. More details about randomness extractor can be found in the full version of the paper [ASN14].

Barak et al. Framework. In [BST03], Barak et al. proposed a framework for randomness extraction with guaranteed statistical property for the output with no need for seed. The motivation of this work is to extract randomness for cryptographic applications where the adversary may influence the output of the entropy source. The adversary's influence is modeled by a class of 2^t possible distributions generated by the source. They proposed a randomness extractor with provable output properties (in terms of statistical distance) for sources that have sufficient min-entropy while the output source symbols may be correlated. The extraction uses *t-resilient extractor* which can extract from 2^t distributions (selected adversarially), all having min-entropy k. Certain hash functions are good *t-resilient* extractors.

Theorem 1 *[BST03]. For every n, k, m and ϵ and $l \geq 2$, an l-wise independent hash function with a seed of length l is a t-resilient extractor, where $t = \frac{l}{2}$ $(k - m - 2\log_2(\frac{1}{\epsilon}) - \log_2(l) + 2) - m - 2 - \log_2(\frac{1}{\epsilon})$.*

An l-wise independent family of hash functions can be constructed using a polynomial $h_s(x) = \sum_{1 \leq i \leq l} a_i x^{i-1}$ of degree l over the finite field $GF(2^n)$, where $s = (a_1, \ldots, a_l)$ is the seed of the extractor and $x \in GF(2^n)$ is the n-bit input.

The t-resilient extractors in Barak et. al's approach reuses a truly random seed that is hardwired into the system (e.g. at manufacturing time) and does not need new randomness for every extraction. Although extractors enjoy sound mathematical foundations, in practice the output of entropy sources are mostly processed using hash functions with computational assumptions and so extractors have not been widely implemented in hardware or software. In this paper we follow the framework of Barak et al.

3   Randomness from User Errors

Consider a computer game in which the player aims to hit a target, and wins if the projectile "hits" the target. There are many factors that contribute to the user missing the target even if they play their "best", making the game result uncertain. *We propose to use the uncertainty in the game's result as the entropy source.* Assuming a human is engaged in the game and plays their best, the uncertainty in the result will be due to a large set of factors including, (1) limitations of human cognitive and motor skill to correctly estimate values, and calculate the best response values, (2) limitation of input devices for inputing the best values when they are known, for example limitation of a mouse in pointing an arrow in a particular direction, and (3) unknown parameters of the game (e.g. game's hidden constants) and variabilities that can be introduced in different rounds. Other human related factors that would contribute to the unpredictability of the results are limited attention span, cognitive biases, communication errors, limits of memory and the like. These uncertainties can be amplified by introducing extra uncertainty (pseudo-randomness) in the game: for example allowing the target to have slow movement. As a proof of concept for this proposal, we designed and implemented an archery game, studied user generated sequences and the randomness extracted from them. Below are more details of this work.

3.1   The Game

Our basic game is a single shooter archery game implemented in HTML5 (available at [Ali13]) in which the player aims an arrow at a target and wins if the arrow hits the target: the closer to the center of the target, the higher the score. A screen shot of the game is shown in Fig. 1. The arrow path follows the laws of physics and is determined by the direction of the shot, initial velocity of the arrow, and the earth gravity pull force. This results in a parabolic path that the arrow will traverse to hit the target. The player chooses an initial speed and angle of throw to hit the target. We will refer to each shot, as a *round* of the game.

The target is shown by a circular disk on the screen. The game records the distance between the center of the target and the trajectory (Fig. 2). To display the trajectory on the screen, graphic engine translates the location of the arrow into pixel values and show their locations on the display. We however use the actual value of the distance between the center of the target and the trajectory calculated using laws of physics (kinematic equations), and then round it off to a 32 bit floating point number (the effective bits). The advantage of using this approach is not only avoiding entropy loss, but also independence of the

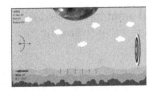
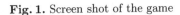

Fig. 1. Screen shot of the game   **Fig. 2.** The measurement of output

implementation and measurements from the screen size and resolution of the end device. For the error variable we use the range $I = [-120, 120]$ with each sample read as a 32 bit floating point number, and represented as [Sign(1bit), Exponent(8bits), Fraction(23 bits)].

3.2 Entropy Source

The distance between the target center and the trajectory is a 32 bit floating point number in I. The human gameplay will produce a sequence of these numbers which we consider as entropy source. Note that one can use multiple seemingly unrelated variables in the game such as the angle and initial velocity of the shot, time that takes for a user to make a shot and the time between two consecutive shots as the entropy source. We only analyze the error variable in this paper though. This entropy source does not produce truly random bits so we followed the randomness extraction framework of [BST03] to extract the entropy from the source. Our randomness extraction and evaluation has three steps. (i) Estimate min-entropy of the sequence; (ii) Given the estimate, apply an appropriate extractor (in our case pairwise independent hash function) on the sequence; and (iii) Use statistical tests to evaluate quality of the final output sequence.

We used the NIST tests [BK12] outlined in Appendix A of the full version of paper [ASN14], to estimate the min-entropy of our sequences. The final output string (after application of extractor) was evaluated using statistical tests. We used the TestU01 framework [LS07b] with an implementation available at [LS07a].

3.3 From the Entropy Source to the Output

We read 32 bit floating point numbers as the output of the entropy source and interpreted each sample as a 32 bit integer as described in Appendix C of the full version of paper [ASN14]. To use a min-entropy test, we needed a sufficiently long sequence over an alphabet. We interpreted each 32 bits block as a collection of subblocks of different lengths. We were limited by available user generated data and so the size of the subblock depended on the experiment to ensure that a sufficiently long sequence was available. We used the min-entropy test outlined in Appendix A of [ASN14] and considered each sample as 32 1bit subblocks, and obtained an estimation of min-entropy per bit. Given the estimate of k bit min-entropy for a single bit, we obtained an approximate value for min-entropy of each sample as $32k$. Here we effectively assumed bits have similar min-entropy which is reasonable since our per-bit min-entropy estimation considered all bits. We performed the above calculations for data from each player including all levels, resulting in minimum estimated min-entropy of 0.626 per bit. For 32 bits, we estimated $32 \times 0.626 \approx 20$ as the minimum min-entropy of the source per 32 bits. Note that this minimum is over the data from all levels for each user, and the minimum we reported earlier (15 bits) is the measured min-entropy for the most skilled user in the simplest level.

We closely followed the framework explained in Sect. 2.1 by using a 32-wise independent hash function, with $\epsilon = 2^{-2}$, and $m = 11$. Using Theorem 1, the extractor was chosen to be t-resilient with $t = 16$. Here 2^t is the number of possible distributions chosen by the adversary. Variations of the distribution due to the players experience could be modeled similarly. The random seed for the extractor was generated from /dev/random in Linux. To examine the properties of the final output sequence, we used the statistical tests Rabbit [LS07b]. Rabbit set of tests includes tests from NIST [ea10] and DIEHARD [Mar98] with modified parameters tuned for smaller sequences and hardware generators. We used an implementation of these tests in [LS07a]. All tests were successfully passed.

3.4   Game Parameters and Levels

Our initial experiments showed that the game parameters affect the final entropy. We designed game levels with varying sets of parameters. The parameters that we alter in the game are: (1) Location of the target, (2) Speed of the target movement, (3) Gravity force with two possible direction, and (4) Wind speed and direction. These parameters can change for every player shot, or stay constant during the game. There were other possibilities such as adding an obstacle (e.g. a blocker wall) to force the player choose angles from a wider spectrum, putting time limit on each shot to force the player to release the arrow faster, smaller target or farther target in the screen that could be considered in future. The final game has 8 levels, 3 of which were used for experiments labeled as A, B and C respectively. In level A, all parameters were "fixed" with no change during the rounds, and so no input is used from the computer. In level B, a subset of game parameters are changed in each round of the game and the values of the parameters were shown in the interface so the player can decide based on that information. In level C, the values of changing parameters of level B were not shown to the user (except the direction of gravity and wind). The high uncertainty in this level of the game makes the players rely on their intuition to play the game.

We did not perform a user study to show attractiveness of these levels but comments from users indicated level B was the most appealing level.

4   Experimental Setup and Results

In this section, we present our experimental results. We asked a set of 9 players to play each of the three levels at least 400 rounds. The rest of the levels were played for learning. Our objective was to answer to the following:

1- *The minimum entropy that can be expected in a single round:* As noted earlier factors such as user's skill level before the game starts, and learning through playing the game, and the match between the skill level and difficulty of the game will affect the final entropy of each round.

2- *The change in min-entropy of a player over time:* We examine how more experience and familiarity with the game would affect the amount of entropy generated in a round.

3- *The effect of the game level on min-entropy:* In this experiment, we determine the best game parameters that maximize the rate of the TRNG.

4.1   Entropy per Round

We performed two sets of experiments to estimate the minimum entropy per round that can be expected from the game.

Entropy of Generated Sequences for One Player. In this experiment we measured the min-entropy of the sequences generated by each player. We partitioned a player's sequence of shots into 20 parts and measured the min-entropy for each part per bit, i.e. considering each bit of a floating point number as one sample which gives us 32 samples per round. The graph in Fig. 3, demonstrates the maximum, minimum and average min-entropy for each player, here a set of 9 players. More details of the experiment can be found on the full version of the paper.

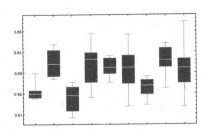

Fig. 3. Min-entropy for players

Sequence Generated by the Population. In this experiment, data from all users were considered as one. We then measured the min-entropy (per bit) for this data set. Our estimation of min-entropy for the population shows that the average min-entropy in the output is 0.643 per bit, so on average, with 5 shots (5×32 bits) one can generate 103 bits of min-entropy. The average time for each shot (over all players) was approximately 2 s. Note that the estimation was higher than the average min-entropy of all users (when min-entropy was measured separately) which is 0.61 because of higher estimation of min-entropy by NIST tests for larger datasets as noted at the end of Appendix A in full version of paper [ASN14].

4.2   Effect of Players' Experience on Min-entropy

An important factor in game design is the effect of players' experience on the generated entropy. Intuitively, we expect the entropy to decrease as players play more. In our game, one expects more experienced players to hit closer to the target center more often and so less observable error, while an inexperienced player's shot to appear more random. We estimated the min-entropy of each of the game levels for 3 different players. Our results confirms this expectation. However it shows that even the most experienced user at the lowest game level can generate good level of entropy.

Figure 4 illustrates the change in min-entropy in each of the three game levels A, B and C, as players gain more experience. Figure 4 also shows how the design of the game neutralizes the affect of player's experience to keep the average min-entropy high enough for randomness extraction.

The graphs of Figs. 4 and 5 are divided into three parts, each consisting of 3 graphs corresponding to the 3 players. The three parts, left (from 0 to 20), middle (21 to 40) and right (41 to 60), correspond to the levels A, B and C, respectively. We used 3 players with the highest (the blue curves marked with letter H), average (the red curves with letter A) and lowest (the yellow curves with letter L) scores for this experiment. An interesting observation about level C is that the min-entropy does not necessarily decrease for a user which is expected from the fact that game parameters are randomly changed and not known by the players.

4.3   Min-entropy and Game Levels

We considered the change in min-entropy over time for a level. That is reduction in entropy as users become more skilled. We used the min-entropy estimation for all player's data, when partitioned into 20 sections as in previous experiment. The data corresponds to the sequence of shots over time and so the first section of the data comes first -that is users starting the game- then the second and the third sections as they get more experienced. We did this experiment for data for all users to find the average trend of min-entropy.

The graph is divided into three parts corresponding to the three levels as in previous section. Figure 5 shows the results of all measurements in the left

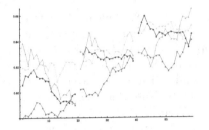

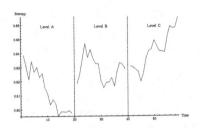

Fig. 4. Min-entropy during level A, B, C for 3 users

Fig. 5. Average min-entropy change during levels over all users

(level A), middle (level B), and right (level C) parts. Level A shows a reduction in the min-entropy as the players become more experienced, and it has the highest min-entropy decrease among the three levels. In level B, the min-entropy fluctuates around the value 0.625 and is relatively stable. For level C however, there is no clear trend in the data and this is true in general for all players, but the average min-entropy is higher than levels A and B. One reason for the increase of min-entropy in level C is probably the reluctance of players to play well over time due to the many unknown variables of the game that makes it hard to win. This confirms the effect of non-deterministic and unknown values of parameters which makes the skill level somewhat irrelevant.

4.4   Randomness Required by Computer

As noted earlier, the least significant bits of the output corresponds to cumulation of small errors in different part of the system and contribute most to the min-entropy. Thus even the sequence collected from level A *without any random input from the computer,* could be used for entropy generation. To confirm this observation we asked the most experienced player (with highest score) to play level A again, after they had played levels A, B and C more than 1200 rounds. We measured the min-entropy for this data. The player had 20 arrows to hit the target and with each shot to the center, a bonus arrow was given. The user played for 3 games, totaling 331 shots to the target. With 83 % of the shots to the center, the estimated min-entropy of the player in this 331 shots was roughly 0.521 per bit.

This suggests that the sequence generated by the game has a minimum min-entropy independent of the randomness used by the game (computer). For higher levels of game that require randomness, one can use pseudorandom generators in real-time or generate the sequences beforehand and use them as needed.

5   Concluding Remarks

We proposed and analyzed a new approach to entropy collection using human errors in video games. We verified the approach by developing a basic intuitive game and studied the sequences generated by users.

Our experiments showed that with this simple design and considering the "worst" case where the user was experienced and made the least error, the rate of entropy generation is at least 15 bits per shot. This rate can be increased by adding variability to the game and also using multiple measurable variables instead of only one. Adding variability to the game increased the min-entropy by 7 bits per round. In choosing parameters one needs to consider attractiveness of the game: increase in entropy can be immediately obtained if game constants such as gravitational force in our case are changed without user's knowledge. However this would decrease the entertainment factor of the game. Studying these factors and in general the randomness generated by users needs a larger user study which is part of our future work. For the randomness extraction we implemented and used t-resilient extractors. The output from extractors passed all statistical tests.

Our work opens a new direction for randomness generation in environments without computational capability or randomness generation subsystems, and provides an attractive solution in a number of applications.

References

[Ali13] Alimomeni, M.: Archery game 2013. http://pages.cpsc.ucalgary.ca/~malimome/game/

[ASN14] Alimomeni, M., Safavi-Naini, R.: Human assisted randomness generation using video games. Cryptology ePrint Archive, Report 2014/045 (2014). http://eprint.iacr.org/

[ASNS14] Alimomeni, M., Safavi-Naini, R., Sharifian, S.: A true random generator using human gameplay. In: GameSec, pp. 10–28 (2014)

[BK12] Barker, E., Kelsey, J.: Recommendation for the entropy sources used for random bit generation, August 2012. http://csrc.nist.gov/publications/drafts/800-90/draft-sp800-90b.pdf

[BST03] Barak, B., Shaltiel, R., Tromer, E.: True random number generators secure in a changing environment. In: Walter, C.D., Koç, Ç.K., Paar, C. (eds.) CHES 2003. LNCS, vol. 2779, pp. 166–180. Springer, Heidelberg (2003)

[C71] Walker, E.C.: DISPLAY DEVICE. Woodspeen, Forest Corner, Ringwood, Hampshire, England Filed Nov. 13, 1968, Ser. No. 775, 401 Claims priority, application Gr/e6a7t Britain, Nov. 14, 1967, 1 Int. Cl. G09f 13/24

[ea10] Rukhin, A., et al.: A statistical test suite for the validation of random number generators and pseudo random number generators for cryptographic applications (2010). http://csrc.nist.gov/groups/ST/toolkit/rng/documents/SP800-22rev1a.pdf

[GPR06] Gutterman, Z., Pinkas, B., Reinman, T.: Analysis of the linux random number generator. In: 2006 IEEE Symposium on Security and Privacy, p. 15. IEEE (2006)

[GW96] Goldberg, I., Wagner, D.: Randomness and the netscape browser. Dr Dobb's J.-Softw. Tools Prof. Program. $21(1)$, 66–71 (1996)

[HDWH12] Heninger, N., Durumeric, Z., Wustrow, E., Halderman, J.A.: Mining your PS and QS: detection of widespread weak keys in network devices. In: Proceedings of the 21st USENIX Conference on Security Symposium, Security 2012, Berkeley, CA, USA, pp. 35–35. USENIX Association (2012)

[HN09]   Halprin, R., Naor, M. Games for extracting randomness. In: Proceedings of the 5th Symposium on Usable Privacy and Security, p. 12. ACM (2009)

[Hot10]   Hotz Console hacking 2010-ps3 epic fail. In: 27th Chaos Communications Congress (2010)

[LHA+12]   Lenstra, A.K., Hughes, J.P., Augier, M., Bos, J.W., Kleinjung, T., Wachter, C.: Public keys. In: Safavi-Naini, R., Canetti, R. (eds.) CRYPTO 2012. LNCS, vol. 7417, pp. 626–642. Springer, Heidelberg (2012)

[LS07a]   L'Ecuyer, P., Simard, R.: Testu01, August 2007. http://www.iro. umontreal.ca/~simardr/testu01/tu01.html

[LS07b]   L'Ecuyer, P., Simard, R.: Testu01: a C library for empirical testing of random number generators. ACM Trans. Math. Softw. 33(4) (2007)

[Mar98]   Marsaglia, G.: Diehard (1998). http://www.stat.fsu.edu/pub/diehard/

[NZ96]   Nisan, N., Zuckerman, D.: Randomness is linear in space. J. Comput. Syst. Sci. 52(1), 43–52 (1996)

[RB92]   Rapoport, A., Budescu, D.V.: Generation of random series in two-person strictly competitive games. J. Exp. Psychol. Gen. 121(3), 352 (1992)

[Wag72]   Wagenaar, W.A.: Generation of random sequences by human subjects: a critical survey of literature. Psychol. Bull. 77(1), 65 (1972)

[ZLwW+09] Zhou, Q., Liao, X., Wong, K.W., Hu, Y., Xiao, D.: True random number generator based on mouse movement and chaotic hash function. Inf. Sci. 179(19), 3442–3450 (2009)

Security Ranking Among Assumptions Within the *Uber Assumption* Framework

Antoine Joux[1,2,3]([✉]) and Antoine Rojat[4]

[1] CryptoExperts, Paris, France
antoine.joux@m4x.org
[2] Chaire de Cryptologie de la Fondation de l'UPMC, Paris, France
[3] Laboratoire d'Informatique de Paris 6, UPMC Sorbonnes Universités, Paris, France
[4] Laboratoire PRISM - Université de Versailles Saint-Quentin-en-Yvelines,
Versailles, France
aro@prism.uvsq.fr

Abstract. In order to analyze a variety of cryptosystems, Boneh, Boyen and Goh introduced a general framework, the *Uber assumption*. In this article, we explore some particular instances of this Uber assumption; namely the n-CDH-assumption, the nth-CDH-assumption and the Q-CDH-assumption. We analyse their relationships from a security point of view. Our analysis does not rely on any other property of the considered group and, in particular, does not use the generic group model.

1 Introduction

There are many different ways of analyzing the security of a cryptographic scheme. One can use a formal proof system (as in [6]) or perform a direct more concrete and computationally oriented proof or use a game based kind of proof (see [4] or [3] for the case of computer-assisted proofs). A difficulty with formal proofs is that the security hypothesis often needs to be stated in an abstract black-box way which can be difficult to verify on a concrete scheme or implementation. For this reason, most proofs of cryptographic schemes emphasize the computational aspect; this is, in particular, the case of reductionist proofs.

In general, a cryptosystem is said to have reductionist or computational security when its security requirements can be stated in an adversarial model with clear assumptions about the adversary, its means of manipulating the system and its computational resources. In this approach, the security of a cryptographic scheme is based on some core algorithmic problem which is assumed to be hard to solve. The scheme should remain secure as long as the chosen instances of the underlying algorithmic problem remain hard.

Among the classical security assumptions used in public-key cryptography, we find the discrete logarithm problem proven difficult in the generic group model by Shoup [17] or the Diffie-Hellman assumption which underlies Diffie-Hellman key exchange protocol [12]. There is a wide variety of more specialized assumptions which have been introduced over the years. In this article, we focus on assumptions related to Diffie-Hellman.

© Springer International Publishing Switzerland 2015
Y. Desmedt (Ed.): ISC 2013, LNCS 7807, pp. 391–406, 2015.
DOI: 10.1007/978-3-319-27659-5_28

These Diffie-Hellman related assumptions can either involve a single group or can be stated in a richer bilinear (or pairing-based) setting. Initially, bilinear pairings were used for cryptanalytic purposes for example the MOV attack [16]. Basically, the attacks using bilinear pairings reduce the discrete logarithm problem on an elliptic (or hyperelliptic) curve to the discrete logarithm problem in a finite field. More recently, bilinear pairings have been used to construct new cryptographic primitives. In [14], Joux showed that the bilinear pairings can be used constructively, proposing to use them to construct a tripartite one-round Diffie-Hellman key agreement protocol. At Crypto 2001, Boneh and Franklin [8] used pairings to propose the first fully functional, efficient and provably secure identity-based encryption scheme. At Asiacrypt 2001, Boneh, Lynn and Shacham [9] proposed a pairing-based signature scheme that features the shortest length among known signature schemes.

One sometime confusing aspect of pairing-based cryptography is that a large number of ad'hoc security assumptions have been introduced in parallel with the new schemes and protocols. In particular, it is not easy to compare the different security assumptions and, thus, to compare the security level of schemes based on different assumptions. As an attempt to simplify the situation, Boneh, Boyen and Goh have introduced the *Uber assumption* in [7]. This assumption offers a general framework which can host all previous assumptions. This assumption is stated as follows:

Definition 1 (Uber Assumption ([10] Sect. 5)). *Let p be some large prime, and let r, s, t, and c be four positive integers. Consider $R \in \mathbb{F}_p[X_1, \cdots, X_c]^r$, $S \in \mathbb{F}_p[X_1, \cdots, X_c]^s$, and $T \in \mathbb{F}_p[X_1, \cdots, X_c]^t$, three tuples of multivariate polynomials over the field $\mathbb{F}_p$, and respectively containing r, s, and t polynomials in the same c variables $X_1, \cdots, X_c$. We write $R = \langle r_1, r_2, \cdots, r_r \rangle$, $S = \langle s_1, s_2, \cdots, s_s \rangle$ and $T = \langle t_1, t_2, \cdots, t_t \rangle$. The first components of R, S, and T are forced to the constant polynomial 1; that is, $r_1 = s_1 = t_1 = 1$. For a set Ω, a function $f : \mathbb{F}_p \to \Omega$, and a vector $\langle x_1, \cdots, x_c \rangle \in \mathbb{F}_p^d$, we use the notation $f(R)$ to denote the application of f to each element of R, namely, $f(R(x_1, \cdots, x_c)) = \langle f(r_1(x_1, \cdots, x_c)), \cdots, f(r_r(x_1, \cdots, x_c)) \rangle \in \Omega^r$; and use a similar notation for applying f to the s-tuple S and the t-tuple T. Let then $\mathbb{G}_1$, $\mathbb{G}_2$, and $\mathbb{H}$ be cyclic groups of order p, and $e : \mathbb{G}_1 \times \mathbb{G}_2 \to \mathbb{H}$ be a cryptographic bilinear pairing. Suppose that $g_1 \in \mathbb{G}_1$ and $g_2 \in \mathbb{G}_2$ respectively generate the groups to which they belong, and set $h = e(g_1, g_2) \in \mathbb{H}$ thus generating $\mathbb{H}$. Together, these form the bilinear context $G = \langle p, \mathbb{G}_1, \mathbb{G}_2, \mathbb{H}, g_1, g_2, e \rangle$. The (R, S, T, f)-Diffie-Hellman problem in G is defined as follows. Given the input vector,*

$$U(x_1, \cdots, x_c) = \left(g_1^{R(x_1, \cdots, x_c)}, g_2^{S(x_1, \cdots, x_c)}, h^{T(x_1, \cdots, x_c)} \right) \in \mathbb{G}_1^r \times \mathbb{G}_2^s \times \mathbb{H}^t,$$

secretly created from random $x_1, \cdots, x_c \in \mathbb{F}_p$, compute the output value,

$$h^{f(x_1, \cdots, x_c)} \in \mathbb{H}.$$

In order to state the difficulty of the *Uber assumption*, Boyen, Boneh and Goh have introduced a notion of dependency as follows:

Definition 2 (Dependence ([10] Sect. 5)). Let $R = \langle r_1, \cdots r_n \rangle \in \mathbb{F}_p[X_1, \cdots, X_c]^r$, $S = \langle s_1, \cdots s_n \rangle \in \mathbb{F}_p[X_1, \cdots, X_c]^s$, and $T = \langle t_1, \cdots t_n \rangle \in \mathbb{F}_p[X_1, \cdots, X_c]^t$ as defined in Definition 1.

We say that a polynomial $f \in \mathbb{F}_p[X_1, \cdots, X_c]$ is dependent on the triple $\langle R, S, T \rangle$ if there exists $rs + t$ constants $\{a_{i,j}\}_{1 \le i \le r1 \le j \le s}$ and $\{b_k\}_{1 \le k \le t}$ and possibly $r^2 + s^2$ $\{d^1_{n,m}\}_{1 \le n,m \le r}$ and $\{d^{1,2}_{p,q}\}_{1 \le p,q \le s}$ additional constants such that:

$$f = \sum_{i=1}^{r}\sum_{j=1}^{s} a_{i,j} r_i s_j + \sum_{n=1}^{r}\sum_{m=1}^{r} d^1_{n,m} r_n r_m + \sum_{p=1}^{s}\sum_{q=1}^{s} d^{1,2}_{p,q} s_p s_q + \sum_{k=1}^{t} b_k t_k$$

When a polynomial f is not dependent from a triple $\langle R, S, T \rangle$, we say that this polynomial is independent from this triple.

Recalling what is stated in the paper of Boyen [10], the constants $d^{1,2}_{p,q}$ models the knowledge of an efficiently computable isomorphism $\varphi : \mathbb{G}_1 \to \mathbb{G}_2$ which exists for pairings of **Type 1** and **Type 2**. While the constants $d^1_{n,m}$ models the knowledge of an efficiently computable inverse isomorphism $\varphi^{-1} : \mathbb{G}_2 \to \mathbb{G}_1$. When neither φ^{-1} nor φ are known, Boyen simply proposed to set the $d^1_{n,m}$ and the $d^{1,2}_{p,q}$ constants to zero which models the pairings of **Type 3**. In there paper, they stated that the *Uber assumption* holds whenever the polynomial f is not dependent from the triple $\{R, S, T\}$. The generic form of the *Uber assumption* introduces a security assumption that allows virtually any of the previous assumptions to be reformulated as a sub-case of it. As a consequence, it suffices to rely on this generic assumption and it is no longer necessary to introduce additional assumptions.

Our Contribution. While the *Uber assumption* appears to be a trustworthy framework for assessing the security of bilinear based assumptions, it does not cover the relative difficulty of such assumptions. In this article, we explore some specific sub-cases of the *Uber assumption* in order to assess the intrinsic hierarchy of difficulty among the different security assumptions that have been introduced over the years. This work is motivated by the fact that the *Uber assumption* has been proven secure only in the generic group model (see the appendix of [7]) and since it subsumed previous assumption, it is very strong and it might feel riskier to rely on it than on a simpler assumption.

Along this article, we focus on sub-cases of the *Uber assumption* where the sets R, S and T are of the following form:

$$S = \{X_1, \cdots, X_n\} \text{ and } R = \{X_{n+1}, \cdots, X_s\} \text{ and } T = \emptyset.$$

We begin by analyzing those assumptions in the group setting, that is $\mathbb{G}_1 = \mathbb{G}_2 = \mathbb{G}_3$ and there is no bilinear pairing. Indeed, the proofs are easier to follow in this setting and furthermore, can be adapted quite easily to the bilinear setting. Thus we discuss the security relationships in the bilinear setting without recalling all the proofs.

We distinguish three kinds of hypothesis depending on the form of the polynomial f. First we consider the case where $f = X_1 X_2 \cdots X_s$ then, we focus on the case where $f = X_1^s$ and finally, we consider the case where f is any arbitrary polynomial of degree less or equal than s.

Throughout the different proofs, we wish to compare the difficulty of an hypothesis H_1 and another hypothesis H_2. More precisely, we want to prove relationships of the form $H_1 \Leftarrow H_2$, i.e. to prove that H_1 is actually harder than H_2. In order to do so, we first assume that we have access to an oracle $\mathcal{O}_{H_1}$ that can solve the H_2 hypothesis for any instance of H_2, $\mathcal{O}_{H_1}$ proposes a solution, which should be correct with probability at least $1 - \varepsilon$. Using this oracle we construct an algorithm that solves H_2.

Along the proofs, we use three types of oracles:

Definition 3 (Perfect Oracle). *A perfect oracle is an oracle that, when queried, always answers the correct solution.*

We can consider another class of oracle that is somehow randomized:

Definition 4 (Almost Perfect Oracle). *An almost perfect oracle is an oracle that, when queried, answers the correct solution with a probability at least $1 - \varepsilon$ such that ε is exponentially small with respect to a parameter $\kappa \in \mathbb{R}_+^*$ that is: $\varepsilon < \exp(-\kappa)$.*

Finally, one can remark that a general difficulty is that an oracle can behave arbitrarily on the ε fraction of incorrect answers. In particular, it may behave in a malicious way designed to adversarily affect our algorithm. This type of oracle can be formally defined as follows:

Definition 5 (Adversarial Oracle). *An adversarial oracle is an oracle that, when queried, answers correctly with a probability at least $1 - \varepsilon$. When the oracle does not answers correctly it can adversarily adapt its answers in a malicious way.*

On can remark that normally, with discrete logarithm based assumptions, the possibly malicious behavior of adversarial oracles can be ignored. This is due to the classical property of random self-reducibility see [1,13]. One of our important contribution is to propose a new form of random self-reducibility versatile enough to deal with the different assumptions we are considering (see Theorem 3). This allows us to reduce the probability of error to $O(1/p)$ were p is the cardinality of the considered groups. This allows us to complete the work done by Bao, Deng and Zhu in [2] where they consider some variations of the Diffie-Hellman problems. We extend their work by considering other kind of problems and furthermore, we do not rely on perfect oracle (see Definition 3) as they did in their paper.

In the group setting, we are able to prove that all the assumptions we are considering are in fact equivalent — in terms of hardness — to the standard computational Diffie-Hellman assumption. Our results are summarized on Fig. 1.

We obtain a very different situation in the bilinear setting: a hierarchy appears between the different assumptions. This hierarchy is based on the degree of the polynomial f. The higher the degree of f is, the harder the assumption. In particular, the case where $f = X_1 \cdots X_S$ cannot be reduced to the classical CBDH-assumption.

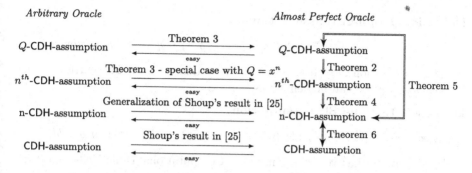

Fig. 1. Security assumptions relations (Group setting)

2   Security Assumptions

As stated in the introduction, we focus on security relationships among several sub-cases of the *Uber assumption*. In this section we define the different assumptions we analyzed as stand alone assumptions. These assumptions make use of the following notion:

Definition 6 (Negligible Function). *A function* $f : \mathbb{N} \rightarrow [0,1]$ *is called negligible if for every positive polynomial* p, *there exists some* $k_0 \in \mathbb{N}$ *such that for every* $k \geq k_0$, $|f(k)| < 1/p(k)$.

We state the different assumptions we are considering below.

Definition 7 (η-CDH-assumption)

$$\forall \mathscr{A}_\eta, \forall x, y \in_R \mathbb{F}_p : \Pr\left[\mathscr{A}_\eta(g^x, g^y) = g^{xy}\right] \text{ is negligible.}$$

This assumption has first been introduced by Diffie and Hellman in [12]. It was the first realisation of a cryptographic protocol allowing secure communication between two parties without requiring prior knowledge. In the bilinear context, this problem has been first introduced by Joux in [14] and is defined as follows:

Definition 8 (η-CBDH-assumption)

$$\forall \mathscr{A}_\eta, \forall x, y, z \in_R \mathbb{F}_p : \Pr\left[\mathscr{A}_\eta(g^x, g^y, g^z) = h^{xyz}\right] \text{ is negligible.}$$

The CBDH-assumption have been widely studied and several cryptographic protocols have been proven secure by reduction to this hypothesis such as the first identity based protocol introduced by Boneh and Franklin in [8]. We consider another problem that is a generalisation of the classical CDH-assumption the n-CDH-assumption in which instead of being given only two quantities, we are given n random elements of a group of the form g^{x_i} and we have to compute $g^{\prod x_i}$. More formally we define then-CDH-assumption as follows:

Definition 9 (η-n-CDH-assumption)

$$\forall \mathscr{A}_\eta, \forall x_1, \cdots, x_n \in_R \mathbb{F}_p : \Pr\left[\mathscr{A}_\eta(g^{x_1}, \cdots, g^{x_n}) = g^{x_1 \cdots x_n}\right] \text{ is negligible.}$$

This assumption have been introduced by Biswas in [5] The corresponding bilinear assumption can be defined as follows:

Definition 10 (η-n-CBDH-assumption)

$$\forall \mathscr{A}_\eta, \forall x_1, \cdots, x_n \in_R \mathbb{F}_p : \Pr\left[\mathscr{A}_\eta(g^{x_1}, \cdots, g^{x_n}) = h^{x_1 \cdots x_n}\right] \text{ is negligible.}$$

In addition to the two extensions of the Computational Diffie-Hellman extension, we have also considered the case of power exponents problem, i.e., given a group element of the form g^x one has to compute g^{x^n}. This problem have been used in [15] and in [11] with $n = 2$ and is called *Square exponent problem* more formally we define the nth-CDH-assumption as follows:

Definition 11 (η-n^{th}-CDH-assumption)

$$\forall \mathscr{A}_\eta, \forall x \in_R \mathbb{F}_p : \Pr\left[\mathscr{A}_\eta(g^x) = g^{x^n}\right] \text{ is negligible.}$$

The corresponding bilinear assumption can be stated as follows:

Definition 12 (η-n^{th}-CBDH-assumption)

$$\forall \mathscr{A}_\eta, \forall x \in_R \mathbb{F}_p : \Pr\left[\mathscr{A}_{(\nu,\eta)}(g^x) = h^{x^n}\right] \text{ is negligible.}$$

More generally, we define the assumption Q-CDH-assumption as follows:

Definition 13 (η-Q-CDH-assumption) *Let Q be a polynomial of $\mathbb{F}_p[X_1, \cdots, X_n]$ of degree d.*

$$\forall \mathscr{A}_\eta, \forall x_1, \cdots, x_n \in_R \mathbb{F}_p : \Pr\left[\mathscr{A}_\eta(g^{x_1}, \cdots, g^{x_n}) = g^{Q(x_1, \cdots, x_n)}\right] \text{ is negligible.}$$

The corresponding bilinear assumption can be stated as follows:

Definition 14 (η-Q-CBDH-assumption). *Let Q be a polynomial of $\mathbb{F}_q[X_1, \cdots, X_n]$ of degree d.*

$$\forall \mathscr{A}_\eta, \forall x_1, \cdots, x_n \in_R \mathbb{F}_p : \Pr\left[\mathscr{A}_\eta(g^{x_1}, \cdots, g^{x_n}) = h^{Q(x_1, \cdots, x_n)}\right] \text{ is negligible.}$$

3   From Polynomials to Powers

In this section, we focus on the main difficulty of the article: the reduction from the Q-CDH-assumption to the nth-CDH-assumption. We conduct our analysis in the group setting since it is easier to follow and the notations are also clearer. The section is organized as follows. First we consider that we are given access to a perfect oracle that solves the Q-CDH-assumption. And we use it to build an algorithm that solves the nth-CDH-assumption. And then, we explain how it is possible to build a random oracle solving the Q-CDH-assumption when having access only to an adversarial oracle that solves the Q-CDH-assumption.

3.1   Using a Perfect Oracle

In this subsection, our goal is to compute g^{x^n} for any $n \leq degree(Q) = d$ knowing g^x and having access to a perfect oracle that on input $g^{x_1}, \cdots, g^{x_n}$ outputs $g^{Q(x_1, \cdots, x_n)}$. Our result is summarized in Theorem 2:

Theorem 1. *Given access to an oracle that solves any instance of the Q-CDH-assumption, we can, after performing $d + 1$ oracle calls, solve any instance of the nth-CDH-assumption with $n \leq d$, where d is the degree of polynomial Q.*

Proof. First, we independently sample n random values $\lambda_1^1, \cdots, \lambda_n^1$ and we call the perfect oracle on the following instance:

$$\left(g^{x + \lambda_1^1}, \cdots, g^{x + \lambda_n^1} \right).$$

This sampling will prove to be essential when dealing with an adversarial oracle. It is not strictly necessary with a perfect oracle, but for the sake of clarity, it is easier to keep the same overall strategy in both cases.

The response of the oracle to this randomized query is, by definition of the oracle,

$$g^{Q(x + \lambda_1^1, \cdots, x + \lambda_n^1)}.$$

As the polynomial Q is formally known, the polynomial $Q(x + \lambda_1^1, \cdots, x + \lambda_n^1)$ can be rewritten as polynomial in x:

$$Q(x + \lambda_1^1, \cdots, x + \lambda_n^1) = \sum_{j=0}^{d} [Q(\lambda_1^1 + x, \cdots, \lambda_n^1 + x)]_j \cdot x^j.$$

Where $[Q(\lambda_1^i + x, \cdots, \lambda_n^i + x)]_j$ denotes the coefficient of x^j in the polynomial $Q(x + \lambda_1^i, \cdots, x + \lambda_n^i)$.

Note that the terms of degree 0 and degree 1 could be removed since they can be computed from the knowledge of the λ_i and g^x. But in order to be able to prove our argument, they are required in the matrix.

By sampling enough values, we can build the following matrix:

$$\mathcal{M} = \begin{bmatrix} [Q(\lambda_1^1 + x, \cdots, \lambda_n^1 + x)]_0 & \cdots & [Q(\lambda_1^1 + x, \cdots, \lambda_n^1 + x)]_d \\ [Q(\lambda_1^2 + x, \cdots, \lambda_n^2 + x)]_0 & \cdots & [Q(\lambda_1^2 + x, \cdots, \lambda_n^2 + x)]_d \\ \vdots & \vdots & \vdots \\ [Q(\lambda_1^{d+1} + x, \cdots, \lambda_n^{d+1} + x)]_0 & \cdots & [Q(\lambda_1^{d+1} + x, \cdots, \lambda_n^{d+1} + x)]_d \end{bmatrix}$$

This matrix is computed without the need to call any oracle, it is derived formally from the known coefficients λ_i^j. In order to be able to prove our result, we need this matrix to be non-singular. We use the following technical lemma:

Lemma 1. *The matrix $\mathcal{M}$ is non-singular with probability at least $1 - 2/p$.*

With reasonnable parameters choices, this probability is non-negligible. Thus, as the λ_i^j are randomly sampled, $\mathcal{M}$ can be assumed to be non singular.

Now, recall that this matrix is formally computed from the randomly sampled values and the knowledge of the polynomial Q. Each time we compute one row of this matrix, we query the oracle in parallel. When computing the ith row, we query the oracle on the following input:

$$\left(g^{x+\lambda_1^i}, \cdots, g^{x+\lambda_n^i}\right).$$

Let $\tilde{z}_i$ be the output of the oracle. We store all those values in a vector:

$$\mathcal{V} = \begin{bmatrix} \sum_{j=0}^{d} [Q(\lambda_1^1 + x, \cdots, \lambda_n^1 + x)]_j x^j \\ \sum_{j=0}^{d} [Q(\lambda_1^2 + x, \cdots, \lambda_n^2 + x)]_j x^j \\ \vdots \\ \sum_{j=0}^{d} [Q(\lambda_1^{d+1} + x, \cdots, \lambda_n^{d+1} + x)]_j x^j \end{bmatrix}.$$

By definition of the matrix $\mathcal{M}$, the following equality holds:

$$\mathcal{V} = \mathcal{M} \begin{bmatrix} x^0 & x^1 & \cdots & x^d \end{bmatrix}^T$$

From the previous technical lemma, we can assume that the matrix $\mathcal{M}$ is non singular with overwhelming probability. By computing the inverse (using the previous technical lemma), of the matrix $\mathcal{M}$ denoted $\tilde{M}$, we can rewrite the previous equality as follows:

$$(E) : \tilde{M}\mathcal{V} = \begin{bmatrix} x^0 & x^1 & \cdots & x^d \end{bmatrix}^T$$

Let $\tilde{m}_{i,j}$ be the element of the ith row and j^{th} column of the matrix $\tilde{M}$. Using the $\tilde{m}_{i,j}$'s, we can compute the following quantities:

$$q_1 = (\tilde{z}_0)^{\tilde{m}_{0,0}} \times \cdots \times (\tilde{z}_d)^{\tilde{m}_{0,d}}$$
$$\vdots$$
$$q_{d-1} = (\tilde{z}_0)^{\tilde{m}_{d,0}} \times \cdots \times (\tilde{z}_d)^{\tilde{m}_{d,d}}$$

By definition, for any k, q_k simplifies to g^{l_k} with:

$$l_k = \sum_{i=0}^{d} \tilde{m}_{k,i} \cdot \sum_{j=0}^{d} [Q(\lambda_1^i + x, \cdots, \lambda_n^i + x)]_j x^j.$$

Using equality (E), we obtain: $q_k = g^{x^{k+1}}$.

Thus, we can obtain all the power of x from 2 to d.   □

The previous result shows that if we have access to an oracle that can compute a polynomial of degree d, it is possible, using $d + 1$ oracle calls to obtain an oracle that compute any n^{th}-CDH-assumption with $n \leq d$. However, the proof is based on the fact that an ideal oracle always outputs the correct evaluation of the polynomial when queried. In the next section we show how to adapt the result in the more general case where we only have access to an imperfect, even adversarial oracle.

3.2 Using an Adversarial Oracle

In this section, we are going to prove the following result:

Theorem 2. *Given access to an adversarial perfect oracle that solves any instance of the Q-CDH-assumption with error probability bounded by ε, we can simultaneously solve instances of nth-CDH-assumption for the same input g^x in all degrees from 2 to $d = \deg Q$.*

This requires $O((d+2)/\varepsilon)$ oracle calls, a computational runtime of $O(\varepsilon^{-d+2})$ and yields a success probability:

$$\frac{p\varepsilon^{d+2}}{p\varepsilon^{d+2} + 1}$$

Proof. First, let us recall that the λ_i^1 are randomly sampled (using the same notations as in the previous subsection), so the $x + \lambda_i^1$ are indistinguishable from random values. In truth, the distribution of tuples of the form $(g^{x+\lambda_i^1}, \cdots, g^{x+\lambda_i^n})$ is identical to the distribution: $(g^{r_1}, \cdots, g^{r_n})$ where $\{r_1, \cdots, r_n\} \in_R \mathbb{F}_p$. As a consequence, the oracle is not able to adapt its behavior depending on the probability distribution of our questions[1].

Thus we safely can assume that every time we submit a query to the oracle the probability that it answers correctly with probability $\geq \varepsilon$. However, if a single answer is incorrect, then our full vector of values g^{x^i} becomes incorrect (at the end of the proof the evaluations of the q_k's are all wrong). This is why we need to propose a way to test whether or not the answers of the oracle are consistent. This is summed up in the following lemma:

Lemma 2 (Adversarial Oracle Testing). *Given a set of $d+1$ answers to randomly chosen queries from an adversarial oracle solving the Q-CDH-assumption, there exists an algorithm that tests whether all the solutions of this set are correct or not and correctly answers with probability:*

$$\frac{\varepsilon^{d+1}}{\varepsilon^{d+1} + (1/p)}.$$

---

[1] Remember that the oracle is stateless and thus not allowed to misbehave by counting the questions and giving an answer that depends on the position of the question. It would be easy to adapt to this case, but we have not considered it.

Assume that we have $d + 1$ answers stored in a vector $\hat{\mathcal{V}}$ from the oracle and that they are all correct. As in the previous case we compute the following matrix:

$$
\hat{\mathcal{M}} = \begin{bmatrix}
[Q(\lambda_1^1 + x, \cdots, \lambda_n^1 + x)]_0 & \cdots & [Q(\lambda_1^1 + x, \cdots, \lambda_n^1 + x)]_d \\
[Q(\lambda_1^2 + x, \cdots, \lambda_n^2 + x)]_0 & \cdots & [Q(\lambda_1^2 + x, \cdots, \lambda_n^2 + x)]_d \\
\vdots & \vdots & \vdots \\
[Q(\lambda_1^{d+1} + x, \cdots, \lambda_n^{d+1} + x)]_0 & \cdots & [Q(\lambda_1^{d+1} + x, \cdots, \lambda_n^{d+1} + x)]_d \\
[Q(\lambda_1^{d+2} + x, \cdots, \lambda_n^{d+2} + x)]_0 & \cdots & [Q(\lambda_1^{d+2} + x, \cdots, \lambda_n^{d+2} + x)]_d
\end{bmatrix}
$$

Note that, compared to the previous case (when we had access to a perfect oracle), the matrix now has an extra line. And we still have the following equality:

$$
\hat{\mathcal{M}} \begin{bmatrix} x^0 \\ x^1 \\ \vdots \\ x^n \end{bmatrix} = \hat{\mathcal{V}}.
$$

Since this matrix has $d + 2$ lines and $d + 1$ columns, we known that, using simple linear algebra, we can obtain a vector $\mathcal{K}$ that is an element of the left kernel of the matrix $\hat{\mathcal{M}}$. By multiplying each part of the previous equality by the vector $\mathcal{K}$, we have:

$$
\left\langle \mathcal{K} | \hat{\mathcal{V}} \right\rangle = 0.
$$

Using the coordinates k_i's of the vector $\mathcal{K}$, we can check whether the oracle's answers are all consistent. Indeed, using the same notation as above, we can compute:

$$
(\tilde{z}_0)^{k_0} \times \cdots \times (\tilde{z}_d)^{k_d}.
$$

And the we test whether or not this value is $1 = g^0$. This can occur in two different ways. The first way occurs when the $d + 1$ answer are correct and has probability ε^{d+1}. The second way occurs when the test equality is satisfied by a vector containing some random values, this occurs with probability $1/p$.

As a consequence, the *a posteriory* probability that the $d + 1$ answers are correct when the test equality is satisfied is:

$$
\frac{\varepsilon^{d+1}}{\varepsilon^{d+1} + (1/p)},
$$

where p is the cardinality of the group. This is close to 1 for reasonable parameter choices. This concludes the proof of the previous lemma.

Remark 1. This probability is close to 1, whenever $\varepsilon^{d+1} > (1/p)$. This requires $(d + 1) \ln \varepsilon$ to remain smaller (and bounded away) from $\ln p$.

In order to obtain a set of $d + 1$ correct answers from the adversarial oracle we submit a large enough amount of queries to the oracle to ensure that the probability of obtaining (at least) d correct answers within the set of all the oracle answers is good enough. By "large enough amount of queries" we mean at least $c.(d+1) \times 1/\varepsilon$ where $c > 1$. With this number of queries, we are almost certain to obtain at least $d + 1$ correct answers from the oracle.

The next set is to extract a subset of $d + 1$ correct answers from the set of all the answers. Since there is no way to get information about the validity of an individual answer, the best approach is to use exhaustive search. Let Q_ε denote the number of correct answers, the fraction of subset of $d + 1$ answer than only contains correct answer is:

$$\frac{\binom{Q_\varepsilon}{d+1}}{\binom{c.(d+1)\times\varepsilon}{d+1}}.$$

Assuming the degree d is not too large, this can be approximated by:

$$\left(\frac{1}{\varepsilon}\right)^d.$$

Thus, the cost of finding a correct subset is ε^{-d}. This is quite high, however, it is a pure computational cost that does not require any extra oracle calls.

Putting it all together, we then delete one row at random in the matrix $\tilde{\mathcal{M}}$ and assume that all the corresponding oracle's outputs are correct. We then proceed as if we had access to a perfect oracle (see Theorem 1).   □

The fact that we are actually able to test the answers given by an adversarial oracle allows us to extend the random self-reducibility result of [1]:

Theorem 3 (Random Self-reducibility of the Q-CDH-assumption). *Given access to an adversarial oracle that solves any instance of the Q-CDH-assumption for a degree d polynomial, we can solve any instance of the Q-CDH-assumption with probability:*

$$\frac{p\varepsilon^{d+1}}{p\varepsilon^{d+1} + 1}$$

using $O((d + 1)/\varepsilon)$ queries and a computational runtime of $O(\varepsilon^{-(d+1)})$.

Remark 2. This probability is close to 1, whenever $\varepsilon^{d+1} > (1/p)$. This requires $(d + 1) \ln \varepsilon$ to remain smaller (and bounded away) from $\ln p$.

In this section, we only considered the group setting. However, in the proof we never had to assume that the inputs or the outputs belong to the same group. Thus everything that has been stated can be straightforwardly adapted to the bilinear setting. This adaptation requires some considerations especially when dealing with pairings of type 2 or 3. The details are given in Sect. 6.

From now on, when we use an oracle, we assume that we are given access to an almost perfect.

4   From Powers to N-product

It is explained in [18] how to solve the n-CDH-assumption using an almost perfect oracle that solves the nth-CDH-assumption with a low probability of failure ε is close to 1. More precisely:

Theorem 4. *Given access to an oracle that solves any instance of the nth-CDH-assumption, we can solves any instance of the n-CDH-assumption.*

This requires 2^n oracle calls and needs all oracle answers to be correct.

5   From N-product to Polynomials

In this section we explain how it is possible to compute in the exponent any polynomial of degree d having access to an almost perfect oracle that solves the d-CDH-problem. We do this for a known polynomial Q whose coefficients are given *in the clear*. Our result is stated in the following theorem:

Theorem 5. *Let m be the number of monomials that appears in Q. Given access to an almost perfect oracle that solves any instance of the n-CDH-assumptionwith probability $\geq \varepsilon$, we build an algorithm that solves any instance of the Q-CDH-assumption for any polynomial Q of degree up to n with probability:*

$$\left(\frac{p\varepsilon^n}{p\varepsilon^n + 1} \right)^m$$

using $O(m \cdot n/\varepsilon)$ queries and a computational runtime of $O(m \cdot \varepsilon^{-n})$.

Even though this reduction need an exponential amount of queries, its exponential dependence is on the degree of the polynomial Q we want to compute and not in the cryptographic parameters (more precisely not in the size of the group). It can thus be considered as efficient.

Proof. The basic is that we can individually compute all the monomials that appears in the polynomial Q, before combining them with their respective coefficients. The monomials of Q are of the form:

$$\alpha_{i_{1,j}, \cdots, i_{2,j}} \cdot x_1^{i_{1,j}} \cdots x_n^{i_{n,j}}, \text{ with } i_{1,j} + \cdots + i_{n,j} \leq d.$$

As the values $\alpha_{i_{1,j}, \cdots, i_{2,j}}$ are explicitly known we only have to be able to compute the product $x_1^{i_{1,j}} \cdots x_n^{i_{n,j}}$ where the $i_{i,j}$ are known. With an ideal oracle, it would suffices to query it on the following input:

$$\underbrace{g^{x_1} \cdots g^{x_1}}_{i_{1,j}} \underbrace{g^{x_2} \cdots g^{x_2}}_{i_{2,j}} \cdots \underbrace{g^{x_n} \cdots g^{x_n}}_{i_{n,j}}.$$

However, since repetitions are extremely rare on randomly generated inputs, nothing prevents an adversarial oracle to answer these specific queries wrongly, without violating its global error bound.

Thus, in order obtain the product, we need to randomize the inputs and derandomize the answer of the oracle. It can be done by sampling independently d random non zero values $\mu_1, \cdots \mu_d$ in $\mathbb{F}_p$ and then querying the oracle on the following input:

$$\underbrace{g^{\mu_1 x_1} \cdots g^{\mu_{i_{1,j}} x_1}}_{i_{1,j}} \underbrace{g^{\mu_{i_{1,j}+1} x_2} \cdots g^{\mu_{i_{2,j}} x_2}}_{i_{2,j}} \cdots \underbrace{g^{\mu_{i_{d-1,j}+1} x_n} \cdots g^{\mu_{i_{d,j}} x_n}}_{i_{n,j}}.$$

From the answer y of the oracle, one can compute $y^{1/\prod_{i=1}^d \mu_i}$ and obtain the expected value.

Finally, using the result of Theorem 3, we can correctly evaluate all the monomials of Q. And thus we can build an algorithm that actually compute correctly the polynomial Q from all its monomials. □

Note that a product oracle for degree d can easily be used to compute monomials of lower degree. Indeed, it suffices to replace some of the variables in the oracle call by randomly sampled constants. This allow us to state the following theorem:

Theorem 6. *In the group setting, all the n-CDH-assumptions are equivalent (w.r.t. n).*

Proof. The proof of the previous theorem relies on the fact that all those assumptions are actually equivalent to the CDH-assumption. Indeed, if we assume that we have access to an oracle solving the n-CDH-assumption, with $n \geq 2$, we can compute the CDH-assumption easily by calling the oracle on the following instance:

$$x_1 = x, x_2 = y, x_3 = \lambda_3, \cdots, x_n = \lambda_n, \text{ with } \lambda_3, \cdots, \lambda_n \text{ being randomly sampled.}$$

Using the same method as the one presented above, we can retrieve the result: g^{xy}.

If we assume that we have access to an oracle solving the CDH-assumption, by repeatedly calling it we can compute the n-CDH-assumption. First, we query the oracle with instance (g^{x_1}, g^{x_2}) and retrieve $(g^{x_1 x_2})$. Then we query the oracle with instance $(g^{x_1 x_2}, g^{x_3})$ and retrieve $(g^{x_1 x_2 x_3})$.

By repeating the process, we can compute $g^{x_1 x_2 \cdots x_n}$. Since this proof does not rely on the value of n (we only require that $n \geq 2$), we can conclude that all the n-CDH-assumptionare equivalent. □

This result should be compared to the result of Maurer and Wolf [15], regarding the equivalence of the CDH-assumption and the discrete logarithm problem. Indeed, this equivalence can be used to show that all the assumptions we are considering are easy when the CDH-assumption is. However, this only covers one direction and the reduction is not explicitly constructive since it relies on the assumption that an auxiliary elliptic curve with smooth cardinality exists and can be found.

In the group setting, as the input and the output of an oracle belong to the same set (actually the same group), we can reuse an answer of an oracle in order to compute more terms: we can iterate the oracle queries and thus from a computational Diffie-Hellman oracle, we can obtain a polynomial of any degree. Whereas, in the bilinear context it is not possible to reuse the output of the oracle as a query but the different relations that we stated in the previous theorems can be adapted to the bilinear context. This adaptation is described in the next section.

6   The Bilinear Setting

All the previous sections focused on the group setting. We now show how our results can be adapted to the bilinear context. The main difference between the two settings is that in the group setting it is possible to actually reuse the output of an oracle to build another query whereas in the pairing setting this is not possible. Indeed, oracle answers do not belong to the same group as queries.

The type of the pairing we are considering is also important, indeed with a type 1 or 2 pairing it is possible to perform some additional operations which are not permitted with a type 3 pairing.

Pairing of type 1

For pairings of type 1, Theorems 2, 3, 4 and 5 can be straightforwardly adapted (the proofs of those theorems are omitted in this paper but will be provided in an extended version). Meaning that in any case, we will have the following relationships: (Fig. 2)

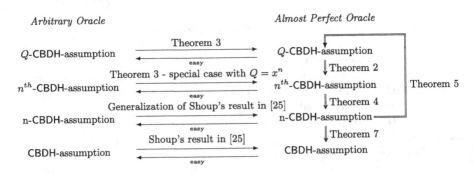

Fig. 2. Security assumptions relations (Bilinear setting)

Theorem 6 can not be stated because in the proof, we need to reuse an oracle output as input. However, we can state that:

Theorem 7. *Given access to an oracle that solves any instance of the n-CDH-assumption, we can solve any instance of the d-CDH-assumption where $d \leq n$.*

This theorem induces a hierarchy within the different class of assumptions. Indeed, the higher n is the harder the assumption is. This can be summarized as follows:

CBDH-assumption $\leq$ n-CBDH-assumption$(n = 4) \leq \cdots \leq$ n-CBDH-assumption$(n = d)$.

Pairing of Type 2 and 3

For pairing of type 2 and 3, once again, Theorems 2, 3, 4 and 5 can be straightforwardly adapted (the proofs of those theorems are omitted in this paper but will be provided in an extended version). In both type of pairings, some computations cannot be done.

For pairing of type 2, assume that we have an oracle that on input $g_1^{x_1}$, $g_1^{x_2}$, $\ldots, g_1^{x_{n_1}}$, $g_2^{y_1}$, $g_2^{y_2}$, $\ldots, g_2^{y_{n_2}}$ outputs $h^{x_1 \cdots x_{n_1} y_1 \cdots y_{n_2}}$. Using this oracle, it is not possible to build an algorithm that can compute $h^{x_1 \cdots x_{n_1} y_1 \cdots y_{n_2}}$ on input $g_1^{x_1}$, $g_1^{x_2}$, $\ldots, g_1^{x_{n_1}}$, $g_1^{y_1}$, $g_2^{y_2}$, $\ldots, g_2^{y_{n_2}}$.

For pairing of type 3, there is no isomorphism between the two base groups and thus some more queries cannot be derived from others.

References

1. Abadi, M., Feigenbaum, J., Kilian, J.: On hiding information from an oracle. J. Comput. Syst. Sci. **39**(1), 21–50 (1989)
2. Bao, F., Deng, R.H., Zhu, H.: Variations of Diffie-Hellman problem. In: Qing, S., Gollmann, D., Zhou, J. (eds.) ICICS 2003. LNCS, vol. 2836, pp. 301–312. Springer, Heidelberg (2003)
3. Barthe, G., Grégoire, B., Heraud, S., Béguelin, S.Z.: Computer-aided security proofs for the working cryptographer. In: Rogaway, P. (ed.) CRYPTO 2011. LNCS, vol. 6841, pp. 71–90. Springer, Heidelberg (2011)
4. Bellare, M., Rogaway, P.: The security of triple encryption and a framework for code-based game-playing proofs. In: Vaudenay, S. (ed.) EUROCRYPT 2006. LNCS, vol. 4004, pp. 409–426. Springer, Heidelberg (2006)
5. Biswas, G.: Diffie-Hellman technique: extended to multiple two-party keys and one multi-party key. IET Inf. Secur. **2**(1), 12–18 (2008)
6. Blanchet, B.: Security protocol verification: symbolic and computational models. In: Degano, P., Guttman, J.D. (eds.) Principles of Security and Trust. LNCS, vol. 7215, pp. 3–29. Springer, Heidelberg (2012)
7. Boneh, D., Boyen, X., Goh, E.-J.: Hierarchical identity based encryption with constant size ciphertext. Cryptology ePrint Archive, Report 2005/015 (2005). http://eprint.iacr.org/
8. Boneh, D., Franklin, M.: Identity-based encryption from the weil pairing. In: Kilian, J. (ed.) CRYPTO 2001. LNCS, vol. 2139, pp. 213–229. Springer, Heidelberg (2001)
9. Boneh, D., Lynn, B., Shacham, H.: Short signatures from the Weil pairing. J. Cryptology **17**(4), 297–319 (2004)
10. Boyen, X.: The uber-assumption family. In: Galbraith, S.D., Paterson, K.G. (eds.) Pairing 2008. LNCS, vol. 5209, pp. 39–56. Springer, Heidelberg (2008)
11. Burmester, M., Desmedt, Y.G., Seberry, J.: Equitable key escrow with limited time span. In: Ohta, K., Pei, D. (eds.) ASIACRYPT 1998. LNCS, vol. 1514, pp. 380–391. Springer, Heidelberg (1998)

12. Diffie, W., Hellman, M.E.: New directions in cryptography. IEEE Trans. Inf. Theor. **22**(6), 644–654 (1976)
13. Feigenbaum, J., Fortnow, L.: On the random-self-reducibility of complete sets. In: Structure in Complexity Theory Conference, pp. 124–132 (1991)
14. Joux, A.: A one round protocol for tripartite Diffie-Hellman. In: Bosma, W. (ed.) ANTS 2000. LNCS, vol. 1838, pp. 385–394. Springer, Heidelberg (2000)
15. Maurer, U.M., Wolf, S.: Diffie-Hellman oracles. In: Koblitz, N. (ed.) CRYPTO 1996. LNCS, vol. 1109, pp. 268–282. Springer, Heidelberg (1996)
16. Menezes, A., Okamoto, T., Vanstone, S.A.: Reducing elliptic curve logarithms to logarithms in a finite field. IEEE Trans. Inf. Theor. **39**(5), 1639–1646 (1993)
17. Shoup, V.: Lower bounds for discrete logarithms and related problems. In: Fumy, W. (ed.) EUROCRYPT 1997. LNCS, vol. 1233, pp. 256–266. Springer, Heidelberg (1997)
18. Young, A., Yung, M.: Relationships between Diffie-Hellman and "Index Oracles". In: Blundo, C., Cimato, S. (eds.) SCN 2004. LNCS, vol. 3352, pp. 16–32. Springer, Heidelberg (2005)

A Secure and Efficient Method for Scalar Multiplication on Supersingular Elliptic Curves over Binary Fields

Matheus F. de Oliveira and Marco Aurélio Amaral Henriques[✉]

Faculty of Electrical and Computer Engineering - FEEC,
University of Campinas - UNICAMP,
Av. Albert Einstein, 400 - Cidade Universitária Zeferino Vaz,
Campinas, SP 13083-852, Brazil
matheus.oliveira@gmail.com, marco@dca.fee.unicamp.br

Abstract. We present a secure and efficient scalar multiplication method for supersingular elliptic curves over binary fields based on Montgomery's ladder algorithm. Our approach uses only the x-coordinate of elliptic curve points to perform scalar multiplication, requires no precomputation and executes the same number of operations over the binary field in every iteration. When applied to projective coordinates, our method is faster than the other typical scalar multiplication methods in practical situations.

Keywords: Elliptic curve cryptography · Scalar multiplication · Supersingular elliptic curves · Binary fields · Side-channel attacks

1 Introduction

The efficiency and security of protocols that employ supersingular elliptic curves, defined over $\mathbb{F}_{2^m}$ and given by Eq. 1

$$E(\mathbb{F}_{2^m}) : y^2 + y = x^3 + x + c, \tag{1}$$

depend directly on the method used to compute scalar multiplications. We propose a method to compute scalar multiplication on supersingular elliptic curves that is efficient and robust against side-channel attacks. These features make our method an option for restricted computational environments like smart cards.

2 Previous Work

To improve efficiency and security of elliptic curve cryptosystems, many researchers have proposed methods to compute scalar multiplication of elliptic curve points. In 1999, López and Dahab [2] proposed a method to efficiently compute scalar multiplication over binary fields on non-supersingular curves.

© Springer International Publishing Switzerland 2015
Y. Desmedt (Ed.): ISC 2013, LNCS 7807, pp. 407–416, 2015.
DOI: 10.1007/978-3-319-27659-5_29

Okeya and Sakurai proposed a similar method for scalar multiplication on prime fields [3]. Fischer et al. showed the implementation of an analogous method to compute scalar multiplication over prime fields in a coprocessor for smart cards [4]. Joye [5] has also showed regular algorithms for scalar multiplication. Our method is analogous to their methods, with the difference that it is specific for supersingular elliptic curves. In spite of our work has reached similar equations to those found in the work of Saeki [6] in the case of affine coordinates, we show how to obtain the y-coordinate and also present the equations for scalar multiplication using projective coordinates. As will be discussed, the method proposed is more efficient then other methods of scalar multiplication when projective coordinates are used. This does not happen with affine coordinates.

3   Multiplication Method: Montgomery's Ladder

Our method is derived from the algorithm to perform exponentiation known as Montgomery's ladder [7], which was adapted to perform multiplication of a elliptic curve point P_0 by the n-bit scalar k(Algorithm 1).

Algorithm 1. Scalar Multiplication using Montgomery's ladder [7]

Input: Elliptic curve point P_0, positive scalar $k = (k_{n-1}, k_{n-2}, \ldots, k_0)_2$.
Output: Elliptic curve point kP_0.
1: $R \leftarrow P_0$, $S \leftarrow 2P_0$.
2: **for** $i \leftarrow n - 2$ **downto** 0 **do**
3:     **if** $k_i = 0$ **then**
4:         $S \leftarrow R + S$, $R \leftarrow 2R$.
5:     **else**
6:         $R \leftarrow R + S$, $S \leftarrow 2S$.
7: **return** R.

An important characteristic of Algorithm 1 is that, for any n-bit positive scalar k, the same number of operations will be performed: one point addition and one point doubling. This does not happen in the widely used double-and-add algorithm [8], where the number of operations performed in each iteration i depends on the bit k_i. Then, the scalar multiplication using Montgomery's ladder is more robust against side-channel attacks. Another characteristic of Algorithm 1 is the invariant $S - R = P_0$, as shown in Lemma 1. This will be important for our method.

4   Group Law

We now present the group law for the supersingular elliptic curve over $\mathbb{F}_{2^m}$ given by Eq. 1 [8], considering affine coordinates.

- **Identity:** $P + \mathcal{O} = \mathcal{O} + P$ for all $P \in E(\mathbb{F}_{2^m})$;
- **Negative:** Let $P_1 = (x_1, y_1) \in E(\mathbb{F}_{2^m})$, then $(x_1, y_1) + (x_1, y_1 + 1) = \mathcal{O}$. The point $-P_1 = (x_1, y_1 + 1)$ is called the *negative* of P_1;
- **Point addition:** Let $P_1 = (x_1, y_1) \in E(\mathbb{F}_{2^m})$ and $P_2 = (x_2, y_2) \in E(\mathbb{F}_{2^m})$, where $P_1 \neq \pm P_2$. Then $P_1 + P_2 = P_3 = (x_3, y_3)$, where:

$$\lambda = \frac{y_1 + y_2}{x_1 + x_2}; \tag{2}$$

$$x_3 = \lambda^2 + x_1 + x_2; \tag{3}$$

$$y_3 = \lambda(x_1 + x_3) + y_1 + 1. \tag{4}$$

- **Point doubling:** Let $P_1 = (x_1, y_1) \in E(\mathbb{F}_{2^m})$, where $P_1 \neq -P_1$. Then $2P_1 = P_3 = (x_3, y_3)$, where

$$x_3 = \left(x_1{}^2 + 1\right)^2 = x_1{}^4 + 1, \tag{5}$$

as the terms with coefficient 2 are null in binary field arithmetic, and

$$y_3 = \left(x_1{}^2 + 1\right)(x_1 + x_3) + y_1 + 1. \tag{6}$$

5 Improved Scalar Multiplication

Let the supersingular elliptic curve points in affine coordinates be $P_1 = (x_1, y_1)$, $P_2 = (x_2, y_2)$ and $P_3 = (x_3, y_3) \in E(\mathbb{F}_{2^m})$, such that $P_1 + P_2 = P_3$. The coordinates x_3 and y_3 may be computed with Eqs. 3 and 4. Now consider another point of the same supersingular elliptic curve given by $P_4 = (x_4, y_4)$, which is the result of $P_2 - P_1$, such that $P_4 = P_2 + (-P_1)$. Because the subtraction may be seen as the addition of P_2 and the inverse of P_1, then $(x_4, y_4) = (x_2, y_2) + (x_1, y_1 + 1)$ and so we have

$$x_4 = (\lambda')^2 + x_1 + x_2, \tag{7}$$

where $\lambda' = \left(\frac{y_1 + 1 + y_2}{x_1 + x_2}\right)$. Notice that $\lambda' = \lambda + \frac{1}{x_1 + x_2}$ and that Eq. 7 can be rewritten as:

$$x_4 = \lambda^2 + \frac{1}{x_1^2 + x_2^2} + x_1 + x_2. \tag{8}$$

Using Eq. 3 in Eq. 8, we obtain

$$x_4 = x_3 + \frac{1}{x_1^2 + x_2^2},$$

which depends only on x-coordinates and can be rewritten as

$$x_3 = x_4 + \frac{1}{x_1^2 + x_2^2}. \tag{9}$$

Now consider the Montgomery's ladder algorithm presented in Sect. 3. In each iteration, the algorithm always performs one point addition and one point doubling. As shown in Eq. 5, the x-coordinate of the point being doubled may be computed using only the x-coordinate before doubling. Equation 9, shows that the x-coordinate of the point resulting from the addition of P_1 and P_2 is a function of x_1, x_2 and x_4. We know that x_4 comes from $P_4 = P_2 - P_1$, and by the Lemma 1, $P_4 = P_0 = (x_0, y_0)$, what means that $x_4 = x_0$. Equation 9 may be rewritten as

$$x_3 = x_0 + \frac{1}{x_1^2 + x_2^2}. \tag{10}$$

Notice that Eq. 10 depends only on x-coordinates of points P_0, P_1 and P_2. So Algorithm 1 can easily be adapted to compute the scalar multiplication of a point P_0 using only the x-coordinates of this point and of the auxiliary points P_1 and P_2, as shown in the next equations. This feature may be advantageous for restricted devices, like smart cards.

Considering $P_5 = kP_0 = (x_5, y_5)$ and $P_6 = (k+1)P_0 = (x_6, y_6)$, at the end of execution of Algorithm 1, we can expect that $x_1 = x_5$ and $x_2 = x_6$. The next equations show how to obtain y_5. We know that $P_6 = (k+1)P_0 = kP_0 + P_0 = P_5 + P_0$, and from Eq. 3 we have:

$$x_6 = \left(\frac{y_5 + y_0}{x_5 + x_0}\right)^2 + x_5 + x_0 = \frac{y_5^2 + y_0^2 + x_5^3 + x_0^3 + x_5^2 x_0 + x_5 x_0^2}{x_5^2 + x_0^2}. \tag{11}$$

The points kP_0 and P_0 belong to the supersingular elliptic curve given by Eq. 1 and so:

$$\left\{\begin{array}{l} y_0^2 + y_0 = x_0^3 + x_0 + c \\ + \ y_5^2 + y_5 = x_5^3 + x_5 + c \\ \hline y_5^2 + y_0^2 + x_5^3 + x_0^3 = y_0 + y_5 + x_0 + x_5. \end{array}\right.$$

We can use the above result in Eq. 11, resulting in

$$x_6 = \frac{y_0 + y_5 + x_0 + x_5 + x_5^2 x_0 + x_5 x_0^2}{x_5^2 + x_0^2}, \tag{12}$$

which can be rewritten as

$$y_5 = y_0 + (x_5 + x_0)(1 + x_0 x_5 + x_6(x_5 + x_0)). \tag{13}$$

Notice that y_5 can be calculated using only the y-coordinate of P_0 and the x-coordinates results available. Based on previous equations, it is possible to adapt Algorithm 1 to compute scalar multiplication of a supersingular elliptic point in $\mathbb{F}_{2^m}$, as shown in Algorithm 2. A comparison between both algorithms is presented in Sect. 7.

6   Using Projective Coordinates

In this section we show how our method can be used with traditional projective coordinates. Considering that addition and squaring can be efficiently computed

---

Algorithm 2. Scalar Multiplication on supersingular elliptic curve using affine coordinates

---

Input: Point $P_0 = (x_0, y_0) \in E(\mathbb{F}_{2^m})$, positive scalar $k = (k_{n-1}, k_{n-2}, \ldots, k_0)_2$.
Output: Point $kP_0 = R = (x_R, y_R) \in E(\mathbb{F}_{2^m})$.
1: $x_R \leftarrow x_0$, $x_S \leftarrow x_0^4 + 1$. {Compute x-coordinates of P and $2P$.}
2: **for** $i \leftarrow n - 2$ **downto** 0 **do**
3:    **if** $k_i = 0$ **then**
4:       $x_S \leftarrow x_0 + \frac{1}{x_R^2 + x_S^2}$.
5:       $x_R \leftarrow x_R^4 + 1$.
6:    **else**
7:       $x_R \leftarrow x_0 + \frac{1}{x_R^2 + x_S^2}$.
8:       $x_S \leftarrow x_S^4 + 1$.
9: $y_R \leftarrow y_0 + (x_R + x_0)(1 + x_0 x_R + x_S(x_R + x_0))$.
10: **return** (x_R, y_R).

---

for binary field [8], we will consider only the cost of the more expensive operations in point addition and doubling, which are the multiplication and the inversion.

It is possible to eliminate the inversion during the computation of point addition using projective coordinates. Let $P_1 = (X_1 : Y_1 : Z_1)$, with $Z_1 = 1$, and $P_2 = (X_2 : Y_2 : Z_2) \in E(\mathbb{F}_{2^m})$ and suppose that $P_1, P_2 \neq \mathcal{O}$, $P_1 \neq P_2$ and $P_1 \neq -P_2$. Then $P_3 = P_1 + P_2 = (X_3 : Y_3 : Z_3)$, where

$$X_3 = \alpha^2 \beta Z_2 + \beta^4 \tag{14}$$

$$Y_3 = (1 + Y_1)Z_3 + \alpha^3 Z_2 + \alpha\beta^2 X_2 \tag{15}$$

$$Z_3 = \beta^3 Z_2, \tag{16}$$

where $\alpha = (Y_1 Z_2 + Y_2)$ and $\beta = (X_1 Z_2 + X_2)$. Note that this addition formula requires 9 multiplications of field elements. For point doubling, 6 multiplications are required. When projective coordinates are used, the result $(X_3 : Y_3 : Z_3)$ can be converted back to affine coordinates by multiplying each coordinate by Z_3^{-1}.

Equations 5 and 9 may be modified to use projective coordinates.

– **Doubling:** from Eq. 5,

$$\frac{X_3}{Z_3} = \frac{X_1^4}{Z_1^4} + 1 = \frac{X_1^4 + Z_1^4}{Z_1^4}, \tag{17}$$

which means that $X_3 = \left(X_1^4 + Z_1^4\right)$ and $Z_3 = Z_1^4$.

– **Addition:** form Eq. 10,

$$\frac{X_3}{Z_3} = x_0 + \frac{1}{\frac{X_1^2}{Z_1^2} + \frac{X_2^2}{Z_2^2}} = x_0 + \frac{Z_1^2 Z_2^2}{X_1^2 Z_2^2 + X_2^2 Z_1^2} = \frac{x_0 t + Z_1^2 Z_2^2}{t}, \tag{18}$$

where $t = X_1^2 Z_2^2 + X_2^2 Z_1^2$. Hence, we have

$$X_3 = \left(x_0 t + Z_1^2 Z_2^2\right), \text{ and } Z_3 = t. \tag{19}$$

In the same way that we have developed Eq. 13 to obtain the y-coordinate of the point $kP_0 = P_5 = (x_5, y_5)$ in the affine case, we can also obtain the y_5 directly in the projective case. By the end of the iterations of the Montgomery Algorithm in projective case we can make $x_5 = X_1/Z_1$, $x_6 = X_2/Z_2$ and use these relations to adapt Eq. 13 and obtain Eq. 20.

$$y_5 = y_0 + \frac{(X_1 + x_0 Z_1)(x_0(X_1 Z_2 + X_2 Z_1) + X_1 X_2 + Z_1 Z_2)}{Z_1^2 Z_2} \tag{20}$$

Algorithm 3 shows how to implement multiplication of point P by scalar k using projective coordinates. We notice that one of the multiplications performed in

---

Algorithm 3. Scalar Multiplication on supersingular elliptic curve using projective coordinates

Input: Point $P_0 = (x_0, y_0) \in E(\mathbb{F}_{2^m})$, positive scalar $k = (k_{n-1}, k_{n-2}, \ldots, k_0)_2$.
Output: Point $kP_0 = R = (x_R, y_R) \in E(\mathbb{F}_{2^m})$.
1: $X_R \leftarrow x_0$, $Z_R \leftarrow 1$, $Z_S \leftarrow Z_R^4$, $X_S \leftarrow X_R^4 + Z_S$.
2: **for** $i \leftarrow n - 2$ **downto** 0 **do**
3:      $t \leftarrow (X_R Z_S + X_S Z_R)^2$.
4:      **if** $k_i = 0$ **then**
5:          $X_R \leftarrow x_0 t + Z_R^2 Z_S^2$, $Z_R \leftarrow t$,
6:          $Z_S \leftarrow Z_S^4$, $X_2 \leftarrow X_S^4 + Z_S$.
7:      **else**
8:          $X_S \leftarrow x_0 t + Z_R^2 Z_2^2$, $Z_2 \leftarrow t$,
9:          $Z_R \leftarrow Z_R^4$, $X_R \leftarrow X_R^4 + Z_R$.
10: $x_R = X_R/Z_R$
11: $y_R = y_0 + \frac{(X_R + x_0 Z_R)(x_0(X_R Z_S + X_S Z_R) + X_R X_S + Z_R Z_S)}{Z_R^2 Z_S}$.
12: **return** (x_R, y_R).

---

each iteration uses the fixed factor x_0. Then, precomputation techniques [1] can improve even more the method's efficiency.

7   Comparison with Double-and-Add

The two steps performed in each iteration of Algorithms 2 (lines 4, 5 or 7, 8) and 3 (lines 5, 6 or 8, 9) are independent and can be parallelized in a hardware implementation or in a software implementation with multiple cores. In this way, each iteration can be performed faster and the overall execution time of the algorithm will be smaller.

We compare our method with the double-and-add method to perform scalar multiplication, since both methods require no pre-computation. For the comparisons, we consider the scalar k with bit length n. In double-and-add, the point doubling is computed at each iteration and if k_i is equal to 1, it is necessary to compute one point addition. In our method, each iteration of the algorithm requires the same number of operations, independently of the value of k_i, a good characteristic as it prevents side-channel attacks. By the end of the algorithm, it must compute a few operations so as to obtain the value of the y-coordinate.

It is known that finite field addition is a low cost operation in binary fields, since it depends only on the number of machine words representing the finite field elements [8]. Analogously, the square operation can use lookup tables and efficient reduction methods. For these reasons, finite field addition and square are operations with low cost in binary fields, and the comparison presented here will consider only the number of multiplications (M) and inversions (I). Finally, we also consider that k has a Hamming weight of 50 %, in average, since in double-and-add algorithm the number of operations varies depending on k_i. Table 1 show the comparisons for affine and projective coordinates.

Table 1. Comparison between methods for affine and projective coordinates.

Coordinates	Method	Operations required
Affine	Double-and-add	$(3n/2)M + (n/2)I$
	Our method	$3M + (n-1)I$
Projective	Double-and-add	$(21n/2)M + 1I$
	Our method	$4(n+1)M + 2I$

Considering the time spent to compute the scalar multiplication of a point, we notice in Table 1 that, for affine coordinates and for large values of n, our method is faster than the traditional double-and-add method if $I < 3\,M$, i.e., when the operation of inversion I costs less than three times the multiplication M, which is hard to find in practical implementations. The relation I/M can vary from 7 to 102 [8]. In the projective case we can consider n large sufficiently to ignore the cost of the terms which are not multiplied by n, such that our method is faster than double-and-add all the times that $(13n/2)M > 1I$, which is always true for practical situations, since n assumes large values (typically, $n > 100$). We have also considered that the cost of inversion algorithm includes the cost of multiplying the numerator by the inverted value. It is important to notice that, while the cost of the double-and-add method depends on the Hamming weight of k, our method requires the same number of operations for all values of k.

Both Algorithms 2 and 3 were implemented and tested, and their results were checked to validate the equations presented in this paper.

8   Comparison with Methods *NAF* and *w-NAF*

It is possible to compare the equations proposed with typical methods of scalar multiplication that employ non-adjacent form (NAF) to represent the scalar. For this purpose, we will consider the methods *NAF* and *w-NAF* of scalar multiplication and the number of operations (multiplications and inversions in binary field) as shown in [8]. We consider a window of length $w = 4$ for w-NAF, which is suitable for devices with constrained memory, like smart cards. First, we present in Table 2 the number of operations for affine coordinates.

Table 2. Comparison between methods for affine and projective coordinates.

Coordinates	Method	Operations required
Affine	NAF	$(4n/3)\text{M} + (n/3)\text{I}$
	w-NAF	$(6n/5)\text{M} + (n/5 + 3)\text{I}$
	Our method	$3\text{M} + (n-1)\text{I}$
Projective	NAF	$(9n)\text{M} + 1\text{I}$
	w-NAF	$(39n/5 + 33)\text{M} + 1\text{I}$
	Our method	$4(n+1)\text{M} + 2\text{I}$

We can notice that, with affine coordinates, our method is more advantageous then NAF and w-NAF when $I < 2M$ or $I < (3/2)M$, respectively, which is hard to find in practical implementations. For the projective case, the number of operations is also shown in Table 2.

As we can notice, with projective coordinates our method is more efficient then NAF and w-NAF for $5n\text{M} > I$ and $(19n/5)\text{M} > I$, respectively, which is always true in practical situations.

9   Further Improvements

To take advantage of the relatively low cost of point duplication for supersingular elliptic curves, the scalar k can be written as

$$k = k_1 + 2^{(n/2)}k_2, \tag{21}$$

where k_1 and k_2 have both the bitlength of $n/2$. In this way, the computation of kP can be performed as two parallel scalar multiplications:

$$kP = k_1P + k_2Q, \tag{22}$$

where $Q = 2^{(n/2)}P$. Even in this way, the proposed method with projective coordinates can still provide efficient computation and robustness against side-channel attacks.

10   Concluding Remarks

We have presented an efficient method for scalar multiplication on supersingular elliptic curves over binary fields based on well known Montgomery's ladder algorithm. In affine coordinates, the efficiency of the method depends of the relative costs of the binary field operations of inversion and multiplication. In projective coordinates and for practical situations, our method is faster than the double-and-add algorithm. The method presented here has important features, considering its use on security applications. Since it is based on Montgomery's ladder algorithm, it is secure against side-channel attacks and can be parallelized. Moreover, the method uses during its iterations only the x-coordinate of the point being multiplied and, by the end of the execution, can easily obtain its y-coordinate.

A   Appendix: Montgomery's Ladder Invariant

Lemma 1. *Every iteration in Montgomery's ladder algorithm to compute* kP_0, *where* $k = (k_{n-1}, k_{n-2}, \ldots, k_0)_2$, *keeps the difference* $S - R = P_0$.

Proof. Before the first iteration, we have $R = P_0$ and $S = 2P_0$, and thus $Q_2 - Q_1 = P_0$. Now let's assume that during an iteration $0 \leq i \leq l - 2$ we have $R = nP_0$ and $S = (n + 1)P_0$, where $1 \leq n \leq k$. The difference $S - R = P_0$ holds. To prove that in iteration $i + 1$ the invariant $S - R = P_0$ is held, we must consider two cases:

- if $k_i = 0$: the values of R and S are updated such that $R = 2nP_0$ and $S = (n + n + 1)P_0 = (2n + 1)P_0$. We can see that the difference $S - R = P_0$ holds in this case.
- if $k_i = 1$: the values of R and S are updated such that $R = (n + n + 1)P_0 = (2n + 1)P_0$ and $S = 2(k + 1)P_0 = (2k + 2)P_0$. We can see that the difference $S - R = P_0$ holds in this case too.

By the end of iterations, we have $i = 0$ and $Q_2 - Q_1 = P_0$ is mantained.

References

1. Cohen, H., Frey, G. (eds.): Handbook of Elliptic and Hyperelliptic Curve Cryptography. CRC Press, Boca Raton (2005)
2. López, J., Dahab, R.: Fast multiplication on elliptic curves over $GF(2^m)$ without precomputation. In: Koç, Ç.K., Paar, C. (eds.) CHES 1999. LNCS, vol. 1717, pp. 316–327. Springer, Heidelberg (1999)
3. Okeya, K., Sakurai, K.: Efficient elliptic curve cryptosystems from a scalar multiplication algorithm with recovery of the y-coordinate on a montgomery-form elliptic curve. In: Koç, Ç.K., Naccache, D., Paar, C. (eds.) CHES 2001. LNCS, vol. 2162, p. 126. Springer, Heidelberg (2001)
4. Fischer, W., Giraud, C., Knudsen, E., Seifert, J.: Parallel Scalar Multiplication on General Elliptic Curves over F_p hedged against Non-Differential Side Channel Attacks. Cryptology ePrint Archive, 2002/007 (2002). http://citeseer.ist.psu.edu/fischer02parallel.html
5. Joye, M.: Highly regular right-to-left algorithms for scalar multiplication. In: Paillier, P., Verbauwhede, I. (eds.) CHES 2007. LNCS, vol. 4727, pp. 135–147. Springer, Heidelberg (2007)

6. Saeki, M.: Elliptic Curve Cryptosystems. Master Thesis. McGill University, Montreal (1997)
7. Montgomery, P.L.: Speeding the Pollard and elliptic curve methods of factorization. Math. Comput. **48**(177), 243–264 (1987)
8. Hankerson, D., Menezes, A.J., Vanstone, S.: Guide to Elliptic Curve Cryptography. Springer-Verlag New York Inc., Secaucus (2003)

Author Index

Printed in the United States
By Bookmasters